WLM 20 GRO

369 0144884

D1426359

Translating Psychological
Research Into Practice

Lisa Grossman, JD, PhD, ABPP, is a clinical and forensic psychologist in private practice in Chicago, Illinois. She also holds a law degree. Dr. Grossman has been very active in both national and state psychology organizations. In the American Psychological Association (APA), she served as a member of their Board of Directors, along with many other leadership positions, including past president of both Division 42: Psychologists in Independent Practice and Division 31: State, Provincial and Territorial Psychological Affairs. She is also past president of the Illinois Psychological Association and has represented the State of Illinois on the APA's Council of Representatives for 6 years and is beginning her second 3-year term representing Division 31. Dr. Grossman has authored and/or coauthored several book chapters and journal articles. She is Board Certified in Clinical Psychology and has been recognized for her excellence and outstanding contributions to the profession of psychology, including the Distinguished Psychological Award from the Illinois Psychological Association, the Outstanding Psychologists Award from APA's Division 31: State, Provincial and Territorial Psychological Association Affairs, the Karl F. Heiser APA Presidential Award for Advocacy, the Association for the Advancement of Psychology Advocacy Award, and a 2010 Presidential Citation. In 2010, she received the prestigious APA Award for Distinguished Professional Contributions to Independent Practice.

Steven Walfish, PhD, is in private practice in Atlanta, Georgia, and a partner at the Practice Institute. He is also a clinical assistant professor in the Department of Psychiatry and Behavioral Sciences at the Emory University School of Medicine. He is coauthor with Jeff Barnett of *Financial Success in Mental Health Practice: Essential Tools and Strategies for Practitioners* (2009), coeditor (with Allen K. Hess) *Succeeding in Graduate School: The Career Guide for Psychology Students* (2001), and edited *Earning a Living Outside of Managed Care: Fifty Ways to Expand Your Practice* (2010). He has published more than 60 papers in peer-reviewed journals in the areas of substance abuse, bariatric surgery, HIPAA, and professional training and practice. He has been the editor of the *Independent Practitioner* and is president of APA Division 42, Psychologists in Independent Practice. He has been a visiting professor/lecturer in the Departments of Psychology at Kennesaw State University and Georgia State University. Prior to moving to Atlanta, Dr. Walfish was in full-time private practice in Tampa, Florida and Edmonds and Everett, Washington.

Translating Psychological Research Into Practice

Edited by

Lisa Grossman, JD, PhD, ABPP
Steven Walfish, PhD

SPRINGER PUBLISHING COMPANY
NEW YORK

Springer Publishing Company, LLC
11 West 42nd Street
New York, NY 10036
www.springerpub.com

Acquisitions Editor: Nancy Hale
Composition: Exeter Premedia Services Private Ltd.

ISBN: 978-0-8261-0942-2
e-book ISBN: 978-0-8261-0943-9

13 14 15 16 / 5 4 3 2 1

The author and the publisher of this Work have made every effort to use sources believed to be reliable to provide information that is accurate and compatible with the standards generally accepted at the time of publication. The author and publisher shall not be liable for any special, consequential, or exemplary damages resulting, in whole or in part, from the readers' use of, or reliance on, the information contained in this book. The publisher has no responsibility for the persistence or accuracy of URLs for external or third-party Internet websites referred to in this publication and does not guarantee that any content on such websites is, or will remain, accurate or appropriate.

Library of Congress Cataloging-in-Publication Data
Translating psychological research into practice / edited by Lisa Grossman, JD, PhD, ABPP, Steven Walfish, PhD.
     p. ; cm.
   ISBN 978-0-8261-0942-2
   1. Clinical psychology.   2. Clinical psychology—Research.   3. Psychotherapy—Research.
   I. Grossman, Lisa R.   II. Walfish, Steven.
   RC467.T724 2014
   616'.890072—dc23
                                                                      2013034845

Printed in the United States of America by Bradford & Bigelow.

To my family for their love, support and unconditional and unwavering faith in my life decisions and career choices,

and to

All the heroic women in the past who dared to insist their voices be heard and who courageously
fought for women's rights, intellectual freedoms and gender equality.

—Lisa

To Steve Tulkin and Jack Tapp, who introduced me to the value of conducting psychological research,

To practitioners and scientists who respect each other and want to get it right for the benefit of those we serve,

and to

Mary, my love and partner in life. She has helped fill my life with warmth, love, and purpose.

—Steve

Contents

Contributors

Brian V. Abbott, PhD   James H. Quillen VA Medical Center, Mountain Home, Tennessee

Andrea Allen, PhD   Independent Practice and Department of Psychiatry, Mount Sinai School of Medicine, New York, New York

Lesley A. Allen, PhD   Department of Psychology, Princeton University, Princeton, New Jersey

Kelly C. Allison, PhD   Department of Psychology in Psychiatry, Center for Weight and Eating Disorders, University of Pennsylvania, Philadelphia, Pennsylvania

Mary Karapetian Alvord, PhD   Alvord, Baker & Associates, LLC, Rockville and Silver Spring, Maryland

Janis L. Anderson, PhD   Department of Psychiatry, Harvard Medical School and Brigham and Women's Hospital, Boston, Massachusetts

Page L. Anderson, PhD   Department of Psychology, Georgia State University, Atlanta, Georgia

Margaret S. Andover, PhD   Department of Psychology, Fordham University, New York

Kevin M. Antshel, PhD   Department of Psychology, Syracuse University, Syracuse, New York

Noelle E. Balliett, PhD   Department of Psychology, University of Tulsa, Tulsa, Oklahoma

Russell Barkley, PhD   Clinical Professor of Psychiatry and Pediatrics, Medical University of South Carolina, Charleston, South Carolina

Donald H. Baucom, PhD   Department of Psychology, University of North Carolina at Chapel Hill, North Carolina

Melanie K. Bean, PhD   Children's Hospital of Richmond at Virginia Commonwealth University, Richmond, Virginia

Lauren J. Behrman, PhD   Independent Practice, White Plains and New York, New York

Deborah C. Beidel, PhD   Department of Psychology, University of Central Florida, Orlando, Florida

Lisa H. Berghorst, PhD   Alvord, Baker & Associates, LLC, Rockville and Silver Spring, Maryland

Marina A. Bornovalova, PhD   Department of Psychology, University of South Florida, Tampa, Florida

Michael S. Boroughs, PhD   Massachusetts General Hospital, Department of Psychiatry, Harvard Medical School, Boston, Massachusetts

Michelle J. Bovin, PhD   Women's Health Sciences Division of the National Center for PTSD, VA Boston Healthcare System, and Boston University School of Medicine, Boston, Massachusetts

Julie Bowman, RD, LMHC   Potomac Behavioral Solutions, Arlington, Virginia

Andrea Bradford, PhD   Department of Gynecologic Oncology and Reproductive Medicine, University of Texas MD Anderson Cancer Center, Houston, Texas

Bethany L. Brand, PhD   Department of Psychology, Towson University, Towson, Maryland

Thomas H. Brandon, PhD   Moffitt Cancer Center, University of South Florida, Tampa, Florida

Christiana Bratiotis, PhD   Department of Health Outcomes and Behavior, Moffitt Cancer Center, and Department of Psychology, University of South Florida, Tampa, Florida

Abigail Brown, MA   Department of Psychology, DePaul University, Chicago, Illinois

Molly Brown, PhD   Department of Psychology, DePaul University, Chicago, Illinois

Colette J. Browning, PhD   School of Primary Health Care, Monash University, Melbourne, Australia

Thomas M. Brunner, PhD   Independent Practice and Center for Character Strength Investment, Tucson, Arizona

Brian E. Bunnell, MS   Department of Psychology, University of Central Florida, Orlando, Florida

Jason Burrow-Sanchez, PhD   Department of Educational Psychology, University of Utah, Salt Lake City, Utah

Martha R. Calamaras, MA   Department of Psychology, Georgia State University, Atlanta, Georgia

Louis G. Castonguay, PhD   Department of Psychology, Pennsylvania State University, University Park, Pennsylvania

Marianne Celano, PhD   Department of Psychiatry & Behavioral Sciences, Emory University School of Medicine, Atlanta, Georgia

Jesse R. Cougle, PhD   Department of Psychology, Florida State University, Tallahassee, Florida

Christine A. Courtois, PhD   Independent Practice, Washington, DC

Colleen M. Cummings, PhD   Department of Psychology, Temple University, Philadelphia, Pennsylvania

Joanne L. Davis, PhD   Department of Psychology, University of Tulsa, Tulsa, Oklahoma

Jerry L. Deffenbacher, PhD   Department of Psychology, Colorado State University, Fort Collins, Colorado

Rayleen V. De Luca, PhD   Department of Psychology, University of Manitoba, Winnipeg, Manitoba, Canada

Alexandra C. De Young, PhD   Centre of National Research on Disability and Rehabilitation Medicine, University of Queensland, Brisbane, Australia

Elaine Ducharme, PhD   Independent Practice, Glastonbury, Connecticut

Christopher I. Eckhardt, PhD   Department of Psychological Sciences, Purdue University, West Lafayette, Indiana

Marion Ehrenberg, PhD   Department of Psychology, University of Victoria, British Columbia, Canada

Lawrence Ellerby, PhD   CPsych, Forensic Psychological Services, Winnipeg, Manitoba, Canada

Brigette A. Erwin, PhD   Executive Director, The Anxiety and OCD Center, Exton, Pennsylvania

Kate M. Esterline, BA   Department of Psychology, University of Kansas, Lawrence, Kansas

Shawn Ewbank, PsyD   Tourette Syndrome Program, Graduate School of Applied and Professional Psychology at Rutgers University, Piscataway, New Jersey; Manhattan Center for Cognitive Behavioral Therapy, New York, New York

Maggie Evans, BA   Department of Psychology, University of Vermont, Burlington, Vermont

Meredyth Evans, MA   Department of Psychology, DePaul University, Chicago, Illinois

Anthony N. Fabricatore, PhD   Nutrisystem, Inc., Fort Washington, Pennsylvania

Antonina S. Farmer, MA   Department of Psychology, George Mason University, Fairfax, Virginia

Erin M. Farrer, PhD   Summa Health System, Akron, Ohio

Todd K. Favorite, PhD   University of Michigan, Psychological Clinic, University of Michigan Medical School, Department of Psychiatry and Ann Arbor VA Healthcare System, PTSD Clinic, Ann Arbor, Michigan

Jonathan M. Feldman, PhD   Ferkauf Graduate School of Psychology, Yeshiva University, Bronx, New York

Lawrence M. Ferber, PhD   Independent Practice, Wantagh, New York

Joseph R. Ferrari, PhD   Department of Psychology, DePaul University, Chicago, Illinois

Kenneth R. Fineman, PhD   Associate Clinical Professor, Department of Psychiatry and Human Behavior, University of California, Irvine, California

John W. Finney, PhD   Center for Health Care Evaluation, VA Palo Alto Health Care System, Menlo Park, California

Erica M. Finstad, PhD   Oregon Research Institute, Eugene, Oregon

Meir Flancbaum, PsyD   Tourette Syndrome Program, Graduate School of Applied and Professional Psychology at the Rutgers University, Piscataway, New Jersey; Behavior Therapy Associates, Somerset, New Jersey

Mark R. Floyd, PhD   North Texas Veterans Healthcare System, Bonham, Texas

Edna B. Foa, PhD   Center for the Treatment and Study of Anxiety, University of Pennsylvania, Philadelphia, Pennsylvania

Gina Fricke, LCSW   Peace and Power Counseling, Omaha, Nebraska

Mary A. Fristad, PhD   Departments of Psychiatry, Psychology, and Nutrition, Ohio State University, Columbus, Ohio

J. Ryan Fuller, PhD   New York Behavioral Health, New York, New York

Tara E. Galovski, PhD   Center for Trauma Recovery, Department of Psychology, University of Missouri at St. Louis, Missouri

Sheila Garos, PhD   Department of Psychology, Texas Tech University, Lubbock, Texas

Gary Geffken, PhD   Division of Medical Psychology, University of Florida, Gainesville, Florida

David Gilfillan, MA   Black Dog Institute, New South Wales, Australia.

Carly M. Goldstein, MA   Department of Psychology, Kent State University, Kent, Ohio

Ruth Golomb, MEd   Behavior Therapy Center of Greater Washington, Silver Spring, Maryland

Rick Goodwin, MSW   The Men's Project, Ottawa, Ontario, Canada

Elizabeth A. Gordon, PhD   Department of Psychology, Temple University, Philadelphia, Pennsylvania

Andrew M. Gottlieb, PhD   Cambridge Cognitive Behavioral Therapy Center, Palo Alto, California

Michael Gradisar, MPsych Clin/PhD   School of Psychology, Flinders University, Adelaide, Australia.

Rachel L. Grover, PhD   Department of Psychology, Loyola University of Maryland, Baltimore, Maryland

Amber Guzman, MA   Department of Clinical Psychology, American School of Professional Psychology at Argosy University, Washington, DC

John Hamel, LCSW   Independent Practice, San Rafael, California

Shane T. Harvey, PhD   School of Psychology, Massey University, Palmerston North, New Zealand

Kirsten A. Hawkins, MS   Department of Psychology, Florida State University, Tallahassee, Florida

Loran P. Hayes, BA   Department of Psychology, University of Utah, Salt Lake City, Utah

Richard G. Heimberg, PhD Department of Psychology, Temple University, Philadelphia, Pennsylvania

Craig E. Henderson Department of Psychology, Sam Houston State University, Huntsville, Texas

Michael B. Himle, PhD Department of Psychology, University of Utah, Salt Lake City, Utah

Laura Hlavaty, BA Department of Psychology, DePaul University, Chicago, Illinois

Clarissa S. Holmes, PhD Department of Psychology, Virginia Commonwealth University, Richmond, Virginia

Jan Paul Hook, EdD The Arlington Center, Arlington Heights, Illinois

Joshua N. Hook, PhD Department of Psychology, University of North Texas, Denton, Texas

Joel W. Hughes, PhD Department of Psychology, Kent State University, Kent, Ohio

Thomas Janssens, PhD Health Psychology, University of Leuven, Belgium

Leonard A. Jason, PhD Department of Psychology, DePaul University, Chicago, Illinois

Lisa Y. Kan, PhD Department of Psychology, Sam Houston State University, Huntsville, Texas

Howard Kassinove, PhD Department of Psychology, Hofstra University, Hempstead, New York

Christopher A. Kearney, PhD Department of Psychology, University of Nevada–Las Vegas, Nevada

Megan Kearns, PhD Department of Psychiatry and Behavioral Sciences, Emory University, Atlanta, Georgia

Allison C. Kelly, PhD Department of Psychology, University of Waterloo, Ontario, Canada

Jennifer F. Kelly, PhD Atlanta Center for Behavioral Medicine, Atlanta, Georgia

Justin A. Kenardy, PhD Centre of National Research on Disability and Rehabilitation Medicine, University of Queensland, Australia

Philip C. Kendall, Ph.D., ABPP Department of Psychology, Temple University, Philadelphia, Pennsylvania

Karen Kleiman, MSW The Postpartum Stress Center, Rosemont, Pennsylvania

Sander J. Kornblith, PhD Allegheny Mental Health Associates, Pittsburgh, Pennsylvania

Phyllis Kosminsky, PhD Independent Practice, Pleasantville, New York and Center for Hope, Darien, Connecticut

Ross Krawczyk, PhD Department of Psychology, College of Saint Rose, Albany, New York

Caleb W. Lack, PhD Department of Psychology, University of Central Oklahoma, Edmond, Oklahoma

Ian Lambie, PhD   Department of Psychology, University of Auckland, New Zealand

Marysia Lazinski, MASc   Department of Psychology, University of Victoria, British Columbia, Canada

Howard A. Liddle, EdD   Department of Epidemiology and Public Health, University of Miami Miller School of Medicine, Miami, Florida

Lisa Rachelle Riso Lilenfeld, PhD   Clinical Psychology Program, American School of Professional Psychology at Argosy University, Washington DC

Heidi M. Limbrunner, PsyD   SoutheastPsych, Charlotte, North Carolina

Wolfgang Linden, PhD   Department of Psychology, University of British Columbia, Canada

Barbara Mackinaw-Koons, PhD   Nationwide Children's Hospital Child Development Center, Columbus, Ohio

Heather A. MacPherson, MA   Departments of Psychiatry and Psychology, Ohio State University, Columbus, Ohio

Kathryn Maher, MS   Children's Hospital of Richmond at Virginia Commonwealth University, Richmond, Virginia

Emily Malcoun, PhD   Department of Psychiatry and Behavioral Sciences, Emory University, Atlanta, Georgia

Michele Many, LCSW   Department of Psychiatry, Louisiana State University Health Sciences Center–New Orleans, Louisiana

Joanna Marino, PhD   Potomac Behavioral Solutions, Arlington, Virginia

Nicole S. Marquinez, BA   Department of Psychology, University of South Florida, Tampa, Florida

Lynne E. Matte, PhD   Ferkauf Graduate School of Psychology, Yeshiva University, Bronx, New York

Alexis K. Matusiewicz, MS   Center for Addictions and Personality Research, University of Maryland at College Park, Maryland

Andrea Barmish Mazza, PhD   Center for Anxiety & OCD, Deerfield, Illinois

Joseph Patrick Hill McNamara, PhD   Division of Medical Psychology, University of Florida, Tallahassee, Florida

Robyn S. Mehlenbeck, PhD   Department of Psychology, George Mason University, Fairfax, Virginia

Alicia E. Meuret, PhD   Department of Psychology, Southern Methodist University, Dallas, Texas

Stephanie Mihalas, PhD NCSP   Independent Practice, Los Angeles, and Department of Psychiatry and Biobehavioral Sciences, David Geffen School of Medicine at UCLA, California

Louis A. Moffett, PhD   Palo Alto University, Palo Alto, California

Christine Molnar, PhD   Mindful Exposure Therapy for Anxiety and Psychological Wellness Center, Abington, Pennsylvania

Rudolf H. Moos, PhD   Center for Health Care Evaluation, VA Palo Alto Health Care System, Menlo Park, California

Arezou Mortazavi, MEd   Department of Psychology, Pennsylvania State University, University Park, Pennsylvania

Suzanne Mouton-Odum, PhD   Clinical Assistant Professor, Baylor College of Medicine, Department of Psychiatry and Behavioral Sciences, Houston, Texas

Greg Murray, PhD   Department of Psychological Sciences and Statistics, Swinburne University of Technology, Melbourne, Australia

Amie C. Myrick, MS   Department of Psychology, Towson University, Towson, Maryland

Douglas W. Nangle, PhD   Department of Psychology, University of Maine, Orono, Maine

Robert A. Neimeyer, PhD   Department of Psychology, University of Memphis, Memphis, Tennessee

Michelle G. Newman, PhD   Department of Psychology, Pennsylvania State University, University Park, Pennsylvania

Lindsey W. North, MA   Department of Psychology, Sam Houston State University, Huntsville, Texas

Michael W. O'Hara, PhD   Department of Psychology, University of Iowa, Iowa City, Iowa

Akiko Okifuji, PhD   Department of Anesthesiology, University of Utah, Salt Lake City, Utah

Mark E. Olver, PhD   Department of Psychology, University of Saskatchewan, Saskatoon, Canada

Lynne S. Padgett, PhD   Division of Cancer Control and Population Sciences, National Cancer Institute, Bethesda, Maryland

David J. Palmiter, Jr., PhD, ABPP   Marywood University, Independent Practice and Department of Psychology, University, Scranton, Pennsylvania

Lindsay Pate, PhD   Department of Psychiatry and Behavioral Sciences, Emory University School of Medicine, Atlanta, Georgia

Michael A. Perelman, PhD   Clinical Professor of Psychiatry, Reproductive Medicine and Urology, Weill Medical College, Cornell University, New York, New York

Marissa N. Petersen-Coleman, PsyD   Department of Psychiatry and Behavioral Sciences, Emory University School of Medicine, Atlanta, Georgia

Steven I. Pfeiffer, PhD   Department of Educational Psychology and Learning Systems, Florida State University, Tallahassee, Florida

Linda J. Pfiffner, PhD   Department of Psychiatry, University of California, San Francisco, California

Priscilla W. Powell, PhD   Department of Psychology, Virginia Commonwealth University, Richmond, Virginia

Andrew Presnell, MA   Department of Psychology, University of Alabama, Tuscaloosa, Alabama

J. Russell Ramsay, PhD   Department of Psychiatry, Perelman School of Medicine, University of Pennsylvania Philadelphia, Pennsylvania

Isabel Randell, BS   Department of Psychology, University of Auckland, New Zealand

Rotem Regev, MSc   Department of Psychology, University of Victoria, British Columbia, Canada

Adam Reid, MS   Division of Medical Psychology, University of Florida, Gainesville, Florida

Rory C. Reid, PhD   Department of Psychiatry and Biobehavioral Sciences University of California, Los Angeles, California

Patricia A. Resick, PhD   Women's Health Sciences Division of the National Center for PTSD, VA Boston Healthcare System, and Boston University School of Medicine, Boston, Massachusetts

Lawrence P. Riso, PhD   Department of Clinical Psychology, American School of Professional Psychology at Argosy University, Washington, DC

Thomas Ritz, PhD   Department of Psychology, Southern Methodist University, Dallas, Texas

Katerina Rnic, BA   Department of Psychology, University of Western Ontario, Canada

Lori Rockmore, PsyD   Graduate School of Applied and Professional Psychology, Rutgers University, Piscataway, New Jersey; Positive Developments, Millburn, New Jersey

Kelly J. Rohan, PhD   Department of Psychology, University of Vermont, Burlington, Vermont

Elisa Romano, PhD   School of Psychology, University of Ottawa, Ontario, Canada

Mary Rooney, PhD   Psychiatry Department, University of California, San Francisco, California

Barbara Olasov Rothbaum, PhD   Department of Psychiatry and Behavioral Sciences, Emory University, Atlanta, Georgia

Linda Sapadin, PhD   Independent Practice, Valley Steam, New York

Michael Scherer, PhD   Center for Sleep Medicine, Chicago, Illinois

Cara Schmid, PsyD   Potomac Behavioral Solutions, Arlington, Virginia

Lori Schwartz, PhD, CST   Independent Practice, Kansas City, Missouri

Forrest Scogin, PhD   Department of Psychology, University of Alabama, Tuscaloosa, Alabama

Golan Shahar, PhD   Department of Clinical-Health Psychology, Ben-Gurion University of the Negev, Israel

Raegan B. Smith, PhD   Child Development and Rehabilitation Center, Oregon Health and Science University, Eugene, Oregon

Douglas K. Snyder, PhD   Department of Psychology, Texas A&M University, College Station, Texas

Melissa Spear, BA   Department of Psychology, University of Nevada–Las Vegas, Nevada

Joel G. Sprunger, MS   Department of Psychological Sciences, Purdue University, West Lafayette, Indiana

Gail Steketee, PhD   School of Social Work, Boston University, Boston, Massachusetts

Phillip Stepka, PhD   Department of Psychiatry, Louisiana State University Health Sciences Center–New Orleans, Louisiana

Eric A. Storch, PhD   Departments of Pediatrics and Psychiatry, University of South Florida, Tampa, Florida

Donald S. Strassberg, PhD   Department of Psychology, University of Utah, Salt Lake City, Utah

Denise M. Styer, PsyD   Alexian Brothers Behavioral Health Hospital, Hoffman Estates, Illinois

Libby Tannenbaum, PhD   Virtually Better, Decatur, Georgia

Anthony F. Tasso, PhD   Department of Psychology and Counseling, Fairleigh Dickinson University, Madison, New Jersey

Daniel J. Taylor, PhD   Department of Psychology, University of North Texas, Denton, Texas

Joanne E. Taylor, PhD   School of Psychology, Massey University, Palmerston North, New Zealand

Shane A. Thomas, PhD   Professor of Primary Health Care Research, Monash University, Melbourne, Australia

J. Kevin Thompson   Department of Psychology, University of South Florida, Tampa, Florida

Christine Timko, PhD   Center for Health Care Evaluation, VA Palo Alto Health Care System, Menlo Park, California

Samantha J. Toale, BS   Center for Character Strength Investment, Tucson, Arizona

Michael A. Tompkins, PhD   San Francisco Bay Area Center for Cognitive Therapy, Oakland, California

Michael J. Toohey, MA   Department of Psychology, Hofstra University, Hempstead, New York

Ari Tuckman, PsyD, MBA   Independent Practice, West Chester, Pennsylvania

Dennis C. Turk, PhD   Department of Anesthesiology and Pain Medicine, University of Washington, Seattle, Washington

Omer Van den Bergh, PhD   Health Psychology, University of Leuven, Belgium

Constance W. Van der Eb, PhD   Independent Practice, Chicago, Illinois

Patti van Eys, PhD   BlueCare Tennessee, Chattanooga, Tennessee

Wendy L. Ward, PhD   College of Medicine, University of Arkansas for Medical Sciences, Little Rocks, Arkansas

Jason J. Washburn, PhD   Department of Psychiatry and Behavioral Sciences, Northwestern University Feinberg School of Medicine, Chicago, Illinois, and Alexian Brothers Behavioral Health Hospital, Hoffman Estates, Illinois

Daniel N. Watter, EdD   Morris Psychological Group, P.A., Parsippany, New Jersey

Rick Weinberg, PhD   College of Behavioral and Community Sciences, University of South Florida, and Independent Practice, Tampa, Florida

Stephanie Y. Wells, BA   Women's Health Sciences Division of the National Center for PTSD, VA Boston Healthcare System, Boston, Massachusetts

Amy Wenzel, PhD   Independent Practice, Rosemont, Pennsylvania

Allison K. Wilkerson, MEd   Department of Psychology, University of North Texas, Denton, Texas

Stephen C. P. Wong, PhD   Institute of Mental Health, University of Nottingham, United Kingdom

Robert L. Woolfolk, PhD   Department of Psychology, Rutgers University, Piscataway, New Jersey

Megan Wrona, PhD   Department of Educational Psychology, University of Utah, Salt Lake City, Utah

Elna Yadin, PhD   Center for the Treatment and Study of Anxiety, University of Pennsylvania, Philadelphia, Pennsylvania

Aimee Yermish, PsyD   da Vinci Learning Center, Stow, Massachusetts; and Massachusetts School of Professional Psychology, Boston, Massachusetts

Matthew S. Yoder, PhD   Department of Psychiatry and Behavioral Science, Medical University of South Carolina and U.S. Department of Veterans Affairs, Mental Health Services, Charleston, South Carolina

Soo Jeong Youn, MS   Department of Psychology, Pennsylvania State University, University Park, Pennsylvania

Virgil Zeigler-Hill, PhD   Department of Psychology, Oakland University, Rochester, Michigan

Elana Zimand, PhD   Independent Practice, Atlanta, Georgia

Jeffrey Zimmerman, PhD   Independent Practice, Cheshire, Connecticut and White Plains, New York

David C. Zuroff, PhD   Department of Psychology, McGill University, Montreal, Canada

Foreword

The idea that psychological practice can be influenced by science is a relatively new phenomenon in psychology with origins in the middle of the last century. Yet enormous progress has been made in the field of clinical psychology in the last 60 years both in our understanding of psychopathology and in advances to research methodologies leading to the development of more efficacious psychological treatments for a variety of mental disorders (Barlow, Bullis, Comer, & Ametaj, 2013). Recently I had occasion to delve deeply into the history of clinical psychology (Barlow, 2011) and once again, came upon the pioneering efforts of David Shakow. As noted in that source, in 1969, Shakow, widely acclaimed as the father of modern clinical psychology, published a book of his collected papers entitled *Clinical Psychology as Science and Profession: A 40-Year Odyssey* (Shakow, 1969). At the time, Shakow had recently retired as the first chief of the Laboratory of Psychology in the Intramural Research Program of the National Institute of Mental Health (NIMH). Prior to that, his career included stints in both departments of psychiatry and psychology in major universities, as well as key leadership positions in prominent clinical settings, including Worcester State Hospital in Massachusetts.

Shakow is one of only two individuals to be honored by the American Psychological Association (APA) over the course of its history with two of its most prestigious awards: the Distinguished Scientific Contribution Award and the Distinguished Professional Contribution Award (Garmezy & Holtzman, 1984). Although he made enormous contributions to our research effort, much of it in the area of schizophrenia, it was Shakow's conceptualization of the role of modern-day clinical psychology that remains his most enduring legacy. He was an early president of the Division (now the Society) of Clinical Psychology of the APA and chaired the very influential Committee on Training in Clinical Psychology that made its report in 1947 defining the Scientist-Practitioner Model of training, a model that was endorsed, broadened, and deepened at the iconic Boulder Conference in 1949 (Raimy, 1950).

Shakow's 40-year odyssey led him to conclude in 1969 that (1) science and practice should be integrated and related parts of training in both PhD programs and professional schools (increasingly true across all models of training [Barlow, 2011]), but (2) that the focus of science in clinical psychology training should be on clinically relevant themes. (In those years, most dissertations focused on basic research, often in animal laboratories.) (3) These training experiences should be firmly grounded in academic psychology, but should be fully integrated into front-line practice settings, with increased attention to organized methods for evaluating quality and competence. And (4) the field should be on the forefront of exploring new systems for delivering broad-based psychological services.

To achieve these goals, Shakow was a strong advocate of integrating clinical settings fully into doctoral clinical psychology programs. This arrangement was rare in those early years, since hardly any in-house training clinics existed, and sites for clinical practica were few and far between. And when they could be procured, psychologists were often limited to roles of administering routine standardized psychological testing. Nevertheless, Shakow, in 1976, stipulated again a suggestion he had been making for 20 years. "My suggestion is that the university (or professional school) and the field-center training activities be as completely integrated as possible. Integration does not mean sameness, which results in a loss of vigor that comes with having the same point of view. . . . The fundamental principle of the plan is that theory and practicum must be constantly associated and tied together, whether in the university or the field station, and that both types of activity—theory and practicum—start with the very beginning of the program. I would suggest as axiomatic: *the greater the degree of integration between theory and practice, and between university and field center, the more effective the program"* (Shakow, 1976, p. 556).

Now several generations have passed and those of us, including myself who were trained in that era are approaching the end of our careers in very different circumstances. Currently, we have a greater understanding of the nature of psychopathology and pathophysiology and as a result we have more precisely targeted treatments. For example, for panic disorder, the discovery of internal interoceptive triggers for fear responses facilitated the development of new psychological treatments targeting these somatic responses and the anxiety focused on them (Barlow & Craske, 2007); in this respect at least, it is clear that Shakow's vision is coming to fruition.

Another important development is that the evidence base of specific psychological procedures and interventions is more important than the theoretical origin grounded in schools of psychotherapy. Hence, while many evidence-based procedures are cognitive behavioral in origin, procedures and techniques from different approaches such as motivational interviewing derived from client centered Rogerian therapy have been found to contribute significantly to treatment (Arkowitz, Westra, Miller, & Rollnick, 2008) as have systems approaches and some psychodynamic concepts. It is likely that schools of psychotherapy will become an anachronism in years to come and theoretical approaches will blur in the face of these developments.

But many barriers remain to Shakow's vision. First, a significant number of patients do not respond adequately to current evidence-based treatments either psychological or drug. While any number of factors such as therapeutic engagement, therapist competence in treatment administration, patterns of comorbidity, and alliance issues have been implicated in less than adequate response to treatment, these factors are not clearly understood and have yet to be extensively investigated (Barlow, in press; Nathan & Gorman, 2007). Perhaps more importantly, dissemination and implementation of evidence-based psychological treatments, while successful in some highly centralized systems, has generally been slow and spotty compared to dissemination of drug treatments. To address these barriers we now have this exciting new volume conceived and edited by Lisa Grossman and Steve Walfish. The format, whereby the evidence for efficacy of psychological interventions for the problem in question is reviewed by an expert followed by a clinician presenting a case where these treatments were actually utilized, and the real-life problems one runs up against in the course of treatment is innovative enough. But then to repeat this for 65 different problems in a manageable and succinct format represents a true integration of science and practice in a way that will move us forward. Clinicians everywhere can become familiar with the evidence and see how these treatments are implemented and problems overcome. Clinical researchers can also note the problems encountered and loop back to investigate these issues in their research efforts in an attempt to further improve our interventions. In this manner will David Shakow's vision on the true integration of science and practice be more fully realized.

David H. Barlow, PhD, ABPP
Center for Anxiety and Related Disorders
Boston University

REFERENCES

Arkowitz, H., Westra, H. A., Miller, W. R., & Rollnick, S. (Eds.). (2008). *Motivational interviewing in the treatment of psychological disorders.* New York: Guilford Press.

Barlow, D. H. (Ed.). (In press). *Clinical handbook of psychological disorders: A step-by-step treatment guide.* New York, NY: Guilford Press.

Barlow, D. H. (2011). A prolegomenon to clinical psychology: Two 40-year odysseys. In D. H. Barlow (Ed.), *The Oxford handbook of clinical psychology* (pp. 3–20). New York, NY: Oxford University Press.

Barlow, D. H., Bullis, J. R., Comer, J. S., & Ametaj, A. A. (2013). Evidence-based psychological treatments: An update and a way forward. In S. Nolen-Hoeksema, T. D. Cannon, & T. Widiger (Eds.), *Annual review of clinical psychology* (Vol. 9, pp. 1–27). Palo Alto, CA: Annual Reviews.

Barlow, D. H., & Craske, M. G. (2007). *Mastery of your anxiety and panic: Workbook* (4th ed). New York, NY: Oxford University Press.

Garmezy, N., & Holzman, P. (1984). David Shakow (1901–1981). *American Psychologist, 39*(6), 698–699.

Raimy, V. C. (Ed.). (1950). *Training in clinical psychology (Boulder Conference).* New York: Prentice Hall.

Shakow, D. (1969). *Clinical psychology as science and profession: A 40-year odyssey.* Chicago: Aldine.

Shakow, D. (1976). What is clinical psychology? *American Psychologist, 31*(8), 553–560.

Acknowledgments

We would first like to thank the contributors to this book. Top flight researchers and high quality clinicians were willing to donate their time and expertise to be part of this project because they believed in the concept. Without their generosity and kindness, this book would not have been possible.

Second, we would like to thank Nancy Hale, Executive Editor at Springer Publishing Company, for seeing the value in a book like this and for her encouragement, patience, and support of our work.

Third, we would like to thank Linda Malnasi McCarter for initially helping to shape the concept for this book. We especially appreciate her idea of having chapters written by clinicians to complement chapters written by researchers. This enriched the volume.

Fourth, Steve Walfish would like to thank his good colleague and even better friend Lisa Grossman for working on this book with him. She has great conceptual skills, is beyond conscientious, is an excellent editor, and she knows how to make me laugh. These are all great skills to have in a collaborator.

Fifth, Lisa Grossman would like to thank Steve Walfish for agreeing to edit this exciting book with her. His experience, judgment, editorial skills and patience are unparalleled, but most importantly, his friendship is a true gift. She is extremely grateful that they traveled together on this incredible journey.

Introduction

There is a well-known split between academics and practicing clinicians. Academics complain that clinicians do not follow, or even care to read about, evidence-based practice (EBP). Practicing clinicians complain that academic research is so tightly controlled and narrow as to not generalize to the types of clients seen in every day practice.

Those who are more centrist about EBP are aware of the strengths and limitations of the quality and generalizability of research from the laboratory to the consulting room. Those in consulting rooms have an appreciation that research generated in clinical trials can guide interventions. As Kazdin (2008) notes, "research and practice are united in their commitment to providing the best psychological knowledge and methods to improve the quality of patient care" (p. 146).

This book is not going to put an end to the philosophical differences between researchers and clinicians. Rather, the purpose of this book is to show how research and practice are, in fact, interrelated and how neither can exist without the other.

THE RESEARCH–PRACTICE DEBATE

Beutler, Williams, Wakefield, and Entwistle (1995) suggest there is always a split between science and practice in whatever field you choose. They note that an article entitled, "The Dilemma of Scientific Knowledge Versus Clinical Management" was published in *The Journal of Prosthetic Dentistry*. One could easily see such a title appearing in the *Journal of Consulting and Clinical Psychology*, *Clinical Psychology: Science and Practice*, or *Professional Psychology: Research and Practice*. Beutler et al. note similar articles regarding the split between scientists and practitioners being published in journals in physics, chemistry, computer science, education, and construction.

In two other papers, Beutler (2009, 2011) points to both camps overstating their claims. In one paper titled, "What if Empirically Supported Psychotherapy Isn't 'Empirically Supported'?," Beutler points to the limitations of the clinical claims of researchers who insist that all treatment be empirically based. On the other hand, he also notes that clinicians may overstate the importance of the therapeutic relationship. Beutler reports that summaries of meta-analytic studies find that the therapeutic relationship accounts for less than 9% of the variance in treatment outcome. The research, according to Beutler, suggests that a 15% increase in outcome between patient–therapist pairs with good and poor relationships. While this is a significant percentage, Beutler notes that the therapeutic relationship is not the largest contributor to client improvement.

Kazdin (2008) summarizes concerns that have been debated between science and practice regarding evidence-based treatments. These include: (a) whether clinical trials in the laboratory generalize to actual clinical practice. He recognizes that clients in clinical trials may have been subject to special selection procedures and the process of enrolling in a clinical trial is different from clients seeking out treatment on their own; (b) the focus of clinical trials on eliminating symptoms as opposed to much of psychotherapy that focuses on the process of teaching coping skills to deal with the trials and tribulations of life; and (c) differing criteria for whether a treatment is indeed evidence based or empirically supported, including comparison groups, statistical methods used, outcome measures that are chosen, and whether results across studies are comparable.

On the other hand, Kazdin (2008) also summarizes concerns regarding clinical practice raised by scientists. These include (a) how clinical decision making is made as it applies to the individual client in the consulting room; (b) the problem of generalization from past clinical experience to the unique client sitting in the consulting room in the current moment; (c) the proliferation of new and untested treatments that may or may not be warranted; and (d) the lack of objective methods for assessing client outcome. If one does not measure treatment progress in a routine manner (Lambert, 2010), Kazdin notes that outcomes are then based on the impressions of the clinician, and these can easily be challenged. To corroborate Kazdin's assertion, Walfish, McAllister, O'Donnell, and Lambert (2012) found mental health professionals' self-assessment of their own skill level, as well as patient outcome data, to be subject to their self-assessment bias. For example, in this study, 25% of clinicians rated their own skill level to be at the 90th percentile or above when compared with their peers (with none "below average"). Clinicians not only tended to overestimate the rates of their clients' improvement, but also tended to underestimate the rates of their clients' deterioration based on the research literature.

However, Kazdin (2008) points out that some tension between research and practice may be a positive thing. He outlines a rapprochement that would focus research on patient care. According to Kazdin, in psychotherapy research, greater priority would be placed on identifying mechanisms of change, identifying moderators of change that would have an impact on clinical practice, and a greater acceptance of qualitative research. In clinical practice, this would include use of systematic measures to evaluate patient progress and allowing clinical work to contribute directly to the knowledge base.

In an early paper, Barlow (1981) discusses the split between researchers and practitioners. He noted an important role for clinicians in the research process and a methodology that would make clinical research more relevant for clinicians. He suggested that front-line clinicians could collect data on their interventions and then collaborate with a clinical research center for data analysis. These analyses could test the effectiveness of the clinical interventions and generate further hypotheses for study. More recently, Barlow (2010) outlines a collaborative methodology in which clinicians could more rapidly identify their patients who are psychologically deteriorating. In this methodology, clinicians could track progress of their patients during the course of treatment and share these data with a clinical research center. Data could be analyzed by the research center and clinicians could hypothesize potential mediator and moderator effects that contributed to the negative outcomes.

Wolfe (2012) presents an interesting two-chair dialog between his researcher side and his clinician side. It is instructive to see this internal dialog that takes place between a long-time National Institute of Mental Health researcher, who is also a private practice clinician. The polarities in his researcher and clinician sides are first presented. These are the traditional scientist–practitioner issues. This is then followed by a discussion regarding the issues that divide them, including conceptions of manualized therapies, the role of comorbid mental health diagnoses in research and treatment, the efficacy of randomized clinical trials (RCTs), and mechanisms of change. Finally, he suggests some solutions to the researcher–clinician dilemma that honors and values the perspective of both sides. These include both sides "recognizing the limitations of their knowledge base, that researchers need the wisdom of clinical experience, and therapists need the fruits of empirical research" (p. 106).

WHAT IS EBP ANYWAY?

The American Psychological Association (2012) approved a resolution recognizing the effectiveness of psychotherapy that stated, in part, "The general or average effects of psychotherapy are widely accepted to be significant and large" and resolved that:

> … as a healing practice and professional service, psychotherapy is effective and highly cost-effective. In controlled trials and in clinical practice, psychotherapy results in benefits that markedly exceed those experienced by individuals who need mental health services but do not receive psychotherapy. Consequently, psychotherapy should be included in the health care system as an established evidence-based practice.

So the science–practice debate is not whether psychotherapy is effective. Rather, the issue has been what constitutes effective psychotherapy? Goldfried (2010) argues that "what takes place in clinical trials does not fully reflect what happens in real-life practice" (p. 203). He further states:

> The APA Task Force has emphasized the central role that clinical expertise plays in implementing intervention procedures or principles of change. Thus, what has been openly acknowledged is what we have all known to be true, namely that when it comes to doing effective therapy, a competent clinician is also needed. (p. 3)

Goldfried warns that what we know to work in psychotherapy must be rooted in clinical observations, but also have empirical verification, and it is important for both the researcher and clinician to acknowledge the contribution that they make to each other.

According to Huppert, Fabbro, and Barlow (2006), treatment efficacy focuses on internal validity, or whether a treatment works in a controlled research setting. However, they note the importance in any discussion of practice to consider clinical utility, or effectiveness, which refers to the generalizability, feasibility, and usefulness of interventions in the local settings where they are offered to the public. Huppert et al. state specifically that EBP should be differentiated from "empirically supported treatments" (EST), which are only one part of EBP.

Goodheart, Kazdin, and Sternberg (2006) point out that the American Psychological Association concurred that evidence-based treatment encompasses more than EST. In 2005, they adopted a policy that stated, "Evidence-based practice in psychology (EBPP) is the integration of the best available research with clinical expertise in the context of patient characteristics, culture, values and preferences." (p. 1)

Bauer (2007) stated that not only are EBP and EST not synonymous, but that "EBP is a much broader concept that refers to knowledge and action in the three essential elements of patient encounters, including (a) the best evidence guiding a clinical decision (the best evidence domain), (b) the clinical expertise of the health care professional to diagnose and treat the patient's problems (the clinical expertise domain), and (c) the unique preferences, concerns, and expectations that the patient brings to the health care setting (the client domain)" (p. 686). According to Bauer, these three elements are often referred to as the three pillars of EBP. He believes that "the fundamental goal of the evidence-based practice movement is to effect a cultural change within health care whereby practitioners will make 'conscious, explicit and judicious' use of current best evidence in clinic practice with individual patients" (p. 685).

The difference between EST and evidence-based treatment (EBT) was also affirmed by Spring (2007) who, again, pointed out that EBP and EST are not the same, although both necessary to care. Spring views ESTs as the best approach for the typical patient presenting for treatment with a specific problem. She believes this is a component of evidence-based practice, but that "psychologists need additional skills to act as creators, synthesizers, and consumers of research evidence, who act within their scope of clinical expertise and engage patients in shared decision-making" (p. 611). Like Bauer (2007), she conceptualizes evidence-based practice as being a three-legged stool. She believes that evidence-based practice matters to improve quality of treatment and provide accountability for interventions delivered to patients. Spring also points to the need for clinicians to engage in lifelong learning as new research evidence may improve clinical practice that has been learned many years ago.

DIALOG, COLLABORATION, AND DISSEMINATION

Clearly, there is now much agreement that science and practice both add necessary components to evidence-based treatments. The next question, then, would be how these two groups can collaborate so that patients truly do obtain the best treatment available? To answer this question, decisions must be made about how scientists can best communicate their research findings to clinicians in manners clinicians can effectively utilize.

Hershenberg and Malik (2008) point to the need for researchers to engage clinicians in dialogs regarding improvement of clinical practice rather than "disseminating to them." They suggest that a dissemination style only perpetuates the "we versus them" split and increases polarization between the two groups. They advocate incorporating clinicians into the design of research studies, as well as in the dissemination phase of the clinical trial.

Similarly, in a presidential address to the Association for the Advancement of Behavior Therapy, Linda Sobell (1996) advises that if researchers want to have an impact on clinical practice, then they will have to do something other than "business as usual." She describes a successful treatment program designed collaboratively by both researchers and clinicians. In this way, they were able to integrate science and practice in developing a treatment protocol for a large sample of patients. Borrowing from a business model, Sobell points to the importance of researchers developing true partnerships with clinicians in the research, development, and dissemination phases of innovation in mental health treatments to help bridge the gap between scientists and practitioners.

Several studies have verified that clinicians typically do not see scientific research published in journals as their primary source of information to guide their clinical practice. Cohen, Sargent, and Sechrest (1986) found that for clinicians, discussions of clinical cases with colleagues were the most highly rated sources of information, followed by workshops on clinical practice and theoretical books on clinical practice. Interestingly, empirical research articles were seen as the least useful source of information to clinicians as they did not view published research as applicable to practice.

Stewart and Chambless (2007) found that private practice psychologists reported that they rely primarily on clinical experience to inform treatment decisions, although they also do consult the EST literature. The most highly rated sources used to increase therapy skills and effectiveness in their sample of private practitioners were past experiences with patients followed far behind by treatment materials informed by psychotherapy outcome research findings, treatment materials based on clinical case observations and theory, and, in contrast to the Cohen et al. (1986) study, discussions with colleagues. However, Stewart and Chambless found that when provided a research summary on an EST, private practitioners reported that they would more likely be in favor of an EST to treat a problem area, when compared to practitioners who did not receive such a research summary.

In a later study with a large sample of private practice psychologists, Stewart and Chambless (2010) examined the impact of willingness to adopt ESTs on the basis of the method of presentation. One portion of the sample read a research review, another portion read a case study, and the other portion received both. These researchers found the inclusion of case studies increased clinicians' interest in obtaining training in the EST.

Stewart, Strirman, and Chambless (2012) present an analysis of 25 interviews with practicing clinicians regarding treatment outcome research and ESTs. While they expressed an interest in the outcome studies, these clinicians were skeptical about the application of the research to their clinical practice and were fearful that they would be dictated to follow treatment manuals, especially by insurance payors. Clinicians were interested in ESTs if they could fit into their existing framework of treatment. These authors suggested that rather than researchers insisting that clinicians abandon what they are doing and follow ESTs, a better method would be "a foot in the door" approach. In this manner, Stewart et al. believe, researchers can help clinicians integrate key ingredients of ESTs into their existing work with clients.

Beutler et al(1995) cite one study which found that clinicians are open to reading about scientific findings, but not in academic journals. Clinicians prefer secondary sources usually written by nonscientists. Beutler et al. conclude that efforts to get clinicians to read academic journals ignore: (a) who clinicians are, (b) their valued sources of knowledge, and (c) the differences in roles of practitioners and scientists. Beutler et al. suggest that research journals may be inappropriate vehicles for guiding clinical practice as articles are written for other scientists. They compared researchers and clinicians regarding their preferred method of receiving information. Clinicians tend to favor professional newsletters as a method of communicating scientific findings. Researchers preferred national conferences. The authors point out that the avenues most preferred by one group was the least preferred by the other. Beutler et al. conclude that the role for researchers to impact clinical practice is not through clinicians reading more primary research articles, but rather for researchers to communicate through channels that clinicians value in their pursuit of knowledge.

Consistent with Beutler et al.'s (1995) findings, Norcross, Klonsky, and Tropiano (2008) conducted a Delphi poll (a survey using a "Panel of Experts" as participants) of independent practitioners and clinical scientists with the purpose of identifying reasons for the researcher–clinician gap and ways to narrow it. Norcross et al. found that both scientists and practitioners insufficiently learn from and engage with each other. Both clinicians and researchers had a consensus that it would be important to make research findings more accessible and relevant for clinicians, and for presenting research findings in outlets that clinicians find more applicable than traditional research journals.

EVIDENCE-BASED TRAINING BEGINS IN GRADUATE SCHOOL

Bauer (2007) notes that while students need practical training in a variety of clinical methods, he feels that one key question to answer is "whether the goal of graduate education is to train students to competency in a critical number of ESTs or whether the goal is to train them in broader principles of evidence-based practice that will enable them to easily adapt to novel demands for new competencies after attaining their PhD?" (p. 688). Hershenberg, Drabick, and Vivian (2012) provide suggestions for both classroom and practicum experiences to optimize graduate student training in these three areas of EBP, (a) the best research evidence; (b) clinical expertise; and (c) patient values, preferences, characteristics, and circumstances. These authors believe that exposure to evidence-based training during graduate education may help to reduce the chasm between research and practice. And, a working draft of a Division 12 Task Force report (Beck et al., undated) noted, "Often mistaken as the same, evidence-based practice and training differ from manualized, empirically-supported treatment. Rather, evidence-based training is a general training approach designed to ensure that doctoral students become proficient in the skills, knowledge and behavior necessary for the study and practice of clinical psychology" (p. 9). A recent paper provides examples of evidence-based training during three phases of professional development, including predoctoral training, internship training, and training for practicing professionals (Leffler, Jackson, West, McCarty, & Atkins, 2013). The predoctoral training example describes coursework and practicum expectations, tools for training, how competency is documented, and the student perspective on the learning experience. At the predoctoral internship level, the example outlines principles of training (including integration of research and practice), providing effective interventions for underserved populations, and the importance of faculty mentoring. At the professional practice level, the intervention is described, the nature of the training discussed, and the results of the training approach are presented. The authors do not mean to be prescriptive of how evidence-based training should take place, but rather, with these examples, to highlight the possibilities for consideration for adoption in other similar settings.

THE PURPOSE OF THIS BOOK

We are both independent practitioners who value scholarly research. We are aware of the chasm between clinicians and researchers and don't believe that it has to exist, or at least be quite so wide. What is clear from the scientific literature is that researchers do not disseminate their research findings in a manner useful to clinicians who actually do desire to apply scientific research data in their practices. In this volume, we bring together researchers and clinicians to discuss their approaches to treating a clinical problem area. We believe this book will be of value to (a) serve as a sourcebook to guide clinical practice for clinicians who are faced with a myriad of client problem areas that present in their offices or clinics on a daily basis; (b) clinicians in training who need to appreciate both the scientific research that has been generated in a problem area, but also the art of clinical practice when dealing with clients; (c) researchers who are wanting to learn what it is like for clinicians to try and implement evidence-based strategies with clients seen by professional psychotherapists in their consulting rooms; and (d) researchers to learn what future research questions clinicians view as important.

We could have edited a volume of researchers summarizing evidence-based research in a variety of clinical problem areas. We could have edited a volume of clinicians presenting clinical case studies in a variety of clinical problem areas. We believe the strength of the current volume is in presenting both the research and clinician perspective side-by-side. Rather than being entrenched in polarities, we hope this volume will make for useful dialog (similar to the internal dialog that Wolfe [2012] presented between his research and clinician selves) between the two camps.

THE STRUCTURE OF THE BOOK

We identified 65 problem areas that are commonly seen in clinical practice. This was not an exhaustive list as there were problem areas that were not included only due to the practical space limitations of a book.

We then sought out researchers who were experts in the particular clinical problem area to summarize the evidence-based research in that area. To promote uniformity in presentation, we offered each researcher a template to follow that included:

1. Description of the clinical problem
2. Prevalence data
3. Cultural diversity issues
4. A summary of evidence-based treatments
5. Suggestions for future research.

Researchers were also asked to identify the three most important references for the interested reader.

We then requested that the researchers identify a psychotherapist who could describe what it is like to apply the evidence-based treatment in actual practice. We debated whether we should pick the psychotherapist or if we would allow the researcher to be involved in this decision-making process. Several researchers voiced concerns about clinician commentators possibly "tearing their work apart" by either explaining why the approach wouldn't work for them because the samples are not representative, comorbidities are not included, the manuals are too rigid, and so forth, or being ambushed because that is what clinical researchers hear all the time when they try to present this material to clinicians. Because we did not want researchers to contribute to the volume and then later feel they were set up for one of these "research bashing ambushes," we solicited their assistance in choosing the psychotherapist who would write the chapter. This is not unlike top journals that have authors suggest potential peer reviewers to evaluate their manuscript submission. Most researchers accepted this invitation. Some indicated they were not tied into the practice community and preferred that we choose a psychotherapist in our professional network. In some instances, the nominated psychotherapists could not contribute owing to other commitments. In these cases we also called on the expertise of our professional networks.

The clinicians were invited to participate because of their expertise in working in the particular clinical problem area. We wanted them to comment on the researchers' presentation of EBP and then to present a case example that applied the evidence-based research to clinical practice. In order to promote uniformity in presentation, we offered each clinician a template to follow that included:

1. Briefly comment on the evidence-based treatment(s) described in the Research Section
2. Describe a case example utilizing this EBT. This included four subheadings:
   a. *Subject information and brief history*
   b. *Presenting problem*
   c. *Treatment intervention and course*
   d. *Outcome*
3. Challenges in applying this evidence-based treatment
4. Cultural diversity issues
5. Suggestions for future research.

Clinicians were also asked to identify the three most important references for the interested reader.

LIMITATIONS OF THE BOOK

Every book has both strengths and limitations. While the readers of this book will form their own opinions, we thought that we would first point out what we considered to be some of the limitations of this volume.

First, as editors, we admit that we are not experts in 65 different clinical problem areas. Therefore, we were dependent upon researchers to present a fair and balanced summary of evidence-based findings and recommendations from the data. We are confident that by choosing high quality research experts to contribute to the volume, the findings presented reflect an accurate representation of the current data-based research. However, we are counting on the intellectual integrity of our contributors to make sure this was the case as we are not in a position to exert quality control over the content of so many clinical problem areas.

Second, because every book has page limitations, and we wanted to present the evidence-based research and the corresponding clinical case presentation in each problem area, all of the chapters are relatively brief. We asked both the researchers and psychotherapists to limit their chapters to four double-spaced typed pages. In some cases, this was accomplished and in others, we allowed for greater length. However, while we were able to accomplish breadth, this came at the sacrifice of depth. For example, in a book on evidence-based treatment, Kazdin (2007) contributed an entire chapter titled, "Psychosocial Treatments for Conduct Disorder in Children and Adolescents." While an excellent resource for both researchers and clinicians, the chapter is also 34 book pages in length. The present book serves as a "quick resource" for clinicians and clinicians in-training in the same vein as the *Ethics Desk Reference* (Barnett & Johnson, 2008) and *Clinical Neuropsychology: A Pocket Handbook for Assessment* (Snyder, Nussbaum, & Robins, 2006). Both researchers and clinicians are encouraged to pursue further knowledge in these areas by following up on the key references suggested by the authors.

Third, we asked clinicians to present a case study that demonstrated the application of evidence-based research in practice. We are aware that most clinical problems are more heterogeneous than homogeneous. For example, not all clients with panic disorder are the same, nor does the panic manifest itself in the same manner for all that carry this diagnosis. Similarly, not all rape victims presenting in clinician's offices or clinics are the same. Some may have recently experienced the assault, some months prior and delayed seeking treatment for a variety of reasons, and some may have experienced the assault many years prior and are seeking treatment for unresolved issues related to the incident. As such, the clinical case presentation should be considered a reflection of what it is like for clinicians to implement evidence-based treatment for the specific problem area and not considered representative of all treatment that should or could take place for clients with similar diagnoses.

Fourth, while not specifically a limitation, we anticipate that one possible criticism of the volume is that most authors cite evidence-based research that is not psychoanalytically oriented. We are aware of research indicating the efficacy of psychodynamic therapies (Shedler, 2010; Summers & Barber, 2009). For example, according to Knekt et al. (2011), short-term therapies, such as Solutions-Focused Therapy for depression or anxiety work faster, but long-term psychoanalysis may yield superior outcomes 5 years post short-term treatment. However, the vast majority of data-based research published on clinical problem areas is not analytically oriented, perhaps because psychoanalytic treatment has historically not been readily compatible with conventional research designs or randomized controlled studies. Recent data have also suggested the predominant theoretical orientation of the faculty in clinical and counseling psychology doctoral programs in the United States to be cognitive behavioral (Heatherington et al., 2012). Thus, the likelihood that other approaches may be empirically tested in clinical research is not strong. We highly encourage our analytic colleagues to continue to build evidence-based research that can show the efficacy of this significant psychological intervention so that future volumes of this book may include more of this work. For example, on one of our professional listservs, we have just learned of an RCT, soon to take place, testing a psychodynamically oriented psychotherapy approach for posttraumatic stress disorder related to childhood abuse. Further, the American Psychological Association has just approved a new journal entitled *Qualitative Psychology* that would focus on a wide variety of methodological approaches in qualitative psychological research other than randomized controlled studies that might encourage research in areas not readily adaptable to RCTs. Such studies are a welcome addition to the literature and the advancement of EBP.

A NOTE ABOUT REFERENCES

The reader will notice two things about the references for each of the chapters that are nontraditional. First, no citations are presented in the body of the chapters. Rather, authors incorporated material from previously published research into their chapters and placed the citations into the Reference sections. This presentation style follows that of Deitel, Gagner, Dixon, Himpens, and Madan (2010). Second, due to the enormous number of citations that are included in 65 research chapters as well as 65 clinician replies, a complete list of references is not included after each chapter. Rather, authors were asked to compile a reference list for each section, although optional for the clinicians.

OUR HOPE

In presenting the best of what researchers and clinicians have to offer side-by-side, we hope to increase dialog and reduce the size of the chasm between these two camps. Excellent clinicians care about high quality research. Excellent researchers want to have an impact on clinical practice. To continue to present the problem in a polarized manner only serves for each camp to dig in their heels and tell the other side why they are right and the other is wrong. In the following chapters, we hope that clinicians will increase their appreciation of the work of researchers and researchers will increase their appreciation of the work of clinicians. Both have similar goals: to help clients with their problems and to reduce the amount of their suffering. Without clinicians and researchers appreciating each other, these goals cannot be accomplished.

REFERENCES

American Psychological Association. (2012). Recognition of psychotherapy effectiveness. Retrieved from http://www.apa.org/about/policy/resolution-psychotherapy.aspx on February 13, 2013.

Barlow, D. (1981). On the relation of clinical research to clinical practice: Current issues, new directions. *Journal of Consulting and Clinical Psychology, 49*, 147–155.

Barlow, D. (2010). Negative effects from psychological treatments: A perspective. *American Psychologist, 65*, 13–20.

Barnett, J. E., & Johnson, W. B. (2008). *Ethics desk reference for psychologists*. Washington DC: American Psychological Association.

Bauer, R. (2007). Evidence-based practice in psychology: Implications for research and research training. *Journal of Clinical Psychology, 63*, 685–694.

Beck, J. G., Castonguay, L., Chronis-Tuscano, A., Klonsky, E. D., McGinn, L., & Youngstrom, E. (undated). *Principles for training in evidence based psychology: Suggestions and models for the graduate curriculum. APA Division 12.*

Beutler, L. (2009). Making science matter in clinical practice: Redefining psychotherapy. *Clinical Psychology: Science and Practice, 16*, 301–317.

Beutler, L. (2010). What if empirically supported psychotherapy isn't "empirically supported"? *The Independent Practitioner, 30*, 71–75.

Beutler, L., Williams, R., Wakefield, P., & Entwistle, S. (1995). Bridging scientist and practitioner perspectives in clinical psychology. *American Psychologist, 50*, 984–994.

Cohen, L., Sargent, M., & Sechrest, L. (1986) Use of psychotherapy research by professional psychologists. *American Psychologist, 41*, 198–206.

Deitel, M., Gagner, M., Dixon, J., Himpens, J., & Madan, A. (2010). *Handbook of obesity surgery: Current concepts and therapy of morbid obesity and related disorder, 2010.* Toronto, Canada: FD-Communications.

Goldfried, M. (2010). What constitutes "evidence" in evidence-based practice? *The Clinical Psychologist, 64*, 1–4.

Goodheart, C. D., Kazdin, A. E. & Sternberg, R .J. (2006). *Evidence-based psychotherapy: Where practice and research meet.* Washington, DC: American Psychological Association.

Heatherington, L., Messer, S., Angus, L., Strauman, T., Friedlander, M., & Kolden, G. (2013). The narrowing of theoretical orientations in clinical psychology doctoral training. *Clinical Psychology: Science and Practice, 19*, 362–374.

Hershenberg, R., Drabick, D., & Vivian, D. (2012). An opportunity to bridge the gap between clinical research and clinical practice: Implications for clinical training. *Psychotherapy, 49*, 123–134.

Hershenberg, R., & Malik, J. (2008). Graduate student's view of evidence-based treatments. *The Clinical Psychologist, 61*, 3–6.

Huppert, J., Fabbro, A., & Barlow, D. (2006). Evidence-based practice and psychological treatments. In C. Goodheart, A. Kazdin, & R. Sternberg (Eds.), *Evidence-based psychotherapy: Where practice and research meet* (pp. 131–152). American Psychological Association: Washington DC.

Kazdin, A. (2007). Psychosocial treatments for conduct disorder in children and adolescents. In P. Nathan & J. Gorman (Eds.), *A guide to treatments that work* (pp. 71–104). New York, NY: Oxford University Press.

Kazdin, A. (2008). Evidence-based treatment and practice: New opportunities to bridge clinical research and practice, enhance the knowledge base and improve patient care. *American Psychologist, 63*, 146–159.

Knekt, P., Lindfors, O., Renlund, C., Sares-Jäske, L., Laaksonen, M. A., & Virtala, E. (2011). Use of auxiliary psychiatric treatment during a 5-year follow-up among patients receiving short- or long-term psychotherapy. *Journal of Affective Disorders, 135,* 221–230.

Lambert, M. (2010). Prevention of treatment failure: *The use of measuring, monitoring, and feedback in clinical practice.* Washington D.C.: American Psychological Association.

Leffler, J., Jackson, Y., West, A., McCarty, C., & Atkins, M. (2013). Training in evidence-based practice across the professional continuum. *Professional Psychology: Research and Practice, 44,* 20–28.

Norcross, J., Klonsky, E. D., & Tropiano, H. (2008). The research-practice gap: Clinical scientists and independent practitioners speak. *The Clinical Psychologist, 61,* 14–17.

Shedler, J. (2010). The efficacy of psychodynamic psychotherapy. *American Psychologist, 65,* 98–109.

Snyder, P., Nussbaum, P., & Robins, D. (2006). *Clinical neuropsychology: A pocket handbook for assessment.* Washington DC: American Psychological Association.

Sobell, L. C. (1996). Bridging the gaps between scientists and practitioners: The challenge before us. *Behavior Therapy, 27,* 297–320.

Spring, B. (2007). Evidence-based practice in clinical psychology: What it is, why it matters, and what you need to know. *Journal of Clinical Psychology, 63,* 611–631.

Stewart, R., & Chambless, R. (2007). Does psychotherapy research inform treatment decisions in private practice. *Journal of Clinical Psychology, 63,* 267–281.

Stewart, R., & Chambless, R. (2010). Interesting practitioners in training in empirically supported treatments: Research reviews versus case studies. *Journal of Clinical Psychology, 66,* 73–95.

Stewart, R., Strirman, S., & Chambless, D. (2012). A qualitative investigation of practicing psychologists' attitudes toward research-informed practice: Implications for dissemination strategies. *Professional Psychology: Research and Practice, 43,* 100–109.

Summers, R., & Barber, J. (2009). *Psychodynamic therapy: A guide to evidence-based practice.* New York, NY: Guilford Books.

Walfish, S., McAllister, B., O'Donnell, P., & Lambert, M. J. (2012). An investigation of self-assessment bias in mental health providers. *Psychological Reports, 110,* 639–644.

Wolfe, B. (2012). Healing the split between the researcher and the practitioner: Let's start with me. *Psychotherapy, 49,* 101–108.

SECTION I: CHILDREN AND ADOLESCENTS

CHAPTER 1

Adjustment to Divorce for Children

Marion Ehrenberg, Rotem Regev, and Marysia Lazinski

CLINICAL PROBLEM

In the 1950s when divorce was a rare event, experiencing a family break-up was considered a form of "family psychopathology" and inevitably damaging to children. Decades of empirical evidence inform the current consensus that parental separation, divorce, and remarriage are a dynamic interaction of family events and individual reactions entailing both risks—including underachievement, internalizing and externalizing problems, and peer disturbance—and opportunities for children's adjustment, such as release from family conflict, enhanced coping capacities, and potentially closer bonds among siblings.

Meta-analyses have demonstrated that negative outcomes stemming from family transitions are relatively small in their effect sizes and not universal; individual factors, such as the child's developmental phase and temperament, and contextual variants, including the level of cooperation and conflict between the divorcing parents, modify the extent to which these risks and resiliencies become apparent. Longitudinal investigations have unraveled the importance of considering children's immediate adjustment to their parents' divorce. These studies also alert us to "sleeper effects" that may not be immediately apparent during childhood but can surface during the teenage years, and to anticipate long-term adjustment into young adulthood when romantic relationships can be affected.

PREVALENCE

The North American divorce rate, particularly involving families with children, rose drastically between 1965 and 1979 and continues to increase gradually. In 2007 alone, 3.6% of legal marriages ended in divorce. The average length of a first marriage is only 8 years, and certain periods during marriages carry higher risk for separation and divorce, with a peak of a 33% chance of dissolution after the 10th year of marriage. More difficult to track systematically are the union and dissolution of common law relationships, although from a child's perspective the psychological consequences of family break-ups are considered to be equivalent regardless of whether their parents were legally married. It is estimated that close to 50% of children born in the early 2000s will experience their parents' separation before reaching adulthood and 35% to 45% will also experience their custodial parent's remarriage. As most divorced parents remarry, and the divorce rate in second marriages is higher than in first marriages, many children live through a series of marital transitions and household rearrangements. Adults with divorced parents are more likely to divorce themselves, but the mechanisms to explain this increased risk remain unclear.

CULTURAL DIVERSITY ISSUES

Internationally, the United States, United Kingdom, and Canada have the highest divorce rates; 4.6, 3.1, and 2.6 per 1,000 marriages per year, respectively. Likely reflecting a myriad of economic, legal, religious, and cultural factors of European countries studied, Greece, Spain, and Italy showed the lowest divorce rates, ranging from 0.5% to 0.7%. Immigrant families in North America bring a diversity of beliefs to their understanding of family conflict and divorce, privacy, and accessing support. However, the study of cultural factors in divorce remains in its infancy such that openness and sensitivity to diverse cultural fabrics will be essential to our understanding of children's adjustment to family stresses and changes.

EVIDENCE-BASED TREATMENTS

Many studies articulate the economic, academic, and psychosocial risks for children experiencing family transitions. Best practices orient toward preventing or minimizing these known risks and facilitating a positive adjustment environment. Parental divorce often entails economic disadvantage with 28% of single mothers and 11% of single fathers living below the poverty line in comparison with 8% of two-parent families. Legal aid, child support and maintenance interventions, and public policy to subsidize these families and their housing are most likely to offset these economic losses. Academic decline and underachievement are additional risk factors for children, often exacerbated by a need to move and change schools, all at a time when newly single parents are distressed and less able to supervise studies and school attendance. Informed teachers and school counselors can play valuable roles in providing additional supports and sensitivity to children to attenuate academic decline and its negative impact on self-confidence. Following parental separation, children experience more life stress, anxiety and depression, and express more avoidant coping and antisocial behavior, than children raised in intact families. Without access to effective family and other supports, more chronic forms of externalizing and internalizing disorders may emerge.

Numerous studies point to exposure to interparental conflict and triangulation of children into their divorcing parents' disagreements as key risk factors for compromising children's adjustment. Although parental separation can afford release from a high conflict family environment, if parents are unable to settle their differences, children can become "caught in the middle," parentified, and develop problems with self-esteem, depression, and anxiety. Similarly, youth who perceive a "pull" to take sides or mediate their divorcing parents' conflicts tend to express dissatisfaction with one or both parents, act out, and show early adolescent problem behaviors. Approximately one quarter of divorces are characterized as medium- to high-conflict, sometimes with many years of legal custody disputes; the children in these families show by far the worst adjustment outcomes. Children whose divorced parents coparent cooperatively and who encourage close relationships with both parents show the most favorable outcomes and are virtually indistinguishable from children raised within intact families.

Research on individual, familial, and extrafamilial risk and protective factors has successfully been translated into divorce intervention objectives. For example,

The Children of Divorce Intervention Program (CODIP) and similar programs are comprised of psychoeducational and supportive groups for children to learn about typical feelings, coping, and asserting oneself against triangulation. These groups are typically comprised of 8 to 10 similarly aged children who are invited to share their feelings and perceptions using developmentally appropriate methods (e.g., speaking, drawing, cartoons, filling in sentence blanks) to normalize and support a wide range of typical reactions. As the group progresses, usually for 6 to 10 sessions, children are also taught relaxation strategies to handle anxiety and other negative feelings, have opportunities to role play self-assertion when faced with parents' inappropriate requests, and are generally exposed to a wide range of coping strategies to manage family changes. These children's groups are coupled with parent groups that educate about children's reactions, stress the importance of reducing interparental conflict, and teach effective coping strategies. For example, parents will be prepared to respond positively when their children assert themselves about not feeling comfortable taking a message from one parent to the other parent. As more chronic adult reactions to the loss of a marriage (e.g., in the forms of clinical depression and substance misuse) can compromise parenting, psychological treatment for individual parents may be needed. Relationships with supportive grandparents show promise for reducing internalizing and externalizing problems among children with divorced parents. Legally based family interventions like mediation for low- to medium-conflict divorcing parents, and custody and access evaluations for high-conflict families, are methods to address entrenched negative patterns that are particularly harmful to children

FUTURE RESEARCH

In addition to studies of cultural factors influencing the dynamics of family transitions and acceptable interventions, research on both the short-term and long-term outcomes of divorce interventions for children and families are needed to further shape best practices standards. Furthermore, while research has focused heavily on risk factors and children's coping with medium- to high-conflict divorces, much is still to be learned from children and low-conflict parents who navigate family transitions in particularly healthful ways. Naturally occurring coping strategies may inform psychoeducation and healthy practices with families who are struggling with divorce and family transitions.

KEY REFERENCES

Goodman, M., Bonds, D., Sandler, I., & Braver, S. (2004). Parent psychoeducation programs and reducing the negative effects of interparental conflict following divorce. *Family Court Review, 42*, 263–279.

Lansford, J. E. (2009). Parental divorce and children's adjustment. *Perspectives on Psychological Science, 4*, 140–152.

Wallerstein, J. S., Lewis, J. M., & Blakeslee, S. (2000). *The unexpected legacy of divorce: A 25 year landmark study.* New York, NY: Hyperion.

Adjustment to Divorce for Children

Lauren J. Behrman and Jeffrey Zimmerman

COMMENT ON THE EVIDENCE-BASED RECOMMENDATIONS

Ehrenberg, Regev, and Lazinski highlight the detrimental effects of ongoing parental conflict on children's adjustment to parental divorce. They note that numerous studies point to "exposure to inter-parental conflict and triangulation of children into their divorcing parents' disagreements as key risk factors for compromising children's adjustment." These authors describe an evidence-based intervention model where children meet with their peers, and parents meet in a group with other parents where they are educated about children's reactions, the stress of interparental conflict, and how to reduce such conflict and build effective coping strategies. The goals for the parents are to help them coparent cooperatively.

Unfortunately, many parents in high conflict need an even more intensive and customized approach to help them develop effective co-parenting skills. They often have difficulty recognizing how the concepts taught actually apply to them and their unique family situation. Parents during and after a high-conflict divorce often respond better to an intensive tutoring approach rather than a classroom model. In this approach, we use the same evidence-based principles to focus with each dyad of divorcing parents. The parents are seen together to help them build more effective communication and decision-making skills and to frame their parental relationship as their primary role, rather than that of "ex-spouses."

We teach parents to reinvent their postdivorce parenting relationships to approximate functional business relationships. By putting structures and ground rules in place for communication, problem solving, and conflict resolution, parents begin to experience the satisfaction of becoming successful, functional coparents while protecting their children from conflict. They begin to function more as a team, in business together, to raise their children. Unlike psychotherapy, the co-parenting counselor does not seek to have the parents engage in emotional disclosure related to their feelings about one another. In addition, there is no attempt to diagnose or treat a psychiatric disorder in either parent, if one is present. Instead, the focus is almost exclusively on directly teaching the parents to focus on communicating effectively about the children, identifying problems to be addressed, and coming to closure on parenting decisions.

CASE EXAMPLE

Subject Information and Brief History

Ron and Pam were a young couple in their early 40s with two sons Jake, age 12, and David, age 9. Pam was a stay-at-home mom, and Ron was a high-powered, successful executive in a fast-paced business arena.

Presenting Problem

Ron had an extramarital affair. When Pam discovered Ron's infidelity, their marriage irretrievably broke down. Pam went through a serious depression. Their children began to show signs of anxiety, aggression, and academic failure. Their high-conflict divorce was bitterly fought out in the courts over a 3-year period, ending up in a trial. As part of these proceedings the judge ordered a parenting plan that included participation in "high conflict coparent counseling." Because the work was court ordered, these parents initially came to the work involuntarily.

Treatment Intervention and Course

From the outset of the first session, these parents were taught to begin to work as a team. For example, when Pam was not able to drive to an appointment, Ron was advised to pick her up without hostility and bring her to the meeting. Early sessions focused on detailing the devastation that their children had suffered, and what Ron and Pam could do to stop the emotional hemorrhaging in order to allow healing to occur. The parents were coached to have a joint meeting with their children to explain that the "war" was over, and to discuss how they would be moving forward as parents, supporting each other's disciplinary efforts and academic priorities. They also decided together to choose a new psychotherapist for the children, as the first clinician had been tainted from being objective when he testified against the mother during the trial. Every effort was made to help these parents avoid hostile and defensive communication, both in and outside the office. The primary focus was on helping them attend to their joint parenting responsibility (rather than their issues with one another). This was accomplished by using a very active engaging approach that was heavily weighted in coaching the interactions and educating the parents about their communication choices and the likely impact of parental conflict on the children. In essence, the focus is on both content and process with a heavier emphasis on making sure the communication process in the office is as healthy as possible (even above dealing with the content of a particular parenting issue).

These parents worked diligently in weekly meetings for close to a year, and accomplished a great deal. They addressed the children's learning disabilities, made educational decisions, and planned a bar mitzvah for their oldest son. When viewing the photographs of the event, it was clear that this family had successfully managed its transition through the divorce and was no longer at war.

Outcome

These parents went on to need less frequent intervention, and eventually agreed after 18 months that they were ready to terminate their period of active intervention. They resumed professional contact 4 years later to deal with a single parental decision about private school for their youngest son, and quickly reached a solution. Follow-up 6 years after the inception of intervention indicated that they had completely stabilized. The children were doing well. Ron and Pam had each moved on in their own lives and continued to work effectively together on behalf of their children.

CHALLENGES IN APPLYING THE EVIDENCE-BASED APPROACH

High-conflict parents may have *DSM* Axis I and Axis II disorders. This requires sensitivity on the part of the clinician, an ability to make appropriate individual referrals for psychotherapy, if necessary, and to maintain good clinical boundaries and techniques to not get caught up in the conflict. It is essential to be able to simultaneously have effective working relationships with two people who are in intense conflict (coincidentally this is somewhat similar to the challenge faced by the child). This professional role requires partnering with other professionals, such as individual therapists for parent(s) and or child, educators, and school personnel, pediatricians, and so forth and the ability to tolerate a great deal of conflict. Clinicians can easily experience vicarious trauma or "second hand shock." This phenomenon, as described by Izzo and Carpel Miller, occurs when clinicians are exposed to and absorb others' trauma while controlling their own emotional response. This process can reportedly gradually alter the structure of the brain, negatively affect the mind, and can ultimately desensitize, numb, and cause a myriad of disturbances. It is essential that clinicians engage in self-care and supportive consultation from peers so as not to get burned out.

Ethically, there are challenges around professional roles and boundaries. In addition, one needs to be aware of and take proactive steps to deal with the possibility of being involved in the parents' litigation. For example, in our work with parents we inform them and counsel at the initial inquiry that we do not testify in court or provide records for the same purpose. At the first visit, parents sign an agreement that outlines this in detail and also states that what they say in the office is not to be used in subsequent litigation. This serves to better keep the process focused on parenting and not legal battles, or convincing the professional as to which parent is better or worse than the other.

It is important to carefully define "success" with each set of parents. During the first meeting, the authors and parents set goals for the work related to general co-parenting skills and specific to the children. Most parents progress at improving their co-parenting relationship, even if that is to different degrees. In some respects it is like learning the skill of playing a musical instrument. While most people can learn to play to some reasonable degree, some can excel in remarkable ways. In this work, it is perhaps best represented by a family in which the parents were literally fighting over basic household items (such as kitchen utensils) when beginning in co-parenting. They later reported that their young child said to them (after a school play where they sat together), "I'm so glad you guys are friends again."

One must be clear that as a mental health professional you are not functioning as a psychotherapist. However, you are functioning in a consulting role under your professional license and have the ethical and other responsibilities incumbent in that role. While there may be some question about the applicability of HIPAA (Health Insurance Portability and Accountability Act) as there is not a diagnosis or treatment of a mental condition being performed, the authors do give the appropriate HIPAA forms to the clients.

When the parents have profound difficulty interacting with some degree of appropriateness, recommendations are made for one or both to seek their own individual psychotherapy to help them focus on keeping their emotional response to the other parent from contaminating the co-parenting interaction(s). At times, contact is made (with appropriate releases in place) with the therapist(s) or a parent's attorney (or attorneys who are present for the children) to help constructively influence the parent to consider ending the "war" for the benefit of the children. Occasionally, the hostility is so intense that this intervention needs to be terminated. However, it is of interest to note that there are certain parents who discontinue at one point, only to return at a later date, apparently more "ready" to begin in earnest.

CULTURAL DIVERSITY ISSUES

In this role, we have worked with families from many different cultural backgrounds as well as LGBT families. There is a need for sensitivity to diverse cultural beliefs and values. This intervention is applicable to families from all cultures and backgrounds, when the clinician has an appreciation and awareness of diversity and can be sensitive to the parenting and role expectations related to each particular family.

FUTURE RESEARCH

Controlled longitudinal outcome studies are needed that examine matched groups of children whose parents underwent coparent counseling, and those who did not. Research on the use of this intervention with different cultural groups is also important to better understand whether there are ways to tailor the approach to increase efficacy. It would also be very useful to develop prediction or screening methodologies to identify which sets of parents are most likely to be responsive to co-parenting; especially as the history of prior conflict does not seem to be a useful predictor of success.

KEY REFERENCES

Baris, M. A., Garrity, C., Coates, C. A., Duvall, B. B., & Johnson, E. T. (2001). *Working with high-conflict families of divorce: A guide for professionals.* New York, NY: Jason Aronson, Inc.

Emery, R. E. (2011). *Renegotiating family relationships: Divorce, child custody, and mediation* (2nd ed.). New York, NY: The Guilford Press.

Thayer, E., & Zimmerman, J. (2001). *The co-parenting survival guide: Letting go of conflict after a difficult divorce.* Oakland, CA: New Harbinger Publications.

CHAPTER 2

Anger Management in Adolescents

Thomas M. Brunner and Samantha J. Toale

CLINICAL PROBLEM

Anger is a "psychological vital sign"; it is a fundamental emotional phenomenon like anxiety or depression, as Darwin recognized. Anger may be defined as a psychobiological state that varies in intensity from mild irritation to intense fury or rage, accompanied by arousal of the autonomic nervous system. Even though the experience and expression of anger have become dominant problems in society, anger has been largely ignored by the clinical world and conceptually oversimplified in the academic realm. One reason for this is researchers have given much more attention to phenomena like anxiety and depression.

While anger is common in youth because it can motivate appropriate goal-directed behavior (e.g., athletic competition), it can be especially intense in the developmental stage of adolescence owing to the convergence of psychological and biochemical characteristics which cultivate tendencies toward more intense emotions. Thus, it is essential to view any particular episode of adolescent anger from a developmental framework that helps us carefully determine to what degree an adolescent's anger may be healthy versus clinically impairing.

Clinical evaluations of anger most often involve interviews and self-report measures. Unfortunately, the vast majority of psychometrically valid screening instruments (whether self, parent, or teacher report) used with adolescents conceptualize anger as a unidimensional phenomenon where one score represents the level of anger. In contrast, there is increasing empirical and conceptual awareness of the complex nature of anger which is driving the use of assessment tools that capture the key clinical facets and dynamics that comprise the multidimensional nature of anger. Advanced clinical assessments of anger are recognizing this complexity as they formulate hypotheses which have to do with certain facets of anger (e.g., trait anger, suppressed anger, or anger control) that comprise an "anger profile."

A review of the literature reveals a growing consensus that there are particular conceptual distinctions that are essential characteristics of anger to understand. It is important to precisely assess these characteristics to produce a meaningful anger profile which will facilitate targeted treatment interventions. The following conceptual distinctions are best understood within an overall theoretical framework that conceptualizes anger as a process with three stages (i.e., experience, expression, and control): (a) state (momentary) anger versus trait (relatively stable) anger; (b) generalized anger (trait anger) versus anger set off by criticism or stress (reactive anger); and (c) suppressed (anger turned inward) versus externalized anger (anger expressed outward). It is also important to recognize what the goal of the anger display is (e.g., vengeance, winning a competition, etc.) to further understand its nature. When these characteristics are together assessed to produce an anger profile, one can begin to capture the adolescent's unique "anger style."

PREVALENCE

Definitive statements about the incidence, prevalence, or epidemiological patterns of anger problems in adolescents have been relatively scarce for many reasons, including the following: the diversity of culturally accepted ways in which anger manifests (e.g., toddler tantrums, competitively focused aggression, etc.), the lack of a *DSM* diagnosis that solely focuses on anger, and the low rate of reporting of anger-based behavior exhibited by youth. Given these realities, many researchers argue that the true magnitude of the anger-based problems are dramatically underestimated.

Several trends in anger-based violent behaviors among adolescents have been reported, suggesting that anger-based violent behaviors have become a serious problem in American society. For example, a U.S. Surgeon General Report found a very significant rise in the total number of school-related violent events with multiple victims. It is concerning to note that the mean age of those who commit violent acts has decreased as larger numbers of children and adolescents are committing violent crimes which seem to have anger-based elements.

CULTURAL DIVERSITY ISSUES

First and foremost, it must be pointed out that what may be considered a "normal" level of anger or aggression can vary according to a number of variables, including age, gender, culture, and situation. Contrary to what folklore or stereotypes might suggest, there are no consistently replicated empirical findings regarding patterns in differences between how girls and boys manifest anger. However, isolated studies have reported higher rates of physical aggression among males than their female peers. Similarly, a few studies have reported that as boys mature, they express anger outwardly less often. Boys and girls seem to be similar insofar as for both sexes, higher scores on scales assessing two facets of anger—trait anger and anger control—have been found to be correlated with depression, suicidal ideation and attempts, and lower mood. Very few studies have examined cross-cultural differences in anger manifestation in adolescents. One study compared style of anger expression between Mexican American and non-Hispanic Caucasian adolescents. This study reported significantly higher rates of all forms of anger-based aggression in the Caucasian males and females as compared to their Mexican American peer group, but this finding has not been replicated.

EVIDENCE-BASED TREATMENTS

It is essential to recognize that a wide range of psychopathology has been associated with anger-based behavior, including oppositional defiant disorder, attention deficit hyperactivity disorder, posttraumatic stress disorder, bipolar disorder, major depressive disorder, substance abuse, psychosis of various types, and personality disorders that may have roots in youth functioning. It is also critical to understand that because anger is a very noticeable problem, it often acts as an "alarm" that finally awakens adults to pay attention to not only the anger problem, but quieter problems like ADHD or anxiety which often co-occur with anger.

Anger is best treated through an approach that targets specific dimensions of anger because, as pointed out previously, anger is complex and multidimensional in nature. One must understand each adolescent's anger style before effective treatment can begin. For example, some adolescents express too much anger whereas others are bullied because they do not express enough anger when criticized or bullied (i.e., low trait anger reactivity). Other adolescents must be treated for too frequently suppressing anger (high trait anger-in) which can lead to a medical problem (e.g., irritable bowel syndrome), while others impulsively strike out at others (high trait anger-out).

Cognitive behavioral therapy (CBT) is the predominant form of therapy which has been investigated by researchers. CBT has been applied to individual and family therapy modalities. CBT has spawned numerous CBT-based offshoots, and one meta-analysis compared four CBT methods with different emphases: skill development, affective education, problem solving, and a more eclectic focus. Results indicate skills development and eclectic treatments are significantly more effective than affective education. The results further suggest that treatments that teach actual behaviors are more effective than treatments that attempt to modify internal cognitive processes believed to be related to targeted behaviors. Several meta-analytic studies showed that CBT-based protocols do significantly reduce the amount of anger experienced and/or the frequency of anger-based impulsivity. The CBT-based family therapy modality includes building skills in anger management, perspective taking, social problem solving, emotional awareness, relaxation training, and social skills enhancement. The goal is to help parents learn to reinforce appropriate adolescent behavior ("catch them being good") while having parents consistently respond to inappropriate behavior in a way that uses these occasions to build skills versus be narrowly punitive.

FUTURE RESEARCH

The next steps for youth researchers should include developing a clinical *DSM* diagnosis that helps those youth with isolated anger problems receive treatment, that is, identifying particular youth anger dynamics that are related to psychological and medical conditions, and building a more precise model of how anger manifests as children grow into adolescence and beyond. In addition, more attention must be paid to the role of anger in other common psychological problems as research already reveals anger is a hidden but under-assessed construct. There has been a paucity of research on suppressed or "hidden anger" that when finally expressed can be explosive and even lethal. For example, overly suppressed anger (even in the face of bullying) appears to be one characteristic of adolescent school shooters who commit mass murder. More research needs to be conducted to examine the anger dynamics of bullies (or cyberbullies) and those who are bullied. The lack of youth anger measures to guide treatment has allowed anger to be under-assessed and this must change, especially given the data that suggest we are living in an "Age of Anger."

KEY REFERENCES

Brunner, T. M., & Spielberger, C. D. (2009). *The State Trait Anger Expression Inventory, Second Edition, Child Adolescent (STAXI-C/A)*. Sarasota, FL: Psychological Assessment Resources.

Feindler, E. L. (2005). CBT and adolescent anger management. In *Encyclopedia of cognitive behavior therapy* (Vol. 8, pp. 11–14). Kluwer Academic Publishers.

Spielberger, C. D., Reheiser, E. C., Owen, A. E., & Sydeman, S. J. (2004). Measuring the psychological vital signs of anxiety, anger, depression, and curiosity in treatment planning and outcome assessment. In M. E. Maruish (Ed.), *The use of psychological tests for treatment planning and outcome assessment* (3rd ed., pp. 421–447). Hillsdale, NJ: Lawrence Erlbaum Associates.

Clinician Application

Anger Management in Adolescents

Gary Geffken and Adam Reid

COMMENT ON THE EVIDENCE-BASED RECOMMENDATIONS

Anger is a transdiagnostic phenomenon in that it often will be the reason adolescents are presenting for treatment, despite other co-occurring psychopathology (e.g., inattention, anxiety, depression). Fortunately, cognitive behavioral therapy (CBT) is effective in treating adolescent anger. As discussed in the Evidence-Based Treatment section, anger is heterogeneous in its clinical presentation (e.g., high trait anger-in, reactive anger-out). Thus, clinicians can easily become baffled when trying to use CBT to treat less common presentations of individuals with anger difficulties, such as those with anger-in forms of anger expression. In these cases, it is important for clinicians to have alternative treatment strategies to add with CBT to maximize clinical outcome. While lacking extensive research, we have found Assertiveness Training as an effective tool to help anger-in individuals properly vocalize their emotions in a healthy manner.

CASE EXAMPLE

Subject Information and Brief History

John was a 17-year-old Caucasian male who was employed as an auto-mechanic assistant and was a senior at a local high school. John was raised in a house where his parents were constantly fighting and he was often physically abused when his father was intoxicated.

Presenting Problem

John presented to our clinic, per his school counselor's recommendation, with a desire to develop ways to control his "ongoing rage problem." He had been fired twice in the past year owing to losing his temper and had never maintained a romantic relationship for more than a few weeks because he would often "frighten girls away," by losing his temper when he felt his girlfriends were being "too controlling." When John was asked to describe what kinds of things made him angry, he replied that "the best defense is a good offense," and elaborated that he became angry in situations where he felt threatened by authority figures, such as his boss and teachers. His anger response had generalized to any individual he viewed as being demanding or controlling, such as romantic partners.

Treatment Intervention and Course

John's presenting symptoms were conceptualized as a reactive, anger-out form of anger expression, in other words, he externalized his anger that was triggered specifically by authority figures. CBT was implemented on a weekly basis to treat John's anger problems. We followed a tailored version of Nelson and colleagues' anger treatment model. During the first session, John was introduced to CBT and was encouraged to conceptualize the thought-feeling-behavior triangle when discussing incidents of anger. The first session was spent discussing the impact of John's anger problems on his quality of life and functioning, as well as aiming to increase treatment motivation. At the end of the first session, John provided an example of losing his temper at work where his boss "exploded" when John forgot to tell his boss he was taking off the following week from work. John reacted by yelling and swearing at his boss about his unapproachable nature and over-reaction to John's mistake. This incident was used as a practice example throughout the remainder of treatment when John was challenged to discuss how to implement CBT techniques in a real-world situation.

John was challenged to achieve three goals in psychotherapy: (a) identify the root of his aggressive response to criticism from authority figures, (b) learn CBT techniques for reducing these outbursts, and (c) role-play situations where he could implement these CBT strategies. John was able to realize that he became defensive when criticized by authority figures because he assumed he would be "run over" if he didn't, as was the case with his father. John identified maladaptive cognitions causing him to become angry such as "jumping to conclusions" and "black-and-white thinking." Challenging his black-and-white thinking, he described a "gray area" when his boss yelled at him about needing to take off work. Specifically, John was able to identify that his boss was worried about losing revenue in John's absence rather than just yelling at him to be malicious. John also was taught several behavioral techniques, such as removing himself from the situation, deep breathing, and finding a healthy outlet to help him control his anger (e.g., exercise). Treatment was terminated when John described a situation at work where he controlled his anger by implementing these CBT strategies rather than losing his temper with his boss. At the same time, he expressed a desire to take time off to continue to practice the skills he learned.

Outcome

John was seen for a total of nine 50-minute CBT sessions. While no well-established assessments of his anger problems provide evidence of improvement, telephone follow-up confirmed that John went from multiple outbursts per month to none over a span of 4 months posttreatment. He also maintained employment and his relationship with his girlfriend he started dating over this period.

CHALLENGES IN APPLYING THE EVIDENCE-BASED APPROACH

John's case exemplifies the effectiveness of CBT, but also highlights some common barriers to treatment that must be maneuvered by clinicians. Motivational interviewing techniques were implemented during the first session when there was a need to increase motivation for treatment, a common obstacle when working with adolescents. Despite his ability to vocalize how to utilize cognitive strategies in-session, John displayed a problem described in the literature in that he was more successful at applying behavioral (e.g., physical removal from triggers, deep breathing) rather than cognitive strategies (e.g., maladaptive thought challenging) of CBT to reduce his anger outbursts. While it is beyond what is outlined in CBT, we found it critical for John to recognize why he was so reactive to any criticism from authority figures in order to increase his awareness and ability to proactively identify potential triggers. Thus, this treatment included several lengthy discussions of the etiology of John's anger outbursts.

CULTURAL DIVERSITY ISSUES

Cultural stereotypes suggest that adolescent anger is a primarily male problem. This is true when defining anger in terms of physical violence. However, adolescent expression of relational aggression (e.g., dating violence) presents in females more frequently. Thus, in a clinical setting, psychotherapists' assessment and treatment of how anger is expressed needs to be guided by an adolescent's gender. It has been our clinical experience that adolescent males are more likely to mitigate their anger through engagement in physical activity as an adaptive coping strategy and to use maladaptive substance abuse as an avoidant coping strategy. Alternatively, we've found females are more likely to employ talking with a friend as an adaptive coping strategy to deal with anger while gossiping is more likely to be used as a maladaptive social coping strategy. "Tunnel vision" can lead the clinician to miss important information regarding the etiology, underlying maintaining mechanisms, presentation, and manifestation of one's anger, subsequently leading to worse treatment outcome. It is important for clinicians to not be influenced by cultural stereotypes when working with adolescent anger. We see a need for additional research in ethnicity and other cultural variables to help clinicians understand how to best implement CBT to treat anger.

FUTURE RESEARCH

Future research will continue to investigate cultural variables in the expression of anger. More research is needed on strategies to help clinicians more effectively use CBT to treat anger in adolescent patients with comorbidities, such as major depressive disorder or oppositional-defiant disorder, which can hinder treatment effectiveness. Case studies and the eventual development of manualized treatments will help clinicians understand how to apply CBT to treat various presentations of adolescent anger.

KEY REFERENCES

Kipnis, A. (1999). *Angry young men: How parents, teachers, and counselors can help "bad boys" become good men.* San Francisco, CA: Jossey-Bass Publishers.

Nelson, W., Finch, A., & Ghee, A. (2006). Anger management with children and adolescents: Cognitive-behavioral therapy. In P. C. Kendall (Ed.), *Child and adolescent therapy: Cognitive-behavioral procedures* (3rd ed., pp. 114–168). New York, NY: Guilford Press.

Potegal, M., Stemmler, G., & Spielberger, C. (2010). *International handbook of anger.* New York, NY: Springer.

CHAPTER 3

Anxiety Disorders in Children

Colleen M. Cummings and Philip C. Kendall

CLINICAL PROBLEM

This chapter focuses on three types of pediatric anxiety disorders: generalized anxiety disorder (GAD), separation anxiety disorder (SAD), and social phobia (SP). Other childhood anxiety disorders, such as posttraumatic stress disorder (PTSD) and obsessive-compulsive disorder, are found to have important differences from GAD, SP, and SAD, suggesting that these disorders benefit from their own focused interventions. Youth with SAD often fear harm will come to either themselves or a caregiver, and may refuse to be away from the caregiver. SP is described as clinically significant anxiety triggered by social and/or performance situations, often leading to avoidance of these situations. Individuals with GAD experience pervasive worries that are difficult to control and often concern performance, family or peer relationships, physical health, or ruminations surrounding past or future events.

PREVALENCE

Anxiety disorders are common in childhood, with evidence indicating that prevalence rates in youth range from 10% to 20%. Further, anxious children experience multiple impairments, including difficulties in peer relationships, and poor academic achievement. Anxiety places children at risk for psychopathology in adulthood, including anxiety, depression, and substance use, as well as suicidal ideation and suicide attempts. Given the prevalence and interference caused by childhood anxiety disorders, research regarding efficacious treatments is warranted.

CULTURAL DIVERSITY ISSUES

Although anxious distress affects youth from a variety of cultural backgrounds, research indicates that inner-city African American children reported higher rates of anxiety sensitivity. In another study that controlled child living arrangements, European American and African American anxious youth were largely similar in terms of symptoms and diagnoses. Hispanic/Latino youth may be more likely to present with somatic symptoms of anxiety, whereas Asian American youth may exhibit somatic symptoms as early signs of anxiety. Lower levels of acculturation toward American culture could be linked with more shyness and overall anxiety among Hispanic American youth. In general, although more research is needed, ethnic minority youth are more frequently diagnosed with PTSD and Anxiety Disorder-Not Otherwise Specified, but less often diagnosed with GAD than

European American youth. Finally, economic disadvantage and ethnic minority status could have an additive effect on anxiety symptoms: ethnic minority anxious youth who live in disadvantaged neighborhoods reported the most severity and impairment when compared to European American anxious youth in both disadvantaged and non-disadvantaged neighborhoods.

EVIDENCE-BASED TREATMENTS

Cognitive behavioral therapy (CBT) for youth with anxiety has been deemed a "probably efficacious" treatment. Reported outcomes from several randomized controlled trials (RCTs) suggest that CBT for youth anxiety is effective in various presentations, including individual treatment, family CBT, and with or without a parent component. Other operationalizations of the CBT approach have also been described as "probably efficacious" for anxious youth, including Group CBT for youth with SP and Social Effectiveness Training for Children.

One version of CBT, the Coping Cat program, consists of 16 sessions, separated into two segments: skills training and skills practice. During the skills training sessions, children learn the "FEAR plan," a four-step approach which involves (a) awareness of bodily reactions to feelings and anxiety-specific physical symptoms; (b) identification of maladaptive, anxious thoughts and replacement with constructive, coping thoughts; (c) problem-solving skills for anxious situations; (d) self-evaluation and reward for effort. In the second segment, children practice the FEAR plan in actual anxiety-provoking situations, or exposure tasks, and learn to face, rather than avoid these situations. Exposure tasks are typically gradual, allowing the child to progress from mild anxiety-provoking to increasingly anxiety-provoking situations, and can be imaginal or in vivo tasks. The Coping Cat program emphasizes therapist "flexibility within fidelity," or tailoring the program to the individual needs of each child, while maintaining the overall goals of each session. The Coping Cat program has also been adapted for adolescents (i.e., The C.A.T. Project).

Several RCTs have examined the efficacy of the Coping Cat program, with sample sizes ranging from 47 to 488 youth. An early investigation involved a modest sample ($N = 47$; ages 9–13) and a waitlist control condition, but found that children who participated showed significant improvements based on child- and parent-report and behavioral observations. Using diagnostic criteria, at posttreatment, 64% of treated children no longer met criteria for their principal anxiety diagnosis, compared with only 5% of controls. Gains were maintained at 1-year and 2- to 5-year follow-ups. A second RCT ($N = 94$, ages 9–13) found comparable gains: for 71% of the treated children, their primary anxiety diagnosis was no longer considered primary at the end of treatment, and 53% no longer met criteria for their primary anxiety diagnosis. A 7.4-year follow-up found that the gains were maintained and that a meaningful percentage of successfully treated participants had reduced problems associated with substance use.

Using a more compelling comparison condition, a third RCT compared the efficacy of individual child CBT (ICBT; Coping Cat program), family CBT (FCBT), and a family-based education/support/attention active control (FESA) among anxious youth ($N = 161$, aged 7–14). At posttreatment, 64%, 64%, and 42% of principal anxiety diagnoses were no longer principal for ICBT, FCBT, and FESA, respectively, and treatment gains were maintained at 1-year follow-up. ICBT children showed a greater reduction in teacher-rated internalizing symptoms compared to FCBT children from pre- to posttreatment, but not at follow-up. FCBT outperformed ICBT when both parents had an anxiety disorder.

The largest RCT, the Child Anxiety Multimodal Study (CAMS), evaluated the efficacy of CBT (the Coping Cat program), sertraline, a combination of the two treatments (CBT + MED), and a placebo drug among 488 youth (ages 7–17). This evaluation was conducted at six different clinics across the United States. Response rates indicated favorable outcomes, with 80.7% of CBT+MED participants, 59.7% of CBT participants, 54.9% of sertraline participants, and 23.7% of placebo participants found to be treatment responders (rated as "very much" or "much improved") at week 12.

Recent efforts developed and then examined the Camp Cope-A-Lot Program (CCAL), a "computer-assisted" intervention program based on the Coping Cat program. The first six sessions are completed by the child, and the remaining sessions (primarily exposure tasks) are completed with the assistance of a coach (therapist). An RCT compared CCAL to ICBT and a computer-assisted education/support/attention condition (CESA) among 49 children with anxiety disorders. Children in the ICBT and CCAL conditions showed significantly greater gains at posttreatment compared to youth who received CESA, and the gains were maintained at a 3-month follow-up.

FUTURE RESEARCH

In sum, evidence indicates that CBT for anxiety in youth is efficacious, alone and when combined with medication, and that gains can be maintained. Computer-assisted CBT will help with dissemination of empirically supported treatments and warrants further exploration. Future research should also examine mediators and moderators of change within CBT, and ways to both personalize treatment and increase response rates for individuals.

KEY REFERENCES

Kendall, P. C., Gosch, E., Furr, J. M., & Sood, E. (2008). Flexibility within fidelity. *Journal of the American Academy of Child and Adolescent Psychiatry, 47*, 987–993.

Silverman, W., Pina, A., & Viswesvaran, C. (2008). Evidence-based psychosocial treatments for phobic and anxiety disorders in children and adolescents. *Journal of Clinical Child and Adolescent Psychology, 37*, 105–130.

Walkup, J. T., Albano, A. M., Piacentini, J., Birmaher, B., Compton, S. N., … Kendall, P. C. (2008). Cognitive behavioral therapy, sertraline, or a combination in childhood anxiety. *The New England Journal of Medicine, 359*, 2753–2766.

Anxiety Disorders in Children

Andrea Barmish Mazza

COMMENT ON THE EVIDENCE-BASED RECOMMENDATIONS

Cognitive behavioral therapy (CBT) for anxiety disorders in youth is an empirically supported treatment that focuses on building coping skills and practicing these skills in feared situations (i.e., exposure tasks). As a clinician, it is particularly important to highlight the researcher's discussion of "flexibility within fidelity." When treating anxious youth, it is crucial to adapt and individualize the way in which coping skills are taught to the individual child. Consideration of the youth's developmental stage, cultural background, and unique symptom presentation, in addition to the youth's interests and hobbies, are all important to incorporate creatively into treatment, and what brings life to the therapeutic process. This, of course, must be done without compromising the main goals of each session.

CASE EXAMPLE

Subject Information and Brief History

Tim is an 8-year-old Caucasian boy who lives at home with his biological parents and 2-year-old sister. He is a second grade student. Tim's parents brought him for evaluation and treatment owing primarily to concerns regarding his separation anxiety.

Presenting Problem

Structured diagnostic interviews with Tim and separately with his parents using the Anxiety Disorders Interview Schedule for Children, Child and Parent Versions (ADIS-IV-C/P) was conducted. Tim clung to his mother for the duration of the consenting procedure and evidenced difficulty separating from his parents for the assessment session. He needed a good deal of persuasion from his parents and from the clinician to separate. However, once separated, Tim was able to complete the 60-minute assessment with three breaks to "visit" his parents.

On the ADIS-IV-C/P, Tim met criteria for a principal *DSM-IV-TR* diagnosis of Separation Anxiety Disorder (SAD). He also met the diagnostic criteria for Social Phobia. According to his parents, Tim has difficulty separating from his mother in almost all situations. He reportedly resists going to school in the morning and his mother needs to walk him to his classroom, rather than dropping him off outside the building like other children his age. Tim does not like school because he "misses [his] parents too much." Tim frequently visits the nurse complaining of a stomachache. He refuses to partake in extracurricular activities or visit friends' homes unless one of his parents accompanies him. Tim also has difficulty being in certain rooms of the house by himself and will not go upstairs alone. His father reported that when Tim is in a separate room, he will call out his parents' names to check that they are still in the house. Tim regularly sleeps in his parents' bed with them because he is scared he will get "stolen from his room by bad guys." Tim refuses to stay with a babysitter and his parents recently had to cancel dinner plans because he was "hysterical crying and screaming" in anticipation of being left with a babysitter. Tim's separation anxiety not only interferes with his ability to get involved in developmentally appropriate activities, it also results in a lot of tension in the house. According to his parents, Tim has "always" been "clingy and anxious," but it was only in the last 4 months when his symptoms have gotten "much worse."

Treatment Intervention and Course

Treatment was cognitive behavioral in orientation and involved both Tim and his parents. The majority of the sessions were spent with Tim individually, although several minutes of each session and two separate sessions were conducted with his parents individually. Treatment consisted of 16 weekly 1-hour sessions with a primary target of his separation anxiety, but some time was also spent addressing his social anxiety. Treatment followed Kendall and Hedtke's *Cognitive-Behavioral Therapy for Anxious Children* manual, known as the Coping Cat program. The primary goal of the Coping Cat was to help Tim identify cues of anxious arousal and use these cues to apply a series of strategies to manage his excessive or unwanted anxiety. Typically, the Coping Cat utilizes a workbook in-session along with take-home tasks to review the content outside of session. Given Tim's reading disorder, these were individualized and altered for Tim to incorporate drawing instead of reading and writing. Tim's parents encouraged him to complete his take-home tasks, but were also urged to allow Tim to complete them independently in order to help develop his sense of self-efficacy.

During the first eight sessions, Tim learned various coping skills, which are captured in an acronym (i.e., F-E-A-R) to facilitate recall. The first step to be implemented was the "F" step of the FEAR plan, "*Feeling frightened?*" in which Tim learned to identify bodily reactions that accompany different emotions, followed by the more specific somatic reactions that characterize his anxiety. Tim was impressively adept at identifying his bodily reactions to anxiety and indicated that he experiences stomachaches and a racing heart when he is anxious. Tim learned and practiced deep breathing techniques and progressive muscle relaxation to manage his body's anxious arousal. He was also given a personalized relaxation recording which he was instructed to use to practice the relaxation skills at home.

In the second step of the FEAR plan (the "E" step; "*Expecting bad things to happen?*") Tim learned to identify and modify anxious self-talk. Tim had difficulty identifying his anxious thoughts, so cognitive restructuring was modified to self-instructional training, where Tim told himself "I can do it!" and "I am brave!" in the face of anxiety-provoking situations. Tim's interest in superheroes was interwoven into the content of these sessions and used as models of individuals who, although fearful, were able to face their fears.

In the third step of the FEAR plan (the "A" step; "_Actions and Attitudes that can help_"), Tim learned how to problem solve to develop a behavioral plan to cope with his anxiety. Tim was encouraged to generate a list of all possible ideas without judging them. After an exhaustive list of possible actions and attitudes was made, he was asked to consider the consequences of each, choose the best option, and follow through with the plan.

In the fourth and final step of the FEAR plan (the "R" step; "_Results and Rewards_"), Tim was urged to identify the favorable aspects of his coping strategies, as well as what could be done differently in the future. Tim was helped to recognize partial success and reward effort regardless of the outcome. He also generated a list of rewards that would be used to reinforce his bravery with exposure tasks.

Tim and his psychotherapist created a "Coping Key Chain" which included a series of images that served as cues for the various coping skills he learned (e.g., lips to indicate deep breathing, and a trophy to indicate rewards). This was provided in an effort to help with retention of the skills and with the generalization of these skills outside of session.

The second portion of the treatment program involved Tim practicing his newly acquired coping skills through in vivo exposures in increasingly anxiety-provoking situations, both in and out of session. In a collaborative effort with Tim and his parents, an individualized hierarchy of Tim's feared situations was created to target his separation anxiety. Exposure challenges began with Tim sitting in the treatment room that is furthest away from the waiting room where his parents sat, without the psychotherapist. Initially, Tim expressed apprehension and made his parents leave their coats in the treatment room to ensure that they would not leave the clinic without him. After several repetitions of this exposure (each increasing in length), these safety objects were removed from the room to ensure that Tim faced his anxiety, utilized his coping skills, and achieve a sense of mastery. Exposures progressed to Tim staying in the room by himself while his parents went to another floor of the building, Tim going to a separate floor with the psychotherapist while his parents remained in the clinic, and eventually his going to a separate floor of the building himself (under the watch of a confederate). Eventually, exposures involved Tim being dropped off to his appointment, and his parents leaving for the duration of the session and returning to pick him up. At home, Tim practiced going upstairs by himself for increasing lengths of time during the daytime, nighttime, and eventually sleeping by himself. Tim also practiced getting dropped off in front of the school and going to a birthday party without his parents. Each time Tim faced a feared situation, he was rewarded for his coping efforts. Tangible rewards offered at the beginning of treatment (e.g., coloring book, candy) were replaced with natural social reinforcers as treatment progressed. In fact, Tim felt proud of himself and frequently shared his accomplishments with his reading teacher.

Throughout treatment, several parenting issues related to Tim's anxiety were addressed. For example, Tim had more frequent tantrums with his mother than with his father. In discussing the function of these tantrums, it became evident that Tim would often "throw a fit" to communicate distress and attempt to avoid an anxiety-provoking situation. His parents differed in how they handled this behavior: Tim's father would encourage him to approach the situation irrespective of his distress, while his mother permitted avoidance behavior. Tim's father reported frustration about his wife's lack of control over Tim and indicated that this was a source of tension between them. Tim's mother indicated that she could not stand to see her son feeling distressed and that she would benefit from her husband's support in implementing exposures, as these are difficult for her as well. Tim's mother was encouraged to utilize aspects of the FEAR plan to help her tolerate her son's distress and manage her own anxiety. To help Tim's parents become a more unified front, they were both asked to model coping behavior, and Tim's father was encouraged to be supportive of his wife during these times. They were also encouraged to redirect their attention from Tim's anxious behavior to his strong points, like his drawing abilities or interest in karate.

Outcome

At the conclusion of treatment, all parties involved in the psychotherapy process noticed significant decreases in Tim's separation anxiety. At posttreatment, the ADIS was readministered and Tim no longer met criteria for SAD. To prevent relapse, the psychotherapist worked with the family to arrange for continued practice of the FEAR plan and brainstormed self-directed exposure tasks that could be conducted in an ongoing way.

CHALLENGES IN APPLYING THE EVIDENCE-BASED APPROACH

Comorbidity can be a challenge in treating anxiety disorders. First, it is important to identify if there are any comorbidities that need to be addressed prior to CBT for anxiety (e.g., principal diagnosis something other than anxiety disorder), or managed in addition to the CBT. For example, adjustments to the Coping Cat workbook were made (i.e., drawing versus writing) owing to Tim's comorbid reading disorder.

In addition, anxiety disorders run in families. Parental anxiety may interfere with a child's treatment if the parent is unable to tolerate the youth's distress and, therefore, accidentally reinforces avoidance or if the parent models anxious avoidance versus coping modeling. Parent anxiety may need to be addressed in the context of treating childhood anxiety and in some cases a referral for individual treatment may be indicated.

CULTURAL DIVERSITY ISSUES

As a clinician, it is important to consider each child/family's culture in the functional assessment of anxiety. For example, in some cultures co-sleeping is normal and may not be a symptom of separation anxiety. As the researchers highlighted, anxiety symptom presentation may vary across cultures; however, treatment outcome research suggests that CBT for youth anxiety is effective across cultures.

FUTURE RESEARCH

Ongoing research to identify the active ingredients in CBT and guidance on how to pace exposure-tasks would be particularly helpful. For example, how would starting exposure-tasks earlier in treatment impact treatment efficacy? How important is it to address exposure tasks hierarchically? In my clinical practice, parents of anxious youth are often eager to "get to it" and research on the relative efficacy of beginning exposure tasks earlier in treatment and more intensively, alongside the skills training, would be helpful. Finally, ongoing research on the predictors of outcome and identification of candidates best suited for CBT with and without medication would be helpful to guide parents accordingly.

KEY REFERENCES

Chansky, T. (2004). *Freeing your child from anxiety: Powerful, practical solutions to overcome your child's fears, worries, and phobias.* New York, NY: Broadway Books, Random House.

Kendall, P. C., & Hedtke, K. (2006). *Cognitive-behavioral therapy for anxious children: Therapist manual* (3rd ed.). Ardmore, PA: Workbook Publishing. www.WorkbookPublishing.com

Kendall, P. C., Robin, J. A., Hedke, K. A., Suveg, C., Flannery-Schroeder, E., & Gosch, E. (2005). Considering CBT with anxious youth? Think exposures. *Cognitive and Behavioral Practice, 12,* 136–150.

CHAPTER 4

Attention Deficit/Hyperactivity Disorder in Children and Adolescents

Kevin M. Antshel and Russell Barkley

CLINICAL PROBLEM

The clinical syndrome of inattention and overactivity dates back over 230 years. Now termed Attention Deficit/Hyperactivity Disorder (ADHD), this clinical syndrome represents *the* most common reason for referral to child/adolescent psychiatry clinics and affects approximately 5% to 9% of youth worldwide.

ADHD diagnostic criteria are described in the American Psychiatric Association's *Diagnostic and Statistical Manual of Mental Disorders* (*DSM-5*). Two categories of symptoms exist: inattention and hyperactivity/impulsivity. Developmentally inappropriate levels of *inattention* (e.g., often easily distracted by extraneous stimuli) and/or *hyperactivity–impulsivity* (e.g., often fidgets with hands or feet or squirms in seat) must be present for 6 months. The *DSM-5* includes three subtypes: primarily inattentive, primarily hyperactive/impulsive, and the combined subtypes.

Other *DSM-5* diagnostic criteria include: (a) the presence of ADHD symptoms prior to age 12 years, (b) that the symptoms occur in two or more settings (e.g., home and school), (c) that the symptoms interfere with or reduce the quality of functioning in life activities (family, school, social), and (d) that the symptoms not be easily attributable to other mental disorders.

PREVALENCE

Prevalence rates of ADHD are not higher in the United States relative to the rest of the world. Boys are diagnosed more frequently with ADHD than girls (2:1 to 9:1 ratios depending on the setting) although there is evidence suggesting that the gender difference is not as significant in community samples. Boys and girls with ADHD are more similar than different. More children are diagnosed with the Combined subtype. More adolescents are diagnosed with the Inattentive subtype.

CULTURAL DIVERSITY ISSUES

While prevalence rates are similar among various ethic/racial groups, African Americans are less likely to be diagnosed with, and treated for, ADHD. There are more similarities among ethnic/racial groups than differences in treatment responsiveness and psychiatric comorbidities.

EVIDENCE-BASED TREATMENTS

ADHD is a chronic disorder and both medication and psychosocial interventions are employed to manage the disorder. Stimulant medications are effective for approximately 70% to 80% of youth with ADHD. While lessening ADHD symptoms, there is less evidence that stimulants normalize functioning. Combining psychosocial treatments with stimulants can result in the need for lower doses of each form of treatment. Parents are also more enthusiastic/interested in treatments that include psychosocial components. For all of these reasons, treatments that include both medication and psychosocial interventions are typically recommended.

Medication

Meta-analyses have shown that the stimulants are more efficacious than nonstimulant medications. The three most common stimulants prescribed are methylphenidate (Ritalin), dextroamphetamine (Dexedrine), and mixed amphetamine salts (Adderall), all of which have a wide assortment of doses and delivery systems. Side effects are common and it is difficult to predict which patients will have side effects. Cardiovascular side effects (e.g., increased blood pressure) are usually of no clinical significance and routine EKG screening prior to stimulant use is needed only in those with positive family or personal cardiac history.

Approximately 20% to 30% of youth with ADHD will not respond to stimulant medications or cannot tolerate the stimulant side effects. Thus, several nonstimulant medications are also employed in ADHD pharmacotherapy. The selective norepinephrine reuptake inhibitor, atomoxetine (Strattera), a long-acting form of guanfacine (Intuniv), and a long-acting form of clonidine (Kapvay) are all effective for treating ADHD. Clonidine and guanfacine have also been FDA approved to be coadministered with stimulant medication.

Psychosocial Interventions

The most common psychosocial interventions for managing child and adolescent ADHD are behavioral parent training (BPT) and training teachers in classroom behavioral management. These are two of the psychosocial interventions that were included in the largest pediatric ADHD treatment study to date, the NIMH Multimodal Treatment Study of Children with ADHD (MTA).

Although there are a variety of ways to interpret the MTA data, for children with uncomplicated ADHD (e.g., no psychiatric comorbidities, adequate social functioning, etc.), the MTA data suggest that medication alone may be the best treatment option. However, for those youth with ADHD complicated by oppositional symptoms, poor social functioning, or ineffective parenting, a combination of medication and psychosocial treatments has the best outcomes.

Behavioral Parent Training

BPT programs are efficacious for youth with ADHD. Rather than ADHD symptom reductions, BPT generally results in decreases in child oppositional behavior, suggesting that the treatment is most useful when parent–child conflict exists. In preschool populations, however, BPT results in significant decreases in ADHD symptoms.

BPT most often consists of teaching parents operant conditioning techniques such as applying consequences following behaviors. Praise and privileges are common reinforcers, and the loss of positive attention, privileges, or time out from reinforcement, are common punishers. Three procedures are generally taught to parents: (a) manipulating the setting so as to increase positive behavior (e.g., parental commands, task demands, etc.); (b) restructuring the tasks (e.g., reduce work demands, inserting more interesting task materials, etc.); (c) and manipulating the consequences for child behavior (e.g., attention, praise, token reinforcement, punishment, etc.).

BPT is more effective for children and less so for adolescents with ADHD. BPT chiefly addresses parent–child conflicts that are often associated with ADHD but does not provide much benefit for ADHD symptoms. Therefore, BPT is often employed in a combined approach with medication (which manages the ADHD symptoms).

Teacher Training in Classroom Behavior Management
Contingency management procedures are the most effective teacher interventions for managing children with ADHD in the classroom. Applying reinforcers for reduced activity level and/or increased attention incorporate more tangible rewards (e.g., increased free time, privileges) as simple praise may not be sufficient to increase or maintain on-task behavior in children with ADHD in the classroom. Home-based contingencies (e.g., daily report cards) for in-class behavior and performance are also effective. Compared to reinforcement, using punishment in children with ADHD has been studied less, yet response cost is the most effective punishment technique.

FUTURE RESEARCH

Compared to what we presently know about childhood ADHD (and even adult ADHD), we know far less about what treatments work for preschool and adolescent ADHD populations. While there has been some research on preschool ADHD (e.g., Preschool ADHD Treatment Study [PATS]), there have been very few treatment studies regarding adolescent ADHD.

Studies considering how to improve medication treatment adherence are also needed. Some epidemiological research suggests that the average stimulant medication therapy duration is 19 months, with a total receipt of fewer than seven prescriptions in a 7-year period. Other epidemiological studies have reported that the most common child age to be taking stimulants is between 7 and 9 years with far lower rates outside of this range. Statistics like these suggest that improving treatment adherence should be a focus of treatment efforts.

KEY REFERENCES

AACAP Work Group on Quality Issues. (2007). Practice parameter for the assessment and treatment of children and adolescents with attention-deficit/hyperactivity disorder. *Journal of the American Academy of Child and Adolescent Psychiatry, 46*, 894–921.

Barkley, R. A. (2005). *Attention deficit hyperactivity disorder: A handbook for diagnosis and treatment* (3rd ed.). New York, NY: Guilford Press.

Barkley, R. A., & Murphy, K. R. (2005). *Attention deficit hyperactivity disorder: A clinical workbook* (3rd ed.). New York, NY: Guilford Press.

Attention Deficit/Hyperactivity Disorder in Children and Adolescents

Mary Rooney and Linda J. Pfiffner

COMMENT ON THE EVIDENCE-BASED RECOMMENDATIONS

Evidence-based treatments (EBTs) for ADHD including medication, behavioral parent training, and behavioral classroom interventions can greatly improve symptoms and impairments associated with ADHD. Although some children and adolescents respond well to either behavioral interventions or medication alone, optimal effects often occur from the combination of treatments. However, parents are often reluctant to medicate their children and frequently prefer to start with nonpharmacological approaches. This sequence of treatments is supported by data showing that some children respond well to behavioral therapy alone, and that for those cases where medication is indicated, the optimal dose may be lower when behavior therapy is provided.

Even though the effects of medication and behavioral therapies for ADHD are well supported in research studies, normalization of functioning may not occur. To improve outcomes, researchers are currently studying adjunctive treatments that address specific impairments (e.g., organizational skills, interpersonal skills). In addition, newer "wrap-around" treatment packages, which include direct interventions with the parents, school, and child, are currently being developed and evaluated.

CASE EXAMPLE

Subject Information and Brief History

Paul[1] was a 13-years-and-1-month-old African American boy adopted into an intact African American family at the age of 16 months following placement in a foster home at birth. His birth mother had received no prenatal care and her history of alcohol and drug use during pregnancy is unknown.

Paul was enrolled in eighth grade at a small parochial school that he had attended since kindergarten. He did not receive special education accommodations. Paul was a gregarious and outgoing boy who considered himself the class clown. He had many acquaintances at school, but felt as though he did not have any close friends.

---

[1]Name has been changed to maintain anonymity.

Presenting Problem

Paul presented to our specialty ADHD clinic when he was at risk for failing eighth grade. He had a history of mild academic underperformance during elementary school, and a significant deterioration in grades during middle school. In the classroom, Paul was easily distracted, disorganized, rushed through his work, and often failed to complete or turn in homework assignments. He was frequently disruptive (speaking out of turn, calling out to other students during lessons, having difficulty remaining seated), and his interactions with peers were often high in conflict. At home, Paul was becoming increasingly noncompliant with instructions, was argumentative during homework time, had difficulty starting his homework and staying on task, and had begun lying about homework assignments and grades.

Treatment Intervention and Course

Following a comprehensive, multi-informant assessment, Paul received a diagnosis of ADHD, Combined Type. Owing to the severity of his symptoms, his recommended treatment plan, designed to target impairments at home, school, and in peer relationships, included all three EBTs for ADHD—behavioral parent training, behavioral classroom interventions, and medication management. Paul's parents expressed strong reservations regarding medication use. Therefore, the initial treatment plan included only behavioral modification, with his parents agreeing to reconsider medication should sufficient gains not be achieved solely through behavioral interventions.

In the home setting, an evidence-based behavior chart/point system was implemented. The behavior chart was adapted to make it more palatable and appropriate for a young adolescent. Paul was included in the identification of target behaviors, rewards were broadened to include more social activities and incremental increases in autonomy/independence, organizational skills were emphasized, and the term "contract" was used in place of "behavior plan."

To effectively include Paul in the selection of target behaviors, the process was completed during a session with Paul and his parents in attendance. Three target behavior priority areas were identified: homework completion, following instructions, and honest communication. The reward selection process was also conducted in-session, and Paul was again given an active role. Rewards included adolescent-appropriate privileges, such as a delayed bedtime on weekends, attending a movie with friends unaccompanied by a parent, and joining the basketball team.

To address problems at school, a behavior plan was implemented with target behaviors that included following classroom rules, being respectful in peer interactions, and handing in homework on time. Points earned at school were added to those earned at home. The plan was implemented across multiple classrooms by having Paul's teachers complete a brief daily report card (labeled "Paul's School Contract") at the end of each period. In order to help Paul maintain his motivation for an improved grade point average (GPA), Paul was allowed to join and remain on the basketball team if he achieved and maintained a GPA of "C" or higher.

After following the behavioral EBTs for 6 weeks, Paul made improvements on his target behaviors. His ADHD symptoms, however, continued to interfere with his ability to pay attention in the classroom. With the clinician's guidance, Paul's parents were able to acknowledge that despite putting forth a good effort, Paul's inattention continued to interfere with his performance. Medication treatment was reconsidered as an adjunct treatment. The empirical evidence regarding medication risks and benefits was reviewed with Paul's parents. Particular attention was paid to parental concerns about stimulant medication increasing substance abuse risks. Empirical evidence indicates that substance abuse risks are not exacerbated by appropriate stimulant medication use, and these findings were described to Paul's parents. Paul also expressed concerns about medication (i.e., stigma, worries about not feeling or acting like himself, and wondering if he would have to take medication for the rest of his life). These concerns were addressed through conversations with the psychotherapist, and Paul indicated that he was willing to trying medication. His parents elected to meet with an experienced psychiatrist affiliated with the clinic who, after a thorough case review, recommended a stimulant medication trial.

Outcome

After 6 months of evidence-based behavioral interventions and 4 months of concurrent stimulant medication treatment, Paul had significant improvement in ADHD symptoms as measured through parent and teacher rating scales. Improvements in impairments at home, school, and with peers were also substantial, as evidenced by ratings on parent and teacher measures, points earned through the behavior plans, a 90% decrease in the number of missing homework assignments, and an improvement in his quarterly GPA from an F to a C. In addition, as a reward for improved behavior with peers, Paul's coach named him co-captain of the basketball team.

CHALLENGES IN APPLYING THE EVIDENCE-BASED APPROACH

Although EBTs for ADHD are effective, the realities of clinical practice often complicate their delivery. Challenges include complex case presentations, financial and logistical barriers, stigma associated with ADHD diagnosis and treatment, variability in parent and/or teacher motivation, and parent preferences regarding treatment modality (e.g., pharmacotherapy, child-directed treatments vs. parenting-focused interventions). In addition, the existing literature largely fails to address key treatment decisions, such as determining which intervention is most appropriate for a particular patient or how to best sequence treatments when multiple treatment modalities are indicated. With little empirical guidance available, clinicians must rely heavily on clinical judgment when addressing treatment challenges and personalizing interventions.

Many of these challenges were addressed in the case example above. In addition, adolescents with ADHD represent an understudied population whose specific needs are not clearly addressed in research on EBTs for ADHD. These needs include unique medication treatment concerns (e.g., noncompliance, stimulant misuse or diversion, co-occurring substance use problems), a desire for autonomy and reduced parental oversight, increased demands on academic, organizational, and interpersonal skills, and college preparation.

CULTURAL DIVERSITY ISSUES

Psychosocial and pharmacological EBTs for ADHD have been found to be effective for children across a range of ethnic, racial, and cultural backgrounds. Evidence suggests that there is variation among ethnic and racial groups regarding access to services, beliefs about the causes of ADHD, and treatment preferences. Research in this area is sparse, however, and findings are mixed. In the absence of clear evidence-based guidelines, clinicians are encouraged to consider each family's treatment preferences, beliefs, and ability to access services as treatment plans are developed and delivered.

FUTURE RESEARCH

For adolescents, additional treatment-outcome research is needed to address the unique developmental, academic, and social needs of this population. Across multiple age groups, future research should examine treatment sequencing, methods of addressing treatment compliance problems or lack of engagement, strategies for generalizing and sustaining treatment gains across settings and across time, and developing and implementing treatment plans for complex cases.

KEY REFERENCES

Children and Adults with Attention-Deficit/Hyperactivity Disorder (CHADD). (2012). http://www.chadd .org

Evans, S.W., & Hoza, B. (Eds). (2011). *Treating attention deficit hyperactivity disorder: Assessment and intervention in developmental context*. Kingston, NJ: Civic Research Institute.

Wolraich, M. L., & DuPaul, G. J. (2010). *ADHD diagnosis and management: A practical guide for the clinic and the classroom*. Baltimore, MD: Paul H. Brookes Publishing.

CHAPTER 5

Bipolar Disorder in Children

Heather A. MacPherson and Mary A. Fristad

CLINICAL PROBLEM

Pediatric Bipolar Disorder (PBD) is a serious psychiatric condition. The manic phase is characterized by periods of elevated mood, irritability, increased energy, grandiosity, decreased need for sleep, and poor judgment. The depressive phase is typically longer lasting and associated with the greatest morbidity and mortality. In contrast to adult-onset bipolar disorder, PBD often consists of mixed moods, rapid cycling, and chronic mood disturbance. Symptoms are associated with significant impairment, including: impaired family/peer relationships; poor academic performance; poor quality of life; substance abuse; legal difficulties; comorbidity; multiple hospitalizations; and suicidality.

PREVALENCE

Epidemiological studies suggest that approximately 1% of adolescents meet criteria for PBD and 5.7% experience symptoms. No epidemiological studies have examined the prevalence of PBD exclusively in children younger than age 12. In specialized psychiatric settings, the occurrence of PBD ranges from 10% to 30% of patients. Although rates of bipolar disorder are equal among sexes, PBD is more commonly diagnosed in males, especially when onset is before age 13.

CULTURAL DIVERSITY ISSUES

Studies have not reported racial or ethnic differences in the prevalence of PBD or treatment response; the majority of studies have utilized predominantly Caucasian samples.

EVIDENCE-BASED TREATMENT

Practice parameters recommend combined psychopharmacology and psychosocial interventions for treatment of PBD. A recent pharmacotherapy algorithm for PBD recommends atypical antipsychotics (i.e., aripiprazole, quetiapine, risperidone, and ziprasidone) as first-line treatment. Mood stabilizers (i.e., lithium and valproate) and olanzapine are second-line treatments because compared with previously mentioned atypical antipsychotics, they are associated with lower effectiveness and weight gain, respectively. Augmentation and combination therapies can be trialed after no or partial response to monotherapy. Clozapine or electroconvulsive therapy should be used only after failure of other interventions. Other considerations when selecting medication include: mood state; clinical variables (e.g., rapid cycling, comorbidities, psychosis); side effects; prior medication response; family history; and patient/family preferences.

Five atypical antipsychotics are approved by the Food and Drug Administration (FDA) for treatment of PBD in youth aged 10 to 17: risperidone, olanzapine, and ziprasidone for acute treatment of manic and mixed episodes; quetiapine for acute treatment of mania; and aripiprazole for acute and maintenance treatment of manic and mixed episodes. All of these atypical antipsychotics have demonstrated efficacy in randomized controlled trials (RCTs). Limited research has investigated optimal maintenance treatment.

Lithium is the only FDA-approved mood stabilizer for treatment of adolescent mania. A discontinuation trial and one double-blind, placebo-controlled trial demonstrated its effectiveness for mania, while one open trial demonstrated its effectiveness for bipolar depression. Efficacy of valproate in treating mania was demonstrated in open trials; however, RCTs yielded mixed results. Open trials support use of carbamazepine in treating mania and lamotrigine in treating depressive and mixed episodes. However, support for oxcarbazepine and topiramate is weak.

Medications may cause serious side effects, most commonly extrapyramidal symptoms, tardive dyskinesia, weight gain, sedation, and metabolic/cardiovascular abnormalities. In addition, lamotrigine has been associated with a potentially lethal skin rash, Stevens–Johnson syndrome. These side effects must be monitored closely.

Comorbid psychiatric disorders are prevalent among youth with PBD. Before treating comorbid psychiatric disorders, symptoms of PBD should be stabilized using aforementioned medications. After mood stabilization, attention-deficit/hyperactivity disorder should be treated with pharmacotherapy (i.e., stimulants, nonstimulants, alpha$_2$ agonists), parent behavior management training, and school consultation/support. Oppositional defiant disorder should be treated with parent behavior management training. Anxiety disorders should be treated with cognitive behavioral therapy (CBT) and/or selective serotonin reuptake inhibitors. Substance abuse should be addressed with integrated treatment (i.e., pharmacotherapy plus family therapies). Management of suicidality requires stabilization of PBD, family and dialectical behavior therapies (DBT), and treatment of risk factors (i.e., substance abuse, behavior problems, stressors, removal of available methods). Autism spectrum disorders require family/school-based behavioral interventions adjunctive to pharmacotherapy.

In addition to medication, psychosocial interventions are essential for treatment of PBD to help the child and family learn to manage what is best conceptualized as a chronic illness, with a waxing and waning course. Psychosocial treatments with empirical support are family based and incorporate psychoeducation, in addition to teaching symptom management skills. Important psychoeducational components emphasize information on etiology, course, prognosis, and treatment of PBD, including school and mental health systems of care. They stress that the *cause* of PBD is likely biological in its basis but that the *course* of illness can be greatly affected by psychosocial circumstances. In families, this translates to not blaming the child or the parents for the condition, but working collectively to manage symptoms effectively. Other important psychosocial treatment components target emotion regulation, impulse control, healthy lifestyles (e.g., sleep, diet, exercise), coping skills, effective communication, problem-solving skills, social/family relationships, academic/occupational functioning, and relapse prevention. Therapies with the most empirical support are drawn from family systems, cognitive behavioral, and dialectical behavioral theories.

Recent research on psychosocial interventions for PBD reveals support for several programs. All treatments have been investigated adjunctive to pharmacotherapy. Three groups developed and tested four psychosocial interventions for children: Family-Focused Treatment (FFT), Child- and Family-Focused CBT (CFF-CBT), Multi-Family Psychoeducational Psychotherapy (MF-PEP), and Individual Family Psychoeducational Psychotherapy (IF-PEP). Four groups developed and tested four psychosocial interventions for adolescents: FFT, CBT, DBT, and Interpersonal and Social Rhythm Therapy (IPSRT). Treatments demonstrated positive results in case studies or open trials. Only MF-PEP, IF-PEP, and FFT have been examined and demonstrated positive results in RCTs.

FUTURE RESEARCH

Despite advances in treatment of PBD, much more research is needed. Limited research provides guidance for treatment of bipolar disorder not otherwise specified, depressive phase of illness, and maintenance treatment. Current interventions provide benefit for some but not all youth who have PBD and the impact of mediators and moderators on treatment outcome is not well understood. Research examining the transportability and dissemination of pharmacologic and psychosocial treatments for PBD in real-world settings is lacking and will be important to inform evidence-based practice efforts. Finally, rigorous evaluation of complementary and alternative interventions utilized by many with PBD is needed.

KEY REFERENCES

Fristad, M. A., Goldberg Arnold, J. S., & Leffler, J. M. (2011). *Psychotherapy for children with bipolar and depressive disorders*. New York, NY: Guilford Press.

Fristad, M. A., & MacPherson, H. A. (2013). Evidence-based psychosocial treatments for child and adolescent bipolar spectrum disorders. *Journal of Clinical Child and Adolescent Psychology*. Advance online publication. doi: 10.1080/15374416.2013.822309

Kowatch, R. A., Fristad, M. A., Findling, R. L., & Post, R. M. (Eds.). (2009). *Clinical manual for management of bipolar disorder in children and adolescents*. Arlington, VA: American Psychiatric Publishing.

Bipolar Disorder in Children

Barbara Mackinaw-Koons

COMMENT ON THE EVIDENCE-BASED RECOMMENDATIONS

The recommendations noted by MacPherson and Fristad in the previous research section are quite comprehensive and take into account all of the comorbid issues typically present when dealing with pediatric bipolar disorder. The complexity of competently attending to all these issues can be extremely complicated and difficult to navigate in routine clinical practice, especially given that all the relevant players may not be aware of all the recent research on the disorder, in such a young population or best supported treatments. Even if mental health professionals are aware of the evidence-based treatments (EBTs) discussed by Macpherson and Fristad, they may not be readily available/accessible to most individuals who need them, especially those families that live in more rural areas.

CASE EXAMPLE

Subject Information and Brief History

"Martin," is a 9-year-old boy initially diagnosed with Bipolar Disorder—Not Otherwise Specified (BP-NOS) by this clinician at age 6 following a comprehensive diagnostic evaluation. Martin was initially referred for behavioral difficulties at home and school, such as defiant and very aggressive behavior.

Presenting Problem

Although Martin was exhibiting many classic symptoms of Oppositional Defiant Disorder, his parents had tried working with a previous psychotherapist on behavior management strategies with little success. They reported feeling inadequate as parents, as they had been told that if they were consistent enough in their behavior management plan, Martin's behavioral difficulties would have improved. However, Martin's extreme mood dysregulation had not been addressed, as further evaluation revealed that Martin was experiencing many symptoms of bipolar disorder, including episodes of elevated and extremely irritable mood, grandiosity, periods of excessive energy with little need for sleep, and periods of increased risky and careless behavior.

Treatment Intervention and Course

Martin was too young initially to fully participate in Multi-Family Psychoeducational Psychotherapy (MF-PEP) or Individual Family Psychoeducational Psychotherapy (IF-PEP), as described in the section by MacPherson and Fristad, which are skill building interventions for prepubertal children with mood disorders, delivered in a group or individual family format. However, the general philosophy and guidelines of the treatment were used with an emphasis on parent education, support, and learning symptom management skills. Martin was not an ideal candidate for individual therapy early in treatment owing to the severity of his symptoms and his young age. Medication management has been ongoing and has presented its own set of challenges, with frequent changes made due to decreasing effectiveness or negative side effects.

One particularly helpful "mindset" for parents that is fundamental to MF-PEP/IF-PEP is the understanding that the cause of the disorder is biological and the course is likely influenced by psychosocial events. However, this guiding principle met continued resistance among other members of the family and school staff who believed that Martin's behavioral challenges were willful and manipulative, rather than the effects of fluctuating mood symptoms. A large focus of treatment throughout the years has been on problem-solving school issues and helping the parents become strong advocates for their son.

Once Martin was old enough to become involved in MF-PEP, which is designed for children ages 8 through 12, the family was eager to participate despite already knowing much of the content from their individual work with this clinician. The parents' hope was that the support from other children and parents might be helpful for themselves as well as Martin. Unfortunately, Martin entered a very difficult-to-manage manic phase soon after his MF-PEP group started. Thus, he was so manic during a good majority of group sessions, that he was unable to process much of the content and quickly alienated many of his peers due to his behavior.

Outcome

Martin continues in therapy and as he gets older, his ability to benefit from individual psychotherapy is improving as he is better able to focus, comprehend, and practice skills being taught in psychotherapy. We have continued to work on coping skills, cognitive restructuring, problem-solving skills, effective communication skills, and his role in preventing relapse when his mood is more stable. We accomplish as much as we can when symptoms are minimal, and switch to parent guidance when symptoms are more severe and he cannot benefit from sessions. His ability to show some knowledge of his own disorder and how to handle it has increased the family's hope for his future.

CHALLENGES IN APPLYING THE EVIDENCE-BASED APPROACH

In addition to the challenges of the disorder itself, treatment has also been difficult, at times, owing to challenges within the mental health system. Martin's parents followed the advice taught in MF-PEP regarding safety planning and need for hospitalization or seeking higher levels of care (such as wrap-around services involving partial hospitalization or community support services where a mental health professional could make home-based visits). However, they have had great difficulty securing these different levels of care due to insurance barriers and lack of understanding of the disorder among other professionals (such as emergency room personnel misunderstanding the child's symptoms during a time of crisis and refusing to admit him). In this particular case, staff believed his symptoms were the result of inadequate parenting or even possible abuse, as he was experiencing some hypersexual symptoms as part of his mania presentation. Treating clinicians were less willing to attend to specific mood symptoms the parents were concerned about, including suicidal ideation, and focused instead on the behavioral aspects of his symptom profile (i.e., being extremely oppositional).

CULTURAL DIVERSITY ISSUES

In this particular case, Martin's grandparents were first-generation immigrants from another country and their cultural beliefs about mental illness were quite different than those of Martin's parents and treatment providers. This posed a problem as his grandparents played a large role in caretaking responsibilities and support for the family. Although this is not a unique problem to pediatric bipolar disorder, it seems especially challenging with this population, given the controversy that sometimes exists even among mental health professionals in this country about this particular diagnosis! Many parents will report a history of providers denying that bipolar disorder can even exist in children and thus postponing the child receiving appropriate treatment.

FUTURE RESEARCH

Further research examining the phenomenology of pediatric mania symptoms longitudinally is ongoing, and it will be interesting to see what effects treatment at an early age might have on the severity of the disease in adolescence and into adulthood. Mary Fristad's research group has already found some initial evidence that participation in MF-PEP may have some preventative effect on transient manic symptoms. Further support for this hypothesis may help many practitioners overcome their reluctance to diagnose pediatric bipolar at such a young age. It seems likely that early intervention will be the best way to prevent a more severe course of the disease throughout the lifetime.

KEY REFERENCES

Fristad, M. A., Goldberg Arnold, J. S., & Leffler, J. M. (2011). *Psychotherapy for children with bipolar and depressive disorders*. New York, NY: Guilford Press.

Nadkarni, R. B., & Fristad, M. A. (2010). Clinical course of children with a depressive spectrum disorder and transient manic symptoms. *Bipolar Disorders, 12*, 494–503.

Pavuluri, M. (2008). *What works for bipolar kids*. New York, NY: Guildford Press.

CHAPTER 6

Conduct Disorder in Adolescents

Craig E. Henderson, Lisa Y. Kan, Lindsey W. North, and Howard A. Liddle

CLINICAL PROBLEM

Conduct Disorder (CD) is characterized by a pervasive pattern of disregard for others and social conventions demonstrated by a pattern of aggressive, deceptive, and destructive behavior. CD symptoms have the distinction of being the primary presenting problem for psychiatric referral among children and adolescents in the United States; however, it is important to note that most adolescents who engage in antisocial behaviors and delinquent acts are not diagnosed with CD. For those who are, compared to youth with other psychiatric disorders, youth diagnosed with CD report higher levels of distress and impairment in multiple life domains. Youth with CD are also at high risk for a constellation of problems, including comorbid psychiatric disorders, legal problems, and early death. Despite the high risk for long-term, maladaptive development such youth face, studies have shown that they frequently do not access services because their mental health care needs often go unrecognized, or, if recognized, they do not receive the care they need. This results in the justice system being the primary point of access for many youths with CD in need of treatment services. Even here, youth frequently do not access services, or continuity of care is lacking when they are released, perpetuating a cycle of more extensive involvement in the criminal justice system. These unfortunate statistics highlight the importance of identifying youth with CD and engaging them in effective treatments before such long-term, maladaptive behavior patterns take hold.

PREVALENCE

The most recent data from the National Comorbidity Survey Replication-Adolescent Supplement (NCS-A) indicate lifetime and 12-month prevalence for CD at 6.8% and 5.4%, respectively. It shares a high degree of comorbidity with many disorders, particularly substance use disorders (SUD) and impulse-control disorders.

CULTURAL DIVERSITY ISSUES

Many studies have documented gender differences in CD, with boys being diagnosed at a rate 3 to 5 times higher than girls. However, girls are more likely to have a childhood onset. Rates of comorbidity with SUD are similar across genders, but recent evidence indicates that comorbidity patterns may manifest differently across genders. For instance, findings from a recent study suggest that substance-abusing females are at greater risk for also having internalizing and externalizing disorders than males. However, at this point, very little is known about the manifestation of CD across adolescents of different ethnicities, with some studies suggesting ethnic differences in prevalence rates and others not. There is next to no research indicating gender or ethnic differences in response to treatment.

EVIDENCE-BASED TREATMENTS

The route to remitting CD through treatment has primarily been through decreasing CD symptoms (e.g., conduct problems) and associated problems such as delinquent behavior. Two treatment approaches that have been effective in treatment trials are cognitive behavioral therapy, usually supplemented with parent training, and family-based treatments. Together, the research underlying these treatments indicates the importance of involving adolescents' family members in treatment. Indeed, at least one study, albeit a study conducted with primarily substance using adolescents, suggests that incorporating families in treatment improves treatment effectiveness, even when CBT was the treatment investigated. There is also emerging evidence that the family-based treatments that have shown promise in decreasing CD symptoms are the same approaches that have achieved success in decreasing adolescent substance use (e.g., Multidimensional Family Therapy [MDFT], Multisystemic Therapy). This is especially important, given the high rates of comorbidity of the two disorders.

As an example of family-based treatments with established empirical support, MDFT is a multicomponent and multilevel intervention system that assesses and intervenes with the: (a) adolescent and parent(s) individually, (b) family as an interacting system, and (c) individuals in the family relative to their interactions with influential social systems (e.g., schools, juvenile justice) that impact the adolescent's development. Interventions are solution focused and strive to obtain immediate and practical outcomes in the most important individual and transactional domains of the adolescent's everyday life—home, school, and justice system. Therapists intervene systematically to help individuals and families develop empirically derived protective and healing factors and processes that offset substance use and behavioral problems, such as decreasing family conflict and improving family cohesion and parental monitoring of their adolescents' activities.

Although it is certainly a positive development that research has identified effective treatment approaches, this may be a "silver lining" in the cloud of problems that currently plague the treatment system. Examples of problems that currently exist is the limited adoption and implementation of evidence-based therapies by community treatment agencies; fragmentation between the mental health and substance use/abuse treatment systems; and funding gaps for youth with co-occurring mental health and substance use disorders. Nevertheless, emerging evidence that treatments initially developed to primarily treat either delinquency/CD symptoms or substance use are decreasing both problem behaviors, as early treatment dissemination efforts are having an impact on the treatment delivery system in spite of the problems mentioned above. These emerging findings provide an empirical basis for adopting policies such as "no wrong door," a policy that moves the burden for finding appropriate services for comorbid problems from the individual/family to treatment agencies that either respond to the adolescent's need through direct service or by linking the individual to partner programs.

FUTURE RESEARCH

Additional research is needed to better understand treatment of CD and its comorbid problems, particularly for girls and diverse populations. Several interventions have been identified as effective, but researchers have not yet identified mechanisms of change (i.e., why the treatment works) or potential moderators of treatment effects (e.g., for whom and under what circumstances is this treatment effective). Future studies should also focus on identifying ways to maintain treatment gains. One obvious method for doing this is extending study follow-up periods during which researchers would examine changes through early, or even middle adulthood. A complementary approach is the development of continuing care models in which one treatment episode would set a foundation for ongoing services and booster sessions, but would not be considered a cure-all for the rest of the teen's life. Such studies are emerging in the field of substance abuse treatment and are rife for testing with CD symptoms. Finally, more attention should be given to examining the impact of treatments on the remission of CD diagnoses and developing treatments to be appropriate for youth with varying severity levels. These studies could assist efforts in matching clients to appropriate treatments/level of intervention, as well as improving the clinical significance of treatment studies.

KEY REFERENCES

Eyberg, S. M., Nelson, M. M., & Boggs, S. R. (2008). Evidence-based psychosocial treatments for children and adolescents with disruptive behavior. *Journal of Clinical Child and Adolescent Psychology*, *37*, 215–237. doi: 10.1080/15374410701820117

Hawkins, E. H. (2009). A tale of two systems: Co-occurring mental health and substance abuse disorders treatment for adolescents. *Annual Review of Psychology*, *60*, 197–227. doi: 10.1146/annurev.psych.60.110707.163456

Woolfenden, S. R., Williams, K., & Peat, J. (2001). Family and parenting interventions in children and adolescents with conduct disorder and delinquency aged 10–17. *Cochrane Database of Systematic Reviews*, *2*, 1–29.

Clinician Application

Conduct Disorder in Adolescents

Rick Weinberg

COMMENT ON THE EVIDENCE-BASED RECOMMENDATIONS

Clinicians who are referred an adolescent with conduct disorder have no easy task ahead of them. These young men and women can be belligerent, deceitful, and disrespectful to authority. Their families are frequently at the end of their rope. Fortunately, clinicians working with these youth and their families have Multidimensional Family Therapy (MDFT) as a foundation on which to base their work. Over the past 20 years Howard Liddle and his colleagues have been developing and refining MDFT, an evidence-based treatment for adolescents with conduct disorder and their families. Numerous studies have found MDFT to reduce psychiatric symptoms, antisocial behavior and drug use, improve grades and family relationships, and increase adolescents' general well-being. While MDFT is a manualized treatment developed in a university clinic, Liddle has emphasized that it is not a one-size-fits-all approach, and should be tailored by the clinician to fit each client and family.

CASE EXAMPLE[1]

Subject Information and Brief History

Joey was a 15-year-old Caucasian boy whose parents brought him in due to a variety of antisocial behaviors. Joey was the youngest of two sons. Bill, his older half-brother, was 21 and away at college during the period when I saw the family. Bill and Joey had the same biological mother, Nancy, who divorced Bill's father before Joey's birth. Bill and Joey were both raised by Frank, who married Nancy when she was pregnant with Joey. Nancy was the primary breadwinner in the family, working as an executive secretary in a large financial services firm. Frank was unemployed at the time of the referral, having recently lost his job as driver for a local delivery company due to the declining economy. In fact, for much of Joey's life, Frank was his primary parent owing to frequent periods of unemployment. In contrast Nancy had always been employed, worked long hours, and made gradual but continued advances in her career. Frank could be described as a rough man—authoritarian, demanding, and punitive as a parent. Nancy was more submissive, kind, fretful, and detail oriented, and seemed somewhat anxious and dysthymic when treatment began.

Presenting Problem

The triggering event for the referral was Joey's expulsion from school due to the discovery of marijuana in his locker and a knife in his backpack. He had been suspended several times over the past few years, mainly for being disrespectful to teachers and fighting with other students. Bringing drugs and a weapon to school, however, were deemed far more serious infractions, and Joey was moved to an alternative education program. Joey was considered by his parents and teachers as very intelligent, and sporadically attained high grades. However, his academic performance was frequently undermined by his failure to study, complete assignments, and prepare for exams. Relations between Frank and Joey were often antagonistic. Frank and Joey would occasionally get into confrontations that turned into shoving matches, but ended before anyone was hurt. A few weeks before the referral, for the first time Joey got the upper hand in the scuffle and pushed his father hard into a wall, hurting his dad's back before Nancy intervened. Frank and Nancy's relationship was also problematic, vacillating between disengaged and frosty. They disagreed on parenting style, with Nancy believing Frank was too harsh and Frank accusing Nancy of being too soft.

---

[1] The case described is an amalgam of three different family cases.

Treatment Intervention and Course

As delivered in the clinic, MDFT has many components. This family was seen in an outpatient office where I emphasized the following subset of MDFT principles: (a) the foundational importance of the treatment alliance; (b) establishing several specific foci for treatment; (c) capitalizing on generic knowledge about the family's life, their strengths, and existing interests; (d) involving relevant extra-familial, community resources; and (e) the establishment and maintenance of hope. In addition to these, I also placed what I believe is more emphasis on tracking and addressing systemic dynamics than is typically employed in MDFT.

Building a rapport was the most difficult of all the components to attain. Joey was not only suspicious of authority, but also contentious. Because so many authority figures in his life had been condescending and critical, his initial expectation was that I would be this way as well. It was a challenge in the early sessions to resist bickering with him. Instead I would try to smile, show affability, and positively reframe his attempts to engage me in arguments—for example, commenting on how smart, quick and verbal he was, and that I appreciated how willing he was to share his thoughts with me. In the first session, partly as an attempt to elevate the conversation and secondly as a way to find something that could be positively reinforcing for him, I asked Joey what activities he enjoyed the most with his dad. His response was pivotal to the success of this family's therapy. He told me that he enjoyed watching mixed martial arts (MMA) matches on TV with his father. When he brought this up, the mood of all three family members quickly changed, particularly father and son. They smiled, playfully teased each other, and spoke with detailed knowledge about the top MMA fighters. Knowing that there was a reputable MMA training academy close to where they lived, that included self-control training and emphasized mutual respect among participants in its philosophy, I inquired about the feasibility of Joey earning a membership in the MMA academy in return for improvement in his grades and more respectful behavior at home. Gradual engagement in this academy and tying participation to treatment goals was critical to the success of the therapy. Consistent with MDFT's suggestion that psychotherapists collaborate with others in client family's social network, I met with the MMA academy owner and helped the family set up a feedback system between Joey's parents, teachers, and the MMA academy whereby Joey's academics, school and at-home behavior determined whether he could participate in MMA training each week.

Another important emphasis was bringing the family's attention to their circular, systemic patterns. Two dynamics in particular were the focus of our analysis and intervention—how Joey and his dad each provoked the other to anger and escalation; and how Nancy's and Frank's criticism of the other's parenting affected the dynamic between each parent and Joey. This was accomplished primarily through asking circular questions, for example, (to Nancy) "Ms. X, what is the impact on you when you see your husband and son get into a shoving match?"; and operational questions, that is, questions that call attention to specific behaviors or processes (operations) that are set in motion by the subject being discussed. An example of an operational question is, "so then, Ms. X, when you say you are distressed by seeing Frank and Joey fight, how does your distress show itself?" These questions continue, directed to other family members, in order to demonstrate how they are drawn into the circular systemic patterns, for example, to Frank, "when Ms. X's distress in seeing you and Joey fight comes out as criticism of your parenting, what does her criticism do to you?", and so forth. Other strategies that were used to focus on systemic dynamics were: approach motivation, for example, to Frank, "when Ms. X is upset by your fights with Joey, rather than criticizing what kind of father you are, how would you prefer she convey her distress with the situation?"; and reciprocal questioning, for example, first to Nancy, "Frank just indicated that he would prefer that you communicate your distress at the fighting by coming to him privately and talking about it calmly. What can Frank do that would make it easier for you to discuss your distress privately and calmly?"; and then to Frank, "Nancy just said that she'd be more likely to approach you calmly if you were generally more responsive and friendly to her. What could Nancy do that would result in you being friendlier and more responsive?"

It became apparent that much of the anger that was displayed in this family was a proxy for considerable historical hurt, disappointment, and sadness that had occurred long ago. Gently approaching and uncovering this pain, enabling the three family members to talk about it constructively with each other, and helping Frank and Nancy to become more soothing and comforting to one another and to their son also became the foci of the later therapy sessions.

Outcome

For the first six sessions, I met with the family weekly. We then went to a biweekly schedule, which lasted another 5 to 6 months. The last two to three sessions were monthly. Almost all of the sessions included all three family members (I never met older brother, Bill). By the end of treatment, Joey was earning As and Bs in school, and the family was in the process of petitioning the school system administration to return Joey to his neighborhood high school. While there continued to be disagreements between his parents and Joey, none escalated to physical violence. Joey continued training at the MMA academy and began mentoring younger boys. He reported that the marijuana smoking had ended within a month or so of beginning MMA training. Nancy and Frank reported more marital satisfaction and in general all three family members' behavior and their prevailing mood during the sessions reflected improved family relations.

CHALLENGES IN APPLYING THE EVIDENCE-BASED TREATMENT

The challenges inherent in working with families having adolescents who are antagonistic, disobedient, and easy to anger far exceed any challenges of using MDFT. However, one area that can present logistical and practical problems is collaborating constructively with other agencies or community professionals who are also involved with the client family. While traveling to meet face-to-face with these providers is more helpful than relying on the phone, for the private practitioner getting away from the office to meet can be disruptive to a calendar full of other clients. Nevertheless the virtues of cooperative engagement among members of the professional network far outweigh the challenges. First, these professionals can have a powerful influence on the adolescent and on family dynamics, and are typically as invested in client progress as the family therapist. Second, teachers, probation officers, coaches, and so forth see the adolescent, and possibly the family, in different contexts than at home and can often provide helpful insights into individual behavior and family dynamics besides those that the family reports to the therapist or those seen in a family therapy session. A second challenge is containing all that one has to do in MDFT into the typical 50–60 minute session of private practice, let alone factoring in the time spent in deescalating raw emotions. The clock moves very quickly in work with these families, and having to do so much can be quite challenging to the clinician who is used to meeting with individual clients.

CULTURAL DIVERSITY ISSUES

My own clinical experience has been primarily with single and two-parent Caucasian families. However, Liddle and his colleagues have written extensively about the importance of incorporating relevant cultural themes in MDFT interventions. Examples include discussing the music and dress of the adolescent's culture; and with African American and Hispanic teens, discussion of salient cultural themes, such as cultural mistrust, anger, respect and disrespect, racism, hopelessness, and the adolescent's ideas about the rites of passage from childhood to adulthood. Idiosyncratic beliefs that appear to foster antisocial behaviors are addressed respectfully. For instance, some of these youth may express the belief that getting arrested or joining a gang is an important rite of passage in their community. When views like these are expressed, Liddle suggests that the psychotherapist openly and thoughtfully confront these beliefs and their implications, and problem solve with the adolescent ways to remain connected with his or her community while avoiding involvement with antisocial youth culture. I would add that including family members in these conversations could also be constructive.

FUTURE RESEARCH

I believe examining the emerging field of Positive Relationship Science and incorporating findings from Positive Psychology could benefit family therapy in general and, in particular, could improve therapy outcomes with the families of adolescents who display conduct disorders. Positive Psychology researchers are studying specific patterns and processes that help family relationships flourish, and are identifying certain skills that can be learned to enhance relational satisfaction and happiness. Specific processes identified by Positive Relationship Science investigators that could be fruitful for future family therapy research are capitalization (i.e., responding with energy and excitement when a loved one relates good news); expressing gratitude; offering apology and forgiveness; sharing novel and fun experiences; the "Michelangelo phenomenon," (i.e., engaging in interactional patterns that bring out the best in others); and participating in deep, meaningful conversations.

KEY REFERENCES

Conoley, C. W., & Conoley, J. C. (2009). *Positive psychology and family therapy: Creative techniques and practical tools for guiding change and enhancing growth.* Hoboken, NJ: John Wiley & Sons.

Liddle, H. A. (2009). *Multidimensional family therapy for adolescent drug abuse: Clinician's manual.* Center City, MN: Hazelden Publishing Co.

Napier, A. Y., & Whitaker, C. A. (1978). *The family crucible.* New York, NY: Harper & Row.

CHAPTER 7

Firesetting in Youth

Ian Lambie and Isabell Randell

CLINICAL PROBLEM

Firesetters are a diverse population within which there exists a wide spectrum of firesetting behavioral severity and variation in the presence and severity of accompanying psychopathology and environmental adversity. Firesetting is typically understood to describe intentional setting of fires by children and adolescents, although some theory and research also addresses "accidental firesetters."

Although empirical studies have identified many risk factors for firesetting behavior, explanations of its development and persistence remain largely theoretical. There is a general consensus within recent research and theory that firesetting, particularly that of individuals whose behavior are more pathological, is the result of a complex interaction of multiple historical and immediate factors which place an individual at risk for, elicit, and possibly maintain firesetting behavior.

Firesetting has been found to be associated with a number of individual and environmental risk factors including family dysfunction and problematic parent–child relationships, experience of abuse and stressful life events, social skills deficits and interpersonal problems, peer rejection, impulsivity and risk taking, anger and aggression, fire interest symptoms of Oppositional Defiant Disorder, Conduct Disorder, depression anxiety and Attention Deficit Hyperactivity Disorder and wide-ranging antisocial behavior. Although the reasons for such a relationship are unknown, firesetting behavior has been found to be associated with particularly severe and persistent antisocial behavior.

PREVALENCE

Studies using community samples indicate that around 5% to 10% of children and adolescents engage in firesetting behavior. However, two recent community studies with adolescent samples found that almost one third of adolescents reported firesetting behavior in the past 12 months. Although recidivism rates vary significantly, the current body of literature reports rates of up to 59%. Of concern, youth are found to account for around one half of all arson offending, indicating the potential seriousness of firesetting behaviors among children and adolescents.

CULTURAL DIVERSITY ISSUES

Firesetting is around two to three times more prevalent among males than females. Although research has largely neglected to investigate characteristics of female firesetters and potential gender differences within firesetting populations, a small number of studies indicate that some firesetting correlates may be gender specific. This suggests that female firesetters may have different treatment needs.

Children and adolescents have been found to be equally likely at risk for firesetting recidivism and to be present in similar numbers across severity groups.

There is no empirical evidence for a relationship between ethnicity or socioeconomic status and firesetting behavior.

EVIDENCE-BASED TREATMENTS

There are two primary treatment approaches for firesetters—fire safety education programs and mental health-based psychosocial interventions. Educational interventions are typically single session, fire service operated, and administered by firefighters. Although common, educational interventions lack standardization, largely owing to a lack of empirical studies to guide practice and program execution. Mental health programs specifically targeting firesetters are rare and firesetters are more likely to be referred to mental health practitioners through fire service programs or other social services.

Psychosocial interventions for firesetters typically employ Cognitive Behavioral Therapy (CBT) techniques such as parent training (including child management, monitoring, reinforcement, and response–cost techniques), identification and challenging of dysfunctional and distorted cognitions, affect regulation, assertion and social skills training, and problem solving. Because firesetting populations are diverse, treatment needs will vary widely and treatment should be individually tailored accordingly. A key aspect of CBT is identifying and addressing relationships between experience, thoughts, emotions, and firesetting behaviors. Graphing is a method of identifying such relationships by visually depicting a timeline of behavior in relation to feelings and external stressors. Older studies suggest the potential usefulness of this technique and it has more recently been used in effective CBT interventions for firesetters.

Research indicates that both fire safety educational interventions and CBT result in a significant reduction in firesetting behavior. However, such studies typically fail to employ control groups and the true extent of program efficacy is therefore unknown. The limited number of studies concerning treatment suggest similar efficacy levels for CBT and fire safety interventions of the same length. CBT does, however, appear to be significantly more effective in reducing fire setting than one- or two-contact fire safety interventions which are typical of current educational intervention practice. Longer fire safety interventions (of eight 1-hour sessions) have been found to be significantly more effective in reducing firesetting than those that involve only one or two contact sessions, indicating the potential benefits of a more intensive educational approach.

Fire safety education, while unlikely to be sufficient in addressing the wide spectrum of problems that some firesetters present with, is considered a potentially important means of addressing fire-specific firesetting correlates. However, there is limited evidence for this, with research indicating that while educational interventions are more effective in increasing fire safety skills and knowledge, they are not necessarily more effective than CBT in reducing curiosity about or attraction to fire. Although multisystemic, multidisciplinary treatments that draw on services such as fire service education, mental health, juvenile justice, and social services are considered "best practice" in firesetting literature, there is a lack of research investigating such a treatment approach. One exception is a study of a 1-day multisystemic, multidisciplinary intervention that resulted in considerably lowered recidivism rates when compared with controls.

FUTURE RESEARCH

Existing research concerning firesetting treatment has typically approached firesetters as a singular population and therefore failed to provide insight into what works for different groups of individuals and why. Future research is needed to investigate the mechanisms involved in the positive effects that can be attained through both extended educational interventions and CBT. In addition, given that researchers and theorists have advocated multicomponent treatment as a "best practice" approach, there is a need for research that assesses the potential benefits of combining CBT with fire safety skills education and whether such interventions would provide additional benefits than those provided by fire safety or CBT interventions alone.

KEY REFERENCES

Kolko, D. J. (Ed.). (2002). *Handbook on firesetting in children and youth.* San Diego, CA: Academic Press.

Lambie, I., & Randell, I. (2011). Creating a firestorm: A review of children who deliberately light fires. *Clinical Psychology Review, 31*, 307–327.

Stadolnik, R. F. (2000). *Drawn to the flame: Assessment & treatment of juvenile firesetting behavior.* Sarasota, FL: Professional Resource Press.

Clinician Application

Firesetting in Youth

Kenneth R. Fineman

COMMENT ON THE EVIDENCE-BASED TREATMENT

The comments made by the researchers concerning the evidence-based treatments most commonly used in the assessment and treatment of youth firesetters is accurate and most helpful. The identification of the relationship between experience, thoughts, emotions, and firesetting, as well as the comment concerning the necessity for multicomponent treatment, is to the point and exceptionally relevant. However, the researcher's comment concerning the assumed, significantly high percentage of firesetters who recidivate should be considered as relevant to those firesetters who are untreated and thus continue to set fires. It is this clinician's experience, from acquiring anecdotal information both in the United States and internationally, that treated child or adolescent firesetters tend to have an exceptionally low recidivism rate, at about a 2% level.

Fire-related issues that will present at the office of a clinician may be a function of fire misuse (exemplified by a minor frequently lighting matches or looking at the flame of a lighter); firesetting (the intentional setting of a fire either by a very young child, or by an older minor that does not reach a level of intensity that would involve law enforcement); or arson (a significant fire that requires the clinician to deal not only with the firesetter and his or her parents, but also with the juvenile justice system). Fire misuse is responsive to fire safety education, and that program, usually facilitated by firefighters or fire educators, is the treatment of choice.

However, firesetting and arson will often require the involvement of the juvenile justice system. As such, the evidence-based treatments must be sometimes viewed within the context of the forensic clinical setting. It must be considered that the content of firesetter treatment, as well as the amount of time required for that treatment, may be significantly influenced, if not mandated, by the juvenile justice system. A case in point: though evidence-based treatments are most frequently focused upon fire safety education programs and psychological intervention, an additional, forensically focused treatment program, concerns diversion groups. Fire diversion groups attempt to divert the less problematic youth offender from the juvenile justice system thus reducing the negative effect of inadvertently stigmatizing youth, while at the same time providing some mental health treatment and fire safety information. Exposure to these groups reduces the impact upon the juvenile justice system and informs the group facilitators about the fire offender allowing for more individualized assessment and referral into the mental health system, if necessary. Firesetters may be placed in a diversion group, with other youth, and possibly with their parents. Those groups will be facilitated by members of the mental health, fire service, and juvenile justice professions.

Fire offender treatment should focus upon "firesetter-specific focused therapy" requiring the minor to create a Relapse Prevention Safety Plan, a document often required of juvenile and adult offenders. To be consistent with best practices for offenders, treatment should focus upon community needs, as well as on individual treatment needs and should incorporate aspects of the Risk-Needs-Responsivity (RNR) model.

CASE EXAMPLE

Subject Information and Brief History

When Bill was initially evaluated at juvenile hall, he presented as a 17-year-old African American male. Both of his parents were engineers. In the past, Bill had received some counseling for his diagnoses of ADHD and Oppositional Defiant Disorder (ODD). He had some difficulties in the past with peers picking on him at school and had a minor history of stealing. During the year prior to his arrest, Bill was doing poorly in school. According to his parents, he had few, if any, friends. It appeared to Bill's parents that he had significant difficulties in establishing a social network.

Presenting Problem

Bill was arrested for igniting paper towels in his high school restroom. During the police interview, he acknowledged setting an additional five or six fires in a low brush area near his home, 2 months prior to the index fire, the fire for which he was arrested. Bill was detained at juvenile hall. The Court ultimately accepted Bill's 6 months spent in juvenile hall as "time served." The Court wished information concerning whether Bill was likely to set more fires, whether he would be positively responsive to treatment, and the specifics of treatment recommendations, if treatment was required. Formal probation was mandated and he was required to engage in psychotherapy.

Psychometric testing using the Minnesota Multiphasic Personality Inventory for Adolescents (MMPI-A) and the Millon Adolescent Clinical Inventory (MACI) were in agreement with regard to Bill having problems in social relationships, preferring to be alone, being anxiously conformist, fearing emotional loss of control, and having marked feelings of personal inadequacy. A major theme with regard to the need to gain peer acceptance was noted. The present clinical assessment suggested the likelihood of Bill being placed on the autistic spectrum (e.g., Asperger's Syndrome). Bill had significant difficulty in accurately reading and interpreting his own emotions, as well as the emotions of others.

With regard to fire-related issues, Bill initially denied, and later acknowledged fire ideation in the form of fantasies, occurring prior to various firestarts. Bill disclosed that he would often think about his peers complimenting him when they found out that it was him who set the fires. He confirmed the significant presence of urges to set fires, his wish for the fires to be somewhat larger as the firesets occurred, and initially acknowledged curiosity and vandalism as major motivational factors. With regard to curiosity, he indicated that he initially wanted to know how the fire would look (how it would change color) as it was consuming a large variety of shrubs. Bill was also curious as to whether or not he could successfully set a fire that would not in his view "get out of hand." Relative to vandalism, he disclosed a positive feeling of superiority when fantasizing that he could break the law by destroying property, and get away with it. Though these may have been initial motivating factors, the manner in which Bill responded during the clinical interviews suggested that a need to express anger, as well as a need to obtain peer attention, also reinforced his firesetting behavior. The interviews suggest that during the duration of his firesetting, Bill was becoming more and more distressed with his life. It was felt that the fire served as a "call for help" ultimately allowing Bill to deal with a variety of issues in therapy.

Treatment Intervention and Course

A mandatory aspect of the treatment of the youth firesetter should be an extensive and two-pronged initial evaluation. The clinician must focus on general psychotherapeutic issues that will help the minor reduce the propensity toward any future maladaptive behavior, but must also provide "firesetter-specific focused therapy" in order to meet the needs of the minor, as well as the needs of the community, sometimes represented by the juvenile justice system.

In addition to uncovering psychopathology in general, and especially psychopathology that may have contributed to firesetting, there must be a focus on fire-related issues. Those issues will concern the qualitative and quantitative aspects of the minor's fire ideation (fascination, obsessions, urges to light, pre-firesetting rehearsal imagery, intent to harm, specific motives); reinforcement issues (i.e., sensory, cognitive, and/or concrete reinforcement); and fire-related behavior issues (frequency of fire misuse or firesetting, accelerants used, intended firesetting severity and dangerousness, the minor's reaction to the firestart and the determination of whether there was an escalating severity of fire offending). When the minor's behavior involves the juvenile justice system, the firesetter should produce a Relapse Prevention Safety Plan where the youth will, for the Court, demonstrate his ability to identify high-risk situations that could lead to continued firesetting and specify the cognitive behavior therapy (CBT) (or other) techniques he used (or will use) to deal with those issues.

Bill required 23 sessions of therapy. Perhaps half of those sessions were focused upon general psychotherapeutic issues and the other half concerned fire-related issues. He initially presented with rather flat affect. He stated that his peer relationships, school relationships, and the relationships in his family were nonproblematic. Although he initially identified only curiosity as the motivator for his firesetting, he soon acknowledged a sense of vandalistic reinforcement for the fires set subsequent to his first fire. He disclosed that he liked the idea of destroying something, and being able to do it in such a fashion as to not get caught. He was reinforced by the idea of outwitting, and thus being superior to authority figures. The assessment suggested that Bill was also reinforced by feelings of power and control. Feelings of power occurred at a vicarious level when he imagined his peers complimenting him on his firesetting activities. Feelings of control were manifested as he perceived himself to be in a superior position because his fires caused extensive movement by police departments and required the fire department to put out his fires.

There were six primary treatment goals that supported the overall goal of no recidivistic firesetting. Various methodologies, primarily cognitive behavioral, were the treatment of choice. The first goal required Bill to identify the relationships between his thoughts and emotions with regard to each of his fires. For each fire he was required to identify these relationships relative to (a) Bill's approach behavior to the fire, (b) during the burning of the property, and (c) after Bill left the fire scene. To accomplish this, a Thought-Feeling-Behavior timeline was used. It is important to note that Bill's treatment assignment was not merely to fill out this timeline during the first therapy session, but rather to provide information concerning this timeline throughout his 23 sessions. Through the use of this cognitive technique, Bill came to realize what reinforced his firesetting and that he sometimes engaged in firesetting rehearsal behavior before setting a fire.

Bill always assumed that there would be a positive outcome to his firesets, namely that he would be able to "get away with it." Thus, it was necessary to reduce Bill's inaccurate ideation. Extensive feedback and advice giving were provided concerning the likelihood of Bill not being able to get away with firesetting if he chose to reoffend. He was provided ample examples of the negative effects of firesetting upon the firesetter, firefighters, and the community at large. He was provided homework wherein he would use cognitive restructuring and thus challenge the inappropriate thought that future firesetting would provide any degree of positive reinforcement. Bill was also given an implosive story to use multiple times during the day wherein a fantasized firesetting scenario would lead to disastrous results for him and his family.

Bill acknowledged that he would feel a significant urge to set fires at least a couple hours prior to his various firesets. Feedback and advice giving, especially with regard to the consequences of reoffending were offered. Bill continued his implosive homework. Bill also continued to challenge these thoughts adding various consequences provided by this clinician. During the early part of therapy, Bill claimed that the urges had gone away. Toward the end of therapy, he acknowledged that there were some urges present during the first third or so of therapy, but eventually they were extinguished.

During the initial therapy sessions, Bill acknowledged having strong needs for peer attention, having never obtained significant peer attention during any of his school years. He was extremely upset that he never had close friends, let alone a best friend. He acknowledged having no interpersonal skills though having developed significant interest in the members of the opposite sex. He came to understand that his inability to have in his view "decent relationships" caused him to be exceptionally angry at his peers, and society in general, and especially at himself. He disclosed a feeling of anxiety when thinking about his discomfort whenever he was in peer groups, and especially when he was around females. He disclosed that the anxiety would often lead to anger. Thus, Bill engaged in significant anxiety management training focusing on breathing techniques, general muscular relaxation, positive self-talk, and thought stopping. Anger management training was also provided along with assertiveness training and social skills training. As this clinician and Bill worked through social skills exercises, it became apparent that Bill had significant difficulty in identifying his own feeling states as well as the feeling states of others on the basis of their verbal behavior or gestural behavior. He was provided awareness training with regard to self and others' feelings as part of his social skills training. He became able to significantly reduce and control his anxiety as well as his anger. Though he developed better social skills, it was clear to Bill that social skills development would be a long-term work in progress.

The fifth goal for Bill was the reduction or elimination of many cognitive distortions. Bill's cognitive errors were primarily based on his inability to develop age-appropriate interpersonal relationships and thus he would engage in *overgeneralizing, jumping to conclusions, catastrophizing,* and *seeing himself as a victim.* Bill focused upon thought-stopping techniques, cognitive restructuring, and rational-emotive therapy. A major focus was to show Bill that his cognitive errors were irrational and how to challenge the cognitive error once it was identified as irrational.

Bill's sixth and final goal was the provision of a written Firesetter Relapse Prevention Safety Plan. Coping skills training was provided so that Bill would be able to identify triggers and high-risk situations associated with his offenses. The analysis of the high-risk situations allowed for the development of coping strategies. The focus of the Risk-Need-Responsivity (RNR) model was to help analyze Bill's past problematic and criminogenic issues and thus set the stage for relevant treatment.

Bill's Firesetter Relapse Prevention Safety Plan consisted of four sections. The first required him to describe the environmental press preceding his fires and the specifics with regard to his offenses. He was required to enumerate offense motives and reinforcement factors. The second section concerned victim issues which included Bill's statements concerning his awareness of the effects (or potential effects) of his offenses, Bill's proclamations concerning responsibility taken and remorse felt. This section also required an apology letter as well as a focus on restorative justice. The third section concerned Bill's proposed changes with regard to his interactions with others. This included information about Bill increasing prosocial influences in his life and decreasing criminogenic influences. These influences included any issues with family, peers, authority figures, or new relationships. The final section concerned Bill's proposed changes with regard to himself. This included his ability to define high-risk situations that could lead to firesetting and a specific description of those psychological techniques that he will use to prevent recidivism. He included a discussion on how deviant thoughts and fantasies, urges, inappropriate ideation,

TABLE 7.1 Treatment Goals and Methodologies

GOALS	METHODS
There were six primary treatment goals supporting the overall goal of no recidivistic firesetting:	The methodologies that effectively dealt with these goals were as follows:
1. Identify the relationships between thought, emotion, and firesetting behavior	A. Use of a firesetter Thought-Feeling-Behavior timeline
2. Reduce inappropriate ideation concerning the positive outcomes of firesetting	A. Cognitive restructuring B. Implosive therapy C. Feedback and advice giving
3. Reduce urges to set fires	A. Feedback and advice giving—regarding the consequences of reoffense B. Implosive therapy C. Cognitive restructuring
4. Reduce anger at society which appeared to be based on the minor's lack of peer attention and significant need for peer attention	A. Anger management training B. Anxiety management training—Focus on breathing, relaxation, assertiveness training, self talk, and thought stopping C. Social skills training D. Awareness of own feelings training E. Awareness of others' feelings training
5. Reduce and eliminate cognitive distortions	A. Cognitive therapy B. Rational-emotive therapy
6. Provide a Firesetter Relapse Prevention Fire Safety Plan, in writing	A. RNR (Risk-Need-Responsivity) therapy B. Coping skills training

This table provides a breakdown of treatment goals as well as CBT techniques that were used to reduce or extinguish maladaptive thoughts, feelings, or behaviors.

as well as fire-related behavior would be dealt with. This section also included Bill's new understanding concerning fire safety issues.

Outcome

Bill ultimately acknowledged as firesetting reinforcers, his seeking of power and control as well as the peer attention needs he initially denied. He ultimately understood that his need for power was based on a need for peer acknowledgement, peer attention, and peer affiliation. His need for control was understood to be a function of the over-control that his parents manifested through his teen years. These issues were uncovered and ultimately "worked through" in treatment. Two years posttreatment he had not recidivated. He was engaging in no maladaptive behaviors. He reported no inappropriate fire-related behaviors, no inappropriate ideation concerning any fire-related issues, and was actively involved with peers. Bill is in his second year of college. He produced a detailed Relapse Prevention Safety Plan which contributed significantly to the minor being taken off probation.

CHALLENGES IN APPLYING THE EVIDENCE-BASED TREATMENT

Within the forensic context, there are challenges in applying the evidence-based treatment described as youths have little reason to be honest during their initial evaluation, especially when that evaluation is mandated by the justice system. In the forensic setting, juvenile firesetters are apprised of the nonconfidentiality of their evaluations and may be told that their treatment is also not confidential, if they are placed on probation. Yet, for those adolescents who come into treatment postsentencing, even as a condition of probation, this clinician perceives a reasonable degree of honesty in their responses.

CULTURAL DIVERSITY ISSUES

There are many myths associated with firesetting. It is incumbent upon the clinician to clarify to the Court and others the dynamics of the youth's firesetting. If these issues are not clarified, those myths and inaccuracies concerning *intelligence, socioeconomic status, ethnicity, recidivism, sexuality, age*, and *gender* are likely to persist. The persistence of some myths concerning the firesetter are counterproductive to treatment, and may impact the willingness of the juvenile justice system itself to believe that a youth is low risk to recidivate when that is the determination of the evaluating clinician. If the Court does not believe that treatment will be of help, the youth may never be given the opportunity to be treated.

FUTURE RESEARCH

It is quite likely that the number of juvenile-caused fires are underrepresented in the available data. Research into the development of a national database is necessary to determine how often and under what circumstances juveniles set fires. A database of this type will also provide additional information concerning the gender issues that were commented upon by the researchers. A more thorough understanding of the circumstances under which adolescent females set fires when compared to their male counterparts will provide information that can be useful both in their assessment and treatment. Few studies have focused upon firesetting recidivism, and have defined empirically, the most effective techniques for dealing with the various categories and subcategories of firesetters. This clinician perceives six major categories which include: *cry for help, delinquent/antisocial, significant emotional dysfunction, cognitively impaired, sociocultural*, and *wildland* types. In addition to these motivational categories, future research should also look at those major qualities of reinforcement such as psychobiological reinforcement, cognitive reinforcement, and concrete forms of reinforcement when considering the treatment methodologies that most effectively reduce recidivism. Moreover, it would be beneficial to more accurately calculate the recidivism rate concerning treated and untreated firesetters, both nationally and regionally. Database information is not available that will allow a researcher or clinician to compare relevant fire-related or psychopathological issues in firesetters to other firesetters in regional communities or to firesetters as a national group.

KEY REFERENCES

Dickens, G., Sugarman, P., & Gannon, T. (Eds.). (2012). *Arson and mental health: Theory, research and practice.* RCPsych Pubs.

Doley, R., Fineman, K., Fritzon, K., Dolan, M., & McEwan, T. (2011). Risk factors for recidivistic arson in adult arson offenders. *Psychology, Psychiatry and Law, 18*(3), 409–423.

Fineman, K. R. (1995). A model for the qualitative analysis of child and adult fire deviant behavior. *American Journal of Forensic Psychology, 13*, 31–60.

CHAPTER 8

Gifted Children

Steven I. Pfeiffer

CLINICAL PROBLEM

As far back as Confucius in China and Plato in Greece, philosophers wrote about "heavenly" children. Early East Asian and classical European traditions both embraced similar views that giftedness constituted a set of special attributes which we today would view as components of intellectual ability. In the United States, we trace early attention to the gifted to the research conducted by Lewis Terman, whose longitudinal study followed high IQ students (higher than 140). Terman collected data on these students over the course of 50 years and concluded that high IQ kids are healthier, better-adjusted, and higher achievers.

Gifted children and youth remain a misunderstood population. Part of the problem is definitional. The federal definition states that the gifted demonstrate outstanding ability or potential and require differentiated educational programs, and includes exceptional intellectual, academic, and leadership ability, creativity, and artistic talent. In clinical practice, however, high IQ remains the predominant definitional criterion. Most psychologists and schools use the criterion of an IQ score of 120, 125, or 130.

A second definitional issue that has contributed to misunderstanding is whether we should narrowly define giftedness as persons of high IQ or more broadly define giftedness as any person with exceptional ability or uncommon talent. A third issue is whether we should restrict our conceptualization to those children with already demonstrated high ability or also consider children with outstanding promise.

Most would agree that the child who is reading at age 3, playing competitive chess at age 6, or performing cello in an orchestra at age 10 is gifted. These examples reflect children who are developmentally advanced, a hallmark of giftedness. Characteristics commonly associated with giftedness include advanced language and reasoning, interests more aligned with older children and adults, impressive memory, intuitive understanding of concepts, insatiable curiosity, uncanny ability to connect disparate ideas and appreciate relationships, rapid learning, heightened sensitivity of feelings and emotions, perfectionism, and asynchrony across developmental domains. However, no gifted child exhibits all of these characteristics and gifted children vary tremendously in core characteristics. Giftedness does not always make an early appearance. For every Mozart, who created masterpieces at an early age, there is the Cézanne, whose great art was completed later in life.

Of course, the gifted, like their nongifted peers, experience typical developmental challenges. Sometimes, developmental milestones occur quite early, which can create unique problems. Some gifted are vulnerable to emotional problems because of the very characteristics that are the hallmark of giftedness. For example, asynchronous development can generate feelings of being out of sync with their peers. Some gifted feel uncomfortably different and have difficulty finding a friend; others experience bullying. Some gifted view their gift as a burden. Difficulty with affect regulation or negative perfectionism increases their vulnerability to psychological problems. An appreciable number of gifted experience a mismatch with their educational environment, which can create boredom, inattentiveness, underachievement, and conduct problems.

The gifted are not immune to the social and emotional challenges that all children face. Some gifted underperform to mask their abilities. A number of gifted struggle with depression, suicide ideation,[1] anxiety, social isolation and feelings of alienation, anger management, neurotic perfectionism, and sexual identity issues. Finally, some gifted are twice exceptional and have sensory, orthopedic, or communication disabilities or psychiatric disorders coexisting with their giftedness, including ADHD, Asperger's disorder, eating disorders, and mood disorders. Experts hypothesize that the majority of twice exceptional gifted/disabled have specific learning disabilities (SLD). There are three types of gifted/SLD. The first type is the gifted with subtle, subclinical learning problems. The second type is diagnosed as learning disabled but rarely identified as gifted. Their learning disability is more pervasive and severe and moderates their academic success. The third type remains unrecognized as either learning disabled or gifted. Their learning disability masks their gift and their gift obscures their learning disability.

Authorities agree that the gifted are those in the upper 2% to 10% compared to their peers in general intelligence, academics, the arts, and leadership. Not surprisingly, there is evidence for a genetic influence. The fields of music and mathematics are rich with child prodigies. Evidence also comes from the unfolding of extraordinary accomplishments among kids from impoverished environments. Most authorities agree that the unfolding of extraordinary talent requires a supportive environment.

PREVALENCE

Giftedness is a social construction, not something real. Prevalence rates, therefore, are always going to be arbitrary and inexact. The number of gifted students reflects how states and schools define giftedness and what criteria they set. Nationwide estimates range from a conservative 3% to as high as 15%. There is no true cutoff between giftedness and nongiftedness, although many would like to believe otherwise.

Research indicates that most gifted are socially well adjusted. Contrary to common stereotype, most gifted are popular, make friends, get along with peers, and do not experience loneliness or depression. Experts estimate that 90% of the gifted are well adjusted and 10% experience some of the difficulties noted above. If we assume that roughly 6% of students are classified as gifted, then there are about 3 million gifted students in the United States. In 2000–2001, there were nearly 6 million students served under the IDEA, equating to approximately 360,000 or 6% of the students served by IDEA as gifted/disabled.

---

[1] Authorities assume that the prevalence of child/adolescent psychiatric problems, such as suicide ideation, gesture, attempts, and successful completions is not markedly different for the gifted and general population. The gifted engage in suicidal behaviors, just like their nongifted peers.

CULTURAL DIVERSITY ISSUES

Prevalence varies along racial/ethnic and socioeconomic lines. This should come as no surprise to the reader as there is a long history of children of color and economically disadvantaged children scoring appreciably lower, on average, on IQ tests. Asian children, however, are disproportionately overrepresented in gifted programs in the United States, likely owing to the high value placed on academics and hard work in the family. The Chinese have a wonderful term for encouraging their children's intellectual development, in fact, "chi ku," translated as "eating bitterness."

EVIDENCE-BASED TREATMENTS

A provocative and even inconvenient question is whether a unique approach is required in psychotherapeutic work with the gifted. Many who write about counseling the gifted feel that this is a basic maxim, that the gifted warrant a unique therapeutic approach. I advocate a slightly different tactic. The approach that I advocate is scientifically defensible and starts from the perspective that the therapist follows a model of evidence-based practice. My approach integrates (a) *the best available research* on the presenting disorder with (b) *clinical expertise* in the context of (c) a *deep understanding of the gifted*. All three components are critical if treatment is to be effective. There exists clinically relevant research on almost every type of psychological problem that a clinician might encounter in work with a gifted child. For example, I report on a case of successfully treating a gifted adolescent with borderline pathology employing dialectical behavior therapy.[2] Cognitive behavior therapy has proven to be an effective intervention for anxiety disorders among gifted children.

Therapeutic work with the gifted should always address the *parents* and *family* and consider *academics and the school situation.* The quality of the *therapeutic relationship* with the gifted client is essential. Clinical expertise in work with the gifted requires compassion, patience, making prudent and well-timed interventions, respecting that change can be difficult and take time, being sensitive to sociocultural nuances and comfortable working with high ability kids. The therapist must be comfortable verbally sparring with the client, because many gifted adolescents relish and are quite adept at debating a point!

FUTURE RESEARCH

The great majority of information on the twice exceptional gifted/disabled and on treating the gifted is based on case study and anecdotal clinical reports. There are few empirical studies where practitioners can turn. There is not even one prospective, epidemiological study that has looked at a large community sample of nonreferred gifted to determine the etiology, pathogenesis, course, or incidence for those who present with psychological disorders. The few treatment studies that exist consist of small clinical samples. Research is needed to determine how widespread misdiagnoses and missed diagnoses are for the gifted. It would be helpful for research to examine the potential value of prevention models, career counseling, and a positive psychology framework in work with the gifted.

---

[2]Pfeiffer, S. I. (2012). *Serving the gifted: Evidence-based clinical and psychoeducational practice* (see Chapter 8: "Counseling Gifted Students"). NY: Routledge.

KEY REFERENCES

Kennedy-Moore, E., & Lowenthal, M. S. (2011). *Smart parenting for smart kids*. New York, NY: Jossey-Bass.
Mendaglio, S., & Peterson, J. S. (Eds.). (2007). *Models of counseling gifted children, adolescents, and young adults*. Waco, TX: Prufrock Press.
Pfeiffer, S. I. (2012). *Serving the gifted: Clinical and psychoeducational practices*. New York, NY: Routledge.

Clinician Application

Gifted Children

Aimee Yermish

COMMENT ON THE EVIDENCE-BASED RECOMMENDATIONS

To a great extent, I find myself in agreement with Dr. Pfeiffer's argument that there does not need to be specifically "gifted therapy" per se, so much as there needs to be skilled psychotherapy that takes into account a deep understanding of giftedness. The clinician needs to consider how all aspects of the context, content, and course of treatment may be affected by the client's high intelligence. Many gifted clients report that issues common within the gifted population—including mismatches with the family, school, occupational, and social environments; developmental asynchronies and interests unusual for age and gender; and the often intense and reactive temperament common in highly intelligent individuals—are either not understood well by psychotherapists, or may even be misconstrued as being "what's wrong with you."

A psychotherapist working with gifted clients needs to be flexible and comfortable with challenge. Techniques often must be adapted to take into account the specific developmental needs of the client. It is easy to be misled, either by a client's young age or by their high verbal skills, into oversimplifying or overshooting what the client is really ready for in treatment. Many gifted individuals explore their internal and external world through questioning and debate, and work best in egalitarian relationships. Psychotherapists must be able to manage the variety of countertransference issues often raised by this population, such as envy, dismissiveness, resentment, competitiveness, and narcissism.

CASE EXAMPLE

Subject Information and Brief History

Zachary was a 10-year-old White male, the only child of warm and supportive suburban middle-class parents. He had been previously assessed, at age 10 years and

5 months, as cognitively gifted, with a somewhat uneven cognitive profile, but no frank learning disabilities. He was evaluated with the Weschler Intelligence Scale for Children, fourth edition (WISC-IV), on which he received a Full Scale IQ score of 132. His Verbal Comprehension factor score was 144, Perceptual Reasoning 117, Working Memory 120, and Processing Speed 115. He demonstrated a relative strength on the tests that tapped into his abilities in problem solving and knowledge of social convention. At the same time, on the Weschler Individual Achievement Test (WIAT-II), he had a Reading Composite of 141, Written Language Composite of 152, and a Mathematics Composite of 114. His mathematical reasoning was in the superior range, but his ability to perform routine calculations was in the average range. He had also qualified for programs run by the Johns Hopkins University's Center for Talented Youth. He attended a private school, which was not specifically focused on gifted children, but had a solid general curriculum. He generally did very well academically, except as noted below. He had strong social skills but reported finding it difficult to find access to people with whom he could be close friends.

Presenting Problem

Zachary's parents referred him for treatment for a variety of concerns related to his cognitive and academic profile. Academically, he had specific problems with handwriting and the memorization of mathematics facts and procedures. However, he was chronically frustrated by what was for him an insufficiently challenging curriculum. In particular, he was a tremendously skilled writer and an avid musician, putting a great deal of effort into improving his craft in both domains. He demonstrated high levels of maladaptively perfectionist expectations for himself, despite constant reassurance from parents and teachers that his work was good enough. Although he had strong levels of social interest and skills, he had difficulty in finding peers with whom he could connect. Zachary also manifested substantial anxiety on a range of topics. For example, in addition to math anxiety, he had never slept away from home, and he worried frequently about existential issues and his own place in the world.

Treatment Intervention and Course

Treatment consisted of weekly individual psychotherapy sessions, with occasional parent guidance sessions for his mother, as well as joint problem-solving sessions with the middle school teaching staff. This continued over the course of several years, with the focus and intensity shifting as Zachary's needs changed. The initial focus was on the remediation of specific problems in mathematics, handwriting, and perfectionist anxiety. Over time, our relationship focused more on meeting Zachary's needs for adult mentoring and helping him connect with resources outside the family.

Zachary found materials designed for children his age to teach simplified penmanship to be demeaning and to interfere with his desire to have his handwriting express his personality. Instead, we took a collaborative approach in which Zachary was guided in designing and practicing his own handwriting, adapting materials designed for adults. He accepted my criteria that it be simple, legible, and consistent, and he was then quite willing to engage in the regular practice necessary to make the handwriting automatic.

Issues around mathematics were handled in a similar fashion. Math anxiety was addressed through direct exposure: he did math work during the sessions. The work combined small but consistent amounts of remedial practice with study in a challenging, conceptually oriented, and structured curriculum designed for students capable of formal operational reasoning. Zachary was included in the process of choosing materials, and we focused on building self-efficacy.

Not surprisingly, Zachary's anxiety, perfectionism, and vulnerability to existential depression were handled through methods informed by typical cognitive behavioral therapy (CBT): for example, building awareness of dysfunctional thoughts and learning to dispute cognitive distortions. However, the traditional approach was constraining in its structure and too similar to the insultingly simple worksheets at school. Materials designed for children his age were rejected out of hand. Furthermore, he recognized that simply knowing that a thought was distorted was not sufficient to make it stop bothering him, and chafed at the idea of having adults essentially dictate that his thoughts were "wrong" and needed to be "fixed." A more relaxed and exploratory approach was important in working with him. Neither CBT, mathematics, nor handwriting was approached through a strict, worksheet-based approach. Curricula were combined, adapted, changed, and created on the fly, in order to provide an appropriate pace and level of academic and emotional challenge. Often, the discussion moved toward a critical examination of the materials themselves and how they did or did not capture the particular nature of his own struggles.

Zachary's existential concerns, in particular, bore thoughtful consideration in psychotherapy. Despite his impressive accomplishments, including numerous awards for his writing, and despite the absence of parental pressure to do more, Zachary still felt that he wasn't "living up to his potential." It was hard for him to avoid holding himself to adult standards. Like many gifted children, it was difficult for him to find valid external reference points and thus to distinguish between "improving his craft" and "setting his sights too high." Within the context of the mentoring relationship, we engaged with the broader philosophical questions these problems evoked. In particular, we deconstructed the idea of "potential" and recognized it as a constantly moving set of goalposts which could never actually be met.

Research findings and clinical lore show that gifted children often struggle to find adults outside the family whom they can see as valid judges, both of their work and of their personal worth. Zachary felt that he could not receive valid judgments from his parents as, after all, unconditional love and validation is what parents do. With his teachers, Zachary believed, rightly or wrongly, that they lacked the intellectual capacity to be valid judges. Based on joint meetings with the middle school staff, Zachary's perceptions seemed accurate: although very well intentioned, the teachers were largely not themselves capable of being valid role models for what it means to be a gifted adult. In part to establish eligibility to serve this role, and in part to offer models of various ways in which developmental challenges could be met, I engaged in substantially more self-disclosure than is common, particularly with a child this age. The role was less of "instructor" or "doctor," and more of "mentor" or "fellow-traveler." Thus, the therapy contained elements both of traditional psychotherapy and of humanistic mentoring.

Outcome

Zachary found the work extremely helpful. He was able to improve his academic skills, manage his anxiety, choose appropriate goals for himself, and seek out social contacts outside the school who were as thoughtful and as engaged as he was, regardless of age. When it came time for Zachary and his family to choose a high school, he had a variety of options, each offering both academic and personal challenge. Despite having never been on a sleep-over until middle school age, Zachary surprised the adults in his life by choosing an elite boarding school, which offered a very high academic level as well as a comparable peer group. Narrative reports from the school consistently indicated that he was an outstanding and joyful student. He and his parents returned for brief consultations periodically, as new developmental stages brought new questions (e.g., adolescent relationships, college choice). At the time of this writing, he is doing very well in his studies at a top-tier college. He reported that when high school and college life became problematic for him, reflecting on the work that he and this therapist had done together helped him to effectively manage the stress and anxiety.

CHALLENGES IN APPLYING THE EVIDENCE-BASED APPROACH

To adapt evidence-based treatments to the gifted population, it is crucial to accept that these individuals often have great needs for autonomy and collaboration within the relationship, even at very young ages. Developmental needs may be sharply different from what the clinician might expect. Some, like Zachary, may need a highly intellectual approach, while others may use overintellectualization to avoid facing their problems, leading psychotherapists to mistakenly treat them as if they were "little adults."

In determining what the nature of the problem is, clinicians must remember that the goal is not for the child to have "a normal childhood" or to force them into a standard model, but rather for them to have their *own* childhood in which their personal developmental needs are met. Because many of the problems arising from giftedness are not seen as problems by the educational system or insurance companies, parents are often confused or frustrated and need thoughtful guidance and advocacy. Clinicians must inform themselves of the myths, hype, and political agendas associated with this population, in order to help the families navigate the complexities of the system.

Research on the experiences of gifted clients in psychotherapy strongly suggests that clinicians must maintain an awareness of their own countertransference regarding the client's high ability. Otherwise, iatrogenic harm can ensue. Examples include such events as a therapist telling a young client that the reason he had no friends was because his being smart was making the other kids feel bad, leading to the client learning to hate himself and to attempt suicide; a play therapist who insisted upon playing chess with a child in every session and beating him in every game they played in order to "put him in his place"; and a series of substance abuse therapists who told a young woman that her intense emotions (a common finding in the gifted population) and non-gender-normative interests were the problem, leading her to increase her substance abuse in an attempt to reduce that intensity.

Training is also an important concern: giftedness is not regarded as a legitimate area about which clinicians must educate themselves in order to provide competent treatment. Because of the common misconceptions that gifted clients suffer only from minor adjustment issues and that their superior cognitive resources will enable them to handle any problem, they are often viewed as easy cases. Thus, more serious issues can be overlooked or casually dismissed.

CULTURAL DIVERSITY ISSUES

The most serious problem with the research on giftedness in psychotherapy is that much of it is based on the erroneous assumption that all gifted clients look like Zachary. The overwhelming majority of the research literature is focused on White middle-class children or adolescents, with no major sociocultural risk factors beyond giftedness itself, dealing with relatively minor adjustment issues related to achievement and social isolation. Although scores on IQ tests may be differentially distributed across sociocultural boundaries, giftedness is found in individuals at all ages, from all ethnic and racial boundaries, and from all economic strata. In fact, those who do not come from such supportive environments as Zachary may be at considerably greater risk for psychological distress. For example, I worked extensively with a 40-year-old gifted low-income male who was in treatment for substance abuse, anger management issues, mood disorder, a history of complex trauma, and existential issues regarding his having been born as a result of his mother's having been raped. This client was constantly being kicked out of court-mandated anger management classes and Alcoholics Anonymous meetings for the same reasons that gifted children often get in trouble in school: he did not accept the pat, simple answers given in group, and the difficult questions that were important to him could not easily be answered within that therapeutic context. The manualized group therapy was like an oversimplified curriculum, and the emphasis within the system on client compliance with therapist and court demands created a strong desire to prove them wrong. As with Zachary, this client benefited from an egalitarian and humanistic approach, in which he could honestly explore what he needed to face in order to make real change.

FUTURE RESEARCH

As Dr. Pfeiffer notes in his summary, most of the research on gifted clients who struggle with serious mental health issues is limited to case reports. Most large-scale studies which suggest that gifted clients are not at risk for psychological disorders are flawed in that the samples were chosen from populations already selected for positive adjustment (e.g., adolescents about to enter governors' schools). All of the arguments about prevalence, however, become moot when gifted clients present in the office: by definition, if they are seeking psychotherapy, they must feel that they have a problem. The research base must be expanded to test the validity of the clinical lore and to provide more concrete guidance for clinicians about how to adapt evidence-based treatments for this population. Furthermore, as noted above, the research base must be expanded to include gifted clients from a broad range of sociocultural backgrounds and those with a wider variety of psychological disorders.

KEY REFERENCES

Mendaglio, S., & Peterson, J. S. (Eds.). (2007). *Models of counseling gifted children, adolescents, and young adults.* Waco, TX: Prufrock Press.

Pfeiffer, S. I. (2012). *Serving the gifted: Clinical and psychoeducational practices.* New York, NY: Routledge.

Yermish, A. (2010a). Cheetahs on the couch: Issues affecting the therapeutic working alliance with clients who are cognitively gifted. Doctoral dissertation. Retrieved from PQDT Open. (AAT 3415722). Available from http://www.davincilearning.org/sketchbook/research.html

CHAPTER 9

Obsessive-Compulsive Disorder in Children

Caleb W. Lack and Eric A. Storch

CLINICAL PROBLEM

Obsessive-Compulsive Disorder (OCD) is a relatively prevalent childhood disorder—affecting approximately 1% to 2% of youth—that has been associated with substantial impairment in quality of life. OCD is characterized by intrusive, troubling thoughts (obsessions), and repetitive, ritualistic behaviors (compulsions) which are time consuming, significantly impair functioning, and/or cause distress. When an obsession occurs, it corresponds with a massive increase in anxiety/distress. Compulsions serve to reduce this associated anxiety/distress. Common obsessions include: contamination fears, worries about harm to self or others, the need for symmetry, exactness and order, religious/moralistic concerns, forbidden thoughts (e.g., sexual or aggressive), and/or a need to seek reassurance or confess. Common compulsions include: cleaning/washing, checking, counting, repeating, straightening, routinized behaviors, confessing, praying, seeking reassurance, touching, tapping or rubbing, and/or avoidance. Although symptoms of pediatric OCD are generally similar to those in adults, children need not view their symptoms as nonsensical to meet diagnostic criteria.

PREVALENCE

In the United States, the lifetime prevalence rate of OCD is estimated at around 1% to 2.3% in children and adolescents under 18, while the 1-year prevalence rate is around 0.7% in children. There is also a fairly substantial number of "subclinical" cases of OCD (around 5% of the population), where symptoms are either not disturbing or not disruptive enough to meet full criteria. Pediatric OCD is heavily male dominated, with some studies showing that there is an evening out within the genders by adulthood, and some showing that the numbers reverse and females become predominant.

CULTURAL DIVERSITY ISSUES

There is strong evidence that cultural differences do not play a prominent role in presence of OCD, with research showing few epidemiological differences across different countries and even between European and Asian populations. There are cultural influences on symptom expression, however. In Bali, for example, heavy emphasis on somatic symptoms and need to know about members of their social network is found. Type of religious upbringing has been related to different types of primary obsessions, such as emphasis on cleanliness and order in Judaism, religious obsessions in Muslim communities, aggressions in South American samples, and dirt and contamination worries in the United States.

EVIDENCE-BASED TREATMENTS

Cognitive behavioral therapy (CBT) is the most well-supported psychological intervention for children with OCD. It is a structured approach to teaching both the client and his or her family skills for responding to symptoms. The short-term efficacy of CBT has been supported in numerous clinical trials, with excellent maintenance of symptom reduction at follow-up up to 7 years in pediatric populations. Effect sizes favor CBT versus antidepressant monotherapy (1.98 versus 1.13). Indeed, a large-scale, multisite randomized placebo-controlled trial found greater symptom reduction in patients receiving either CBT alone or in combination with sertraline relative to sertraline and placebo (sertraline was superior to placebo in outcomes). Recent work suggests group-administered CBT to be as effective in improving symptoms as individual CBT in children although this requires further verification and may present logistic challenges when considering the heterogeneous nature of OCD.

The central component of CBT for OCD is exposure and response prevention (ERP), although cognitive restructuring can also be incorporated in an adjunctive basis. Exposure with response prevention is a behavioral technique based on learning theory, namely Mowrer's two-stage theory for fear acquisition and maintenance. To eliminate the fear, persons with OCD must first be exposed to the fear-causing stimulus and then prevented from engaging in rituals which serve to reduce distress (and thus, are negatively reinforcing). Exposure relies on the gradual decrease in anxiety after being exposed to a feared or ritual-provoking stimulus. This leads to decreased anxiety and more rapid attenuation of distress in future exposures. Exposures are typically performed in vivo, using real-life settings and situations. Using imaginal exposures may be required in some situations, such as addressing feared consequences of not performing a ritual. One aspect of performing exposures to be aware of is that the psychotherapist should first model each exposure before having the client perform it. This will not only provide evidence that doing the exposure is safe, but it will serve as an exposure in and of itself that will be less distressing than when the client performs the exposure. When dealing with living creatures (e.g., insects, snakes, dogs) or potentially dangerous situations (e.g., heights), the psychotherapist must take precautions to ensure the safety of the client (e.g., using nonpoisonous snakes). Response prevention is based on the assumption that rituals and compulsions serve to reduce anxiety in the short term through negative reinforcement (i.e., escaping and/or avoiding distress). Individuals with OCD perform rituals to relieve anxiety, and do not have the experience of anxiety reduction naturally. Response prevention does exactly this, requiring the patient to avoid performing their compulsion so the anxiety can be reduced through the process of habituation. Cognitive restructuring involves teaching youth how to challenge anxious thoughts, as these involve inaccurate interpretations of events. Commonly seen themes in children with OCD include inaccurate estimates of danger, responsibility, and likelihood. Cognitive techniques demonstrate to the client how to effectively argue with obsessions, helping to recognize and reframe those obsessions in a realistic manner.

Extensive research has been performed examining the most effective ERP strategies. Response prevention after exposure is a necessary treatment component as findings suggest that exposure alone is not sufficient for clinical benefit. Mixed results have been reported in terms of the use of imaginal exposure as a supplement to in vivo exposure, even though it tends to be recommended by clinical experts.

Gradual exposure, working up from least distressing to most distress situations, is also recommended, as this can assist in building success early in treatment, increasing motivation for more difficult exposures. The optimal frequency of therapy for OCD has not been conclusively determined. Both intensive (e.g., daily sessions for 3–4 weeks) and weekly or twice-weekly sessions show excellent results and no differences in effectiveness. The most highly motivated individuals, or those with very strong support systems, may require less frequent clinical contact, while those with more severe symptoms or low motivation may benefit from more intensive treatment. The involvement of family members for both adults and children, including spouses, parents, and siblings, has been associated with better long-term outcomes and is highly recommended.

Antidepressant medications involving serotonin reuptake inhibitors (SRI) have shown efficacy relative to placebo in pediatric OCD treatment. However, response rates across antidepressant trials are modest, with about 50% to 60% of youth considered treatment responders and average response rate being approximately 35% reduction in symptoms. Clinical remission with SRI monotherapy is rare as many patients do not prefer pharmacological approaches, and there is a real concern for side effects. Thus, practice parameters suggest CBT alone for mild and moderate cases, and conjoint CBT and antidepressant therapy for severe cases.

FUTURE RESEARCH

There are a number of areas in need of empirical attention. First, treatment dissemination, particularly for CBT, remains an issue. The average latency between symptom onset and provision of any treatment is quite long, with some estimates in adults suggesting over 10 years. Efforts have been made to incorporate technology into the treatment of OCD in general, with recent efforts to extend into the realm of pediatric OCD. For example, Storch et al. (unpublished data) reported on a randomized trial of web camera-delivered CBT, finding robust outcomes relative to a waitlist control. Second, although many youth respond to first-line interventions, partial response is frequent with many youth continuing to exhibit residual symptoms, particularly to medication monotherapy. Augmentation options remain limited and under-researched. One approach involves targeting extinction learning core to ERP with D-cycloserine (DCS), a partial agonist at the N-methyl-D-aspartate (NMDA) receptor in the amygdala. Preliminary results in youth with OCD show promising results and are suggestive of further work. Third, given the frequency of comorbidity in pediatric OCD presentation (~75%) and the impact certain comorbid conditions might have on outcome, attention should be given to personalizing treatment approaches to address comorbidity patterns (e.g., combining parent management training with CBT for youth with OCD and disruptive behavior). Finally, further understanding about the relevance of immune factors in the etiology and treatment of pediatric OCD is needed given recent clinical attention in this domain.

KEY REFERENCES

Barrett, P. M., Farrell, L., Pina, A. A., Peris, T. S., & Piacentini, J. (2008). Evidence-based psychosocial treatments for child and adolescent obsessive-compulsive disorder. *Journal of Clinical Child and Adolescent Psychology, 37*, 131–155.

Mancuso, E., Faro, A., Joshi, G., & Geller, D. A. (2010). Treatment of pediatric obsessive-compulsive disorder: A review. *Journal of Child and Adolescent Psychopharmacology, 20*, 299–308.

Storch, E. A., Murphy, T. K., & Geffken, G. R. (Eds.). (2007). *Handbook of child and adolescent obsessive-compulsive disorder*. Mahwah, NJ: Lawrence Erlbaum.

Obsessive-Compulsive Disorder in Children

Raegan B. Smith

COMMENT ON EVIDENCE-BASED TREATMENTS

As described by Drs. Lack and Storch, the evidence-based treatment (EBT) for the treatment of pediatric Obsessive-Compulsive Disorder (OCD) is cognitive behavioral therapy (CBT) with exposure plus response prevention (ERP). This mode of treatment is useful in that it is a direct intervention upon the anxiety experienced by the client and has good ecological validity. That is, this form of treatment provides a sometimes rare opportunity to create and treat the same situations in psychotherapy as the client experiences in their natural environment.

Although this clinician does not always begin exposure treatments immediately in the course of therapy, it is always the ultimate objective in achieving the identified treatment goals for pediatric OCD. More specifically, ERP may be preceded by other treatment modalities, such as play therapy or parent training. However, neither of these approaches is typically sufficient for full elimination of OCD symptoms.

CASE EXAMPLE

Subject Information and Brief History

The client is an 11-year-old boy presenting for treatment with multiple diagnoses, including ADHD and Bipolar Disorder-Not Otherwise Specified. He presented a complicated clinical case for which empirically supported interventions were used. He had significant learning problems and was receiving special education services. The client had begun having significant difficulties maintaining friendships and was functioning poorly in peer interactions. His social history was significant for repeated disruptions in the family environment and an enmeshed mother–child dynamic. In addition, there was a family history positive for OCD and Bipolar Disorder with psychotic features. Prior to treatment, OCD symptoms caused significant psychological distress for the client and led to remarkable parent–child relational problems. For example, the parent often became frustrated in response to the client's compulsive question asking and reacted punitively. The client, in turn, grew more anxious, as evidenced by withdrawal and tearfulness.

Presenting Problem

This client presented with recurring fears of overestimated dangers and threats, contamination fears, food-related obsessions and compulsions (i.e., food items having to remain separate on the plate, refusal to eat casserole-type dishes due to fears of foods mixed in unfamiliar ways or with gooey substances, and insisting on using separate utensils for separate dishes), obsessions about going to hell, compulsive apologizing, and compulsive question asking with the primary caregiver. His mother was concerned about the amount of time OCD symptoms consumed for her son, as well as the level of disruption to their routine owing to OCD symptoms. Also, as is typical of pediatric OCD, the client exhibited little insight into the nature of his anxiety symptoms.

Treatment Intervention and Course

This client presented as a complicated clinical case for which empirically supported cognitive therapy interventions were employed. Cognitive interventions were used to challenge overestimated dangers and threats and to help the client view obsessions as "false alarms" his mind was giving him. That is, the client was instructed and learned that obsessions were like fire alarms sounding when there is no fire. Put another way, they are thoughts that send threat messages when there is actually no true or probable threat in the current environment. The client was taught how to discriminate OCD thinking from healthy, adaptive thinking. Specifically, the client was taught to identify obsessive thoughts and label them as such for himself. He was also instructed on how to identify his basic goals/values in various situations when obsessions tended to disrupt his ability to function adaptively. When obsessions were a problem, he learned to refocus his thoughts onto self-talk intended to help him do what he really wanted or needed to do instead of the obsessions. ERP was implemented in two phases. First, the primary caregiver was taught the skills necessary for extinguishing reinforcement of compulsive question asking and apologizing. Specifically, the caregiver's feelings about the compulsive question asking and apologizing were identified and the motivation to respond differently was established. Following this, the caregiver was instructed to cease answering compulsive questions and providing reassurance in response to compulsive apologies. Instead, the caregiver was instructed to say "That sounds like OCD to me," or "This sounds like an opportunity to stand up to OCD. I wonder if there's anything I can do to help." The client was also involved in a therapeutic agreement about how compulsive behaviors would be handled within the parent–child interaction. However, owing to the complexity of the client's individual and family issues and in order to ensure the success of the behavioral intervention at home, a great deal of time was devoted to parent training to address coercive interaction styles (i.e., gradual escalations in conflict behaviors, such as yelling and threats, which had developed over time and were reinforced by the child's history of escaping demands initially but then complying eventually with increased parental negativity).

The second phase of treatment was devoted to doing in vivo ERP during office visits to treat food-related obsessions and compulsions. After creating a hierarchy of food-related fears and compulsions, exposures were designed to gradually increase the level of anxiety provoked by the stimuli presented in session. To create the hierarchy of fears, the client, therapist, and parent worked collaboratively to establish a list of all food-related fears and compulsions. The client then rated his fears according to intensity (e.g., on a scale of 1–10 with 10 being the highest intensity). An agreement regarding the exposures was made such that the least intensely feared stimuli (e.g., trying a different brand of preferred food) were presented in the first exposure session. Subsequent sessions were devoted to doing exposures with feared stimuli associated with more intensely feared stimuli (e.g., allowing familiar foods to touch, combining familiar foods, taking bites from all sides, using a single utensil for multiple foods, and eating casserole-type foods). The client was given full control over the pace at which he graduated to the next level intensity exposure until he completed the entire hierarchy of fears with success.

A playful approach was used at various times to help the client understand the work of cognitive restructuring. For example, activities included doing hands-on worksheets and games designed to cast OCD as a separate entity with whom the client must do battle in order to gain the freedom to fully enjoy childhood. The client's interest in videogames was used on occasion to increase motivation and understanding, mainly serving as a reward for efforts to doing exposures but also to develop a metaphor for thinking about OCD (i.e., viewing OCD as a video-game type "enemy" which one must try to conquer). Ongoing problems with ADHD, mood-related difficulties, and frequent family disruptions meant there was a need for periodically reviewing previously taught cognitive skills. However, as the client moved into the maintenance phase of treatment, he expressed great pride in his new ability to try and accept new foods, and spent more time on fun activities instead of compulsively asking the same questions repeatedly.

Outcome

The client was helped most by the EBT to eliminate compulsive question asking, fears about overestimated dangers and impairment due to food obsessions and compulsions. The client was highly eager to begin exposure sessions for food compulsions. However, slower progress was made with compulsive question asking given the long history of reinforcement by his mother (i.e., prior to treatment, the mother would always answer the client's compulsive questions and had done so for a long time). Furthermore, a prolonged maintenance phase was necessary for this particular client given the comorbidities observed.

As is typical in pediatric OCD, obsessions and compulsions wax and wane over time. This was observed in this particular case when some of obsessions which presented at referral (e.g., about going to hell) remitted spontaneously over time. In addition, compulsive apologizing was treated with a pure behavioral intervention in session (e.g., Functional Analytic Psychotherapy), such that compulsive apologizing was extinguished by removal of reinforcement (i.e., strategic ignoring) and adaptive responses were positively reinforced (i.e., with therapist attention). In other words, after establishing the compulsive nature of the client's apologizing, the therapist withheld socially indicated responses to compulsive apologies made in session (e.g., not saying "That's o.k.") and reinforced other client responses (i.e., responded verbally and positively to all other responses).

CHALLENGES IN APPLYING THE EVIDENCE-BASED APPROACH

Some of the challenges with treating this population are evident in the case example outlined above. These include those related to treating clients with multiple diagnoses, such as ADHD and Learning Disorders, as well as the challenges of delineating family systems issues from OCD symptoms. Oftentimes, pediatric clients presenting with unidentified OCD symptoms are perceived by parents and/or treatment providers as oppositional defiant when the true motivations behind their difficult behaviors are actually based upon their obsessive fears and related compulsions. In addition, pediatric clients often exhibit little insight into their OCD symptoms. For these reasons, it can be challenging to establish the diagnosis of pediatric OCD in the first place.

Establishing a therapeutic alliance for ERP can be challenging if the client lacks awareness about the problem or feels stigmatized by the diagnosis. CBT in general is often highly focused on logic. Therefore, delivering CBT to the pediatric population can present challenges if the client's attitude toward therapy is guarded. Children often benefit from knowing the experiences of children like themselves and can be disarmed by learning they are not alone. However, other challenges may involve difficulties understanding the logic of the intervention or deficits in executive function capacities (e.g., self-awareness, meta-cognition) that impair the client's ability to implement cognitive behavioral skills in their daily lives.

In addition, there are special considerations when delivering treatment for OCD to clients who present with Autism Spectrum Disorders, such as Asperger's syndrome. Oftentimes, clients with this dual diagnosis will require extra care in the manner in which metaphors are used and in the delivery of family-based behavioral interventions.

CULTURAL DIVERSITY ISSUES

Sensitivity to cultural diversity is particularly important when assessing pediatric clients for OCD. The culture of childhood is, in and of itself, a remarkable component of the assessment process in that children are often more profoundly affected by systemic issues than adults. Thus, it is important to consider whether there are any other explanations for the presence of symptoms that may otherwise indicate OCD, such as the religious beliefs of family in a child who prays compulsively.

FUTURE RESEARCH

Clinicians would be served well by additional research with pediatric clients who present with comorbid diagnoses, such as ADHD and Asperger's disorder. In addition, there is much to learn about pediatric OCD in children whose parent(s) also have mental health conditions. For example, it would be helpful to learn whether the course of OCD, response to treatment, or pathways to diagnosis are significantly different for these populations of children with OCD compared with the population of children who present with OCD only and/or with parents who have no mental health history.

KEY REFERENCES

Chansky, T. E. (2000). *Freeing your child from obsessive-compulsive disorder.* New York, NY: Three Rivers Press.

Huebner, D. (2007). *What to do when your brain gets stuck: A kid's guide to overcoming OCD.* Washington, DC: Magination Press.

March, J. S. (2007). *Talking back to OCD: The program that helps kids and teens say "No Way" – and parents Say "Way to Go."* New York/London: The Guilford Press.

CHAPTER 10

Posttraumatic Stress Disorder in Children

Alexandra C. De Young and Justin A. Kenardy

CLINICAL PROBLEM

Classified as an anxiety disorder, Posttraumatic Stress Disorder (PTSD) consists of three core symptom clusters—reexperiencing of a traumatic event, emotional numbing and avoidance of reminders of that event, and physiological hyperarousal. Young children with PTSD also commonly present with increased separation anxiety, new fears, new aggressive and oppositional behavior, and regression in developmental skills. Importantly, recent research has indicated that children demonstrating what is referred to as "partial PTSD"—that is, meet two of the three symptom clusters—are as functionally impaired as those with the diagnosis of PTSD. Furthermore, it has been argued that the PTSD diagnostic criteria are not developmentally sensitive, particularly for infants and preschoolers, thus alternative criteria have also been proposed. Careful assessment is needed as the presentation of PTSD can mimic other disorders, such as Attention Deficit/Hyperactivity Disorder, oppositional defiant disorder, or other anxiety disorders.

Children with PTSD are at increased risk for comorbid depression, and anxiety and behavioral disorders. In addition, traumatic experiences are linked with harmful effects on brain function and structure as well as worse social, physical, and academic outcomes. Furthermore, trauma during childhood has been associated with the onset of psychiatric disorders, health risk behaviors, and physical health conditions in adulthood. Therefore, the early identification and treatment of PTSD and comorbid conditions, across the developmental spectrum from preschool through adolescence, is important.

PREVALENCE

The incidence of PTSD varies greatly (6%–90%) depending on trauma type, methodology used, and sample characteristics. In the general population, the prevalence of PTSD among children and adolescents has been reported to range from 1.6% to 9.2%, and 0.6% in preschool children. Most children are resilient or recover over time following trauma. However, without treatment, approximately 10% to 30% of children are at risk of following a chronic and debilitating trajectory for at least 2 years after the event.

CULTURAL DIVERSITY ISSUES

Generally, research findings are not consistent for demographic variables as risk factors for PTSD. However, results from recent meta-analyses indicate that girls may be more at risk than boys for developing PTSD following trauma exposure. Small effect sizes have been found for race and younger age as risk factors for PTSD. Cultural and socioeconomic differences have not been significantly associated with long-term posttraumatic stress reactions.

EVIDENCE-BASED TREATMENTS

In addition to children reaching full diagnostic criteria, it has been suggested that those children who meet partial PTSD criteria and are functionally impaired should be considered for treatment. The inclusion of parents in treatment should be considered, particularly when working with young children. This is owing to the close association between parent and child distress following trauma and evidence of improved outcome when parents are included. Furthermore, given the high rate of comorbidity with PTSD, assessment and treatment planning need to be guided by established treatment guidelines for comorbid conditions.

Overall, few controlled trials evaluating clinical interventions for PTSD in children and adolescents have been published. Of those studies, most have examined the subgroup of traumatic events associated with sexual abuse. However, it has been noted that child survivors of sexual abuse appear to represent a very different population (in terms of symptom profile) compared with youth who experience a single traumatic event. Single incident traumas represent a subgroup of more frequently occurring traumatic events affecting children and adolescents, however fewer trials have been reported.

In adults, trauma-focused cognitive behavioral therapy (CBT) has received the strongest level of empirical support for treatment of PTSD. In the child and adolescent literature, the evidence base is also strongest for PTSD-targeted CBT models and is recommended as first-line treatment. Trauma-focused CBT (TF-CBT) is a manual-based program that has been the most widely tested of these models. Effectiveness has been demonstrated in diverse cultural and socioeconomic groups. In addition to reductions in PTSD symptoms, TF-CBT can also lead to improvements in depression, anxiety, behavioral problems, shame, guilt, grief, and adaptive functioning. Research has demonstrated that developmentally modified CBT is also feasible and effective for treating PTSD in young children (3–6 years).

Models of the psychological impact of trauma suggest that the way in which people remember and recount threatening events significantly affects how well they manage and adjust to those experiences. These models propose that PTSD and other negative psychosocial outcomes are maintained by a sense of serious current threat which arises as a consequence of: (a) a disturbance of autobiographical memory (i.e., an individual's "story" about what happened to them) characterized by poor elaboration and contextualization, strong associative memory, and strong perceptual priming, and (b) excessively negative appraisals of the trauma event and/or its consequences (e.g., symptoms of PTSD may be interpreted negatively—"I keep having all these thoughts about the accident that I don't want to have—I must be going crazy!"). Adaptive changes in the trauma memory are prevented by certain behavioral (e.g., avoidance of trauma-related stimuli) and cognitive (e.g., distraction) coping styles. PTSD-targeted CBT aims to challenge unhelpful appraisals and provide exposure to the trauma memory. Other components of CBT for PTSD include psychoeducation, relaxation, in vivo exposure, and affect regulation skills.

A smaller number of studies have investigated psychodynamic and attachment-oriented approaches. These approaches have shown promise, especially child–parent psychotherapy which utilizes cognitive behavioral, attachment, and psychodynamic components. Preliminary evidence suggests that medication may be effective for complex presentations and when used in combination with psychotherapy. Group- and school-based interventions, in particular Cognitive Behavioral Intervention for Trauma in Schools, have demonstrated good outcomes. These approaches are delivered to school groups usually as indicated interventions.

FUTURE RESEARCH

Important areas for future research include conducting larger-scale, well-designed randomized control trials for evaluating psychotherapies for single incident traumas, minority populations, and traumatized preschool children. In addition, research is needed to help identify potential mediators and moderators for therapeutic change. Finally, further research is needed to identify the optimum time to provide treatment following trauma exposure.

KEY REFERENCES

Cohen, J. A., Bukstein, O., Walter, H., Benson, R. S., Chrisman, A., … Stock, S. (2010). Practice parameters for the assessment and treatment of children and adolescents with posttraumatic stress disorder. *Journal of the American Academy of Child & Adolescent Psychiatry, 49*, 414–430.

Njoroge, W. F. M., & Yang, D. (2012). Evidence-based psychotherapies for preschool children with psychiatric disorders. *Current Psychiatry Reports, 14*, 121–128.

Silverman, W. K., Ortiz, C. D., Viswesvaran, V. C., Burns, B. J., Kolko, D. J., … Amaya-Jackson, L. (2008). Evidence-based psychosocial treatments for children and adolescents exposed to traumatic events: A review and meta-analysis. *Journal of Clinical Child & Adolescent Psychology, 37*, 156–183.

Clinician Application

Posttraumatic Stress Disorder in Children

Patti van Eys

COMMENT ON THE EVIDENCE-BASED RECOMMENDATIONS

De Young and Kenardy emphasize several important points in the overview of the clinical research for treating Posttraumatic Stress Disorder (PTSD) in children and adolescents, particularly: (a) the central role of assessment in discerning various developmental presentations of trauma symptoms; (b) the importance of treating "partial" PTSD; (c) the critical role of caregivers in treatment, particularly for young children; and, (d) the evidence for specific trauma-based treatments designed for children.

Focused assessment creates a roadmap for successful trauma treatment and should ideally include a trauma exposure scale[1] followed by a PTSD symptom checklist[2] through child interview and/or caregiver report, a general measure for discerning comorbid conditions, and a caregiver measure of functioning when judged as necessary.[3] Gathering clinical information from the child, caregiver, and collateral sources (e.g., teacher, case worker) gives rise to an individualized treatment plan that acknowledges symptoms in light of developmental, family, and community contexts.

The caregiver role is *essential* in treating young children, and *ideal* when treating older children and adolescents. The Trauma-Focused Cognitive Behavioral Therapy (TF-CBT) model emphasizes caregiver involvement throughout treatment; research has shown value added when the caregiver component is included. Although the caregiver acts as a "coach" for the child throughout the course of therapy, a particularly salient part of TF-CBT is the later session in which the young client shares his or her trauma narrative with the caregiver. Caregiver validation and support of the child's perception of the traumatic event has been proven to predict a better prognosis for trauma resolution.

The role of evidence-informed *trauma-specific therapy* in treating children with traumatic events and resulting symptoms cannot be overemphasized. Nondirective trauma work does not offer the ingredient of *gradual exposure* that is a necessary component of trauma treatment. Models such as TF-CBT, Child–Parent Psychotherapy (CPP), and Attachment, Self-Regulation and Competency (ARC) are trauma-specific models that include caregiver–child relationship variables and emphasize not only gradual exposure, but also psychoeducational and skill-based coping work.

CASE EXAMPLE

Subject Information and Brief History

Katie was a 12-year-old Caucasian girl from the rural South who was placed in foster care along with her only sibling, Dave, age 14. The siblings had been removed from their neglectful birth home when Katie was 3, they were in foster care, adopted, and then lived with their new family for 5 years at which time they were removed following physical abuse by their adoptive father. In the 4 years after the adoptive placement, the children lived in 10 foster placements that were often disrupted due to the children's fighting or general disobedience. One placement ended when a favorite foster mother died suddenly. Katie experienced great loss in these many transitions and her schooling was disrupted by every move. Seen as a bright student, but not achieving to her potential, she was perceived as restless and willfully defiant in the home setting. She was generally compliant, but isolative in the school setting. She had never been in mental health treatment.

---

[1] Examples include the Northshore Long Island Jewish Health System Trauma History Checklist and Interview (NLIJHS) or the Trauma History Questionnaire (THQ).
[2] Examples include the UCLA PTSD Index for *DSM* or the Trauma Symptom Checklist for Children.
[3] Examples include the Parent–Child Relationship Inventory or the Parenting Stress Inventory.

Presenting Problem

Katie was referred by her child welfare case worker because of her frequent anger outbursts that resulted several times in abrupt temporary removals from her foster home into foster homes designed for crisis stabilization. It was the case worker's impression that Katie had strengths such as academic prowess, natural social skills, and a caring heart that were being overshadowed by her noncompliant behaviors. The case worker realized that Katie had unresolved losses, adding, "She's a good kid underneath." Assessment with the Northshore Long Island Jewish Health System Trauma History Checklist and Interview trauma exposure scale and the UCLA-PTSD index indicated that Katie had experienced a number of traumas over the course of her life. She reported that her criterion trauma was the physical abuse of her brother by her adoptive father. She witnessed her father beating Dave's head into the floor. She reported incomplete memory before and after the trauma; however, she did recall the police coming to the home and she clearly remembered when the children were taken away from their adoptive home. Her UCLA PTSD Severity Score was 45, well above the cut-off of 38. Further, her UCLA PTSD cluster scores were all above threshold. Together, her UCLA scores met full diagnostic criteria for PTSD. Katie was a bright and creative child. Her foster mother complained about her noncompliant behaviors in the home, and particular complaints were about Katie and her brother "constantly fighting."

Treatment Intervention and Course

Although the typical course of TF-CBT is 16 to 20 sessions, the complexity of Katie's previous life circumstances, several placement changes during our psychotherapy course, and the uncertainty of her future created the need to extend TF-CBT to a year of weekly sessions, followed by 4 months of sibling/family therapy. Katie appeared eager to be involved in treatment, seemingly owing to her need for attention and support; rapport was easily established, although trust was later tested. For example, Katie sometimes purposely disappointed me or misbehaved to see if I'd remain accepting or she tested by becoming angry with me and overtly rejecting me when I made a mistake such as forgetting to follow up with something. Repairing these ruptures added both strength to the relationship and insight for Katie regarding her issues with past and present maternal figures. Initially "antsy" in session, Katie vacillated between hyperarousal (e.g., fidgety, bouncing around the office, unable to participate in relaxation techniques) and avoidance (e.g., asking for help with homework or organizing colored markers instead of settling into planned therapy activities). Katie's treatment progressed through all of the *PRACTICE* components of the TF-CBT model, that is: *P*sychoeducation/*P*arenting, *R*elaxation, *A*ffect Regulation, *C*ognitive Coping, *T*rauma Narrative, *I*n Vivo, *C*onjoint Sharing, and *E*nhancing Future Safety. The first four components (*PRAC*) are the grounding skills mastered in preparation for the deeper trauma narrative writing and processing (*T*: Trauma Narrative). PRAC skills entail learning about trauma (*P*: Psychoeducation), educating caregivers about how to best parent traumatized children (*P*: Parenting), learning skills for physical and mindful relaxation (*R*: Relaxation), general emotional regulation (*A*: Affect Regulation), and coping with negative thoughts (*C*: Cognitive Coping). In Vivo work (*I*) is used after the trauma narrative is processed and only if there are still triggers causing impairment (e.g., child cannot sleep in room alone). Conjoint Sharing (*C*) allows the caregiver and/or other important adult figures to hear the child's trauma narrative and further process with the child. Finally, the child and caregiver are guided through the important features of personal safety (including emotional safety around possible future trauma triggers) as they plan for the future (*E*: Enhancing Future Safety).

Katie readily understood the connection between her assessment results and the concepts of trauma triggers and trauma symptoms. She enjoyed mastering a puzzle of the brain whose various structures cut from colored felt (e.g., cortex, limbic system parts) showed how the amygdale becomes triggered by a stressor (often related to trauma) and the "amygdale alarm" sounds (a felt star was used to depict the alarm), shutting off the thinking part of the brain—shown by a black puzzle piece with a symbolic lock and key that covers the cortex when the amygdale alarm piece is placed on the amygdale. Katie was able to identify how her anger eruptions that were "quick and like a volcano in Hawaii" were linked to her past trauma in connection with caregivers who raised their voices or gave authoritarian commands. She began listing her "triggers" such as her brother's provoking and was eager to figure out ways to "cope" with trauma symptoms. Katie was especially adept in the area of cognitive coping, mastering the cognitive triangle concept (e.g., a triangle model with the three points showing how various thoughts produce various feelings and consequential behaviors). She routinely filled out "triangle homework sheets" upon which she noted, for example: *Trigger*: brother teases > *Thought*: "I hate him!" > *Feeling*: "anger" > *Behavior*: "hitting him" and > *Consequence*: sent to her room. The homework sheets encouraged her to rethink each scenario and change the triangle sequence in a "redo" scenario such as: *Trigger*: brother teases > *Thought*: he's trying to provoke me; I can stay in control > *Feeling*: proud to be in control > *Behavior*: ignore him > *Consequence*: he stops; foster mom praises me for self-control. She further practiced these concepts through role plays in response to various scenarios provided on index cards to master how thoughts, feelings, and behaviors are linked. In session, she and I took on various roles; she practiced and I modeled various responses to challenging scenarios like failing a test or getting into an argument. She enjoyed card and board games that illustrated the connections among thoughts, feelings, behaviors, and consequences,[4] and was adept at *feelings charades* (choosing a feelings face card and acting out the feeling for others to guess) and *feelings concentration* (turning over cards of feelings faces to find matches and then describing a scenario regarding that feeling) which she liked to play jointly when caregivers and/or Dave came in at the end of sessions. These games that aided her "emotional literacy" paved the way to more controlled emotion regulation and capacity to articulate accurate emotions in her later trauma narrative. Katie was exposed to a number of affect regulation coping strategies including basic relaxation techniques like progressive muscle relaxation, mindfulness (e.g., focusing solely on something such as an M & M melting in her mouth, a serene musical selection, a smooth stone in her hand, or her own breathing while allowing all her thoughts to drift by), grounding activities (e.g., listing favorite songs or sports figures, listing the colors seen in the room, or noticing how the chair and floor feel), and active techniques like coloring. Perhaps due to her restlessness and need for control, Katie was less apt to engage in mindfulness or formal relaxation and more inclined to active ways of coping such as creating a "cool down kit" that included items such as bubble wrap to pop, lotion, colored pencils, and coloring

---

[4]Examples of games used in this therapy course included Dr. Playwell's Don't Stress and Think Positive games and the Talking, Feeling, and Doing Anger Card Game.

sheets with mandala designs,[5] a journal, balloons, bubbles, Play-doh, stress balls, and her favorite music.

Katie's trauma narrative was a highlight of her work. Her narrative, though featuring the criterion trauma (abuse of her brother and the subsequent removal from her adoptive home), included her many placements and her choppy journey from birth home to final adoptive home. As part of her TF-CBT psychoeducation component, she had read a book about a youngster in foster care which prompted her to write a paper for her English class and provided insight to her own trauma narrative process. Katie was integrating her new understandings into active parts of her life.

Trauma processing of the narrative elucidated dynamics that were to become a turning point for Katie in terms of her sense of having appropriate power and accepting her larger identity rather than defining herself as a "weird, unwanted foster kid." Her grief over her birth parents centered on her wish that they could have been better parents, her anger over their drug use, and wondering if they had truly loved her and now continued to miss her. She drew pictures of the apartment where she had lived with them and wrote memories, both positive and negative, about her birth parents. She processed overwhelmingly sad, angry, and yearning feelings about her adoptive mother, and wrote a letter to her that she chose not to send, but included in her trauma narrative. Trauma processing centralized, though, on her relationship with her brother, as her contentious relationship with Dave continued to cause significant problems in the home. In the processing of her trauma, Katie demonstrated this sibling conflict through a technique called "Responsibility Pie." She divided a circle on paper (i.e., "pie") into colored sections to show her perception that she blamed Dave for the abusive incident and the disrupted adoption. Had he not misbehaved, she believed, they would still be with that family in the lovely home. The Responsibility Pie showed that she also partially blamed herself for "stirring Dave up" the night he was abused, causing him to be irritable and act up. She also blamed her adoptive mother, in part, because she had left the children alone with the father. Through psychoeducation about parenting and the responsibility of adults to correctly discipline children, Socratic questioning, and perspective shifting through use of the "best friend role play" (a technique wherein the therapist takes the role of the client's best friend who has a similar problem and the client "helps" her friend), Katie changed her perspective about blame and began to soften her attitude regarding her brother and herself. Subsequent Responsibility Pie sections changed dramatically to reflect her new understanding. At the same time, work with Katie's current caregiver was focused on that caregiver being a more regulated, nurturing parent so as to support positive behavioral change through attunement and nurturing communication. The caregiver–child dynamics had remained a significant challenge attributed mainly to a poor match of foster parent whose rigidity made the caregiver work unsuccessful.

In vivo work between Katie and Dave solidified their burgeoning collaboration as friendly siblings. The two psychotherapists had the siblings act as a team in several competitive games (e.g., feelings charades) against the two of them and

---

[5] The word mandala comes from the classical Indian language of Sanskrit and loosely translated means "circle." Mandala designs represent wholeness—they are integrated structures organized around a unifying center. Used for grounding youngsters as they color the intricate inner details, mandala coloring sheets can be located free of charge on the internet by searching for "mandala."

sometimes the caregivers. This practice shaped them into getting along in sessions and they were given activities to practice at home (e.g., the "Don't Stress" board game focused on positive alternative solutions to stressful situations).

Outcome

Some months into treatment, both psychotherapists advocated for the children to be removed from the current foster home due to a growing sense that the caregiver was a "red light parent," that is, she was not able to execute the needed caregiving skills with these children. Toward the conclusion of TF-CBT, an adoptive family was secured. Caregiver work was actively begun and these caregivers were eager recipients of the model and their roles. Katie shared her trauma narrative with her new "mom" and "dad." The sharing was a time of needed validation, bonding, and healing. Katie, Dave, and their new family continued in family therapy for several months following the conclusion of the formal TF-CBT work. Katie was now a participant in the cheerleading program at her school, had several good friends, was making solid grades in school, was happy, and was not a behavior problem at home or school. She and Dave were getting along reasonably well. The children were formally adopted and we had a large celebration and closure of treatment party with their child welfare workers, guardian ad litem, previous in-home counselors, the adoptive family, and the clinic staff. Four years later, the report is still positive and neither Katie nor Dave have needed further therapy, however, booster sessions were offered on an as-needed basis.

CHALLENGES IN APPLYING THE EVIDENCE-BASED APPROACH

A significant challenge in this approach is working with a caregiver who is resistant to change or simply unable to make needed changes, like the foster mom in this case. Another challenge to TF-CBT is complex or "developmental" trauma, wherein the developing brain has been adversely affected by early and significant family adversity. TF-CBT can take longer in these complex cases, as it did with Katie. Early attachment trauma often causes issues of control and distrust within the therapy relationship which is of paramount importance. Thus, the psychotherapist must engage in behaviors with heightened attunement to attachment trauma. Finally, for the same reasons, there may be more family issues to work out following the completion of TF-CBT.

CULTURAL DIVERSITY ISSUES

TF-CBT has been researched across races, ethnicity, gender, and ages in the United States in multisite, randomized controlled trials in the last decade and has shown generalized effectiveness. However, more recent efforts to better understand how cultural differences affect the successful delivery of TF-CBT have resulted in promising modifications across a broader range of cultures.

TF-CBT has been recently employed and evaluated internationally in a number of countries including: Western Europe (Germany, Norway, Sweden, Italy, and the Netherlands), Africa (Zambia Tanzania, and Democratic Republic of Congo), southeast Cambodia, Japan, China, Greenland, and Australia. Various cultures concentrate more heavily on certain trauma types such as HIV illness/deaths, violence, sexual assault, and traumatic loss that leaves children orphaned (e.g., Africa); starvation, sexual trafficking, forced labor, executions (e.g., Cambodia); and domestic violence (e.g., Greenland). Immigrant cultures in the United States show a higher concentration of trauma exposure of certain types in children/teens (e.g., war violence, sexual assault), yet, they are less likely to seek out mental health treatment. For example, foreign-born Latino adolescents utilize health services at a significantly lower rate than U.S.-born Latinos.

Research to date indicates that Western European countries, as a group, are adhering closely to TF-CBT, with only slight modification to the Parenting component by toning down the use of *praise* to fit more within their culture. In contrast, more significant cultural adaptations to TF-CBT in a number of low-resource countries are proving successful, as are cultural adaptations for U.S. Latino families, American Indian, and Alaska Native Children, children with developmental disabilities, military families, and children in foster care or with complex trauma. These recent and growing studies indicate that necessary modifications, such as using lay persons as psychotherapists in low resource countries can be successful. The Honoring Children-Mending the Circle (HC-MC) enhancement for Native American cultures emphasizes indigenous knowledge known as "Old Wisdom" that, for example, relates to the connection between thoughts, feelings, and behaviors, upholds the centrality of the family, and emphasizes the interconnectedness of all things. The HC-MC model relates the trauma narrative to the traditional value of storytelling. The HC-MC enhancement uses the traditional concept of a circle to define well-being as a balance and harmony both within and between one's spiritual, relational, emotional, mental, and physical dimensions. Culturally Modified TF-CBT (CM-TF-CBT) for Latino culture that includes modifications such as using *dichos* (short phrases depicting cultural values) and *cuentos* (folklore and storytelling to teach therapeutic skills) do not interfere with the fidelity or effectiveness of TF-CBT according to both quantitative and qualitative research efforts.

FUTURE RESEARCH

Continued efforts regarding culturally specific TF-CBT research and "what works for whom" will benefit clinicians. Further, TF-CBT research is needed specific to settings (e.g., psychiatric residential treatment centers, schools, juvenile justice settings, and intensive in-home settings). Finally, trauma researchers need to determine effective and efficient adaptations for addressing complex (i.e., developmental) trauma in youngsters. How well does TF-CBT work for children with early developmental trauma and what adaptations might be needed in terms of working with disturbed attachment systems?

KEY REFERENCES

Cohen, J. A., Mannarino, A. P., & Deblinger, E. (2006). *Treating trauma and traumatic grief in children and adolescents.* New York, NY: The Guilford Press.

Cohen, J. A., Mannarino, A. P., & Deblinger, E. (2012). *Trauma-focused CBT for children and adolescents: Treatment Applications.* New York, NY: The Guilford Press.

Deblinger, E., & Heflin, A. H. (1996). *Treating sexually abused children and their nonoffending parents.* Thousand Oaks, CA: Sage Publications.

CHAPTER 11

School Refusal Behavior

Christopher A. Kearney and Melissa Spear

CLINICAL PROBLEM

School refusal behavior (SRB) entails refusal to attend school as well as difficulties remaining in classes for an entire day. SRB may include full absences from school, missed classes, tardiness, morning misbehaviors to stay home, and school attendance under great duress that precipitates pleas for future nonattendance. SRB may be especially problematic if a youth (a) has missed at least 25% of total school time for at least 2 weeks, (b) has severe difficulty attending classes for at least 2 weeks with significant interference in a youth's or family's daily routine, and/or (c) has been absent from school for at least 10 days during any 15-week period while school is in session, with an absence defined as 25% or more of school time missed.

SRB can lead to family conflict, legal trouble, declining grades, social alienation, and distress. Potential long-term problems include extended absenteeism, delinquency, school dropout, and occupational, economic, and social problems in adulthood. Extended absenteeism has also been linked to suicide attempt, risky sexual behavior, teenage pregnancy, violence, injury, driving under the influence of alcohol, and substance use and abuse. SRB is commonly associated with various medical and psychiatric conditions as well as mixed internalizing and externalizing symptoms.

PREVALENCE

SRB affects as many as 28% to 35% of youths at some point. This figure includes formal absenteeism as well as behaviors designed to try to miss school (e.g., noncompliance in the morning before school). SRB affects boys and girls equally though school dropout rates are higher for boys (9.1%) than girls (7.0%). The most common age of onset for SRB is 10 to 13 years but youths entering a new school building for the first time (e.g., kindergarten, high school) are also at elevated risk for SRB.

CULTURAL DIVERSITY ISSUES

Studies involving clinical samples of youth with SRB have included primarily European American students or have found no ethnic differences. Studies involving community samples of youth with SRB, however, have included high rates of ethnic minorities and especially Hispanic youth. In related fashion, Hispanic youth have the highest school dropout rate in the United States (22.1%). This compares to rates for African American (10.7%) and European American (5.8%) youth.

EVIDENCE-BASED TREATMENTS

Successful treatment for SRB typically involves a short-term, intensive approach to restore full-time attendance with reduced distress. Cognitive behavioral and family systems approaches have been most useful. Clinical researchers have focused on anxiety and contingency management techniques as well as family-based practices to boost problem-solving and communication skills. Such work involves parents and children but usually includes consultation with school officials as well.

Anxiety management techniques apply best to youths who find aspects of school distressing, such as peer interactions or performance before others. Several anxiety management techniques are described here. Psychoeducation involves teaching youth and parents about the primary components of absentee and anxiety-based behaviors and providing a rationale for treatment. Somatic control exercises involve relaxation training and breathing retraining to reduce physical symptoms of anxiety associated with school attendance. Cognitive restructuring involves identifying and modifying maladaptive thoughts about school-based social and evaluative situations to develop more adaptive and realistic thinking. Exposure-based practice involves gradual reintegration of a youth into school, such as one class or hour at a time, in conjunction with an anxiety hierarchy. Anxiety management techniques for youths with SRB are sometimes supplemented with social skills or assertiveness training.

Contingency management techniques, or parent-based training, apply best to youths who demonstrate substantial attention-seeking behavior, separation anxiety, or general noncompliance regarding school attendance. Contingency management for this population involves teaching parents to establish regular morning and daily routines, alter commands toward brevity and clarity, ignore SRBs such as tantrums, and provide consequences for attendance and nonattendance. Contingency management is often conducted in conjunction with consultations with school officials regarding a child's daily academic and behavioral performance at school.

Family-based approaches to treatment apply best to youths who refuse school for substantial tangible reinforcement outside of school and to families with limited problem-solving and communication skills. Contingency contracting is commonly used in these cases and involves written contracts between parents and a youth to increase incentives for school attendance, disincentives for school nonattendance, and daily supervision of the youth. Peer refusal skills training is sometimes employed as well to help youths refuse offers to miss school or avoid high-risk situations that provoke absenteeism.

Cases of SRB can be urgent and complex. Treatment thus requires ongoing consultation with school officials (regarding attendance and other key behaviors), frequent therapy sessions, daily assessment and attendance journals, and quick response to emerging obstacles to school attendance. Treatment should begin very soon after assessment completion. Relapse prevention is also important for this population and can involve booster sessions and reminders for family members to practice specific techniques that were found most effective for helping a child resume full-time school attendance.

FUTURE RESEARCH

Researchers will need to consider broader contextual variables that can impact cases of SRB. Examples include pregnancy, comorbid health and mental health conditions, transportation problems, poor parent involvement, family-based stressors, deviant peer influences, school-based threats and climate, and even economic pull factors. Protocols for treating complex cases of SRB require further development but will likely include more systemic approaches conducted in conjunction with school officials, legal officials such as truancy and probation officers, and medical professionals. One systemic approach could involve a multitiered model of preventative practices, immediate intervention for emerging cases, and alternative school placements and extensive services for chronic cases. Such a model will also require researchers to develop common definitions of problematic absenteeism as well as standardized assessment practices for youths with SRB.

KEY REFERENCES

Bye, L., Alvarez, M. E., Haynes, J., & Sweigart, C. E. (2010). *Truancy prevention and intervention: A practical guide.* New York, NY: Oxford University Press.

Heyne, D., & Rollings, S. (2002). *School refusal.* Malden, MA: BPS Blackwell.

Thambirajah, M. S., Grandison, K. J., & De-Hayes, L. (2008). *Understanding school refusal: A handbook for professionals in education, health and social care.* Philadelphia, PA: Kingsley.

Clinician Application

School Refusal Behavior

Stephanie Mihalas

COMMENT ON THE EVIDENCE-BASED RECOMMENDATIONS

The prevalence for school refusal behavior (SRB) is considerably moderate, ranging from 28% to 35% for youth at some point during development. Notably, research indicated a disproportionate rate of SRB in Hispanic youth which may be linked to a higher percentage of school dropout rates for these youth (22.1%).

Applied clinical research for SRB firmly supports what is found to be effective in real-world clinical settings (e.g., family therapy, contingency management, stress-reduction practices). Unfortunately, while best practice suggests that relapse prevention is indicated, many families discontinue treatment when their child finally achieves success and negate the importance of booster and maintenance sessions.

CASE EXAMPLE

Subject Information and Brief History

Henry was a 6-year-old Caucasian male referred by his pediatrician for primary concerns related to somatic complaints, inflexible thinking, atypical behaviors, and general hypersensitivity to his environment. Notably, his parents remained married; however, his father traveled for work frequently and as such, Henry did not see him often. Henry attended a small parochial school with strict guidelines and expectations for behavior and development.

Presenting Problem

Henry appeared to have a number of presenting concerns related to a developmental disability, but a formalized assessment was not completed during the course of treatment with this psychologist. Henry's mother reported that at night he required her to sleep in his bed or a tantrum would ensue. She reported that he feared "bad men" would enter his room. Likewise, each morning prior to school, Henry spoke incessantly about the school day, demanded that his mother dress him, and refused breakfast. Reportedly on the way to school, retching would occur, in addition to obsessive discourse about activities Henry's mother would be engaging in while he was in school. Upon arrival at school, Henry would ask questions such as "When will this day be over?" or "Can you pick me up early?" In addition, he would compulsively tell his mother how much he loved her and would fawn over her on the playground before the bell rang prior to school starting. As soon as his mother would attempt to leave the playground, Henry would either start falling to the ground, crying and screeching loudly, or run after her. Henry was able to remain in school approximately 0 to 0.5 days when treatment started.

Treatment Intervention and Course

The course of treatment followed Kearney and Albano's (2007) cognitive behavioral therapy (CBT) approach for school refusal. Initially, the psychotherapist conducted a multidimensional assessment to gain an accurate picture of the contributing variables (e.g., medical, school, family, and life events). The psychotherapist attempted to conduct a school functional assessment but the parent refused as she felt it would call too much attention to Henry. However, a school observation on the playground at drop-off in the morning was observed. Based on the data, the primary function of the SRB was attention seeking and gaining reinforcement from his mother which guided the course of intervention toward: (a) family intervention, (b) contingency management, and (c) relaxation training. The psychotherapist met with Henry's mother for one psychoeducation session to discuss etiology of school refusal and general issues pertaining to child development and behavioral family therapy. Two sessions were dedicated to parent training related to positive and negative reinforcement/punishment and how differential forms of reinforcement and punishment could be used to shape behavior, and more specifically, Henry's school attendance. For example, Henry could spend time with his mother after school reading, pending completion of the morning routine by himself. Between sessions, his mother kept a log of Henry's behaviors, the time he spent at school (and out of school) so that progress could be monitored. For session 3, the psychotherapist accompanied the family in the home, car, and at school to observe Henry, his mother, and the parent–child interaction to further guide intervention planning. Session 4 was spent with his mother providing her feedback regarding an extinction protocol, ways to transition Henry's focus in the car, and how to leave the playground at school without providing excess attention. Sessions 5 through 10 were spent providing Henry with tools to calm himself which included relaxation through breathing, imagery, private self-talk, and the use of a sensory ball. Sessions 10 through 14 were spent on reviewing what the family had learned in addition to focusing on bullying issues that Henry was facing that the family believed was compromising the outcome of treatment. As such, assertiveness techniques were taught which notably, is not part of the treatment protocol for school refusal.

Each week, Henry had a "Show-That-I-Can" (STIC) task that progressively became more difficult. The STIC tasks ranged from practicing walking to the car by himself every night five times to repeating 10 times at night "I feel confident that I can succeed tomorrow driving to school without throwing up." Each STIC was aimed at building the client's self-efficacy toward accomplishing a subgoal of the final goal of staying at school the entire day.

Outcome

At the end of week 14, Henry was able to attend school and remain for the entire day 85% of the time. Tantrums decreased from 100% of the time to 50% of the time. His mother terminated treatment prematurely because school was coming to a close for the year. Remaining issues included perseverative talk about what his mother would engage in during the school day; separation anxiety at drop off; and rigidity about the morning routine. Notably, the course of treatment was compromised by a clear developmental disability that the family was unwilling to recognize or treat.

CHALLENGES IN APPLYING THE EVIDENCE-BASED APPROACH

The first challenge as a private practitioner is the feasibility of conducting a functional-based assessment (FBA) in the school setting. A proper FBA requires multiple times of observation which presents numerous obstacles including: (a) gaining access to a student (multiple times) as an outside provider in public school settings, which is often not allowed as much as it once was because of stricter district guidelines; (b) the time to and from the location, plus the observation requires a practitioner to have excess time in his or her practice to accommodate the completion of an FBA; (c) cost of this time is transferred to the patient which may not be an option for families financially. Therefore, oftentimes the best practice in terms of assessment cannot be completed by the private practitioner who has expertise in this area of assessment and treatment. The second challenge is that some schools do not provide accommodations for students who present with school refusal. One of the main ways of working through this presenting problem is home–school collaboration and for the parent and school to problem solve together. However, as is the case with Henry and his family, the school stated that he would need "outside help" and they were not open to changing their practices or procedures to support what was transpiring in the therapeutic arena.

CULTURAL DIVERSITY ISSUES

With this particular family, culture-bound issues played an integral part in treatment. The family was from a country outside the United States where "guilt" and "shame" are phenomena (per the report from the mother) that play into child rearing. As such, the mother had a difficult time implementing strategies that required boundaries, ignoring poor behavior, and removing preferred activities or items. Thus, some of the best approaches to helping this patient, in particular, were not used consistently. Second, psychotherapy was deemed unfavorable to the country-of-origin for this particular family. Therefore, the family felt very conflicted about attending treatment in the first place. This psychotherapist attempted to make the process more "scientific" to meet the needs of the family and their cultural background, which reportedly helped them cope with the stigma of seeing a psychologist. Nevertheless, the resistance and defensiveness was ever-present in the therapeutic relationship and implementing specific techniques for eradicating school refusal.

FUTURE RESEARCH

Qualitative research that could elucidate schools' hesitancy to engage in problem solving with families and psychologists would be helpful. This realm of suggested research would identify how practitioners could overcome barriers to working with schools. The second line of research that would be helpful is how to specifically alter the school refusal protocol to work with children with a variety of developmental disabilities. Different manualized treatments would be helpful for children with intellectual disabilities, children on the autism spectrum, and those with attention deficit/hyperactivity disorder (ADHD). Finally, clinically speaking, the access to health care for Hispanic youth and the mental stigma surrounding mental health services may stymie the treatment of SRB in this population. This is an area of research that needs further exploration and has not been addressed to date.

KEY REFERENCES

Kearney, C. A., & Albano, A. M. (2007). *When children refuse school: A cognitive behavioral therapy approach* (2nd ed.). New York, NY: Oxford University Press.

Moffitt, C. E., Chorpita, B. F., & Fernandez, S. N. (2003). Intensive cognitive-behavioral treatment of school refusal behavior. *Cognitive & Behavioral Practice, 10*, 51–60.

Wimmer, M. B. (2003). *School refusal: Assessment and intervention within school settings*. Bethesda, MD: National Association of School Psychologists Publications.

CHAPTER 12

Social Phobia in Children

Brian E. Bunnell and Deborah C. Beidel

CLINICAL PROBLEM

Children presenting with social phobia (also known as Social Anxiety Disorder) experience an intense fear, along with apprehension, about social situations. More specifically, the child fears social situations during which his or her performance might be evaluated by peers. Children suffering from social phobia often experience physiological symptoms such as restlessness, stomachaches, blushing, palpitations, muscle tension, sweating, and trembling/shaking. Along with the distress associated with social situations, social phobia is often marked by avoidance of the anxiety-provoking situation (e.g., avoiding speaking in front of a group). This distress, anticipatory response, and behavioral avoidance creates significant functional impairment.

Social phobia is typically diagnosed in early to mid-adolescence (age 11 to 15), but earlier onset is possible, with symptoms presenting as early as age 8 and even before age 5. Earlier onset social phobia has been associated with more negative outcomes, including additional anxiety disorders, depression, and conduct problems. An early history of social phobia also may result in dysfunctional social skills. As children with social phobia increasingly avoid social situations, they inadvertently sacrifice opportunities to develop and establish the social skills necessary for effective social interaction. This pattern of inadequate skill and social distress associated with social phobia, in turn, may result in additional negative effects on the child including additional anxiety disorders, depression, substance abuse, and behavioral problems.

PREVALENCE

The prevalence of social phobia ranges from 1% to 15% of the general population. These rates increase to 18% to 32% when examining clinical populations of patients seeking treatment for anxiety disorders. Incidence rates are reported to be approximately 3%. Sex differences in the prevalence of childhood social phobia have yet to be established; however, current data suggest higher prevalence among adult females when compared to adult males.

CULTURAL DIVERSITY ISSUES

There are limited data examining ethnic/racial differences in childhood social phobia. Specifically, one investigation examining differences between Caucasian and African American children diagnosed with social phobia found no differences in their severity of illness, level of social anxiety, level of impairment, observed anxiety and social effectiveness, or self-reported anxiety during tasks requiring social interaction. In the examination of these variables following treatment, no significant differences were found between these two groups, although a higher percentage of African American children responded to treatment when compared to Caucasian children, which held at 6-month follow-up. Thus far, it is unknown whether rates differ among different socioeconomic statuses.

EVIDENCE-BASED TREATMENTS

In the realm of psychosocial interventions, there are two empirically supported treatments for childhood social phobia: cognitive behavioral therapy (CBT) and Social Effectiveness Therapy for Children (SET-C). Both interventions view anxiety as a tripartite model including physiological, cognitive, and behavioral symptoms. These interventions attempt to target social fears using different methods such as relaxation training, cognitive restructuring, exposure therapy conducted either imaginally or in vivo, and/or social skills training.

One empirically supported CBT protocol is Coping Cat, which consists of approximately 14 to 18 sessions over a 12 to 16 week period. The first half of the program (6 to 8 weeks) focuses on the acquisition of new coping skills such as relaxation training and cognitive restructuring. The second half of the program includes both in-session and in vivo exposures to anxiety-provoking stimuli. Coping Cat and its variations are considered to be an efficacious treatment for childhood anxiety disorders, although results from a recent investigation suggest that sertraline, Coping Cat, and the combination were all less effective with children who had a diagnosis of social phobia when compared to children who did not have a diagnosis of social phobia (i.e., they had a different anxiety disorder diagnosis).

Although CBT produces some reduction in anxiety levels in children suffering from social phobia, most interventions do not specifically target a key component of social phobia (social skills deficits). In contrast, SET-C focuses on reducing social anxiety and fear, improving social skill and interpersonal functioning, and increasing participation in social activities. SET-C incorporates four major components: Child and Parent Psychoeducation, Social Skills Training, Peer Generalization Experiences, and In Vivo Exposure. Child and parent education occurs during a single session, while the latter three components are incorporated simultaneously and constitute the vast majority of the program. Treatment is provided twice weekly (one group session and one individual session) over a 12-week period of time. Social Skills Training is conducted in groups of four to six children and includes training in greetings and introductions, starting conversations, maintaining conversations, listening and remembering skills, skills for joining groups, positive assertion, negative assertion, and telephone skills. Peer Generalization sessions are 90 minutes, occur immediately following the social skills group, and include practicing social skills with nonanxious peers in community settings such as bowling alleys, pizza parlors, and miniature golf courses. In Vivo Exposure is conducted once a week in individual sessions and uses activities constructed specifically to address the child's unique pattern of social fears. SET-C is more efficacious than an active nonspecific psychological treatment, pill placebo, and the active pharmacological treatment, fluoxetine. For example, in one study, both SET-C and fluoxetine decreased anxiety in social situations whereas only SET-C resulted in improved social skills. Furthermore, improvement is maintained 5 years later with less than 10% relapse. At posttreatment, 53% to 63% of participants no longer met diagnostic criteria for social phobia. A version of SET-C adapted for schools (e.g., SASS) also has efficacy for the treatment of social phobia.

FUTURE RESEARCH

There are several key areas of research that remain to be addressed. First, it is still unclear if CBT without social skills training produces efficacy rates that are (a) equal to the rates reported for other diagnostic groups, and (b) if the cognitive element of CBT is a necessary component of the intervention, particularly for younger children where negative cognitions are uncommon. Second, the need for parental involvement is unclear and merits further investigation. Finally, enhancing current interventions to reach even more children and adolescents suffering from this disorder will be the focus of ongoing research efforts.

KEY REFERENCES

Beidel, D. C., & Alfano, C. A. (2011). *Childhood anxiety disorders: A guide to research and treatment* (2nd ed.). New York, NY: Taylor and Francis/Routledge.

Kendall, P. C. (2000). *Coping Cat workbook*. Ardmore, PA: Workbook Publishing.

Clinician Application

Social Phobia in Children

Lisa H. Berghorst and Mary Karapetian Alvord

COMMENTS ON THE EVIDENCE-BASED TREATMENT RECOMMENDATIONS

Empirical evidence supports various treatment protocols for pediatric social phobia that are rooted in cognitive behavioral therapy (CBT), social skills training, or a combination of these techniques. In addition to Coping Cat and Social Effectiveness Therapy for Children (SET-C) described by Bunnell and Beidel, there are other evidence-based protocols, including various group CBT interventions with either a social skills or cognitive focus, and one CBT intervention with a brief 3-week format. Of note, a combination of CBT with a selective serotonin reuptake inhibitor (SSRI) may be particularly helpful for some children struggling with social phobia. However, given the possibility of medication side effects, psychotherapy without pharmacotherapy is preferred as an initial treatment strategy.

In light of equivocality regarding whether children experience negative cognitions, it is clinically relevant to highlight that multiple studies report significantly greater negative cognitions in children with high social anxiety as compared to less anxious children. Moreover, there are empirical data to support that CBT with a cognitive focus can significantly improve social anxiety symptoms in children. In line with these findings, in clinical practice, negative cognitions are often prominent in socially phobic children, and addressing these as part of treatment is recommended. Clinical experience also underscores the importance of parental involvement in treatment (e.g., having parents model and reinforce positive social skills and nonanxious behavior). Although empirical data are limited, CBT with parental involvement has been linked to greater improvement in socially anxious children than CBT alone.

CASE EXAMPLE (COMPOSITE OF MULTIPLE 8- TO 10-YEAR-OLD CHILDREN WITH SOCIAL PHOBIA)

Subject Information and Brief History

At the time of intake, John was a 9-year-old Caucasian male in the fourth grade. He had a history of social isolation—withdrawing in environments where other children were present and avoiding potential play dates with peers. He did not want to attend any organized group activities with peers, including birthday parties and Cub Scout events. Although he was intellectually bright, John's teachers reported that he regularly refused to participate in class and "froze" when asked to present in front of the class.

Presenting Problem

John's parents sought treatment for him because they were concerned about his social and school functioning. They reported a deterioration in his behavior and mood at home over the past year. When asked by his parents to attend a social event, John would immediately refuse, sometimes slamming the door and yelling (although he usually spoke in a very quiet voice), other times crying and pleading not to go. Moreover, he often did not want to go to school, usually claiming a somatic symptom such as a stomachache.

Treatment Intervention and Course

- *Psychoeducation:* Throughout the course of treatment, John was provided with a rationale for each component to help him understand the connections between his thoughts, behaviors, feelings and physiological symptoms, and why modifying his thoughts and behaviors could improve his functioning. The CBT triangle was visually illustrated on a whiteboard with arrows going both directions between "thoughts," "feelings/sensations," and "behaviors," while discussing the ways in which the CBT model could be applied to John's experiences. For example, it was explained to John that dealing with anxiety-provoking social situations and related fearful thoughts by avoiding those situations might make him feel less anxious in the moment but actually strengthen his anxiety over time (by reinforcing his thoughts about not being able to handle social situations, which likely increases his anxiety the next time he is faced with such situations, and continues the cycle with avoidance, etc.). It was also explained that John would learn new skills and ways of coping with anxiety-provoking social situations in order to help him face those situations, build more rational thoughts, and reduce his feelings of anxiety over time.
- *Cognitive Restructuring:* A developmentally appropriate form of cognitive restructuring was implemented with John to challenge his fears about social situations

Situation	Negative Automatic Thoughts (NATs)	Feelings with NATs (Rate intensity: 1-10)	Rational Thoughts (RTs)	Feelings after RTs (Rate intensity: 1-10)
Sitting in the school cafeteria at lunchtime. Five other boys at the table; three of them are talking together and two of them are quietly eating lunch next to me.	I can't talk to anyone because I don't really have anything to say and I might make a mistake and say something stupid. Other kids will laugh at me and think I am stupid, and everyone will hate me.	Anxious (8) Sad (8)	Some other kids might be just as nervous as I am about having a conversation. I could try talking to the kids next to me and telling them about my new video game and see if they have ever played it. I could ask about their favorite video games. I do not know for sure what will happen or how other kids will react. They might think my video game sounds really cool. Even if I do make a mistake, it might not be a big deal because everyone makes mistakes sometimes. If another kid made a mistake, I wouldn't think he was stupid or decide to hate him. If someone was that mean to me, I wouldn't want to be friends with that person anyways.	Anxious (5) Sad (3)

FIGURE 12.1 Example of cognitive restructuring with John.

(e.g., "other kids will think I am stupid"), reduce associated feelings of anxiety, and increase the frequency of rational and helpful thoughts. Common categories of cognitive distortions (also referred to as "thinking errors" or "off the mark" thinking) were discussed (e.g., "catastrophizing," "mind reading," "all-or-nothing" thinking); concepts were illustrated visually in an effort to make sessions interactive (e.g., dart board to show "on the mark" vs. "off the mark" thinking, balloons to show thoughts "blowing up"). John was also taught ways to challenge his "off the mark" thinking: examine the evidence for/against his thoughts, consider the realistic chances of the worst case scenario happening and his ability to deal with it, generate alternative explanations/outcomes, and so forth. As situations were discussed, the psychotherapist recorded John's negative automatic thoughts/cognitive distortions, the situations in which they occurred, associated feelings (with intensity ratings on a scale of 1 to 10), and rational responses/alternative thoughts (with a second intensity rating of feelings afterward to emphasize any mood shift resulting from reframing his thoughts); see Figure 12.1 for an example. In an effort to underscore self-efficacy, John was also guided to make his own book (entitled *Facing My Fears*, illustrated using clip-art with a dragon representing his fears) about challenging his "off the mark" thinking in order to face and overcome his fears.

- *Anxiety Management Skills:* In order to help John build coping skills to handle anxiety-provoking situations, he was taught relaxation techniques (e.g., deep breathing, progressive muscle relaxation, visualization, self-talk), often guided by an audio CD developed by the second author.
- *Behavioral Exposure:* A graduated exposure approach was used to help John face previously avoided social situations by building up to his most feared situations one step at a time. First, John worked with his psychotherapist to create a list of scenarios that instilled fear in him (e.g., starting a conversation, asking a question to someone sitting near him in class). Next, these were organized into a fear

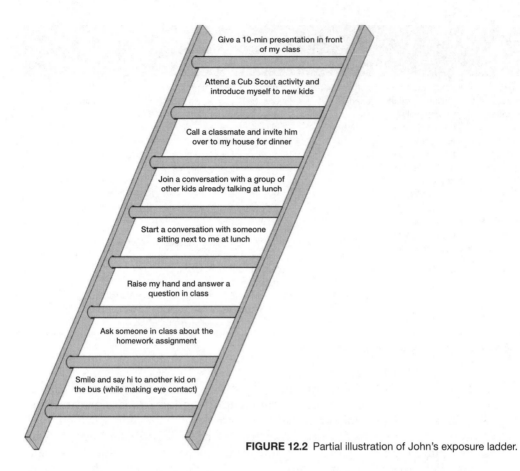

FIGURE 12.2 Partial illustration of John's exposure ladder.

hierarchy by writing each of his fears on one rung of a large paper diagram of a ladder, from least to most anxiety provoking; see Figure 12.2 for an example. Exposure practice began at the bottom of the ladder and John moved up the ladder to progressively more challenging situations over time. A "subjective units of distress" (SUDs) picture with a large colorful thermometer was used to help him communicate his "anxiety temperature" and determine when to move to the next rung in the ladder (e.g., after a ~50% drop in "temperature"); see Figure 12.3 for an example.

- *Social Skills Training:* Given that John typically spoke in a barely audible voice, a sound meter was used in session as a feedback device to help him learn an appropriate sound level for everyday speech. Eye contact was practiced using timed staring contests. John also worked with his psychotherapist to compile a list of "what, where, when, how" questions that he then used to practice initiating and maintaining conversations. The majority of social skills training for John took place through his participation in a group CBT program (described below).
- *Contingency Management:* Throughout treatment, John was reinforced verbally for practicing social skills, using adaptive coping skills, and engaging in planned exposures. Intermittently, he was presented with "bravery awards" for his efforts and accomplishments. In addition, John put sports stickers next to each rung on his exposure ladder after he accomplished that goal. The stickers had point values that were redeemable for special activities with a parent (e.g., playing board games, going bowling) or tangible prizes (e.g., bouncy balls, Legos).

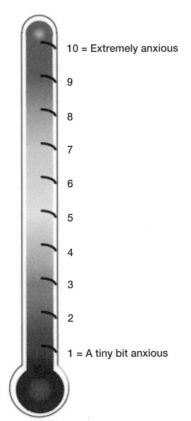

10 = Extremely anxious

9

8

7

6

5

4

3

2

1 = A tiny bit anxious

FIGURE 12.3 Anxiety thermometer.

- *Parental Involvement:* John's parents attended the final 10 to 15 minutes of each session in order to learn the skills he was acquiring. To reinforce his learning and application of the skills, John was encouraged to explain his understanding of the skills to his parents in session and they were all encouraged to continue related discussions at home. His parents also learned how to model and reinforce positive social skills and nonanxious behavior.
- *Group Treatment/Peer Interaction:* In addition to individual treatment, John participated in the Resilience Builder Program®, a resilience-based group CBT approach designed to improve social, emotional, and family functioning with heterogeneous groups of children. This 12-week manualized program focused on self-efficacy, affect and behavior regulation, flexibility/adaptability, social problem solving, and proactive orientation. Strategies included engaging in interactive didactic lessons, role-play, behavioral rehearsal during a playtime, self-regulation techniques, home assignments (discussed in group each week), and a session in the community (e.g., bowling alley, mini-golf).

Outcome

After 3 months of treatment, John evidenced significant improvement in his social competence, including speaking in an audible voice, making eye contact, and initiating and maintaining conversations. His tantrums at home had subsided and he was beginning to use his anxiety management skills without prompting. He willingly attended a few Cub Scout activities with peers and invited a classmate over to his house twice. John was voluntarily going to school and participating more in class, although he was still working toward giving a 10-minute presentation in front of the class. His parents were also actively implementing the skills learned, modeling positive social interactions, and problem solving social-related dilemmas in front of John (e.g., whether to attend a party where only know one person).

CHALLENGES IN APPLYING THE EVIDENCE-BASED APPROACH

One of the challenges inherent to treating social phobia in children is that exposures can be difficult to design and implement, particularly if parents display social impairment as well (and inadvertently reinforce social anxieties or avoid fostering skills practice at home). In developing a behavioral plan, exposures need to be titrated to each child and the ability for generalization to nonstructured settings (e.g., school recess) is a key consideration from the outset.

Another challenge revolves around the feasibility of implementing empirically supported treatment protocols in real-world clinical settings. For example, provider availability, time commitment required from the client, and cost may be limiting factors for a treatment program that dictates multiple weekly sessions. There is also the challenge of dissemination with regard to the imbalance between the availability of providers trained in empirically supported treatments and the need for services, which may be mitigated in part through the use of new technology. For example, computer-assisted CBT programs for children with anxiety disorders (e.g., Camp Cope-A-Lot) appear promising as treatment approaches; moreover, a new CBT-based smartphone app—the Mayo Clinic Anxiety Coach—is now available to guide exposure therapy.

CULTURAL DIVERSITY ISSUES

The few studies to date that have specifically examined ethnicity in pediatric social phobia suggest that it does not contribute to significant differences in symptom presentation or treatment response. Social phobia in children may be slightly more prevalent in females than males, but evidence is limited. In clinical practice, there do not appear to be notable differences in pediatric social phobia based on ethnicity, gender, sexual orientation, socioeconomic status, or religion, although providers need to be sensitive to all of these factors in treatment endeavors.

FUTURE RESEARCH

In order to increase generalizability of the empirically supported treatments for child social phobia to date, future research efforts should examine treatment outcome in real-world clinical settings, which often include more severe and heterogeneous case presentations. To gain a better understanding of how these treatments lead to improvement, research efforts also need to focus on identifying the key underlying mechanisms of change. Furthermore, a recent review of evidence-based treatments for pediatric anxiety disorders indicated that researchers often fail to include measures of cognition (e.g., the Children's Automatic Thoughts Scale) and physiology (e.g., electrodermal response of the hand). It will be important for future studies to assess these variables along with diagnostic, emotional, and behavioral measures of treatment outcome.

KEY REFERENCES

Albano, A. M., & DiBartolo, P. M. (2007). *Cognitive-behavioral therapy for social phobia in adolescents: Therapist guide*. New York, NY: Oxford University Press.

Alvord, M. K., Zucker, B., & Grados, J. J. (2011). *Resilience builder program for children and adolescents*. Champaign, IL: Research Press.

Zucker, B. (2008). *Anxiety-free kids: An interactive guide for parents and children*. Waco, TX: Prufrock Press.

CHAPTER 13

Substance Abuse in Adolescents

Jason Burrow-Sanchez and Megan Wrona

CLINICAL PROBLEM

Substance use can become a clinical disorder for adolescents and is diagnosed according to the severity of the problem using behavioral criteria set forth in the *Diagnostic and Statistical Manual of Mental Disorders* (*DSM-5*). The vast majority of adolescents who experiment with or use substances do not go on to develop a substance use disorder. In 2009, according to the Substance Abuse and Mental Health Services Administration (SAMHSA), approximately 7% of youth in the United States aged 12 to 17 could be diagnosed with a substance abuse or dependence disorder. An adolescent will meet diagnostic criteria for a *substance abuse disorder* when he or she develops a maladaptive pattern of substance use that has led to clinically significant impairment in one of the following areas in the past year: problems with fulfilling role obligations at school (e.g., constant tardiness, missing class), work, or home; engaging in physically hazardous situations (e.g., driving while intoxicated); recurrent legal problems related to substance use; or continued use despite interpersonal (e.g., constant arguing with parents) or social problems (e.g., losing friends) related to his or her use. A more severe diagnosis, *substance dependence*, exists if an adolescent demonstrates at least three of the following: signs of tolerance (i.e., using more of the drug to achieve intoxication); signs of withdrawal (i.e., negative physical symptoms when stopped using the drug); use of substances in larger amounts or for a longer period of time; frequent and unsuccessful attempts to reduce use; a great deal of time spent in obtaining substances; reduction in important social activities (e.g., not attending school, giving up sports); or continuing to use the drug despite problems related to the use (e.g., continued use despite court involvement) over the past 12 months.

PREVALENCE

Data from the 2011 report on the national *Monitoring the Future* (*MTF*) study indicate that by the time adolescents complete 12th grade, the majority (71%) report having used alcohol in their lifetime and more than one half (54%) report they have been drunk on at least one occasion. Further, more than one third (41%) of high school seniors report the use of some alcohol in the past month. Recent *MTF* data indicate that 36% of 8th grade students report having used alcohol in their lifetime and 16% of these students report being drunk at least once. Marijuana is the most commonly used illicit substance by adolescents and *MTF* data indicate 43.8% of 12th graders and 17.3% of 8th graders report having tried marijuana in their lifetimes. Smaller but significant numbers of adolescents report daily marijuana use: 6.1% of 12th graders, 3.3% of 10th graders, and 1.2% of 8th graders.

Among adolescents, a growing concern is the use of prescription medications for nonmedical reasons. *MTF* data indicate that 21.6% of 12th graders report having used prescription medication at least once in their lifetime with 15.0% also reporting the use of such medication in the past year. In general, the *MTF* data reveal that adolescent males tend to have higher rates of illicit substance use than females, especially related to frequency of use. However, regarding alcohol use, 8th grade females have higher rates of alcohol use over the prior 30 days than their male counterparts, and rates of use over the prior 30 days are nearly equivalent for 10th grade females and males.

CULTURAL DIVERSITY ISSUES

According to data from the *MTF* study, there are differences in use patterns across grades 8, 10, and 12 for the three largest ethnic groups in the United States— Caucasians, African Americans, and Hispanics. In 8th grade, Hispanic students report higher levels of substance use compared to their African American and Caucasian counterparts in nearly all drug categories (except amphetamines). By 12th grade, this pattern of use shifts with Caucasian students reporting the highest use rates followed by Hispanic students. In general, African American youth report lower substance use rates compared to their Caucasian and Hispanic counterparts across all grade levels and for most drugs, including illicit drugs, alcohol, and cigarettes. The *MTF* data are school based and provide good estimates of drug use levels for youth in school; however, these data may underestimate substance use for adolescents who have dropped out of school.

EVIDENCE-BASED TREATMENTS

The use of preventive and treatment interventions are important for dealing with adolescent substance abuse depending on the severity of the problem. Preventive interventions typically occur in school settings and target all students (i.e., universal prevention) or groups of "at-risk" students (i.e., secondary/tertiary prevention) with the goal of preventing substance abuse problems from developing in later adolescence or adulthood. Treatment interventions typically occur in community or medical clinics and are designed for adolescents who have been diagnosed with a substance use disorder and need more than a school-based intervention can provide.

Substance abuse prevention programs generally target a wide range of adolescents, in hopes of strengthening protective factors while reducing risk factors for substance use. Adolescents exposed to such programs may or may not have a history of drug use. More specifically, primary or universal prevention programs are geared toward all students in a given school, whereas secondary or targeted prevention programs focus on youth who are exhibiting specific risk factors for substance use (e.g., tardiness, failing grades, school suspension). The more successful prevention programs typically focus on providing adolescents with ways to enhance their problem-solving, decision-making, and coping skills for daily living. More information on specific research-based prevention programs can be found through SAMHSA's National Registry of Evidence-Based Programs and Practices (SAMHSA, nrepp.samhsa.gov).

Adolescents who do not respond to preventive interventions, or have developed a substance use disorder, should be referred to a treatment program. Such programs typically occur in the community settings and cover a range of services including detoxification, residential treatment, and outpatient treatment. By far, the majority of adolescents receive outpatient treatment services compared to either residential or inpatient treatment. The three most common formats for delivering outpatient treatment, in order, are individual, group, and family based. Individual and group approaches with a cognitive behavioral foundation have shown the most success in reducing adolescent substance abuse. Cognitive behavioral interventions are based on theories of learning with the goal of helping the individual identify and then change maladaptive thoughts and behaviors. These types of interventions typically fit well with adolescents because they are time limited, present, and problem focused. In addition, family-based interventions have also demonstrated success for treating adolescent substance abuse. From a family treatment perspective, the problem is typically viewed from the context of the larger family system and thus, the identified adolescent as well as his or her family members is needed to participate in treatment. Some of the more successful research-based family treatments for adolescent substance abuse include: Functional Family Therapy, Multidimensional Family Therapy, and Multisystemic Family Therapy.

In general, the findings on evidence-based substance abuse prevention and treatment interventions are based on studies that have included larger samples of White adolescents compared to youth from other racial and ethnic groups. Thus, less is known about the efficacy of such interventions for ethnic minority adolescents. There is some encouraging evidence to suggest that certain ethnic minority adolescents respond positively to evidence-based interventions for substance abuse. On the other hand, there is too little research to determine if ethnic minority adolescents benefit from culturally adapted versions of evidence-based substance abuse interventions. Research in this area continues to emerge but it will be difficult to draw firm conclusions until more is known about how ethnic minority adolescents respond to substance abuse interventions.

It is important to note that regardless of the specific treatment modality selected, relapse is a common occurrence when treating substance abuse. Research suggests that about 50% of adolescents will relapse within 3 months after completing treatment, so the need for additional services is highly likely.

FUTURE RESEARCH

Three important areas for future adolescent substance abuse research include prevention, treatment, and determining the efficacy of interventions for ethnic minority adolescents. First, more substance abuse prevention research is needed to examine ways that current school-based interventions can include larger support systems for students (e.g., families, communities) in order to delay the onset of substance use and prevent substance use problems from becoming worse. Second, more substance abuse treatment research is needed to determine effective methods for reducing the risk of relapse and increasing support for adolescents after treatment completion. Finally, more research is needed to determine the efficacy of prevention and treatment interventions for ethnic minority adolescents.

KEY REFERENCES

Burrow-Sanchez, J. J., & Hawken, L. S. (2007). *Helping students overcome adolescent substance abuse: Effective practices for prevention and intervention.* New York, NY: Guilford Press.

Huey, S. J., Jr., & Polo, A. J. (2008). Evidence-based psychosocial treatments for ethnic minority youth. *Journal of Clinical Child and Adolescent Psychology, 37,* 262–301. doi: 10.1080/15374410701820174

Waldron, H. B., & Turner, C. W. (2008). Evidence-based psychosocial treatments for adolescent substance abuse. *Journal of Clinical Child and Adolescent Psychology, 37*(1), 238–261. doi: 10.1080/15374410701820133

Clinician Application

Substance Abuse in Adolescents

Erica M. Finstad

COMMENT ON THE EVIDENCE-BASED RECOMMENDATIONS

As noted in the research section, marijuana and alcohol are the most commonly misused (non-tobacco) illicit substances by adolescents. In contrast to adults, the type of substance used is frequently based on availability among their friends, at parties, or in their home, as in the case of experimentation with prescription medications and inhalants. Burrow-Sanchez and Wrona also noted that most adolescents who use substances do not go on to develop a substance use disorder. Although any drug use during adolescence has the potential for serious negative consequences, many young clients are not necessarily "addicts" with a lifelong struggle for sobriety ahead. Adolescents are often referred or even pressured into treatment by family members, their school, or the juvenile justice system rather than presenting voluntarily. They generally have a lower level of motivation to change than their adult counterparts.

The authors also noted the demonstrated efficacy of cognitive behavioral therapy (CBT) and family therapy, two developmentally appropriate approaches that are well accepted by our clientele. I regularly utilize a CBT approach with my adolescent substance-using clients. A focus on developing critical thinking skills and helping youth understand the connections between their thoughts, feelings, and subsequent behaviors is particularly useful for young people whose mental capacities are not yet fully developed in these areas. Further, specific training on recognizing high-risk situations and triggers for use is helpful for youth who often use in response to peer influences and social situations.

CASE EXAMPLE

Subject Information and Brief History

Eduardo, a 16-year-old Mexican American male, was referred to our clinic by a county juvenile probation officer for outpatient treatment of alcohol dependence and marijuana abuse.

Presenting Problem

Eduardo reported that he began using substances at age 9 and had a history of being charged with assault and theft. He noted that substance use is commonplace among his friends and "is like a tradition in my family." His motivation for entering treatment was to "get clean" in order to be eligible to enter a residential alternative high school completion program.

Treatment Intervention and Course

Treatment was offered in the context of a federally funded treatment research study. It involved a 14-session, individual, manualized CBT approach, with exercises adapted to be appropriate for adolescent clients and introductory sessions guided by Motivational Interviewing techniques. Required CBT topics included a functional analysis (e.g., triggers, consequences) of substance use, a functional analysis of non-using behaviors (e.g., positive activities that serve to interfere with use), coping with drug cravings, substance refusal, and HIV-risk education. The functional analysis exercises were borrowed from the Adolescent Community Reinforcement Approach, a manualized treatment similar to CBT but with a particular emphasis on positive reinforcement and contingency management for reducing substance use and increasing non-using activities. Additional topics included communication skills training, anger management, identifying social support resources, and learning to cope with negative emotions.

Eduardo responded well to the structured approach of CBT. Adolescents are familiar with the concept of having homework assignments, so he was compliant in completing written CBT exercises between sessions. Although he moved to a new home environment where alcohol and marijuana were no longer available, he reported having no sober friends and continued to associate with deviant peers. Therefore, significant time was spent on coping with high-risk situations, such as substance refusal skills (e.g., different ways to say "no" or redirect his peers to alternative activities) and relapse prevention (e.g., carrying an index card with his list of reasons to stay clean).

Outcome

Eduardo's initial motivation to change seemed primarily based on external factors, such as "getting (his) Probation Officer off (his) back." During the course of treatment, he began to speak more clearly about goals he would like to achieve and came to understand that his previous lifestyle and behaviors were interfering with achieving these goals. Eduardo noted that he found the particular skills taught in CBT useful and was finding it easier to resist substance use over time. He stayed clean from marijuana and alcohol and completed his application for the residential program.

CHALLENGES IN APPLYING THE EVIDENCE-BASED APPROACH

While CBT will teach valuable skills for changing thoughts, feelings, and behaviors, it may not be appropriate or even feasible to jump into this content if an adolescent lacks initial motivation to change. Many adolescent clients are referred, or even mandated, to substance abuse treatment by outside forces (e.g., parents, schools, juvenile justice) rather than by a personal desire for change. To address this issue, CBT can be enhanced by starting first with one or several sessions of another evidence-based practice, Motivational Interviewing (MI). MI is a particularly good match for adolescents because it takes the client's level of motivation into consideration and does not assume that he or she is ready to make a change in behavior. The collaborative atmosphere created by a skilled MI therapist who is able to "roll with resistance" is an appropriate choice for youth who might resist the advice of an adult. Furthermore, MI focuses on increasing clients' feelings of self-efficacy to change, helping to build confidence before introducing CBT.

CULTURAL DIVERSITY ISSUES

Meta-analyses of the treatment literature indicate that evidence-based treatments for adolescent substance abuse are effective for the three largest ethnic groups represented in the samples: Whites, Hispanics, and African Americans. However, some findings suggest that for Hispanic youth, family-based interventions may be more efficacious than CBT. There is also preliminary evidence that therapist–client ethnic matching may produce greater reductions in substance use for Hispanic youth.

FUTURE RESEARCH

Given that the vast majority of youth with drug problems never receive the help they need, I would like to see future research focus on psychotherapy approaches designed to identify and engage unmotivated, "treatment-refusing" adolescents with substance use problems into treatment. One approach we have found particularly effective for this purpose is Community Reinforcement and Family Training (CRAFT). In this manual-guided treatment approach, the psychotherapist works first with a willing parent who is concerned about the substance use of a treatment-elusive adolescent. Behavioral skills are taught to help parents change communication skills and behaviors at home to reduce substance use, even if their child never attends treatment. Ideally, families will be assisted with rapid entry into a treatment program if the adolescent later agrees. Such approaches hold promise for helping individuals who are very unlikely to voluntarily seek needed help on their own.

KEY REFERENCES

Miller, W. R., & Rollnick, S. R. (2013). *Motivational interviewing, third edition: Helping people change.* New York, NY: The Guilford Press.

Smith, J. E., & Meyers, R. J. (2007). *Motivating substance abusers to enter treatment: Working with family members.* New York, NY: The Guilford Press.

Springer, D. W., & Rubin, A. (2009). *Substance abuse treatment for youth and adults: Clinician's guide to evidence-based practice.* Hoboken, NJ: John Wiley & Sons, Inc.

CHAPTER 14

Tic Disorders

Loran P. Hayes and Michael B. Himle

CLINICAL PROBLEM

Tic disorders (TDs) are characterized by sudden, rapid, recurrent, nonrhythmic movements and vocalizations (i.e., tics). The severity of TDs vary along several dimensions including number, frequency, and intensity of tics, the degree of interruption the tics cause, and tic complexity. Tics can be simple or complex. Simple tics are discrete, rapid, meaningless movements and/or sounds (e.g., blinking, twitching, sniffing) whereas complex tics are slower and orchestrated and may be construed as purposeful (e.g., patterned touching or tapping, shouting/saying words or sentences). In addition to the tics, many people with TDs report aversive premonitory urges that precede tics. These urges are often described as localized feelings of discomfort, such as tingling or itching, or a generalized feeling that something is "not just right." Some individuals also report that premonitory urges are worsened by attempts to suppress tics and are alleviated by performance of the tic. This has led some to suggest that some tics are "semivolitional." Tic severity is highly variable and typically takes a naturally fluctuating course. Tics also fluctuate in response to various external (e.g., stressful events, tic-related talk) and internal triggers (e.g., mood states).

The *DSM-5* recognizes three main TDs that are differentiated by the duration and type of tic(s) present. Tourette's Disorder is diagnosed when multiple motor tics and at least one vocal tic have been present (though not necessarily concurrently) for 1 year. Persistent Motor or Vocal Tick Disorder is diagnosed when only motor or vocal tics (but not both) have been present for 1 year. Provisional Tic Disorder is diagnosed when motor and/or vocal tic(s) have been present less than 1 year. Provisional (transient) tics typically take a fluctuating course and often remit spontaneously.

Chronic tic disorders are associated with increased risk for several comorbid conditions. Most common are obsessive-compulsive disorder (OCD, 30%–40%) and attention deficit/hyperactivity disorder (ADHD, 40%–50%). The co-occurrence of Tourette disorder, OCD, and ADHD is common and has been dubbed the "Tourette Triad." In addition, TDs are associated with increased risk for mood and anxiety disorders and impulse control problems (e.g., anger or rage attacks). Though not all individuals with tics experience impairment, many report problems with social, educational, and occupational functioning and diminished quality of life. Severe tics can cause pain, discomfort, and physical complications. Comorbid conditions often contribute to greater functional impairment than the tics themselves and are often the first target for intervention.

PREVALENCE

Estimates of the prevalence of TDs vary considerably. When only a full diagnosis of Tourette's syndrome is considered, point prevalence estimates range from 0.1% to 1%. When Chronic Motor and Vocal Tic Disorders are included estimates center between 1% and 2%. If broadened to include simply the presence of tics, studies indicate that 5% to 15% of children display one or more transient tic(s) at some point during childhood. Tics typically onset in early childhood with motor tics (usually of the face) preceding vocal tics and simple tics preceding complex tics. Tics typically peak in severity in early adulthood with most adults reporting significant improvement or remission. When tics persist into adulthood, they typically become less variable.

CULTURAL DIVERSITY ISSUES

Tic disorders occur more commonly in males than females by a ratio of about 5:1. There is scant research on how race and ethnicity influence TDs; however, a small number of studies showed higher rates in Caucasian and European American than in Latino, African American, and sub-Saharan Black African samples.

EVIDENCE-BASED TREATMENTS

Empirically supported treatments (ESTs) for tics include pharmacological and behavioral interventions, usually used in combination. The rationale for behavioral interventions is that although tics are caused by biological dysfunction, they are influenced by contextual factors such as specific settings, activities, and mood states. The degree to which specific antecedents impact tics is idiosyncratic, but with an individualized and systematic assessment and treatment plan, tic exacerbating antecedents can be identified and altered (or eliminated) for therapeutic gain. Tic-contingent consequences can also impact tic severity and include both internal (private) and external (social) factors. Regarding internal factors, it is believed that some tics are strengthened because they remove an aversive urge (i.e., negative reinforcement). Procedures designed to interrupt or prevent the tic would "expose" the individual to the premonitory urge thereby allowing habituation to the urge and extinction of the negative reinforcement cycle. Social contingencies, such as tic-contingent attention or escape from aversive tasks, have also been shown to exacerbate tics in some cases. Like antecedents, tic-contingent consequences can be identified and modified to reduce tics.

The behavioral treatments with the most empirical support are Habit Reversal Training (HRT) and the recently expanded version Comprehensive Behavioral Intervention for Tics (CBIT, which includes HRT as a primary component). HRT uses three primary techniques: Awareness Training (AT), Competing Response Training (CRT), and social support. During AT, the therapist teaches the individual to recognize tic occurrence and tic warning signs, such as initial tic movements or a premonitory urge. During CRT, the therapist teaches the individual to engage in a response that is directly incompatible with performance of the tic. For example, an individual experiencing a head-jerking tic may tense muscles in the neck that are antagonistic to the tic and thus will not allow the tic to occur. The CR is held until the premonitory urge dissipates thus breaking the urge reduction (negative reinforcement cycle). Social support is included to reinforce and prompt use of the CR. The effectiveness of HRT has been shown in numerous studies, including several randomized controlled trials with children and adults with TDs.

CBIT was developed and tested in two large multisite randomized controlled trials, with both children and adult clients. CBIT is a multicomponent treatment delivered over 10 to 12 weekly sessions with a new tic targeted each week. In addition to HRT, CBIT uses a personalized, systematic, function-based assessment to identify environmental factors that exacerbate tics and teaches function-based strategies to eliminate or alter them. In both the chid and adult trials, CBIT was shown to reduce tics more than supportive psychotherapy. Tic severity was reduced by 31% (effect size, 0.68) in children who received CBIT and 26% (effect size, 0.57) in adults who received CBIT. Treatment gains were maintained at 6 months post treatment in both trials.

FUTURE RESEARCH

More research is needed in a number of areas concerning TDs. Given the relatively high percentage of children who show transient tics at some point in their lives, identifying those who are likely to develop chronic TDs will be a goal of future research and may guide early intervention efforts. As previously noted, studies related to factors of diversity in TDs are sorely needed. On the treatment front, research on mediators and moderators of treatment outcome, strategies for addressing comorbid symptoms, and research to address treatment barriers and improve treatment dissemination are needed.

KEY REFERENCES

Cook, C. R., & Blacher, J. (2007). Evidence-based psychosocial treatments for tic disorders. *Clinical Psychology: Science and Practice, 14*(3), 252–267. doi: 10.1111/j.1468-2850.2007.00085.x

Woods, D. W., Conelea, C. A., & Himle, M. B. (2010). Behavior therapy for Tourette's disorder: Utilization in a community sample and an emerging area of practice for psychologists. *Professional Psychology: Research and Practice, 41*(6), 518–525. doi: 10.1037/a0021709

Woods, D. W., Piacentini, J. C., Chang, S., Deckersbach, T., Ginsberg, G., ... Wilhelm, S. (2008). *Managing Tourette's syndrome: A behavioral intervention for children and adults (therapist guide)*. New York, NY: Oxford University Press.

Tic Disorders

Lori Rockmore, Shawn Ewbank, and Meir Flancbaum

COMMENT ON THE EVIDENCE-BASED RECOMMENDATIONS

Evidence-based treatments (EBTs) for tic disorders (TDs) include pharmacological and behavioral interventions. While medications have traditionally been the treatment of choice for reducing tics, many individuals discontinue their use owing to aversive side effects. There has been a resurgence of research and a growing empirical support for the use of Habit Reversal Training (HRT), a behavior therapy for the management of tics, either alone or in conjunction with medication management. From a clinician's perspective, the accessibility of HRT was punctuated by the publication of a user-friendly treatment manual by Woods and colleagues in 2008, which provides an expanded version of HRT called Comprehensive Behavioral Intervention for Tics (CBIT).

Based on the large catchment area which our clinic serves and based on the data from survey studies of mental health practitioners nationally, it appears that there are very few therapists with expertise in providing HRT or CBIT for TDs. Furthermore, our experience indicates that many parents and practitioners—mental health and medical—often misunderstand the complex presentation of individuals with TDs. The resulting confusion can delay proper identification of tic symptoms and associated disorders, and delay the initiation of effective treatments.

CASE EXAMPLE

Subject Information and Brief History

Graham was an 11-year-old Caucasian boy who lived with his parents and younger sister in a suburban, middle-class neighborhood. He was referred to a university-based tic disorder specialty program by a local organization that provides support to individuals with TD and their families. Graham was previously diagnosed with a TD by his neurologist. He was on several medications that remained stable throughout treatment, including guanfacine for tics.

Presenting Problem

Graham presented with TD and obsessive-compulsive disorder. Problematic tics consisted of numerous motor tics, including a side-to-side head shake and jaw snapping, as well as phonic tics, such as a deep "huh" sound and throat clearing. His score on Yale Global Tic Severity Scale (YGTSS), a clinician-administered interview used to assess tics, indicated severe tic symptoms (total tic score of 40). One month prior to Graham's evaluation, he experienced a sudden and severe exacerbation of motor and vocal tics which interfered with his ability to participate in both academic and social activities. When the family was interviewed about potential antecedents to this episode and no identifiable stressors were reported, the exacerbation was attributed to the natural waxing and waning course of tics. In addition, he reported some symptoms of anxiety and depression related to his current level of tic symptoms. As a result, Graham's parents, in cooperation with his school, decided to place him on homebound instruction.

Treatment Intervention and Course

Treatment consisted of 12 weekly 50-minute sessions, followed by one booster session. Session content was based on the CBIT treatment manual authored by Douglas Woods and colleagues (2008), with some variations to session structure and format as was deemed clinically appropriate. Treatment began by explaining the rationale for CBIT, creating a tic hierarchy, and conducting a functional assessment of the headshaking tic. Graham and his parents were then assigned to monitor the frequency of the identified tic.

During session 2, Graham and his parents reported a significant decrease in the headshaking tic. Graham stated that as he became more aware of engaging in the tic, he was able to "control it more." To further increase motivation, the clinician facilitated a discussion about the impact of tics on Graham's life using the Tic Hassles Form. Next, HRT was introduced for the headshaking tic. This consisted of identifying the onset of the premonitory urge that preceded the tic, becoming more aware of the onset of the tic, identifying and practicing the competitive response (pulling chin back, tensing neck, deep breathing), and instructing the parents on how to support Graham's efforts in using the competitive response.

At session 3, Graham and his parents reported that his headshaking tic was no longer as frequent, intense, or distressing. Thus, treatment shifted to the second tic identified on the hierarchy (jaw snapping) and the treatment procedures were repeated (functional assessment, monitoring, awareness training, and competitive response training) with similar results. During session 4, a third tic (a deep "huh" sound) was targeted in the same fashion. During session 5, Graham and his parents reported that they felt comfortable implementing the treatment for additional tics at home. The remaining seven sessions were spent working with Graham and his parents on the anxiety he was experiencing as a result of this recent exacerbation of tics and how he was going to handle returning to school. Strategies utilized during these sessions were psychoeducation about anxiety, cognitive restructuring, relaxation techniques, and behavioral practice/exposure.

Outcome

Graham and his parents were able to successfully implement CBIT for his tics. His score on the YGTSS decreased from 40 (severe symptoms) to 23 (moderate symptoms) based on lower ratings in tic number, frequency, intensity, and interference. Graham also returned to school after session 10.

CHALLENGES IN APPLYING THE EVIDENCE-BASED APPROACH

Several challenges may arise when treating individuals with TD. Although most clients seeking HRT or CBIT report interference as a result of their tics, they may nonetheless have difficulty consistently implementing competitive responses. In our experience, this is often a motivation-related problem that is best addressed using antecedent interventions, including reviewing treatment rationale, motivational interviewing, and using sessions to practice tolerating the urge to tic.

More generally, treatment of individuals with TDs is challenging owing to the high rate of co-occurring psychological disorders, particularly attention deficit/hyperactivity disorder and obsessive-compulsive disorder. When working with individuals with TDs, therefore, a thorough assessment and collaborative discussion to prioritize treatment goals is critical. It is important to consider treating comorbid conditions first, as they may be more impairing than the tics themselves, or hinder a client's ability to effectively utilize HRT strategies. In addition to management strategies for tics and co-occurring disorders, many clients and their families can benefit from support around the acceptance of a TD diagnosis, and from skills to navigate the social and functional challenges commonly associated with these disorders.

CULTURAL DIVERSITY ISSUES

In addition to the diversity issues discussed in the research section, it is important to be sensitive to cultural norms when discussing a TD diagnosis and its treatment recommendations. Understanding a client's perspective on his or her diagnosis is a critical first step in collaborating to promote acceptance, reduce stigma, and determine treatment.

FUTURE RESEARCH

Future research is indicated in several areas. First, while HRT and medications have both been found to be effective, studies comparing the efficacy of these two commonly used treatments is needed. Second, given the importance of bolstering dissemination efforts, further research on the effectiveness of HRT in community-based clinic settings is needed. Finally, research should focus on better understanding the specific components—mediators and moderators—that are most critical for successful behavioral treatment of tics.

KEY REFERENCES

Woods, D., Piacente, J., Chang, S., Deckersbach, T., Ginsberg, G., ... Wilhelm, S. (2008). *Managing Tourette syndrome: A behavioral intervention for children and adults – Therapist guide*. New York, NY: Oxford University Press.

Kurlan, R. (2010). Tourette's syndrome. *New England Journal of Medicine, 363*, 2332–2338.

Woods, D., Piacentini, J., & Walkup, J. (2007). *Treating Tourette syndrome and tic disorders: A guide for practitioners*. New York, NY: Guilford Press.

Attention Deficit/Hyperactivity Disorder in Adults

J. Russell Ramsay

CLINICAL PROBLEM

Attention Deficit/Hyperactivity Disorder (ADHD) is a neurodevelopmental disorder characterized by age-inappropriate levels of inattention, hyperactivity, and impulsivity. More specifically, ADHD is currently understood as a developmental disorder of impaired executive functioning that underlies the observed impairments. Executive functioning has been defined in many ways, with a useful definition by Russell Barkley being "self-regulation across time for the attainment of one's goals (self-interests), often in the context of others." In fact, recent research has indicated that skill deficits associated with the executive functions—self-management to time, self-organization/problem solving, self-restraint (inhibition), self-motivation, and self-regulation of emotion—are more specific and consistent predictors of ADHD's persistence into adulthood than are inattention/restlessness and impulsivity factors.

Studies of the life outcomes of adults with ADHD, either longitudinal studies tracking children with ADHD to adulthood or cross-sectional studies of recently diagnosed adults, indicate that ADHD is associated with a profile of persistent difficulties affecting most domains of adult life, such as academic, workplace, and relationship functioning, placing the disorder among the most impairing seen in outpatient psychology and psychiatry. Fortunately, ADHD also has been found to be responsive to treatment, though treatment response may be affected by factors such as severity of ADHD symptoms and impairment, comorbidity, and other complicating factors.

PREVALENCE

ADHD is estimated to affect 3% to 7% of school-aged children in the United States with international rates averaging 5.29%. Longitudinal studies of children and adolescents with ADHD tracked into adulthood indicate that "syndromatic" persistence rates of around 40% while "symptomatic" persistence rates, reflecting ongoing residual symptoms, and functional impairment, fall in the 65% to 90% range.

Prevalence rates for adult ADHD fall around 4%. A national survey study in the United States estimated a 4.4% prevalence rate for adult ADHD, the equivalent of about 8 million U.S. adults. The prevalence rates for U.S. college students were 2.9% for males and 3.9% for females. Whereas there is a significantly higher male-to-female ratio of clinic-referred children with ADHD, adult samples usually indicate ratios that are closer to being equal, usually falling around 2:1 or 1.5:1 with males outnumbering females with ADHD.

CULTURAL DIVERSITY ISSUES

An international survey conducted in the Americas, Europe, and the Middle East found a prevalence rate for adult ADHD of 3.4% and an international study of college students found a prevalence range of 0% to 8.1%, with differences across different countries (i.e., United States, Italy, and New Zealand). Studies of adult ADHD in China, Mexico, South Africa, and various other countries further indicate that the symptoms and impairments of ADHD know no geographic cultural boundaries. Moreover, there may be underserved populations, such as minority groups in the United States, for whom the effects of ADHD have not yet been well documented. Similarly, there may be subpopulations of adults with ADHD in substance use treatment programs or in the criminal justice system for whom adequate assessment and treatment may lead to decreased relapse and recidivism rates, respectively.

EVIDENCE-BASED TREATMENTS

Based on the extant clinical research, pharmacotherapy for ADHD stands out as the treatment option with the strongest evidence base for patients of all ages. Stimulant medications have been found to be particularly effective in treating the core symptoms of ADHD. There also are effective nonstimulant options. Although medications are effective, it is estimated that medications alone may represent insufficient treatment for many adults with ADHD. That is, while providing symptom improvements, medication alone may not necessarily result in normalization or adequate improvements in domains of daily functioning. Similarly, a clinically significant treatment response, which is typically defined as a 30% reduction in symptoms, may not translate into sufficient improvements in the day-to-day lives of patients.

There is increased interest in adjunctive treatments for adult ADHD. While medications directly treat the symptoms of ADHD, most adjunctive treatments for adult ADHD target areas of life impairment. The adjunctive treatment with the strongest evidence base to date has been psychosocial treatment, primarily characterized by cognitive behavioral therapy (CBT) approaches. CBT approaches adapted for adult ADHD have been well studied in many uncontrolled studies, though there has been a recent increase in randomized controlled trials that have yielded positive results when compared with educational support and relaxation treatments. CBT can be offered in both individual and group formats and there are available treatment guides.

ADHD Coaching has emerged as an applied psychoeducational support service designed to help individuals with ADHD to implement coping strategies in their daily lives. Drawn from the field of life coaching, ADHD Coaching involves regular contact (including through the use of e-mail, texting, videoconferencing, and other technologies) with a coach who helps the individual with ADHD identify specific areas of difficulty and to develop and implement corresponding solutions and coping skills to more effectively manage them. The field is still defining itself and its training requirements, ethics, and so forth. Preliminary outcome research evidence indicates the benefits of academic coaching for college students with ADHD, with one other published outcome study of ADHD Coaching for nonstudent adults with ADHD.

Findings from studies of complementary-alternative medical (CAM) treatments for adults with ADHD have been equivocal at best. There have only been a handful of published studies of neurofeedback that have included adult ADHD patients and no published studies of computerized working memory training for adults with ADHD. The available outcome data are insufficient to recommend any CAM treatments as a viable complement to standard treatments, much less as stand-alone treatments for adult ADHD. Promising areas for further research include mindfulness meditation and supplementation with essential fatty acids, as well as well-designed studies of neurofeedback and working memory training for adults. Although not constituting "treatments" per se, good health practices, such as healthy diet, regular physical exercise, and adequate, regular sleep habits are commonly recommended to manage the effects of ADHD.

FUTURE RESEARCH

There are other areas of treatment, such as academic or workplace interventions, couples or family therapy for relationships involving an adult with ADHD, that simply have not yet been studied. ADHD is currently viewed as a lifelong condition that will require ongoing efforts to effectively manage, akin to managing diabetes or hypertension. Although medications currently form the foundation of treatment, they do not necessarily solve all of the problems experienced by adults with ADHD. Various adjunctive, nonmedication treatments for adult ADHD are being developed and studied. Future research will explore their efficacy in combination with medications and as stand-alone treatments in the relatively few cases in which medications are ineffective, intolerable, medically contraindicated, or declined. The focus of future outcome research is to provide treatment protocols for which the goal is not achieving symptom improvement but rather normalization of functioning and well-being.

KEY REFERENCES

Barkley, R. A., Murphy, K. R., & Fischer, M. (2008). *ADHD in adults: What the science says*. New York, NY: Guilford Press.

Ramsay, J. R. (2010). *Nonmedication treatments for adult ADHD: Evaluating impact on daily functioning and well-being*. Washington, DC: American Psychological Association.

Weiss, N. (2011). Assessment and treatment of ADHD in adults. *Psychiatric Annals, 41*, 23–31. doi: 10.3928/00485713-20101221-05

Attention Deficit/Hyperactivity Disorder in Adults

Ari Tuckman

COMMENT ON THE EVIDENCE-BASED RECOMMENDATIONS

Ramsay rightly identifies Attention Deficit/Hyperactivity Disorder (ADHD) as a disorder of executive functions. Despite their inconsistent track record, adults with ADHD tend to know quite well what they should do, how to do it, why they should do it, and even when and where they should do it. Unfortunately, it is their weak executive functions that interfere with their reliably acting on these intentions. A long history of suboptimal performance and confusing setbacks, despite good effort and fervent promises to do better next time, predictably leads to higher rates of anxiety, depression, and substance use among adults with ADHD. These conditions further impair their performance.

Therefore, the most effective treatments address the executive functioning weaknesses with skill building, while also using more traditional cognitive behavioral therapy (CBT) to address the psychological fall-out of living with ADHD. These two components are often blended together in practice, but can be explained separately. The first involves teaching life management habits, such as using a calendar to track appointments, using a to-do list to track obligations, getting organized, time management, and so forth. Medication improves the executive functions and allows clients to better manage their daily responsibilities. These habits are easier to learn and maintain when appropriately medicated. The second component involves addressing the psychological fall-out from a lifetime of ADHD-based struggles, including common self-limiting beliefs (e.g., "I won't be able to stick with this"; "These sorts of thing never work out well" etc.).

CASE EXAMPLE

Subject Information and Brief History

"Paul" is a typical client in many ways. He is 36 years old and works in sales. He was diagnosed with ADHD 6 years earlier, although his educational, occupational, and social history makes it clear that he has struggled with distractibility and impulsivity throughout his life. He is bright and likeable but has never achieved his potential. He enjoys going out with his friends, but can get carried away with his drinking which then leads to regrettable actions.

Presenting Problem

Paul sought treatment at this time because his life felt out of control and he was worried about the potential consequences at work and in his personal life. He was worried about being fired from his job owing to his inconsistent performance and had cheated on his girlfriend with a woman that he met at a bar.

Treatment Intervention and Course

A practical, skills-based CBT model was used with Paul. Because it posed the greatest risk, initially, treatment focused on curbing his impulsivity, especially when alcohol was involved. We identified his priorities (doing well at work, strengthening his relationship with his girlfriend, and handling the various responsibilities at home) and discussed how his actions either supported these priorities or undermined them. We also discussed how some behaviors (such as starting Saturday night festivities early or with certain friends) tend to make other outcomes more likely (such as being too tired on Sunday to clean up his house, get the bills out on time, etc.). We focused on making better choices early on rather than counting on making the right choices in the heat of the moment. This involved challenging some beliefs, such as his role within his group of friends to be "the life of the party" and, therefore, what the implications might be for him in stepping back from that role.

Psychotherapy also focused on practical matters related to staying organized, self-activating (i.e., breaking procrastination) to make sales calls, and pushing himself to complete the necessary reports after sales meetings. Although some of this involved practical advice (e.g., "turn off email alerts to eliminate those distractions"), this often led to more psychological discussions (e.g., What does it mean for his self-concept that he needs to use some strategies that some other people don't?).

Although he admitted that medication had been helpful in the past, he was resistant to taking it consistently. He was concerned that it changed his personality by making him less spontaneous (even though this spontaneity also got him into trouble). The use of medication raised questions about free will and self-determination which is a common theme for many individuals with ADHD. In sessions, discussions addressed these irrational beliefs about "being controlled by his medication" and thereby enabled him to see more clearly that the benefits outweighed the costs.

Outcome

Paul made good progress in treatment by putting himself into fewer situations that tended to elicit problematic impulsive behavior and also was able to apply himself more diligently to the important but less interesting aspects of his job. He currently returns once every couple months for a tune-up. He changed jobs to what is hopefully a better fit for him and also eliminated some personality conflicts with his prior boss. ADHD is a lifelong condition so it is not uncommon to have ongoing or episodic contact with clients.

CHALLENGES IN APPLYING THE EVIDENCE-BASED APPROACH

Structured programs such as the research-validated CBT programs can be difficult to apply in private practice. Although clients may initially appreciate the highly structured format, they may also find it to be overly rigid, particularly when it requires a high level of effort to complete homework and then maintain the habit changes. This is partially due to executive function-based challenges with consistency and repetition, but it may also elicit psychological avoidance reactions to possible failure.

CULTURAL DIVERSITY ISSUES

Ironically, perhaps the greatest concern regarding diversity in the diagnosis and treatment of ADHD has less to do with culture than it does with age. ADHD is diagnosed much more often in children and teens, whereas, it is far too often missed in adults. Culturally and ethnically, ADHD is diagnosed much more often among Caucasian Americans than in other ethnic groups.

FUTURE RESEARCH

Although more research is needed in general on ADHD in adults, a relatively untapped area is that of couples therapy for adult ADHD as couples where one partner has ADHD have been shown to have lower marital satisfaction and higher divorce rates. It would also be helpful to have more information on predictors of early therapy drop-out and ways to prevent it.

KEY REFERENCES

Ramsay, J. R., & Rostain, A. L. (2008). *Cognitive behavioral therapy for adult ADHD: An integrative psychosocial and medical approach*. New York, NY: Routledge.

Solanto, M. V. (2011). *Cognitive behavioral therapy for adult ADHD: Targeting executive functions*. New York, NY: Guilford Press.

Tuckman, A. (2007). *Integrative treatment for adult ADHD: A practical, easy-to-use guide for clinicians*. Oakland, CA: New Harbinger.

CHAPTER 16

Alcohol Abuse

John W. Finney, Christine Timko, and Rudolf H. Moos

CLINICAL PROBLEM

Problems associated with alcohol consumption cover a broad spectrum—from misuse leading to accidents and/or longer-term medical consequences, to alcohol use disorders (AUDs; abuse and dependence) that may be further complicated by co-occurring conditions, such as psychiatric disorders and/or significant life problems. A treatment provider should assess where a client lies along this spectrum, determine whether detoxification is required, and select an appropriate evidence-based intervention or set of practices in conjunction with client preferences for specific interventions and treatment goals, while taking the client's cultural background into account.

PREVALENCE

According to the Substance Abuse and Mental Health Services Administration, almost 60 million people in the United States engaged in binge drinking in 2010 and about 18 million met diagnostic criteria for an AUD. In a 2000–2001 national survey, alcohol abuse was more prevalent among adult men (6.9%) than among adult women (2.6%), as was alcohol dependence (5.4% versus 2.3%, respectively). Alcohol abuse was more widespread among Whites (5.1%) than among African Americans (3.3%), Asians (2.1%), or Hispanics (4.0%), but less common than among Native Americans (5.8%). The prevalence of alcohol dependence was greatest among Native Americans (6.4%), followed by Hispanics (4.0%), Whites (3.8%), African Americans (3.6%), and Asians (2.1%). Although 5.2% of U.S. adults in 2010 without mental illness had a past-year diagnosis of alcohol abuse or dependence, the percentages were 13.8%, 17.8%, and 18.9%, respectively, for adults with mild, moderate, and serious mental illness.

CULTURAL DIVERSITY ISSUES

The American Psychiatric Association recommends that providers treating individuals with AUDs determine their cultural identity and cultural explanations for their presenting problems. The provider should consider the client's language, social norms, beliefs, and behaviors relevant to AUDs in planning the type and course of treatment. Providers may opt to apply AUD practices that are effective with the general population, but in a form that is adapted and culturally sensitive to members of specific cultural groups. Alternatively, if they regularly see members of a specific cultural group, providers may apply an empirically based, culturally specific treatment approach. Culturally sensitive treatment can explore linkages between the development and maintenance of the AUD and any stressors related to discrimination, language barriers, or acculturation conflicts.

EVIDENCE-BASED TREATMENTS

Alcohol Misuse

Brief interventions (BIs) for alcohol misuse are cost-effective. Although some BIs simply advise a client to reduce or abstain from alcohol use, the "FRAMES" acronym, captures six active ingredients that appear to characterize effective BIs: **F**eedback on impairment or risks, personal **R**esponsibility, **A**dvice to change, a **M**enu of change strategies, therapist **E**mpathy, and enhancement of the client's **S**elf-efficacy. Another common BI component involves reviewing the pros and cons of drinking, but it is best directed toward persons who are ambivalent about changing their drinking behavior, rather than those already committed to change.

Alcohol Use Disorders

Pharmacotherapy

Medications to treat AUDs include disulfiram (Antabuse), acamprosate, and two forms of naltrexone (oral and injectable). However, compliance problems and health risks have limited the use of disulfiram. Consistent with their presumed mechanisms of action, acamprosate has been more efficacious with respect to abstinence outcomes whereas oral naltrexone has shown greater efficacy in reducing craving and relapse to heavy drinking. Thus, naltrexone may be the better choice for patients who are less committed to abstinence.

Psychosocial Treatments

In contrast to such widely used approaches as general alcohol counseling, alcohol education, and confrontation that have little empirical support, several psychosocial treatments for AUDs are evidence based.

Cognitive-behavioral treatments enhance clients' sense of self-efficacy and build skills to cope with life circumstances, usually following a functional analysis to identify triggers and high-risk situations for relapse. The overall goal of the *community reinforcement approach* (CRA) is to encourage alternative behaviors that make a sober life style more rewarding than one involving alcohol use. CRA employs familial, social, recreational, and vocational rewards for sobriety, trains clients in communication, problem solving, and drink-refusal skills, and focuses on providing job skills and sober social activities.

Contingency management (CM) reinforces new behaviors in the treatment setting. Once a contingency (e.g., a series of alcohol-free screens) is met, it is reinforced by providing something of value, such as (a drawing for a chance at) a voucher to purchase desirable items. Immediate and higher-value rewards have been shown to be more effective. CM enhances treatment attendance and medication compliance, mechanisms that may account for its positive effects on drinking outcomes. Combining CM with some other psychosocial treatment may extend CM's initial benefits.

The first stage of *behavioral couples treatment* is a thorough assessment of the targeted individual's drinking behavior and of the marital relationship. Interventions to address drinking include behavioral contracts and contracts for taking medications in the presence of the spouse. Increasing caring behaviors, planning joint recreational activities, enhancing communication skills, and developing behavior change agreements are interventions used to improve marital or family relationships.

Motivational interviewing (MI), which is used to treat both AUDs and alcohol misuse, follows four core principles: (a) empathizing with the client; (b) highlighting discrepancies between the client's alcohol use and desired outcomes; (c) rolling with (i.e., not directly confronting) the client's resistance to change; and (d) supporting the client's sense of self-efficacy that he or she can change. MI helps clients resolve their ambivalence about changing their alcohol use, reinforces stated reasons for change, and strengthens clients' commitment to change. *Motivational enhancement therapy* (MET) draws on principles of MI and normative assessment feedback (i.e., letting clients know how their drinking behavior compares to norms) and is as efficacious as other evidence-based treatments, such as cognitive behavioral treatment.

Twelve-step facilitation (TSF) treatment is based in part on principles of Alcoholics Anonymous (AA) and the "disease model" of addiction. It helps patients accept their powerlessness over substances, surrender control to a Higher Power and work a 12-step program by attending 12-step group meetings and obtaining sponsors.

Although much attention has been given to the implementation of complete evidence-based treatments, such as those described above, an alternative and more flexible approach is to provide therapeutic processes that are common across some or all of these treatment approaches and address clients' particular needs. Examples of such processes include promoting support, goal direction, and structure in clients' life contexts, enhancing clients' involvement in new rewarding activities, and building their self-efficacy and coping skills.

Maintaining Treatment Gains

Continuing Outpatient Care
After an initial episode of inpatient, residential, or intensive outpatient treatment, additional outpatient treatment may be needed to maintain or enhance therapeutic gains. A recent review noted that continuing care is most likely to be effective when it is active and engaging, and lasts longer. Connecting patients to community resources, maintaining contact with patients over time, and ensuring continuity in providers can lead to longer periods of continuing care. A specific, effective intervention for facilitating engagement in continuing care is "contracting, prompting, and reinforcement." Finally, telephone sessions can be used effectively to extend care.

Mutual Help Organizations
Twelve-step mutual help groups, such as AA, can positively impact patients' functioning and recovery. In addition, other organizations, such as Women for Sobriety, Moderation Management, and Double Trouble in Recovery are available for persons who do not resonate with the 12-step approach, have drinking goals other than abstinence, or have co-occurring psychiatric conditions, respectively.

FUTURE RESEARCH

Instead of only evaluating complete treatment approaches, future research could focus on identifying effective therapeutic treatment processes, such as building support and enhancing coping skills, as well as combinations of therapeutic processes that can be tailored to individual patients. In addition, given the chronic, relapsing nature of some individuals' AUDs, more research is needed on the role of primary medical care providers in encouraging individuals with AUDs to seek treatment, monitoring their functioning, and re-engaging them with treatment, as needed. More generally, it is important to identify sensitive and specific indicators of the need for "stepped-up" care, as well as for when "stepped down" care is sufficient. Research to identify alternative low-intensity intervention options for engaging individuals who opt not to participate in specialty treatment programs or mutual help groups also would be beneficial. Finally, the effectiveness of more culturally sensitive treatments versus "standard" treatments needs to be evaluated.

ACKNOWLEDGMENTS

Preparation of this chapter was supported by NIAAA Grants AA008689, AA015685, and by a VA Health Services Research and Development Research Career Scientist Award to Dr. Timko. The views expressed are those of the authors and are not necessarily those of the U.S. Department of Veterans Affairs or any other U.S. Government entity.

KEY REFERENCES

Finney, J., Wilbourne, P., & Moos, R. (2007). Psychosocial treatments for substance use disorders. In P. E. Nathan & J. M. Gorman (Eds.), *A guide to treatments that work* (3rd ed., pp. 179–202). New York, NY: Oxford University Press.

Leggio, L., & Addolorato, G. (2010). Pharmacotherapy of alcohol dependence: Past, present and future research. *Current Pharmaceutical Design, 16,* 2074–2075.

Moos, R. H. (2007). Theory-based active ingredients of effective treatments for substance use disorders. *Drug and Alcohol Dependence, 88,* 109–121.

Clinician Application

Alcohol Abuse

Louis A. Moffett

COMMENT ON THE EVIDENCE-BASED RECOMMENDATIONS

The different evidence-based treatments for alcohol misuse, abuse, and dependence are compatible and can be combined in clinical practice, although contingency management and community reinforcement are difficult to implement outside of a specialized clinic or program. Still, as noted, clinicians can incorporate the principles of these methods in the processes of treatment. Couples therapy may enhance outcomes over individual therapy. Also, these same psychosocial treatments are effective for patients who misuse other substances in addition to alcohol. Finally, some clinicians are not familiar with the range of mutual-help groups available (e.g., Women for Sobriety, Secular Organization for Sobriety) besides 12-step fellowships, or they may object to the ideology or practices of some recovery groups and consequently could either overlook this resource or not effectively integrate mutual-help participation in treatment.

CASE EXAMPLE

Subject Information and Brief History

Mr. K was a 36-year-old, married (9 years), Korean businessman. He had immigrated to the United States 13 years earlier, intentionally severing his ties with his family of origin. Quite unexpectedly, Mr. K was sued by a former business associate. He felt betrayed by a man whom he had recruited, mentored, and befriended. Mr. K was ashamed, humiliated, and feared that the suit would damage his reputation. He was preoccupied with the lawsuit, had difficulty concentrating on his business, was unable to fall asleep easily or to remain asleep, and was tired throughout the day. For the past 5 years, he and his wife had been drinking wine with dinner almost daily, with Mr. K drinking four glasses over the course of the evening. Now, in order to fall asleep, he was drinking nearly two bottles of wine per night. Still, he remained anxious and depressed and sought help from his physician who informed Mr. K that his abnormal liver function was likely due to his drinking and advised him to stop drinking. He prescribed an antidepressant and referred Mr. K to psychotherapy for his depression.

Presenting Problem

In psychotherapy, Mr. K complained that for the prior 2 months he had not been sleeping through the night, had been waking up too early, had been fatigued, had lost his appetite, worried constantly, and had not been able to concentrate on his business. He had no current or prior suicidal ideation. When asked about his physician's advice to stop drinking, Mr. K dismissed it, indicating that, unlike many other Koreans, he did not experience an alcohol flush and was therefore convinced that he was immune from alcohol's damaging effects, despite his abnormal liver function and his physician's opinion. He was certain that drinking was the only way for him to fall asleep. Mr. K was diagnosed with major depression, mild, and alcohol dependence, mild. He had no other mental disorders and no history of prior disorders or treatment.

Treatment Intervention and Course

Outpatient psychotherapy focused on his depression using cognitive therapy and behavioral activation. His drinking to fall asleep was acknowledged, and yet he was repeatedly reminded that his drinking was likely disturbing his sustained sleep, increasing his depression, and posing a risk for liver damage. Mr. K was not ambivalent; he was confident in his judgment and adamant that his drinking was necessary for his sleeping and not detrimental.

After five sessions, Mr. K reported having thought about how he might kill himself. This experience frightened him and his wife. In collaboration with her, the therapist reiterated that Mr. K's drinking was likely contributing to his depression and restless sleep. Mr. K agreed to reduce his drinking by one less glass of wine per day per week (a rate that would minimize aversive withdrawal symptoms) and to monitor his quality of sleep.

Over the next few weeks, Mr. K became less anxious, less ashamed, more energized, and increasingly angry about being sued. He began to view the lawsuit as an unprovoked attack to which he would respond as if he were in combat with his adversary. This emerging attitude was used as additional motivation to stop drinking (i.e., as an abstinent combatant, he would be more alert and focused).

With his wife's support and encouragement, his discovery that he could still sleep relatively well with much less nighttime drinking, diminishing depression, and his investment in being alert and energetic, all converged in fostering Mr. K's willingness to reduce his drinking even further. Within 6 weeks, he had stopped drinking completely, and he did so with little apparent effort once he decided that it was in his best interest.

Outcome

Mr. K continued in therapy for 2 years, continuing to address his depression, replacing his father's devaluing of him with his own more realistic self-evaluations, and being supported throughout the lawsuit which was eventually resolved in his favor. Over the next 5 years, Mr. K met periodically with the therapist for relapse prevention of depression. Except for an occasional glass of wine with his wife, he was content with no longer drinking regularly.

Of the evidence-based treatments, brief intervention alone had not helped. Instead, motivational enhancement was the key intervention: evoking and emphasizing Mr. K's motivations for outcomes (e.g., restorative sleep, his wife's approval, reduced depression, and being maximally fit for an adversarial process) that were incompatible with continued drinking.

CHALLENGES IN APPLYING THE EVIDENCE-BASED APPROACH

Unlike symptoms of anxiety or depression, drinking alcohol is not distressing, and patients are most invested in reducing the problems associated with alcohol misuse rather than in reducing drinking itself. Consequently, motivational considerations, constructive coping skills, and social support are relevant throughout engagement, primary treatment, and continuing care. Patients with chronic alcohol dependence are likely to have serious additional problems relating to health, family, work, and finances, and many patients will also have co-occurring psychiatric disorders. These complex patients require comprehensive interventions, and few solo practitioners are able to provide or even coordinate the full range of services over the length of time required for recovery.

CULTURAL DIVERSITY ISSUES

The drinking norms in a person's surrounding subculture (e.g., college, military, gay) pose a major difficulty in treatment because the person not only has to change a pattern of drinking but may also have to change a whole network of social relations and activities. Ultimately, once a person's alcohol dependence has become chronic, the culture of drinking trumps all other diverse ethnic identities and affiliations.

FUTURE RESEARCH

Alcohol use disorders are one of the most prevalent lifetime psychiatric disorders for men in the United States, and the long-term outcomes of treatment are modest. For persons with severe and chronic alcohol dependence or co-occurring disorders, treatment outcomes are even less positive. Continuing research on prevention and early intervention is critical. Treatment effectiveness research using combined treatments with representative clinical populations including the multiply-disordered are needed to inform practice. Given the role of urges in the high rates of relapse, research on interventions that are accessible at any time, such as portable Internet devices, holds promise for brief interventions, core treatment, and continuing care.

KEY REFERENCES

Carroll, K. M., & Kiluk, B. D. (2012). Integrating psychotherapy and pharmacotherapy in substance abuse treatment. In S. T. Walters & F. Rotgers (Eds.), *Treating substance abuse* (3rd ed., pp. 319–354). New York, NY: Guilford Press.

Margolis, R. D., & Zweben, J. E. (2011). *Treating patients with alcohol and other drug problems: An integrated approach* (2nd ed.). Washington, DC: American Psychological Association.

McCrady, B. S. (2008). Alcohol use disorders. In D. H. Barlow (Ed.), *Clinical handbook of psychological disorders: A step-by-step treatment manual* (4th ed., pp. 528–542). New York, NY: Guilford Press.

CHAPTER 17

Anger Management

Howard Kassinove and Michael J. Toohey

CLINICAL PROBLEM

Anger is a negative, phenomenological feeling state that motivates desires for actions, usually against others, that aim to warn, intimidate, control, attack, or gain retribution. As a precursor to motor aggression, it is part of the "fight or flight response" that was critical for survival in the prelinguistic animal world. Animals might growl, hiss, puff out their bodies, or spit, to signal that they want intruders to back off. For similar purposes, we become angry.

As a phenomenological state, it begins with awareness and subjective labels such as "I feel furious about that!" It is associated with cognitive misappraisals about the importance of events (e.g., "It's so terrible"), about personal ability to cope (e.g., "I just can't take this stuff anymore"), personal mandates about justice (e.g., "He should treat his employees with more respect"), demands about how others are to act (e.g., "She should have known better than to cheat on me"), and difficulty differentiating what people do from global statements about who they are (e.g., "She's a total dope!"). Anger is also associated with dichotomous thinking (e.g., "Either you are my friend or you are not"), overgeneralizations (e.g., "Since he didn't invite me, he clearly doesn't want to be my friend"), and attributions of blame (e.g., "It's all her fault"). At the cognitive level, there may be fantasies of revenge and punishment (e.g., "Now, I'll teach her a *real* lesson!"). In addition, anger is associated with physiological changes (e.g., heart rate and sweating) and with patterns of verbal and motor behavior (e.g., yelling, profanity, sarcasm, pointing fingers, glaring, crossing arms, smirking, and breaking objects). These cognitive, imaginal, physiological, and motor behaviors can be maladaptive and often become targets for change in anger management programs.

Adults are, more or less, able to regulate their angry responses to aversive events. This variation is important because anger management therapy is warranted when responses to common aversive stimuli are too strong, endure beyond a short time, and when anger appears as a reaction to an excess number of stimuli. These people are often referred to as "hot headed," and are frequently said to "fly off the handle." They may be secretive and vindictive, or they may use anger to intimidate and control others. Although the variation in anger reactions among people could be genetic in origin, anger dysregulation can also be a function of poor environmental learning, inadequate parental modeling, and other forms of inappropriate socialization. Proper regulation of anger is a critical element of successful life functioning.

PREVALENCE

Humans have many ways to resolve conflicts including mediation, the legal system, treaty provisions, government regulations, religious advice, and in-house judicial boards extant in colleges and universities. Most anger, which was critical in the animal world, is simply no longer needed to live a happy and successful life. Nevertheless, it is still very common. For example, adults have reported an average of 7.3 incidents of anger and 23.5 incidents of annoyance episodes in 1 week. In one study, community adults were divided into those with higher trait anger (HTA) or lower trait anger (LTA). HTA adults reported anger about once per *day* and 86% reported anger at least a few times per week. In contrast, only 7% of LTA adults had anger episodes a few times a week or more. Also, HTA adults reported that their anger was more intense and lasted longer than episodes of LTA adults. Other studies have shown group differences in anger regulation. As people become older, they tend to become less reactive to aversive triggers and less angry in general. Also, anger seems to be experienced with equal frequency by men and women, as both genders are subject to blocked personal goals and the aversive behavior of others. However, anger regulation varies by context partially because of differing social appraisals of its expression. In partner relationships, some evidence indicates that women, overall, express anger more than men. Angry men may use more directly aggressive acts, such as throwing objects, whereas women often use more defusing acts, such as talking to a friend to calm down.

CULTURAL DIVERSITY ISSUES

Regarding ethnic differences, in a young adult sample (ages 18 to 30) it was found that Asians were less assertive than Blacks or Whites. Blacks reported less agreeableness, and more negativism and cynical hostility, than Whites and Asians. Whites had lower anger-in scores and higher scores on assertiveness. In a different study using a sample of marital batterers (mean age = 41), it was found that Korean Americans experienced more anger and controlled it less than European Americans.

EVIDENCE-BASED TREATMENTS

In order to help people who present in professional settings with anger problems, a number of treatment programs have been developed. Although they differ somewhat, their commonalities address the most important issues in anger management. Generally, the programs include a phase in which the patient is prepared for treatment, a phase for changing behavior, a phase for accepting what cannot be changed, and a phase for preventing future anger episodes.

Anger patients differ from those who present with anxiety or depression in that they typically blame others for their problem and are resistant to change. This is a significant treatment issue for court-mandated patients or those referred by family members or employers. For this reason, the programs include a preparation phase in which the goal is to increase both awareness of personal anger and motivation to work on this problem area. To increase awareness, the programs use a psychoeducational segment to explore components of anger episodes. In addition, patients are often asked to monitor their episodes by keeping an anger journal. To increase motivation, programs often use a Motivational Interviewing approach in which there is reinforcement for patient verbalizations about anger reduction, while maintaining a nondirective stance. At present, however, there is little research about the effectiveness of the preparation phase in managing anger.

After increasing awareness and motivation, most anger programs begin with techniques to change behaviors of the patient. Some, however, first work on helping patients accept what they can't change. In order to change behavior, interventions such as Progressive Muscle Relaxation, Assertiveness Training, and Escape and Avoidance strategies are used, which have all been shown to be effective for managing anger. Progressive Muscle Relaxation increases awareness of muscle tension and increases the conscious use of relaxation. Assertiveness Training helps the patient learn to express annoyance and anger in a direct, honest, and appropriate manner. This reduces the tendency to hold anger in and ruminate, in addition to not expressing it aversively (e.g., yelling and using sarcasm). Finally, most therapists discuss the importance of avoiding situations that are likely to increase anger or escaping from situations that are already leading to increases in anger. Although avoidance and escape are considered to be temporary solutions for more chronic problems, they are important in the early phase of intervention because they are simple solutions that can be easily implemented.

In the stage that addresses the acceptance of aversive anger triggers, cognitive restructuring and exposure to anger-evoking situations are useful. Both have been found to be beneficial in anger therapy. Anger reduction programs also use perspective taking and forgiveness interventions. Cognitive restructuring involves changing rigid and demanding beliefs to those that are more flexible and realistic. Exposure decreases sensitivity to anger triggers by giving patients graduated experience with them. Finally, if there is difficulty letting go of grudges, a forgiveness intervention may be appropriate in which the patient is asked to step out of the victim role and let go of the emotional reactivity to the perceived injustice.

In the final stage, relapse prevention, the techniques are reviewed and discussion centers on potential future anger triggers and how to react to them. The patient becomes aware of the importance of continued work on his or her anger.

FUTURE RESEARCH

Studies certainly support the efficacy of some anger interventions and some show positive results in as little as eight sessions. However, because it is not recognized as a disorder in the *DSM-5* or the ICD-10, there has been much less research on anger interventions than those for other human problems. It would be beneficial for future studies to attempt to validate those interventions for which there is a lack of empirical data and to examine manualized and self-help programs.

KEY REFERENCES

Feindler, E. (2006). *Anger-related disorders: A practitioner's guide to comparative treatments.* New York, NY: Springer Books.

Kassinove, H., & Tafrate, R. (2002). *Anger management: The complete treatment guidebook for practitioners.* Atascadero, CA: Impact Publishers.

Tafrate, R., & Kassinove, H. (2009). *Anger management for everyone: Seven proven ways to control anger and live a happier life.* Atascadero, CA: Impact Publishers.

Anger Management

J. Ryan Fuller

COMMENT ON THE EVIDENCE-BASED RECOMMENDATIONS

Dr. Kassinove and Mr. Toohey concisely explained critical elements of anger and its psychological treatment. They identify four general phases of treatment: preparation, change, acceptance, and prevention. They also specify empirically based techniques utilized at each phase, for example, Motivational Interviewing (MI), relaxation, assertiveness, and cognitive restructuring. Practitioners treating clients with anger problems will benefit from this scientific review.

Although my experience may not generalize to every population, I have found evidence-based treatments to be applicable to my patients. The good news for clinicians is that cognitive, skills-based, relaxation, and combined interventions can all benefit angry clients. Therefore, treatment planning can incorporate any or all of these based on the needs of each client. Understanding the general phases of treatment and the corresponding techniques and skills will aid practitioners in efficiently utilizing evidence-based treatments for anger disorders.

CASE EXAMPLE

Subject Information and Brief History

The client, a 46-year-old White man, employed at a large financial institution, lived with his wife of 18 years, his son (14 years old), and daughter (11 years old). His anger episodes often included passive-aggressive comments, yelling, and, at times, property destruction. The most serious behaviors typically occurred in front of his wife at home, but more moderate symptoms were displayed to direct reports at work. The client reported the presence of symptoms for more than 15 years.

Presenting Problem

A recent incident directed at his wife occurred in front of his son and a school friend. He reported yelling profanities at his wife at high volume with an enraged tone, threatening posture, and gestures in response to what he called a "small thing." His son later acknowledged fear of his father to his mother and inquired about the possibility of divorce. His wife had urged him to seek treatment in the past, but this time threatened a trial separation unless he enrolled in psychotherapy.

Treatment Intervention and Course

A semistructured clinical interview, intake questionnaires, and anger logs were used to identify antecedents and consequences of anger episodes, and other relevant client and environmental characteristics (e.g., work stressors, commute time, social support, etc.). Ongoing assessment, rapport building, and motivational enhancement were emphasized early. A number of behavioral deficits and physiological vulnerabilities were identified that put him at risk for intense anger reactions. He appeared to be overworked, chronically stressed, frequently worried, and often suppressed or avoided his feelings. He slept and exercised insufficiently, was rarely assertive or relaxed, and did not utilize traditional problem-solving skills at home, or address interpersonal issues at work. He also held a number of irrational beliefs, cognitive styles, and behavioral scripts which were associated with anger episodes. Examples included, "People must always meet the standards they set," "I can't stand it when people make excuses," and "When people let me down, I have an obligation to let them know immediately." While his worries and anxiety appeared to put him at risk for anger problems, these symptoms did not meet criteria for an Axis I or Axis II diagnosis or warrant a psychopharmacological referral.

An overview of treatment was provided, along with psychoeducation related to anger, which included the anger chain created by Howard Kassinove, and the cognitive ABC model of emotions developed by Albert Ellis. Self-monitoring, goal setting, crisis management, and homework were all regularly utilized. Specific barriers to goals were identified and framed in the cognitive ABC model (i.e., Activating Events, Beliefs, and Consequences). The functions of his behaviors were explained to him by first identifying the accompanying antecedents and consequences. Likewise, the clinician conducted similar functional behavioral assessments (FBA) throughout treatment in order to constantly guide treatment planning. Cognitive and behavioral interventions were utilized together. A typical trigger for anger was his perception that his son was not studying enough or efficiently. Irrational beliefs to this and other activating events (As or triggers) were identified and disputed. Adaptive or rational alternative statements were created and rehearsed, and alternative behaviors such as assertive communication and behavioral contracting with his son were developed. During one session, the client revealed that even though he no longer exercised, he had experienced benefits to his mood from exercising in the past. Therefore, aerobic exercise was introduced into his weekly routine, along with recommendations to improve his sleep habits. "Stop and Think" exercises, along with paced respiration (a relaxation exercise), assertiveness, and problem solving, were taught and incorporated into homework assignments. Although compliance was poor for paced respiration, and formal problem solving (i.e., orienting, defining the problem, brainstorming, decision making, and verifying), he frequently reported stopping to think before acting and practiced assertiveness in a variety of contexts.

Outcome

With significant improvements in 18 sessions, and the tight time constraints of his work schedule, it was determined that he would commit to continuing to practice his new coping skills, better self-care, use his relapse prevention plan, and would schedule a booster session in 3 months after an upcoming work project concluded. Although room for improvement existed at termination, overall, the frequency, intensity, and duration of anger experiences were significantly reduced, along with guilt, shame, anxiety, and embarrassment that were consequences of what he considered his inappropriate angry behaviors. Goal congruent behaviors had increased as well. These targets were recorded on worksheet logs by the client in between sessions and reviewed during sessions. He still became angry at times, but the intensity was rarely as high, there were a few common triggers that no longer resulted in any significant anger, and even when intensely angry, he typically behaved in socially appropriate and adaptive ways. He had begun to approach previously avoided situations, emotions, and thoughts. Family relationships had also significantly improved.

CHALLENGES IN APPLYING THE EVIDENCE-BASED APPROACH

Precisely applying evidence-based protocols in clinical practice may be challenged by client characteristics and the interpersonal nature of anger. My clients often fit into three categories: (a) highly ambivalent, encouraged/ordered to treatment, (b) emotionally dysregulated with comorbidities (e.g., Borderline Personality Disorder, Major Depressive Disorder, Generalized Anxiety Disorder, Substance Abuse diagnoses), or (c) highly motivated, achieving, with treatment conflicting work schedules. All three types of clients have strained relationships. Therefore, a greater number of sessions and technical deviations in form and order from standard protocols are often necessary. As cognitive techniques, skills training, and relaxation are all effective; I have found the use of clinical judgment and ongoing FBA helpful in customizing treatment plans.

CULTURAL DIVERSITY ISSUES

Many anger stereotypes exist regarding gender, sexual orientation, culture, race, ethnicity, and so forth. Although Kassinove and Toohey describe some cultural/ethnic differences in the previous section, my clinical experience is more congruent with previous research by Kassinove, which indicates that similarities are more common than gender or cultural differences. Even though our personal learning histories, which include cultural, racial, ethnic, and sexual factors, may shape our anger triggers and behavioral scripts, I have found the best practice is to develop individual hypotheses and collaboratively test them with each client.

FUTURE RESEARCH

There is a great deal of research indicating that accumulating negative affect of any kind can ultimately result in aggression. Clinically, I have frequently targeted guilt, anxiety, shame, embarrassment, and jealousy when treating anger problems. I believe these are often peripherally addressed in clinical trials. I am curious if this could impact the amount of anger change or reduce relapse rates. Likewise, understanding the mechanisms involved, such as experiential avoidance (i.e., avoidance of internal experiences including thoughts, feelings, sensations, urges, cravings, etc.) may help improve treatment. I have often found it helpful for collaterals (e.g., spouses, siblings, parents, etc.) to attend individual therapy sessions, to refer clients for couples or family therapy in addition to, or instead of, individual therapy to address anger issues, depending on the role of the dyad or family system. But I am unaware if efficacy rates for these compared to individual psychotherapy or combined treatments exist. Research evaluating the value and role of pharmacotherapy, aerobic and anaerobic exercise, yoga, diet, sleep, socialization, sex/affection, bibliotherapy, and alternate delivery formats of therapy (e.g., telephonic therapy, etc.) in anger treatment could also be useful to practitioners.

KEY REFERENCES

Fuller, J. R., DiGiuseppe, R., Fountain, T., O'Leary, S., & Lang, C. (2010). An open trial of a comprehensive anger treatment program in an outpatient sample. *Behavioural and Cognitive Psychotherapy, 38*, 485–490.

Kassinove, H. (1995). *Anger Disorders: Definition, diagnosis and treatment.* Philadelphia, PA: Taylor & Francis.

Kassinove, H., & Tafrate, R. C. (2002). *Anger Management: The complete treatment guidebook for practitioners.* Atascadero, CA: Impact Publishers.

CHAPTER 18

Bereavement

Robert A. Neimeyer

CLINICAL PROBLEM

Although bereavement, in the form of the loss of a loved one to death, is a common life transition rather than a clinical disorder, research has documented that adaptation in its wake varies considerably. On the one hand, a substantial minority of the bereaved display resilience, defined as transitory distress with reestablishment of one's emotional baseline within a few months. Others demonstrate an active course of grieving over the course of several months, but ultimately adapt to the changed circumstances of their lives. A few—especially those whose relationships with the deceased were troubled or who experienced the stressors of prolonged caregiving— even display *improved* functioning following the death. But bereavement can also exacerbate distress for those with a history of psychological difficulties such as major depression, as well as trigger a chronic and disabling course of grieving that can last for years if left untreated. This latter condition, variably termed *complicated grief* or *prolonged grief disorder*, warrants clinical assessment and intervention.

Complicated grief (CG) has as its core feature a marked and unremitting preoccupation with the loss, often reflected in overwhelming yearning for the deceased or rumination about the death to a degree that compromises the survivor's functioning in occupational, familial, or broader social roles. Other common symptoms include shock, disbelief and anger about the death, loneliness and isolation, a feeling that a part of the self has also died, and the sense that the future holds little prospect of purpose or fulfillment. Because CG represents an intensification and prolongation of symptoms that might be commonplace in the immediate aftermath of loss, it cannot be reliably diagnosed until several months have passed with little evidence that the survivor is experiencing less anguish and reengaging important life roles. Importantly, CG has displayed "incremental validity" in predicting a variety of serious psychosocial and medical outcomes even after depression and anxiety are taken into account.

Prevalence

Several studies have placed the frequency of CG in nonclinical populations in the neighborhood of 10% of bereaved adults, although risk of the condition varies depending on the nature of the lost relationship and the manner of death. Parents who have lost children and adults who have lost intimate partners are at greatest risk, with a rate of CG as high as 30% in some samples. Similarly, cause of death has been found to predict incidence of CG in various studies, with levels of complication approaching 50% in the case of death of a loved one to suicide or homicide.

Some evidence also suggests that younger widows and widowers report more complications than those who are older.

CULTURAL DIVERSITY ISSUES

A growing body of research has documented CG across a wide range of cultural contexts, despite the diverse customs and rituals shaping the bereavement experience in different countries and ethnic or religious traditions. Within the United States, some studies suggest that African Americans may be at higher risk of CG than Caucasian Americans, although how much of this may be accounted for by differential exposure to violent death, and especially homicide, remains to be determined. Likewise, women report more CG symptoms than men in most studies that make this comparison.

EVIDENCE-BASED TREATMENTS

Quantitative reviews of many dozens of controlled studies raise questions about the efficacy of psychotherapy in mitigating normative grief symptomatology in adults, such as crying or missing the deceased. This is because most of those who are bereaved ultimately adapt well to the loss with or without professional treatment. When grief is profound, unremitting, and complicated, however, there is evidence that specialized forms of psychotherapy can be quite effective. At this point, evidence-based treatments include attachment, coping, cognitive behavioral, and narrative constructivist models, which differ in their emphases but tend to converge in key therapeutic strategies. These include: (a) fostering confrontation with the story of the death in an attempt to master its most painful aspects and integrate its finality into the mourner's internalized models of the deceased, the self, and the world, (b) encouraging engagement with the image, voice, or memory of the deceased to facilitate a sense of ongoing attachment while allowing for the development of other relationships, (c) gradually challenging avoidance coping and building skill in emotion modulation and creative problem solving, and (d) helping the bereaved to review and revise life goals and roles in a world without the deceased person physically in it.

In the first instance, psychotherapists might invite clients to introduce the deceased, perhaps providing some orientation to their relationship with them as a backdrop for a detailed retelling of the event story of the death itself. This form of revisiting of the loss is akin to prolonged exposure treatments for trauma, in which the psychotherapist fosters "containment" of difficult emotions as clients slowly unfold their reactions to witnessing or learning about death, gradually expressing and exploring the troubling images, events, and feelings that they customarily avoid in accounts of the experience to others. Although such retelling across periods ranging from 15 minutes to one or more full sessions is typically highly evocative, it also helps clients achieve a greater sense of mastery over aspects of the story that had previously haunted them. Close review of the story helps them make sense of the experience and assimilate more fully the emotional reality of the loved one's physical absence from their lives. In addition, psychotherapy often facilitates renegotiation of the terms of attachment to the deceased, not so much "letting go" of the loved one as much as finding a sustainable way of maintaining the bond. Symbolic "empty chair" conversations or correspondence with the loved one can provide means of addressing troubling concerns in the relationship such as caregiver guilt, and ultimately reaffirm love in a way that survives death. As the psychotherapist helps the client identify and surmount cognitive, behavioral, and relational obstacles to addressing the loss and its implications, clients commonly are able to find ways to honor the loved one's presence in their lives and conversations, while reaffirming or reconstructing a life of meaning that was challenged by the death. The Complicated Grief Therapy of Katherine Shear and her colleagues exemplifies one evidence-based therapy that includes retelling, symbolic conversations with the deceased, and revision of life goals, and has been found to outperform interpersonal psychotherapy in a randomized controlled trial.

FUTURE RESEARCH

Although the key features of CG are well documented, more research is needed to document its relationship to such factors as insecure attachment, cognitive and behavioral avoidance strategies, and a struggle to find spiritual and secular meaning in the loss and in one's life in its aftermath, all of which are receiving increasing scientific attention. Unlike static risk factors focusing on the character of the relationship to the deceased or the circumstances of the loss, those linked to renegotiating the bond to the deceased, developing more adaptive strategies for emotion regulation, and reconstructing the meaning of the loss in the context of one's changed life are potentially modifiable, and thus carry clear implications for psychotherapeutic strategies and techniques. In addition, investigators are only beginning to delineate the impact of the psychotherapeutic relationship in providing a surrogate "secure base" as the client reworks his or her attachment to the deceased and other living figures. Further attention to such factors holds promise for the ongoing refinement of grief therapy, whether conducted in an individual, family, or group format.

KEY REFERENCES

Neimeyer, R. A. (Ed.). (2012). *Techniques of grief therapy: Creative practices for counseling the bereaved*. New York, NY: Routledge.

Neimeyer, R. A., Harris, D., Winokeur, H., & Thornton, G. (Eds.). (2011). *Grief and bereavement in contemporary society: Bridging research and practice*. New York, NY: Routledge.

Stroebe, M. S., Schut, H., & van der Bout, J. (Eds.). (2012). *Complicated grief: Scientific foundations for health care professionals*. New York, NY: Routledge

Bereavement

Phyllis Kosminsky

COMMENT ON THE EVIDENCE-BASED RECOMMENDATIONS

As a clinician, I can attest to, and heartily endorse, Dr. Neimeyer's opening observation that while most people are able to accommodate to significant loss with time and support from those close to them, a substantial percentage of grievers continue to experience profound sadness, longing, and compromised functioning for months or years after the loss. My experience over the past 17 years suggests that many, if not most of the people who seek bereavement therapy do so because they are part of this subgroup. That is, the trajectory of their grief is not identifiable as a set of stages; it is, rather, a seemingly endless and even chaotic process that offers no hope of resolution. The divergence of their own experience from the experience described in many books about loss is a frequent source of distress, leading the grieving person to fear that they are not mourning in the proper way. The conclusion that they should be making a more concerted effort to get over their loss is often supported by family and friends who urge the bereaved to set aside their grief and get on with the business of living, perhaps supporting their presciption by referencing the supposed endorsement of the deceased ("That's what he would have wanted you to do"). The idea that the loss of a loved one is, after all, an inevitable part of life and one that it is therefore only reasonable to expect a more or less complete recovery from such an event within a matter of months is one that the clinician should address early on in treatment. As is the case with many kinds of emotional distress (Posttraumatic Stress Disorder [PTSD], for example) psychoeducation is the first step in helping someone who is experiencing grief. Even so called normal grief is a shock to the system, and a simple explanation of the range and severity of responses that can accompany such loss can go far in easing the anxiety of a newly bereaved client. Likewise (and the timing here is very much a matter of clinical judgment), bereaved individuals can benefit from an explanation of the factors that make some losses harder to cope with than others (conflicted relationships, abuse, trauma). Such information, provided in a way that normalizes but does not minimize their own distress, can serve as ballast for someone who is confused and frightened by the intensity of their feelings. For someone whose nervous system has been on overload for weeks or months, this alone can be a great relief, and it provides a firmer base on which to proceed with the types of interventions described in the research section of this chapter.

As Dr. Neimeyer's recommendations regarding treatment suggest, work with the bereaved must be tailored to the individual; there is no "one size fits all" treatment for grief, and clinicians typically use a variety of interventions and clinical approaches to support healing. One approach to providing support is to help the client integrate the loss into the ongoing internally constructed narrative of their life. Narrative approaches help the individual to reestablish a sense of meaning, and can also serve to bring to the surface thoughts and feelings that are causing problems for the bereaved (for example, misplaced feelings of responsibility for the death, guilt in relation to the deceased). In that the description of treatment by Dr. Neimeyer emphasizes the use of narrative. I will introduce a case that utilizes this approach.

CASE EXAMPLE

Subject Information and Brief History

The client, Sylvia, was a 74-year-old woman whose 34-year-old daughter had died 18 months previously following a lengthy illness, and whose husband died 4 months prior to her beginning treatment. Sylvia missed her husband, but she felt they had had a good life together, and his death was less distressing to her than the death of her daughter.

Presenting Problem

Sylvia was referred by her physician and friend, who reported that she seemed "very down and maybe depressed." Sylvia confirmed that she was not feeling like herself, and noted that since her daughter's death, she had not been able to forgive herself for failing to be more available to her daughter during her illness.

Treatment Intervention and Course

Based on information collected in the first and second sessions, it became clear that Sylvia had endeavored to be more of a presence in her daughter's life, but that her daughter had in fact resisted her interventions. Subsequent sessions focused on identifying Sylvia's interpretation of her daughter's response, and what became clear was that to Sylvia, her daughter's refusal to accept her help "proved that she didn't love me."

This discussion helped pave the way to Sylvia's understanding that her pain was a composite not only of grief and guilt, but of resentment and a feeling of rejection. She mourned the lost opportunity to build a better relationship with her daughter, one that would have allowed her to be closer to her during the final stages of her illness. During our psychotherapy, Sylvia was invited to describe her daughter's personality and disposition to the therapist, and in the course of doing so, she talked about her fierce independence and her refusal to be "pitied or babied" by friends and family. As she talked about her, Sylvia came to realize that her daughter's behavior was not a personal rejection, but more a reflection of a lifelong pattern of wanting to take responsibility for herself and not be dependent upon others. Sylvia was able to see that in in complying with her daughter's requests that she not be involved in the management of her illness, Sylvia had honored her daughter's wishes, even though this had been hard for her to do.

Following this work, during one session Sylvia was able to have an imaginal conversation with her daughter, in which she was able to express what she believed her daughter would have to say about her steadfast refusal to accept help. Moreover, she was able to recall many instances in which her daughter had clearly communicated love for her mother and gratitude for her support and care.

Outcome

The work described above took place over 2 months, with Sylvia attending every 2 weeks. She took notes during the intervening weeks to keep track of her thoughts, and frequently returned to psychotherapy with new questions and concerns. She reported feeling "much more at peace" about her daughter, having realized that "a lot of what was hurting so much was the feeling that my daughter didn't love me, and now I realize that that just isn't true."

CHALLENGES IN APPLYING THE EVIDENCE-BASED TREATMENT

Not all clients are as able as Sylvia to access positive feelings about a loved one and the relationship they shared. For clients lacking in a capacity to realistically reflect on the nature of a deceased loved one and to fairly assess their responsibility for problems in the relationship, there can be a tendency to loop back to familiar narratives that do not serve the desired purpose. When, for example, a client says "I understand intellectually that what I think is not true but I still *feel* that it is," clinical work must focus on identifying the experiences and beliefs that keep these narratives locked in place. The clinician should be empathic regarding the difficulty of letting go of long-held beliefs about the self while at the same time remaining hopeful that change is possible, communicating that attitude to the client, and enlisting the client's commitment to letting go of mistaken or exaggerated beliefs that cause them distress.

CULTURAL DIVERSITY ISSUES

Narrative, imaginal conversation and relationship appraisal are techniques widely employed with a variety of populations. For some clients, the invitation to engage in "make believe" may not be well received. However, if properly introduced, imaginal techniques, including empty chair, imagery, and so forth can be of benefit.

FUTURE RESEARCH

As noted above, there is no one size fits all treatment for bereavement. There is, however, evidence that with individuals who suffer from problematic grief, timely and tailored intervention can facilitate healing. Case formulation and treatment planning will be best served by research that offers guidance as to what kinds of clients are most likely to benefit from treatment and what kinds of treatment are best suited to addressing the factors complicating their bereavement. The work of Lichtenthal exemplifies this approach. Finally, there is growing evidence that early attachment experiences impact how people manage emotion, their capacity to form and maintain healthy relationships, and their ability to adapt to significant loss. It is hoped that future research will expand our understanding of the impact of attachment status on adaptation to loss and that this knowledge will be a useful in guiding clinical practice.

KEY REFERENCES

Neimeyer, R. (Ed.). (2012). *Techniques of grief therapy*. New York, NY: Routledge.

Neimeyer, R. A., Harris, D., Winokur, H., & Thornton, G. F. (Eds.). (2011). *Grief and bereavement in contemporary society*. New York, NY: Routledge.

Rubin, S. S., Malkinson, R., & Witzum, E. (2012). *Working with the bereaved: Multiple lenses on loss and mourning*. New York, NY: Routledge.

CHAPTER 19

Bipolar Disorder

Greg Murray

CLINICAL PROBLEM

We all experience variations in mood and energy. For a minority of the population, however, complex variations in mood and energy are very pronounced, becoming clearly dysfunctional. Until recently, psychiatry was the discipline that paid most attention to these extreme states, so they are typically framed in medical terms, and for about 30 years have been given the name Bipolar Disorder (BD).

Diagnosable BD is probably an extreme form of normal human variation, rather than the distinct diseaselike entity implied by the *DSM*. There appear to be two quantitative traits underpinning the BD syndrome, namely, depression-proneness and mania-proneness. Depending partly on how they respond to environmental contingencies, people with high levels of these traits may manifest the symptoms labelled as BD. This diathesis–stress formulation underpins all psychosocial treatments for BD (see subsequent sections).

The categorical BD diagnoses provided by current taxonomies, therefore, have debatable validity, but remain useful communication tools. For *DSM*, the bipolar disorders are diagnosed on the basis of manic symptoms of varying severity. *Bipolar I Disorder* (BD I), defined by at least one episode of mania (labeled a "mixed" episode when a depressive episode is concurrent), receives most research and clinical attention. There is growing appreciation that *Bipolar II Disorder* (BD II, defined by hypomanic episodes and depressive episodes) generates comparable impairment and suicide risk to BD I. While BD I and BD II are conceptualized as episodic disorders, *Cyclothymic Disorder* is a milder chronic variant.

PREVALENCE

Defined by *DSM* criteria, the bipolar disorders are not common, with lifetime prevalence of BD I typically estimated at approximately 1% to 2%, and all bipolar disorders at approximately 4% to 5%. Unlike unipolar depression, there are no significant gender differences in prevalence of BD. However, BD II is somewhat more common in women than men, the frequency of depressive compared to manic episodes is higher in women and women are more likely to experience rapid cycling and mixed episodes. In terms of management, gender becomes important around the life events of childbirth and menopause.

CULTURAL DIVERSITY ISSUES

The simple prevalence of BD is relatively stable across cultures. There is a dearth of research into how culture interacts with the expression of the disorder and its outcomes, but there is no evidence that race or ethnicity impact prevalence rates.

EVIDENCE-BASED TREATMENT

Medications are the first-line treatment for acute and maintenance phases of BD, but outcomes are significantly improved with the addition of psychological interventions. Most of what we know about pharmacological and psychosocial treatments for BD refers to BD I, and evidence-informed practice for BD II and Cyclothymic Disorder must rely on extrapolations from relevant data and theory.

More than 20 randomized controlled trials (RCTs) of adjunctive psychosocial interventions have now been published along with a number of scholarly reviews. The particular interventions tested are family-focused therapy (FFT; family psychoeducation focusing on family dynamics and emotional expression), adaptations of cognitive behavioral therapy (CBT; skill development using cognitive and behavioral strategies for responding to triggers), interpersonal and social rhythm therapy (IPSRT; skills around stabilizing social rhythms and managing relationships), integrated treatments (psychosocial intervention embedded into routine care), and group psychoeducation (teaching patients about the nature of the disorder and ways of avoiding relapse). All of the tested therapies are highly structured, and not surprisingly, have significant overlaps in content (Box 19.1).

BOX 19.1 SHARED CONTENT OF EFFECTIVE PSYCHOSOCIAL TREATMENTS FOR BD

- Addressing biological rhythm instability (particularly IPSRT).
- Prodrome/warning signs identification and early intervention.
- Medication adherence.
- Communication and managing interpersonal stress (particularly FFT).
- Activity regulation and mood monitoring skills.
- Critiquing unproductive thoughts and beliefs (particularly CBT).
- Education about BD and risks.
- Addressing substance use.

Empirical research supports the efficacy of adjunctive psychosocial interventions, as measured in decreased relapse rates, quicker stabilization from acute episodes, reduced symptom severity, or enhanced psychosocial and family functioning. Effect sizes are not large, but consistent findings of added benefit have led to the inclusion of adjunctive psychosocial interventions in recent consensus treatment guidelines. Best practice treatment of BD is undoubtedly a combination of pharmacotherapy and psychotherapy.

The active ingredients of psychosocial interventions are not known, and there is no systematic evidence for preferring one treatment (FFT, IPSRT, etc.) over another, so the literature does not directly lead to a prescription for psychotherapists working with a particular client with BD. However, a defensible assumption is that

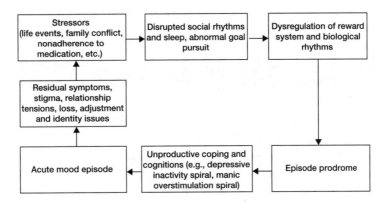

FIGURE 19.1 An integrative model of BD (after Steven Jones, Dominic Lam, and others).

core components shared across the branded interventions (see Box 19.1) should be part of any treatment package. The therapeutic importance of these specific elements is corroborated by recent qualitative research with people who manage their BD well—wellness strategies spontaneously reported by these "lived experience experts" overlap substantially with the specific content elements in the branded psychological treatments.

It is useful for psychologists to work from a simple treatment-leaning model of BD. As shown in Figure 19.1, this evidence-informed model characterizes BD from a diathesis–stress framework and highlights opportunities for psychological intervention.

FUTURE RESEARCH

The optimal description, explanation, and management of BD is a work in progress. Fundamental questions remain about the evolution of BD across development, and the relationship between BD and related conditions (particularly unipolar depression and psychosis). A first wave of adjunctive psychological treatments has demonstrated efficacy, but understanding of active ingredients is limited. Further research into the psychological treatment of BD in the context of common comorbidities is urgently needed. Similarly, systematic investigation of moderators of outcome (duration of illness, patient preference, medication, phase of illness, etc.) is needed to determine who benefits when. On another front, future psychological treatments may bypass diagnosis, instead targeting relevant transdiagnostic processes (e.g., substance use, anxiety, impulsivity). Research and practice in BD will also be impacted by consumers' calls to prioritize subjective quality of life as an outcome measure.

KEY REFERENCES

Lam, D., Hayward, S., & Jones, S. (2010). *Cognitive therapy for bipolar disorder: A therapist's guide to concepts, methods and practice*. Chichester, UK: Wiley-Blackwell.

Miklowitz, D. J., & Scott, J. (2009). Psychosocial treatments for bipolar disorder: Cost-effectiveness, mediating mechanisms, and future directions. *Bipolar Disorders, 11*, 110–122.

Young, A., Ferrier, N., & Michalak, E. E. (Eds.). (2010). *Practical management of bipolar disorder*. Cambridge, MA: Cambridge University Press.

Bipolar Disorder

David Gilfillan

COMMENT ON THE EVIDENCE-BASED RECOMMENDATIONS

The suggestion that Bipolar Disorder is "probably an extreme form of normal human variation" is controversial and suggests that the condition is a response to "environmental contingencies." This ignores the strong genetic factors inherent in the condition and its well-researched links to other psychiatric illnesses. Psychosis, the severity of the depressions, and the altered state often described in hypomania are just some of the characteristics qualitatively different from "normal human variation."

The shared content of treatments referred to in the evidence-based section represent a sound structure for working with BD, although there appears to be one component missing, namely the damage caused by the condition, frequently prior to it being diagnosed. The stress–diathesis diagram in the research section has some value but appears limited on three levels, namely, (a) some bipolar episodes, particularly those characteristic of rapid cycling, do not have a clear trigger, (b) the reactions are multidirectional (e.g., biological rhythms may disrupt social rhythms), and (c) it ignores the damage or "debris" created by the condition.

CASE EXAMPLE

Subject Information and Brief History

The client is a 35-year-old Caucasian woman first diagnosed with BD 3 years prior to referral, with a history of mood instability dating back to her early teenage years. During the years before diagnosis, her condition had severely affected her life resulting in a marriage failure, an avoidance of further close relationships, periods of drug and alcohol abuse, anorexic behavior, and employment instability. She had reacted reasonably positively to mood stabilizing medication, gained stable employment, and was no longer using drugs and alcohol at the time of her referral.

Presenting Problem

On presentation, the client described still frequently experiencing periods of depression and hypomania that at times threatened her capacity to perform her work duties and affected her relationships with others. She felt powerless to control these episodes, although acknowledging that medication had reduced the severity of the symptoms. She also described strong guilt feelings about past behaviors, with these feelings becoming excessive during depressive episodes, and which severely affected her perception of herself and of her future. While her condition was being managed by an eminent psychiatrist, she felt too intimated by him to question him in depth about her condition.

Treating Intervention and Course

Initial treatment focus was on the client's understanding of her disorder. During this period, she was (a) offered the opportunity to discussion her condition; (b) educated as to its nature in a nondidactic fashion; (c) provided with reading and other resources to increase her knowledge; and (d) helped to formulate questions that she could discuss with her psychiatrist.

Simultaneously with the above, mood monitoring routines were implemented with the focus on discovering the triggers and early warning signs for her bipolar episodes. Using this information, together with collateral information that highlighted patterns of which she was not aware, and her personal insights, a well-being plan was developed in which she learned to identify her triggers and pattern of entering mood episodes (her "relapse signature"), and was assisted in developing immediate remedial strategies that included increasing stimulatory behaviors when becoming depressed and reducing these behaviors when becoming hypomanic. General lifestyle changes were directed at regulating her sleep, diet, exercise, medication-taking, and work (working more regular hours rather than doing excessive shift work) with the focus on creating greater stability, while she was also assisted in developing additional coping strategies such as mindfulness and behaviors that calmed her and gave her intrinsic satisfaction (such as taking guitar lessons and doing volunteer work with children).

As the above became entrenched, attention was given to the "debris" of the preceding years, covering such issues as her sense of failure and guilt, her schemas of lack of self-worth and values, her doubts about the future, her anger at past treatments that had failed and had neglected to assess her for BD, her impaired relationship with her family, and her fears of never again being able to have a relationship. Family were involved in some of the sessions and also contributed to the well-being plan.

The treatment initially comprised 10 sessions, but during each of the subsequent 2 years, there were intermittent sessions related to arising issues or dealing fully with those previous discussed. She is currently seen approximately twice a year. The education and well-being issues were dealt with fully in the initial sessions (note: with other clients, group sessions have proved valuable in dealing with these areas, enabling the individual sessions to be more focused), while work was commenced on the "debris" and she was encouraged to continue dealing with this on her own. She also learned meditative strategies independent of the counseling and was assisted in finding a support group.

Outcome

During the last 3 years, in stark contrast to the 15 preceding years, she has had no major bipolar episodes. Her relationship with her family has been fully restored and is supportive. She has received promotions in her work, is active socially, and has become involved in charity work that she finds immensely satisfactory. She is also open to the possibility of a long-term relationship although this has not as yet materialized.

CHALLENGES IN APPLYING THE EVIDENCE-BASED APPROACH

The first and obvious challenge in applying evidence-based psychological treatment is that the evidence base is still weak and definitive treatments have not been fully defined. In the above case study, all of the areas outlined in the research section were addressed to a greater or lesser extent, but would not have been sufficient without dealing with the effect of the condition on the client's life, identity, and ability to function. However, it was necessary to control and tame the BD, as much as possible, by use of education, medication, mood monitoring, and well-being strategies in order to give her the psychological space, previously absent, to work on the debris caused by the disease. Dealing with these issues in turn reduced the internal triggers for her disorder, thereby indirectly adding to her mood stability.

The second challenge to evidence-based therapy relates to the goals of treatment. BD is not cured, so the aim of treatment is to reduce the frequency and intensity of episodes, limit the disruption that it causes, and to assist the sufferer to lead a productive life despite and because of the condition.

CULTURAL DIVERSITY ISSUES

Cultural diversity research in BD is lacking in quantity. There have been suggestions that the manifestations of mania and hypomania may differ across cultures, and that the degree of acceptance of the condition within a culture may affect the prognosis.

FUTURE RESEARCH

It appears that an integrated model to dealing with BD is still lacking. There is a need for researching a broader, more integrated approach, possibly one that combines individual and group consultations, as well as reference to the pretreatment consequences of the condition.

KEY REFERENCES

Colom, F., & Vieta, E. (2006). *Psychoeducation manual for bipolar disorder.* Cambridge, MA: Cambridge University Press.

Goodwin, F. K., & Jamison, K. R. (2007). *Manic-depressive illness.* Oxford, UK: Oxford University Press.

Parker, G. (Ed.). (2012). *Bipolar II disorder: Modelling, measuring and managing.* Cambridge, MA: Cambridge University Press.

CHAPTER 20

Body Dysmorphic Disorder

Ross Krawczyk, Michael S. Boroughs, and J. Kevin Thompson

CLINICAL PROBLEM

Body Dysmorphic Disorder (BDD) is characterized by marked preoccupation with an imagined or slight defect in physical appearance. To warrant diagnosis, this preoccupation must cause clinically significant impairment and/or distress. Though BDD has been systematically researched in recent years, the presentation of the disorder has been documented for over a century and labeled dysmorphophobia or dermatologic hypochondriasis.

BDD has several key clinical features that are typically present. First, the patient may be preoccupied with one or more aspects of appearance with commonly cited areas of concern that include the face, head, skin, hair, or nose. A second clinical feature is the presence of rituals or compulsive behaviors that involve examining, improving, and/or concealing the perceived defect. These behaviors may include frequent mirror checking, wearing clothing that camouflage the defect, or frequent clothing changes to make sure the defect is concealed. A few other important clinical features should be noted. Many sufferers of BDD chronically avoid social situations owing to the anxiety surrounding their perceived defect. BDD is typically very impairing and comorbidity with other mental disorders is common, especially depression, substance abuse, social phobia, and Obsessive-Compulsive Disorder (OCD). Finally, and of great importance, suicidal ideation and attempts are common among patients with BDD. Approximately 80% of BDD sufferers exhibit suicidal ideation at some point in their lifetime, while approximately 25% attempt suicide. Therefore, clinicians must often monitor and manage the greater risk for suicidal thoughts and attempts while simultaneously attending to direct treatment of the presenting symptoms.

PREVALENCE

BDD occurs in approximately 0.7% to 2.5% of the general population. This percentage appears somewhat higher among college students; estimates among American, Australian, German, and Turkish college samples are approximately 2% to 5%. Prevalence of BDD appears to be much higher among psychiatric inpatients, approximately 16%, but this is believed to be a low estimate owing to possible underreporting. Among seekers of cosmetic surgery, the prevalence of BDD appears to be approximately 6% to 15% across samples in the United States, France, and Japan.

CULTURAL DIVERSITY ISSUES

While relatively few studies have been conducted, BDD research has examined group differences between genders, and among racial, ethnic, and sexual orientation groups. BDD occurs more frequently among women though the presentation of symptoms is similar for both genders. Research into racial and ethnic differences suggest that, among women, Caucasians and Latinas exhibit similar and significantly higher prevalence of BDD when compared to African American women. Researchers have also investigated group differences between heterosexual and sexual minority groups, finding that sexual minority women have the highest prevalence rates of BDD, followed by heterosexual women and sexual minority men who do not differ, followed finally by heterosexual men with the lowest BDD prevalence rates. Overall, BDD is a relatively common, yet understudied, psychological disorder with important demographic group differences that should be considered.

EVIDENCE-BASED TREATMENTS

There are two common approaches to treating BDD, cognitive behavioral therapy (CBT) and pharmacotherapy, that can be used independently or in conjunction. CBT for BDD typically consists of both cognitive and behavioral strategies to reduce anxiety about appearance, challenge faulty and maladaptive cognitions, decrease social avoidance, and prevent compulsive behaviors. For example, a psychotherapy session using CBT for BDD may include exposure to anxiety-provoking stimuli coupled with response prevention.

Treatment efficacy studies examining CBT for BDD have shown positive and consistent results for both individual and group treatment formats. Psychopharmacotherapy has demonstrated efficacy in treating BDD. The class of medications with the most empirical support for treating BDD are selective serotonin reuptake inhibitors (SSRIs).

Although CBT and pharmacotherapy are the only empirically supported treatments for BDD, it appears that a great number, possibly even a majority, of individuals with BDD seek cosmetic medical treatments such as plastic surgery, dermatologic treatment, or cosmetic dental interventions. These cosmetic treatments rarely result in a reduction of BDD symptoms and often lead to increased appearance preoccupation and cosmetic surgery seeking. When deciding upon treatment for BDD, one or both CBT and pharmacotherapy are empirically supported and should be utilized, but cosmetic surgery is not recommended.

FUTURE RESEARCH

Additional research is needed to better define and understand BDD, study its prevalence, examine its features, and determine effective treatment. First, more work must be done to further define and more accurately diagnose BDD. As currently defined in the *Diagnostic and Statistical Manual of Mental Disorders-5*, BDD is in need of differentiation from eating disorders as there is currently some overlap between symptoms. Also, little is known about the primary influences on the development of BDD, be they genetic, biological, psychological, or sociocultural. Very importantly, future research is needed to further examine gender, racial, ethnic, cultural, and sexual orientation group differences. Finally, further efforts are needed in determining and evaluating the most effective psychological and pharmacological treatments of

BDD. Some treatment strategies, such as CBT or SSRIs have shown good efficacy, but other treatments may be evaluated. For example, Acceptance and Commitment Therapy for body image dissatisfaction is one avenue for future investigations. Should it prove efficacious for body image dissatisfaction, research into its efficacy with BDD patients will be needed. In addition, though SSRIs have shown success in treating BDD, there is some evidence supporting the use of other medications such as serotonin-norepinephrine reuptake inhibitors and the antiepileptic medication, levetiracetam. These potential future avenues of research and treatment should be explored. Considering its high prevalence and the severity of impairment caused, a great deal of future work is needed in order to better understand and treat BDD.

KEY REFERENCES

Phillips, K. A. (2009). *Understanding Body Dysmorphic Disorder: An essential guide.* New York, NY: Oxford University Press.

Thompson, J. K., Heinberg, L. J., Altabe, M., & Tantleff-Dunn, S. (1999). Exacting beauty: Theory, assessment, and treatment of body image disturbance. *American Psychological Association.* Washington, DC: doi: 10.1037/10312-000

Wilhelm, S., Phillips, K. A., & Steketee, G. (2012). *A cognitive behavioral treatment manual for Body Dysmorphic Disorder.* New York, NY: Guilford Press.

Clinician Application

Body Dysmorphic Disorder

Andrea Allen

COMMENT ON THE EVIDENCE-BASED RECOMMENDATIONS

As noted in the research summary, Body Dysmorphic Disorder (BDD) is an often severe disorder characterized by compelling obsessive thoughts and time consuming behavioral rituals related to distress about a physical feature patients incorrectly perceive as horribly unattractive. It is heartening that there are now demonstrated treatments for this serious disorder that previously had been considered treatment refractory. As reported in the research review, the first-line evidence-based treatments are Cognitive Behavior Therapy (CBT) and antiobsessional medications (selective serotonin reuptake inhibitors [SRIs]). These approaches also seem effective for BDD in practice. The focus here is on CBT, however, it is notable that SRIs are typically used in higher doses than for depression, perhaps above FDA-approved doses, and therapeutic effects are not expected for 8 to 12 weeks.

CBT is a broad approach based in learning theory and employing an unlimited array of behavioral and cognitive techniques. Psychoeducation is an essential component and CBT also often incorporates aspects of Acceptance and Commitment

Therapy (e.g., mindfulness), Dialectical Behavior Therapy (DBT) (e.g., distress tolerance training), and other enhancements of basic CBT. This provides a rich and broad base of practical techniques to apply to the many symptoms of BDD.

CASE EXAMPLE

Subject Information and Brief History

Gary, an attractive, 25-year-old White male graduate student, contacted me for treatment of self-diagnosed BDD. He reported a 7-year history of concern with his facial complexion that began at age 17 when he developed acne. The acne was successfully treated and no longer active by age 19. He remained as concerned about residual redness and scarring as he had been over the acne, and his concern escalated over time. Neither redness nor scarring was visible on casual examination in office lighting.

Gary could not tolerate SRIs. At the time he began CBT, he had a prescription for clonazepam (Klonopin), an anxiolytic, which he took as needed for extreme BDD episodes.

Presenting Problem

Gary sought CBT specifically (because he knew that it was the recommended treatment for BDD) owing to disabling distress over his facial complexion. Because he believed that appearance was extremely important, not just in romantic relationships but in friendships and for a successful career, he felt hopeless about his life. He had persistent, distressing thoughts, virtually nonstop, ranging from nagging worry to cascades of catastrophizing that led to anxiety attacks, often more than once per day. He performed many behavioral rituals and avoided many situations. Although he was able to go to school most of the time and perform adequately, the BDD limited his academic success (by preventing him from participating in classes, impairing his presentations and networking, and interfering with his ability to focus on his studies), and led to severe impairment in social and general functioning. He had moderate insight most of the time: (a) he firmly believed that his skin was red and scarred, but accepted that he had BDD owing to the level of distress and impairment he experienced, and (b) he thought it was possible that his skin was not quite as bad as it looked to him.

Treatment Intervention and Course

Many different CBT techniques were used. In addition to psychoeducation, the most valuable techniques seemed to be: (a) exposure and response prevention, using both planned exposures and ritual reduction, and, (b) mirror retraining. Other techniques included deep breathing and muscle relaxation training, mindfulness, and cognitive restructuring.

Mirror retraining consisted of Gary looking at himself in a mirror and describing his head and face in detail from top to bottom using basic, nonevaluative descriptions, such as those a physician might use, not emotional or dramatic, terms. First, Gary did this in low lighting with the mirror a few feet away and positioned so he saw his "better" side. Initially, this was a very anxiety-provoking exercise, but after doing it 4 times per week for a few weeks in session and at home, Gary experienced no anxiety and the areas of concern were less noticeable at the start of each exercise and indistinguishable by the end. At this point, the exercise was made more difficult by changing the distance, lighting, and/or angle of the mirror relative to his face. These new conditions were maintained until Gary had minimal anxiety, then made more difficult again, until he had normal mirror behavior.

A typical planned exposure involved a social situation that was designed to arouse some anxiety and, over time, was repeated in circumstances of increasing difficulty. For example, Gary went to a club with a friend and sat in a dim area. Over time, this was made more difficult by having him talk in lighted areas. Later exposures required Gary to start a brief conversation with women he didn't know in a dim area, and, over time, having longer conversations and/or conversations in areas with better lighting.

All of Gary's rituals and avoidance were gradually and systematically reduced. Examples of targeted behaviors included concealer on the red areas of his face, mirror checking, and taking new photos of himself and comparing them to old photos.

Outcome

When Gary left psychotherapy, he had no behavioral rituals under normal circumstances. Further, thoughts and feelings about his skin were absent in all his typical day-to-day activities. At times, he believed he might have redness or minor scarring, but usually thought that was entirely a BDD misperception and the idea of flawed skin now did not ordinarily result in emotional distress. He accepted that any problems with his skin were unlikely to have an impact on his work success or friendships, though he occasionally thought some people might be less interested in him as a good friend or romantically because of his skin. He occasionally had intrusive thoughts and distress in social situations, such as clubs or big parties where there were a lot of new people, but not at work, with friends, nor at smaller parties, and he was in a romantic relationship. Gary returned for one booster session and is continuing to do well with BDD virtually absent most of the time, but appearing at a manageable level in particularly challenging social situations.

CHALLENGES IN APPLYING THE EVIDENCE-BASED APPROACH

Poor insight is the most problematic issue when treating BDD patients. The majority of BDD patients have poor insight at least some of the time and many have little or no insight most of the time, being convinced that their perception of their appearance is totally accurate. This is just the reality of BDD and such patients can be successfully treated, but the psychoeducation and cognitive work needs to be changed to be compatible with the patient's reality. Psychiatrists should be aware that research shows even delusional patients respond to treatment with SRIs. Thus, antipsychotics may not be necessary. Augmentation of an SRI with atypical antipsychotics is an appropriate second-line treatment if an adequate dose of the SRI brings an unsatisfactory response. Research does not support their use as a monotherapy, regardless of degree of insight.

The severity of BDD also influences the way techniques can be applied. Many BDD patients are besieged constantly by distressing thoughts and urges that can lead to multiple anxiety attacks per day. Typical recommended strategies, such as sitting with the distressing thoughts and accepting uncertainty without engaging in rituals, are likely to be impossible for these individuals. In such cases, accepting the thoughts, but then distracting themselves may be a better early strategy.

CULTURAL DIVERSITY ISSUES

Diversity issues are important in BDD because the specific concerns differ across groups as do the physical ideal and the importance of attractiveness. Sex differences tend to be obvious. Females are likely to be concerned about femininity (e.g., being too muscular, having small breasts, or being too hairy). Males are more likely to be concerned about masculinity (i.e., concern about muscularity or penis size). Social and cultural groups may have their own issues that influence the BDD experience.

FUTURE RESEARCH

The most important research needs are to better understand how to conduct psychotherapy with patients with poor insight and otherwise severe BDD. Additional work is also needed on characterizing the symptom subgroups. For example, when treating men with concerns about muscularity, the clinician needs to be aware of the likely use of supplements, steroids, and so forth. When dealing with skin picking, the clinician needs to be aware of the possible use of implements to gouge the skin. In both these cases, if the clinician doesn't ask, the patient might not volunteer the information. Many gay men live in a subculture in which appearance is actually much more important than the one heterosexual men experience. It would be valuable to know more about these social and cultural factors. Finally, clinical samples tend to have equal numbers of males and females while prevalence in some nonclinical samples shows differences, possibly owing to subclinical and mild cases. Further work on this would be valuable.

KEY REFERENCES

Veale, D., & Neziroglu, F. (2010). *Body Dysmorphic Disorder: A treatment manual.* Chichester, UK: Wiley-Blackwell.

Wilhelm, S. (2006). *Feeling good about the way you look.* New York, NY: Guilford Press.

Wilhelm, S., Phillips, K. A., & Steketee, G. (2013). *A cognitive behavioral treatment manual for Body Dysmorphic Disorder.* New York, NY: Guilford Press.

CHAPTER 21

Borderline Personality Disorder

Alexis K. Matusiewicz and Marina A. Bornovalova

CLINICAL PROBLEM

Borderline Personality Disorder (BPD) is a severe, persistent disorder characterized by disturbances in emotional, interpersonal, and behavioral functioning. The symptoms of BPD include (a) frantic efforts to avoid abandonment, (b) a pattern of unstable and intense interpersonal relationships characterized by alternating extremes of idealization and devaluation, (c) markedly and persistently unstable self-image or sense of self, (d) chronic feelings of emptiness, (e) transient, stress-related paranoid ideation or severe dissociative symptoms, (f) affective instability due to a marked reactivity of mood, (g) inappropriate, intense anger or difficulty controlling anger, (h) impulsive behavior, and (i) recurrent suicidal behavior, gestures, threats, or deliberate self-harm. Self-harm and suicidal behavior have been described as the "behavioral specialty" of BPD, and occur in 50% to 80% of people with the disorder. Between 3% and 9.5% of people with BPD eventually die by suicide. BPD is associated with high rates of psychiatric comorbidity, poor physical health, and diminished academic and professional attainment. Further, despite extensive utilization of outpatient mental health services and the increasing accessibility of empirically supported treatments for BPD, these individuals frequently demonstrate poor response to treatment and are more likely to utilize costly emergency and inpatient psychiatric services.

PREVALENCE

The prevalence of BPD in the general population is estimated to range from 1% to 5.9%, whereas approximately 10% to 20% of mental health outpatients and up to 50% of psychiatric inpatients have a BPD diagnosis. Traditionally, it was believed that BPD could not be diagnosed prior to adulthood. However, temperamental precursors of BPD, which include impulsivity and affective instability, are observable in preschool-age children. BPD can be diagnosed in adolescents without modification of the diagnostic criteria.

CULTURAL DIVERSITY ISSUES

Most epidemiologic studies indicate comparable rates of BPD among men and women, however, in clinical studies, between two thirds and three quarters of those diagnosed with BPD are women. Because of the preponderance of women in treatment-seeking samples, much of the treatment outcome research has focused on women. Nonetheless, there is reason to believe that efficacious treatments for women with BPD are similarly effective for male clients. Men and women experience comparable levels of functional impairment and endorse similar symptom profiles and patterns of comorbidity. However, women are more likely to have co-occurring Posttraumatic Stress Disorder (PTSD) and eating disorders, and men with BPD are more likely to have substance use disorders and comorbid personality disorders. There is little evidence of racial or ethnic differences in the prevalence, clinical presentation, or treatment outcome of BPD.

EVIDENCE-BASED TREATMENTS

Among psychosocial treatments for BPD, Dialectical Behavior Therapy (DBT) has amassed the greatest empirical support. DBT is a highly structured cognitive behavioral treatment delivered over 12 to 18 months, consisting of: individual therapy, group skills training, phone consultation, and therapist supervision. DBT is structured around a hierarchy of targets: reducing suicidal behavior, reducing therapy-interfering behaviors, reducing behaviors that interfere with quality of life, and finally, fostering the client's ability to develop a meaningful and valued life. Techniques include functional analysis, exposure, contingency management, cognitive restructuring, and problem solving. The therapeutic alliance is considered a fundamental aspect of the treatment approach.

The efficacy of this treatment package for clients with BPD has been demonstrated in a total of nine randomized controlled trials (RCTs) spanning different patient populations and clinical settings. Of these, seven studies compared DBT to low-intensity control treatments (e.g., unstructured nonbehavioral therapy). DBT was superior to low-intensity treatments in reducing nonsuicidal self-injury (NSSI) and suicidal behavior. DBT was also associated with diminished impulsivity/impulsive behavior, improved interpersonal functioning, diminished anger (although one study favored supportive counseling), and decreased affective disturbances. DBT was more effective than lower-intensity control treatments in terms of treatment-related factors (e.g., treatment retention, use of inpatient psychiatric or emergency services) and global functioning. However, when comparing DBT to more rigorous control treatments (i.e., psychodynamic psychotherapy with medication management), there was comparable improvement across domains of functioning.

The effectiveness of DBT has been demonstrated in a range of clinical settings and patient populations, including community mental health centers, a Veteran's Affairs hospital, and private practice. Efforts to adapt DBT for use with inpatients have also met with preliminary success in four nonrandomized controlled trials. In these studies, DBT was associated with decreased frequency of NSSI, decreased depression and anxiety, improved social functioning, and decreased dissociative symptoms. With regard to comorbid psychopathology, there is some evidence that DBT is more effective than low-intensity control treatments in reducing co-occurring depression and substance use. In studies specifically designed to target BPD-substance use disorder (SUD) comorbidity, DBT was associated with decreased substance use, improved social functioning and, albeit inconsistently, decreased dropout. Findings are mixed as to whether standard DBT, which does not have content specific to abstinence or relapse prevention, affects substance use outcomes. Finally, the efficacy of DBT has been examined among patients with co-occurring eating pathology (binge eating disorder or bulimia nervosa) in two open trials. DBT was associated with decreased binge eating, decreased NSSI, improved social functioning, and fewer inpatient days. Although DBT has garnered the most robust empirical support of any treatment for BPD, a number of other psychosocial treatments, including cognitive behavioral interventions, psychodynamic psychotherapy, and adjunctive skills-based groups have shown promising results in certain symptom domains.

Psychopharmacological interventions are commonly used, either independently or in combination with psychotherapy, to treat BPD. Currently, no psychopharmacological agent has been approved by the FDA for the treatment of BPD. However, the existing literature lends support to the practice of symptom-targeted pharmacotherapy. In total, 28 RCTs have been conducted to examine the effect of various psychopharmacological agents on BPD symptomatology.

First-generation antipsychotics have been evaluated in four RCTs and have shown limited efficacy in the treatment of BPD. Haloperidol was associated with decreased anger as compared to placebo, and did not differ from the tricyclic antidepressant amitriptyline or the second-generation antipsychotic olanzapine in any symptom domain. Flupentixol decanoate was associated with reduced suicidal behavior, whereas thiothixene did not differ from placebo on any outcomes. Second-generation antipsychotics have been evaluated in nine RCTs and have demonstrated efficacy across a range of symptoms. Aripiprazole was superior to placebo in terms of reducing anger, psychotic symptoms, impulsivity, and interpersonal problems. Olanzapine has been shown to decrease affective instability, anger, and psychotic symptoms in individuals with BPD; however, findings are mixed as to its effect on suicidal behavior. Olanzapine did not differ from antidepressant fluoxetine on any outcome, nor did the combination of fluoxetine + olanzapine differ from olanzapine alone. Ziprasidone failed to show significant effects on any outcome. Mood stabilizers have been compared to placebo in seven RCTs. Valproate semisodium was found to improve interpersonal functioning and anger. Lamotrigine was associated with decreased impulsivity and anger. Topiramate was associated with improved interpersonal functioning and impulsivity. Antidepressants have been evaluated in seven RCTs. Amitriptyline and phenelzine sulfate yielded improvements in depression, anxiety, and general psychiatric severity, but did not have an effect on BPD symptoms. Compared to placebo, the SSRIs fluvoxamine and fluoxetine were not associated with improvements in any domain. Finally, omega-3 fatty acid supplementation, which was compared to placebo in two trials, was associated with reduced suicidality and depression.

FUTURE RESEARCH

Current evidence indicates that clients with BPD can benefit from psychotherapy and pharmacotherapy, yet despite these advances, many empirical questions remain. A critical limitation in the treatment research for BPD is discrepancy across studies in how outcomes are selected, measured, and reported, which makes it difficult to determine whether the absence of findings in a particular symptom domain reflects a null effect, or, rather, that a particular outcome was not assessed. Another critical question pertains to the feasibility of implementing complex, intensive, multicomponent interventions in private practice and other community-based treatment settings. Given the costs and practical problems associated with this type of intervention, future research might examine whether, or for whom, treatments can be shortened without compromising their effectiveness.

KEY REFERENCES

Binks, C., Fenton, M., McCarthy, L., Lee, T., Adams, C. E., & Duggan, C. (2006). Psychological therapies for people with borderline personality disorder. *Cochrane Database Systematic Review, 25,* CD005652.
Lieb, K., Völlm, B., Rücker, G., Timmer, A., & Stoffers, J. M. (2010). Pharmacotherapy for borderline personality disorder: Cochrane systematic review of randomised trials. *British Journal of Psychiatry, 196,* 4–12.
Lieb, K., Zanarini, M. C., Schmahl, C., Linehan, M. M., & Bohus, M. (2004). Borderline personality disorder. *The Lancet, 364,* 453–461.

Clinician Application

Borderline Personality Disorder

Heidi M. Limbrunner

COMMENT ON EVIDENCE-BASED RECOMMENDATIONS

Borderline Personality Disorder (BPD) is a difficult to treat and complex disorder. Dialectical Behavior Therapy (DBT) demonstrates the greatest empirical support and provides a framework for practitioners on how to best help these patients who often have life-threatening behaviors and multiple psychological issues and concerns. In practice, one of the many benefits of DBT is that it provides a hierarchy of targets to guide clinicians in their treatment. For instance, when a patient presents with multiple concerns (e.g., suicidal ideation, relationship struggles, and poor treatment adherence), DBT provides guidance on which area to address first. This therapy approach also provides several helpful strategies to engage patients in therapy and remain motivated for change. Finally, DBT provides support for practitioners working with this challenging population through routine consultation team meetings with colleagues.

CASE EXAMPLE

Subject Information and Brief History

Emma was a 21-year-old, single, Caucasian female who attended classes part-time at a local community college. She resided at home with her parents and had few friends. Emma had been in psychotherapy since she was a teenager for difficulty with relationships, self-harm behavior, and disordered eating. Over the previous 18 months, she had been hospitalized three times for suicide attempts.

Presenting Problem

Emma presented for a psychological evaluation after being discharged from an inpatient hospital. She had been hospitalized for taking an overdose of her prescribed medication after a breakup with her boyfriend of 3 months. She shared that she engaged in self-harm behaviors via cutting several times a week and reported constant strain in her relationship with her parents. Emma indicated that most days she feels depressed and suicidal. At the end of her initial evaluation, Emma stated that she typically does not like therapists, but was willing to try DBT as she was embarrassed of her scars from self-harming.

Treatment Intervention and Course

Emma agreed to participate in DBT which consisted of weekly individual and group sessions. Emma cancelled her third and fourth individual appointments one hour prior to their scheduled time. The psychotherapist contacted Emma to remind her of the treatment agreement and Emma then attended the remainder of her appointments on time.

In sessions, Emma learned the biosocial theory for the development of BPD and concepts related to states of mind and mindfulness. She completed diary cards on a weekly basis, which kept track of her mood, skill use, and self-harm behaviors. Emma also completed behavior chains each time she engaged in self-harm or therapy-interfering behaviors. Through this exercise, Emma was able to identify several trends in her behaviors including her tendency to isolate prior to cutting and listening to sad music in an effort to cope. Emma found that listening to the sad music was intensifying her desire to cut. Her frequency of self-harm behaviors decreased as she began to use effective coping skills such as writing in her journal, distracting herself from emotions by watching TV, and calling a friend.

Emma also participated in a weekly DBT group with peers. During this group, Emma learned ways to cope with stress, increase mindfulness, communicate effectively, build healthy relationships, and understand and identify her emotions. In practicing interpersonal effectiveness skills with group members, she was able to identify effective ways of communicating with her parents at home.

Through her treatment, Emma also utilized the on-call pager (telephone support) when she was having strong urges to overdose. Emma was encouraged to utilize the pager only after she had attempted three skills independently and found these skills to be ineffective. In using the pager, she was able to receive coaching for skill use in a moment of difficulty. Emma utilized the pager once to twice a month throughout treatment.

After a year of treatment, Emma had completed the DBT skills group and was completing her diary cards on a daily basis. Although she occasionally engages in self-harm behavior, the frequency decreased from several times a week at the start of therapy to less than once a month at the end of treatment. Emma continues to report suicidal ideation on a frequent basis, but she has remained out of the hospital for the past 6 months and is able to identify coping skills should her urges increase. Emma remains in psychotherapy to address relationship concerns and work on building self-esteem.

CHALLENGES IN APPLYING THE EVIDENCE-BASED APPROACH

One of the main challenges in providing DBT is having access to all treatment components. For instance, not all communities have DBT groups. In addition, providing 24-hour telephone crisis access is difficult to offer as an independent practitioner. Working with individuals that struggle with BPD can be a very rewarding, but stressful undertaking. Having frequent treatment team consultation, and having a support system in place for psychotherapists are essential, but can be difficult to find especially in smaller community settings.

Although DBT has demonstrated greater treatment adherence, it is often difficult for patients to remain invested in psychotherapy and motivated to change. DBT is a time-intensive treatment and requires at least two therapy hours a week and time spent independently working on homework assignments and diary cards. In addition, treatment duration is often well over a year. Not all patients are able or willing to make this time commitment. Finally, DBT can be costly for patients and some are not able to afford (or insurance does not cover) all aspects of treatment. For example, some insurance companies will not cover group treatment or for adolescent group treatment, the parent component of DBT treatment is not covered.

CULTURAL DIVERSITY ISSUES

There are no diversity issues related to the treatment of BPD.

FUTURE RESEARCH

As stated previously, it can be difficult to provide all treatment components of DBT. Studies that examine which components of DBT are the most effective and/or whether DBT is as effective when only certain aspects of treatment are provided (for instance, not having phone pager access) would be beneficial. Further research would also be helpful to identify which patients may necessitate the need for all components of DBT as compared to those who may benefit from single components. While most studies have been focused on women, as they have the highest rate of BPD, it would be helpful to know how DBT fares in the treatment of males. Additional research would be helpful to examine effectiveness with different ethnic groups and individuals of various sexual orientations.

KEY REFERENCES

Linehan, M. (1993a). *Cognitive behavioral treatment of borderline personality disorder*. New York, NY: Guilford Press

Linehan, M. (1993b). *Skills training manual for treating borderline personality disorder*. New York, NY: Guilford Press

Miller, A., Rathus, J., & Linehan, M. (2007). *Dialectical behavior therapy with suicidal adolescents*. New York, NY: Guilford Press

CHAPTER 22

Depression

Lawrence P. Riso and Amber Guzman

CLINICAL PROBLEM

Depressive disorders are among the most common of all psychiatric problems, and they can be extremely debilitating. According to the World Health Organization (WHO), depression is the number one cause of disability worldwide.

The most frequently diagnosed form of depression is Major Depressive Disorder (MDD). MDD is a broad diagnostic category encompassing depressions that are short lived, chronic, mild in intensity, and severe with prominent psychotic features. The broad nature of this category limits its clinical utility, to some extent.

The comorbidity between depression and other disorders is considerable. Nearly three quarters of those with MDD have a lifetime history of another psychiatric disorder. The most common comorbid disorders are anxiety disorders and substance use disorders.

PREVALENCE

Over 30 million adults in the United States have a lifetime history of depression. Thirteen million people suffer from depression in any given year and the lifetime risk for developing depression is a staggering 23%. Women are at twice the risk for depression compared to men. Depression tends to begin early in life with a median age of onset of 32.

Once depression strikes, it is very likely to recur. Over half of those who experience an episode of depression will suffer a recurrence. The median number of episodes is seven. The time to recovery is highly variable, although the great majority of patients recover within one year. Five percent of those who become depressed will develop a chronic course. The high prevalence rate, early onset, and chronic and recurrent nature of depression contribute to its rank as the most burdensome disease in the world.

CULTURAL DIVERSITY ISSUES

In 2001, the U.S. Department of Health and Human Services expressed concerns over the inadequate representation of ethnic minority and immigrant populations in efficacy studies. However, there is increasing evidence that our empirically supported treatments for depression are just as effective with minority and immigrant groups. Nonetheless, there are a number of research findings that stress the importance of taking cultural context into account when planning treatment. For instance, African Americans and Hispanic Americans tend to find antidepressant medication less acceptable than Caucasian Americans. Moreover, some cultural groups may be more inclined to turn to family members (such as South Asians) or religion (such as Black Caribbeans) to deal with emotional and psychiatric problems instead of relying on mental health professionals.

EVIDENCE-BASED TREATMENTS

Antidepressant medication is the most commonly used treatment for depression and the most extensively studied. The major classes of antidepressant medications include tricyclic antidepressants, monoamine oxidase inhibitors, and selective serotonergic reuptake inhibitors. All antidepressants are thought to alter the regulation of the neurotransmitters norepinephrine, serotonin, or both, in the brain. However, these effects may not actually represent the therapeutic mechanism of antidepressant medications. For instance, while antidepressants impact these neurotransmitter systems almost immediately, their therapeutic effects may not be seen for weeks. Other mechanisms under investigation include intracellular protein synthesis, neuronal growth, and dendritic sprouting.

The efficacy of a number of antidepressants has been demonstrated in numerous studies. The superiority of any particular class of antidepressant or of any specific medicine, however, has not been demonstrated. Consequently, the choice of an antidepressant medication is typically based upon the patient's history of previous response, side-effect profile, cost, and at times, subtype of depression. Recently, some authors have made controversial, although empirically supported to some extent, claims that the apparent efficacy of antidepressant medication is largely a placebo response for depressions in the mild to moderate range. However, even those skeptical of antidepressant medication note that they offer considerable benefit for patients suffering from severe depression. Depressions that are severe and associated with psychotic features are also responsive to electroconvulsive therapy.

In addition to medication, a number of other somatic treatments have demonstrated efficacy in at least some studies including St. John's wort, vagal nerve stimulation, and transcranial magnetic stimulation. These treatments, however, are not as well studied as antidepressant medications and electroconvulsive therapy, and they may not be as efficacious.

Cognitive therapy (CT) for depression is the most well-studied psychotherapy for depression. The great majority of clinical trials demonstrate its superiority over pill placebo. The efficacy of CT is similar to that of antidepressant medication for outpatients, even for those outpatients who are severely depressed. Some studies found that the level of clinical experience and expertise in administering CT may be critical for its efficacy. Behavior therapy is also well studied and has recently received renewed interest. The most recent incarnation of behaviorally based approaches is known as "behavioral activation" (BA). BA is a freestanding therapy that focuses on the environmental context of depression and involves a functional analysis of the behaviors that may keep an individual depressed. It seeks to identify and eliminate avoidance behaviors that are blocking potential sources of reinforcement in the patient's life and attempts to get the patient more active and engaged with their environment. BA appears to be as efficacious as CT and some evidence suggests that it may be superior to CT for more severely depressed outpatients.

Other psychotherapies with considerable support in the literature include the cognitive behavioral analysis system of psychotherapy, interpersonal therapy, problem-solving therapy, and self-control therapy. There is modest empirical support for some insight-oriented and emotion-focused approaches including short-term psychodynamic therapy, emotion-focused therapy, and reminiscent/ life review therapy (specifically for older adults). Finally, a growing body of evidence suggests that mindfulness-based cognitive therapy, which integrates meditation with traditional CT, can help to prevent relapse of depressive episodes. At this point, there is little evidence for the efficacy of mindfulness-based cognitive therapy as an acute phase treatment.

For decades, the field has worked to match treatments to patient characteristics (i.e., determine which treatments work for whom). Unfortunately, there is little consistent evidence to decide which treatment to employ among the many empirically supported treatments (whether somatic or psychosocial). Although the endogenous/ melancholic subtype of depression was traditionally thought to be more responsive to somatic treatments, clinical research has not consistently borne this out.

Some research suggests that combining medicine with psychotherapy can increase efficacy, although the increase in efficacy is quite modest. One advantage of medication is the speed of its response. CT, on the other hand, has the advantage of offering protection against relapse of depressive episodes, even after treatment has ended. This is in contrast to medication treatment alone. After antidepressant medication is discontinued, it offers no further protection. Thus, combining medication with CT may offer the rapid response of medication with the enduring protection of CT.

FUTURE RESEARCH

One of the most challenging and important areas for future research is the effort to better understand the mechanisms of change for our treatments—both somatic and psychosocial. Better understanding of the active ingredients will not only tell us what to emphasize when administering our current treatments, but will also limit the proliferation of purportedly new therapies and medications. Many newly introduced treatments are likely to be redundant in their mechanisms of change with existing treatments, and thus, needlessly complicate the field. A related growth edge for the field is to improve our ability to match patient characteristics with treatments (i.e., better understand which treatments work for whom).

KEY REFERENCES

Gelenberg, A. J., Freeman, M. P., Markowitz, J. C., Rosenbaum, J. F., Thase, M. E., ... Silbersweig, D. A. (2010). Practice guideline for the treatment of patients with major depressive disorder (Third edition). *American Journal of Psychiatry, 167*(10 Suppl), 1–3, 9–11, 13–118.

Hollon, S. D., Thase, M. E., & Markowitz, J. C. (2002). Treatment and prevention of depression. *Psychological Science in the Public Interest, 3*(2), 39–77.

Young, J. E., Rygh, J. L., Weinberger, A. D., & Beck, A. T. (2008). Cognitive therapy for depression. In D. H. Barlow (Ed.), *Clinical handbook of psychological disorders: A step-by-step treatment manual* (4th ed.). New York, NY: Guilford Press.

Depression

Sander J. Kornblith

COMMENT ON THE EVIDENCE-BASED RECOMMENDATIONS

The literature indicates that patients are more likely to access medication than psychotherapy for the treatment of depression, which is the number one mental health problem. Yet, those treated with medication for mild to moderate depression fare no better than those on placebo, and recurrence of a depressive episode is likely when medication is stopped. Research has shown that psychosocial treatments such as cognitive behavioral therapy (CBT) and behavioral activation are generally effective and produce a greater level of improvement than placebo. As depression intensifies, the use of combined treatments (medication plus psychosocial treatment) appears to generate symptom reduction sooner than when either is used alone.

Together, these observations suggest that such individuals can be better served by a treatment that trains them to examine the cognitive and behavioral features of their emotional vulnerability and develop tools for mood control, symptom relief, and relapse prevention in practical, problem-solving ways. Such a strategy, when combined with antidepressant medication, may facilitate the pace of improvement for many suffering severe depression.

CASE EXAMPLE

Subject Information and Brief History

Molly is a 29-year-old Caucasian married female in a biracial marriage. She had been a child of divorced parents by age 11 and reported a history of 15 recurrent episodes of depression with self-injurious behavior dating back to high school and college. She had successfully ceased self-cutting on her own after college and was in remission of such behavior before she married.

Presenting Problem

Initially, Molly presented with symptoms of a Major Depressive Disorder (MDD), recurrent episode, severe type without psychotic features, characterized by depressed mood, decreased interest in previously pleasurable activities, chronic attention and concentration problems, hypersomnia, fatigue, amotivation, guilt, chronic low self-esteem, thoughts of worthlessness, and passive thoughts of suicide. She also evidenced Attention Deficit/Hyperactivity Disorder, but had not been treated with stimulant medication since adolescence.

Molly reported that this episode of clinical depression was triggered one year ago by moving away from friends and family for the purpose of her husband's professional training. She found it additionally stressful to have to take a job unrelated to her professional training and career goals while her husband finished his training.

Treatment Intervention and Course

In our initial treatment session, we identified five goals for treatment:

1. Reduce/eliminate the symptoms of severe depressed mood and anxiety
2. Improve productivity at work and at home
3. Help resolve unhappiness with her current job
4. Help cope with feeling disconnected from family and friends.
5. Help replace a tendency to be passive-aggressive/hostile submissive with an expressive and assertive pattern in response to conflicts with others.

Treatment was provided twice weekly for 8 weeks (16 sessions) and once weekly for the remaining four sessions. Initially, Molly tended to be disorganized regarding what was covered in sessions and in complying with plans for homework. We decided to regularly write down what was covered in session as summary points including what we collaboratively designed for her to do as tasks between sessions. As a result, her compliance improved. Using the Weekly Activity Schedule, we began to examine her activities in terms of mood, mastery, and pleasure. Time spent with her husband was viewed as enjoyable, while time at work was stressful and draining. We listed the pros and cons of staying in her current job versus going part-time versus seeking another position. As her husband had begun a work assignment that generated income, she chose to discuss reducing her hours at work to part-time status with him and subsequently with her employer. We rehearsed how she wanted to present this proposal to her employer and how she might respond to his questions and concerns.

By the third week of treatment (at the fifth session), we were able to examine her success at asserting her preference and renegotiating her hours. She reported experiencing feelings of guilt that accompanied her reduced workload. By examining her automatic thoughts and the actual facts in the situation, she was able to reduce the credibility of her guilty thoughts from 80% true to merely 20% true, and experienced genuine relief. Feedback at the end of each session indicated that she appreciated the empirical approach of spotting and evaluating her distressing thinking with facts.

Continuing the exploration of her thought process, we found that guilt and shame were common themes following the divorce of her parents, and had been a trigger in her earlier pattern of self-injurious behavior. She learned in our sessions to ask the question, "Is this a problem to solve, or a measure of my entire self-worth?" Given her history of chronic low self-esteem, Molly discovered this to be a novel and productive way for her to think about challenges she encountered.

We discerned that "mind-reading" and "fortune–telling" (e.g., "He'll be angry with me and think I'm worthless if I say my preference") was a common way in which she had coped with her childhood, putting others' needs above hers. As it still occurred in her marriage, we began to promote a more expressive strategy for resolving frustrations. We began to identify how to use "I" messages to clarify observations, feelings, and preferences. As her mood improved, Molly wrote a summary of the changes she'd learned to make in her thinking and behavior that promoted her healthy mood.

Outcome

Molly achieved a successful remission of most depressive symptoms and improved communication and negotiating skills with her husband. She no longer met criteria for Major Depressive Episode. Her Hamilton Interview Rating Scale 17 item score substantially decreased from 15 to 4. She was able to summarize key cognitive and behavioral changes in her recovery as well as key relapse prevention elements.

Molly had explicitly modified her beliefs and practices regarding how she managed distressing emotions. This had previously served as a major source of her vulnerability to stressful events. She resumed planning and engaging in pleasant events such as dinner with friends, going to the gym, and discussing starting a family with her husband.

CHALLENGES IN APPLYING THE EVIDENCE-BASED APPROACH

Challenges to treating Molly's mood disorder included her prior history of family upheaval and self-harm following her parents' divorce; her attention deficit disorder features combined with the decreased concentration notable in depression that would require more redundancy (e.g., writing things down); her recent losses including the lack of proximity of family and friends due to being transplanted to a part of the country in which she didn't wish to reside, and being obliged to take a job that was not consistent with her postgraduate training and career aspirations.

A limitation of the therapy as provided in this research study was that it was offered as 20 sessions over 12 to 14 weeks. Twice weekly sessions of CBT for the first 2 months requires both a patient and therapist commitment to a schedule not everyone may be able to do. This therapy can be conducted using a more common weekly schedule but with potentially less potency.

In addition, the patient's improvement by session 15 afforded a modest opportunity to gradually taper treatment in this 3-month contract. More time is preferable in maintenance sessions to promote durable relapse prevention skills and greater confidence in her emerging emotional resilience.

CULTURAL DIVERSITY ISSUES

There are no aspects of this clinical treatment program which present problems regarding the issue of diversity. CBT for depression has been demonstrated to be effective with patients in childhood, adolescence, and adulthood and across a wide range of racial and ethnic groups.

FUTURE RESEARCH

CBT therapists working with adult children of divorce seeking treatment for depression often examine the dysfunctional strategies such patients used as children to help them spot and revise maladaptive beliefs about themselves and how they interact with others. Future research is needed to examine how these revised, more helpful core and intermediate beliefs can be made more durable once treatment has been terminated, as well as the kinds of subsequent practices (e.g., dysfunctional thought records) after treatment has concluded which may be associated with the maintenance of benefits.

KEY REFERENCES

Beck, J. (1995). *Cognitive therapy: Basics and beyond*. New York, NY: Guilford Press.

McCullough, J. P. (2000). *Treatment of chronic depression: Cognitive behavioral analysis system of psychotherapy (CBASP)*. New York, NY: Guilford Press.

McGoldrick, M., Pearce, J. K., & Giordano, J. (1982). *Ethnicity and family therapy*. New York, NY: Guilford Press.

CHAPTER 23

Dissociative Disorders

Bethany L. Brand and Amie C. Myrick

CLINICAL PROBLEM

Dissociation is a disruption of the integration between consciousness, memory, awareness of body and/or self, environment, and identity. Dissociative Identity Disorder (DID) and Dissociative Disorder, Not Otherwise Specified (DDNOS) have similar symptomatology, history, and treatment response and have been described the most extensively; therefore, they are the focus of this chapter.

DID and many cases of DDNOS begin in childhood following early exposure to severe, chronic trauma or severe attachment difficulties. When fight or flight is not possible, dissociation protects the child from the emotional and/or physical pain caused by trauma. When used repetitively, dissociation can result in fragmented memories and the development and persistence of discrete behavioral states that may become elaborated into dissociated self-states found in DID. Despite the media portrayal of such self-states, obvious presentations only occur in about 6% of DID patients; more commonly, these states present in subtle ways including sudden shifts in mood accompanied by alterations in the individual's characteristic style of behaving, thinking, speaking, and relating to others, often co-occurring with depersonalization and derealization, as well as poor recall for some aspects of recent and childhood events.

Comorbidity with other psychological disorders is common among those with DD including severe, treatment-resistant depression, posttraumatic stress disorder (PTSD) as well as other anxiety disorders, eating disorders, and substance abuse disorders. Typically, these patients struggle with destructive behavior patterns (e.g., self-injury, suicidality, dysfunctional relationships, repeated hospitalizations) and complex dissociated self-states. Medical disorders including fibromyalgia, chronic fatigue syndrome, gastrointestinal problems, gynecological problems, and conversion disorders are also frequently present. Given the complexity of their psychiatric difficulties, these patients usually require long-term treatment.

PREVALENCE

Studies of DD have been conducted in North America, Europe, and Asia and have identified DDNOS as the most prevalent DD, with rates of about 9.5% in inpatients and outpatients. DID prevalence rates vary across samples with ranges between 1% to 5% in most psychiatric inpatients. Four general population prevalence studies have found rates between 0.4% and 1.5% for DID and between 1.7% and 18.3% for any dissociative disorder.

CULTURAL DIVERSITY ISSUES

Women present more often with DD symptoms than do men. This gender difference is thought to be due to cultural factors such as men being less comfortable reporting childhood sexual abuse and men with DD being more likely to present to the criminal justice rather than the mental health system. Racial differences have not yet been adequately studied.

EVIDENCE-BASED TREATMENTS

Research for DD is still in its infancy. Studies examining specialized treatment for DD have considerable methodological limitations including noncontrolled designs, small samples, and reliance on inpatient and/or small samples of patients and therapists. Nonetheless, these studies provide preliminary evidence that specialized treatment for DD is associated with reductions in symptoms and, in some cases, reductions in Axis I and II disorders. Effect sizes for a variety of symptoms in DD treatment studies are in the moderate to large range, using within patient designs. There are no controlled trials for DD owing to the logistical challenges of designing short-term, controlled treatment for these complex patients.

Using a prospective, naturalistic design with the largest sample to date, the Treatment of Patients with Dissociative Disorders (TOP DD) Study collected data from 280 DD patients and 292 therapists. The majority of therapists reported having had specialized training in treating DD and appeared to use DD-focused interventions such as stabilizing safety, educating patients about dissociation and its management, and increasing patients' awareness and understanding of dissociated self-states. The cross-sectional results indicated that patients in the later stages of treatment had less dissociation, PTSD, and general distress symptomatology and better adaptive functioning (e.g., GAF scores) compared to those in the beginning stages. After 30 months of treatment, the DID/DDNOS patients demonstrated decreases in dissociation, PTSD, general distress, depression, self-harm, suicide attempts, hospitalizations, drug use, and a variety of risky behaviors as well as improved functioning, including GAF scores according to therapist and patient reports. In light of the personal suffering and economic cost associated with DD, it is noteworthy that DD treatment is associated with improved social and occupational functioning, as well as decreases in self-destructive behaviors, suicide attempts, and hospitalizations.

FUTURE RESEARCH

Expert consensus guidelines for treating DID have been published by the International Society for the Study of Trauma and Dissociation (ISSTD) that advocate using a carefully paced, staged approach to treatment. Furthermore, a survey of DD experts found that a core set of treatment techniques were consistently recommended for treating DID and DDNOS patients, including developing skills in grounding, emotion regulation, impulse control, managing relationships, and containment of traumatic intrusions; these recommendations are consistent with the ISSTD treatment guidelines. In addition, a recently published manual for assisting DID patients in early stabilization provides useful treatment guidance for patients and therapists. Finally, a prognostic model for patients in the earliest stage of DID treatment has been developed as well.

Future treatment studies could combine the prognostic model, the core treatment techniques recommended by experts, and the published manual to develop and investigate the efficacy of systematic treatment for DID/DDNOS. Given the severity of symptoms, the degree of impairment, and the economic costs associated with DD, rigorous research on the treatment of DD is urgently needed.

KEY REFERENCES

Brand, B., Classen, C. C., McNary, S. W., & Zaveri, P. (2009). A review of dissociative disorders treatment studies. *Journal of Nervous and Mental Disease, 197*, 646–654.

Brand, B. L., McNary, S. W., Myrick, A. C., Classen, C., Lanius, R., ... Putnam, F. W. (2013). A longitudinal naturalistic study of patients with dissociative disorders treated by community clinicians. *Psychological Trauma: Theory, Research, Practice, and Policy, 5*, 301–308.

International Society for the Study of Trauma and Dissociation. (2011). Guidelines for treating dissociative identity disorder in adults, third revision. *Journal of Trauma & Dissociation, 12*, 115–187.

Clinician Application

Dissociative Disorders

Elaine Ducharme

COMMENT ON THE EVIDENCE-BASED RECOMMENDATIONS

As noted in the Research Section, dissociation is a disruption of the integration between consciousness, memory, awareness of body and/or self, environment, and identity. A number of types of dissociative disorders have been identified. These include: Dissociative Amnesia, Dissociative Fugue, Depersonalization Disorder, Dissociative Identity Disorder (DID), and Dissociative Disorder, Not Otherwise Specified. Some professionals also consider possession states and out-of-body or near-death experiences to be dissociative states. The researchers identify age, attachment issues, gender, and culture as contributing factors. As a clinician, it is important to note that for DID to develop, the severe and generally ongoing trauma must occur before the age of 9 or 10. After that, although the person may suffer from Posttraumatic Stress Disorder (PTSD) or even have some dissociative experience related to the actual trauma, the ego structure is generally strong enough to avoid the fracturing that occurs in DID. Not pointed out by the researchers is that patients diagnosed with DID have spent an average of 6.8 years from initial presentation in the mental health system to the time they typically receive the correct diagnosis. Although the researchers note the cultural impact/comfort levels of reporting sexual abuse on men and women, there are different manifestations of symptomatology in diverse cultures. For example, what is seen as spirit possession in India may be considered DID in Western cultures.

The researchers correctly note that although research for Dissociative Disorders (DD) is in its infancy, specialized treatment is definitely associated with symptom reduction and, in some cases, reduction in Axis I and Axis II disorders. The Research Section points out that the expert consensus guidelines established by the International Society for the Study of Trauma and Dissociation (ISSTD) recommends a carefully paced, staged approach to therapy. The core techniques identified are developing skills in grounding, emotional regulation, impulse control, managing relationships, and containment of traumatic intrusions. Clinicians must remember that safety, both physical and emotional, must be at the center of all treatment. This includes finding any internal self-helping alters, identifying the patient's external support system, and establishing safety contracts with alters both inside and outside of the body. Other safety issues include things such as making sure patients with DID undergoing medical treatment communicate their diagnosis with the medical team as different alters may respond very differently to medications and even anesthesia. Patients have been known to have the body put to sleep under an anesthetic only to have an alter wake up in the middle of surgery completely unaffected by the medication. Presence of a coexisting substance abuse problem and highly suicidal alters further complicate treatment. It is important to note that medications may be used to treat various symptoms such as depression or anxiety and even nightmares (prazosin). Talk therapy is the primary mode of treatment.

CASE EXAMPLE

Subject Information and Brief History

Leslie was a 32-year-old Caucasian woman who had recently lost her job as a secretary at a small company. She had completed an inpatient treatment program for opiate abuse and was maintained on Suboxone, which is a combination of buprenorine and naloxone used to treat opiate addictions. She was dealing with legal issues related to taking Ritalin from a friend's home. She reported a history of sexual abuse by her grandfather, occurring from age 4 until his death when she was 13. She also experienced several rapes in her later teens and early 20s. She had been divorced from a verbally and emotionally abusive husband and was raising her son from this first marriage with her new husband. She reported seeking help for what she felt was increasingly disorganized behavior during the previous 4 years.

Presenting Problem

Leslie indicated she was exhausted from constant problems that were being created by her behaviors and actions. She had never had any legal problems prior to this drug issue. Prior to the first session, she had worked with another psychotherapist for about 3 years and had been diagnosed with PTSD, depression, anxiety, and opiate dependency. She gave me a journal written earlier in her life that identified several suicide attempts of which she had no memory. When she began our treatment she was also participating as the only female in a support group for drug abusers. She felt unsafe as the group engaged in trust exercises of falling into each other's arms, and so forth. Ultimately, the psychologist running the group was found to be in relapse and engaging in unethical behaviors, such as consistently being very late for meetings, not showing up at all scheduling meetings at his home while recovering from surgery, and making inappropriate comments.

Treatment Intervention and Course

The beginning of treatment clearly involved facilitating a safe environment for her. We also worked on teaching her relaxation techniques. During this first year, I began to notice Leslie wearing different styles of clothing and having slightly different speech patterns. She reported "losing time" on a fairly regular basis. About 5 months into treatment, several alters made an appearance and I made a diagnosis of DID. About 9 months into treatment, during the fall, a time identified for increased abuse in her past, Leslie developed severe depression and anxiety. We agreed on psychiatric hospitalization for stabilization and adjustment of her medication. Unfortunately, the hospital, after admission, made it clear they did not believe in the diagnosis of DID. They engaged in group treatment that involved convincing her that the alters did not exist. She ultimately developed "seizures" and became catatonic as a way of removing herself from the treatment. She eventually left the hospital after 1 week and against medical advice. From this negative experience, trust in me and psychotherapy was severely compromised.

As her comfort level with me returned, about 1 year into therapy, alters expressed a desire to tell their stories and we began memory work. Leslie struggled with the idea that she might have "parts." However, she acknowledged that it helped make sense of her experiences. During this time her husband reported that her behavior was becoming increasingly bizarre. Her son found her hiding in a closet, crying and speaking in a child's voice. Her husband found her in the kitchen in the middle of the night climbing onto the counter and trying to make a peanut butter and jelly sandwich. This little girl alter was happily comforted by her husband. But the next day, she had no memory of these events. As parts pushed forward to talk in session, Leslie's home life seemed even more disorganized. Interestingly, her older teen part was very helpful in calming some of the younger parts who reported being very scared that the abuse was going to continue.

Gradually, Leslie began to accept her diagnosis. We explored who knew about each other "inside" and developed ways the parts could communicate with each other and me. We utilized relaxation techniques for grounding at the end of sessions, especially after different parts had been "out." As with many patients I have treated with DID, these relaxation techniques proved helpful in calming the system during the inevitable crises in the evening or weekends during some of the very difficult memory work. She generally held a blanket that was in my office to help her remember we were here in the present, not back when she was a child. We utilized previously identified safe places inside the system for parts to rest and a safe place for Leslie to go when other parts were out. We worked on more comfortable transitions. We also met two to three times per week during the intense memory work.

It was during the second and third years of treatment that most of the memory work took place. Six major parts, including two teens, two preteens, and children, ages 4 and 6, took turns talking about horrific experiences with the grandfather and uncle, as well as other men in her church. She also reported feeling the presence of an "entity." She felt it was her grandfather and was terrified that she was possessed. Her husband reported finding his wife smoking a cigar on their porch and speaking in a husky voice. Shortly after, I received a call from this part telling me that he was the one in control of the body. He did not like being talked about as a bad guy, he had the ability to hurt Leslie and he certainly was not dead! I invited him to come to our next session after getting him to agree not to hurt Leslie before then. He arrived for the next session, sat in my chair and tried hard to intimidate me. Ultimately, he acknowledged he was tired and wanted to give some control back to

Leslie. Working with parts that have developed with an identity of the perpetrator (persecutors) is difficult but critical work. It is important to remember that all parts developed to protect the individual in some way. A huge clinical error occurs when psychotherapists, frightened by the threats of these persecutors, try to get rid of them or lock them up. They must be heard and generally have useful information.

Treatment is generally difficult with patients with DID. It is especially so if there is an accompanying substance abuse problem. Throughout treatment, we had to deal with cravings and drug seeking behaviors to handle her high levels of anxiety. There were also financial crises related to Leslie's inability to hold a job and difficult relationships with extended family. These issues needed to be dealt with as they arose and therefore slowed the process of memory work. As she became healthier, she was able to set clear boundaries with her family of origin. They accepted her diagnosis and her memories of what had happened. Her mother had also been sexually abused by this same man (her father), and the family was able to talk about her parents' inability to protect her. She refused to attend family functions where other abusive relatives would be present. Throughout treatment, Leslie was a protective and loving mother, determined to nurture her son.

Outcome

Leslie experienced several health issues during treatment, including a miscarriage, episodes of endometriosis, and thyroid cancer. In spite of this, during the third year of treatment, Leslie was able to obtain and maintain a job. Her dissociative episodes were rare and if they happened during very stressful times, her behavior was never out of control and she could look inside and piece together what had happened. She and her husband continued to work on developing better communication skills, coparenting techniques and finding ways to cope with her DID. In particular, her husband had developed a fondness for one of her young child alters and seemed to encourage her "coming out." This was very difficult for Leslie who tried hard to stay in control. She reported feeling much more in control of her behaviors. At this point she began to discuss integration. Although there were lots of fears about what this would mean to each part, she decided that she definitely wanted to integrate her parts. As of this writing, she is preparing to work on this.

CHALLENGES IN APPLYING THE EVIDENCE-BASED APPROACH

Treatment of DID is complicated by many factors, including presence of substance abuse, numbers and types of alters, family relationships, and contact with the abusers. However, the basic factors identified by the ISSTD guidelines are critical in providing the safety for this type of treatment. One important concern for psychotherapists relates to whether the memories discussed are true. I maintain that this is not a critical part of treatment. If it is discussed as an experience without judgment, the patient experiences relief in the telling and gains an increased sense of safety; that is what matters. A manual for assisting patients in early stabilization may be useful for some patients. For many, however, establishing a safe and trusting relationship with the psychotherapist is the most critical piece in early treatment.

CULTURAL DIVERSITY ISSUES

A cross-cultural perspective is particularly important in the evaluation of DD because dissociative states are a common and accepted expression of cultural activities or religious experience in many societies. In most instances, dissociative states are not pathological and do not lead to significant distress, impairment, or help-seeking behavior. However, a number of culturally defined syndromes characterized by dissociation do cause distress and impairment and are recognized indigenously as manifestations of pathology. The symptomatolgy may take different forms in different cultures, such as recurrent brief episodes of dissociative stupor, or spirit possession in India. This may explain the reason that the disorder tends to be most frequently diagnosed in North America. Though, research suggests that DID is diagnosed much less frequently in countries other than the United States.

FUTURE RESEARCH

Clearly, patients suffering from DID respond well to treatment in a safe environment. Most clinicians utilize a psychodynamic approach to treatment. Treatment is generally long term and expensive. Thus, future research should focus on finding more efficient and less stressful ways to help process trauma. Memory work is generally very painful even when a therapist tries hard to limit the reexperiencing of traumatic memories/events. In the past, some therapists engaged patients in abreaction, a process involving hours of "reliving the trauma." Although patients generally must go back and talk about the trauma, much can be done to help the patient feel safe. Techniques such as letting the patient "put the memories onto a video/DVD which can be stored safely in the office" provides a sense of control and establishes boundaries for where the memories can be viewed. Limiting sessions to 1½ hours also allows for a manageable amount of memory work to be done and gives the patient time to have an appropriate alter be back in charge of the body before leaving the session. Guidelines to help provide for the safety and comfort of the psychotherapists treating these individuals, and helping them avoid the vicarious traumatization which can occur when they listen and try to provide a container for the patient's horrific experiences, would also be beneficial. It is really critical for therapists specializing in the treatment of trauma to maintain good self-care. Future research should also focus on the discrepancy of prevalence of this disorder between cultures. It will be important to determine whether or not the diagnosis of DID is being missed, identified as something else (e.g., possession state) or overdiagnosed. Viewing this diagnosis within the criminal justice system is also important and should consider assessment of underdiagnosis as well as malingering.

KEY REFERENCES

International Society for Study of Dissociation. (2005). Guidelines for treating dissociative identity disorder in adults. *Journal of Trauma & Dissociation, 6*, 69–149.
Putnam, F .W. (1989). *Diagnosis and treatment of multiple personality disorder*. New York, NY: Guilford Press.
Spanos, N. P. (1996). *Multiple identities and false memories*. Washington, DC: American Psychological Association.

CHAPTER 24

Gambling

Shane A. Thomas and Colette J. Browning

CLINICAL PROBLEM

The *DSM-5* (American Psychiatric Association, 2013) defines Gambling Disorder as "Persistent and recurrent gambling behavior leading to clinically significant impairment or distress" with at least 4 out of 9 associated criteria required to be attained in order to merit the diagnosis. There are now 3 levels of severity of this disorder specified in *DSM-5* ("mild," "moderate," and "severe"). In the United States, problem gambling is often considered to be a subclinical form of pathological gambling but in many other jurisdictions, the term "problem gambling" (PG) is used to encompass all people with a significant gambling problem. Although problem gambling can be expressed in a variety of gambling modalities, the evidence is that electronic gaming machines figure prominently among the gambling patterns of problem gamblers and there is concern that online gambling forms may lead to even more problem gambling in the future.

Problem gamblers often experience important social consequences. Divorce rates are high, family violence and relationship problems more generally are common sequelae. Bankruptcy rates and participation in criminal activity related to money are also higher among this group than in the general community.

PG has been demonstrated to have a high prevalence of comorbidity with other psychological problems, mental health disorders, and addictions with highly elevated rates of a range of disorders including alcohol use disorders, mood disorders and depression, bipolar disorder/manic episodes, substance use disorders, illicit drug abuse/dependence, nicotine dependence, anxiety disorders, and antisocial personality disorder. However, evidence is limited for the causal nexus in these comorbidities. The etiology of PG is poorly understood with some claiming that PG is actually a loose cluster of conditions with varying etiologies.

PREVALENCE

The prevalence of PG is affected by the measurement tools used and the study methodology. There has been some controversy about the validity of some of the study methods used in various epidemiological studies. In studies using the Canadian Problem Gambling Index as the classification tool, the rates of PG have been found to vary quite widely across different jurisdictions between 0.4% and 1.4% of the adult population with a mean of 0.9% across all studies. The variations may reflect methodological differences in the studies, different regulatory systems, as well as the maturity of the gambling industry in the different jurisdictions. Problem gambling rates have been shown to grow steadily following legalization of gambling and to then plateau 15 to 20 years later.

Globally, the liberalization of access to gambling opportunities has seen a steady increase in the rates of PG in many jurisdictions over the last several decades. PG is frequently underdiagnosed and undertreated with only 7% to 12% of people with PG ever having sought help for their condition and PG is frequently treated in isolation from the patient's other comorbid mental health problems perhaps because of lack of screening and missed diagnosis.

CULTURAL DIVERSITY ISSUES

The distribution of PG within the communities in different jurisdictions is somewhat affected by different regulatory systems in local access to gambling opportunities. The evidence base for differential effectiveness of treatments for different groups of patients is generally weak in this field. However, there is good evidence globally that adolescent and young adult males are more at risk of PG than other groups. While globally men generally have higher rates of PG than do women, the differential rates of problem gambling between males and females seem to be affected by access to Electronic Gaming Machines (EGMs). Higher relative female rates appear to be related to higher access to EGMs. Evidence concerning cultural and racial differences in problem gambling rates is limited and somewhat contradictory, but indigenous peoples seem to have higher rates. PG can occur in any social, gender, and cultural grouping.

EVIDENCE-BASED TREATMENTS

A recent Australian National Health and Medical Research Council-approved clinical guideline has extensively reviewed the global evidence for effectiveness of different treatments for PG. A total of 34 randomized controlled trials, reported in 37 articles, met the inclusion criteria for the clinical questions posed in the guideline review, although significant methodological shortcomings were noted in many of the studies including randomization inadequacies and short follow-up and study length. Appropriate high-quality evidence could be found to address only 6 of the 22 clinical questions regarding treatment in the guideline review. The guideline used a four level strength of evidence classification scheme as follows:

GRADE	EVIDENCE GRADE DESCRIPTION
A	Body of evidence can be trusted to guide practice
B	Body of evidence can be trusted to guide practice in most situations
C	Body of evidence provides some support for recommendation but care should be taken in its application
D	Body of evidence is weak and recommendation must be applied with caution

The treatment recommendations and their associated evidence grades were as follows:

Individual or group cognitive behavior therapy (CBT) should be used to reduce gambling behavior, gambling severity, and psychological distress in people with gambling problems (Grade B evidence)

Motivational interviewing and motivational enhancement therapy should be used to reduce gambling behavior and gambling severity in people with gambling problems (Grade B evidence)

Practitioner-delivered psychological interventions should be used to reduce gambling severity and gambling behavior in people with gambling problems (Grade B evidence)

Practitioner-delivered psychological interventions should be used over self-help psychological interventions to reduce gambling severity and gambling behavior in people with gambling problems (Grade B evidence)

Group psychological interventions could be used to reduce gambling behavior and gambling severity in people with gambling problems (Grade C evidence)

Antidepressant medications should not be used to reduce gambling severity in people with gambling problems alone (Grade B evidence)

Naltrexone could be used to reduce gambling severity in people with gambling problems (Grade C evidence)

In summary, there is credible evidence for the effectiveness of CBT and Motivational Interviewing in the treatment of PG and for the lack of utility of the sole use of antidepressants in treating people with PG.

FUTURE RESEARCH

Further credible and methodologically robust randomized controlled trials are necessary to establish the efficacy and effectiveness of both psychological and pharmacological treatments for PG. Further work is also required to demonstrate whether treatment matching of treatment modalities to specific types of patients is appropriate. While the utility of CBT and to a lesser extent Motivational Interviewing approaches have been established in the treatment of PG, there is considerable work yet to be done in establishing whether the use of pharmacological treatments for treatment of PG is appropriate. Naltrexone may be a useful pharmacological therapy for PG but cannot be recommended as a front-line therapy under current evidence. The utility of screening in terms of increasing rates of treatment uptake is also yet to be established, although the current consensus position is that screening for PG in mental health treatment settings is useful as is screening for mental health disorders among those presenting for treatment of PG.

KEY REFERENCES

Blaszczynski, A., & Nower, L. (2002). A pathways model of problem and pathological gambling. *Addiction, 97,* 487–499.

Lorains, F. K., Cowlishaw, S., & Thomas, S. A. (2011). Prevalence of comorbid disorders in problem and pathological gambling: Systematic review and meta-analysis of population surveys. *Addiction, 106,* 490–498.

Thomas, S. A., Merkouris, S. S., Radermacher, H. L., Dowling, N. A., Misso, M. L., ... Jackson, A. C. (2011). Australian guideline for treatment of problem gambling: An abridged outline. *Medical Journal of Australia, 195,* 664–665.

Gambling

Gina Fricke

COMMENT ON THE EVIDENCE-BASED RECOMMENDATIONS

In my experience, cognitive behavioral therapy (CBT) is quite effective in working with those diagnosed with pathological gambling. I also find that motivational interviewing and motivational enhancement therapy are useful daily in my practice with gamblers. As stated in the review of the research, those with gambling problems vary significantly. In my experience, these treatment approaches allow for the therapeutic joining or the necessary relationship building process that encourages trust by the client in the therapist that is necessary for those with gambling problems to make changes. While working with those with gambling problems, it is imperative to allow the client to be in control of the change process, with the psychotherapist acting as an educator and a guide.

CASE EXAMPLE

Subject Information and Brief History

Sally was a 55-year-old married female, with two adult children and three grandchildren. She was employed in a professional position in a large business. She reported a history of enjoying gambling, but her husband had recently threatened to end the marriage as a result of her gambling and lying. Sally reported that the first time she gambled was while on vacation when she was 21 years old. She spent $30 on gambling at that time. At 23 years old, she gambled again on vacation. Twenty years later she gambled while on vacation. She spent $30 per day for three days on slots and video poker. About five years later, she gambled again while on vacation, this time spending $50 per day over the three-day vacation. Sally continued to gamble on slots and video poker. Five years later, Sally, on vacation, gambled $100 per day over three days. Each of the next 11 years, she gambled $100 per day on a three-day vacation. During the beginning of these years, Sally came home with winnings, but later she began spending more money than she brought with her. At one point, she remembers winning $600 two years in a row. She remembers gambling that money back before leaving the video poker machine. During this time, Sally began gambling closer to home. At first, she brought $10 to $20 to the local casino to play video poker one to two times per year. Later she began taking between $100 and $1000 to gamble on video poker once or twice a month. Sally was keeping this gambling from her husband by having a secret bank account. Her husband knew how much time she was spending gambling but had no idea how much money she was gambling.

Sally recognized that her gambling had increased significantly as a result of her children leaving home and the fact that her identity as a mother was not the same as it had been in the past. This was a serious loss in identity for her. Sally made it clear during her treatment that gambling allowed her to not have to think or feel about her own mother's death. It was a way to escape from the reality that hurt so much. Prior to treatment, Sally had made no connection between these two losses and their connection to the onset of her problem gambling.

Presenting Problem

Sally reported a history of enjoying gambling. However, her husband had recently threatened to end the marriage of 35 years as a result of her gambling and lying. Sally's husband had experienced long nights waiting up for his wife to come home from the casino, sometimes two to three nights a week. As often as once a week he would go to the casino and coax Sally out so that they could go home and go to bed. He had also become aware of the secret account and had an idea of the large amount of money she had been spending over the last several years. He had asked her to stop gambling but she was unwilling to commit to abstinence. He was concerned that his wife's gambling would prevent them from retiring when they were ready, and that time was not far. Sally self-identified that she saw only limited problems with her gambling behavior.

She was given two gambling assessment instruments. She scored 13 out of 20 on the South Oaks Gambling Screen—a score of 5 or more indicates that the client is a probable pathological gambler. Sally scored 12 on the Gamblers Anonymous 20 questions—a score of 7 or more indicates a client might be a compulsive gambler. She met 7 of the *DSM-5* criteria for gambling disorder, with the presence of 6 or more indicating a diagnosis of Gambling Disorder moderate severity. Sally identified being preoccupied with gambling, increasing the amounts of money gambled, trying to limit or stop gambling without success, chasing losses, gambling to escape from problems, lying about gambling, and jeopardizing a significant relationship owing to gambling.

Treatment Intervention and Course

Sally's first session involved a comprehensive psychosocial gambling evaluation. This included the gambling assessment instruments noted above, the taking of her gambling history, family history, and medical history, as well as information about any other chemicals or behaviors that were being used compulsively. The evaluation also included a suicide assessment, noting of current medications, and any other information from her history or current life circumstances that appeared relevant. As part of this session, Sally said that she wanted to limit her gambling. She decided to limit her gambling because she did not want to give up her gambling but was recognizing she was spending more money than she intended when she gambled and she wanted to get her husband off her back. Sally was not ready to let go of her one and only coping skill that helped her feel better, at least temporarily, every time she went.

We began her treatment with a harm reduction approach. Harm reduction is an approach that allows the client to determine, within the treatment setting, if she is able to continue doing the behavior in a limited or controlled way. Sally set rules for her own gambling: how much money to risk, how often to gamble, how much time to spend gambling, and considered accountability options. Some options for accountability are telling someone before she gambles and when she plans to return, taking someone with her, or planning her gambling in advance and sharing that plan with another person. Sally attempted to limit her gambling for approximately 11 months. The amount of time necessary for this process to happen will be different for each client. It took her 11 months to determine harm reduction to be unsuccessful and she changed her goal to abstinence. Sally learned she was unable to control gambling through a process of trial and error while experiencing the support of treatment. This was a challenging process for Sally because she wanted to maintain her relationship with gambling as it was the one thing that consistently helped her feel better. (Sally was avoiding the feelings she had as a result of her children leaving home and her mother's death. Gambling gave her the experience of temporarily not having to feel the sad, isolated, and anxious feelings that resulted from these stages of life shifts. Sally was assessed for anxiety and depression and had obvious symptoms. As she began addressing the losses she had experienced, she had an easier time coping with her gambling and with other stressors as they came.) She needed those 11 months to develop trust in her psychotherapist, and to be willing to let go of the fantasy associated with wanting to gamble in a controlled way. During those 11 months, Sally learned about addiction, expanded her social support system, used spiritual coping mechanisms, worked toward being honest with her husband, and told her husband about her secret bank account.

Sally accomplished each one of these steps. I had originally suggested that she close the secret bank account but Sally decided rather than closing the account she would begin showing her husband statements from this account. This was an acceptable compromise. A Motivational Interviewing approach was used with Sally. This allowed her to move at her own pace through the change process. I have found that when an adult is told to do something, they generally find a way to rebel against it. However, when the same adult is given flexibility, patience, and choices, he or she is much more likely to move through the change process. Sally was given this latitude and was respected along the way. If I would have attempted to rush her, she may have gotten stuck trying to defend her gambling rather than accepting that gambling was out of her control.

During Sally's psychotherapy, she was taught several CBT techniques to encourage her to think about her gambling and the reasons that she gambled. She was taught several Dialectical Behavioral Therapy (DBT) skills. These DBT skills include chain analysis, which is making a connection between cognitions, emotions, and behaviors in the process from trigger or initial thought through the entire situation to the outcome. Another DBT skill Sally learned is called PLEASE MASTER; this skill teaches very basic self-care skills and encourages individuals to do something that creates a sense of mastery every day. Sally also learned a DBT skill called Wise Mind, where she learned to differentiate her rational mind or factual mind from her emotional mind and then determine a healthy response to a situation rather than an impulsive reaction. Although an executive at work, Sally demonstrated poor planning, follow through, and self-care skills in her personal life. The impulsivity associated with pathological gambling causes this to be quite common. Part of our work with clients is to teach basic self-care skills. It is important to discover what they are already doing well and then build on it. As part of gambling treatment, it is important to teach scheduling or filling time so that the client is able to understand, especially early in recovery how to prevent unscheduled time from leading her back to gambling. This can involve having the client write a schedule on a piece of paper or a calendar between or during sessions., Another important component of gambling treatment is teaching accountability. Many gamblers have been hiding what they have been doing with their time from their family and friends. I teach a concept I heard about through the Alcoholics Anonymous program which is called "living a transparent life." It is important that gamblers be willing to only do things that they would be proud to share with others rather than doing things they believe they have to hide from others. The next important area to cover in gambling treatment is financial protections. Clients must find a way to protect their income, home, and family from the consequences that pathological gambling can cause. This may include developing a specific budget, telling another person the financial plan, having someone else hold the money, getting a payee. Gamblers can be very creative about how they address financial protections. Healthy coping skills is an important topic to cover in gambling treatment. It is important to recognize that gambling is an unhealthy coping skill because it creates significant consequences, but it does temporarily make the gambler feel better. Teaching gamblers about healthy coping skills, which are things that make us feel better when we are doing them and after as well, is very important. It is also useful to teach this and time management simultaneously. Spiritual connectedness is imperative as a component to gambling treatment. From my perspective, the client having any belief in a power greater than him or her is sufficient. This is covered thoroughly in Gamblers Anonymous steps 2 and 3. The importance of a social support system is an integral component to gambling treatment. Many gamblers feel lonely and isolated like Sally, they may have friends but they do not talk with their friends about their problems. It is important that they develop some authentic relationships where they can be themselves rather than having to hide themselves from others. Sally was also exposed to the Gamblers Anonymous 12 steps during her treatment. Sally worked through the GA 12 steps in treatment and attended GA meetings in the community. Although daily meetings are available in this community, Sally attended these meetings once a week.

Outcome

At this time, Sally has over one year of abstinence from gambling and is well on her way to recovery. Sally continues to attend treatment on an as-needed basis about once every 4 to 6 weeks. She has worked through her grief in several areas of her life and even addressed feelings that her husband was trying to control her. She has worked to improve her relationships with others and has developed effective boundary-setting skills. Her mood has improved significantly and her feelings about herself and her relationships with others have also improved. I believe that without Motivational Interviewing, Motivational Enhancement, and CBT, a multi-method approach, this would not have been possible for Sally.

CHALLENGES IN APPLYING THE EVIDENCE-BASED APPROACH

Motivational interviewing and motivational enhancement therapy are effective treatment approaches, but require the psychotherapist to be quite patient. These approaches, in my opinion, are more effective than confrontation style therapies because they allow the client to be approached in a way that develops the treatment relationship and prevents defensiveness that can cause the client to avoid change. It is important to not create a situation where the client feels "shamed."

The only challenge I see in applying CBT—especially at the beginning of treatment—is that some clients with gambling problems have little self-awareness.

It is our job as clinicians to help them increase self-awareness about distorted thinking and how this effects emotions and behaviors. Doing so, especially about thoughts and emotions that they are having at the time that they experience the urge to gamble, is imperative for the client to have a successful outcome in treatment. It is helpful to use a DBT chain analysis. The DBT chain analysis is a process used to help the client gain insight into his or her thoughts, emotions, and behaviors. It involves writing down each of the components of the problem in a systematic way. For example, "I was at work when I began thinking about gambling after work, I was stressed about making a mistake that my boss pointed out. I felt that stress in my chest and all I could think to do is to get away from this feeling by gambling" and so forth.

CULTURAL DIVERSITY ISSUES

Cultural aspects can be very important when working with gamblers. The most important, in my opinion, is the lack of availability of a diverse workforce that is working with gamblers. The psychotherapists in the state I work in are all Caucasian and middle class. It is important that we expand the services, so they are being offered by and to individuals who represent the diversity of our state.

Different families have different levels of exposure to gambling. Some children grow up with gambling happening during holidays or even every weekend and/or week day as family and friends get together. Others are only exposed to gambling in their church or at carnivals and others are only exposed on television and in the movies and billboards. In our society, everyone is exposed to gambling at one level or another. I believe the level has more to do with the family the individual grows up in than it has to do with the color of a person's skin or their family's historical connections. However, generally, what we are taught is that those of African American, Asian American, and Native American descent are more likely to develop addictive gambling behaviors than the general population. It is unclear the reason, it may be that more families with these cultural backgrounds have early and frequent exposure to gambling in their home as a socially acceptable activity.

FUTURE RESEARCH

Further research to determine why these three cultural groups seem to have a higher rate of problem or pathological gambling than the general population would be helpful. It is possible that it has more to do with the early exposure but it is also possible there is an additional cultural vulnerability. Research on the effectiveness of prevention efforts in the area of pathological gambling would also be helpful. It would also be helpful to learn the most effective way to help those with major psychiatric diagnosis who also have gambling problems in the most effective and efficient way because, these populations tend to be some of the most challenging clients to treat.

KEY REFERENCES

Hotchkiss, S. (2002). *Why is it always about you? The seven deadly sins of narcissism.* New York, NY: Free Press.

Linehan, M. (1993). *Skills training manual for treating borderline personality disorder.* New York, NY: Guilford Books.

Whelan, J., Meyers, A., & Steenbergh, T. (2007). *Problem and pathological gambling.* Cambridge, MA: Hogrefe & Huber.

CHAPTER 25

Generalized Anxiety Disorder

*Arezou Mortazavi, Soo Jeong Youn, Michelle G. Newman,
and Louis G. Castonguay*

CLINICAL PROBLEM

Generalized Anxiety Disorder (GAD) is defined in the *DSM-5* as persistent and excessive anxiety and worry about a number of domains in the person's life, present for at least 6 months. The worry and anxiety are difficult to control and cause significant distress and/or impairment in the individual's functioning. In addition, in order to meet *DSM-5* criteria, at least three of the following symptoms must also be present for at least 6 months: restlessness, being easily fatigued, difficulty concentrating, irritability, muscle tension, and disturbed sleep. The symptoms cannot be better explained by another mental disorder, medical disorder, and/or substance abuse/dependence. The course of this disorder is chronic and often debilitating, and is associated with reduced quality of life. Diagnosis in children follows similar criteria with the exception of one associated symptom being present rather than the three required for adults. This disorder is commonly seen in primary care settings as compared with other anxiety disorders and results in higher utilization and cost of health care resources.

Comorbidity with Major Depressive Disorder (MDD) and other anxiety and psychiatric disorders may be as high as 90%. There has already been some investigation done on different conceptualizations of GAD, such as viewing GAD and MDD as a unified disorder or classifying GAD as a mood disorder. The basis of these arguments stems from the high overlap in symptoms between these conditions and their high comorbidity. However, exploration in this area has yielded mixed theories. Angst, Gamma, Ajdacic, Rossler, and Regier suggest that GAD and Bipolar Disorder may share more similarities than GAD and MDD. Further, a review by Hettema found no basis for unifying MDD and GAD. He argues that although the two share characteristics, these are diagnostically unspecific. Kessler et al. found that while GAD and MDD may have a possibly identical genetic basis, they greatly differ in their environmental determinants. GAD has also been shown to be frequently comorbid with substance abuse. It may be aggravated by poor family environment, comorbidity with Cluster C personality disorders, and comorbid Axis I disorders.

GAD is one of the least reliably diagnosed anxiety disorders, perhaps owing to cultural and developmental factors. Evidence suggests that the use of structured assessment measures complements clinical judgment and assists in differential diagnosis. GAD is also unique from other anxiety disorders in that the worry is future-focused rather than related to past events and these individuals view worry as having positive utility for their coping. Assessment may be improved by determining the focus of the worry for the individual as well as inquiry regarding current and lifetime symptoms of depression.

PREVALENCE

GAD has been found to have an incidence of 5% in the general population. It has a lifetime prevalence of 5% to 6.1%, 12-month prevalence of 3.1%, and a current prevalence of about 2% to 3%. Projected lifetime prevalence at age 75 is 8.3%. Current comorbidity for GAD has been reported to range from 8% to 22% for dysthymia, 8.6% to 46% for major depression, 10.7% to 27% for social phobia, and 11% to 36% for panic disorder—the four most common comorbid Axis I diagnoses. Women are affected more than men with a ratio of 1:1.9 for lifetime and 1:2.2 for 12-month prevalence; however, men show higher comorbidity with substance abuse.

CULTURAL DIVERSITY ISSUES

Individuals with GAD may present different symptoms or manifestations of the disorder across cultures, with variation observed in rates, clinical presentation, and interpretation of symptoms. GAD also presents differently among gender, ethnic, and social groups. For example, individuals from Asian cultures and women tend to present with more somatic symptoms, whereas Americans and men tend to present with more psychological symptoms. Some of the proposed explanations for the cultural differences may be due to the variance in assessment and diagnostic criteria validity, and perception and experience of the disorder.

EVIDENCE BASED TREATMENTS

A recent review conducted by Turk and Mennin indicates that GAD is the least researched of the anxiety disorders. GAD has also been found to be the most resistant to treatment among the anxiety disorders, with remission rates of 0.38 at 5 years post treatment. Acute treatment of GAD targets reduction of symptoms while long-term care focuses on full remission.

Cognitive behavior therapy (CBT) has been extensively researched for treatment of GAD and found to be more effective compared to waitlist, pill placebo, placebo treatment, and analytic psychotherapy. However, the success of this treatment remains at 50% symptom reductions with high rates of relapse. CBT for GAD is currently informed by four different conceptual models of GAD: Cognitive Avoidance Theory, Metacognitive Model, Intolerance of Uncertainty Model, and Emotional Dysregulation Model. These models overlap in that they view worry as a persevering type of thought that occurs following a triggering thought, feeling, or event. Furthermore, all of these models conceptualize worry as a means for coping with future negative events that may arise.

The investigation of the impact of comorbidity on GAD treatment outcome has yielded inconclusive results. A study conducted by Newman, Przeworski, Fisher, and Borkovec has shown that comorbidity is associated with greater severity of symptomatology at treatment entry. However, these comorbid clients show greater change and thus, the efficacy of CBT for these individuals is not reduced. However, another study conducted by Provencher, Ladouceur, and Dugas found that CBT is less effective for patients with a diagnosis of GAD and other comorbid diagnoses, including panic disorder, at 6 months follow-up.

Medications for treatment of GAD may be used either alone or in adjunction with psychotherapy. The use of antidepressants such as selective serotonin reuptake inhibitors (SSRIs, such as sertraline, paroxetine, escitalopram) or serotonin–norepinephrine reuptake inhibitors (SNRIs, such as venlafaxine or duloxetine) is considered to be the first line of treatment. These have been shown to have limited efficacy, with less than 40% remission rates, with a high risk of relapse and adverse effects. Current research is exploring the effects of atypical antipsychotics, either as monotherapy or as augmentation in the treatment of GAD.

Other empirically supported treatments include mindfulness, relaxation techniques through the use of meditation, yoga, biofeedback, and exercise.

FUTURE RESEARCH

Future research should address the changing theoretical conceptualizations of GAD. For example, a new model has been proposed by Newman and Llera that depicts GAD as an attempt by the individual to use chronic worry as a means for avoiding an emotional contrast from a positive state to a negative state. Another area for further exploration should focus on the development of more effective treatment options for GAD, such as mindfulness-based CBT, focus on interpersonal styles within GAD treatment, Cognitive Bias Modification interventions, and Acceptance-Based Behavioral Therapy. Research should also focus on the identification and application of the effective components of CBT. Integration of interpersonal and emotional processing has been investigated through client recognition of interpersonal needs and behavior patterns, development of more effective processing skills and exposure to avoided emotional content. This area holds particular promise given that individuals with GAD report difficulty experiencing uncomfortable emotions as well as difficulty in interpersonal relationships. However, investigation thus far of the effects of adding these components to treatment for GAD has provided mixed results. A recent study by Newman et al. found effect sizes for integrative therapy that were higher than average results for CBT alone, while another study found no significant differences when interpersonal and emotional processing techniques were added to standard CBT.

KEY REFERENCES

Borkovec, T. D., & Ruscio, A. M. (2001). Psychotherapy for generalized anxiety disorder. *Journal of Clinical Psychiatry, 62*(Suppl. 11), 37–45.

Katzman, M. A. (2009). Current considerations in the treatment of generalized anxiety disorder. *CNS Drugs, 23*, 103–120.

Newman, M. G., & Llera, S. J. (2011). A novel theory of experiential avoidance in generalized anxiety disorder: A review and synthesis of research supporting a contrast avoidance model of worry. *Clinical Psychology Review, 31*(3), 371–382. doi: 10.1016/j.cpr.2011.01.008

Generalized Anxiety Disorder

Christine Molnar

COMMENT ON THE EVIDENCE-BASED RECOMMENDATIONS

Cognitive behavior therapy (CBT) alone is insufficient to meet the treatment needs of about half of the clients who seek therapy for Generalized Anxiety Disorder (GAD) at our outpatient clinic. When the Interpersonal and Emotional Processing (IEP) Therapy strategies developed by Newman and her colleagues are added to CBT, along with a brief Mindfulness-Based Stress Reduction (MBSR/MBCT) protocol, about 80% of the clients meet the treatment goal of no longer meeting diagnostic criteria for GAD and the disorders that are so often comorbid with it, such as other anxiety disorders, cluster B and C personality disorders, and depression. Brief MBSR (bMBSR) is based upon the longer MBSR and related MBCT protocol that reduces symptoms of a range of emotional disorders. Regarding pharmacotherapy, it is rare that clients have not already exhausted multiple pharmacotherapy options without adequate relief before presenting for psychotherapy.

It is agreed that GAD is often not diagnosed reliably and standardized assessment measures can complement clinical judgment and assist in differential diagnosis. Owing to inadequate clinical assessment, many with GAD and comorbid personality disorders have been misdiagnosed with either Bipolar Disorder or Attention Deficit Disorder (ADD) and do not receive treatment matched to their needs. Often, clients have received non-evidence-based therapies (EBT) from previous providers who have incorrectly diagnosed their concentration difficulties and "rushing thoughts" (worries) and associated behavioral reactivity as ADD or mania. Moreover, even if GAD is diagnosed, it is common for clients to have actually learned to strengthen rumination in response to anxiety symptoms in non-EBTs. For example, in a typical story, one woman spent 9 years with a therapist who described her as "damaged and manipulative" and who focused therapy time almost exclusively on past explanations for current anxiety symptoms. The client learned to become more internally focused on questions such as "Why am I so anxious and what does it mean about me?" This client worried about the catastrophic consequences for her future if she could not "figure it out" with more thinking. She presented with comorbid depression, as would be predicted from findings about rumination.

CASE EXAMPLE

Subject Information and Brief History

Steve, a single Caucasian male, presented for intake during a fall break 2 weeks before his 21st birthday. He wanted to complete intensive and short-term treatment, specifically mindfulness-based CBT (m-CBT), over the upcoming winter break because he and his family had heard about the mental and physical benefits of mindfulness meditation. Steve was unhappy at the undergraduate school where he was enrolled and in the process of applying for entrance to an Ivy League University. His grades were excellent but his life was unbalanced and did not give him the chance to learn he could function well without what he called a "one-dimensional" focus on academics. Steve defined one-dimensional as an exclusive focus on academic work above all else. He did not allow himself to engage in potentially enjoyable activities when his school work was not completed. He was on a stable dose of daily Wellbutrin and took Adderall as needed for ADD. His parents participated in the first 20 minutes of the initial 2-hour intake interview. After his parents left, Steve spoke with goal direction and organization about the symptoms he wanted to target. It was apparent from his verbalizations that his intellectual ability was above-average and this was confirmed by review of prior neuropsychological assessment reports that his parents had requested at multiple points in his life. The reports showed no evidence for ADD, but did identify some specific learning disorders that the therapy plan accommodated. Steve had participated in psychotherapy for anxiety when he was in high school, including 4 months of weekly CBT and family therapy, with a psychologist who described the past treatment as targeting family dynamics, perfectionism related to those dynamics, and obsessive-compulsive disorder (OCD) that focused on school work and excessive exercise. He repeated a year of high school owing to interference from the OCD and GAD but did not meet criteria for OCD at our intake. Steve reported that CBT psychotherapy in the past "didn't really work" and that he "didn't do the homework." He had also seen a psychodynamic psychiatrist who "tried to delve into the past" and whom he "tuned out." Steve reported a brief history of both alcohol and cannabis abuse in high school that was not currently a problem area.

Presenting Problem

Steve described elegantly what he wanted treatment to target: "I am a perfectionist and I am constantly working to avoid the feeling I get if I have not done my very best. I cannot relax if there is still more to do. Everyday I feel on edge, driven, hyped-up, restless, frustration, irritation…I've been boiled down to a grade-creating machine….I want a more balanced life. I want to focus on something other than good grades. I want my sense of self to be about more than academics. I want to be open to relationships with others. I am utterly unable to connect with people. I should be more social than I am." Steve listed his main problem on an intake questionnaire as "social anxiety" and rated its severity as an 8 (severe) on a 10 point scale. He met current *DSM-5* diagnostic criteria for Social Anxiety Disorder; Major Depressive Disorder secondary to chronic anxiety; and GAD, the latter of which best captured his current presenting concerns. Primary worry domains included being judged negatively in all kinds of relationships with peers and those he did not know well; not performing exceptionally academically; and choosing the wrong major and future career. Steve reported the following GAD criterion C symptoms as being present for him for years: feeling keyed up and restless; difficulties with sleep; irritability and concentration; and being easily fatigued. He also reported avoidant (*DSM-5* criteria 2–5) and obsessive-compulsive (criteria 1–4 and 8) personality traits.

Treatment Intervention and Course

Psychotherapy was conducted during the winter break because it created too high of a stress level for Steve not to focus exclusively on academics when classes were meeting. He completed a total of ten 50-minute sessions. Two were right after the intake during his fall break, seven were during his winter break, and the final session was during a visit home in the spring. Relaxation was anxiety provoking for Steve, thus it was decided that mindfulness training, which strengthens one's ability to relate with experience with curiosity and compassion without changing it, would replace relaxation training initially. Thus, he began the bMBSR protocol using CDs, a video, and a workbook between sessions to guide him. Each of the four bMBSR sessions focused on one of four "objects in the field of awareness" that one notices during meditation. Objects include emotion and the three elements that compose it: mental events (thoughts and attention processes), physiology, and urges for behavior or the actual behavior that is served and influenced by physiological activity (including how one relates to experience and what gets attention). Through instructions in guided meditations and both modeling and prompting in the therapy relationship, Steve learned to relate with friendliness and without excessive control with experience intra- and interpersonally and to maintain short- and long-term awareness of the consequences of the mental and behavioral habits in which he engaged. One specific example of how this learning occurs is during or after meditations in sessions when the therapist teaches alternate ways of relating with the material to which the client attends. Thus, if during meditation a client reports, "I can't focus on my breath...I keep thinking about what a loser I am for being so anxious. I shouldn't get so sweaty when I go to meetings. I'm hot and sweating just anticipating it. I can't do it. I am not going," the therapist can respond, "So there are these *judging thoughts* in the mind about being a loser and about how you cannot focus on breath sensations and this *mental activity* is part of this *emotion* of anxiety. This anxiety is also composed of the *thought* that you cannot do it and the *behavioral urge* to avoid as well as the *behavior* to keep giving attention to these *thoughts*. And *thoughts* in the mind are accompanied by *sensations* of heat in the body." With curiosity the therapist can ask, "I wonder what experience would be like if you noticed what else is here right now along with all of this?" with a curiosity and compassion in her tone.

The bMBSR protocol overlaps with Newman and colleagues' CBT-IEP protocol. Some examples of overlap include the following: (a) adoption of the construct of emotion as composed of thoughts, physiology, and behavior that reciprocally influence each other to maintain what is called the "anxiety spiral" in CBT-IEP; (b) using the elements that compose negative emotion as cues to prompt more adaptive responses such as cue-controlled relaxation in response to the occurrence of unpleasant body sensations or cue-controlled mindfulness in bMBSR; (c) education about the difference between primary emotions such as fear and sadness and secondary emotions such as anxiety and depression; (d) focus on awareness of intra- and interpersonal wants and needs that are signaled by primary emotion or obscured by secondary emotion; and (e) the maladaptive consequences of behavioral reactivity that is often driven by unpleasant emotions in an ineffective effort to get what is desired in relationships or to do something about or get rid of unwanted internal experience. The bMBSR program was designed for busy people with high stress levels who were not willing to commit to the longer mindfulness training protocols and practices.

Treatment for Steve also included traditional CBT. He completed a CBT workbook for clients from Newman et al.'s protocol for homework that included the following: (a) self-monitoring and logging of the cognitive, physiological, and behavioral elements present during specific worry-provoking situations; (b) systematic tracking of worry predictions and how often these were discrepant from actual outcomes; and (c) generation of nonthreatening and even positive alternative predictions about future outcomes. Through the CBT protocol Steve learned to treat worries and other anxiogenic beliefs as hypotheses and not facts and to view worry as a conditioned mental habit that is modifiable. With practice and attention to actual experience Steve learned how reciprocal interactions between the elements that composed anxiety could be both strengthened (via "the worry spiral") and weakened (via application of m-CBT responses) GAD.

Mindfulness was combined with CBT in Steve's therapy. For example, Steve learned the CBT technique of self-control coping desensitization (SCD) in which one repeatedly images an anxiogenic situation and identifies the elements of the anxiety spiral and how they interact until he could have the image with lessened physiological activation. At this point, he envisioned a mastery image of how he wanted to respond to both specific anxiety cues and in the situation. For example, Steve imagined himself attending an upcoming orientation at the new university to which he was accepted. He identified thoughts such as, "No one will like me or want to talk to me"; physiological sensations such as heart pounding and sweating; and the behaviors of avoiding eye contact, not talking, and holding his breath during interactions. First he rehearsed noticing one anxiety cue, such as avoiding eye contact, and replacing it with making eye contact. He then imaginally practiced responding to anxiogenic thoughts with three alternative nonthreatening and even positive thoughts that were generated via cognitive therapy (CT). For example, Steve rehearsed explaining silence in conversations with the thoughts, "They may be tired and preoccupied. Most of the time others' behaviors are not about me." In traditional CBT, after he can envision this scene without physiological activation, he then imagines a mastery image of people approaching him with interest, himself honestly disclosing reasons he decided to transfer, and breathing freely when interacting. To address the fact that not all clients desensitize to anxiety-provoking scenes, mindful responses such as pausing and staying present and listening and looking even when distressed are practiced. Some other mindful alternatives to anxiety cues include allowing the experience of unwanted sensations with compassion without "getting rid" of or trying to immediately change experience and expanding the field of attention to allow for the presence of other possible foci such as nonthreatening interpretations, internal pleasant or neutral sensations, and external attention to actual sound and sight sensations in the moment. In Steve's words, "I have shifted perspective in relationship with thoughts—now I hold many different nonthreatening perspectives at once in situations where there is uncertainty. I remind myself when I notice the immediate worry thought that I may be missing something important. I notice sensations of my lungs expanding to let the breath in and this reminds me to let in three more nonthreatening thoughts and the sensations of my feet on the ground. I can trust sensations of touch and sound and sight... I cannot always trust the thoughts..."

Steve also practiced planned exposures imaginally using SCD. Before exposures, he identified alternative and nonthreatening interpretations and possible outcomes and he specified the actual behaviors he wanted to exhibit, such as staying for a minimum of 45 minutes at orientation or asking open-ended questions of fellow students about reasons for declared majors. He agreed that he would consider exposures "successful" if he met these criteria regardless of how he felt or how others responded. Finally, he developed awareness of the consequences of avoidance intra- and interpersonally and began to discover that his efforts to protect himself in relationships were interfering with creating the very connection that he both feared and wanted. For example, if he never went to orientation he never would have learned people can be kind and sources of joy and if he did not connect to primary emotions he would not know what brought him joy and what did not meet his needs.

Outcome

At his final session, Steve no longer scored at clinical levels on measures of anxiety and depression. Standardized scores on two scales indicated that he changed from below to above average, compared to other college students, on level of mindfulness. Neff's Self-Compassion Scale indicated that he went from a low to a moderate level of self-compassion, nonidentification with thoughts and feelings, and common humanity and reported a much lower level of self-judgment than he had pretreatment. Scores on the Mood and Anxiety Symptom Questionnaire revealed that he no longer scored at clinical levels as he had pretreatment. Some of Steve's words at his final session described the insights he derived from psychotherapy and associated behavior changes: "Worry doesn't protect or prepare me. Anxiety interferes with remembering and learning"; "The barriers erected to avoid pain get in the way of experiencing pleasure." He ended the session by describing how his parents worried about him and called him constantly to see if he was working hard enough. He noted that their actions were sometimes discrepant from their claim that they wanted him to be happy. He asserted, "I am allowed to relax!" and reported that sometimes he chose not to answer their calls and rather he made time to go out to socialize even when all of his work was not done.

CHALLENGES IN APPLYING THE EVIDENCE-BASED APPROACH

Clients who have been misdiagnosed with Bipolar Disorder or ADD, or those with comorbid Panic Disorder with Agoraphobia, often must wean off of sometimes addictive medications. The resultant withdrawal symptoms can interfere with information processing in therapy. Such clients may also cling tightly to a medical model of mental illness when asked to engage in challenging behavioral experiments that evoke discomfort and attribute their GAD symptoms to a "broken brain." In such cases, the addition of motivation enhancement therapy, which results in identification of the short- and long-terms costs and benefits of staying the same verses changing in order to live in alignment with a valued life, can motivate difficult behavior changes. For especially severe clients stuck in the maladaptive intra- and interpersonal relating styles that are a relic of their developmental learning history, the addition of Interpersonal Reconstructive

Learning Therapy (IRT) usually supports modification of the mental and behavioral habits that are keeping them stuck. In IRT, loyalty to the internalized rules and values of caregivers are hypothesized as a mechanism that interferes with modification of mental and behavioral habits and therapy aims to create friendly differentiation from internalized representations of caregivers.

CULTURAL DIVERSITY ISSUES

In cases where issues arise as a function of cultural diversity, the diversity is understood in the context of learning history, and the usual goal of understanding the client's perspective empathetically still applies. Worth mentioning are religious beliefs that reflect an external attribution of control and/or a dependency on an external entity such as God to guide important life choices. In the face of uncertainty about the future and difficult decisions, both of which trigger the worry habit, clients often say, "Things will turn out as God plans" or, God is giving/will give me a sign regarding how to act." In such cases the client is encouraged to also have a sense of agency in affecting important outcomes in ways that are in alignment with nonreligious values that have been identified through awareness of primary emotion. Take for example the case of a religious woman with GAD who worries she will never meet a life partner with whom to have children and share her life. She is encouraged to connect with the sadness of lacking these sources of reinforcement and to let this primary emotion signal to her that she values relationship. She is encouraged to brainstorm about how she can engage actively in social activities at events that reflect her interests (dance) and to volunteer to become a mentor to children in need as a dance coach so that she can take an active role in creating the life she values rather than passively waiting for God to provide signs of what she should do or to provide reinforcers without her engagement in life.

FUTURE RESEARCH

Several areas of inquiry have the potential to improve psychotherapy outcome for those with GAD. These include: (a) Identification of factors that contribute to experiential avoidance (e.g., interpersonal learning history) and further development of the related contrast avoidance model of worry and its treatment implications. This latter model hypothesizes that clients maintain worry activity to generate a chronically negative emotional state because they are motivated, for reasons as yet unidentified, to avoid positive emotional states. Clinical researchers can usefully identify reasons for this theory that is embraced by those with GAD. Clients often report reasons that include attachment to caregivers who worried and communicated messages about being too happy and fear of loss of reinforcements. Theories about strength of conditioning in the face of contrasting expectations may also be relevant because they describe how stimuli associated with a positive valence can become even more strongly conditioned fear stimuli for negative emotions than stimuli that are neutral or negative at baseline. One important source of conditioning that may result in experiential avoidance is when caregivers, presumed to be a source of safety, behave in hostile or neglectful ways when children exhibit negative emotions. This may result in the expectancy that both relationships and negative emotions are a source of potential threat and it can chronically activate threat physiology. Indeed, most worry domains have a basis in intra- and interpersonal relating. Other areas of useful research include (b) the development of refined assessment tools with which clinicians can make accurate differential diagnosis between GAD and the disorders with which it is often confused; and (c) exploration of the neuropsychological factors that enhance learning of new mental and behavioral habits.

KEY REFERENCES

Benjamin, L. S. (2003/2006). *Interpersonal reconstructive therapy: Promoting change in nonresponders*. New York, NY: Guilford Press.

Molnar, C., Marks, D., Gardner, F., Brewer, J., & Klatt, M. (2012). How much is enough? Designing "low-dose" mindfulness-based stress reduction programs for crowded schedules and busy lives. Presented at the 46th Annual conference of the Association for the Advancement of Cognitive and Behavior Therapy (ABCT), National Harbor, MD.

Newman, M. G., Castonguay, L. G., Borkovec, T. D., Fisher, A. J., Boswell, J., ... Nordberg, S. S. (2011). A randomized controlled trial of cognitive-behavioral therapy for generalized anxiety disorder with integrated techniques from emotion-focused and interpersonal therapies. *Journal of Consulting and Clinical Psychology, 79*, 171–181.

CHAPTER 26

Geriatric Depression

Forrest Scogin and Andrew Presnell

CLINICAL PROBLEM

Depression in late life is one of the most common psychological disorders faced by older adults. Many controlled investigations have examined the treatment of the disorder, providing for a rich foundation for determining the best course of treatment. Central to the issues of treatment is the diagnosis of the disorder in this population.

Depression in late life may not manifest itself with the same symptom pattern seen in younger individuals. Older adults are more likely to focus complaints on somatic concerns, such as sleep problems or loss of appetite, fatigue, and cognitive concerns, than to present affective complaints. Older adults may also have a variety of medical issues that complicate treatment. These special issues make the treatment of depression in late life nuanced and therefore require techniques specifically studied within the population for best practices to be established.

PREVALENCE

Estimates suggest that up to 5 million Americans over the age of 65 may suffer from depressive symptoms. The prevalence of major depression and significant depressive symptoms in community-dwelling older adults is no greater than the rates in middle-aged adults. Estimates for clinically significant symptoms range from 8% to 16% and this drops to 1% to 4% for diagnosable major depression. Estimates increase when the populations are drawn from primary care settings (5%–10%), hospitalized individuals (10%–12%), and in long-term care facilities (up to 20%). Higher prevalence is seen in the oldest old (85 years and older) but can be accounted for by other factors associated with depression, including a higher proportion of women, increased disability, cognitive impairment, and lower socioeconomic status (SES). The incidence of major depression in older adults during a 1-year period is similar to younger adults at 0.15%. This rate increases in sub-populations with long-term care facility residents showing an incidence rate of up to 6.4%.

CULTURAL DIVERSITY ISSUES

There is a high level of disparity in the treatment of depression across minority groups in older adults. The primary factor in the successful treatment of minority elders is the cultural competency and skill of the therapist. Disparities are largely attributed to underutilization of services. Sensitivity to barriers to treatment for minority groups is important. These barriers can include: stigmatization of mental health treatment, believing depression is part of old age, culturally specific shame, and lack of acculturation. For example, a depressed client who is a Chinese immigrant may have difficulty with language, an issue of acculturation, and culturally specific issues of shame and guilt associated with mental illness that can make seeking and receiving treatment difficult. Sensitivity to issues like these may help a therapist overcome barriers to treatment.

As for matching specific treatments to various demographic groups, there is a dearth of evidence to suggest that a modality should be selected on that basis of race/ethnicity, sexual orientation, religious background, and so forth. A clinician should use sensitivity to the issues described above in addition to an evidence-based treatment when working with clients of diverse backgrounds.

EVIDENCE-BASED TREATMENTS

A review of literature established six psychological treatments as evidence based for use in this population. Recently, we have reexamined the literature produced between 2005 and 2008 and found that while significant studies have been published on the treatment of late-life depression, these studies have not established any new evidence-based treatments. The six therapeutic techniques supported by the literature are briefly presented below.

Treatment using behavior therapy techniques has been shown to be an efficacious treatment in multiple studies. The treatments used in these studies are largely based on the work of Peter Lewinsohn. In this model, depression is seen as an abundance of negative events and lack of positive events. The goals of treatment are to reverse these, lowering the negative stimuli and increasing the engagement of the older adult in positive, meaningful events.

Cognitive behavior therapy (CBT) is the most researched modality of treatment for late-life depression. CBT for older adults is based upon the work of Beck and his colleagues and has been modified into a protocol for older adults by Gallagher-Thompson, Thompson, and colleagues. The goals of CBT are to challenge maladaptive thinking and to use behavioral techniques such as behavioral activation and relaxation training in combination. The research supports the use of this treatment for late-life depression.

Cognitive bibliotherapy is a self-administered form of treatment consistent with the goals of cognitive behavior treatment. In the literature, the studies providing evidence to support this treatment use the book *Feeling Good: The New Mood Therapy* by David Burns. The treatment has individuals participate by reading and completing written exercises over a 4-week period of time. These exercises focus on challenging maladaptive thought processes. The role for therapists in these studies is as support through weekly phone contacts.

Problem-solving therapy (PST) teaches skills that make participants focus on taking active and adaptive approaches to solving problems in their lives. This modality is best represented in the protocol produced by Nezu and colleagues. Research supports the effectiveness of this approach and it is quickly gaining popularity as a treatment.

Brief psychodynamic psychotherapy has demonstrated effectiveness with older adults. The primary focus of this treatment is on identifying conflicts, exploring unconscious processes, and assisting the client with insight. The techniques used in the above studies are based upon the work of Horowitz and Kaltreider and Rose and DelMaestro.

Reminiscence therapy is unique among these techniques in that it was specifically designed for work with older adults. Individuals are asked to review their past, placing special emphasis on significant positive and negative life events, with the goal of gaining a better sense of perspective and resolving conflict through acceptance. Multiple studies have supported the use of this treatment for older adults with depression.

FUTURE RESEARCH

Though there are a variety of treatments established as evidence based, there are several areas that need to be further addressed within the literature. These areas include using diverse population samples, including "older" older adults, treatment of depression in individuals with Mild Cognitive Impairment and dementia, and overcoming barriers to access. Findings in these areas will further improve the ability of clinicians to effectively treat real world samples of older adults.

KEY REFERENCES

Gallagher-Thompson, D., & Thompson, L. W. (2010). *Treating late life depression: A cognitive-behavioral therapy approach, Therapist Guide*. New York, NY: Oxford University Press.

Scogin, F., Welsh, D., Hanson, A., Stump, J., & Coates, A. (2005). Evidence-based psychotherapies for depression in older adults. *Clinical Psychology: Science and Practice, 12,* 222–237.

Zeiss, A. M., & Steffen, A. (1996). Treatment issues with elderly clients. *Cognitive and Behavioral Practice, 3,* 371–389.

Clinician Application

Geriatric Depression

Mark R. Floyd

COMMENT ON THE EVIDENCE-BASED RECOMMENDATIONS

As noted in the Research Section, depression is a significant problem in the older adult population and is more pronounced in specific subpopulations (e.g., nursing home resident) or when comorbid with conditions common in the elderly (e.g., chronic pain). The diagnosis of depression is, indeed, challenging when there are multiple illnesses, medications are involved, and/or the patient is reluctant to admit to feeling sad. However, these patients can still be helped if the problem is framed as "coping" rather than "depression." A more difficult differential diagnosis is the lack of activity observed in patients with comorbid depression and dementia. That is, it can be impossible to determine whether the lack of activity is a depression-related anhedonia or a dementia-related failure to initiate. The inability/failure/refusal to increase activity does not bode well for psychotherapy success.

Regarding treatment, it is beneficial to have several different treatment techniques because it is not possible to use only one technique with everyone. Although I most often use cognitive behavior therapy (CBT), there are some patients who have trouble identifying their emotions, do not like rational disputation regardless of how it is done, or do not want to do homework. Other patients naturally engage in reminiscence and respond well to processing their life events.

CASE EXAMPLE

Subject Information and Brief History

"Jim" is an 82-year-old Caucasian male who is married but living alone and apart from his wife for the past 18 months because she has dementia and is living with her daughter from a previous marriage. Jim has a history of depression, including one hospitalization at age 35, and has received both psychotherapy and pharmacotherapy in the past. Prior to the current depressive episode, he has been free of depression for 15 years.

Presenting Problem

Jim is currently depressed and states that he feels lonely. He endorses symptoms of depressed mood, guilt, and cognitive slowing, meeting criteria for Depressive Disorder-Not Otherwise Specified (*DSM-IV*). His Geriatric Depression Scale (GDS-15) score was 11 out of 15, a moderate level of depression. He reports the symptoms gradually started after his wife moved in with her daughter and recently became bad enough that he recognized he needed help. He explains that he has accepted his wife's condition and understands there is nothing he can do to cure her. He attributes his current depression to loneliness more than anything else. It is important to note his feelings of guilt are not related to his inability to be a 24/7 caregiver for his wife, but, rather, are long-standing guilt feelings for a wide variety of events in his life. The mental status examination on intake showed mild memory impairment consistent with a diagnosis of Cognitive Disorder-Not Otherwise Specified. In spite of cognitive impairment, I thought he would be appropriate for CBT because he had good insight and prior experience in psychotherapy. Furthermore, his memory impairment was primarily in working memory (he had trouble with serial 7s and spelling words backward) and I had confidence we could find ways to compensate for this in each session.

Treatment Intervention and Course

We began CBT and although Jim reported he had never done cognitive therapy, he seemed to quickly grasp the concepts and was a willing participant in homework. Review of his activity record indicated he was active in a variety of tasks each day, including some activities he enjoyed. However, every activity was done by himself. As one of his primary complaints was loneliness, we discussed why he kept to himself. He explained that there are more women than men at his age, "and a lot of these women won't take no for an answer and are pretty aggressive about seeking a husband." I asked if there was a problem with having a platonic relationship, and he answered he does not want to do anything that could resemble infidelity. During the course of this discussion, Jim voiced his strong Christian beliefs and his guilt about adultery in a prior marriage and fornication prior to his current marriage. We discussed how it may be unrealistic to avoid women altogether and encouraged him to consider participation in the local senior center as he had done many years before.

In sessions 3 to 8, we focused on using the three-column technique. The three-column technique is a way to increase awareness of the connection between thoughts and emotions. On a sheet of paper there are three columns titled "event," "emotions," and "thoughts." Whenever the patient encounters a situation and experiences a negative emotion (e.g., sadness, anger, frustration, guilt, shame, fear, etc.) the patient writes a brief description of the event under the event column, lists the emotions experienced in the emotion column, and the corresponding thoughts in the thought column. In CBT, it is not so much what actually happens that matters as much as how the person interprets what happens—thus the focus on thoughts. Jim was able to accurately identify his emotions, thoughts, and the interconnection. He started going to the local senior center and enjoyed it. However, he reported occasional conversations with people who said something to offend him. For example, Jim is an accomplished musician and when he arrived at the senior center, one of his friends asked him to play a song on the piano. Jim did and enjoyed it until someone else was critical of his performance. Another time a person said to him: "You could not have been very successful in life because you live in a small run-down house." Jim was so hurt by these comments that he was considering not returning to the senior center. We used the five-column technique to identify the evidence and dispute his negative thoughts using the evidence. The five-column technique is an expanded form of the three-column technique that adds two additional columns for "rational response" and "outcome." The rational response is essentially a revision of what is written in the "thought" column based upon a review of the available evidence. The outcome then is an evaluation of the intensity of his emotions after reviewing the evidence and developing a rational response. In the course of discussing this, we discovered one of his core dysfunctional beliefs was the need for everyone to approve of him. We also noted how Jim had trouble saying "no," and this was the reason that in spite of earning an excellent salary during his career, he had no significant savings and truly did live in a small run-down house. We used the "downward arrow technique" to examine the significance of his financial situation and identified that he did not consider himself to have much value as a human being and was not worthy of love. The downward arrow technique is effective at examining the significance of what appears to be a sad but true statement, as in this case he didn't have much money. In the downward arrow technique, the sad statement is written at the top of the page and the patient is asked: "What is the significance of this?" The patient's answer is then written on the line below with an arrow drawn to it from the statement above. The patient is asked for the significance of each answer he provides until we reach something that seems fundamental to his depression. In this case, Jim answers were successively: "I do live in a run-down house," "I didn't manage my money well," "I have been a failure," "I did not achieve my potential," "I'm not worthy of love or respect." Had I pressed him again, he may have said "I can never be happy" or something similar but I thought I had identified his core negative belief at this point so I did not persist. The downward arrow technique is a very powerful tool because it shows exactly why his house bothered him. Some people think having an inexpensive house is the best option financially, but for Jim, it was a highly visible indication of how he was an utter failure in life. We discussed how his basic negative beliefs about himself set him up for the need to have approval from others.

In sessions 9 to 16, we repetitively addressed negative thoughts associated with the need for approval from others and his lack of self-acceptance. He continued to go to the senior center and enjoyed the social interactions most of the time. We used cognitive therapy techniques to process his negative social interactions. I attempted to utilize his faith to increase his basic feelings of self-worth by stressing how God loves and accepts him in spite of his shortcomings. However, Jim was quick to cite several scriptures indicating he was not a very good practicing Christian. Because he rejected such a basic concept as forgiveness, I concluded I would not succeed with this line of evidence and suggested he might benefit from talking about this with his minister. We also devoted a session to the principles of assertiveness and practiced working through his guilt and other negative emotions arising from his saying "no."

Outcome

Jim reported a significant reduction in depressive symptoms (GDS-15 = 4) and felt like he was no longer at risk for sliding into a serious depression. He became a regular at church and at the senior center and participated in all their social events. He was able to develop some platonic relationships with the women he met there but he continued to have reservations and worried about how some would think he was acting inappropriately for a married man. He continued to struggle with saying "no" and had to work through the negative feelings each time, but he considered himself to be doing much better. We have planned a follow-up session in 2 months.

CHALLENGES IN APPLYING THE EVIDENCE-BASED APPROACH

Working with older adults is a delightful experience and I have no regrets about specializing in this field. However, there are some characteristics of older adults that can be frustrating and limit the speed of progress in psychotherapy. Notably, older adults tend to be loquacious and it is sometimes difficult to know when to bring them back on topic without offending them or possibly losing some valuable information. I typically allow loquaciousness to go unchecked for the first few sessions until I have developed a rapport and have a sense of when he or she is straying off-topic. Another issue is the age-related change in mental ability. The normal changes in attention, working memory, and information processing speed can limit the amount of progress made in a single session. To compensate, it is usually necessary to frequently repeat major points, to write down summaries at the end of each session, and to work through multiple examples of the same problem. These issues are even more salient in older adults with memory disorders. The psychotherapist must be understanding and not jump to the conclusion that this is a form of resistance.

CULTURAL DIVERSITY ISSUES

Strong religious beliefs are commonplace in the South and among the elderly. Research on faith/religion demonstrates it is generally a positive source of coping and it can be used with positive effect in psychotherapy. However, some people acquire religious beliefs that promote negative self-regard. And because it is a matter of faith, it is by definition outside of logic/reason and, therefore, potentially at odds with CBT. The therapist must be careful when challenging the patient's beliefs. Not only is there risk of weakening the therapeutic relationship, there is also a risk of termination due to being identified as too secular to be helpful.

FUTURE RESEARCH

My experience with CBT for geriatric depression is that behavioral activation is critical. Behavioral activation is the intervention designed to: (a) increase pleasant events just for the sake of increasing enjoyment, (b) increase activity levels to gather evidence to disprove negative thoughts such as "life is not fun" or "I can't do much of anything," and (c) to increase activity levels in general to increase energy levels and vitality. The lack of willingness to increase activity levels is the common thread among the patients I count as treatment failures. As we become progressively older, we are more likely to have significant physical limitations that make behavioral activation increasingly difficult. I routinely encounter patients who cannot move around owing to chronic pain and also have impairments of vision and/or hearing. Thus, sedentary activities such as reading, watching TV, and/or listening to music may provide limited pleasure. It is a challenge to help such individuals overcome depression. I hope our science can identify methods to improve mood without reliance on behavioral activation and can be effective even in the face of significant disability.

KEY REFERENCES

Beck, A. T., Rush, A. J., Shaw, B. F., & Emery, G. (1979). *Cognitive therapy of depression.* New York, NY: Guilford Press.

Burns, D. (1980). *Feeling good.* New York, NY: Signet.

Smith, M. J. (1975). *When I say no I feel guilty.* New York, NY: Bantam Books.

CHAPTER 27

Hoarding Disorder

Christiana Bratiotis and Gail Steketee

CLINICAL PROBLEM

Hoarding is defined as the acquisition of and failure to discard a large number of possessions that appear to be useless or of limited value, impairment of living spaces so as to preclude the intended use, and distress or impairment in functioning. Until recently, hoarding was categorized diagnostically as a subtype of Obsessive Compulsive Disorder (OCD). However, it is now included in the fifth edition of the *Diagnostic and Statistical Manual of Mental Disorders* (*DSM-5*). Recent research has shown that while hoarding and other forms of OCD have some similarities, there are a significant number of distinguishing features. The proposed diagnostic criteria for Hoarding Disorder include difficulty discarding or parting with objects due to strong urges to save items, accumulation of possessions that clutter living areas, and distress or interference in functioning caused by the hoarding. Hoarding behavior must not be better accounted for by another medical or mental health condition. Two specifiers are proposed: (a) with excessive acquisition and (b) with poor insight.

Hoarding Disorder is characterized by three main manifestations: acquisition, difficulty discarding, and clutter. Acquisition and saving are often fueled by strong beliefs about an object's usefulness, sentimental value, or intrinsic worth. Difficulty parting with objects commonly results in a cluttered home environment which may create impairment in carrying out daily life activities and elicit feelings of distress, as well as endanger the safety and health of occupants, neighbors, and the surrounding community.

PREVALENCE

Within the United States, hoarding is estimated to have a prevalence rate ranging from 2% to 5% of the population. Epidemiological studies in other industrialized nations such as the United Kingdom (2%) and Germany (4%) show similar rates. Nearly 60% of clinical hoarding onsets in childhood and adolescence between the ages of 11 and 20 years. These studies show that hoarding occurs as often, if not more commonly, in men than in women, but most clinical studies contain many more women than men. This suggests that women are more willing to participate and to seek clinical treatment. People who hoard marry at lower rates than the general population and divorce at higher rates, a situation which may lead to social isolation in older adult years.

In a clinical sample (N = 217) of people who met diagnostic criteria for Hoarding Disorder, 69% also met criteria for major depressive disorder (MDD) during their lifetime. Approximately 28% of the sample met criteria for social phobia and 25% for generalized anxiety disorder (excessive worry). Less commonly associated with hoarding were other forms of OCD, approximately 17%. Attention Deficit (but not hyperactivity) Disorder was present in approximately 28% of woman and 25% of men. In addition to the prevalence of significant Axis I comorbidity, common personality traits identified among people who hoard are difficulty making decisions, perfectionism, procrastination, and low insight, all challenges to clinical treatment.

CULTURAL DIVERSITY ISSUES

The predominant amount of hoarding research has been conducted in North America, although research and practice colleagues from Asia, Europe, and Australia also recognize hoarding as a significant problem. Within North America, most of the empirical evidence about Hoarding Disorder and its treatment derives from studies conducted at academic institutions and research centers. The voluntary participants at these sites may not accurately represent a cross-sample of the population of people with significant hoarding problems. Increasing focus on community-based research may provide access to and information about more diverse groups of people who hoard.

Sensitive intervention for hoarding and its co-occurring conditions will likely benefit from understanding the influences of culture on thoughts, behaviors, and emotions. Understanding the diverse practices and traditions of a particular racial or ethnic group can be helpful in assessing reasons for acquiring, saving, and difficulty parting with items and in resolving problematic beliefs and emotions associated with hoarding behavior. However, focusing on the meaning of hoarding behavior based on culture alone is not likely to be useful.

EVIDENCE-BASED TREATMENTS

To date, the most commonly studied treatment for hoarding is based on a conceptual model described in a book by Steketee and Frost. This model suggests that a person's genetic, neurobiological, and environmental vulnerabilities, combined with deficits in information processing (i.e., attention, categorization, association, perception), contribute to the formation of distorted beliefs about possessions. Attachment to objects elicits emotions, both positive and negative, which together with the distorted beliefs, are maintained through positive and negative reinforcement.

The specialized cognitive and behavioral treatment (CBT) derived from Steketee and Frost's model consists of 26 sessions of individual outpatient therapy delivered both in office and at the client's home (every fourth session). The treatment modules include: assessment; case formulation and goal setting; motivational enhancement; skills training—organizing, problem solving, decision making; challenging beliefs about possessions; practice sorting, discarding and nonacquisition (exposure); and relapse prevention. An open trial of 10 treatment completers demonstrated a strong therapeutic effect, with 50% rated much or very much improved on a clinical global improvement (CGI) scale. In a waitlist comparison trial of CBT for hoarding with a sample of 37 treatment completers, CBT was superior to waitlist after only 12 weeks and when all patients completed 26 sessions. In this study, approximately 75% of the patients were rated much or very much improved. CBT methods to treat hoarding were also studied in older adult samples (ages 60 and older) with somewhat conflicting findings. It appears that the effects of CBT for older adults may be somewhat attenuated. Additional clinical trials are needed to better understand the specific needs of older adults who hoard and to enhance treatment response.

Twenty sessions of group CBT produced good effects, almost at the level of individual treatment. Research on the effects of mutual-help groups is very limited, although findings are promising with regard to the degree of improvement in discarding clutter for those participating in such groups.

FUTURE RESEARCH

While the empirical research on Hoarding Disorder has grown exponentially over the past two decades, further study is still needed. For example, at this time there is little or no information about the influence of race and culture on hoarding symptoms and on intervention methods and treatment outcomes. As hoarding appears to be substantially different from OCD, it is not surprising that serotonergic medications do not appear to work well. However, some studies contradict this finding. Studies of other types of medication, or combinations of medications, are also needed.

With its multidimensional symptoms, many associated features, and high rate of co-occurring Axis I disorders, Hoarding Disorder is a challenging problem to treat. Among the most difficult hoarding clients are those who have low levels of insight into the impairment caused by the hoarding and low motivation for treatment. Researchers and practitioners alike are working to increase the benefits of treatment while simultaneously testing methods of treatment delivery that require less time and are practical in a range of community treatment settings.

KEY REFERENCES

Mataix-Coles, D., Fernandez de la Cruz, L., Nakao, T., & Pertusa, A. (2011). Testing the validity and acceptability of diagnostic criteria for Hoarding Disorder: A *DSM 5* survey. *Psychological Medicine, 41*, 2475–2484. doi: 10.1017/S0033291711000754

Steketee, G., & Frost, R. O. (2007). *Compulsive hoarding and acquiring: A therapist guide.* New York, NY: Oxford University Press.

Steketee, G., Frost, R. O., Tolin, D. F., Rasmussen, J., & Brown, T. A. (2010). Waitlist controlled trial of cognitive behavior therapy for Hoarding Disorder. *Depression and Anxiety, 27*, 476–484.

Hoarding Disorder

Michael A. Tompkins

COMMENT ON THE EVIDENCE-BASED RECOMMENDATIONS

At this time, cognitive behavior therapy (CBT), delivered in individual or group formats, is the psychological treatment of choice for Hoarding Disorder. Several points raised by the researchers are particularly relevant to clinicians treating Hoarding Disorder. First, Hoarding Disorder is a low-insight condition with multiple comorbidities. In order to be effective with this population, clinicians require considerable expertise and experience in applying the basic principles and strategies of CBT, as well as motivational enhancement strategies. Second, home visits are a central component to this treatment and some research suggests that the greater the number of in-home sessions, the better the treatment outcome. Therefore, in order for clinicians to be effective with this population, they must be willing and comfortable leaving their offices to provide as much treatment as possible in the hoarding environment. Finally, because many with the most severe symptoms of Hoarding Disorder are older adults on fixed incomes, the field would benefit from treatments that are not only evidence based but also that are cost-effective.

CASE EXAMPLE

Subject Information and Brief History

Gloria is 57 years old and retired early from her career as a classroom art teacher. Gloria is divorced and lives alone. She has an adult son and daughter who live nearby. Gloria's daughter called the clinician to make an appointment for her mother. Gloria reluctantly agreed to the consultation and was pleasant but a bit perplexed stating, "What is all of the fuss about my stuff?"

Presenting Problem

As an art teacher Gloria acquired and kept a large variety of art supplies, as well as anything she might use for an art project—an egg cartoon, broken plastic pipe, or piece of dirty string. Gloria acquired art supplies at garage sales and art supply stores. She had filled her small two-bedroom home with possessions such that she no longer was able to sleep on her bed, sit on her furniture, or move easily around her home. Using the Clutter Image Rating (CIR) scale, Gloria rated the rooms of her home from 6 to 7 on a 9-point scale, where 9 is the most cluttered.

Treatment Intervention and Course

This treatment targets a number of variables hypothesized to maintain the condition: (a) distorted beliefs about possessions, (b) information-processing deficits (e.g., difficulties with attention, categorization, and perception), and (c) positive and negative reinforcers. The clinician began the first appointment with motivational interviewing to engage Gloria in the assessment process. Gloria completed a number of measures (Saving Inventory-Revised, Saving Cognitions Inventory, Activities of Daily Living-Hoarding, and Obsessive-Compulsive Inventory-Revised) to assess hoarding-related symptoms. With the clinician, Gloria completed the Clutter Image Rating scale to assess the level of clutter in her home. The clinician then arranged a home visit, where he photographed each room in Gloria's home and identified areas of the home on which to focus first.

In the early and middle phases of treatment, the clinician focused on enhancing Gloria's ability to organize her possessions, such as categorizing her art supplies and developing a plan that identified where she would store each category of possession. Together, the clinician and Gloria developed a plan that identified which supplies she would donate and to whom. Focusing on donating rather than discarding her possessions, as well as motivational interviewing strategies, increased Gloria's trust in the clinician and enhanced her motivation to work collaboratively on the problem. Because of her difficulty with sustained attention, the clinician taught Gloria several strategies to manage inattention and distraction, such as stimulus control (minimizing distractions when she worked on organizing her possessions, covering the area adjacent to the one on which she is working) and prompting to sustain task engagement (timers). Throughout this phase, as well as throughout the treatment, Gloria's motivation wavered and the clinician quickly shifted to motivational enhancement strategies (e.g., decisional analysis, motivational interviewing) to get Gloria back on track with the task at hand.

The middle phase of treatment targeted Gloria's beliefs that maintained her hoarding behavior, such as she could not tolerate discarding an item that she or someone else might possibly use. For example, Gloria believed that if she discarded an item she would be tormented "forever" by the thought of that item and the accompanying distress. Gloria and the clinician then devised an experiment to test this prediction, whereby Gloria discarded an item and she monitored over several days the frequency with which she thought about the item and her level of distress. Gloria was surprised to learn that by the next day, she thought very little about the item, which increased her willingness to discard other items.

In the final phase of treatment, the clinician targeted the beliefs that maintained her excessive acquiring. Gloria and the clinician created a "resisting the urge" hierarchy, which listed the ways Gloria acquired art supplies. For example, one of Gloria's hierarchies included the following steps: (a) stand outside the art store and look in the window, (b) enter the art store and stand for several minutes and then exit, (c) enter the art store and pick up an item then put it down and exit. The clinician initially accompanied Gloria on these exposures. Later, Gloria completed the exposures with the assistance of her daughter. Gloria made good progress over the course of 8 months of treatment. She and the clinician developed a plan to taper meetings and decrease the likelihood of relapse. The clinician telephoned Gloria several times during the tapered treatment phase to review her relapse management plan and to check on her progress.

Outcome

At the end of treatment, although Gloria retained more art supplies than she would ever use, she was sleeping in her bed, sitting on her furniture, and hosting arts and crafts parties for her friends where she provided all of the art supplies. The clinician and Gloria rated the rooms of her home from 4 to 5 on the CIR scale (it was initially 6 to 7 on this 9-point scale). With constant encouragement from her daughter, Gloria resisted urges to acquire more supplies and slowly decreased the level of her collection through these parties.

CHALLENGES IN APPLYING THE EVIDENCE-BASED APPROACH

Clinicians face a number of challenges when treating Hoarding Disorder. Perhaps the foremost challenge is the low insight of many clients who hoard, even those who are open to treatment. For this reason, it is essential that clinicians are highly skilled in motivational enhancement strategies. Clinicians will depend on these strategies to engage the client throughout the treatment, and in particular, with the more difficult aspects of the treatment, such as letting go of possessions and resisting urges to acquire.

The high likelihood that clients with Hoarding Disorder have one or more additional psychological conditions means clinicians may need to treat multiple conditions, either concurrently or prior to treating Hoarding Disorder. For this reason, it is important that clinicians who treat Hoarding Disorder have expertise in evidence-based treatments for other disorders, in particular, depressive and anxiety disorders, and attention-deficit disorder. Many clients with Hoarding Disorder are older adults. Clinicians effective in treating Hoarding Disorder are also knowledgeable about the unique developmental needs of older adults and with adjusting typical cognitive behavioral interventions for the age-related deficits in an older population.

CULTURAL DIVERSITY ISSUES

Little research is available on the prevalence of Hoarding Disorder across cultures or on the applicability of the cognitive behavioral model of hoarding behavior and CBT for the condition within various cultures. Research focused on understanding the cultural influences on the thoughts, beliefs, and behaviors hypothesized to maintain hoarding behavior might lead to culturally sensitive interventions for the disorder.

FUTURE RESEARCH

At this time we do not understand the nature of insight for those who hoard. Researchers might look at theories of insight in other low-insight psychological disorders, such as bipolar disorder and schizophrenia, for models that may help to elucidate the low or limited insight in certain clients who hoard. A clearer understanding of the factors that influence low insight and the development of methods to assess for level of insight may increase the ability of clinicians to engage a broader range of clients with this condition.

Many people who hoard are frail older adults. We know little about the interface between hoarding behavior, squalor, and self-neglect. Clinicians would benefit from research on assessment and intervention strategies for clients who present with both hoarding behavior and squalor.

Currently, effective CBT for Hoarding Disorder is a time-intensive treatment that requires highly skilled clinicians. Clinicians would benefit from additional research focused on treatments that require less time, are more cost-sensitive, and are effective with clients across a range of insight and age.

KEY REFERENCES

Ayers, C. R., Wetherell, J. L., Golshan, S., & Saxena, S. (2011). Cognitive-behavioral therapy for geriatric compulsive hoarding. *Behaviour Research and Therapy, 49*, 689–694.

Muroff, J., Steketee, G., Rasmussen, J., Gibson, A., Bratiotis, C., & Sorrentino, C. (2009). Group cognitive and behavioral treatment for compulsive hoarding: A preliminary trial. *Depression and Anxiety, 26*, 634–640.

Steketee, G., & Frost, R. O. (2007). *Compulsive hoarding and acquiring: A therapist guide*. New York, NY: Oxford University Press.

CHAPTER 28

Nightmares

Joanne L. Davis and Noelle E. Balliett

CLINICAL PROBLEM

Nightmares are typically defined as dreams involving negative emotions that wake the sleeper. Idiopathic nightmares are those that have no known specific trigger but may increase during times of stress, be associated with physical illness, typically peak during middle childhood, occur during rapid eye movement (REM) sleep, and occur toward the end of the sleep cycle. Trauma-related nightmares have a clear precipitating event, are a symptom of Posttraumatic Stress Disorder (PTSD) but may occur in the absence of PTSD, and are often accompanied by panic-like symptoms. Trauma-related nightmares are associated with greater sleep difficulties and daytime dysfunction perhaps in part because they occur earlier in the sleep cycle and are associated with difficulties returning to sleep. People experiencing both idiopathic and trauma-related nightmares may not benefit from the restorative function of sleep as they lose a significant quantity of sleep and have poor quality of sleep.

Nightmares are pernicious, pervasive, and persistent. They are associated with a number of negative health outcomes such as depression, suicidal ideation, anxiety, difficulty concentrating, irritability, and sleep disordered breathing, and are associated with distress above and beyond that accounted for by PTSD. While many trauma-exposed individuals report nightmares in the acute aftermath of a traumatic event, these tend to be transient, dissipating in the weeks following the event. For others, however, nightmares and related sleep disturbances become chronic conditions. Increasingly, nightmares and sleep disturbances are thought to be the "hallmark" of PTSD as they are thought to play a role in the development and maintenance of PTSD. Trauma-related nightmares may include content that replicate to varying degrees the actual traumatic event. Nightmare content closer to the trauma is associated with greater distress.

PREVALENCE

While most people experience occasional nightmares, in the United States, 1% to 8% of the general population report frequent nightmares. Although nightmares peak during childhood, they reemerge in early adolescence. Girls begin to report more problems with nightmares than boys in adolescence and this trend continues into adulthood. Persons exposed to traumatic events report significantly higher rates of frequent nightmares than those not exposed to trauma. Indeed, nightmares are among the most prevalent symptoms following a traumatic event, reported by 50% to 88% of trauma survivors, and are more frequent and severe among those suffering from PTSD. Nightmares are reported at even higher rates in the presence of psychiatric disorders comorbid with PTSD. Untreated, nightmares may persist for decades following a traumatic event.

CULTURAL DIVERSITY ISSUES

Sleep, dreaming, and nightmares are subject to considerable variation across cultures in prevalence, associated distress, interpretation, and response to treatment. For example, a study of American Indian Vietnam Veterans found a higher base rate of nightmares and higher rates among those with trauma and PTSD than non-American Indian Veterans. Culture and spirituality may play an important role in the interpretation of nightmares and other distressing sleep events. For instance, a study of Cambodian refugees found that they treat nightmares by seeking spiritual advisors to create additional protection around the self during sleep. Native American trauma survivors may prefer to involve shamanic practices in the treatment of nightmares. While in Aceh, Indonesia, discussion of dreams and nightmares is typically perceived as taboo. In summary, treatment providers should explore the role of culture in sleep and dreaming and proceed with treatment in a respectful and collaborative fashion. There are no known differences in the prevalence of nightmares based on race.

EVIDENCE-BASED TREATMENTS

Some evidence suggests that nightmares and sleep disturbances may be resistant to pharmacological and psychological interventions that broadly target PTSD symptomatology and may not remit to subclinical levels. Contrarily, cognitive behavioral treatments that directly target nightmares and sleep problems consistently find positive treatment effects for nightmares and associated sleep impairments as well as other mood symptoms not directly targeted. Together, these findings suggest that for some individuals, nightmares and sleep impairments may be primary conditions.

Two cognitive behavioral treatments are promising for alleviating nightmares and related problems: Exposure, Relaxation, and Rescription Therapy (ERRT) and Imagery Rehearsal Therapy (IRT). ERRT includes psychoeducation regarding trauma, PTSD, and sleep problems, behavioral relaxation techniques, sleep hygiene education, modification of sleep habits, exposure to the nightmare, identification of trauma-related themes (e.g., safety, esteem, trust, intimacy, power/control) within the nightmare, modification of nightmare content based on the themes, and imaginal rehearsal of the modified content. Currently two versions have been developed and tested empirically, including a three-session version for civilians and a four-session version for military personnel and veterans. IRT is a variable-length treatment ranging from one to six sessions. Treatment components include imagery exercises, modifying the content of a nightmare, and visualizing the new content vividly. It may also include cognitive restructuring and education about sleep.

Both ERRT and IRT are found to be effective with survivors of civilian traumas and demonstrate robust effects on nightmares and sleep impairment. Although these treatments do not directly address other symptoms, a generalized impact is found in reductions of symptoms of depression, anxiety, and PTSD following treatment. ERRT has also been shown to significantly reduce physiological fear reactions to nightmare-related imagery. Treatment gains are typically well maintained over time. Evidence suggests that ERRT is also promising in military samples, while equivocal findings are reported for IRT.

Prazosin, an antihypertensive pharmacological agent, has been demonstrated to be effective for trauma-related nightmares. It is unclear whether the effects of prazosin are only palliative, however.

FUTURE RESEARCH

No evidence currently exists distinguishing trauma-exposed individuals for whom nightmares and sleep impairments are primary versus secondary conditions. This research will be important in informing treatment planning for trauma-exposed individuals. If nightmares are the primary condition, driving and maintaining other difficulties, a treatment directly targeting nightmares may be the best initial approach. If nightmares are a secondary condition, just one of many symptoms of PTSD, then a treatment targeting PTSD may be the first choice.

Future research will also need to compare promising treatments with active control conditions to determine the specificity of their efficacy for nightmares. It will also be important to compare medications and psychotherapy and their combination to ascertain differential efficacy. Further, while the treatments are promising, little is known about the potential mechanisms of change. Many theories have been proposed regarding the development and maintenance of nightmares, which may suggest important possible mechanisms to target.

KEY REFERENCES

Davis, J. L. (2009). *Treating post-trauma nightmares: A cognitive behavioral approach*. New York, NY: Springer.

Krakow, B., Hollifield, M., Johnston, L., Koss, M., Schrader, R., ... Prince, H. (2001). Imagery rehearsal therapy for chronic nightmares in sexual assault survivors with posttraumatic stress disorder: A randomized controlled trial. *Journal of the American Medical Association, 286*, 537–545.

Levin, R., & Nielsen, T. A. (2007). Disturbed dreaming, posttraumatic stress disorder, and affect distress: A review and neurocognitive model. *Psychological Bulletin, 133*, 482–528.

Clinician Application

Nightmares

Todd K. Favorite

COMMENT ON THE EVIDENCE-BASED RECOMMENDATIONS

The authors of the Research Section describe two categories of nightmare presentation in the clinical population, those without discernible precipitating events and nightmares that are a consequence of traumatic experiences. The adverse effects of both types of nightmares on sleep continuity and efficiency can be equally profound. However, in the case of trauma-based nightmares, there is a significantly higher rate of frequency, intensity, and persistence over the life span. The authors articulate that higher rates of nightmares are reported by patients with Posttraumatic Stress Disorder (PTSD) and comorbid psychiatric disorders. There is increasing evidence that these psychiatric disorders are exacerbated by, if not caused by, persistent loss of sleep in which disruptive nightmares play a central role. In the veteran population, particularly combat veterans, frequency of trauma-based nightmares are widely reported. Nightmares are included in the diagnostic criteria for PTSD and, it is often the case, that nightmares persist even after first-line PTSD treatments have successfully concluded.

There are two evidence-based treatments available for trauma-focused nightmares. Both methods utilize a brief sequential approach that incorporates psychoeducation on trauma nightmares, sleep hygiene, relaxation and visual imagery practice, and, finally, rewriting the nightmare based on specific themes (rescripting). Although Imagery Rehearsal Therapy (IRT) and Exposure, Relaxation, and Rescripting Therapy (ERRT) share these foundational aspects, they diverge in significant ways when it comes to the theory, structure, and application. IRT has adopted an approach to intervention that is grounded in "systematic desensitization" and creates a hierarchy of nightmares in which the patient moves from a moderately intense nightmare toward more distressing ones over the course of treatment. IRT focuses attention on changing the imagery system, which is hypothesized as an entrenched, habitual process that is altered through practiced alternative or competing imagery and relaxation. ERRT has developed as a cognitive behavioral, exposure-based approach to nightmare reduction that targets the most intense nightmare as the focus of treatment and assists the patient in identifying core themes (i.e., safety, trust, power/control, intimacy, self-esteem) manifested in the nightmare content and modifying the nightmare by addressing the theme. This is followed by relaxation exercises. To outline the application of each of these models, I have provided a case illustration for each method. The cases were chosen on the basis of the similarity of demographics and nightmare presentation in terms of frequency, intensity, and previous trauma-focused treatments.

CASE EXAMPLE 1

Subject Information and Brief History

Jack is a 66-year-old married, Caucasian Vietnam War veteran. He retired from an automotive factory job 4 years ago, where he frequently worked overtime or double shifts over the 34 years that he was employed there. He has been married for 35 years and has two adult children and three grandchildren. He describes his family relationships as emotionally distant, but supportive, and he and his wife sleep separately owing to his protracted nightmares and violent movements during sleep. Jack reports that he has few friends and avoids social activities and public events. He used alcohol for several years to reduce stress and promote sleep. When alcohol abuse threatened his marriage and job, Jack stopped drinking and began working overtime as often as he could in an attempt to exhaust himself so he could sleep. This provided limited results as he aged and he was asked to take an early retirement when his company began to lay off workers.

Presenting Problem

Jack presented at the Veteran's Association Health care System, initially for medical problems related to high blood pressure and diabetes, but also reported that his sleep was poor and that he experienced multiple nightmares about the war each night. Jack was referred to the PTSD clinic for evaluation and treatment. On the Clinician Administered PTSD Scales (CAPS), Jack obtained a total score of 106, which is a high score on this scale, and he met criteria for all three PTSD symptom clusters, that is, reexperiencing, avoidance, and hyperarousal. He reported that he was sleeping 2 to 3 hours each night and that he had vivid, recurrent nightmares each night when he did fall asleep. His nightmares and other PTSD symptoms had noticeably increased since his retirement, and he reported feelings of hopelessness and depression as a consequence. He reported that his nightmares typically involved responding to several men screaming for a medic and working frantically to stop bleeding or close wounds only to have the soldier die in each nightmare.

Treatment Intervention and Course

Jack was engaged in Prolonged Exposure Therapy to address his PTSD symptoms and he was prescribed citalopram and trazodone to address his PTSD, depression, and insomnia. He was able to complete psychotherapy and reported a moderate reduction in his PTSD symptoms (CAPS = 84), primarily with regard to avoidance behaviors, which serve to reduce anxiety by withdrawing from the source of distress. He adhered to his medication regimen, which afforded two to three more hours of sleep some nights; however, he continued to report frequent nightmares. He was referred to group psychotherapy for Imagery Rehearsal Therapy (IRT) in which five Vietnam War combat veterans were seen weekly for a period of 6 weeks to address trauma-related nightmares. He completed all sessions and was engaged and compliant with treatment, which provided a description of the nightmare process as a cognitive habit involving expectations and associations. The rationale for IRT was provided and breathing techniques, sleep hygiene principles, and mental imagery exercises were introduced. Jack was asked to complete a list of his nightmares from the most distressing to the least, and from this hierarchy he chose a nightmare that was in the middle range of intensity using a subjective unit of distress (SUD) rating scale. He then wrote out the nightmare in detail and provided an SUD rating upon completion. He was asked to rescript this nightmare with a description of more pleasant sequence of mental images that he chose to replace the existing nightmare with. He wrote this out in detail, and gave an SUD rating. His homework for the week was to practice diaphragmatic breathing, rehearse the rescripted imagery by reading it and visualizing it as well as practice sleep hygiene principles. Each week progress was checked by reviewing practice and SUD levels. When SUD levels for the target nightmare was reduced by 50%, the next nightmare in the hierarchy was rescripted and practiced in the same fashion.

Outcome

Jack was able to complete the six sessions of IRT and was adherent with between-session practice and rescripting assignments. He was unable to reduce his SUD from his target nightmare to move to a higher level nightmare, and this impeded his progress in psychotherapy. He chose to rescript his nightmare with a mental

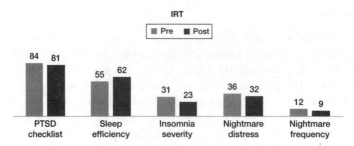

FIGURE 28.1 Outcome Scores for Imagery Rehearsal Therapy.

Note: Symptom reduction is indicated by a decrease in scores with the exception of sleep efficiency. Increase in sleep efficiency denotes improvement in symptoms of insomnia.

image of fishing on a lake rather than content that reflected the subject matter of the nightmare. This rescripting appeared to reflect his avoidance of traumatic content. He stated that he could not change what happened in Vietnam and he believed he had nightmares, "so that those soldiers would not be forgotten." He improved his sleep hygiene by reducing caffeine intake at night and establishing a regular bedtime and an optimal bedroom environment. His pretreatment and posttreatment scores are reflected in Figure 28.1. He was then referred for depression treatment and a medication evaluation as he continued to complain of low mood and insomnia. Jack continued to report nightmares at the end of treatment.

CASE EXAMPLE 2

Subject Information and Brief History

Charles is a 68-year-old Caucasian Vietnam War veteran in his second marriage of 23 years, with an adult daughter from his previous marriage. He has been self-employed as a plumbing subcontractor for the last several years and has had a number of skilled labor jobs. He decided that he is better off working for himself. Charles has received treatment through the VA Health Care System ever since his return from Vietnam in 1968 where he was severely wounded when his squad of 19 Marines walked into an ambush and only six survived.

Presenting Problem

Charles was referred for nightmare treatment by his primary clinician after he completed 12 sessions of Cognitive Processing Therapy (CPT) for PTSD. He was able to complete first-line group psychotherapy and reported a moderate reduction in his PTSD symptoms, evidenced by a reduction in his CAPS total score of 18 points. However, he continued to struggle with repetitive nightmares of the ambush he had survived in Vietnam. His sleep was interrupted on a nightly basis and when he attempted to return to sleep, the nightmare would continue where it left off. Charles typically experienced 3 to 4 hours of sleep per night and would stay up late to avoid the nightmare. Charles was having difficulty working owing to fatigue and his family relationships were strained due to his irritability.

Treatment Intervention and Course

Charles was engaged in a group ERRT with four other combat veterans and was seen weekly for a period of 6 weeks to address trauma-related nightmares. Treatment followed the ERRT protocol developed by Dr. Joanne Davis for trauma-related nightmares. Initial sessions provided psychoeducation on trauma-related nightmares and sleep hygiene, and relaxation methods that were practiced daily. Treatment followed the ERRT protocol which were practiced daily prior to sleep. He was asked to provide a detailed description of the most frequent and intense nightmare as well as an SUD rating before and after writing the description. Upon review of the scripted nightmare, Charles was asked to identify the predominant theme of the nightmare (i.e., safety, trust, power/control, intimacy, self-esteem) for which he identified safety and control as central themes in his nightmare. While maintaining the basic content of the nightmare, Charles worked with the psychotherapist to construct new elements to the nightmare that addressed safety and control. Again, SUD ratings were established for the rescripted dream. These elements were included in a rescripted dream that Charles then practiced 1 hour prior to a set bedtime, for 15 to 20 minutes, followed by relaxation techniques for 10 minutes, each night for six weeks. Weekly sessions provided a review of the daily practices, troubleshooting around sleep hygiene, relaxation methods, and dream rescripting.

Outcome

Charles completed each of the six sessions of ERRT and was adherent to the between-session practice. After his initial rescripting of the entire nightmare, he decided that there was one part of the nightmare that was the most difficult and he focused on this with a more circumscribed theme identification and rescripting. He showed improvement on each of the pretreatment measures (see Figure 28.2). The most significant outcome for Charles was the change in his attitude toward his sleep and dreaming. This was evidenced in his reduced anxiety, agitation, and fear about having a nightmare about the ambush and his increased sense of efficacy when these nightmares occurred less often. He reported that he was better able to stay asleep longer while dreaming and that he dreamt about smaller portions of the ambush. He also reported that he found he could return to sleep without the dream repeating.

CHALLENGES IN APPLYING THE EVIDENCE-BASED APPROACHES

The challenge in applying each of these approaches to nightmare treatment is that the clinician needs to be reasonably knowledgeable about sleep science, relaxation methods, and trauma treatment. These are brief treatments and each session requires sufficient structure and preparation in order to obtain the maximum psychotherapeutic benefits. This also applies to the between-treatment portion as patients are encouraged to contact the psychotherapist during the week if they are having difficulty practicing the methods. The IRT method presents particular challenges in that it is more difficult to address avoidance behaviors that are hallmarks of PTSD. Patients who utilize avoidance and/or safety behaviors in the rescripting process limit the therapeutic effect of the treatment. In addition, it is difficult to move a patient up the nightmare hierarchy in six sessions. ERRT adopts an exposure-based approach in identifying the most difficult nightmare first. This may present a challenge for psychotherapists who are less familiar or uncomfortable with this method. Although the ERRT has a more structured protocol, there is a significant degree of abstract thinking, creativity, and nuance in the use of narrative themes, while assisting patients in rescripting of nightmares.

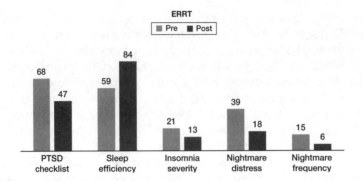

FIGURE 28.2 Outcome Scores for Exposure, Rescripting, Relaxation Therapy.

Note: Symptom reduction is indicated by a decrease in scores with the exception of Sleep Efficiency. Increase in Sleep Efficiency denotes improvement in symptoms of insomnia.

CULTURAL DIVERSITY ISSUES

Nightmare treatment is applicable to a diverse group of patients who have experienced trauma. The case examples used in this response depict a military culture that has its own values, beliefs, code of behavior, and lexicon. The application of psychological treatments for mental health disorders for this population is highly relevant at this time, and yet it can be problematic. The very nature of military training is predicated on self-reliance, tolerance of adversity and pain, and a heightened sense of caution. This does not make engaging in psychotherapy with a civilian professional particularly easy or straight forward. This becomes even more pronounced when treatments are shorter and time for developing a working alliance is restricted. It is critically important for therapists to be aware of the cultural meaning and importance of dreaming and nightmares for each of their patients. For many veterans, nightmares represent a traumatic reexperience, but also a memorial of those friends who died, and of their own survival.

FUTURE RESEARCH

While these psychosocial treatments for nightmares demonstrate efficacy, there is a poor understanding of the mechanisms of change they provide. This suggests that future dismantling studies would be an instrumental next step in the research on nightmare treatments. Future research on nightmares would also be well served by investigations comparing psychosocial treatments with pharmacological interventions to better understand the benefits of both as well as a combined approach to treatment. Improving our understanding of changes in the CNS during sleep/wake cycles before and after treatment could lead to better application, combinations and sequencing of interventions.

KEY REFERENCES

Davis, J. L. (2009). *Treating post-trauma nightmares: A cognitive behavioral approach.* New York, NY: Springer.

Krakow, B., Johnston, L., Melendrez, D., Hollifield, M., Warner, T. D., ... Herlan, M. J. (2001). An open-label trial of evidence-based cognitive behavior therapy for nightmares and insomnia in crime victims with PTSD. *American Journal of Psychiatry, 158,* 2043–2047.

Swanson, L. M., Favorite, T. K., Horin, E., & Arnedt, J. T. (2009). A combined group treatment for nightmares and insomnia in combat veterans: A pilot study. *Journal of Traumatic Stress, 22,* 639–642.

CHAPTER 29

Non-Suicidal Self-Injury

Margaret S. Andover

CLINICAL PROBLEM

Non-suicidal self-injury (NSSI) is defined as deliberate injury to the body without intent to die and includes behaviors such as cutting, burning, hitting, carving, scratching, or skin picking. Negative consequences of NSSI include physical injury varying in severity that may result in infection, scarring, and physical disfigurement, social stigma, guilt, shame, and social isolation.

Although both NSSI and attempted suicide involve deliberate, self-inflicted injuries, the behaviors differ in suicidal intent, perception, function, lethality, and chronicity. However, NSSI and attempted suicide tend to co-occur. A significant number of individuals with a history of NSSI report past suicide attempts, and history of NSSI is a risk factor for attempted suicide. Despite the distinction between behaviors with and without suicidal intent, individuals who engage in NSSI should be assessed for suicidal ideation and behaviors as they may be at greater risk for attempted suicide.

NSSI is associated with a range of disorders, including Major Depressive Disorder, Dysthymia, Depressive Disorder NOS, Posttraumatic Stress Disorder, substance abuse, eating disorders, and Borderline Personality Disorder (BPD). NSSI is also associated with increased symptomology in the absence of a diagnosis, including depressive and anxious symptoms and symptoms of BPD. It is important to note that NSSI is not associated with any one disorder; rather, the behavior occurs across psychiatric disorders.

PREVALENCE

NSSI is prevalent among both clinical and nonclinical samples. Between 21% and 44% of clinical samples and 7% to 38% of nonclinical samples report a history of NSSI. Young adults are thought to be at the highest risk for engaging in the behavior. Although NSSI generally onsets in early adolescence, a recent study reported that nearly 8% of third graders in the United States engage in NSSI. Prevalence of NSSI has not been studied extensively in older adults, but the behavior does occur in this age group. Men and women are equally likely to engage in NSSI, although there may be gender differences in method of NSSI, age of onset, and medical severity of NSSI.

CULTURAL DIVERSITY ISSUES

Although the association between ethnicity and NSSI has not been extensively studied, the prevalence of NSSI appears to be similar across ethnicities. In addition, preliminary research suggests that individuals with a sexual minority orientation may be at higher risk for engaging in NSSI, although further research is necessary.

EVIDENCE-BASED TREATMENTS

The negative consequences associated with NSSI and the behavior's alarming prevalence mandate its treatment. However, no empirically supported treatments have been identified specifically for NSSI. Further, relatively few treatment outcome studies have specifically investigated NSSI as an outcome measure. Therefore, we inform our understanding of treatments for NSSI with treatments for deliberate self-harm (DSH), a construct that includes both NSSI and attempted suicide.

Research suggests that treatments for DSH that focus on cognitive behavioral strategies, specifically Dialectical Behavior Therapy (DBT) and Problem-Solving Therapy, hold the greatest promise for decreasing NSSI. Marsha Linehan developed DBT as an outpatient treatment for individuals with BPD that included DSH as a treatment target. The treatment incorporates cognitive behavioral techniques, Eastern philosophy, and a focus on validation and acceptance. Treatment generally lasts for a minimum of one year and includes individual therapy, group therapy, telephone consultations for clients, and case consultations for psychotherapists. Several randomized controlled trials of DBT have specifically investigated NSSI as an outcome measure. These studies have shown DBT to be effective at decreasing NSSI among women with BPD; gains have also been reported at 1-month and 6-month follow-up. Researchers have also evaluated modifications to DBT, including: (a) a 6-month DBT intervention, Brief DBT (DBT-B), that reported significant decreases in NSSI behaviors and urges, and (b) treatment with adolescents, also with effective results.

Problem-Solving Therapy and problem-solving techniques have also been used to treat DSH. The goal of Problem-Solving Therapy is to teach alternative methods of identifying and resolving problems, especially those that ordinarily would have resulted in the use of DSH as a coping strategy. Manual Assisted Cognitive Therapy (MACT) is a cognitive behavioral intervention with a focus on problem solving developed for the treatment of DSH. MACT is a 6-session intervention that incorporates elements of DBT, cognitive behavioral therapy, and bibliotherapy. Following workbook chapters specifically developed for MACT, sessions address DSH functions, emotion regulation and problem solving skills, the management of cognitions and substance use, and relapse prevention following termination. While some researchers have reported significant decreases in DSH frequency and severity, others have not. One study specifically investigated MACT for the treatment of NSSI among women with BPD. They found that MACT, in addition to treatment as usual, was more effective than treatment as usual alone at decreasing NSSI. Although additional research is necessary, Problem-Solving Therapy appears to be a promising intervention for reducing DSH and NSSI, especially when combined with other cognitive behavioral techniques.

Researchers suggest that successful treatments for DSH should focus on emotion regulation, as this appears to play an important role in the decrease of DSH, and emotion regulation difficulties are associated with NSSI. Development of emotion regulation skills is a strong component of DBT. Researchers have also developed an acceptance-based emotion regulation intervention. The goal of this 14-week group intervention is to decrease NSSI by targeting emotion dysregulation and emotional avoidance. Specifically, the intervention aims to provide psychoeducation regarding self-injury, address the functions of NSSI and emotions, increase emotional awareness and understanding, and identify life values and goals. Further, the intervention addresses the benefits of emotion regulation and emotional acceptance and consequences of emotional avoidance, as well as strategies for emotion regulation and impulse control. Investigations of the acceptance-based emotion regulation group intervention have demonstrated decreases in NSSI among women with BPD and subclinical BPD.

Although difficult to treat, NSSI does respond to treatment. An empirically supported treatment for NSSI has not yet been identified, but general guidelines for treatment have been suggested. Behavioral assessment strategies are recommended in order to ascertain the specific functions of and reinforcements for NSSI. Behavioral intervention strategies can then be used to target the factors reinforcing NSSI behaviors. Cognitive restructuring techniques may be used to address distortions that may be associated with NSSI, such as the cognition of needing to be punished. In addition, a strong relationship and alliance between psychotherapist and client is an important component of the treatment process.

FUTURE RESEARCH

Research on the treatment of NSSI is in its infancy. Although NSSI and attempted suicide are distinct behaviors, much of the research that informs the treatment of NSSI has focused on the treatment of DSH. In addition, most interventions for DSH were developed for and evaluated with individuals with BPD, although NSSI occurs across psychiatric diagnoses. Future research is necessary to determine whether interventions for DSH are effective for NSSI specifically and if interventions generalize beyond the treatment of individuals with BPD. Evidence supports DBT as a promising intervention for NSSI; however, DBT may be more intensive a treatment than is necessary for decreasing NSSI in non-BPD samples. The field would benefit greatly from the development of interventions specific to NSSI that are informed by an empirically based model of NSSI as well as existing interventions that have shown promise for the treatment of this serious behavior.

KEY REFERENCES

Klonsky, E. D. (2007). Non-suicidal self-injury [Special issue]. *Journal of Clinical Psychology, 63*, 1039–1143.
Nock, M. K. (2009). *Understanding nonsuicidal self-injury: Origins, assessment, and treatment*. Washington, DC: American Psychological Association.
Walsh, B. W. (2006). *Treating self-injury: A practical guide*. New York, NY: Guilford Press.

Non-Suicidal Self-Injury

Jason J. Washburn and Denise M. Styer

COMMENT ON THE EVIDENCE-BASED RECOMMENDATIONS

The evidence base for the treatment of non-suicidal self-injury (NSSI) is clearly in its infancy. Although no empirically supported treatments exist specifically for NSSI, people needing treatment specifically for NSSI do exist. Without an evidence base, clinicians must inform their treatment of NSSI by referencing treatments developed and evaluated on other conditions, such as suicidal self-injury, Borderline Personality Disorder, or depression. As noted in the Research Section, cognitive behavioral treatments, such as Dialectical Behavior Therapy (DBT) and Problem-Solving Therapy (PST), offer promise in informing the treatment of NSSI. Yet, the data are inconclusive for the effects of DBT specifically on NSSI, and the contradictory findings of PST suggest caution in relying on this treatment approach. From a clinical perspective, neither of these treatments offer a satisfactory, comprehensive treatment package for NSSI: PST is too simplistic for the majority of individuals who seek treatment for NSSI, whereas a full DBT treatment program is typically unnecessary for the large proportion of individuals with NSSI that do not have a Borderline Personality Disorder.

CASE EXAMPLE

Subject Information and Brief History

Jessica was a 15-year-old Caucasian female with a history of multiple self-inflicted lacerations of her skin in the past year. Jessica was an only child who lived with her father; her mother left the family when Jessica was 5 years old with no further contact.

Presenting Problem

Jessica was referred by her high school counselor after she was discovered cutting her arm at school. During the intake interview, Jessica acknowledged using a razor blade to cut her skin on her upper thighs and arms an average of two or three times per week for the last 3 months. She reported experiencing social isolation and other symptoms of depression. Although she denied current suicidal behavior, she reported attempting to kill herself in the last month by overdosing with Tylenol.

Treatment Intervention and Course

Due to the severity of Jessica's self-injury and recent suicide attempt, she was admitted to a partial hospital program designed specifically to treat self-injury. Jessica's treatment was directed by a case formulation which hypothesized that her self-injurious behavior functioned to regulate her affective distress. This was hypothesized to be largely driven by interpersonal difficulties with her father.

Jessica was initially resistant to engaging in treatment, stating that her father should be in treatment instead of her. Understanding that Jessica was at a precontemplative stage of change, her initial treatment relied heavily on motivational interviewing techniques and psychoeducation regarding self-injury. As Jessica acclimated to the program and began to participate in the groups, she acknowledged that self-injury was not the most effective way for her to regulate her emotions. With greater engagement in the program, treatment focused on identifying triggers for Jessica's self-injury as well as healthy alternatives to regulate her affect. For example, Jessica identified arguments with her father as a trigger for self-injury. Treatment focused on helping her to regulate her affective responses and "sit through" uncomfortable feelings during arguments with her father by engaging in diaphragmatic breathing, challenging cognitive distortions (e.g., catastrophic and black-and-white thinking), and engaging in physical exercise (e.g., yoga). As she improved her affect tolerance, treatment also focused on recognizing and challenging cognitive distortions, particularly self-derogatory beliefs.

Despite Jessica's progress in treatment, she continued to experience significant affective distress due, in part, to her father's refusal to participate in treatment. Indeed, Jessica's father indicated treatment was "a waste of time" and expressed anger that Jessica's problems interfered with his personal life. Using a variety of approaches, such as motivational interviewing and providing psychoeducation on the long-term consequences of Jessica's self-injury, Jessica's treatment team was eventually able to engage Jessica's father in treatment. Family and individual sessions with Jessica's father helped him to identify that his anger toward Jessica was largely driven by his anger toward Jessica's mother for leaving him. He eventually accepted a referral for individual psychotherapy to address his anger, and Jessica and her father agreed to a basic set of rules for family roles and communication.

Outcome

Jessica was successfully discharged from the partial hospitalization program after 12 days of treatment. She began outpatient psychotherapy that involved individual and family sessions. Jessica also attended a posthospitalization aftercare group at the hospital. Approximately 3 months after discharge from the partial hospitalization program, Jessica continued to experience occasional urges to self-injure but had not engaged in self-injurious behaviors. She also reported moderate improvements in her depression and no suicidal behavior, although only modest improvements in her relationship with her father.

CHALLENGES IN APPLYING THE EVIDENCE-BASED APPROACH

NSSI is a functional behavior, and, as such, it is perceived as useful or helpful by many people who routinely engage in the behavior. A skilled clinician with the most efficacious treatment for NSSI will still face difficulty in achieving treatment success if her or his patient is not motivated for treatment. Clinicians must assess and address motivation for change when treating persons with NSSI, and it may be necessary to adjust treatment strategies based on an individual's current stage of change.

Because existing empirically supported treatments were not designed specifically for NSSI, they often don't address factors that specifically contribute to and maintain NSSI. For example, the ideal treatment of NSSI would assess for and treat the function(s) of NSSI, target the influence of self-derogation on emotional dysregulation, address physical factors such as pain tolerance and body image, and tackle family contributors and/or peer influences that maintain NSSI. Consequently, treatments for NSSI must flexibly integrate cognitive, behavioral, dialectical, interpersonal, and family systems strategies based on a coherent, theoretically sound case formulation. Such a treatment has yet to be clearly articulated and evaluated in the literature.

CULTURAL DIVERSITY ISSUES

The majority of persons with NSSI who need treatment are female. However, in our experience, approximately 10% will be males. NSSI among males may manifest differently than females, such as engaging in fighting to cause pain, punching walls, or purposely getting hurt when participating in sports or hobbies. Although NSSI has been found to occur across racial/ethnic groups, acculturation can be an important part of treatment of NSSI. Acculturative stress is often a trigger for self-injury, especially among individuals who experience marginalized cultural identities. As such, acculturative stress and family conflicts related to intergenerational differences in acculturation must be assessed and addressed in order for successful treatment of NSSI. Finally, we also find that many of the youth we treat for NSSI express fluid and sometimes confused sexual identities. Although sexual identity development is not always a critical moderator of treatment outcome, for some youth it is a part of a larger concern with sense of self and acceptance, and requires direct attention.

FUTURE RESEARCH

The explosion of research on NSSI in the last decade has greatly expanded our understanding of this disorder, yet we still lack any data on the efficacy of treatments designed specifically for NSSI. Put simply, we need to create the evidence base for the treatment of NSSI. Although treatments of related conditions can inform the treatment of NSSI, even powerful treatments such as DBT for borderline personality disorder fail to demonstrate consistent effects on NSSI. The first priority of clinical research in the field of NSSI must be the development and evaluation of comprehensive treatments specifically designed to treat NSSI.

Future research must also move beyond aggregating of all persons with NSSI into one group. Individuals with NSSI are not a homogenous group; some may be experimenting with NSSI and are relatively straightforward to treat with evidence-informed approaches, whereas others may have long-term, entrenched patterns of self-injury that are complicated by co-occurring conditions, such as eating disorders, substance abuse, PTSD, and Borderline Personality Disorder. Although some research has explored latent classes of NSSI among nonclinical samples, we need to better understand the multiple ways in which individuals with NSSI present in the clinical setting. Our clinical experience suggests that most individuals with

NSSI can be grouped into several classes, and that these classifications can inform treatment. However, data are needed to verify these observations.

KEY REFERENCES

Klonsky, E. D., Muehlenkamp, J. J., Lewis, S. P., & Walsh, B. (2011). *Nonsuicidal self-injury: Vol. 22. Advances in psychotherapy—evidence-based practice.* Cambridge, MA: Hogrefe.

Nixon, M. K., & Heath, N. (2009). *Self-injury in youth: The essential guide to assessment and intervention.* New York, NY: Routledge.

Nock, M. K. (2010). Self-injury. *Annual Review of Clinical Psychology, 6,* 339–363.

CHAPTER 30

Obsessive Compulsive Disorder

Edna B. Foa

CLINICAL PROBLEM

Obsessive Compulsive Disorder (OCD) is characterized by recurrent obsessions and/or compulsions that interfere substantially with daily functioning. Obsessions are persistent ideas, thoughts, impulses, or images that are experienced as intrusive and inappropriate and cause marked anxiety or distress. Obsessional content is frequently categorized into six areas including: aggression, contamination, sex, hoarding/saving, religion, and symmetry/exactness. What distinguishes OCD obsessions from nonclinical obsessions are the greater frequency, intensity, and discomfort of the former.

In addition to frequent obsessions, most individuals with OCD (98%) engage in actions (compulsions) to reduce discomfort from obsessions. Compulsions are repetitive behaviors or mental acts of which the goal is to prevent or reduce anxiety or distress. As in the case of obsessions, compulsions are also often classified into six categories including: cleaning, checking, repeating, counting, ordering/arranging, and hoarding/collecting. The most common compulsion reported by patients with OCD is checking.

OCD results in severe personal distress and interferes with employment, relationships, and the daily activities of living in adults and children/adolescents. Between 80% and 100% of individuals with severe OCD report significant impairment in home, work, relationships, and social life. One study showed that 22% of treatment-seeking participants with OCD were unemployed compared to the 6% unemployment rate for the U.S. general population at the time. Another study showed an even higher unemployment rate (40%) among patients with OCD. OCD patients are also overrepresented in health care populations. One survey showed that OCD patients saw dermatologists and cardiologists more often than the general public and even more than individuals with panic disorder or GAD. Such high medical utilization, unemployment, and lost productivity due to OCD cost the U.S. economy billions of dollars each year. It is estimated that in 1990, the direct and indirect cost of OCD to the U.S. economy was $8.4 billion. Indeed, OCD is considered one of the top ten causes of disability worldwide.

PREVALENCE

It is estimated that between 2 and 3 million people are suffering from OCD in the United States. The National Comorbidity Survey Replication (NCS-R) showed that approximately 1.6% of the U.S. population reported OCD at some point in their lives with 1% of the sample experiencing OCD within the last year. The average onset of the disorder in males is earlier than the onset in females, but in adulthood the prevalence is the same in males and females.

CULTURAL DIVERSITY ISSUES

Interestingly, studies on the general population in the United States suggest that the prevalence of OCD among African Americans is similar to that of Caucasians. However, very few African Americans seek treatment in OCD clinics. The percentage of African Americans in major OCD clinics in the United States is between 1% and 2%.

EVIDENCE-BASED TREATMENTS

The first real breakthrough occurred in the 1960s, when Meyer described two patients successfully treated with a behavioral therapy program that included exposure to distressing objects and situations, coupled with prevention of the associated compulsions or rituals. This treatment program has become known as "exposure and response prevention" or EX/RP. The word "Response" in EX/RP is often replaced by "Ritual" as the word "Response" is too broad—not all responses to obsessions are compulsions. Though behaviorally based, EX/RP includes both behavioral and cognitive techniques. A more cognitive approach, that is cognitive therapy (CT), is advocated by some and may be appropriate for patients who are not responsive to behavioral strategies. However, EX/RP and CT both typically include behavioral and cognitive elements. EX/RP has been used in a variety of formats, including individual and group treatment, family-based treatment, computer-based treatment, self-help techniques, and intensive programs.

EX/RP treatment program includes the following procedures:

- *Exposure in vivo* (i.e., exposure in real life), involves helping the patient confront cues that trigger obsessive thoughts. Cues include objects, words, images, or situations.
- *Imaginal exposure* involves asking the patient to imagine in detail the distressing thoughts or situations. It is used primarily to help patients confront the disastrous consequences that they fear will occur if they do not perform the rituals.
- *Ritual prevention* involves instructing the patient to abstain from the ritualizing that he believes prevents the feared disaster or reduces the distress produced by the obsession (e.g., washing hands after touching the floor and fearing contracting a disease). By practicing ritual prevention, the patient learns that the anxiety and distress decrease without ritualizing and that the feared consequences do not occur.
- *Processing* involves discussing with the patient what happened during the exposure as it relates to experiencing changes in anxiety levels, as well as to gaining insights about feared consequences.
- *Home visits* involve planning and executing visits to the patient's home environment, to both collect important information about the patient's OCD symptoms and to aid in transferring and implementing treatment gains.

The bulk of the treatment program involves the practice of exposure and ritual prevention exercises, both in session and as homework assignments, working through more difficult exposures as treatment progresses. During the sessions, an emphasis is placed on relapse prevention and future maintenance of gains. These sessions can be conducted once a week, twice a week, or daily in an intensive treatment program, depending on symptom severity and logistical considerations. Treatment includes both therapist-supervised exposures and ritual prevention and self-monitored exposure and ritual prevention at home.

Since 1966, after Victor Meyer's initial positive report of the efficacy of EX/RP with two OCD patients who suffered contamination obsessions and rituals, numerous controlled studies of EX/RP treatment have been conducted around the world with thousands of OCD patients. Results clearly indicated that EX/RP is quite effective in significantly reducing OCD symptoms; moreover, most patients maintain their gains following treatment termination. A number of randomized controlled trials have found that EX/RP is superior to a variety of control treatments, including placebo medication, relaxation, and anxiety management training. Importantly, studies have indicated that the successful outcomes of EX/RP are not limited to highly selected samples of OCD patients who participate in controlled studies, but are also obtained in clinical samples.

Pharmacotherapy

Research in the past three decades has provided a large body of knowledge about the efficacy of medications for OCD symptom reduction, such as the tricyclic antidepressants, including clomipramine (CMI), and the selective serotonin reuptake inhibitors (SSRIs). In controlled trials, CMI has been found consistently superior to placebo. Similar positive results versus placebo have been obtained with the SSRIs such as fluvoxamine, fluoxetine, sertraline and paroxetine. Indeed, the FDA has approved each of these medications as treatments for adult OCD. Compared to tricyclic antidepressants, SSRI medications have shown superior results, with clomipramine (an SRI) showing stronger and more consistent therapeutic effect than other tricyclics.

Overall, medication studies suggest that up to 60% of OCD patients benefit from treatment with medication. However, because of the difficulties in treating OCD, medication trials have used a definition of response that is more liberal than that used in, for example, depression studies. An OCD patient is considered to have a positive response to medication if symptoms decrease by 25% to 35%. Although these reductions reflect meaningfully clinical improvement, many OCD sufferers who respond to medication continue to have clinically significant symptoms, which considerably affect their functioning and quality of life. Moreover, a substantial relapse has been found when medication treatment is discontinued.

Augmenting Medication Effects With EX/RP

In a well-controlled study, patients on a stable and therapeutic dose of an SRI medication, who experienced only partial response, were given either EX/RP or Stress Management Training (SMT) while being maintained on their medication. At the end of treatment and at follow-up, EX/RP was significantly superior to SMT in further reducing patients' OCD symptoms. Adding EX/RP also improved patients' functioning and quality of life. In other words, continued symptoms of SRI-treated OCD can be significantly reduced by adding EX/RP.

FUTURE RESEARCH

While we have effective treatments for OCD, most patients remain somewhat symptomatic and only about 40% have excellent response or achieve remission. As excellent outcomes are associated with general functioning and quality of life, future research should focus on further improving treatment efficacy by studying mechanisms underlying the treatments and moderators and mediators of treatment efficacy.

KEY REFERENCES

Abramowitz, J. S., McKay, D., & Taylor, S. (2008). *Clinical handbook of obsessive compulsive disorder and related problems.* Baltimore, MD: Johns Hopkins University Press.

Foa, E. B., & Wilson, R. (2001) *Stop Obsessing! How to overcome your obsessions and compulsions* (2nd ed.). New York, NY: Bantam Doubleday Dell.

Foa, E. B., Yadin, E., & Lichner, T. K. (2012). *Exposure and ritual prevention for obsessive compulsive disorder therapist guide.* London, UK: Oxford University Press.

Clinician Application

Obsessive Compulsive Disorder

Elna Yadin

COMMENT ON THE EVIDENCE-BASED RECOMMENDATIONS

The extensive research on Exposure and Response (Ritual) Prevention (EX/RP) treatment for Obsessive Compulsive Disorder (OCD) has clearly demonstrated the effectiveness of this therapeutic approach. Clinical application of EX/RP in people with OCD with a large variety of OCD presentations has often resulted in noticeable and quantifiable improvement in their daily functioning and overall quality of life, with many continuing to maintain their gains for years. Adherence to the principles of EX/RP while utilizing creative tailoring to the individual patient is what helps solidify the effectiveness and long-term benefit of this treatment. Given the research and clinical track record of this evidence-based treatment, the scarcity of available clinicians providing EX/RP in their own practices or referring patients to receive it elsewhere is rather puzzling. The goals going forward will be to increase awareness among OCD patients and their families about the disorder in its recognizable, as well as its more subtle forms, to educate them about the treatment for it, and to improve dissemination of EX/RP to clinicians who see patients with OCD.

CASE EXAMPLE

Subject Information and Brief History

Linda is a 38-year-old Caucasian woman, married with four children ranging from 2 years to 14. She and her husband owned a small family business. She reported suffering from OCD symptoms on and off over the years since her early teens, and had received treatment in a variety of clinical settings, including medication. She reported that although there were times when her OCD subsided somewhat, she had never achieved a level of remission that was satisfactory. Her OCD symptoms tended to shift and "to latch on to a new focal point," which meant that any personal incident or a news report entailing socially inappropriate or undesirable behavior could become the focus of her obsessions, triggering renewed distress that required avoidance or ritualizing.

Presenting Problem

Linda presented for evaluation owing to a recent major exacerbation of her symptoms after a fender-bender experience with a motorist on the highway near her home that was not her fault. Her symptoms included obsessions about being contaminated by germs and dirt from other people, and especially being "emotionally" contaminated by badness and evil. Her main fear was that by coming in contact with anything associated with "bad people" she would contract or acquire their undesirable qualities. Her compulsions included washing and cleaning, designating "clean" and "dirty" zones, neutralizing "badness" by replacing it with "goodness," and engaging in major avoidance of words, places, and people that were associated with the incident that triggered the flare up. Linda realized that her life had become consumed by her OCD and that she, as well as her family, was suffering. She had been on a selective serotonin reuptake inhibitor (SSRI; Zoloft) for some years. Upon assessment, her OCD was found to be in the severe range and EX/RP was recommended. She decided to take time out of her busy schedule to focus on the treatment. She opted for the intensive treatment format that entailed daily 2-hour therapist-guided sessions for 3.5 weeks.

Treatment Intervention and Course

In session 1, information on Linda's OCD symptoms and history was collected. In addition, explanation about OCD and the rationale for and description of the treatment were presented. Self-monitoring was introduced, which included noting the triggers that produced the urge to avoid or to ritualize, the degree of distress associated with them, the types of compulsions she engaged in, and the length of time spent doing so. Session 2 entailed continued gathering of relevant information in order to generate a treatment plan and a hierarchy of triggers and relevant exposure exercises. The monitoring sheets from the previous session were examined and information based on them was incorporated into the treatment plan. An extremely important component of this process was to explore and identify the core fear that was feeding many of Linda's avoidances and rituals. It was clearly identified as fear of becoming or being perceived as an "irresponsible and evil person." This is why her OCD often shifted from one trigger to another over the course of her illness. The scale of Subjective Units of Discomfort or Distress (SUDs) was introduced, and a hierarchy of items for exposures was created. Examples of just a few of the items on Linda's hierarchy included buying foods in bulk at the supermarket; pumping gas at the service station and driving home without washing or sanitizing her hands; parking in a lot at the local hardware chain store where she had pulled over after the fender-bender incident; using the motorist's name; mixing her old contaminated and new uncontaminated makeup products; imagining herself being rejected by her family and community because they thought of her as being an irresponsible and evil person.

Starting with session 3, exposure and ritual prevention were practiced at each visit with increasingly difficult exposures. Linda acknowledged that for the first time in her illness history she truly understood the treatment rationale and the consequences of not applying the principles fully. She was, therefore, very motivated to get her OCD under control once and for all which made her approach the exposures and ritual prevention exercises with vigor and resolve. She was able to see that when she deliberately confronted the triggers that she had previously avoided or ritualized, she experienced some initial increased anxiety, but was able to tolerate it and, consequently, feel a reduction in her anxiety. In processing the exposure and ritual prevention experience, Linda often commented on the desirable sense of freedom resulting from not having to perform a ritual or needing to avoid the triggers. This allowed her peace of mind and increased precious time for her to engage more fully in her family's life. Around session 8, the highest items on Linda's hierarchy were confronted both as in vivo and imaginal exposure exercises. Those included touching many "contaminated" items without washing, showering, or neutralizing, as well as conducting imaginal exposures to scenarios where she was responsible for the death of her children due to inadvertent negligence or outright blatant lack of parental caring that then resulted in imprisonment and isolation from her family and friends.

During the remainder of the sessions, exposures were repeated and varied to include possible future variations, and relapse prevention strategies were introduced. Thus, Linda was given several descriptions of potential incidents or stimuli that could trigger her obsessional distress in the future and asked to tailor specific in vivo and imaginal exposure and ritual prevention exercises to address them. Linda did not require home visits as she was successfully able to implement the exposures designed during treatment in her home environment. The final session included an evaluation of Linda's progress in treatment and preparation for return to her regular routine, with discussion of strategies to maximize relapse prevention. Lastly, follow-up weekly phone calls were scheduled with Linda for the next 6 weeks to help ease her transition from the active treatment phase to the maintenance phase.

Outcome

At the end of the full course of EX/RP, Linda had achieved a level of partial remission. Her Yale-Brown Obsessive-Compulsive Scale scores went from 28 (Severe) to 12 (Mild). In the months following the active treatment phase, Linda's OCD continued to improve and she recently reported that in spite of experiencing occasional intrusive obsessional thoughts, she never engages in any form of avoidance or ritualizing in response to them. She has since offered support to other people with OCD who have had difficulty deciding whether or not to undertake EX/RP or in the early stages of the treatment when encouragement to fight the OCD is most needed.

CULTURAL DIVERSITY ISSUES

In spite of the fact that the prevalence of OCD is similar across cultural groups, there is a clear underrepresentation of minorities with OCD seeking treatment of any kind, including EX/RP. This is true not only for African American populations but also for people of Hispanic, Asian, and other minority populations. Increasing awareness and reducing the stigma about having OCD and seeking treatment for it remain an ongoing outreach goal.

CHALLENGES IN APPLYING THE EVIDENCE-BASED APPROACH

Potential challenges in the treatment of OCD include: lack of personal motivation to get well, overvalued ideation or poor insight (i.e., a strongly held belief that a feared consequence will indeed come true), intense fear of experiencing symptoms of anxiety, and long-term disastrous consequences that cannot be easily disconfirmed during an exposure. Most of these challenges can be addressed with: (a) providing psychoeducation in patient-friendly language about OCD and EX/RP at the evaluation phase and at the beginning of treatment; (b) individual tailoring of the pace and nature of exposures; (c) involvement of family members in an appropriate and helpful manner; and (d) examining the cost–benefit ratio of living a healthy life now with the chance of a potential, vague disastrous consequence in the remote future.

FUTURE RESEARCH

Clinically, some patients require more help developing successful strategies for ritual prevention during treatment, and some patients do better with scheduled follow-up booster sessions after the active phase to help them solidify their gains. Future research should examine augmentation strategies to improve the achievement of good end state results in the treatment phase and to help maintain gains after treatment termination.

KEY REFERENCES

Foa, E. B., Yadin, E., & Lichner, T. K. (2012). *Exposure and response (ritual) prevention for obsessive compulsive disorder.* New York, NY: Oxford University Press.

Penzel, F. (2000). *Obsessive-compulsive disorders: A complete guide to getting well and staying well.* Oxford University Press.

Yadin, E., Foa, E. B., & Lichner, T. K. (2012). *Treating your OCD with exposure and response (ritual) prevention.* New York, NY: Oxford University Press.

CHAPTER 31

Perfectionism

Allison C. Kelly and David C. Zuroff

CLINICAL PROBLEM

There has been general agreement since the 1990s that perfectionism is a multidimensional construct with both adaptive and maladaptive components. Factor analytic studies of North American measures reveal two broad dimensions of perfectionism, and similar factors have emerged with different measures in Hindu, Indian, and Chinese samples. The first, often termed *personal standards perfectionism* (PS-PFT), is characterized by the setting of and striving toward ambitious goals, and involves a preference for order and organization. The second, often called *evaluative concerns* or *self-critical perfectionism* (SC-PFT), is characterized by harsh self-criticism when one fails to meet self-imposed standards, worries about making mistakes, chronic fears of being criticized, and failing to meet others' expectations. We use the term PS-PFT when referring to questionnaire subscales that routinely load onto the former latent factor and SC-PFT for those which typically load onto the latter.

SC-PFT has been associated with negative self-representations, disturbed interpersonal relationships, avoidant coping, low positive affect and high negative affect, and is elevated in major depressive disorder, eating disorders, anxiety disorders, and obsessive compulsive personality disorder. It is even more elevated in individuals suffering from comorbid psychiatric disorders. PS-PFT, however, has been linked to adaptive processes like problem-focused coping, conscientiousness, positive affect, and well-being. Although some studies, particularly in the field of eating disorders, suggest that PS-PFT may be maladaptive, its relationship to Axis I symptoms tends to disappear when SC-PFT is controlled. For instance, one study found that among individuals with binge eating disorder, SC-PFT explained the relationship between perfectionism and eating disorder symptoms, and the same pattern has been found in depression. The research therefore suggests that treatments for perfectionism should intervene less with the tendency to set high personal standards and more with the propensity to self-criticize and fear judgment when these standards are not met.

PREVALENCE

Data on the prevalence of perfectionism are limited both because perfectionism is typically conceptualized and assessed dimensionally rather than categorically, and because there are numerous measures of perfectionism making it difficult to compare across studies and derive normative data. One approach has been to categorize individuals as either SC or PS perfectionists if their scores on the relevant measure(s) are more than one standard deviation above the sample mean. This method results in prevalence rates of approximately 15% no matter the sample or measure, and might thus be considered artificial. Attempts to categorize perfectionists using cluster analyses reveal slightly higher prevalence rates. A study of 1,537 college students yielded three clusters, with 34% of the sample considered adaptive perfectionists (high PS-PFT), 29% maladaptive perfectionists (high PS-PFT and high SC-PFT), and 37% nonperfectionists. The authors uncovered these same clusters among 875 ninth graders, who showed similar prevalence rates of 30.2%, 34.8%, and 35%, respectively. In earlier research using a different measure of perfectionism, cluster analyses revealed these same three categories among 800 academically talented sixth-grade students, with 32.8% emerging as PS perfectionists, 25% as SC perfectionists, and 41.7% as nonperfectionists. A follow-up study found that prevalence rates did not differ between sixth graders who had been identified as academically talented and those who had not. Although the conceptualization and measurement of perfectionism limit research on prevalence rates, the few existing studies suggest that one quarter to one third of people across age groups could be classified as either a PS or SC perfectionist. Whether it is meaningful to study perfectionism in this categorical way nevertheless remains a contentious issue.

CULTURAL DIVERSITY ISSUES

Cross-cultural researchers suggest that people from more collectivistic societies are more self-critical and biased toward negative self-relevant information than those from more individualistic societies, who self-enhance and focus more on positive self-relevant information. Indeed, it is thought that in certain Eastern cultures, the interdependent construal of self may be associated with a propensity to critically assess one's own upholding of social norms, and correct substandard behaviors. Several studies have offered indirect support for this theory. One found that Japanese individuals held a more pessimistic bias about encountering negative events, taken to be a sign of higher self-criticism, than did European Americans. In another study, individuals from East Asia reported being aware of their negative attributes for more years than Westerners were, and indicated a greater motivation to improve upon these attributes. Using more traditional measures of SC-PFT, several empirical studies of American college students have found SC-PFT to be higher among Asian Americans compared to their Caucasian American peers, and sometimes African American peers. One study found, however, that Black college students in South Africa had higher SC-PFT than their White and Asian counterparts. Indeed, a study among children aged 11 to 14 similarly found that African American girls had higher levels of SC-PFT than Caucasian girls. The literature therefore suggests that there appear to be cross-cultural differences in SC-PFT, with more collectivistic cultures showing higher levels of the trait. Future research would benefit from examining cultural differences and similarities in the antecedents and consequences of SC-PFT.

EVIDENCE-BASED TREATMENTS

Treatment studies underscore the importance of targeting SC-PFT. It has been associated with poor prognosis across a range of treatments and diagnostic categories, including anorexia nervosa, social anxiety, and depression. Promising, however, is that reductions in SC-PFT during treatment for depression predict larger and faster subsequent improvements in depressive symptoms, suggesting that the successful treatment of SC-PFT may allow changes in presenting psychopathology.

Various psychological interventions have proven effective at reducing SC-PFT. Cognitive behavioral therapy (CBT) has been associated with reductions in SC-PFT in individuals with social anxiety disorder and depression. In a group of psychiatric patients, compassion-focused therapy (CFT), which teaches self-compassion—a kind, accepting attitude toward oneself in response to distress and disappointments—promoted reductions in SC-PFT and shame. It has also been found that teaching students to meditate daily for 4 months was associated with a decline in SC-PFT cognitions two semesters later.

A handful of studies have compared treatments for perfectionism with scarce evidence of differential efficacy. In a large sample of depressed outpatients, researchers found significant and equivalent reductions in SC-PFT across four treatment conditions: CBT, interpersonal therapy (IPT), imipramine plus clinical management, and placebo plus clinical management. Another study found that therapist-guided and client-directed cognitive behavioral self-help interventions both reduced SC-PFT and associated dysfunction among adults who self-identified as having problems related to perfectionism. In a similar sample, a study comparing no treatment, stress management, and stress management plus CBT, found that improvements in SC-PFT and distress were greater the more intensive the treatment. Another study compared equally intensive treatments for bulimia nervosa (BN) varying in content (CBT for BN, CBT for perfectionism, and mindfulness training) and there were no Treatment × Time effects for SC-PFT or eating disorder symptoms. These studies cast doubts on the differential efficacy of one class of therapeutic interventions over another, with one study suggesting that treatments for SC-PFT may be more efficacious the more intensive and active the intervention.

Common factors in treatment offer another perspective from which to understand how best to intervene with perfectionism. The therapeutic relationship, in particular, appears to play an important role. One study found that individuals high in SC-PFT struggle to form a strong alliance, which in turn explained their poorer prognosis. Indeed, a strong therapeutic alliance facilitates not only reductions in Axis I complaints, but also reductions in SC-PFT. There is also some empirical evidence that a strong therapeutic relationship allows self-critical perfectionists to internalize a supportive other and rework their models of others as critical and self as unworthy. In fact, recent research suggests that certain therapists are more effective than others in part because of their ability to share the goals of their patients, and bond with them. Research has found that patients whose therapists had higher overall ratings of warmth, nonjudgment, and positive regard showed faster reductions in SC-PFT and depressive symptoms across three treatment conditions. Although more research on mechanism is needed, studies to date suggest that treatment-providers who excel at forming constructive relationships with their patients may provide the conditions necessary for SC-PFT to abate.

Another mechanism by which SC-PFT may dissolve is through increased self-compassion, which may be facilitated by a strong therapeutic relationship and/or specific interventions. Regarding the latter, researchers found that mindfulness exercises can increase self-compassion. CFT-based interventions, which involve imagery and letter-writing, have also been found to increase the capacity for self-compassion. It has, in addition, been found that among self-critical individuals, CMT exercises may facilitate constructive behavior change. Self-compassion therefore appears to be a promising treatment target for those high in SC-PFT.

FUTURE RESEARCH

Research to date reveals a range of therapies (e.g., CBT, IPT, CFT) and therapist qualities that can help to reduce SC-PFT. A crucial next step is to determine whether there are facets of perfectionism which are especially important to target in treatment. Various features and correlates of perfectionism—mental representations, rumination, coping styles, perceptions of support, self-compassion, and resilience to self-attacks—have been identified as candidate targets and warrant empirical testing. Another important research avenue is to shed further light on the role of common factors in psychotherapy. On the patient side, researchers have found preliminary evidence that helping perfectionists to develop less external, guilt-focused reasons for entering treatment could improve outcomes. On the psychotherapist side, there is a need for more research into the features of treatment providers who succeed at lowering the SC-PFT of their patients. Yet another next step might be to study the interaction of common and specific factors in treatment. It could be, for instance, that certain interventions are effective at reducing SC-PFT only when psychotherapists focus on delivering them in a compassionate, de-shaming way.

KEY REFERENCES

Dunkley, D. M., Zuroff, D. C., & Blankstein, K. R. (2006). Self-critical perfectionism and daily affect: Dispositional and situational influences on stress and coping. *Journal of Personality and Social Psychology, 84*, 234–252.

Gilbert, P., & Procter, S. (2006). Compassionate mind training for people with high shame and self-criticism: Overview and pilot study of a group therapy approach. *Clinical Psychology and Psychotherapy, 13*, 353–379.

Zuroff, D. C., Kelly, A. C., Leybman, M. J., Blatt, S. J., & Wampold, B. E. (2010). Between-therapist and within-therapist differences in the quality of the therapeutic relationship: Effects on maladjustment and self-critical perfectionism. *Journal of Clinical Psychology, 66*, 681–697.

Clinician Application

Perfectionism

Golan Shahar

COMMENT ON THE EVIDENCE-BASED RECOMMENDATIONS

Kelly and Zuroff highlight a unique but frequently overlooked issue in clinical psychology, namely, the efficacy of evidence-based therapy, not for a diagnosable psychiatric disorder, but for *psychological vulnerability*. Neither perfectionism in general, nor self-critical perfectionism (SC-PFT) in particular, appear in the *DSM* or ICD, other than "between the lines" where the patient's sense of self lies. While the role of SC-PFT in various forms of psychopathology is well established in research, evidence-based treatments geared specifically toward perfectionism or self-criticism are relatively rare.

My reading of the literature, empirical research, and clinical practice with adolescents and young adults unanimously suggest that the problem is linked to self-criticism rather than perfectionism, or even "self-critical perfectionism." All my experience leads to the conclusion that individuals are at risk for developing psychopathology not owing to their drive to maximize or perfect performance, but rather, when they adopt a punitive, accusatory stance toward the self. I also fully concur with Kelly and Zuroff's stress on the psychotherapeutic relationship as a focal and, in my opinion, the most central, point in treatment for self-criticism. One of the prerequisites for the successful implementation of any evidence-based intervention is the patients' sense that they are cared for (as opposed to being overlooked), appreciated (in contrast to being denigrated), and nurtured (rather than being undermined).

CASE EXAMPLE

Subject Information and Brief History

Twenty-five-year-old Ilan has been in therapy with me for the past 4 years. He is a brilliant, articulate, hardworking, and successful professional student with excellent career prospects, echoing previous performance during elementary and high school and in the Israeli Defense Forces.

Ilan's parents divorced when he was 5 years old. Even prior to the divorce, Ilan reported, he had felt neglected and marginalized in the family. This feeling was significantly exacerbated following the divorce. His parents had joint custody, thus, Ilan and his older brother spent part of the year with their mother and part with their father. When the father remarried, the turbulent relationship the two boys experienced with their stepmother further contributed to Ilan's sense of being overlooked. To ease his mental pain, Ilan sought comfort in food. However, the mockery his increasing obesity exposed him to at school only aggravated his distress. Having made a conscious, committed decision to diet, Ilan is successfully breaking this cycle. His strong will, indeed, together with his talents, are substantially responsible for his academic and professional success.

Presenting Problem

Ilan reported being depressed (i.e., sad, agitated, anhedonic, pessimistic) for as long as he could remember. Upon clinical inquiry, he was able to differentiate between long periods of comparatively low-level depression and more circumscribed periods, usually lasting for months, during which his depression peaked and he also became suicidal. He made a single, relatively nonlethal, suicide attempt during his teens. On intake, he conveyed clear suicidal ideations and plans. However, the plans were not immediate, but rather projected into the future (e.g., "Unless I find someone to love by 36, I am probably going to kill myself"). Despite these thoughts, Ilan was determined to give treatment a chance, and an evidence-based suicide risk assessment using several test instruments established a moderately high level of risk. Because he was not an imminent danger to himself, outpatient treatment was considered feasible. My diagnosis was Recurrent Major Depressive

Episode superimposed upon Dysthymic Disorder. The following scores were obtained via standard assessment: Beck Depression Inventory-II = 40, Beck Anxiety Inventory = 18, an elevation (more than 3) on the depression subscale of the Brief Symptoms Inventory, clear indications of suicide ideations on the Suicide Behavior Questionnaire, and very few suicidal mitigators as gleaned from the Reasons for Living Scale.

Underlying all of Ilan's symptoms and diagnoses was a clear, highly ominous level of self-criticism. Ilan used to spontaneously and excessively berate himself, declaring himself "unlovable and deficient." He bluntly overlooked his talents and accomplishments, defining them both as trivial and meaningless. These self-evaluations served as the foundation for a profound sense of hopelessness, at times escalating into suicidal ideations. Tackling Ilan's self-criticism was thus determined as a central treatment goal.

Treatment Intervention and Course

I decided to adopt a cognitive behavioral treatment integrating two evidence-based components: behavioral activation, aimed at alleviating Ilan's depressive anhedonia, and acceptance/mindfulness to help him combat self-critical and self-derogatory thoughts. The rationale and evidence of both interventions being explained to him, he hesitantly agreed to give the treatment a try. Concurrently, I referred him for a psychiatric consultation, emphasizing the importance of medication for chronic and severe depression (and suicidality). Ilan was very suspicious about the prospect (and cost) of seeing a psychiatrist, and it took considerable persuasion on my part to convince him to do so. The (very able) psychiatrist prescribed a course of Wellbutrin, which took the edge off his depressed mood and increased his energy level. However, despite the initiation of this medication trial persistent depressive symptoms remained and Ilan's self-criticism was also unaffected, feeding his ongoing thoughts of death and prospects of future suicidality.

Although I thought the first sessions, which focused on behavioral activation and acceptance/mindfulness, were going well, Ilan quickly expressed his pessimism with respect to psychotherapy. He was adamant not only that the sessions were not beneficial, but also that, in principle, I was incapable of helping him. He experienced me as a smug, know-it-all psychologist who cared little about him as a person. I was surprised and somewhat taken aback. Initially, I tried to inquire about the specifics of my intervention in the hope of identifying elements which Ilan might have found offensive or adverse. When none were pinpointed, I made the mistake of proposing that Ilan would perhaps be best off seeking another psychotherapist. To this he responded indignantly: "This is it? You're giving up on me that quickly?!" It was only then that I understood that Ilan might be testing my commitment in the face of *his own self-criticism and hopelessness*. A trial of substance, in fact, Ilan's demeanor indeed evoked my own self-doubt and self-criticism. I raised this possibility with Ilan. "You got me," he said. "I have to test people before I let them in." True to his word, he has done so repeatedly and meticulously over the course of the psychotherapy.

During treatment, we employed *evidence-based techniques*, primarily behavioral activation, mindfulness, and a mild form of cognitive restructuring (conceptualizing Ilan's self-criticism as an internal voice and encouraging him to locate other voices which might challenge the self-critical ones) in order to help Ilan fight off gnawing self-criticism, depressive symptoms, and suicidality.

These techniques have been implemented, however, with a constant, twofold relational focus: (a) on the way in which Ilan's depression adversely impacts his social environment, and (b) on his experience of the psychotherapeutic relationship, ensuring that he feels supported, understood, seen, and respected. These processes are ongoing.

Outcome

The last formal assessment taken with Ilan 3 months ago revealed a precipitous decline in depressive symptoms (BDI-II = 10) and anxiety (BAI = 6). Although some suicidal thoughts remained, they were weaker and lacked intent and plans. Marked interpersonal developments took place in Ilan's work, both within and without treatment. In psychotherapy, Ilan has repeatedly expressed his trust in my candor and commitment (as well as ability) to help him, which has been deeply gratifying. Outside treatment, he has reported an improved ability to negotiate conflict with friends and family members, forming some new—and serious—romantic relationships. Despite these ending frustratingly, causing Ilan considerable pain, he has not sunk into depression or self-criticism.

CHALLENGES IN APPLYING THE EVIDENCE-BASED APPROACH

As should be clear from the discussion and case presentation, self-criticism is unlikely to be amenable to a *straightforward implementation of evidence-based intervention*. Self-critical patients experience any and all interventions, and most occurrences in the world, as potential evidence for their inadequacy and as proxies for criticism from others. On occasion, they endeavor to provoke this criticism or rejection both in the hope that they will fail and in an attempt to preempt it. As Kelly and Zuroff outline, these interpersonal patterns are likely to generate interpersonal strife, contributing to the patient's distress.

I believe that the only way around this obstacle is to confront it head on—that is, to expect to experience and endure mistrust on the part of self-critical patients and know that it will activate my own self-critical faculties. I am finding it helpful to constantly remind myself that these patients are in treatment because they want to experience themselves and their relationships differently. With time and patience—and the *timely and delicate use of evidence-based intervention*—I am convinced that they can achieve this goal.

CULTURAL DIVERSITY ISSUES

Cross-cultural studies have questioned the universality of positive self-regard, arguing that, at least in Japan, self-criticism is not only socially approved but also culturally adaptive. As measured by the same questionnaire assessing this trait in North America, Europe, and Israel, however, self-criticism correlates with depressive symptoms amongst Japanese and Chinese participants, as well as in another collectivistic culture, namely, Bedouin participants. I thus regard self-criticism as a universal stance toward the self that, in its more punitive form, is universally deleterious.

FUTURE RESEARCH

Future research should: (a) further substantiate the differences between self-criticism and perfectionism, particularly adaptive forms of the latter trait; (b) examine interpersonal processes underlying the links between self-criticism and suicidality; (c) examine developmental trajectories of self-criticism across the life span, and (d) conceptualize and operationalize specific behaviors launched by self-critics, which derail their psychotherapy.

KEY REFERENCES

Blatt, S. J. (2004). *Experiences of depression*. Washington, DC: American Psychological Association Press.

Shahar, G. (2004). Transference-countertransference: Where the political action is. *Journal of Psychotherapy Integration, 14,* 371–396.

Shahar, G. (In press). *Erosion, self-made: The psychopathology of self-criticism*. New York, NY: Oxford University Press.

CHAPTER 32

Procrastination

Joseph R. Ferrari

CLINICAL PROBLEM

Chronic procrastination is the dispositional tendency to postpone tasks and decisions in a variety of situations that seem necessary to reach goals. It should be noted, however, that procrastination is not the same as personality disorders such as obsessive compulsive and attention deficit disorder (ADD) tendencies. Procrastination, scholars report, may in some cases be found as a symptom for persons diagnosed with such disorders. However, procrastination is separate and distinct, becoming a clinical problem for individuals who are easily bored and distracted. *Academic procrastination*, while related to chronic tendencies, is more situational in that university students may delay a school-related task but not delay for their work or social engagements.

Previous regression studies found that both forms of procrastination are complex and comprised of distinct personality traits. Focused on *chronic procrastination*, research found that self-reported procrastination positively correlated with extraversion, and had a curvilinear relationship with neuroticism (such that high and low scores positively associated with higher procrastination scores) within Eysenck and Eysenck's three-facet personality model. Procrastination also may be linked to the Big-five model proposed by Costa and McCrae, specifically to neuroticism and conscientiousness. Other studies indicated that chronic procrastination is related to a variety of variables, including low states of self-confidence and self-esteem and high states of depression, stress, self-awareness, social anxiety, worry, forgetfulness, disorganization, noncompetitiveness, dysfunctional impulsivity, behavioral rigidity, lack of energy, and even physical illness. Chronic procrastinators, but not nonprocrastinators, claim a self-concept focused on being unreliable, and self-presentation styles displaying self-sabotaged tasks with justification and excuses for performance failure. In essence, chronic procrastinators reflect extreme concern over their social, public image suggesting they seek approval and want to be liked by others.

In terms of *academic procrastination*, neuroticism (specifically, underlying facets of impulsiveness and vulnerability) were significant predictors of this behavior. Strong neuroticism has been found as a predictor, adding depression and self-consciousness facets. Low conscientiousness from the Big-five model was the overall strongest predictor of procrastination.

PREVALENCE

Prevalence studies indicate that at least 20% of normal, adult women and men in such diverse countries as the United States, Canada, England, Spain, Peru,

Venezuela, Italy, Poland, Turkey, and Saudi Arabia all report a maladaptive chronic procrastination lifestyle. In fact, studies in these countries found no significant sex difference in prevalence rates, contrary to popular perception.

Studies report prevalence of academic procrastination in the United States to be as high as 70%, but no major prevalence rates between and within nations has been reported by researchers on academic-related procrastination . Those few studies conducted in countries other than the United States find academic procrastination rates similar to the United States.

CULTURAL DIVERSITY ISSUES

Within the United States, there seems to be no significant racial/ethnic differences in chronic procrastination, and the diverse set of nations assessed for procrastination prevalence suggest no significant international differences in self-reported procrastination. Unfortunately, a body of published research on cross-cultural treatment outcomes and effectiveness for chronic or academic procrastination types does not exist.

EVIDENCE-BASED TREATMENT

For the 20% of adults who are chronic procrastinators, it is suggested that professional therapy with a cognitive behavioral approach is warranted. Changing the thoughts and the actions of persons with this disposition is needed. In other words, sending the chronic procrastinator to time management classes or life coach training in better organizational skills will have little to no long-term, lifestyle change effectiveness.

For everyone else (i.e., the 80% of more situational procrastinators such as students with academic tasks), a few suggestions for intervention include:

- *Time Telling* = procrastinators are poor estimators of how long a task may take, either under or over estimating the time. Having procrastinators learn to practice time estimates seems desirable.
- *Use of Prompts and Notes* = Simple, physical reminder notes (e.g., Post-it notes) placed in overt locations to remind them to finish a particular project may be effective.
- *Organizational Skills* = Related, learning to be more organized is a requisite skill for procrastinators. Learning to prioritize, in terms of task importance, helps procrastinators tackle the first most important things first.
- *"Bits & Pieces"* = Teach procrastinators not to focus on the entire task, but to focus on smaller subunits. In essence, focus on the chain of tasks that need to be met and teach to accomplish one at a time.
- *Structure the Setting* = Find a place where the procrastinator may focus exclusively on the target task. For instance, if writing is a student problem, find a designated table and chair only for studying, reading, and writing.
- *"5-Minute Planner"* = Instead of focusing on the task in entirety, focus on the amount of time needed to meet the completion of the task. Then, break it into small "doable" minutes and accomplish one unit at a time.
- *Models of Nonprocrastination* = Because procrastinators are so concerned with their social image, pair procrastinators with peers who accomplish tasks—with doers as role models for task completion.

- *Social Support* = Build a social network for procrastinators of nonprocrastinators. These individuals would not let the procrastinator "slide" and get away with tasks not completed. In other words, create a social network that holds the procrastinator accountable for task completions.

These interventions are only a few suggestions. All are based on cognitive-behavioral approaches, raising the issue whether other therapeutic interventions (e.g., psychodynamic or humanistic) are effective. There seems to be no systematic, published outcome study on procrastination (especially chronic types) that compares or contrasts therapeutic techniques.

FUTURE RESEARCH

Clearly, additional research on chronic and situational procrastination is needed. Moreover, reporting on the effect of varied treatment programs seems to be void. A few studies examined how to treat study skill issues, but there has not been widespread embrace by scholars on interventions beyond time management training. In the area of chronic procrastination, it would be effective to examine traditional and nontraditional treatment modes for individuals and couples. For instance, there does not seem to be any empirical-based published study focused on couple treatment when one or both partners are chronic procrastinators. A few studies examined developmental issues fostering procrastination tendencies, but more research is needed to examine family dynamics and developmental components of procrastination. Both chronic and academic procrastination tendencies are learned. Still, no neuropsychiatric study on procrastination seems to be reported in the published literature. Thus, there remains much needed to be known about the cause, consequences, and cures of procrastination.

KEY REFERENCES

Ferrari, J. R. (2010). *Still procrastinating? The no regrets guide to getting it done.* New York, NY: J. Wiley & Sons, Inc.

Ferrari, J. R., Johnson, J. L., & McCown, W. G. (1995). *Procrastination and task avoidance: Theory, research, and treatment.* New York, NY: Springer Science Publications.

Schowuenburg, H. C., Lay, C., Pychyl, T. A., & Ferrari, J. R. (Eds.). (2004). *Counseling the procrastinator in academic settings.* Washington, DC: American Psychological Association.

Procrastination

Linda Sapadin

COMMENT ON THE EVIDENCE-BASED RECOMMENDATIONS

The interventions that Dr. Ferrari described are definitely useful in clinical practice. However, for these techniques to be most effective, they must be tweaked toward the specific personality style triggering the delay tactics. Once aware of the dominant style, the clinician can develop a tailor-made program for change, teaching specific skills and strategies to help the patient develop more effective ways of thinking, speaking, and acting.

Six personality styles (*perfectionist, dreamer, worrier, crisis-maker, defier, and pleaser*) trigger most procrastination behavior. These six styles represent the outer polarities of three traits:

1. *Attention to Details*: The *perfectionist* finds it difficult to begin or complete a task as he gets bogged down with excessive attention to nonessential details, while the *dreamer's* projects rarely get off the ground owing to a lack of attention to essential details that must be addressed to transform dreams into reality.
2. *Focus on the Future*: The *worrier* is so concerned about "what might happen if" that he or she becomes inhibited from taking action, while the *crisis-maker* only begins to focus on "what might happen if" when it's crunch time and he's under the gun with an immediate deadline staring him in the face.
3. *Relationship With Others*: The *defier* (including the *passive-aggressive defier*) *pays little attention to what others want*, while the *pleaser* is excessively oriented to what others want, leaving little time and energy for accomplishing one's personal goals.

CASE EXAMPLE

Subject Information and Brief History

Lindsey, a 28-year-old Ivy League graduate, was born into a family of high achievers. Doing well in school was an expectation which she happily met, though it wasn't unusual for her to feel agitated about the amount of work she had.

Shortly after graduation, Lindsey landed an ideal job, working as an investor relations manager for a hedge fund. Surrounded by "movers and shakers," Lindsey felt an enormous pressure to succeed. Her idealized self-image made things worse. "I'd rather not do anything at all than do something just mediocre," she quipped. Though Lindsey felt compelled to meet the highest possible standards in her work, she had neither the time nor energy to accomplish it all. Her solution was to relieve the pressure by "getting to it tomorrow." Too often, however, tomorrow never arrived.

Presenting Problem

When I first met Lindsey, she described her problem as a growing lack of self-confidence. She was feeling overwhelmed by the high expectations that others had of her and she kept doubting whether she could handle it all.

Treatment Intervention and Course

To help Lindsey develop ways to moderate her impossibly high standards, and hence her need to put tasks off, we focused on developing more effective ways to think, speak, and act. Here's an example of each:

Thinking Patterns
As Dr. Ferrari stated, procrastinators are poor estimators of how long a task will take. This was absolutely true for Lindsey. Due to her excessive attention to detail, most tasks took her longer to do than she expected, resulting in her frequently feeling frenzied and frantic. Though Lindsey was working hard, she wasn't working smart. Hence, we brainstormed together to establish a realistic estimate of what needed to be done to complete a project, as well as the approximate time it would take her to complete it. We then added 20% extra time to that estimate. If she completed her project earlier, she'd be ahead of the game, with a chance to relax, review or catch up on something else.

Speaking Patterns
Lindsey's frequent use of the word "should," (i.e., this "should" be done a certain way) was a mirror into Lindsey's mind. Tyrannized by the pressure of "one more thing" she "should" do to get it "just right," she found it impossible to complete many a task. We experimented with substituting the word "could" for "should." Lindsey "got it" right away. "Shoulds" drained her energy; "coulds" empowered her. "Could" carried the mature message that she has the right, capacity, and obligation to decide when and how to take care of her responsibilities.

Acting Patterns
Lindsey's to-do list was way too long, too detailed, and too intimidating. No way could she accomplish everything on her list. Hence, she felt like a failure. Always more to do but never enough time to do it all is a great recipe for procrastination. We worked together to create a shorter, less detailed, more down-to-earth to-do list. This helped Lindsey prioritize her responsibilities and be more realistic about what she could complete in one day.

Outcome

In a word, "successful." She claimed that it was liberating to be a "regular" person who was not always reaching for unattainable goals and failing in the process. She relished living a life without over-the-top expectations constantly swirling about in her head. She learned to take on responsibilities that she could handle and delegated what she couldn't, both at work and at home. By setting time budgets up front, she was able to create realistic estimates for how long a task would take. This resulted in her being able to complete the vast majority of work assignments on time. Less hassled, she was now able to enjoy life more. Last time we met, she had a big smile on her face as she told me she's no longer a "human doing," but is now a "human being," taking the time to enjoy family and friends, music, and just letting herself "be."

CHALLENGES IN APPLYING THE EVIDENCE-BASED APPROACH

Though people have struggled with procrastination since the beginning of time, the digital age has made it harder to overcome. Accessible, appealing, affordable, addictive distractions are everywhere. If a task doesn't grab us, our mind gravitates to other matters. What we were "going to do" gets put off or completely forgotten.

Hence, today's greatest challenge in treating procrastination is teaching people how to responsibly manage their use of technology. Though the hypnotic allure of the web will always be there, self-regulation strategies need to be taught. The web, itself, can actually help people resist the temptation to put things off. Sites can help a person block distractions, track time, make to-do lists, take notes, create reminders, bookmark sites (to prevent getting distracted from the task at hand), and more.

CULTURAL DIVERSITY ISSUES

As Dr. Ferrari reported, procrastination is an equal opportunity problem. Studies have not found any significant differences between the sexes or cultural groups. The diversity that does need to be addressed, however, is the diversity in personality styles. Giving generic advice to procrastinators is likely to be less than helpful.

FUTURE RESEARCH

Most procrastination studies use college students as their subjects. I'd like to see more research done with adult groups facing real-life, real-time problems. Here are a few suggestions:

- Comparing procrastinators' use of technology with those who don't typically procrastinate.
- Researching which parental strategies are most effective for children who are prone to procrastination.
- Examining how procrastination patterns undermine a marriage and delineating the actions a spouse can take to deal with it without becoming an enabler.
- Researching how the web can help procrastinators become more focused, less distracted.

KEY REFERENCES

Ferrari, J. R. (2010). *Still procrastinating? The no regrets guide to getting it done.* Hoboken, NJ: Wiley & Sons.

Sapadin, L. (2012). *How to beat procrastination in the digital age: 6 unique change programs for 6 personality styles.* Long Beach, NY: PsychWisdom Publishing.

Sapadin, L. (2013). *Procrastination busting strategies for perfectionists.* Long Beach, NY: PsychWisdom Publishing.

CHAPTER 33

Posttraumatic Stress Disorder

Kirsten A. Hawkins and Jesse R. Cougle

CLINICAL PROBLEM

Posttraumatic Stress Disorder (PTSD) is a disorder that may emerge following a traumatic event. It is characterized by four different symptom clusters: (a) reexperiencing of the trauma in the form of recurrent thoughts, nightmares, flashbacks, and intense reactions to reminders of the event; (b) avoidance of reminders of the trauma; (c) changes in cognitions and mood following the event; and (d) heightened arousal or feeling "keyed up." These symptoms must last at least one month to receive a diagnosis. Unlike other psychological disorders, PTSD must have its onset tied to a specific traumatic event. What events are considered "traumatic" has been a matter of considerable debate and controversy because a PTSD diagnosis cannot be given if a trauma did not occur. *DSM-5* PTSD diagnostic criteria state that traumatic events must involve "exposure to actual or threatened death, serious injury, or sexual violence," that is experienced in one of four ways: (1) directly experienced; (2) witnessed in person; (3) learning that the event happened to a close family member or friend; or (4) experiencing exposure to aversive details of the event.

PTSD is associated with high rates of comorbidity and marked impairment. Some have argued that it is the most costly of anxiety disorders in terms of its impact on overall mental health care expenses. Research suggests a strong relationship between PTSD and risk for suicide (i.e., suicidal ideation and attempts) that is independent of co-occurring psychiatric disorders, including depression.

PREVALENCE

Population-based surveys indicate that most Americans (over 80%) will experience a traumatic event at some point in their lives, though the percentage that develop PTSD is much lower (approximately 6.4%). The most commonly referenced traumas among people with PTSD include unexpected death of a loved one, serious illness or injury to someone close, and sexual assault. Research indicates 5% to 20% of military personnel who served in Iraq or Afghanistan met criteria for PTSD postdeployment. Among men with PTSD, 16.2% report combat as their worst event. Many who develop PTSD will experience natural recovery without any treatment. For example, one longitudinal study found that two thirds of individuals meeting for PTSD 1 to 4 months following a car accident had remitted by the 1-year follow-up assessment. Childhood trauma and interpersonal violence are associated with more chronic PTSD. Some have cautioned against treating PTSD soon after a trauma as this may interfere with the natural recovery process. There is little evidence of efficacy and some evidence of harm associated with psychological debriefing, a commonly used early intervention for recently traumatized people.

CULTURAL DIVERSITY ISSUES

Epidemiological studies have found that PTSD prevalence rates are higher for women than men. Though men are more likely to experience traumatic events than women, women are approximately twice as likely as men (20.4% versus 8.2%) to develop PTSD following trauma exposure. Other established risk factors for PTSD are low socioeconomic status and younger age. In the United States, lifetime prevalence of PTSD is highest among Blacks, and ethnic minorities are less likely than Whites to seek treatment for PTSD. Unfortunately, much of the PTSD treatment outcome literature consists of predominantly White samples lacking in diversity.

EVIDENCE-BASED TREATMENTS

A large body of evidence supports the use of exposure-based therapies in the treatment of PTSD. Exposure therapy for PTSD consists of in vivo and imaginal techniques. In vivo exposure involves direct confrontation of fear-provoking trauma-related situations, while imaginal exposure involves repeatedly imagining cues related to the traumatic event. Imaginal exposure is especially useful when in vivo is not possible (for example, if it is difficult to return to the scene of the trauma). The goal of both procedures is to reduce avoidance of reminders of the trauma and to facilitate adaptive processing of the trauma. By purposefully confronting reminders of the trauma, individuals learn that their anxiety will naturally decline and the fear associated with these memories will weaken. Despite evidence for the efficacy of exposure therapy, many clinicians are reluctant to employ these techniques for fear of the high level of distress that they will cause the clients. Researchers surveyed 852 psychologists and found that very few used exposure therapy for PTSD, and approximately one half thought the use of exposure would increase the likelihood of client dropout. However, a review of published treatment studies for PTSD found no differences in dropout rates between exposure therapy and treatments that do not involve extensive fear confrontation.

Prolonged exposure (PE) is a manualized exposure-based treatment for PTSD, and its efficacy has been demonstrated with a wide range of populations (e.g., assault victims, combat veterans, motor vehicle accident survivors). PE typically consists of 9 to 12 90-minute treatment sessions. Treatment begins with education regarding symptoms of PTSD. Goals of treatment and rationale behind the use of exposure are discussed. In addition, breathing retraining is introduced as a method to manage distress. After a few introductory sessions, clients are directed to perform in vivo and imaginal exposures in session and for homework. Memories of the traumatic event (including thoughts and feelings associated with it) are discussed extensively during sessions.

A recent meta-analytic review found that PE was associated with significantly better outcomes than either waitlist or placebo conditions. The average participant who received PE achieved better symptom reduction than 86% of those in control conditions. Significant differences were not found between PE and other active, trauma-focused treatments. However, the comparison treatments included elements of exposure therapy, so they may work through similar mechanisms to reduce PTSD symptoms. Studies have investigated the benefits of combining PE with either cognitive restructuring or stress inoculation training and found that the addition of these strategies did not enhance treatment outcomes.

Randomized controlled trials have found that selective serotonin reuptake inhibitors (SSRIs) reduce some symptoms of PTSD (mainly the numbing and arousal symptoms). However, the level of improvement is not as great as that produced by trauma-focused treatments. Research is currently being conducted to examine whether the addition of specific medications to exposure-based treatments for PTSD may lead to better outcomes, though this work is still in its infancy.

FUTURE RESEARCH

Further research is necessary to better understand factors contributing to the development of PTSD, as there is currently no dominant theoretical model of the disorder. Research on the mechanisms associated with symptom reduction will likely yield significant insights into factors that contribute to the disorder. In addition, given the heterogeneity of traumatic events that may lead to PTSD, more treatment studies are needed that focus on specific populations and symptom presentations (e.g., PTSD from unexpected death of a loved one). Given the low rates of treatment utilization among minorities with PTSD, greater understanding of treatment perceptions among different ethnic groups would be beneficial. Lastly, work is needed to evaluate the efficacy of combined medication and psychotherapy treatments.

KEY REFERENCES

Brewin, C. R., & Holmes, E. A. (2003). Psychological theories of posttraumatic stress disorder. *Clinical Psychology Review, 23*, 339–376.

Foa, E., Hembree, E., & Rothbaum, B. O. (2007). *Prolonged exposure therapy for PTSD: Emotional processing of traumatic experiences (client workbook and therapist guide)*. New York, NY: Oxford University Press.

Hembree, E. A., Rauch, S. A. M., & Foa, E. B. (2003). Beyond the manual: The insider's guide to prolonged exposure therapy for PTSD. *Cognitive and Behavioral Practice, 10*(1), 22–30.

Clinician Application

Posttraumatic Stress Disorder

Matthew S. Yoder

COMMENT ON THE EVIDENCE-BASED RECOMMENDATIONS

As noted in the research section, posttraumatic stress disorder (PTSD) is a well-defined, debilitating disorder affecting significant numbers of trauma survivors. As a clinician, there are two points made by the researchers that are particularly noteworthy. First, the definition of "trauma" is subjective and may differ between patient and provider. It is often necessary to rely on self-reports when attempting to assess whether a patient's experience during a particular event was subjectively "traumatic." However, it is important to do a thorough assessment of presenting symptoms when working with a potential PTSD patient, rather than assuming a diagnosis based on a history of surviving events that may be thought of as traumatic. A comprehensive assessment is additionally important as the large majority of survivors of severe events go on to recover without treatment.

The second point made in the Research Section that is particularly worth noting is the availability of effective treatment. Over the past 25 years, evidence of exposure-based treatments for PTSD have greatly expanded and they are now the widely considered the front-line treatment for patients with this diagnosis. In particular, Prolonged Exposure (PE) has been found to be remarkably effective in treating PTSD. Clinical lore that PE is too difficult for many patients, that it cannot be used in certain populations (elderly, mild traumatic brain injury, etc.), or that it results in high levels of dropout are unfounded.

CASE EXAMPLE[1]

Subject Information and Brief History

Don was an 87-year-old married Caucasian army veteran of World War II. He was referred to the Posttraumatic Stress Clinical Team (PCT) at his local Veterans' Association medical center by a primary care physician. Don was a paratrooper who, during the course of his service, landed behind enemy lines in France after D-Day (June 6, 1944). He was captured by the German military and spent 8 months as a prisoner of war (POW) in Germany and Poland in 1944–1945 before escaping and making his way to North Africa where he reunited with American forces. He eventually returned to America where he had a successful civilian career as an engineer.

Presenting Problem

Don presented to the PCT clinic with chronic, moderately severe symptoms of PTSD. He reported weekly intrusive memories and weekly nightmares. He also reported an exaggerated startle response, hypervigilance in crowds/public settings, irritability, and insomnia. Don's most impairing set of symptoms, however, were associated with avoidance. At the initial assessment, Don reported he had not told the full story of his capture and escape to anyone since his debriefing in 1945. He avoided settings where he may be asked about his experience in WWII and became very skilled at deflecting questions regarding his war experiences in general. He kept most people at an arm's length, rebuffing invitations to be part of veteran groups and to attend parades or other celebrations for veterans. As a result, Don reported feeling isolated and often lonely. Internally, he maintained self-critical beliefs globally, and specifically he carried significant guilt from his interpretations of his behavior after capture. At session 1, Don scored a 51 on the PTSD Checklist Military Version and a 15 on the Beck Depression Inventory-2.

---

[1] A full version of this case study has been published elsewhere (Yoder, Tuerk, & Acierno, 2010).

Despite reporting mild symptoms of depression, Don did not meet full criteria for depression or other comorbid psychiatric disorders. He had Axis III diagnoses of disc disease, polyneuropathy, and tinnitus. Of concern to this case study, Don also suffered from atrial fibrillation. As part of the routine care for this condition, he was monitored by a cardiologist for abnormal EKGs prior to and throughout the course of exposure therapy.

Treatment Intervention and Course

Treatment followed the PE manual designed by Edna Foa and colleagues with minor variations to address idiosyncrasies of Don's progress. Therapy was initiated after routine medication management appointment with a psychiatrist in which Don reported a desire to "talk more about what happened." Treatment consisted of seven 75- to 90-minute sessions of PE which included psychoeducation about PTSD and anxiety (session 1), orientation to exposure therapy and rationale for treatment (session 2), four imaginal exposure sessions (sessions 3–6), and a treatment wrap-up/follow-up session (session 7). Don also started a course of 10 mg of citalopram hydrobromide, an SSRI antidepressant, during treatment. He was monitored by a psychiatrist during treatment but no changes were made, and at the conclusion of treatment, Don discontinued medication.

Outcome

Don completed seven sessions of PE therapy for PTSD. At the beginning of session 7, Don inquired about terminating treatment, given his progress and the attainment of his goals stated during the first session. Assessment measures completed at the beginning of session 7 showed significant improvement (PCL-M = 30, BDI-II = 8). He reported no nightmares in over 5 weeks, along with noticeable improvements in social anxiety and avoidance. He described attending several holiday functions with decreased anxiety compared to recent years. He also accepted invitations to several events which he avoided during previous holiday seasons. Don completed one imaginal exposure trial to his traumatic memory during which he reported Subjective Units of Distress (SUDS) of 20 to 35. After the exposure trial, Don described "bewilderment" at his response to the capturing German officer, but noted little guilt, saying he believed his response was submissive but also life-saving. Don's request to terminate treatment was discussed, and it was agreed that he would be discharged from PCT services, with the option for restarting treatment in the future, if needed.

CHALLENGES IN APPLYING THE EVIDENCE-BASED APPROACH

There are several challenges in applying this treatment approach. First, the treatment requires weekly appointments. For many patients, regular, weekly appointments are difficult to attend on a consistent basis, especially if they are employed. In order to accommodate patients' schedules it is extremely helpful to have clinician time that is flexible and to empower clinicians to schedule their own appointments. Second, as noted above, there is often significant clinician resistance to employing PE in their practice. Despite decades of research and clinical experience to the contrary, the myth that encouraging patients with PTSD to retell their trauma story is in somewhat "retraumatizing" or dangerous, remains. This may be, in part, to the directive nature of exposure therapy, and that confronting anxiety-provoking (but safe) stimuli is often against what the patient wants to do when initially engaging in treatment. Strong training, consistent peer support, and ongoing supervision is helpful as clinicians integrate this powerful treatment approach into their clinical toolbox.

CULTURAL DIVERSITY ISSUES

There are no apparent diversity issues related to clinical treatment in this area. Exposure-based therapies have been found to be effective across multiple types of traumas, with many different age and ethnic groups, and in various settings.

FURTHER RESEARCH

More research on the impact of exposure-based therapies on patients' long-term mental health and PTSD symptomotology is needed. Longer-term follow-up with patients 12+ months post treatment will help elucidate the effect treatment has on a condition that continues to be conceptualized by many clinicians as chronic and "incurable." In addition, it continues to be extremely important to do further research on the 10% to 25% of patients who do NOT respond to PE or other exposure-based treatments. Discovering ways to improve care for this subgroup of patients should be a priority, given the large numbers of the population who will be diagnosed with PTSD during their lifetime.

KEY REFERENCES

Foa, E., Hembree, E., & Rothbaum, B. O. (2007). *Prolonged exposure therapy for PTSD: Emotional processing of traumatic experiences (client workbook and therapist guide)*. New York, NY: Oxford University Press.

Hembree, E. A., Rauch, S. A. M., & Foa, E. B. (2001). Beyond the manual: The insider's guide to Prolonged Exposure therapy for PTSD. *Cognitive and Behavioral Practice, 10*, 22–30.

Yoder, M. S., Tuerk, P., & Acierno, R. (2010). Prolonged exposure with a WWII veteran: 60 years of guilt and feelings of inadequacy. *Clinical Case Studies, 9*, 457–467.

Yoder, M. S., Tuerk, P. W., Grubaugh, A., Price, M., Strachan, M., ... Acierno, R. (2012). Prolonged exposure for combat-related posttraumatic stress disorder: Comparing outcomes for veterans of different wars. *Psychological Services, 9*, 16–25.

CHAPTER 34

Public Speaking Anxiety

Martha R. Calamaras and Page L. Anderson

CLINICAL PROBLEM

Public speaking anxiety (PSA) involves a central fear of being scrutinized or negatively evaluated by others in a public speaking situation. Commonly feared situations include giving a speech in public and speaking in a meeting or class. This fear is often accompanied by a variety of physical and emotional reactions, including intense feelings of anxiety, worry, nervousness, trembling or shaking, sweating, and/or dizziness. People with such fear are often afraid that they will do or say something embarrassing, that other people will notice their trembling hands or voice, or will be puzzled or insulted by their speech.

Because most people experience some degree of anxiety when faced with the task of speaking publicly, PSA has often been viewed as "normative"; however, clinical levels of PSA are associated with significant negative consequences including lower income, decreased education, and increased unemployment.

PREVALENCE

Public speaking is the most feared social situation among the general population, with an estimated prevalence ranging from 20% to 34%. Onset of public speaking fears is typically early (i.e., 50%, 75%, and 90% by the ages of 13, 17, and 20 years, respectively). The intensity and impact of PSA can lead to a diagnosis of social phobia. Approximately 3% to 5% of the general population has social phobia that consists purely of public speaking fears. Compared to socially phobic individuals who have at least one nonspeaking fear, those with pure speaking fears are less likely to have comorbid mood, anxiety, and personality disorders and are less impaired. It would be a mistake, however, to conclude that social phobia with pure speaking fears is not real social phobia, as some persons with pure speaking-fear social phobia do experience considerable impairment.

CULTURAL DIVERSITY ISSUES

Any visible cultural identity that may lead a person to be vulnerable to scrutiny from others may be relevant for PSA. For example, it has been hypothesized that sexual minorities (i.e., gay, lesbian, bisexual, transsexual individuals) may expect rejection by the heterosexual majority, which may translate into symptoms of social anxiety, including PSA. Outward symptoms of a physical disability may also lead to fear of scrutiny by others; however, individuals with physical disabilities often do not receive a diagnosis of social phobia because their anxiety is judged to be secondary to their self-consciousness and embarrassment about their symptoms being visible to others. A single case study of a 60-year-old male with Parkinson's disease who feared speaking in front of other people and on the phone reported that after 12 sessions of cognitive behavioral group therapy (CBGT), the patient showed significant short- and long-term reductions in his social anxiety symptoms. These findings are encouraging because they suggest that cognitive behavior therapy (CBT) may be an effective treatment for social anxiety and PSA, even when that anxiety is related to Parkinson's disease or some other disability.

EVIDENCE-BASED TREATMENTS

Most of the empirical research on PSA occurs in the context of treatment for social phobia. The treatment of choice for PSA is CBT, which is a combination of exposure and cognitive therapies. The behavioral component in CBT is exposure to feared stimuli. However, simply facing a fear does not lead to recovery. Many people must give presentations as a part of life through school, work, or volunteering. If simply doing it eliminated fear, PSA would not be so common. Effective exposure therapy must be repeated, prolonged, and controlled. That is, the person should face the fear repeatedly, stay in the feared situation long enough to learn something new (e.g., that one's anxiety does decrease over time), and should face the fear in a gradual manner (e.g., starting with smaller challenges before facing one's worst fear). People with PSA may not avoid public speaking entirely, but if they give a talk only on rare occasion, rush through it before they have a chance to learn something from the exposure, or only tackle a highly feared situation, public speaking fears can persist. The conditions for effective exposure therapy explain why people with PSA who meet criteria for social phobia may not benefit from skills-based groups like Toastmasters International© as a first step for overcoming their fears.

Exposure therapy for PSA has been examined in several formats: in a natural setting (in vivo), by imagination (in vitro), or through virtual reality exposure therapy (in virtuo; VRE). Though in vivo exposure is superior to imagination, it can be costly, time consuming, and the situational elements are difficult to control. For example, for people with PSA, it may be logistically difficult to gather an audience for a client to practice a classroom presentation. Virtual reality exposure therapy allows a person to face his or her fears virtually by wearing a head-mounted display that immerses the person in a computer-generated virtual environment that moves in a natural way. Advantages of VRE are that it can be conducted with a high degree of control and that it can be conducted repeatedly. A handful of small uncontrolled studies and one large trial comparing VRE to traditional CBT suggest that it can be effective for treating public speaking fears.

FUTURE RESEARCH

In spite of the substantial research on the treatment of PSA, several important questions remain. Recently, some researchers have argued that PSA may represent a distinct subtype of social phobia that is qualitatively and quantitatively different from other subtypes of social phobia. Conceptualizing PSA as a distinct subtype of social phobia has implications for the validity of speech tasks, which have historically been used as a behavioral assessment of social anxiety in research testing the efficacy of treatments for social phobia. An intriguing line of recent research has focused on the role of attention biases in social phobia and the effects of computerized attention retraining programs that essentially train people not to attend to threatening faces. One study found that after only one session of attention retraining, participants in the experimental condition showed significantly lower levels of anxiety in response to a public speaking challenge than did the participants in the control group. Moreover, blind raters judged the speeches of those in the attention retraining group as better than those in the control group. Another issue is that the majority of research on PSA has been conducted with European American samples. Little research has examined whether and how racial identity may impact the course and outcome of treatment for PSA. As such, it is unknown whether research findings generalize to diverse populations. Lastly, though PSA is common and consequential, it is rarely a presenting problem in a therapist's office. It is important to educate health professionals and the lay public alike to recognize that PSA is a real, potentially debilitating problem with effective treatments. Thus, a final important area of research is investigating how to broadly disseminate effective treatments to service providers and those suffering from PSA.

KEY REFERENCES

Clark, D. M., & Wells, A. (1995). A cognitive model of social phobia. In R. G. Heimberg, M. R. Liebowitz, D. A. Hope, & F. R. Schneier (Eds.), *Social phobia: Diagnosis, assessment, and treatment* (pp. 69–93). New York, NY: Guilford Press.

Heimberg, R. G., Dodge, C. S., Hope, D. A., & Kennedy, C. R. (1990). Cognitive behavioral group treatment for social phobia: Comparison with a credible placebo control. *Cognitive Therapy and Research, 14*(1), 1–23.

Moscovitch, D. A., Antony, M. M., Swinson, R. P., & Stein, M. B. (2009). Exposure-based treatments for anxiety disorders: Theory and process. In *Oxford handbook of anxiety and related disorders* (pp. 461–475). New York, NY: Oxford University Press.

Clinician Application

Public Speaking Anxiety

Libby Tannenbaum and Elana Zimand

COMMENT ON EVIDENCE BASED RECOMMENDATIONS

As mentioned in the Research Section, public speaking anxiety (PSA) can be considered a "normative" fear, as most people suffer to some degree from this problem. Although highly prevalent as a fear, it is fairly uncommon for this nongeneralized form of social phobia to appear as a singular presenting problem in the clinician's office. As PSA does frequently occur within the context of more generalized social phobia, evidence-based public speaking interventions must be incorporated into an overall treatment plan for generalized social phobia. Unfortunately, the very few controlled research trials have tended to test interventions that are logistically or financially difficult to arrange in private practice (e.g., generating an audience, virtual reality). As such, videotaped exposures and speeches given in front of a mirror or family members serving as an audience, though not tested in research, are much more likely to be conducted by clinicians in private practice.

CASE EXAMPLE

Subject Information and Brief History

Brian was a 52-year-old Caucasian married male employed in the field of finance in a metropolitan area. He reported a lifelong fear of public speaking beginning in childhood, becoming an impairment in adulthood that followed a single panic attack during a work presentation. Years after this panic attack, he sought a first round of therapy which reportedly focused primarily on "relaxation techniques." He described this as helpful, though he continued to avoid any public speaking situations (e.g., wedding toasts, eulogy at funeral, son's college events), declined board memberships, and resigned from a previous job due to his fear.

Presenting Problem

The current impetus for his seeking treatment was an upcoming ceremony honoring his son with his desire to speak "just a few sentences" at this event. He expressed much regret for having avoided similar events in the past owing to fear. In addition, because Brian experienced extreme daily preoccupation with the fear of public speaking, though it was not at all a part of his job, he hoped that through the treatment, he would no longer be tormented with this irrational fear.

Treatment Intervention and Course

Phase 1 of treatment (sessions 1–6) consisted of information gathering, providing a treatment rationale (describing the three components of anxiety disorders as relates to PSA: the *physical* component (e.g., shortness of breath, increased heart rate, sweating, shaking), *cognitive* component (mindreading, fear of evaluation, perceived social threat and cost/rejection), and *behavioral* component (avoidant behavior, including the role of safety behaviors), with treatment designed to target each component), psychoeducation regarding the nature of panic symptoms and PSA, followed by teaching anxiety management techniques (e.g., breathing retraining, creating a fear hierarchy, cognitive restructuring), including a videotape "self-perception check," designed to shift cognitions regarding the visibility of anxiety symptoms. This exercise proved effective and pivotal, as this was the first time the client had seen himself speak on video, and upon review, was able to observe the absence of obvious (feared) signs of anxiety. This task helped solidify the precept that using one's internal experience of anxiety as a "measuring tape" for performance evaluation is often fraught with bias and perpetuates fear.

Phase 2 of treatment (sessions 7–14) focused on exposure therapy, continuing with videotaped speeches, in vivo speeches (e.g., from a balcony overlooking the building atrium, presentations given outdoors with potential of passersby stopping), and to a small group assembled in our office), and introducing virtual reality exposure as another cognitive behavior therapy (CBT) tool, given its availability at the therapy clinic. Using this medium, the client completed speeches in front of virtual small- and large-sized audiences, with the gradual introduction of audience disruption and distraction (e.g., cell phones ringing, audience members whispering or nodding off) via therapist manipulation of the software program, all demonstrating to the client his ability to continue speaking (without getting "derailed") despite an increase in his anxiety. The client made progress through homework assignments as well. After years of avoidance, he began leading the family dinnertime prayers, also disclosing for the first time his fear of public speaking to his family. Upon discovering that his family was much less critical and judgmental of his fears than predicted, he had further evidence challenging his long-held assumptions of social threat and cost.

Outcome

With the progression of treatment, the client reported much less anticipatory anxiety and much less preoccupation with his fear. He accomplished his goal of attending and speaking at his son's ceremony. And while very proud of these successes, he admitted to continued anxiety regarding the prospect of leading a work training, thus this remained as an identified posttreatment goal. Overall, the client reported much improvement post treatment, not only in the arena of public speaking, but generalizing to his sense of self-worth, decreased shame, and improved family intimacy.

CHALLENGES IN APPLYING THE EVIDENCE-BASED APPROACH

Like with all exposure-based treatment, effectively treating PSA requires repetition of the exposure, control of exposure conditions, and prolonging the individual's experience in the exposure, in order to move through the fear hierarchy. There is an array of PSA exposure techniques, but each has limitations in meeting the requirements of effective exposure. Virtual Reality, as an exposure tool, can provide a medium in which all three conditions (repeat, control, and prolong) are met, yet its accessibility to clinicians is limited. Videotaping speeches can also meet the exposure conditions; however, there is no audience (other than the therapist) which reduces the quality of the exposure. Group-based treatment can provide clients with real audience members; however, habituation to the same audience can occur without generalization to unknown audiences. Therefore, the real challenge to effective treatment of PSA is completion of speech exposures outside of sessions, where there is unfortunately less control, less ability to prolong, and repetition is difficult. Ideas for homework exposures can include: sitting in a room location where it is more likely to be called on and/or escape (i.e., a door) is more difficult, asking or answering questions out loud in a group setting (classroom, meeting), and giving a speech in front of friends or family members. Although the therapist should be creative and inventive with speech ideas in session, it is much more important that clients complete increasingly more challenging exposures out of session. Like any learning-based treatment, the more motivated the client is to seek out speaking opportunities, the more positive the treatment prognosis.

CULTURAL DIVERSITY ISSUES

Diversity and multicultural issues can be more relevant to PSA than some other disorders because of the public nature of speaking in front of others. Any differences that an individual perceives as distinguishing him/her from the majority can increase a general sense of insecurity and fear of judgment. As pointed out by Calamaras and Anderson, the fear of scrutiny and evaluation inherent in PSA may lead to increased vulnerability for the client regarding any sense of "difference," be it visible or invisible. Racial differences, physical disability, foreign accent, cultural norms, or geographic dialect all lend themselves as markers that have been known to cause bias and prejudice in our society, and at the very least may draw attention. When an anxiety disorder is added on to these other factors, the individual may suffer from the perception that the "differences" are "broadcast" to the audience, which will disproportionately magnify and intensify their fear. A combination of clinician awareness, empathy, and cognitive- and acceptance-based approaches may offer tools and strategies to manage the anxiety provoked by these cognitive, though natural, triggers for internal fears. It is critical that the therapist conduct a thorough assessment and help the individual explore all triggers to anxiety, including individual idiosyncrasies, personal history, and societal norms and expectations. The therapist must be sensitive to these issues, while also considering with the client their functionality in the context of treatment aims.

FUTURE RESEARCH

One of the known ways to prevent anxiety disorders in adulthood is to provide treatment during childhood and adolescence. PSA, in particular, is one of the anxiety disorders that is likely to emerge during early years when presentations and performances are school requirements. As such, it would be beneficial to conduct research on PSA with children and adolescents wherein exposures are more easily developed in the classroom setting. In addition, we must conduct PSA clinical trials on more diverse populations in order to address the issues related to the vulnerability associated with an individual in a minority group facing public scrutiny.

KEY REFERENCES

Antony, M. M., & Swinson, R. P. (2000). *The shyness & social anxiety workbook.* Oakland, CA: New Harbinger Publications.

Hofmann, S. G., & Otto, M. W. (2008). *Cognitive behavioral therapy for social anxiety disorder: Evidence-based and disorder-specific treatment techniques.* Routledge Taylor & Francis Group.

Hope, D. A., Heimberg, R. D., & Turk, C. L. (2010). *Managing social anxiety workbook, 2nd edition: A cognitive-behavioral therapy approach (Treatments that work).* New York, NY: Oxford University Press.

CHAPTER 35

Seasonal Affective Disorder

Maggie Evans and Kelly J. Rohan

CLINICAL PROBLEM

Seasonal Affective Disorder (SAD) is a subtype of recurrent depression characterized by a regular seasonal pattern of Major Depressive Episode (MDE) onset and remission. In *DSM-5*, SAD is diagnosed using the Seasonal Pattern Specifier, which is applied to Major Depressive, Bipolar I, or Bipolar II Disorder when there is a temporal relationship between MDE onset, remission, and time of year. The Specifier requires seasonally linked MDEs and an absence of nonseasonal MDEs in the past 2 years, no extraneous seasonally linked stressor causally implied in the pattern, and substantially more seasonal than nonseasonal MDEs over the lifetime. In the general population, the number and severity of seasonal symptoms lies on a continuum, with SAD at the pathological extreme. Subsyndromal SAD (S-SAD) is a milder form of SAD with fewer symptoms and less impairment (i.e., not fulfilling MDE criteria).

The most common pattern in SAD[1] is fall and/or winter MDEs, although a minority of cases experiences MDEs in the spring and/or summer. SAD and nonseasonal MDEs share many presenting symptoms such as depressed mood, loss of interest/pleasure, worthlessness, and fatigue. SAD patients are more likely to endorse atypical symptoms including hypersomnia, increased appetite, weight gain, and carbohydrate craving than insomnia and appetite loss, which are more common in nonseasonal MDEs. Relative to nonseasonal MDEs, worsening of mood in the morning versus evening is more common and suicidal ideation is less severe in SAD.

The following biological vulnerabilities have been examined in SAD with mixed support: circadian rhythm disruptions (i.e., the onset and/or offset of nocturnal melatonin release in relation to the timing of dusk and dawn or the sleep–wake rhythm); a summer versus winter difference in the duration of nocturnal melatonin release; diminished retinal sensitivity to light involving abnormalities in rods, cones, or photoreceptors; serotonin deficiencies; and genetic variants in serotonin, dopamine, G-protein, photoreceptor, and clock genes. In addition, psychological factors involving maladaptive cognitions (i.e., rumination, dysfunctional attitudes, and negative attributional style), low positive reinforcement during winter, and emotional and psychophysiological reactivity to light, and season-related stimuli correlate with SAD. Biological and psychological factors most likely interact in SAD onset and maintenance.

---

[1] The term "SAD" will be used to refer to winter-type SAD from this point on.

PREVALENCE

An estimated 10% to 20% of patients with recurrent MDEs have a seasonal pattern to their syndrome. In population surveys of U.S. adults, SAD prevalence estimates vary by latitude and range from 1.4% in Florida to greater than 9% in New Hampshire and Alaska, implying that photoperiod (i.e., day length) is related to onset. The relationship between latitude and SAD prevalence is statistically significant in North America, but not in European countries. Most research on the epidemiology of SAD, including the findings reported above, used retrospective questionnaire measures. Studies using interviews with *DSM*-defined criteria report lower lifetime SAD prevalence, in the range of 1% to 2% nationwide.

CULTURAL DIVERSITY ISSUES

Most epidemiological surveys find a sex difference, with SAD prevalence at least two times higher in females than in males. Mechanisms behind this difference are unknown and warrant future study. The average age of SAD onset is between 23 and 27 years, although SAD has been reported in children and adolescents at a lower prevalence. Data on racial differences in SAD prevalence in the general population are not available, underscoring the need for future exploration. A study in the Washington, DC area found that the prevalence of summer-SAD was higher among African immigrants (2.35%) than African Americans (0.55%), whereas the prevalence of winter-SAD did not differ between these groups (6.08% vs. 5.38%, respectively).

EVIDENCE-BASED TREATMENT

Efficacious treatment options currently available for SAD include light therapy, antidepressant medications, and cognitive behavioral therapy (CBT), as well as alternative possibly efficacious treatments such as dawn simulation, negative ions, and exercise. Treatments, in general, are aimed at reducing current symptoms with adherence crucial in effectiveness. Most treatments are palliative with effects not sustained after treatment has stopped, and retreatment is generally recommended every fall/winter season. The possible exception to this is CBT, which may have longer-term effects after cessation of initial treatment.

Clinical practice guidelines for light therapy recommend scheduled daily exposure to 10,000-lux of white light with an ultraviolet filter to block UV rays. Light therapy devices are commercially available without prescription, and it is best to use one that has demonstrated efficacy in a peer-reviewed clinical trial. Light therapy should begin with the onset of first symptoms and continue until the time of year when symptoms spontaneously remit. The starting dose is typically 30 minutes daily upon waking, although a minority of SAD patients (i.e., those who have difficulty staying awake in the early evening) benefit from evening light therapy. For Bipolar SAD, the starting dose is typically lower (5–10 minutes per day) and increased slowly to avoid switching to mania/hypomania. Supervision by a mental health professional is necessary to make individual adjustments to the prescription (i.e., time of day and number of minutes per day) based on side effects and sleep changes. Side effects are usually mild and include headaches, eye strain, irritability or anxiety, insomnia, and fatigue.

Light therapy is an empirically supported treatment for SAD. Meta-analyses concluded that SAD symptoms significantly improved during light therapy as compared to credible controls and that 53% of light therapy patients met remission criteria at posttreatment. The following have been associated with better light therapy outcomes: atypical symptoms (e.g., weight gain, increased appetite, hypersomnia), younger age, a comorbid anxiety disorder, and a larger phase-advance with treatment. A comorbid Axis II disorder is related to worse light therapy outcomes.

Antidepressant medications are commonly used as a first-line treatment for SAD, alone or combined with light therapy. Buproprion XL is the first FDA-approved drug for SAD. A multisite trial found a lower proportion of winter depressive recurrences after prophylactic treatment with Buproprion XL than placebo. Sertraline and fluoxetine have documented efficacy over placebo in treating acute SAD. Possibly efficacious medications that require more research include citalopram, Reboxetine, moclobemide, and modafinil.

A form of CBT tailored specifically for SAD, which uses cognitive restructuring and behavioral activation to cope with winter symptoms has growing support. Preliminary studies found that CBT was comparably effective to light therapy and more effective than a wait-list control in treating acute SAD symptoms. Furthermore, CBT has the potential to prevent future winter depressive episodes with preliminary research finding that 7% of patients treated with CBT had a recurrence in the winter following treatment compared to 37% in patients treated initially with light therapy. CBT-treated patients also had less severe self- and interviewer-rated symptoms the next winter as compared to the light therapy group.

FUTURE RESEARCH

An approach that integrates biological and psychological vulnerabilities is needed to inform research toward understanding, treating, and preventing SAD. Given the predictable course of SAD, studies can use prospective, longitudinal designs to test interactions between vulnerabilities in SAD onset and maintenance and to examine long-term treatment outcomes. Preventing recurrence should be the primary aim of effective SAD treatments.

KEY REFERENCES

Lam, R. W., & Levitt, A. J. (1999). *Clinical guidelines for the treatment of seasonal affective disorder.* Vancouver, Canada: Clinical & Academic Publishing.

Rohan, K. J., Roecklein, K. A., & Haaga, D. A. F. (2009). Biological and psychological mechanisms of seasonal affective disorder: A review and integration. *Current Psychiatry Reviews, 5*, 37–47.

Rosenthal, N. E. (2006). *Winter blues: Everything you need to know to beat seasonal affective disorder* (Revised ed.). New York, NY: Guilford Press.

Seasonal Affective Disorder

Janis L. Anderson

COMMENT ON THE EVIDENCE-BASED RECOMMENDATIONS

It is challenging to evaluate treatment techniques during a time when the underlying scientific knowledge changes rapidly, and assumptions behind clinical evidence are called into question. Seasonal Affective Disorder (SAD) was characterized by Rosenthal et al. in 1984 with light as the first-line treatment, and has developed alongside a dramatically expanding basic science of chronobiology. Meta-analyses and consensus guidelines for light treatment of SAD date back to the 1990s, yet key discoveries in physiology of the eye were announced in 2002 by Berson et al. and Hattar et al., with their discovery of light-sensitive ganglion cells in mammalian retina that respond preferentially to short-wavelength light.

Light treatment continues to be clinically effective and treatment recommendations from the Canadian Consensus Guidelines remain useful, even as many assumptions about mechanism of action have proven to be incorrect or incomplete. This particularly affects choice of light treatment device and recommendations for "dosing" of light exposure. Lam and Leavitt suggest using light in conjunction with mood-stabilizing medications in Bipolar I along with close attention to dose. They did not suggest dosing bipolar patients with only 5 minutes of light, and it is difficult to find scientific evidence to support such a conservative recommendation.

Confusion has arisen following scientific reports and commercial claims regarding short-wavelength "blue" light versus more traditional "white" broad-wavelength devices as the buzz has outpaced relevant clinical trials. Using short-wavelength LED light of only 98 lux, we observed a robust antidepressant effect. Meesters et al. reported blue-enriched white light of 750 lux compared favorably to 10,000 lux white. More data are needed for a thorough vetting of novel light sources such as blue LEDs. It is unfortunate that the pace of clinical trials has slowed even while increasing knowledge of the underlying physiology provides new treatment options to consider.

The development of increasingly potent light sources has allowed larger numbers of patients to improve with shorter daily durations of exposure. Along with size and price of a device, relative strength can make one device more convenient than another for a given patient. As a clinician, I have familiarized myself with several widely available research-tested products of varying price, size, and light intensity so that I can assist patients in choosing on the basis of practical considerations of affordability and usability. The availability of alternative treatments such as cognitive behavioral therapy is another practical consideration.

An additional limitation of the clinical research on SAD is the emphasis on subjects screened to exclude comorbid conditions. In clinical practice, many, if not most, patients present with comorbid nonseasonal mood disorder, eating disorder, anxiety disorder, or addiction.

CASE EXAMPLE

Subject Information and Brief History

Daisy is a 44-year-old married African American mother of three who works as a TV producer. She felt well in the summer and had no trouble getting to work in the morning. She would work 10 hours per day, use the gym or have family time, and have energy to socialize. As autumn arrived, she began having greater difficulty getting up in the mornings, had intense cravings for starchy foods and gained 8 pounds with only one trip to the gym in several weeks. She enlisted the help of her family to get up in the morning and to go to bed at night. However, she still felt very sluggish, was napping at times in her office and awakening in the middle of the night. Her husband suggested, because this was a recurring pattern, that she look into possible treatment for Seasonal Affective Disorder. She was referred by her primary care physician, who had completed a physical exam and notes normal blood levels of thyroid-stimulating hormone.

Presenting Problem

Daisy reported, "Every November my depression gets significantly worse...this mood of 'hibernation,' as I call it, brings me down. When it's gray, I don't want to get out of bed. I just lie around and eat snacks. I'm a summer person. The kids and I pack up and stay at the beach. I get outside as much as I can 8 to 10 hours each day and go biking with the kids. I've always had this—like clockwork...the day we change the clocks I have a meltdown...I'm about one quarter less productive, have tremendous difficulty getting out of bed, and feel a constant dull headache."

Daisy and her siblings remember her having this fall/winter problem since childhood (Northern Ohio). She did not have these episodes when she was in college (Los Angeles), but the Portland area (where she has lived since 2000) is worse for her. Daisy was first treated for depression 5 years ago in the context of bereavement, and since takes citalopram 20 mg. In college, she had 2 years of psychotherapy and felt cognitive behavioral therapy (CBT) was extremely helpful, particularly with issues of fitness and weight loss. She describes herself as an energetic, very productive individual in spring and summer. She is interested in bright light therapy, and it is indicated to help ameliorate her fall/winter symptoms. She scored a total of 28 on the Structured Interview Guide for the Hamilton Depression Rating Scale with Atypical Depression Supplement (SIGH-ADS). This is indicative of moderate severity. It was important to note that she did *not* have a personal or family history suggestive of Bipolar Disorder, because this would increase the need to closely monitor potential overactivating effects of light treatment.

Treatment Intervention and Course

We discussed alternative treatments including light therapy, CBT, and medication. She was particularly interested in a trial of light treatment. We reviewed alternative options for using light (10,000 lux vs. dawn simulator vs. LED device) and discussed potential adverse effects, as well as costs and insurance coverage for each modality. In view of her hallmark difficulty getting out of bed on time in fall/winter, we discussed a long-term strategy that might include beginning in late September with a dawn simulator (if agreeable to her spouse) to help her maintain wakefulness at her summer hour of 6:30 a.m. She could then add bright light morning exposures if symptoms develop as the days shorten. At present, given the progression of her symptoms, it would make sense to begin with a trial of bright light treatment in the morning before work. Potential contraindications were considered: she has no history of rash/hives in sunlight; her ophthalmic history is significant for lasix "a couple of years ago" and she has been followed by her Ophthalmologist annually. There is no other personal or family history of eye injury or diseases. She is scheduled to see a new ophthalmologist and I advised her to discuss with them the plan for light therapy before she initiates the treatment. Light treatment devices that have been used in research at reputable institutions have been evaluated for safety of the eyes, but some eye injuries or diseases can elevate risk.

Daisy has looked online and is interested in purchasing a Northern Light Technologies SADelite. We reviewed descriptive material for the product to find the distance at which it reportedly produces 10,000 lux illuminance. We reviewed optimal strategy for using a light device, and I demonstrated positioning of light device, provided written instructions, reviewed potential adverse effects (e.g., feeling "wired," awakening too early, transiently experiencing headache or nausea), and discussed how to deal with them. It is important that she avoid awakening extra early in the morning as she begins light treatment, because that dramatically increases the effect of light on the circadian "body" clock. If cleared ophthalmologically, she will begin 30 minutes each morning of 10,000 lux white light for 7 days.

Daisy used light first thing in the morning for 30 minutes uninterrupted over 2 days and reported, "I really did feel good all day; with more energy today." She noted no adverse effects such as being overenergized, disrupted sleep/wake schedule, dyspepsia, or headache.

Outcome

Daisy returned after 2 weeks of light treatment. She reported a reduction in symptoms and her SIGH-ADS total was 8, which is in the normal nondepressed range. Her wakeup time was back on target and she had improved energy and concentration. Within 20 minutes of awakening, she goes to a built-in desk in the kitchen area where she can use the light device as she has breakfast and examines her children's homework. She is not sleeping in on weekends and has maintained regular bedtime with limited light exposure in the hour prior to bedtime. Her sleep quality has improved and the amount of time she spent in bed or taking a nap decreased.

CHALLENGES IN APPLYING THE EVIDENCE-BASED APPROACH

An important barrier to successful light treatment is attitudinal. Light exposure via the retina produces relevant physiological effects, but light treatment ultimately is a behavioral intervention. The patient must incorporate light treatment into his or her daily routine and appropriately use the light to realize the therapeutic benefit. Most people have limited knowledge regarding physiological actions of light, and often a kind of magical thinking invests specific light-emitting devices with exceptional powers, leading patients and clinicians to center their efforts on finding THE device and put less effort into how it is used. Lax regulation of the marketplace heightens confusion regarding choice of a device. Some devices on the market have never been used in objective clinical trials and have few of the characteristics which science suggests would make them useful. On the other hand, many devices have been developed in collaboration with knowledgeable clinicians, cited in clinical trials literature, reported in reputable peer-reviewed journals, and demonstrated as effective by those standards. Among the latter devices which have been supported by credible data, the differences may only be marginally important. They differ in relative potency, but the range of "doses" in research trials has been relatively broad and many patients in studies with less intense light sources did achieve remission. No evidence suggests that any specific device was crucial to the success of treatment. Hence, it is important clinically to focus more attention on how to incorporate supplemental light into a healthy winter lifestyle and away from investing a light device per se with all the healing power. Evidence from Rohan and colleagues strongly suggests that group cognitive behavioral therapy also is a potent intervention for treating SAD.

The diagnosis of SAD ultimately is based on personal history and the annual interval between episodes. This places a premium on long-term self-monitoring. The greater the stress and disruption faced by an individual on a day-to-day basis, the more difficult it is to discern an annual pattern. This favors detection in individuals with steady employment, stable housing, consistent interpersonal relationships, and observant friends and relatives. The extent of symptoms within an individual also can be affected by geographic location, with worsening as one moves farther from the equator. Limited available data suggest the vast majority of SAD patients go undetected and untreated. Charting tools that show the timing of past episodes across months of the year can help document the specific chronology of a patient's episodes, rather than relying on generalizations.

A converse diagnostic problem—false-positives—also occurs. SAD has relative social acceptability. Some individuals present with self-diagnosed SAD, but on closer evaluation their symptoms extend throughout the year. In some cases, this represents a "double depression" with an SAD component reliably exacerbating symptoms during fall/winter. A goal for light treatment is to return the patient to his or her summer level of functioning. At times, the recognition of depression during fall/winter months and experience of some symptom relief leads a patient to realize that he or she is more depressed at other times of year than formerly appreciated.

CULTURAL DIVERSITY ISSUES

Epidemiologic and comparative studies have suggested some intriguing differences among ethnic groups, such as a relatively low prevalence of SAD among individuals of Icelandic heritage, and also a relatively equal prevalence between men and women in Japan. At present, the pathophysiology of SAD and genetic contribution to risk are unknown. The importance of behavioral factors has been further highlighted by studies at far northern latitudes suggesting much greater prevalence of SAD in those with a modern versus a traditional indigenous lifestyle.

FUTURE RESEARCH

Greater incorporation of patients, families, primary care providers and other stakeholders in a patient-centered outcomes research framework could be important in advancing the clinical utility of light treatment, CBT, and pharmacological modalities. During its early years, SAD research was facilitated by public outreach and patient support groups that were nurtured by Dr. Norman E. Rosenthal and his colleagues at the NIMH Intramural Branch. A new framework is needed to capitalize on the collective wisdom of SAD patients, and to clarify the questions of greatest importance to those patients, their families, and their primary medical providers. As technological advances in lighting, and scientific discoveries in physiology and medicine, raise new hypotheses to be investigated, the availability of a patient network could establish mechanisms for collecting data in an efficient and less expensive manner. Hopefully, advances in social networking and electronic communication can help to foster such productive and forward-thinking collaborations.

KEY REFERENCES

Anderson J. L., Glod C. A., Dai J., Cao Y., & Lockley S. W. (2009). Lux versus wavelength in light treatment of Seasonal Affective Disorder. *Acta Psychiatrica Scandinavica, 120*, 203–212. PMID: 19207131. doi: 10.1111/j.1600-0447.2009.01345.x

Gordijn, M. C., t' Mannetje, D., & Meesters, Y. (2012). The effects of blue-enriched light treatment compared to standard light treatment in seasonal affective disorder. *Journal of Affective Disorders, 136*, 72–80. doi: 10.1016/j.jad.2011.08.016

Meesters, Y., Dekker V., Schlangen, L. J., Bos, E. H., & Ruiter, M. J. (2011). Low-intensity blue-enriched white light (750 lux) and standard bright light (10,000 lux) are equally effective in treating SAD. A randomized controlled study. *BMC Psychiatry, 11*, 17.

Dr. Anderson has received research funding from Philips Healthcare Solutions and formerly Apollo Light Systems, through projects conducted at the Brigham & Women's Hospital.

CHAPTER 36

Self-Esteem

Virgil Zeigler-Hill

CLINICAL PROBLEM

Self-esteem refers to the evaluative aspect of self-knowledge that reflects the extent to which individuals like themselves. Self-esteem is typically assessed through the use of direct self-report measures that ask respondents to report their level of agreement with statements such as "I feel that I'm a person of worth, at least on an equal plane with others" or "On the whole, I am satisfied with myself." Individuals who report high levels of self-esteem tend to possess generally positive attitudes about themselves. However, it is important to note that individuals with low levels of self-esteem tend to be uncertain about their self-evaluations rather than clearly disliking themselves.

The considerable interest that researchers have shown with regard to self-esteem is most likely due to the fact that self-esteem was once believed to be a means to deal with many of the challenges facing society including issues such as drug abuse, unemployment, academic underachievement, and violence. Although self-esteem has not emerged as the sort of panacea that many had once hoped it would be, it has been found to be associated with a range of subjective outcomes (e.g., life satisfaction) as well as some important objective outcomes (e.g., academic achievement). An example of the connection between self-esteem and important outcomes is the considerable body of research demonstrating that self-esteem—and the pursuit of self-esteem—is tied to both the development and expression of psychopathology. The link between self-esteem and psychopathology is evident in the *DSM-5* which contains various references to self-esteem and related terms (e.g., self-image, sense of self). Low self-esteem is included as a diagnostic criterion or associated feature for a variety of psychological disorders including most mood disorders, many anxiety disorders, some eating disorders (e.g., anorexia), a few personality disorders (e.g., avoidant personality disorder), various learning disorders, stuttering, attention deficit-hyperactivity disorder, substance abuse disorders, gender identity disorder, and elimination disorders (e.g., encopresis). It is important to note that there are also psychological disorders that refer to elevated or fragile forms of self-esteem such as narcissistic personality disorder, borderline personality disorder, the manic phase of bipolar disorder, antisocial personality disorder, conduct disorder, and oppositional defiant disorder. The *DSM-5* continues to highlight the important connection between self-esteem and psychological adjustment.

Self-esteem has been shown to be associated with various forms of psychopathology but the underlying reason for this link remains unclear. The most prominent explanations for this connection are known as the *vulnerability model* and the *scar model*. The vulnerability model suggests that low self-esteem serves as a risk factor for various forms of psychopathology. This vulnerability may be clearest in the case of depression. It is believed that low self-esteem may contribute to the development and maintenance of depression through both intrapsychic processes (e.g., rumination) and interpersonal strategies (e.g., excessive reassurance seeking). In contrast to the vulnerability model, the scar model suggests that low self-esteem is a consequence of psychopathology rather than one of its causes. According to this model, psychological disorders tend to erode psychological resources and leave "scars" that distort how individuals feel about themselves through intrapsychic processes (e.g., altering how individuals process self-relevant information) or by damaging interpersonal relationships (e.g., a child being mocked because of a stuttering problem).

PREVALENCE

It is difficult to estimate the prevalence of low (or high) levels of self-esteem in the population because self-esteem is almost always conceptualized as a dimensional construct rather than as discrete categories. Despite difficulties with determining the prevalence of low self-esteem in the population, group differences in self-esteem have been extensively studied. For example, sex differences have consistently emerged such that men tend to report slightly higher levels of self-esteem than women. There are also predictable changes in self-esteem across the life span with self-esteem being high during childhood, dropping during adolescence, rising gradually throughout adulthood, and dropping precipitously in old age. Although age-related patterns in self-esteem changes are clear, it has been difficult to establish a consensus concerning generational shifts in self-esteem because some studies have found modest increases during recent decades, whereas others have argued that the observed changes are not large enough to be considered meaningful.

CULTURAL DIVERSITY ISSUES

Culture plays an important role in shaping how individuals feel about themselves. For example, individuals from East Asian countries (e.g., China) consistently report lower levels of self-esteem than do those from Western countries (e.g., United States). Converging evidence suggests that this cultural difference in self-esteem is due in large part to the modesty of East Asians (i.e., they appear to feel as positively toward themselves as Americans but are less willing to report excessively positive self-evaluations). Cultural differences in self-esteem can also be observed among the various racial–ethnic groups in the United States. The pattern shows that Black individuals (i.e., African Americans of sub-Saharan biological ancestry) report higher levels of self-esteem than White individuals (i.e., non-Hispanic Caucasians of European heritage). In turn, White individuals tend to report higher levels of self-esteem than Latino(a)s or Asians. The fact that Black individuals report such high levels of self-esteem despite their stigmatized status has intrigued researchers and various explanations have been offered ranging from the idea that stigma actually protects the self-esteem of some groups to the recent observation that the feelings of self-worth reported by Black individuals tend to be somewhat fragile and vulnerable to challenge.

EVIDENCE-BASED TREATMENTS

Self-esteem plays a key role in many types of psychotherapy and it is a commonly used outcome measure in psychotherapy treatment studies. Feelings of self-worth are considered to be an integral component of modern treatment approaches including humanistic therapy, motivational enhancement therapy, and cognitive behavioral therapy. For example, cognitive behavioral therapy influences self-esteem by focusing attention on the recognition and correction of negative "self-talk" as well as correcting errors such as all-or-none thinking, overgeneralization, and selective attention to negative life experiences. This is important because these cognitive distortions may underlie how those with low self-esteem view themselves. Humanistic approaches, in contrast, often try to help clients find sources of self-esteem that are consistent with their internal needs, as well as assist clients in aligning their actual and ideal selves in order to reduce discrepancies between the person they currently believe themselves to be and the person they would like to be in the future. In addition to therapeutic approaches that address self-esteem as part of a larger goal, there are a number of therapeutic techniques that specifically target self-esteem. As an example, the therapeutic program developed by Christopher Mruk includes a psychoeducational component that increases awareness of self-esteem and addresses issues related to self-esteem such as resistance to change, alteration of self-defeating behaviors, and acquisition of new competencies. Interventions such as this have a great deal of potential to improve the lives of those diagnosed with various forms of psychopathology given the intimate connection between self-esteem and psychological adjustment. The results of interventions that directly target self-esteem appear promising but it is important that clinicians remain sensitive to the multifaceted nature of self-esteem and the function that self-esteem serves in the lives of their clients. There are also therapeutic techniques that are concerned with self-esteem solely as a means for enacting behavioral change or that help clients focus less attention on the pursuit of high self-esteem. For example, certain treatments for eating disorders emphasize the enhancement and stabilization of self-esteem in order to effect changes in eating behavior.

Interventions that target self-esteem have been shown to be at least as effective as other treatments for modifying behavior. However, elevating self-esteem may not always lead to positive outcomes because high self-esteem is a heterogeneous construct that consists of a *secure* and a *fragile* form. Secure high self-esteem reflects positive attitudes toward the self that are realistic, well-anchored, and resistant to threat. The feelings of self-worth possessed by those with secure high self-esteem do not require constant validation and their well-anchored feelings of self-worth allow these individuals to recognize and acknowledge their weaknesses without feeling threatened by their own lack of perfection. In contrast, fragile high self-esteem refers to feelings of self-worth that are vulnerable to challenge, require constant validation, and rely upon some degree of self-deception. It is often assumed that self-esteem enhancement programs promote the development of secure high self-esteem but this needs to be examined more directly in future research to make sure that these programs do not unintentionally foster fragile feelings of self-worth.

FUTURE RESEARCH

The close association between self-esteem and psychological adjustment may explain why so many treatment programs focus either directly or indirectly on feelings of self-worth. However, it is important for future researchers to clarify three important issues concerning the connection between self-esteem and psychological adjustment. First, the causal link between self-esteem and psychological adjustment needs to be clarified. It is important to determine whether low self-esteem actually causes certain types of psychopathology or if some other pattern of causation best fits the data (e.g., low self-esteem may be a consequence of psychopathology, rather than a cause). Second, researchers should focus more of their attention on examining the potential role of fragile self-esteem in the development of various forms of psychopathology. This is likely to be important because a rapidly growing body of literature suggests that accounting for markers of self-esteem fragility allows for a more thorough and nuanced understanding of the connections between self-esteem level and related constructs. Third, therapeutic techniques and programs that focus on enhancing self-esteem should be evaluated to determine whether they aid individuals with developing secure feelings of self-worth or if they unintentionally foster fragile self-esteem. Research concerning the link between self-esteem and psychological adjustment has a great deal to offer in terms of theoretical insights into the etiology and consequences of psychopathology, as well as suggesting intervention strategies that may either improve existing therapeutic techniques or suggest new approaches for future interventions.

KEY REFERENCES

Baumeister, R. F., Campbell, J. D., Krueger, J. I., & Vohs, K. D. (2003). Does high self-esteem cause better performance, interpersonal success, happiness, or healthier lifestyles? *Psychological Science in the Public Interest, 4,* 1–44.

Kernis, M. H. (2006). *Self-esteem issues and answers: A sourcebook of current perspectives.* New York, NY: Psychology Press.

Zeigler-Hill, V. (2013). *Self-esteem.* London: Psychology Press.

Clinician Application

Self-Esteem

Lawrence M. Ferber

COMMENT ON THE EVIDENCE-BASED RECOMMENDATIONS

The researcher discusses several critical components regarding the therapeutic value of clinicians targeting evidence-based interventions that have been specifically designed to address "self-esteem" issues. They view this focus on self-esteem as one of the key components in the development of treatment plans.

As the researcher points out, clinical interventions designed to improve patients' self-esteem are well known for lowering and/or extinguishing a variety of symptoms that have assisted the perpetuation of numerous negative maladaptive behavioral patterns, including improved academic outcomes and reduced psychopathology. These patterns appear to play a major role, as well as one of the central themes, for individuals with a variety of disorders that meet *DSM-5* criteria.

From a clinical perspective it is critical for mental health professionals to understand that there is little chance for a "one size fits all" paradigm when utilizing interventions designed to raise one's feelings of *self-worth*. As the researcher discusses, this appears to be owing to two major factors. The first and foremost being the presenting symptom, or chief complaints, that motivate the client into treatment. In other words, if the patient presents with anxiety or depression, the nature of the intervention would be quite different than if the presentation is Narcissistic Personality Disorder. The second reason may simply be owing to the transient, fluctuating nature of self-esteem that has made it difficult for researchers to define as a concrete operational construct. Without establishing a global definition, there is less validity and reliability, therefore making it difficult to study as an isolated variable.

CASE EXAMPLE

Subject Information and Brief History

James is a 23-year-old single Caucasian male graduate student at a highly respected university. He was ranked at the top of his class with a number of his professors agreeing that that he was doing stellar work. James reported experiencing feelings of depression and anxiety since he was in his early teens. Although his symptoms seem to "come and go," he had never experienced a period of total remission. James had previously been in therapy from ages 17 to 19 when he began his academic career. However, psychotropic medication had not been recommended at that time due to what his treatment provider believed was a "typical developmental stage" that James had been experiencing. According to his psychotherapist, it was not unusual for anyone to feel the way he felt.

Presenting Problem

When James started psychotherapy, he stated that his depression and anxiety had "hit a new level" in that he was waking up each morning in a state of despair and/or panic because he was telling himself, "I can't figure out anything" and "I'm so stupid and incapable." He also told himself, "There is really nothing special about me and without my academic achievements, I am just average and, no doubt, when people look close enough, they will see that I am a fraud." James stated that he realized that his life had become unmanageable at school, as well as in his interpersonal relationships owing to the recent exacerbation of his symptoms. Therefore, he decided to seek treatment.

Although James had initially stated that he sought treatment owing to increased symptoms that appeared to significantly affect his performance academically as well as in interpersonal relationships, upon further analysis, we hypothesized that it was James' lack of coping skills that exacerbated the situation, thus causing an increase in symptoms and not the other way around. This is an important point regarding the provision of treatment. If we can notice signs before the exacerbation of symptoms, we can treat the condition while the patient is in a less heightened state of mind. This provides a better chance of treatment interventions being successful owing to moderate symptomology being targeted as opposed to severe symptomology.

Treatment Intervention and Course

Treatment consisted of twenty-four 50- to 60-minute weekly psychotherapy sessions. Session 1 was devoted to a clinical interview as well as some diagnostic assessment with the knowledge of establishing a base line that would be quantitative and, therefore, progress would be able to be measured statistically. However, prior to us beginning our work, it was standard procedure to ask when the last time James had been to see his personal medical internist and had a medical physical examination. James stated he had seen his family doctor approximately 1 year prior and, at that time, no medical issues were identified. James was then asked to complete the Burns Depression Inventory (BDI), Burns Anxiety Inventory (BAI), and the Relationship Satisfaction Scale (RSS), along with a comprehensive biological, psychological, and social clinical interview. His scores on the BDI, BAI, and RSS all fell within the "severe" to "extremely dissatisfied" range. Toward the end of the first session, there were psychoeducational materials that James and I both read aloud in order to provide rational reasons for the presence of his symptoms and to help foster hope that his dilemma was solvable as long as he was willing to commit to the treatment. This commitment would be demonstrated by attending weekly sessions, staying proactive in all areas of our treatment together (i.e., doing homework assignments, participating in the role playing, and staying vigilant to our work together). In addition, he agreed to see a psychiatrist to be further evaluated if we decided that there was not a significant change within the first two to three sessions. Sessions 2 to 6 were devoted to building a collaborative relationship. This was accomplished by demonstrating empathy as well as genuine care and concern by active listening and taking a nonjudgmental view of James and his problems. In this process, there were moments in numerous sessions where James started to recognize a number of automatic negative thoughts that contained cognitive distortions such as "Black–White thinking" (sometimes referred to as "all or none thinking") and negative self-statements (e.g., "I'm so stupid"; "I can't figure anything out"; and, "There really is nothing special about me"). By paying conscious attention to this negative self-talk, it started to become apparent to him that this pattern might be the cause of his continual negative perspective and affect.

The materials were first worked on together in sessions. At the start of each session, we would go over his homework for the week. This included a review of his *automatic thought records* (a method from cognitive behavioral therapy in which maladaptive thought patterns are identified and replaced with more adaptive thought patterns), and the practicing of *daily affirmations* (positive self-statements targeting the enhancement of self-esteem, e.g., "While not perfect, I am a worthwhile person"; "I am talented in many ways"). He was asked to say these out loud in front of a mirror.

Most sessions consisted mainly of the discussion and processing of his thoughts, as well as the changes that were taking place for James. At home he was also asked to practice relaxation exercises, as well as personal growth writing exercise. Every third session, the assessment measures completed in session 1 (BDI, BAI, RSS) were completed by James in order to assess his symptoms and to assure he was making progress.

Outcome

By the 24th and final session, James had self-reported his overall feeling of self-esteem had changed from what he considered to be "low" to become "healthy." He indicated that he no longer was "crippled" by feelings of depression and anxiety. At the onset of treatment, his BDS, BAI, and RSS scores fell within the "severe" to "extremely dissatisfied" range. The change in his scores was clinically significant in that they fell within the "mild" to "somewhat satisfied" range at the end of treatment. Treatment ended because he was comfortable with the gains that had been attained in treatment and he was aware that he could return to see me at any time in the future should he feel the need.

CHALLENGES IN APPLYING THE EVIDENCE-BASED APPROACH

To reiterate an earlier point made, it appears as though the biggest obstacle in applying this evidence-based approach may be the transient nature of self-esteem. Therefore, because we are humans studying human nature, we cannot escape a certain amount of psychological vulnerability. The amount of self-esteem that we possess as individuals will vary to certain degrees at different times in our lives. The researcher also notes there to be two types of self-esteem, secure and fragile. Those with "fragile" self-esteem may be more vulnerable to external challenges or situational events when compared to individuals with a more "secure" self-esteem.

The good news is that no matter how transient or difficult it may be to define universally, the one thing we do know about self-esteem, according to Chris Mruk, one of the leading authorities on self-esteem research, is that "competence" and "worthiness" play an integral role in its makeup. Knowing this as clinicians provides us with the ability to communicate the importance of developing an underlying sense of competence and worthiness. Once accepted by our clients, they may be more capable of rejecting negative thought patterns and correcting distorted thinking. If, in fact, we as clinicians can convince our patients that although it may be natural to think negative thoughts, such thoughts do not necessarily constitute "the truth." Thoughts are not facts; they are merely thoughts. Until further examination, such as through the utilization of "automatic thought records" they are thoughts that may not be logical or make any objective sense. By reviewing our patients' thought records with them, we can help them better discern how much of one of their actuals thoughts are factual and/or what the evidence is that helps support or not support the thought. We are then better prepared to help our patients discover what is real and what may be a cognitive distortion. They can then change their perspective, thus having a positive impact on their underlying beliefs and feelings regarding their own competence and worthiness.

CULTURAL DIVERSITY ISSUES

Clinicians need to be aware of the needs of a number of ethnic groups, gender, socioeconomic status and cross-cultural differences regarding treatment of self-esteem deficits. Indeed, the role that self-esteem and worthiness plays may vary from culture to culture. In individualistic societies, it may be fine for an individual to live and thrive in a "dog-eat-dog" world to better himself. However, in a collectivistic culture, the importance of family and bringing honor to the family is a higher order value. Thus, the role of self versus the role of others in the development and maintenance of self-esteem is important for the clinician to understand in the client.

FUTURE RESEARCH

The main focus of future research needs to examine two apparent unanswered questions. First, there are two types of self-esteem problems, these being situational and characterological. Situational, low self-esteem tends to show up only in specific areas of a person's life, such as expecting to fail in work or social domains, but at the same time, having confidence in other parts of one's life (e.g., parenting and being a sexual partner). Characterological issues of low self-esteem are derivatives of a basic identity statement. A basic identity statement is a simple assessment of how one feels about himself or herself regarding how worthy and competent that individual feels. Differential interventions must be identified that effectively target each type of self-esteem difficulty. Second, the question of "What came first? Was it the chicken or the egg?" must be addressed. In other words, researchers need to focus on studies that attempt to isolate specific variables of low self-esteem that may shed light on it either being a cause consequence or cause of specific pathology, or if specific elements of specific pathology may be a cause of low self-esteem.

KEY REFERENCES

Burns, D. (1999). *Ten days to self-esteem*. New York, NY: Harper Collins Publishers.

McKay, M., & Fanning, P. (1992). *Self-esteem*. Oakland, CA: Harbinger Publications.

Orth, U., Robins, R. W., & Roberts, B. W. (2008). Low self-esteem prospectively predicts depression in adolescence and young adulthood. *Journal of Personality and Social Psychology, 95*, 695–708.

CHAPTER 37

Social Anxiety Disorder

Elizabeth A. Gordon and Richard G. Heimberg

CLINICAL PROBLEM

Social Anxiety Disorder (SAD; also known as social phobia) is a chronic and debilitating disorder characterized by a fear of embarrassing or humiliating oneself in front of others. It is typically understood as an extreme fear of negative evaluation from others; however, recent research highlights that those with SAD fear social scrutiny in general, including that which may result in positive evaluation from others. Physiological symptoms such as sweating, tachycardia, and nausea often accompany evaluative fears and may present in the form of a panic attack. As a result, persons with SAD avoid or experience intense distress during social situations or performance situations. Those who fear most social situations are diagnosed with the generalized subtype of SAD and typically experience greater distress and more impairment compared to those with less pervasive fears.

SAD is associated with high levels of comorbidity and functional impairment. For example, individuals with SAD are at increased risk for comorbid anxiety, mood, and substance abuse disorders, and they are more likely to commit suicide than individuals without the disorder. They also demonstrate significant impairment in many life domains, including educational attainment, occupational functioning, physical health, and interpersonal functioning. Not surprisingly, this last domain is particularly affected. Compared to healthy individuals, those with SAD or high levels of social anxiety report low social support, have poorer quality friendships, are less likely to be married, and, if married, report more marital distress.

PREVALENCE

SAD is among the most common psychiatric disorders. Data from U.S. National Comorbidity Survey Replication estimate lifetime prevalence at 12.1%, making it the fourth most common psychiatric disorder after specific phobia, Major Depressive Disorder, and alcohol abuse. During a given year, SAD is second in prevalence only to specific phobia, affecting an estimated 6.8% of the population. Although SAD typically emerges by early adulthood, individuals may suffer from clinically significant symptoms for decades before seeking treatment. If left untreated, SAD tends to follow a chronic and unremitting course.

CULTURAL DIVERSITY ISSUES

Epidemiological studies suggest that women suffer from SAD more often than men. However, men may be more likely to seek treatment, possibly because SAD interferes more directly with male gender roles. Although there are little data on how race or ethnicity may influence prevalence of SAD, there is some indication that SAD may manifest differently as a function of cultural context. For example, researchers have identified a social fear expressed in Japanese culture, *Taijin Kyofusho*, which refers to a fear of embarrassing or causing discomfort to *others* owing to the offensiveness of one's presence. This manifestation is consistent with more collectivist cultures such as Japan. However, symptoms of *Taijin Kyofusho* are not uncommon among persons with SAD in the United States.

EVIDENCE-BASED TREATMENTS

Cognitive behavioral treatments (CBT) for SAD are among the most researched and empirically supported. The cognitive models of SAD (put forth by David M. Clark and Adrian Wells and by Ronald Rapee and Richard Heimberg), on which many of these treatments are based, emphasize the reinforcing relationships between thoughts, feelings, and behaviors. These models posit that individuals with SAD have dysfunctional beliefs about themselves and others (e.g., "I am inept"; "people are critical") that promote a sense of danger in social situations. Individuals in turn approach social situations with hypervigilance, paying particular attention to threatening information, be it internal (e.g., physiological signs of anxiety) or external (perceived looks of boredom or disappointment by others). These processes serve to distract the individual and may impair social performance, leading to negative social outcomes that support original beliefs. Overt avoidance and safety behaviors further interfere with the opportunity to reconsider accuracy of maladaptive beliefs. Subsequent "postevent processing" may distort and magnify negative aspects of social encounters even further, bolstering maladaptive beliefs and making the next social situation just as, if not more, anxiety provoking.

Different versions of CBT for SAD vary in emphasis and detail, but they share common components of cognitive restructuring and exposure, with some incorporating social skills or relaxation training techniques as well. Heimberg and colleagues developed CBT protocols for both group and individual settings. Session number and length vary by format (group: 12 2.5-hour sessions; individual: 16–20 1-hour sessions). Treatment begins with psychoeducation about SAD. Next, cognitive restructuring helps patients build awareness of thinking patterns and learn skills to challenge their maladaptive thoughts. In-session exposures (e.g., role-plays) follow, starting with situations that feel more manageable for the patient (e.g., small-talk conversation) and building up to those that evoke more intense fear (e.g., making a formal speech in front of a group). Exposures serve as an important opportunity to evaluate automatic thoughts, practice social behavior, and to habituate to anxiety. In addition, patients are asked to conduct exposures between sessions within the context of their own lives. The end of treatment is an opportunity to examine deeper core beliefs and to consolidate gains made throughout the psychotherapy process.

Several studies demonstrate the efficacy of CBT for SAD. In an initial examination of group CBT, we randomly assigned 49 patients with SAD to 12 weeks of CBT or an educational–supportive control group. Both groups showed significant improvement. CBT was superior to the control group as assessed by clinician interview and equivalent by self-report at post treatment. However, 5-year follow-up revealed that CBT patients were less anxious than those who had been in the control condition. Subsequent research demonstrated that the individual form of CBT produced effect sizes similar to the group format and was superior to delayed treatment.

Other studies have compared both individual and group CBT to medication treatment with the monoamine oxidase inhibitor phenelzine, the high potency benzodiazepine clonazepam, and the selective serotonin reuptake inhibitor, fluoxetine. Combined treatment with CBT and medication was superior to either medication or CBT alone in one study. However, when medication and CBT monotherapies are compared, they tend to yield roughly equivalent results, with medication sometimes producing faster and stronger effects at post treatment, and CBT resulting in lower likelihood of relapse in the long term. However, newer approaches to combination treatment, such as the use of the antibiotic D-cycloserine to consolidate learning during CBT exposure exercises, hold great promise.

FUTURE RESEARCH

Further research is needed to understand basic facets of social anxiety, including its manifestation and prevalence among ethnic minorities and its impact on interpersonal functioning. Applied research will help clarify mediators and moderators of change in the therapeutic process. In addition, there are several promising advances in treatment research that may expand options for psychotherapists with additional empirical support. For example, there is a growing research literature examining interpersonal therapy for SAD as well as therapies, such as Acceptance and Commitment Therapy, which emphasize the acceptance of anxiety and living according to deeply held personal values. Together with current knowledge, these advances provide clinicians and their patients with much hope for addressing this painful and debilitating disorder.

KEY REFERENCES

Heimberg, R. G., Brozovich, F. A., & Rapee, R. M. (2010). A cognitive behavioral model of social anxiety disorder: Update and extension. In S. G. Hofmann & P. M. Dibartolo (Eds.), *Social anxiety: Clinical, developmental, and social perspectives* (2nd ed., pp. 395–422). Amsterdam, The Netherlands: Elsevier. doi: 10.1016/B978-0-12-375096-9.00015-8

Hope, D. A., Heimberg, R. G., & Turk, C. L. (2010). *Managing social anxiety: A cognitive-behavioral therapy approach (client workbook and therapist guide)* (2nd ed.). New York, NY: Oxford University Press.

Pontoski, K., Heimberg, R. G., Turk, C. L., & Coles, M. E. (2010). Psychotherapy for social anxiety disorder. In D. Stein, E. Hollander, & B. Rothbaum (Eds.), *Textbook of anxiety disorders* (2nd ed., pp. 501–521). Washington, DC: American Psychiatric Press, Inc.

Social Anxiety Disorder

Brigette A. Erwin

COMMENT ON THE EVIDENCE-BASED RECOMMENDATIONS

A wealth of empirical evidence suggests that cognitive behavioral treatment (CBT) is the first-line treatment of Social Anxiety Disorder (SAD). The effectiveness of CBT is maximized when treatment targets both situation-specific triggers (for instance, "If I give my opinion at this meeting, I'll look stupid") and core triggers (for instance, fear of rejection, worthlessness, and shame). When constructing the hierarchy of feared situations, it is important to assess specific situations that trigger anxiety, along with cognitive and behavioral responses to those triggers. These items on the hierarchy are useful precisely because they trigger anxiety currently and because they are tools through which core beliefs and emotions can be accessed and processed.

Core beliefs and emotions are the driving force behind disparate situation-specific triggers, and therefore behind the anxiety disorder as a whole. Anxiety is not always the only core emotion. In fact, emotions such as shame, regret, guilt, or resentment are commonly associated with SAD. Awareness that situation-specific triggers emanate from the same core beliefs and emotions improves treatment compliance and distress tolerance. Core beliefs and emotions may be apparent at the outset; however, exposure to situation-specific fears accesses, identifies, and processes core fears that are not initially apparent. Treatment outcome is maximized when all core beliefs and emotions are identified and processed.

CASE EXAMPLE

Subject Information and Brief History

Ann was a 33-year-old woman who met criteria for the generalized subtype of SAD. She had been shy for as long as she could remember. Despite her social anxiety, she functioned well. She was married with three children and she worked full-time at a financial institution. Ann was a perfectionist and adept at hiding her social anxiety. As a result, she received numerous promotions and was highly regarded by her colleagues.

Presenting Problem

Ann's social anxiety suddenly increased and began to make her life very difficult after she was offered a high-level position at a prestigious accounting firm. Once Ann began this new job, she realized that she was responsible for managing many more employees than she initially thought, and that most of her work was conspicuous and would be critiqued by superiors. In addition, her bonuses and advancement in the company were directly related to yearly evaluations performed by her superiors. Ann was preoccupied with overwhelming anxiety and with her belief that she could not make mistakes and still be successful in this position. Ann worried about saying or doing things that would lead her employers to conclude that she was not as smart or talented as they had believed. These fears caused Ann to over-prepare, to speak minimally during meetings, to call in sick on days when she had to make presentations, and to avoid social interactions with her superiors. Ann's supervisors were perplexed by her behavior. When assigned a task, she did a wonderful job. Yet, she hesitated to suggest new ideas or even chat casually about her weekend.

Ann's social anxiety began to affect her social relationships outside of work. She worried that her heightened and unmanageable anxiety would be noticed. She found that her mind went blank with increasing frequency, which also increased her anxiety. Ann began to avoid interactions with friends, neighbors, and her children's teachers and coaches. Family gatherings were starting to become difficult. Ann began to worry that her anxiety was going to spiral out of control and that she would lose her job. She regretted her decision to take this new job and she grew increasingly depressed.

Treatment Intervention and Course

Ann received a trial of CBT and the selective serotonin reuptake inhibitor, fluoxetine. Ann was provided with psychoeducation about SAD. In individual psychotherapy she participated in cognitive restructuring, graduated in-session exposures (e.g., role-plays), and graduated in vivo exposures. Ann started with easier exposures such as sharing opinions and being assertive with friends and neighbors, chatting casually with teachers and parents at her children's school, and speaking so that she was the center of attention in social groups. She then began working on more challenging exposures at work such as sharing opinions, speaking casually with superiors, and conducting presentations.

Through these exposures Ann and her psychotherapist were able to identify automatic thoughts such as, "I can't make a mistake," "if someone disagrees with me, it means that I am wrong or dumb," "everyone is giving me dirty looks," and "I could lose my job if I don't impress my bosses." Core beliefs also became clear. Ann believed that she had to be perfect and please others in order to be accepted and successful. When she wasn't perfect, Ann believed that others rejected her. Ann identified shame and dread as core emotions.

Outcome

Over the course of 16 sessions, exposure goals were modified to target and process core beliefs and emotions more directly. Ann developed insight into her automatic thoughts, core beliefs, and core emotions. Her awareness that core fears and emotions (shame at imperfection and dread) drive disparate situation-specific fears improved treatment compliance and distress tolerance.

CHALLENGES IN APPLYING THE EVIDENCE-BASED APPROACH

One of the most common challenges in applying CBT is managing a client's distress. In order to meet personal and professional responsibilities, clients frequently need to engage in high-distress situations while they are working in treatment on lower-distress situations. Participating in situations with extreme anxiety will likely impair performance and reinforce negative automatic thoughts. Combining CBT with acceptance-based strategies has been associated with clinically significant improvement among patients with generalized anxiety disorder. The goal of acceptance-based strategies is awareness of the present moment that is intentional and nonjudging. These strategies ask clients to intentionally make a choice about where to focus attention, to selectively deploy attention broadly or narrowly depending on their level of distress, and to never shut anything out of awareness. Acceptance-based strategies have been implemented in SAD, but their combination with CBT is an area that needs to be examined. Providing acceptance-based strategies to persons with SAD will likely improve distress tolerance, treatment compliance, and outcome.

CBT for social anxiety disorder activates maladaptive emotions and beliefs with the goal of habituation to excessive emotion and acceptance of uncertainty regarding feared consequences (for instance, "I need to speak up at meetings without knowing what my boss thinks of me"). Selectively deploying attention narrowly or broadly can facilitate coping and tolerating distress, awareness of symptoms, and acceptance of symptoms and feared consequences. This distress tolerance strategy imparts warmth and compassion.

When distress is highest, the treatment goal is to cope and to minimize reinforcement of negative automatic thoughts. Without avoiding cognitive or physiological symptoms, attention is focused narrowly on the environment ("I'm in the conference room") and on nonsymptom internal information ("I'm sitting with my hands on the conference table"). Narrowly focusing attention prevents catastrophic fears and distress from escalating and increases the effectiveness of the exposure as anxious thoughts and symptoms are still within peripheral attention.

When distress is manageable, the treatment goal shifts to awareness. Attention is focused on symptoms and feared stimuli. For example, physical symptoms ("my heart is racing") and cognitive symptoms ("I'm afraid I will panic"; "I'm afraid I will look stupid and lose my job") are attended to. This more direct exposure improves awareness and allows for exposure to disconfirmatory information and habituation.

With greater tolerance of symptoms and feared consequences, attention is focused on accepting the possibility of current and long-term fears. For instance, the following imaginal exposure is incorporated into an in vivo exposure: "If I speak up at this meeting I am risking rejection, shame, and uncontrollable panic. I'm going to picture and accept this risk because I will have fear if I don't accept this possibility, and because I need to improve my social anxiety in order to function at this job." Using this strategy, exposure effectively identifies and processes situation-specific and core fears and emotions with the goal of acceptance of the worst case scenario.

CULTURAL DIVERSITY ISSUES

The prevalence of social anxiety disorder varies by culture. In addition, cultural norms and values may influence the symptom profile of persons with SAD. For instance, *Taijin Kyofusho* is a Japanese culture-specific expression of SAD and is characterized by a fear of offending or embarrassing others. Social anxiety should be evaluated in the context of an individual's cultural background in order to most accurately assess the nature and scope of the SAD.

FUTURE RESEARCH

Despite the demonstrated efficacy of CBT for SAD, a number of patients either drop out of treatment or do not achieve clinically significant improvement by the end of treatment. A pretreatment trial of motivational interviewing has been associated with increased compliance and treatment response among persons with SAD. Motivational interviewing is a form of treatment in which clients are asked to attend to patterns of high, medium, and low motivation for change. The therapist is typically directive and goal oriented. The goal of motivational interviewing is to resolve ambivalence by engaging and activating intrinsic motivation. The integration of acceptance-based techniques with CBT may also improve compliance and treatment response among persons with SAD. Further research is needed to explore psychotherapeutic augmentation of CBT.

Persons with social anxiety disorder may inherit a general tendency to become anxious in novel situations (behavioral inhibition; shyness) that may become exacerbated and circumscribed to social situations with repeated exposure to certain environmental factors. Consistent with this notion, certain parental factors have been found to be associated with social anxiety. Specifically, lack of parental support, expectations of perfection, high parental social anxiety, isolation of their children from peer social interactions, low responsiveness to their children, emphasis on the importance of the opinions of others, the use of shame as a method of discipline, and deemphasis on family socialization have been found to be associated with greater social anxiety, though some of these associations may be culturally specific. Prevention studies should explore interventions designed to educate parents about anxiety, about strategies to manage anxiety, and about parenting techniques in order to lower the incidence of SAD in their children.

KEY REFERENCES

Heimberg, R. G., Brozovich, F. A., & Rapee, R. M. (2010). A cognitive behavioral model of social anxiety disorder: Update and extension. In S. G. Hofmann & P. M. Dibartolo (Eds.), *Social anxiety: Clinical, developmental, and social perspectives* (2nd ed., pp. 395–422). Amsterdam, The Netherlands: Elsevier.

Hope, D. A., Heimberg, R. G., & Turk, C. L. (2010). *Managing social anxiety: A cognitive-behavioral therapy approach (client workbook and therapist guide)* (2nd ed.). New York, NY: Oxford University Press.

Ledley, D. R., Erwin, B. A., & Heimberg, R. G. (2008). Social anxiety disorder. In W. E. Craighead, D. J. Miklowitz, & L. W. Craighead (Eds.), *Psychopathology: History, theory, and empirical foundations* (pp. 198–233). New York, NY: John Wiley & Sons.

CHAPTER 38

Trichotillomania (Hair Pulling Disorder)

Michael B. Himle and Loran P. Hayes

CLINICAL PROBLEM

Trichotillomania (TTM, also known as Hair Pulling Disorder) is characterized by repetitive pulling out of one's own hair, despite repeated attempts to stop, resulting in noticeable hair loss and significant distress or impairment (APA, 2013). Although no longer part of the formal *DSM-5* diagnostic criteria, many pullers (especially adults) report a sense of tension before, or when resisting, pulling as well as pleasure, gratification, or relief during/after pulling.

TTM is a heterogeneous disorder in regard to manifestation, severity, and impairment. The most common pulling sites are the scalp, eyelashes, and eyebrows, though pulling can occur from anywhere on the body. Approximately one third of individuals pull from multiple sites. Research has traditionally dichotomized pulling as focused or automatic. Focused pulling is done intentionally and with awareness. This type of pulling has been described as goal directed, usually to reduce tension, an aversive urge, or regulate a negative emotional state. In contrast, automatic pulling occurs outside of immediate awareness, usually during mundane or sedentary activities and is typically not recognized until after the pulling episode ends. Only 25% of individuals report primarily focused pulling, with the majority reporting automatic or mixed (focused and automatic) pulling.

Individual variations in pulling behavior are also important for conceptualization and treatment. Pulling is usually conducted using the fingers; however, some individuals use instruments and accessories (e.g., tweezers). Some individuals have elaborate pre- and postpulling rituals such as searching for particular hairs (certain texture, color, etc.), stroking the hair prior to pulling, and examining or manipulating the hair (usually with the fingers and/or mouth) after it has been pulled.

In addition to cosmetic damage, chronic pulling can damage hair follicles and disturb hair regrowth (alopecia) and cause musculoskeletal problems (e.g., carpal tunnel syndrome). A small percentage of pullers consume their hair, which can cause severe medical problems. Hair pulling may result in significant time loss and pullers often spend considerable time and money concealing hair loss. Avoidance of social activities (e.g., dating) and academic and occupational interference is common. In addition, TTM is often accompanied by psychological distress, especially shame, embarrassment, and guilt, which is complicated by high rates of comorbid psychopathology. Adult samples suggest that 80% of pullers meet lifetime criteria for another Axis I disorder, especially depression (57%–65%), anxiety (27%–57%), eating disorders (20%), and substance use disorders (16%–22%). While less is known about children with TTM, it is apparent that mood and anxiety disorders are common.

PREVALENCE

The true prevalence of TTM is unknown. Lifetime prevalence estimates range from 1% to 4% depending upon sample characteristics, ascertainment methods, and diagnostic criteria used. TTM is more common in females by a ratio of about 2:1; however, this may represent a gender reporting bias. There is some evidence that the prevalence may be slightly higher, and the gender distribution more balanced, in children. Pulling usually begins around puberty and takes a waxing and waning course. A small percentage of children display hair pulling very early (ages 0–6; referred to as "baby-trich"). This appears to be a distinct entity with a different longitudinal course.

CULTURAL DIVERSITY ISSUES

Little is known about ethnic and racial factors in TTM, however, a recent (predominantly female) Internet survey found that African American and Latino/a respondents, compared to Caucasian respondents, reported pulling from different sites, were less likely to report tension prior to pulling, reported less daily stress, and were less likely to seek/utilize treatment.

EVIDENCE-BASED TREATMENTS

Treatment of TTM usually includes a combination of pharmacological and behavioral interventions. Selective-serotonin reuptake inhibitors (SSRIs) have been shown to be effective for managing comorbid conditions, but the evidence is less encouraging for reducing actual pulling. More recently, clomipramine, olanzapine, and N-acetylcysteine have shown some promise in adults. There are no FDA-approved medications for TTM.

Cognitive behavioral therapy (CBT) techniques have garnered strong empirical support in both adults and children. From a CBT perspective, the goal of treatment is to identify and manipulate antecedent (e.g., triggers, prepulling behavior) and consequence (e.g., urge reduction, postpulling behavior) variables that maintain the pulling. There is evidence that focused and automatic pulling serve different behavioral functions. Focused pulling reduces or otherwise regulates aversive private experiences (e.g., urge, drive, cognition, emotion) and thus is negatively reinforced. In contrast, automatic pulling is likely maintained via tactile consequences (e.g., stimulation from rolling hair between fingers) or increased stimulation in an otherwise sedentary environment. CBT attempts to systematically analyze and interrupt these processes.

Usually delivered as an intervention package, key CBT techniques include self-monitoring, awareness training, stimulus control, and Competing Response Training (CRT). Collectively, these interventions are referred to as Habit Reversal Training (HRT). During HRT, self-monitoring and awareness training help the individual to identify functional antecedent variables and to recognize initial elements of the hair-pulling behavior chain. These techniques are especially important for individuals engaging in automatic pulling. Stimulus control introduces practical strategies to prevent pulling (e.g., placing bandages on the fingers) or as a functional alternative to postpulling behavior (e.g., rolling dental floss between fingers). During CRT, the therapist teaches the individual to engage in a response that is directly incompatible with pulling (e.g., clench fists) and hold the competing response until the urge dissipates, thus breaking the urge-reduction (negative reinforcement) cycle in focused pulling and the habitual pattern of automatic pulling. Social support is often included to reinforce and prompt use of the competing response. The effectiveness of CBT has been shown in numerous studies with both children and adults. It has been shown to be more effective than waitlist/minimal attention control (adults and children), supportive psychotherapy (adults), and pharmacotherapy (adults).

FUTURE RESEARCH

A better understanding of the phenomenology and underlying etiology of TTM will likely lead to enhanced treatments. To date, no treatment has been shown to be effective for all pullers and treatment gains are often moderate, suggesting the need for additional treatment development. Add-on techniques such as cognitive restructuring, motivational strategies, and acceptance-based techniques (e.g., Acceptance and Commitment Therapy) are designed to enhance treatment, and have shown to be effective, though their incremental benefit is unclear. In addition, although TTM typically begins in childhood, few treatment studies have been conducted with children. There is a dire need to better understand TTM from a family-based perspective and to develop and enhance treatments for TTM early in the course of the disorder.

KEY REFERENCES

Bloch, M. H., Landeros-Weisenberger, A., Dombrowski, P., Kelmendi, B., Wegner, R., ... Coric, V. (2007). Systematic review: Pharmacological and behavioral treatment for trichotillomania. *Biological Psychiatry, 62*, 839–846. doi: 10.1016/j.biopsych.2007.05.019

Franklin, M. E., & Tolin, D. F. (2007). *Treating trichotillomania: Cognitive-behavioral therapy for hairpulling and related problems*. New York, NY: Springer Science + Business Media.

Stein, D. J., Grant, J. E., Franklin, M. E., Keuthen, N., Lochner, C., ... Woods, D. W. (2010). Trichotillomania (hair pulling disorder), skin picking disorder, and stereotypic movement disorder: Toward *DSM-V*. *Depression and Anxiety, 27*, 611–626. doi: 10.1002/da.20700

Clinician Application

Trichotillomania (Hair Pulling Disorder)

Suzanne Mouton-Odum and Ruth Golomb

COMMENT ON THE EVIDENCE-BASED RECOMMENDATIONS

Trichotillomania (TTM) is a complex disorder with increasing treatment outcome research. Although Habit Reversal Training (HRT) has been empirically researched and outcomes are documented, clinicians who regularly treat TTM have found that HRT, as it was originally conceptualized by Azrin and Nunn (1973), required modification in order to increase both applicability to hair pullers and to improve effectiveness of treatment. These modifications include stimulus control, aversion, negative practice, over-correction, and covert sensitization. HRT, with these additions, is commonly referred to as "HRT Plus." Although these additions greatly improved the efficacy of HRT, "HRT Plus" still produces results that are inconsistent across subjects and not terribly durable over time.

CASE EXAMPLE

Subject Information and Brief History

Natalie was a 38-year-old married female with two children (ages 6 and 8 years). She was a stay-at-home mom who, prior to having children, was an attorney at a large law firm. Natalie began hair pulling at age 12, while in the seventh grade. She did not report any significant, current life stressors. She described pulling primarily from the crown of the head as evidenced in a large (4 inch diameter) bald spot on the top of her head. She also pulled from her eyelashes and eyebrows resulting in thin lashes and brows. Natalie had never sought treatment for TTM.

Presenting Problem

Natalie presented for treatment of TTM reporting feeling frustrated with her pulling behavior and was concerned that she might pull her hair in front of her children, perhaps "teaching" them the same behavior. She also felt that at times she became preoccupied with her pulling and was not as attentive to her children as she would like. Finally, she reported that she was tired of having to spend time and money to "camouflage" her bald spot or to pencil in her eyebrows.

Treatment Intervention and Course

Information gathered during the first several sessions revealed that Natalie pulled in both "focused" and "automatic" situations. Focused pulling occurred in front of the mirror and automatic pulling tended to take place while driving, lying in bed late at night while trying to fall asleep, and while watching television. She did report that when in front of the mirror her pulling was more goal-directed or "focused." Thus, in this situation, her awareness was high. Natalie reported pulling occasionally in response to tension, but that her pulling also occurred in response to boredom, fatigue, and insomnia. Natalie was instructed to wear gloves while

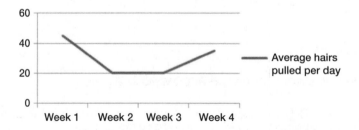

FIGURE 38.1 Average hairs pulled per day from week 1 to week 4.

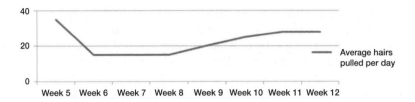

FIGURE 38.2 Average hairs pulled per day from week 5 to week 12.

driving and finger bandages on her fingers while lying in bed at night to increase awareness of pulling urges. Further, she was taught diaphragmatic breathing to address feelings of tension and anxiety while she was in the bathroom. Initially, her pulling decreased from an average of 45 hairs a day to about 20 hairs a day as measured with a self-report monitoring form designed to track pulling behavior and increase awareness of behavior. This decrease lasted for 2 weeks and then increased to 35 hairs a day during week 4 (Figure 38.1).

Natalie was then taught to use alternate competing response strategies; one involved clenching her fists while the other involved playing with a "koosh" ball to keep her hands occupied. She and her psychotherapist also identified activities she could engage in when she was feeling "bored." About one half of Natalie's residual pulling occurred while looking in the mirror in the bathroom. To address this, she was instructed to limit her time in the bathroom by using a kitchen timer. As a result of these interventions, Natalie's pulling decreased to an average of 15 hairs a day which lasted for the next 3 weeks with a slight pulling increase during weeks 9 to 12 (Figure 38.2).

Outcome

At this point, Natalie's 12 sessions were complete and she experienced some initial hair regrowth. She was pleased with her symptom improvement and sessions were scheduled on an "as-needed" basis.

CHALLENGES IN APPLYING THE EVIDENCE-BASED APPROACH

Probably the most limiting factors in adhering strictly to "HRT Plus" are the categorization of pullers into dichotomous categories and the lack of attention to both the sensory and cognitive aspects inherent in hair pulling behavior. First, looking at hair pulling in a dichotomous fashion by categorizing people as either "focused" or "automatic" pullers oversimplifies the behavior and, thus, can lead to oversimplification of the treatment. Because 75% of people with TTM report a mixture of both types, it is important to look comprehensively at each individual before making clinical decisions about treatment. As demonstrated in the Case Example, Natalie engaged in both focused and automatic pulling so appropriate interventions were needed for each scenario.

Second, HRT and "HRT Plus" do not consider the roles that sensory experiences and cognitive errors play in this disorder. TTM is a complex, idiosyncratic behavior that requires a highly individualized treatment package. Had this psychotherapist inquired about these important modalities, he might have learned that Natalie rubbed the cool, wet root along her mouth following pulling and squeezed it between her fingers to experience a popping sensation (sensory). Further, he may have learned that Natalie believed that pulling the coarse or different looking hairs would ultimately lead to a "perfect" head of hair (sensory and cognitive). Knowing this type of functional information adds intrinsic value to the treatment plan and leads to the use of strategies that better address the needs of this client.

There is a treatment package that addresses these multiple components and guides the clinician to create an individualized treatment program derived from a thorough functional analysis of the behavior. The Comprehensive Behavioral Model for Treating Trichotillomania (ComB Model) is an individualized treatment package that uses a five modality approach (Sensory, Cognitive, Affective, Motor [awareness], Place [environment]) to understand and treat hair pulling. This functional analysis then guides the selection of strategies. The ComB Model is highly individualized and comprehensive, providing a better alternative to the current research standard of HRT. Each modality of the ComB Model incorporates components that are evidence based; however, the treatment package as a whole has yet to be researched.

CULTURAL DIVERSITY ISSUES

Historically, TTM was believed to affect predominantly female populations. It is unclear whether more females indeed engage in pulling behavior or perhaps males are more able to hide their pulling behavior by removing hair from parts of the body that are less noticeable, thus causing minimal distress.

Although little is known about racial factors and TTM, a study by Neal-Barnett et al. indicated that African American women reported less distress as a result of hair pulling in part because it is more acceptable to wear wigs or to have hair extensions within this culture. It is also unclear whether or not hair pulling is less common in non-White populations, or if this discrepancy is due to reduced willingness within non-White cultures to seek psychological treatment.

FUTURE RESEARCH

More research is needed to evaluate the complex nature of hair pulling behavior including the sensory and cognitive contributions. Until then, interventions to address these areas will not be included in the empirically supported treatments and evaluation of the efficacy of these strategies will remain unknown outside of clinical observation. A treatment outcome investigation is currently underway to systematically evaluate the ComB Model. However, until this approach has been validated scientifically, evidence for its utility, as compared to other validated treatment options, will remain largely clinical in nature.

KEY REFERENCES

Christenson, G. A., & Mansueto, C. S. (1999). Trichotillomania: Descriptive characteristics and phenomenology. In D. J. Stein, G. A. Christenson, & E. Hollander (Eds.), *Trichotillomania*. Washington, DC: American Psychiatric Press.

Mansueto, C. S., Golomb, R. G., McCombs-Thomas, A., & Townsley-Stemberger, R. M. (1999). A comprehensive model for behavioral treatment of trichotillomania. *Cognitive and Behavioral Practice, 6,* 23–43.

Mansueto, C. S., Townsley-Stemberger, R. M., McCombs-Thomas, A., & Goldfinger-Golomb, R. (1997). Trichotillomania: A comprehensive behavioral model. *Clinical Psychology Review, 17,* 567–577.

Part III: Health Concerns

CHAPTER 39

Asthma in Adults

Thomas Janssens and Omer Van den Bergh

CLINICAL PROBLEM

Asthma is a chronic inflammatory condition characterized by inflammation of the airways, airway hyperreactivity, bronchoconstriction, and symptoms such as dyspnea (breathlessness, chest tightness), wheeze, and cough, with nightly symptoms often disturbing sleep. Asthma symptoms are usually associated with a variable degree of airflow obstruction, which is reversible, either spontaneously, or with the help of asthma treatment. The general aim of asthma treatment is to control disease manifestations. Poor asthma control is associated with limitations in daily activities and a negative impact of the disease on emotional well-being. Nonadherence to asthma medication further complicates the treatment of asthma. However, the addition of psychological interventions to asthma treatment may help to improve asthma control and reduce the burden of asthma.

PREVALENCE

In Western countries, physician diagnosed asthma has a prevalence ranging from 4% to 10%, while the prevalence of self-reported asthma-like symptoms ranges from 10% to almost 30%. Asthma control is surprisingly poor: more than 50% of patients with asthma do not achieve asthma control. About 50% of persons with asthma show nonadherence to asthma treatment.

Persons with asthma show a high prevalence of mood disorders and anxiety disorders. The high prevalence is especially striking for Panic Disorder (12%), with bidirectional longitudinal associations between Panic Disorder and asthma. Furthermore, there is a considerable prevalence of generalized anxiety in asthma (9%), which also has an impact on asthma morbidity.

CULTURAL DIVERSITY ISSUES

There are ethnic/cultural differences in asthma prevalence and morbidity, with asthma prevalence and morbidity being greater when comparing individuals from different ethnic/cultural subgroups to non-Latino White individuals. Although the mechanisms behind these disparities are not well understood, we want to single out two contributing factors that may have an impact on asthma management and therefore merit special attention during asthma treatment.

There have been observed ethnic/cultural differences in asthma symptom perception. For example, Latino children have been shown to overestimate their degree of airway compromise, which is associated with greater morbidity and health care use compared to non-Latino White children.

Apart from differences in asthma symptom perception, there are also ethnic/cultural differences in the identification of asthma triggers. These differences may be related to culturally idiosyncratic trigger beliefs that are often tied to beliefs about the efficacy of traditional asthma remedies. Examples are exposure to cold foods in south Asian cultures, or imbalances in hot and cold elements often endorsed in Guatemala and Mexico.

EVIDENCE-BASED TREATMENTS

Guidelines emphasize that optimal asthma treatment should include education on asthma and asthma treatment, a discussion of treatment goals, the development of a personalized, written self-management plan (often including self-monitoring of asthma symptoms or lung function), and periodical follow-up appointments with an asthma care provider. Self-management and education have been shown to reduce exacerbations, improve lung function, asthma symptoms and quality of life, improve adherence to inhaled corticosteroid medication, and reduce unscheduled medical appointments and emergency room visits.

Several psychological factors may influence the course of asthma. Anxiety and depression have a negative impact on asthma control and quality of life, while stress and negative emotions have been shown to increase airway inflammation and asthma symptoms. Patients with poorly controlled asthma may therefore benefit from additional psychological interventions. Despite the limited number of high quality studies on psychological interventions for asthma, a meta-analysis did show consistent beneficial effects of cognitive/behavioral interventions. A prototypical intervention complementing self-management and education includes cognitive restructuring, self-monitoring of antecedents and consequences of symptoms and medication intake, stimulus control and response control in a 6-session individual therapy format. Compared to a waiting-list control group, this program reduced asthma symptoms and negative emotions and increased quality of life, lung function, adherence and self-efficacy, showing medium to large effect sizes.

Furthermore, relaxation training, surface electromyography (EMG) biofeedback and heart-rate variability (HRV) biofeedback have been used to reduce the influence of stress on asthma. Overall, these interventions seem to produce small but significant effects. In contrast, direct biofeedback of respiratory parameters has failed to produce consistent beneficial effects in persons with asthma.

Asthma and panic disorder often co-occur, and symptoms of both disorders can be rather similar (e.g., chest tightness). However, treating a panic disorder symptom as an asthma symptom or vice versa may worsen both conditions. A pilot study of a treatment program that included education and training on differences in panic symptoms and asthma symptoms, combined with self-management training, progressive relaxation training, breathing training, cognitive restructuring, problem solving, exposure and assertiveness training has shown a large (d = 1–1.7) decrease in both asthma and panic symptoms, a reduction in rescue medication use, and an increase in quality of life.

Hyperventilation-related symptoms and reductions in carbon dioxide partial pressure (PCO_2) have been frequently observed in persons with asthma and can lead to symptom exacerbations. PCO_2 biofeedback and breathing training interventions have been proposed to change maladaptive breathing behavior, and initial studies have shown promising results.

FUTURE RESEARCH

Studies on psychological treatment of asthma are usually limited to small-scale efficacy studies. Therefore, there is a need for large-scale efficacy studies, as well as studies evaluating the day-to-day effectiveness of interventions in clinical practice. In addition, studies investigating underlying assumptions and specific (mediating) mechanisms involved in various treatments are needed. For example, an increase in self-efficacy has been suggested as a potential mediator in most nonpharmacological interventions for asthma. Furthermore, the study of symptom perception in asthma can act as a framework to help to understand the discrepancy of asthma symptom reports and physiological indices of asthma severity. Obesity and ethnicity, but also attentional mechanisms, mental representations of asthma symptoms, and concurrent emotional and contextual information have been implicated in this discrepancy. The addition of measures of proposed treatment mediators to clinical trials may inform us about the role of these specific mediators. Furthermore, owing to the packaged nature of psychological interventions for asthma, dismantling studies are needed to identify necessary and sufficient components of asthma treatment. Finally, the influence of stress on asthma-related inflammatory mechanisms calls for the construction and evaluation of psychological interventions aimed at reducing asthma-related inflammation.

KEY REFERENCES

Kotses, H., & Creer, T. L. (2010). Asthma self-management. In A. Harver & H. Kotses (Eds.), *Asthma, health and society* (pp. 117–139). New York, NY: Springer.

Lehrer, P. M., Feldman, J., Giardino, N., Song, H. S., & Schmaling, K. (2002). Psychological aspects of asthma. *Journal of Consulting and Clinical Psychology, 70,* 691–711.

Yorke, J., Fleming, S. L., & Shuldham, C. (2007). Psychological interventions for adults with asthma: A systematic review. *Respiratory Medicine, 101,* 1–14.

Clinician Application

Asthma in Adults

Lynne E. Matte and Jonathan M. Feldman

COMMENT ON THE EVIDENCE-BASED RECOMMENDATIONS

Janssens and Van den Bergh conclude that there are a limited number of well-designed, large-scale studies examining psychological interventions for asthma. Therefore, clinicians working with asthma patients with comorbid psychiatric disease may, at times, need to rely on data from other chronic diseases or the general psychological treatment literature. However, applying efficacious psychological interventions (e.g., cognitive behavior therapy [CBT] for panic disorder) to patients with asthma may require modifications. Overlap in symptoms between asthma and anxiety (e.g., difficulty breathing) presents additional challenges for patients who first need to identify correctly whether they are experiencing asthma or panic attacks in order to treat their symptoms appropriately. Certain interoceptive exposure exercises, such as voluntary hyperventilation, might actually trigger bronchoconstriction in patients with asthma. Therefore, we present a case example below of a patient with asthma and panic disorder, and apply a CBT and asthma education protocol and heart rate variability biofeedback.

CASE EXAMPLE

Subject Information and Brief History

Edna was a 23-year-old, single, Puerto Rican American female who lived in the inner city with her parents, twin sister, and three other siblings. She and her mother were both disabled owing to a muscle disorder. Edna completed high school and had a desire to attend a training school. She reported being diagnosed with asthma when she was 10 years old. She was never formally diagnosed with panic disorder but remembers having attacks as young as 17 years old. Her stressors included chronic medical diseases, several somatic complaints (e.g., stomach pain, dental problems, etc.), a recent move to an unsafe neighborhood after living in a shelter for almost 9 months, and problems in her relationship with her mother.

Presenting Problem

Edna was self-referred to our clinic as she was looking for treatment for her panic attacks. She presented with uncontrollable panic attacks, which began as a teenager, occurring four to five times weekly with moderate to extreme worry about the occurrence of future panic attacks. She was not able to work or attend school owing to agoraphobia, which started about 3 years ago. She was afraid of traveling owing to fear that she would experience a panic attack, not be able to escape the situation, and then experience embarrassment. She feared having a panic attack in trains or in airplanes. She reported her asthma triggers included strong odors, pollen, and upper respiratory infections. Edna's symptoms during panic attacks included heat behind her neck, tachycardia, tingling in fingers, and rapid breathing. These panic symptoms were sometimes exacerbated by her poorly controlled asthma, which required her to use quick-relief medication frequently to alleviate her asthma symptoms. She was not taking any controller medication for asthma, which works to reduce airway inflammation and helps prevent asthma symptoms. Edna was using her quick-relief medication four to six puffs per day. Her last medical appointment for asthma treatment was over a year ago owing to her agoraphobia and feelings of frustration with getting an appointment in a timely manner.

Treatment Intervention and Course

Session 1 focused on Edna's understandings of her symptoms of asthma and panic and how they affected each other. She was aware that some of the symptoms of asthma were similar to her panic. At times she was confused whether symptoms such as "breathing hard" were indicative of an asthma or panic attack. She was taught how to complete a daily record of symptoms, actions, and event records. Edna learned how to use a peak flow meter, which provides an objective measure of airflow, to help her distinguish between asthma and panic attacks. Asthma attacks are more typically characterized by wheezing, coughing, mucus production, and reduced peak flow values. Panic attacks have a more rapid onset, shorter overall duration, and may include symptoms of hyperventilation. Self-monitoring forms helped Edna to see how often she was confused as to whether she was experiencing asthma or panic attacks. The first treatment session also focused on asthma education and medications. Edna revealed that she had been undertreating her asthma because she could not get a timely appointment at her inner city hospital clinic owing to overcrowding and was afraid of leaving her home. Thus, she was only relying on her quick-relief medication for asthma treatment.

The second session focused on education regarding the panic cycle and how her thoughts affect her physical symptoms, which in turn lead to maladaptive behaviors such as avoidance. For example, explaining the cognitive component of panic helped Edna connect her perceived thoughts with increases in her panic level and subsequent avoidance behavior. During sessions 3 to 5, Edna learned about her cognitive response to panic symptoms and how to stop the cycle of panic. She was taught cognitive monitoring, self-statement analysis, and how to examine the evidence for and against her thoughts. Heart rate variability biofeedback was used during sessions 3 to 5. This form of biofeedback focuses on increasing the amplitude of heart rate oscillations and has been shown to be beneficial for the treatment of asthma. Edna practiced breathing at her resonance frequency, which is the rate of respiration corresponding to maximal heart rate variability. She was given homework to practice breathing at this rate at least twice a day at home. Motivational interviewing was employed to help Edna deal with her resistance to seeing her primary care provider to treat her asthma symptoms and other physical symptoms (e.g., stomach pain). This component focused on Edna's ambivalence about seeking health care owing to her past negative experiences and agoraphobia versus a desire to improve her asthma control. Edna's twin sister attended session 6 and was engaged in the treatment protocol to help Edna with interoceptive exposure and to understand other components of treatment (e.g., the difference between panic and asthma, avoidance of asthma triggers vs. exposure to panic triggers). Her sister was selected as the family member to attend this session because Edna felt that her sister could help the most with her panic attacks and the two had a very close relationship.

Outcome

Edna's Panic Disorder Severity Scale rating decreased from severe (23) to moderate (16) from her initial session to the last session 8 weeks later. Her Clinical Global Impression Scale of global improvement from session 1 to session 8 showed "much improvement." By her fifth session, Edna started taking controller medication for asthma and was adherent with taking it as prescribed. She decreased her use of quick-relief medication and she now relied on using her asthma action plan. This individually tailored plan is a written summary of when to use preventive and rescue asthma medications, zones of peak flow, and when to seek medical attention. Edna practiced heart rate variability biofeedback at home on a regular basis. She reported experiencing higher levels of relaxation and less frequent panic attacks at post treatment.

CHALLENGES IN APPLYING THE EVIDENCE-BASED APPROACH

The challenges that may affect treatment of inner-city patients with asthma include lack of access to medical care and poor understanding of asthma medications and how to take them. Therefore, psychological interventions for asthma patients may first need to address poor asthma control and lack of inhaled corticosteroids, which is the first-line medical therapy for asthma. Poorly controlled asthma and its life-threatening symptoms can naturally lead to higher levels of anxiety, panic, and depression. Therapists may need to address this issue by providing patients with proper referrals for asthma care and working with patients on skills to improve communication with providers (e.g., assertiveness training, writing questions in advance). Other challenges in applying evidence-based approaches include unsafe neighborhood and the many stressors inherent when living in inner-city neighborhoods. For example, exposure therapy has to be modified to take into account safety issues, such as traveling alone.

CULTURAL DIVERSITY ISSUES

Cultural factors and beliefs about asthma and panic play a major role in the interpretation of body sensations and potential catastrophic thoughts. Training patients to discriminate between asthma and panic symptoms is an important first step in self-management of both diseases. More specifically, Latinos tend to be family-oriented and thus, inviting a family member or close friend to a session may help to increase the family's understanding of asthma and panic disorder. Family stressors may also interact with limitations of inner-city living, which may include many individuals living in a small apartment and family members not understanding the person's panic attacks and how treatment works. The challenges posed by participants of low socioeconomic status may include medical care access, comorbid health issues, unsafe neighborhoods and limited privacy to practice CBT exercises. Motivational interviewing may be useful in working with inner-city minorities who might be frustrated by the lack of access to medical care and perceptions that providers do not understand their condition.

FUTURE RESEARCH

The asthma field would benefit from additional large-scale, randomized controlled trials on psychological interventions. First, efficacious treatments for psychiatric disorders should be applied to patients with asthma to determine whether specific modifications are required. Second, intervention research focused on techniques for improving treatment adherence, such as motivational interviewing, and asthma symptom perception are needed to improve asthma self-management. Finally, more intervention research is needed on ethnic minority populations given the disparities in asthma outcomes that exist between Puerto Rican and African American adults versus Caucasian adults.

KEY REFERENCES

Feldman, J. M., Giardino, N. D., & Lehrer, P. M. (2000). Asthma and panic disorder. In D. I. Mostofsky & D. H. Barlow (Eds.), *The management of stress and anxiety in medical disorders* (pp. 220–239). Needham Heights, MA: Allyn & Bacon.

Lehrer, P. M., Karavidas, M. K., Lu, S. E., Feldman, J., Kranitz, L., ... Reynolds, R. (2008). Psychological treatment of comorbid asthma and panic disorder: A pilot study. *Journal of Anxiety Disorders, 22,* 671–683.

Lehrer, P. M., Vaschillo, E., Vaschillo, B., Lu, S. E., Scardella, A., ... Habib, R. H. (2004). Biofeedback treatment for asthma. *Chest, 126,* 352–361.

CHAPTER 40

Blood-Injection-Injury Phobia

Thomas Ritz and Alicia E. Meuret

CLINICAL PROBLEM

Blood-injection-injury (BII) phobia is a distressing condition with far-reaching consequences for patients' well-being and health. Patients experience intense fear when seeing blood or injuries, or when receiving injections or other invasive medical procedures. Usually, these stimuli or situations are avoided at all cost resulting in an inability to watch movies of accidents, violence or surgeries, talk about medical conditions and treatments, or even smell detergents used in medical settings. Associated cues also trigger fears, such as hospital or physician visits, and in some cases even more distant reminders, such as red paint or ketchup, can also trigger fears.

BII phobia is unique among the specific phobias in that it elicits a characteristic physiological response pattern that can culminate in vasovagal syncope or presyncopal states. Patients feel faint, start sweating and trembling, turn pale, and may lose consciousness. Usually, these episodes resolve within minutes of removal from the stimulus, although there is an obvious risk of injuries from falls and a strong feeling of weakness and embarrassment. The typical response pattern in these patients has been described as an initial fight–flight response that is shared with other fear states, followed by a unique stage of sympathetic withdrawal and/or parasympathetic discharge. This leads to peripheral blood vessel dilation and heart rate slowing, with the consequence of blood pooling in the periphery, a fall in blood pressure, and reduced cerebral blood flow.

BII phobia is associated with great impairments on many levels. Patients will refuse important medical procedures and avoid regular preventative care or chronic disease management (e.g., for diabetes), which constitutes a substantial threat to patients' personal health and poses a substantial burden on health care systems. The inability to confront BII stimuli may also affect others, in that patients may be unable to assist in cases of injury or other threats to health. Long-term professional or personal life choices are guided by such fears, in that patients may avoid entering health-related professions or becoming pregnant. Daily life activities can also be limited when avoidance of such stimuli is strongly generalized, with associated consequences for social quality of life.

PREVALENCE

BII phobia is one of the most common specific phobias. Lifetime prevalence estimates vary between populations but are typically estimated around 2% to 5%. Age of onset is often early—within the first 20 years of life. Female gender and lower educational level are associated with higher reports and older age with lower reports of lifetime prevalence. Comorbidity is also substantial, with elevated rates of other anxiety disorders, substance abuse or dependency, and depression. An additional percentage of the population reports substantial fears of BII stimuli but does not necessary qualify as phobic, typically because of lack of interference in life and/or apparent avoidance of the stimuli. Further substantial numbers experience fainting when confronted with these stimuli (particularly with injections, blood draws, and blood donations) without reporting fear. Both conditions may also complicate medical treatments and may constitute the initial stages of a phobia development.

CULTURAL DIVERSITY ISSUES

The literature has only sporadically reported about diversity aspects in BII phobia. There is some evidence from questionnaire studies that medically related fears are stronger in Asian cultures and weaker in African Americans as compared to Caucasians.

EVIDENCE-BASED TREATMENT

Psychological treatments for BII phobia are notoriously understudied, partly owing to a common misconception that the ideal treatment has been found. The "golden standard" treatment technique for BII phobia is Applied Tension, which consists of two distinct components: the training of brief sequences of muscle tension and exposure to the feared stimulus. The tension component emphasizes brief, 10- to 15-second sequences of voluntary contractions of the arm, leg, and chest muscles followed by 20 to 30 seconds of release of tension (not relaxation). As a rule of thumb, tension should be long enough to feel sensations of warmth in the face. Such sequences are typically repeated a number of times in session and additional homework assignments instruct patients to practice these sequences daily five times. The exposure component resembles typical procedures for other specific phobias, with the important difference that tension is applied as a coping technique when patients feel the development of presyncopal symptoms (i.e., sweating, feelings of dizziness, nausea). Part of the session is dedicated to training of the perception of these early warning signs of faintness. Both one- and five-session protocols have been described in the literature. The one-session protocol lasts approximately 2 hours, with an introduction to the rationale and subsequent training of the tension technique, followed by exposure practice using pictures of BII stimulus material, viewing test tubes of blood, and/or receiving a finger prick. The five-session protocol can culminate in more challenging exposure settings such as visits to blood donor centers or observations of surgeries. A maintenance program can be offered that includes regular exposure to BII stimuli and a contract to not avoid feared situations.

Empirical evidence for the efficacy of Applied Tension comes from only five published clinical trials, all with small patient numbers and by a Swedish group led by Lars-Göran Öst. A critical examination of this literature shows that although generally strong effects are observed at post and follow-up assessments, the technique is not necessarily superior to other treatment approaches, such as exposure treatment alone. Whereas somewhat higher effects sizes are observed for in-session anxiety reduction, a general tendency to respond phobic to BII stimuli, as measured by questionnaire inventories, is equally reduced by the different treatment techniques. Interventions with multiple sessions appear to be somewhat more efficacious than single sessions and maintenance programs improve outcomes at follow-up. Most notably, patients who report a history of fainting improved equally well as patients without such a history, raising doubts over the integrity of the Applied Tension treatment rationale, which is geared toward counteracting physiological disturbances that are characteristic for a vasovagal syncope. It is also unknown how many patients refuse exposure due to high fear or avoidance.

FUTURE RESEARCH

The underlying causes and mechanisms of BII phobia have been subject to much speculation but little empirical research. Existing research has only provided partial insights into relevant physiological processes. Much of the focus has been on aberrations in the autonomic regulation (e.g., blood pressure). A critical role of hyperventilation has been illustrated recently. Patients confronted with feared stimuli (e.g., surgery film) hyperventilate by taking deep breaths even before autonomic dysregulation (such as massive drops in blood pressure and/or heart rate) occurs. Hyperventilation is a potent stimulus for the cerebral blood vessels to constrict and it is strongly correlated with a range of characteristic fear symptoms of these patients, including lightheadedness, dizziness, and faintness. These findings motivate designing new treatment approaches that include elements of breathing retraining with an effort to reverse hyperventilation (or low carbon dioxide levels). A recent experimental intervention trial tested instructions in breathing slow, abdominally, and most importantly, shallowly to reduce hyperventilation and found similar reductions of in-session anxiety as for Applied Tension instructions. In addition, because a number of patients also report pronounced feelings of disgust in response to BII stimuli, preliminary studies have begun addressing disgust with exposure techniques. Overall, problems with the rationale and outcomes of the Applied Tension technique should motivate further exploration of basic mechanism and treatment techniques in BII phobia.

KEY REFERENCES

Ayala, E. S., Meuret, A. E., & Ritz, T. (2009). Treatments for blood-injury-injection phobia: A critical review of current evidence. *Journal of Psychiatric Research, 43,* 1235–1242.

Marks, I. (1988). Blood-injury phobia: A review. *American Journal of Psychiatry, 145,* 1207–1213.

Öst, L. G., & Sterner, U. (1987). Applied tension. A specific behavioral method for treatment of blood phobia. *Behaviour Research and Therapy, 25,* 25–29.

Blood-Injection-Injury Phobia

Mary Karapetian Alvord

COMMENTS ON THE EVIDENCE-BASED RECOMMENDATIONS

Cognitive behavioral therapy (CBT), in particular exposure therapy, is an empirically supported approach to overcoming phobias. While Applied Tension as described by Ritz and Meuret has been shown in small studies to be effective with people suffering from Blood-Injection Injury (BII) phobia who faint, exposure therapy, alone, is the most accepted form of treatment in practice. Clinicians who gradually habituate a phobic person to feared situations, in this case to the drawing of blood or to the sight of blood, through the use of increasingly demanding exposures, have a high success rate in helping their patients reduce their avoidance. It is important to assess whether fainting is a symptom. In this case, Applied Tension should be incorporated into the treatment. In addition to exposure therapy, a clinician might use several techniques that are found to be helpful in practice, but which are minimally discussed in the literature. These include: interoceptive exposure for panic symptoms (for example, hyperventilating with a client to show that it is harmless), teaching calm breathing, and/or exploring cognitive distortions associated with blood, injuries, and needles.

While research has supported one- and five-session protocols, it is more typical in practice to carry out a 1-hour intake plus 5 to 10 50-minute sessions. In this way, other comorbid anxieties may be addressed, and exposures may be paced so that an individual is willing to gradually face fears and thus continue treatment. Greater numbers of sessions also allow for more practice with settings in which the difficulties arise.

CASE EXAMPLE (COMPOSITE OF SEVERAL FEMALES, LATE ADOLESCENCE THROUGH EARLY ADULTHOOD)

Subject Information and Brief History

Lauren is a 20-year-old Caucasian female college student. From childhood, she experienced great distress when faced with the need for injections, or with the drawing of blood. On one occasion, she fainted at the mere sight of blood.

Presenting Problem

Lauren was referred by her physician. She was required to have blood tests for a medical procedure and had repeatedly rescheduled the tests. She was further motivated to seek help with this phobia, as she planned to enter her junior year abroad and anticipated that she might need blood work and/or immunizations prior to being allowed to travel.

Treatment Intervention and Course

The practitioner will require medical supplies for office exposures. These may be obtained from a physician or pharmacy. Fake blood can be made from recipes found on the internet or obtained from novelty stores. Depending on the patient's specific fears, supplies might include: syringes and needles of various sizes/lengths, tourniquets, alcohol swabs, IV needles, latex gloves, cotton balls, bandages, blood collection tubes, and fake blood. Treatment may also include exposure to movies and/or websites showing injections and blood. Home exposures may include pictures, movies, and visits to actual medical settings.

Session 1 involved discussing Lauren's specific fears, her physiological reactions to and thoughts about those fears, her avoidance behaviors, and her motivation for change. Because of her history of fainting, she was also taught the Applied Tension technique, and was asked to practice it between sessions. At Session 2, Lauren enumerated a list of scenarios that precipitated her fear (e.g., seeing a needle with its cap on, holding a needle, and seeing blood). These were recorded on index cards so that a hierarchy could be developed. The hierarchy was recorded into a computer (Word) document that allowed "track changes" so that a hierarchy could be adjusted as treatment progressed (see Table 40.1). In each following session, Lauren was exposed to progressively more difficult situations until her "subjective units of distress" (SUDS), which were graphed on a scale from 1 to 10, were reduced by approximately half. When it became obvious that a given exposure was too difficult to be accomplished within the 50-minute session, the exposure sequence was broken into smaller steps. Most exposure sessions involved the use of medical supplies and/or visual depictions (e.g., watching injections/medical procedures in YouTube clips). Hyperventilating with the client ("interoceptive exposure") and later, "calm" breathing exercises, were introduced. Other sessions involved imaginal exposures (e.g., "visualizing" fear-invoking situations). Applied Tension was necessary in only two sessions. Lauren was routinely assigned homework consisting of planned exposures, such as watching a bloody movie, or sitting in the waiting room of a medical lab. She was asked to record her SUDS, at 5-minute intervals, on a graph (see Figure 40.1).

TABLE 40.1 Lauren's Hierarchy

10 Having blood drawn and looking at the blood vials
 9 Sitting in the waiting room of a medical lab
 9 Going with mom to a medical lab added 6/05
 8 Going with friend to a medical lab
 8 Seeing someone injured and bleeding
 *
 5 Visualization of getting a blood draw
 4 ~~Watching video clip of someone getting a shot~~ ◊ 6/05
 2 ~~Picture of a syringe with the cap on~~ ◊ 6/05

*partial hierarchy for illustration.
◊ = successful habituation and date.

Name: Lauren............

Date:... xx........

(Home) Office Exposure activity: Looking at a picture with human blood

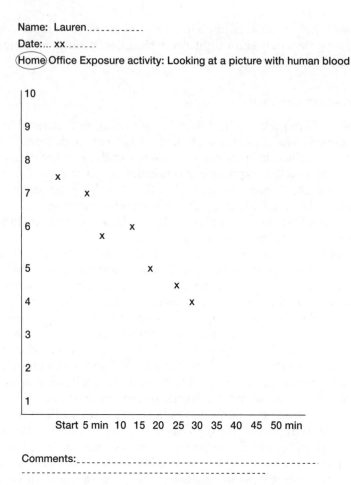

FIGURE 40.1 Anxiety ratings for exposure (SUDS).

Outcome

After several unaccompanied visits to the medical facility, which included sitting in the waiting room, Lauren was able to complete the required blood tests. Two more sessions were scheduled so that she could complete the medical procedure, which required receiving anesthesia through an IV.

CHALLENGES IN APPLYING THE EVIDENCE BASED APPROACH

One challenge to be solved is motivation. Unless a patient is confronted with the absolute need for getting injections or blood draws, his or her motivation to deal with BII is often low. Another challenge is to develop a specific plan that incorporates all the important elements of fear for exposure for *that* particular individual, for example, smells, images, feelings of disgust, and fear of touch.

A further challenge is to accommodate a patient in the event that she faints or experiences dizziness/lightheadedness during a session. A final challenge is to ensure that the specific "exposure" provided significantly reduces the client's anxiety *within* the 50-minute session.

CULTURAL DIVERSITY ISSUES

Although the literature does not point to cultural differences, in clinical practice it appears that primarily females seek treatment for blood-injection phobia. I have no direct knowledge of religious or cultural groups where this is a specific problem.

FUTURE RESEARCH

A better understanding of the utility of Applied Tension is required. The literature speaks of how "disgust" is an important component in blood-injection phobias. It would be helpful if practitioners were to better understand how the "anticipation of pain" also plays a role in such phobias. Interoceptive exposure, breathing retraining, and cognitive restructuring as an addition to exposure therapy should be further studied.

CLINICIAN APPLICATION

Antony, M. M., & Watling, M. A. (2006). *Overcoming medical phobias.* Oakland, CA: New Harbingers Publications. Out of print and available from the author: http://www.martinantony.com/downloads

Leahy, R. L., Holland, S. J. F., & McGinn, L. K. (2011). *Treatment plan and interventions for depression and anxiety disorders* (2nd ed). New York, NY: Guilford Press.

Mednick, L. M., & Claar, R. L. (2012). Treatment of severe blood-injection-injury phobia with the applied-tension method: Two adolescent case examples. *Clinical Case Studies, 11,* 24–34. Retrieved June 1, 2012, http://ccs.sagepub.com/content/11/1/24

CHAPTER 41

Bulimia-Binge Eating

Lisa Rachelle Riso Lilenfeld

CLINICAL PROBLEM

Bulimia Nervosa (BN) and Binge Eating Disorder (BED) both share in common the problem of recurrent binge eating, that is, eating a large amount of food in a discrete period of time, marked by a loss of control over eating. BN is additionally accompanied by recurrent compensatory behavior (e.g., vomiting, laxative abuse, excessive exercise, fasting) in an attempt to counteract the effects (e.g., weight gain) of repeated binge eating. Individuals with BN also have a significant portion of their self-worth strongly influenced by body shape or weight. A final distinction between these two eating disorders that is not reflected in the diagnostic criteria, but is well known to clinicians, is that individuals with BN typically significantly restrict their food intake outside of their bulimic episodes in a relentless attempt to decrease their weight. This is not typically the case for those with BED.

PREVALENCE

Reliable lifetime prevalence data for BN and BED emerged from the 2007 National Comorbidity Survey-Replication Study, which was a nationally representative, face-to-face household survey of nearly 10,000 individuals in the United States. From this study, we learned that the lifetime prevalence rate for BN is 1.5% for females and 0.5% for males. This 3:1 ratio came as a shock to most researchers and clinicians in the field, who now appreciate how much more common eating disorders are in males than previously thought.

The lifetime prevalence rate for BED is 3.5% for females and 2.0% for males. By contrast, this closer than 2:1 gender ratio was not a surprise to researchers and clinicians in the field. When considering this lifetime prevalence statistic obtained from a community sample, it is important to note that estimates of BED among weight-loss treatment seeking individuals have been found to be much higher, with up to one third of such individuals currently or previously having met criteria for BED.

There is significant diagnostic cross-over among eating disorder diagnostic categories, such that changing from one eating disorder diagnosis to another (and often more than one such transition) over time, is actually the norm. In addition, eating disorder not otherwise specified (NOS) is actually the most common eating disorder diagnosis in clinical settings. Both of these facts have led some to suggest that the most valid depiction of the entirety of eating pathology would be one broad diagnosis. It is clear from theoretical models of the development and maintenance of eating pathology that there are many more overlapping features than distinct ones.

CULTURAL DIVERSITY ISSUES

It is important to note that despite the important realization that one third of all individuals with BN are male, nearly all treatment studies have involved only women. Treatment trials of BED are slightly more representative, but still have primarily female participants, despite the fact that nearly one half of all individuals with BED are male. This must be rectified in order for our treatment studies to more accurately represent those afflicted with these disorders. Likewise, the typically overwhelmingly Caucasian samples in treatment studies are not at all representative of what is now known about the occurrence of eating disorders across racial groups. African American, Asian American, and Latino individuals are afflicted with BN and BED less often than European Americans, but they are by no means immune. In fact, compared to White female adolescents, it has been found that Hispanic female adolescents more often abuse diuretics, Black female adolescents more often induce vomiting, and Asian female adolescents report more binge eating. Among adolescent boys, African American and Asian American boys have been found to be at greater risk for harmful weight control behaviors than White boys.

EVIDENCE-BASED TREATMENTS

BN is the eating disorder for which treatment has been the most widely studied, with more than 30 randomized controlled trials having been conducted. Regardless of the treatment approach being utilized, one must be sure to have an appropriate medical evaluation at the start of treatment and as often as needed during treatment, as there are significant medical complications that may occur with BN.

The National Institute for Clinical Excellence (NICE) guidelines in the United Kingdom assigned a grade of "A" for cognitive behavioral therapy (CBT) for BN, indicating that this very specific tailoring of CBT for this condition is considered the first-line treatment for BN. Early focus in CBT for BN is normalization of food intake. Maladaptive beliefs are challenged through cognitive restructuring and behavioral experiments. It is important to note that if significant (i.e., 70% reduction in purging) is not seen by session 6, the likelihood of remission is greatly diminished.

Serotonin-specific reuptake inhibitor (SSRI) antidepressants have been demonstrated to be slightly less effective than CBT for BN and are considered a second-line evidence-based treatment. The risk for relapse after discontinuation of treatment is much greater, whereas treatment gains are well maintained after CBT treatment ends. There is no compelling evidence that combining SSRIs and CBT is more effective than CBT for BN alone. It is useful for the clinician to know that the effective dose for treating BN with fluoxetine (considered the "gold standard" of pharmacological treatment for BN) is higher (i.e., 60 mg) than the dose typically used for the treatment of depression.

Interpersonal Psychotherapy (IPT) for BN has likewise been shown to be comparably effective to CBT in achieving remission, though it takes longer to achieve this outcome, which is why it is considered a useful second-line treatment. IPT, originally developed as a treatment for depression, is not at all symptom focused as in CBT, but rather focused upon interpersonal factors that are thought to maintain the disorder. IPT is the only psychological treatment that has been shown to have outcomes comparable to CBT at 1- and 6-year follow-ups since the end of treatment.

A few studies of Dialectical Behavior Therapy (DBT) have shown some early evidence of efficacy for BN. DBT for BN shares some features in common with CBT for BN and is an additional evidence-based treatment approach for BN, but has been studied far less than CBT, pharmacotherapy, and IPT.

Owing to the very impressive outcome of Maudsley-model family-based therapy for adolescent anorexia nervosa, it has now been adapted for adolescent BN and there are preliminary data supporting the efficacy of this treatment. This warrants further study as nearly all other treatment trials of BN involved only adults and although the average age of onset of BN is young adulthood (e.g., age 18), there are many cases of earlier onset during adolescence that may be responsive to this promising family-based treatment.

Other treatment approaches are in widespread use for eating disorders, such as psychodynamic and psychoanalytic approaches, though at present, these have comparatively little, if any, empirical support for their use with either BN or BED. Fairburn has developed an expanded version of CBT, called CBT-Enhanced (CBT-E), which is applicable to all forms of eating disorders. It is grounded in the CBT–BN underlying theoretical and resulting treatment model, but has been adapted to apply to restrictive, bulimic, and pure binge eating forms of disorders, as it targets the common underlying pathology (e.g., overvaluation of shape and weight). At the time of this writing, there is promising preliminary empirical support for CBT-E. Other novel treatments for bulimia nervosa are also under study, such as integrative cognitive-affective therapy.

Fewer treatment studies of BED have been conducted despite the fact that BED is more prevalent than BN. Similar to findings with BN, CBT for BED has the most evidence of efficacy, though IPT for BED (delivered in group format) is equally effective. In addition, self-help versions of CBT for BED do appear to have some utility as a first step in treatment or a potential alternative if therapist-delivered CBT is not available. IPT for BED yields comparably significant and well-maintained improvement as has been found with IPT for BN. As with BN, there is a smaller, but growing, body of evidence supporting DBT as an effective treatment for BED, usually delivered in group format. Finally, many pharmacotherapy attempts to treat BED have met with modest success. There have been mixed results regarding the efficacy of SSRIs in reducing the frequency of binge eating and little evidence of a clinically significant weight loss effect. There is evidence that CBT alone is more effective than medication alone in reducing BED symptoms.

FUTURE RESEARCH

In addition to diversifying the nature of the participants in treatment studies, two important areas of research needing further attention are a better understanding of: (a) early predictors of treatment response, and (b) predictors of who is most likely to respond to self-help treatment delivery. Ultimately, this may allow us to improve upon the roughly 50% response rate to the best treatments currently available for adults with BN or BED.

KEY REFERENCES

Fairburn, C. G. (2008). *Cognitive behavior therapy and eating disorders.* New York, NY: The Guilford Press.

Grilo, C. M., & Mitchell, J. E. (Eds.). (2010). *The treatment of eating disorders: A clinical handbook.* New York, NY: The Guilford Press.

Le Grange, D., & Lock, J. (2007). *Treating bulimia in adolescents: A family-based approach.* New York, NY: The Guilford Press.

Clinician Application

Bulimia-Binge Eating

Joanna Marino, Cara Schmid, and Julie Bowman

COMMENT ON THE EVIDENCE-BASED RECOMMENDATIONS

Fortunately, the research literature on Bulimia Nervosa (BN) has demonstrated that psychotherapeutic interventions tend to be successful, and opportunities for second-line approaches are available (e.g., fluoxetine). As Binge Eating Disorder (BED) has received somewhat less research attention owing to its more recent identification, the disconnect between research and practice appears somewhat larger. For example, it remains unclear as to whether psychopharmacological agents may support psychological interventions. It appears thus far that CBT is effective for treating BED. For clinicians, self-help and group settings may be used to supplement individual therapy as a backup method of intervention for treatment-resistant cases, although additional research is needed to support this therapeutic approach.

CASE EXAMPLE

Subject Information and Brief History

Anna was a 23-year-old, single female who was employed as a consultant at a major firm in a metropolitan area. She reported a history of obesity, but had recently lost weight (BMI = 25) through exercise with a personal trainer three to four times weekly and by reducing her caloric intake.

Presenting Problem

Anna presented for psychological evaluation because she was unable to control binge eating episodes which occurred four to five times weekly. She reported a history of previous "family dieting" in which her mother, father, and sister would follow a "fad diet." She indicated that these diets never produced lasting results for her. Anna denied a history of compensating (e.g., purging, laxatives, diuretics, etc.) for her binge episodes. She indicated that she enjoyed yoga as a means of relaxation and also enjoyed exercise to maintain her weight. She indicated that her exercise was not directly related to binge eating episodes. Also of note, Anna reported consuming four to six alcoholic beverages several times per week when attending social activities with coworkers.

Treatment Intervention and Course

Session 1 included gathering Anna's relevant background information and introducing her to the cognitive behavioral therapy (CBT) model. Anna was able to articulate her "all or nothing thinking" related to her binge episodes. Specifically, after eating three cookies which she did not plan to eat, she would often tell herself, "Well, I blew it, I might as well over-indulge and start fresh tomorrow." Anna was encouraged to complete daily meal records (Figure 41.1) to raise awareness of eating patterns, begin to generalize concepts discussed in psychotherapy, and provide "data" on specific eating-related situations to collaboratively review with the therapist. Anna created a goal of three binge episodes or less between sessions in order to gain some success in the initial weeks of treatment. During sessions 2 through 4, the therapist and Anna collaboratively reviewed the meal logs to assess her thoughts and beliefs about eating. Anna was also encouraged to develop alternative behaviors, including walking her dog, talking on the phone, or painting her nails, which helped her to identify methods for distracting and delaying her binge episodes. The number of binge episodes was recorded on a graph to clearly depict improvements or set-backs (Figure 41.2). Anna was referred to a dietician to aid her in meal choices and timing. The dietician introduced concepts such as scheduling five or six smaller meals throughout the day, meal planning, and meal preparation.

By session 5, the frequency of Anna's binge episodes had been reduced to twice a week. She had a slight set-back at session 6, when her romantic relationship ended and she worried about her upcoming yearly review at work. Anna began to see that the development of interpersonal and situational stressors led to feeling less in control and "triggered" her to binge. This was an opportunity for the therapist to provide Anna with education about lapses and relapses, and also provided an opportunity for Anna to learn about "triggers" from the lapses she experienced. She also began to recognize her pattern of consuming alcohol and how it related to set-backs in her eating and self-esteem.

Time/Place	Food & Beverage Consumed	Thoughts/Feeling/Interpersonal Context	Binge/Vomit/ Restrict

FIGURE 41.1 Example meal log.

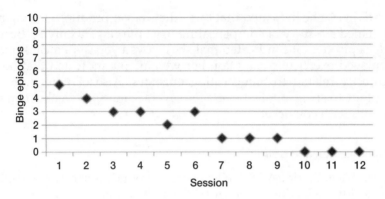

FIGURE 41.2 Example behavior chart.

Outcome

By session 8, Anna maintained once weekly binge episodes. As can be seen in Figure 41.2, these gains were maintained through to session 12, and her binge eating felt "controlled."

CHALLENGES IN APPLYING THE EVIDENCE-BASED APPROACH

Motivation for change is often a leading concern in treating BN and BED. Many patients seem to report distress caused by binge eating (e.g., loss of control, weight gain, or feeling overly full). A patient who engages in compensatory measures tends to become frustrated by the behavior, experience medical complications, and/or have negative emotions (e.g., guilt, depression, shame) following episodes of purging. Psychoeducation is often a helpful way to increase motivation to cease the binge/purge behavior. For example, informing the patient that binge–purge behavior can decrease metabolism, vomiting may cause permanent damage to the teeth, and purging can lead to life-threatening electrolyte imbalances.

In addition, motivation is difficult for patients with BN or BED who are significantly preoccupied with weight loss or who believe that purging or other compensatory measures help to maintain weight. These patients seem to have difficulty exercising cognitive flexibility related to eating disordered thoughts and behaviors. That is, many individuals have rigid rules related to "safe foods and bad foods" or difficulty engaging in behavioral experimentation (e.g., increasing the frequency of eating or attempting to add variety to a diet).

Psychiatric comorbidities can also present difficulties in treating BN and BED. At times, the focus of therapy can change as it becomes apparent that mood, anxiety, substance, or personality concerns are affecting the patient's ability to fully address the eating disorder. Clinical judgment is needed to determine if the comorbidities can be treated simultaneously. Referral to another provider such as a psychiatrist or therapist to address the comorbid disorder may also be effective in helping the primary therapist refocus on the eating disorder.

CULTURAL DIVERSITY ISSUES

Historically, eating disorders were believed to affect largely female populations. More common in current clinical practice is the increased number of male patients with BN or BED. Some males with BN appear to have difficulty discussing their preoccupation with weight, fear of weight gain, or compensatory measures used in attempt to maintain body image, perhaps owing to the stigma of eating disorders being associated with females. Males with BED seem to respond to CBT equally as well as females, although further research support is needed to confirm this observation.

Additional research is needed to inform clinicians of the particular needs of various ethnic groups. Similarly, research support that identifies treatment considerations of homosexual, bisexual, or transgender individuals will allow for refinements in evidence-based treatment for these groups. In the meantime, current methods of evidence-based treatment for BN, as well as CBT for BED, are used to address eating concerns, while overt consideration of specific diversity needs is essential in tailoring the treatment appropriately.

FUTURE RESEARCH

Two areas of research may help clinicians refine therapeutic interventions. First, prevention research may help to identify disordered body image or eating and allow individuals to preempt the development of additional eating disorder concerns or behaviors by early enrollment in psychotherapy. Second, research regarding methods for supplementing individual therapy (e.g., group therapy, dietician consultation, self-help, etc.) may offer techniques for addressing the needs of treatment-resistant individuals. This research may also include clinical techniques for tailoring evidence-based treatment to atypical or subthreshold eating disorders, such as purging disorder.

KEY REFERENCES

Fairburn, C. G. (1995). *Overcoming binge eating*. New York, NY: The Guilford Press.

Grilo, C. M., & Mitchell, J. E. (Eds.). (2010). *The treatment of eating disorders: A clinical handbook*. New York, NY: The Guilford Press.

Mitchell, J. E., Devlin, M. J., de Zwaan, M., & Peterson, C. B. (2007). *Binge-eating disorder: Clinical foundations and treatment*. New York, NY: The Guilford Press.

CHAPTER 42

Chronic Fatigue Syndrome

Leonard A. Jason, Molly Brown, Laura Hlavaty,
Meredyth Evans, and Abigail Brown

CLINICAL PROBLEM

Chronic fatigue syndrome (CFS) is a chronic, debilitating illness that is poorly understood in terms of etiology and pathophysiology. The most commonly used international definition of CFS requires a new onset of fatigue lasting at least 6 months that is not caused by ongoing physical exertion and not substantially alleviated by rest. In addition, four out of eight definitional symptoms must be present including sore throat, tender lymph nodes, muscle pain, pain in multiple joints, headaches, postexertional malaise, memory and concentration problems, and unrefreshing sleep. Fatigue-inducing medical or psychiatric illnesses are exclusionary for a diagnosis of CFS.

PREVALENCE

Patients with CFS experience a greater level of disability compared to other illness groups such as those with acute infectious mononucleosis, type II diabetes mellitus, and multiple sclerosis. Patients experience a severe exacerbation of symptoms after even mild exertion. Few patients recover from CFS, and the illness renders most unemployed or underemployed.

Prevalence estimates for CFS vary on the basis of sampling methods used and case definition applied. Jason et al. conducted a community-based epidemiological study in which stratified random sampling was used to screen 18,675 individuals in Chicago, Illinois, for CFS. The prevalence rate was estimated at 0.42% using the Fukuda et al. case definition. Prevalence estimates were substantially higher when a broader case definition developed by the Centers for Disease Control and Prevention was applied. Accurate sampling methods are critical in estimating prevalence rates, as many individuals with this illness may not be sampled if they lack access to health care, and broader case definitions might include many individuals with primary psychiatric disorders.

CULTURAL DIVERSITY ISSUES

CFS has historically been perceived as an illness occurring predominantly among White upper-class women, but Jason et al.'s community-based study found that women, Latinos, middle-aged individuals, and persons of middle to lower socioeconomic status were at higher risk for this illness. Treatment effects for men and women are most often evaluated together, so it is unclear whether gender moderates treatment outcomes. The vast majority of randomized treatment trials for CFS have been conducted in Europe. Therefore, it is unclear how findings might generalize to other geographic areas. Furthermore, the ethnic composition of clinical trial samples is not frequently reported. Most randomized treatment trials recruit participants from primary or tertiary care settings, and these sources tend to target a higher prevalence of White, middle-class samples that are not representative of the broader CFS population. Consequently, it is unknown how interventions need to be tailored to optimally benefit ethnically diverse groups.

EVIDENCE-BASED TREATMENTS

Owing to the complex nature of this illness, curative somatic treatments are unavailable, and patients rely on pharmacologic, nonpharmacologic, and alternative medicine interventions for illness management. Several clinical trials have evaluated the efficacy of nonpharmacologic interventions for CFS, such as cognitive behavioral therapy (CBT) and graded exercise therapy (GET). While studies have shown that nonpharmacologic interventions can produce health-related quality of life improvements for those with cancer, the use of CBT and GET for CFS have been extremely controversial. Activity-based interventions may be inappropriate for participants with CFS owing to their level of disability. A worsening of symptoms can occur after exercise for patients experiencing postexertional malaise. Results from a survey of individuals with CFS suggest that GET can influence symptom flare-ups. High dropout rates in some clinical trials may signify these treatments are not properly suited for this patient group.

Given the incapacitating nature of postexertional malaise, a cardinal symptom of CFS, illness management techniques, such as pacing, have been developed to prevent symptom exacerbation due to overexertion. According to the Envelope Theory, patients are encouraged to estimate their amount of daily perceived available energy on a 0 to 100 scale and to exert no more energy than they perceive they have available to them. In doing so, patients can remain within their "energy envelope" and prioritize a day's activities on the basis of their self-estimated available energy. Jason, Benton, Torres-Harding, and Muldowney found that patients who remained within their energy envelope after participating in nonpharmacologic interventions experienced lower fatigue than those who did not.

A number of studies have evaluated the efficacy of pharmacologic treatments for CFS, however, some of these approaches have not shown promising findings and some are associated with adverse effects. Yet, Lerner et al. found antiviral treatments were associated with improved functioning among a subset of patients presenting with several types of viral infections, highlighting the importance of identifying subtypes of CFS patients in treatment research. Patients with CFS were found to use several medications including pain relievers, antidepressants, and hormones, at a higher rate than nonfatigued controls. Many patients with CFS also utilize complementary and alternative medicine (CAM) such as dietary supplements, acupuncture, or meditation. Few studies have rigorously evaluated the effectiveness of CAM treatments, but the majority of controlled clinical trials have shown at least some positive outcomes.

In conclusion, the most consistent positive treatment effects have been revealed from nonpharmacologic intervention trials, deeming these the best practice approaches for treating CFS. Yet, some patients experience symptom relief from individualized pharmacologic and alternative medicine treatment approaches as well. Given no single intervention has been found to restore most patients to their premorbid level of functioning, nonpharmacologic interventions are likely most appropriate for use within a multidisciplinary treatment program. Moreover, nonpharmacologic interventions should take into account individual differences in available energy so patients are not at risk of overexertion and adverse effects of treatment.

FUTURE RESEARCH

Nonpharmacologic interventions have evidenced positive improvements among individuals with CFS, yet these approaches are far from curative. Research in this area should continue to explore aberrant biological systems and etiological factors based on clearly defined, diagnostically homogeneous samples to promote development of targeted treatments. More studies should explore the efficacy of pacing interventions, as pacing is favored among patients compared to activity-based interventions. Further investigation is warranted for identifying mediators and moderators of pharmacologic and nonpharmacologic treatment effects. A range of factors must be considered in order to optimally tailor interventions for patients with this illness.

KEY REFERENCES

Drachler, M. L., Leite, J. C., Hooper, L., Hong, C. S., Pheby, D., ... Poland, F. (2009). The expressed needs of people with chronic fatigue syndrome/Myalgic Encephalomyelitis: A systematic review. *BMC Public Health, 9*, 458. doi: 10.1186/1471-2458-9-458

Jason, L., Benton, M., Torres-Harding, S., & Muldowney, K. (2009). The impact of energy modulation on physical functioning and fatigue severity among patients with ME/CFS. *Patient Education and Counseling, 77*, 237–241. doi: 10.1016/j.pec.2009.02.015

Price, J. R., Mitchell, E., Tidy, E., & Hunot, V. (2008). Cognitive behaviour therapy for chronic fatigue syndrome in adults (Review). *The Cochrane Library, 3*, 1–98.

Clinician Application

Chronic Fatigue Syndrome

Constance W. Van der Eb

COMMENT ON THE EVIDENCE-BASED RECOMMENDATIONS

Chronic fatigue syndrome (CFS) is an "invisible illness." The adult or youngster ill with CFS struggles with flulike symptoms, postexertional malaise, unrefreshing sleep, debilitating fatigue, pain, and often encounters skepticism from others (even family members). This is in stark contrast to the instrumental and social support that is so necessary both at onset and over time. Symptoms are worse following physical, intellectual, and social forms of exertion beyond what the body can handle at the time.

Adaptation to life with CFS is challenging, but possible. Over time, reduced resilience becomes the "new normal" for many children and adults living with this illness. The patient's external environment (relationships, financial issues, physical sensitivities) will have a strong influence of the youth's health status. The prospect of pursuing goals and losing the capacity to fulfill expectations for oneself in current roles may constitute a resource or a challenge to the patient. As indicated in the accompanying Research Section by Jason and colleagues, Envelope Theory focuses on helping patients exert no more energy than they perceive they have available to them, and therefore prioritize a day's activities on the basis of their self-estimated available energy. Staying within one's energy envelope, or pacing, combined with ongoing reflection about one's priorities, concerns, and resources can be a very productive therapeutic approach. Pacing is very helpful to guide future expenditures of physical, intellectual, and social energy in a safe way, especially if combined with collaborative "exploration of data" gathered by patient and others caring for/living with the adult or youth living with CFS.

CASE EXAMPLE

Subject Information and Brief History

From the northern suburbs of Chicago, two Caucasian children diagnosed with CFS and their families participated in a treatment intervention. The intervention focused on helping these two families come to terms with a very sick child, and all family members needed to participate to better understand how progress could occur. Both families were treated separately, but the overall goals, as described below, were similar. In regard to the target children, Susan was a 17-year-old female ill with CFS approximately 7 years. Robert was a 12-year old male sick for 2 years and was receiving home-tutoring since he was unable to attend school. Susan had been sick for 6 years, and Robert had been sick for 4 years. Both families were Caucasian, and they could be described as being within the middle class. There were two parents within each family. Susan had two older siblings, one male and the other female. Robert had one older sister and two older brothers (one of the older brothers lived out of the house as he was over 18 years of age).

Presenting Problem

Both children with CFS were brought for treatment because they were having difficulties attending school fulltime and they were missing important opportunities for social growth. Both children experienced worsening of symptoms following exertion be it physical activity, cognitive effort, or social effort (interactions/relationships). Their physical health and stamina, quality of sleep, capacity to function independently, and to pursue meaningful activities were all being adversely affected. In particular, their cognitive functioning was severely challenged, as fatigue and other symptoms accumulated leading to "brain fog," the common term for these problems. Especially unwelcome was "postexertional malaise" a distinct, very unpleasant physical response that occurs about 48 hours following overexertion. At the beginning of treatment, Robert only engaged in quiet activities when awake, experienced high levels of body/muscle and stomach pain and headaches, and engaged in minimal exercise. Susan had significant sleep difficulties, high levels of fatigue, and low activity levels.

Treatment Intervention and Course

For both children, family sessions occurred every 2 weeks over a 6-month period. In working with the two youth, it was important to involve all family members rather than just the affected ill child. I tried to have open lines of communication in order to resolve a number of social and educational issues. With both youth, I found the staff at their schools were not sure about how to deal with the ill youth. I, as well as the other family members, reached out to these personnel so that both children could participate in school. On some days, both children had more energy and on other days less energy, and this is very typical for youth with this illness. So, in my treatment approach, depending on their level of energy, it was critical to help teachers and other school personnel change their expectations to accommodate to the daily energy levels of both youth. For Robert, we focused on doing work at home whereas for Susan the focus was attending school on a limited basis. During these treatment plans, I kept as a primary goal allowing the child to not go beyond his or her daily energy envelope, so that continued improvements could be made. As one of the most important parts of my role, I helped to educate several teachers and family members about the importance of learning the day-to-day monitoring of health energy expenditure. As an example, there were several days that both Susan and Robert felt extremely low energy and lacked any stamina. In these instances we were able to help both family members and school personnel to recognize these limitations and not push the children on those days. For Robert, he just did some light reading and sat quietly, whereas for Susan, she did not go to school that day and rested. Sometimes she would just attend school in the morning and rest in the afternoon. After a few days, we were able to get back to the more usual activities for both youth, and this was owing to them being able to rest when really not feeling well. Had the family or school pushed that youth at this time, both would have had more postexertional malaise and could have been set back for a longer period of time.

In our therapeutic work, the primary goals for the two children were to learn from them what symptoms were most troubling and what were his or her priorities for treatment focus. For Robert, it was high levels of body/muscle and stomach pain and headaches, and postexertional malaise. For Susan it was sleep difficulties and high levels of fatigue with low activity levels. I tried to get all family members to express their concerns and questions about how life may be different at home with someone sick with CFS. The family members were not sure whether to push their children to be more active or to respect their limitations and reduced energy levels. Our approach that we worked out was to accept their current energy levels and when they felt better, to use those times to push them a little. This was something that they were able to work on as a team. The focus through our sessions was helping them understand the variable nature of CFS along with the importance of pacing one's activities (physical, cognitive, social) to keep expenditure of energy within an "envelope" of safe functioning

If I were to describe the core of my treatment with both families, it was to teach the concept of each of us having a unique "battery size" that describes our available energy. I would tell the families that most healthy people have a D-size battery, but their child with CFS had only an AAA battery for available energy. Staying within the available energy supply is important for reducing crashes and experiences of postexertional malaise. This is what is meant by staying within the "Envelope Theory," and the youth were helped to see this concept clearly by each day keeping recordings of his or her choice and intensity of activities along with notations about symptoms. The two children and the family members found this information extremely helpful. Each child had a personal record of symptoms and symptom severity in relation to exertion/energy expenditures over time. This was a valuable technique for identifying what helped and what hindered each child's health status. Susan and Robert learned how to record energy and to adjust exertion (activity) to keep themselves within a "safe" range. Throughout treatment, Susan and Robert were encouraged to become more active, as long as they stayed within their energy envelopes. In this way, they were able to not overdo it when they felt good, but also not push themselves on those days that they had little energy or felt sick. In a sense, both the children, as well as the families, were learning through the therapeutic treatment how to both monitor energy expenditures, as well as symptoms on a daily basis so as to titrate their activities with available energy resources.

Outcomes

Both families perceived the nonpharmacologic intervention as being extremely helpful. Over time, with support from the family and altering school schedules, Robert was able to do gentle stretching, balancing a ball, and some walking and swimming. He learned to have more control over his pain by not engaging in activities that intensified these sensations. Over the course of the intervention, Susan was able to consolidate her sleep routine and become more active with improved strength and stamina. Follow-up assessments at 1 year postintervention revealed that benefits of the pediatric family-oriented program were sustainable. Compared with preintervention status, both adolescents showed improvement in measures of activity levels, as well as physical and social role functioning. Susan was able to more regularly attend school, and Robert continued to be home schooled but was able to attend one class in school each day. They began to spend more time with adolescents their own age. Both became more aware of current events as well as technological innovations that continue to capture the attention of youth. The impact of being able to successfully navigate school and social networks led to improvements in their sense of self-efficacy. Anecdotally, Susan and Robert commented that intervention discussions facilitated their understanding of the relationship between severity of CFS-related symptoms and levels of activity and/or stress (physical, mental, emotional). The interventions empowered these adolescents to acquire skills needed to assume increased responsibility for managing their own health care and pursuit of educational, social, and other goals. These children had not been referred for emotional issues, as their primary concerns were physical so that was the focus of the interventions.

CHALLENGES IN APPLYING THE EVIDENCE-BASED APPROACH

CFS routinely impacts almost every facet of the individual's life and triggers ripple effects within the family, the workplace, and/or school due to fluctuating symptoms that require new or revised accommodations (if available). The adult or youngster with CFS may experience skepticism from others about the medical validity of his or her reports of symptoms. By the time a clinician is consulted, the client may be frustrated, depleted and very worried about his or her capacity to carry on with obligations and personal goals. A child may wish to be well enough to be in school with peers.

A respectful approach to the patient (whether adult or youngster) is essential both to offset some of his or her accrued stress and to promote an effective patient–practitioner collaboration for symptom management. It is also important to ask the patient about the frequency, severity and timing of symptoms in order to identify patterns of activity that should be modified so as to protect patient health going forward. For example, in my work with Robert and Susan, it was not uncommon for them to experience postexertional malaise (a biologic response to excess exertion) when they did too much. I found it important for them to understand that it made matters worse when they tried to exercise more to "work through" the discomfort. Patient education about such a pattern and other forms of overexertion/effort must be addressed and modified in favor of careful pacing.

CULTURAL DIVERSITY ISSUES

Children and adolescents are susceptible to CFS but present symptoms somewhat differently from those in adults. Adults and children ill with severe symptoms of CFS may become house- or bed-bound. Adults with less severe CFS and/or greater skills in pacing activity may venture out of the home on a limited basis or even manage part-time work. A child with unrecognized CFS is disadvantaged for health, educational, and social development. A youth who has been accurately diagnosed with CFS qualifies for educational accommodations such as home tutoring, modified class scheduling, and other supports to help the student pursue academic potential and to retain opportunities to interact with peers to facilitate social growth. Unfortunately, there are no data on racial differences in treatment, as almost all samples have consisted of primarily White youth. We also do not know if there are differences in socioeconomic status (SES) among youth treated for CFS.

FUTURE RESEARCH

Prevalence data are available for other childhood illnesses but lacking for pediatric CFS. Epidemiologic research is essential to identify untreated pediatric CFS and mobilize necessary supports for the child with CFS and his or her family.

KEY REFERENCES

Brown, M., Bell, D. S., Jason, L. A., Christos, C., & Bell, D. E. (2012). Understanding long-term outcomes of chronic fatigue syndrome. *Journal of Clinical Psychology, 68*, 1028–1035.

Crawley, E. M., Emond, A. M., & Sterne, J. A. C. (2011). Unidentified chronic fatigue syndrome/myalgic encephalomyelitis (CFS/ME) is a major cause of school absence: Surveillance outcomes from school-based clinics. *BMJ Open, 1*, e000252.

Jason, L., Benton, M., Torres-Harding, S., & Muldowney, K. (2009). The impact of energy modulation on physical functioning and fatigue severity among patients with ME/CFS. *Patient Education and Counseling, 77*, 237–241.

CHAPTER 43

Chronic Pain

Akiko Okifuji and Dennis C. Turk

CLINICAL PROBLEM

Pain is a complex perceptual experience involving psychosocial and behavioral components, as well as physiological ones. In this chapter, we focus on chronic non-cancer pain (CNCP) characterized as pain lasting longer than 3 months or beyond the expected period of healing. CNCP is a large and growing public health concern in the United States. Recently, the Institute of Medicine (IOM) estimated that more than one third of the U.S. population experience some form of chronic pain, costing between $565 billion and $635 billion per year in direct health care expenditures and associated indirect costs (e.g., lost tax incomes). This amount is expected to grow further as the population ages.

PREVALENCE

Chronic pain is common. The IOM estimates the chronic pain prevalence of 116 million adults in the United States. The recent report from the National Health Interview Survey reports that in the past 3 months, 16% experienced severe headaches, 15% experienced neck pain, and 28% experienced back pain. Chronic pain appears to be more prevalent among the geriatric population. Persistent pain is reported by approximately 50% of community-dwelling geriatric persons.

CULTURAL DIVERSITY ISSUES

A large volume of research suggests that chronic pain is typically more common in women than in men, with some exceptions of cluster headaches and back pain. Minority status may be associated with pain. A large population study of the community dwelling people over age 51 shows that troublesome pain, particularly severe pain, is reported more commonly by non-White people. For arthritis, although minority individuals do not have higher rates of physician-diagnosed pain disorders, pain seems to impact minorities more adversely (e.g., work limitation, greater pain intensity). It is however possible that racial/ethnic status may be serving as a proxy measure for more general socioeconomic status, such as educational, financial, and occupational disadvantages.

EVIDENCE-BASED TREATMENTS

Behavioral health treatments can generally be separated into theoretically based approaches and specific techniques. The most common theoretical approaches are cognitive behavioral therapy (CBT). CBT for chronic pain evolved from behavioral theory, but with an emphasis on the role of patients' attitudes, beliefs, and expectations that are related to pain and health. It typically includes psychoeducation regarding pain and disability, acquisition of self-management skills (e.g., relaxation, problem solving), and cognitive therapy to address maladaptive thought processes that often contribute to the perpetuation of pain and disability cycle. The ultimate goal is for patients to become active and resourceful in coping with their pain and associated functional disability.

Overall, stand-alone CBT treatments for chronic pain seem to improve cognitive-affective well-being. CBT may also improve pain and disability to some extent although the effects seem much weaker for those with significant emotional distress. A systematic analysis suggests that CBT, compared to active controls, yields greater benefit in pain, disability, and mood in chronic pain patients albeit the effects are limited. In contrast, interdisciplinary rehabilitative approach that incorporates CBT typically shows strong clinical benefit. Indeed, there is a wealth of evidence supporting the efficacy and effectiveness of integrated care with CBT-based rehabilitation (e.g., including physical activation, medication management) for pain, function, quality of life, and other associated disabilities. Thus, CBT works best when it is well integrated in the frame of interdisciplinary rehabilitative model of treating chronic pain.

Recently mindfulness-based therapies have gained increasing attention. Often called mindfulness-based stress reduction (MBSR) approach, it comes from the attempt to integrate western clinical practice with Buddhist meditation practice. It typically aims at achieving open and accepting awareness of sensory and emotional experience. Earlier studies testing MBSR for chronic pain were typically uncontrolled with promising results. Results from the controlled trials testing MBSR however, have shown no or limited efficacy in management of chronic pain. The inconsistency in the research results may stem from various methodological issues as well as the lack of rigor in study procedures in general. The intensity of therapy, for example, varies across the studies. Integration of home practice is critical in deriving benefit from MBSR while many studies do not include systematic ways to measure this effort. Given the popularity of the approach, future research with proper methodological rigor is warranted.

FUTURE RESEARCH

Managing patients with chronic pain can be a daunting task because of the complexity of the condition. Past research has shown unequivocal evidence that the cognitive, affective, and behavioral factors play an important role in chronic pain and associated disability. Incorporation of psychological approaches is, as we reviewed above, critical in successful pain rehabilitation.

Another important, yet often neglected aspect of clinical outcomes for pain treatment, is the large individual differences in treatment response. This likely reflects the ubiquitous assumption of "patient uniformity." Pain patients are typically bundled into a classification by pain location (e.g., head, neck, back) and/or known pathology (e.g., neuropathic) and treated as a homogeneous group. We believe that chronic pain patients are psychosocially heterogeneous. Indeed, patients' responses to a standardized interdisciplinary treatment vary on the basis of the psychosocial and behavioral characteristics of patients. Future studies need to focus more on patient-centered approaches to tailor our treatment approaches.

In addition, there are needs for better understanding of how psychological approaches may be integrated with commonly used invasive therapies for chronic pain, such as nerve blocks, intrathecal therapies, and pharmacotherapy. In today's clinical reality, the majority of patients receive a monomodal medical approach, at least at the beginning of their pain care. Unfortunately, the efficacy of those approaches is not well understood and the outcomes evaluation typically have narrow focus without much consideration for the quality of life of the patients. Given the pervasive service provisions of those approaches, however, it would be important for the field of behavioral medicine to evaluate if and how our approach may contribute to the better outcomes.

A general caution about all treatments that we described is that of maintenance. Those treatments that are tested in clinical trials are rehabilitative, not curative. It is reasonable to assume that patients continue to manage some pain, disability, and inevitable flare-ups. Maintenance of therapeutic efforts from patients is critical for long-term success. However, it is naïve to assume that benefit from brief treatments will be maintained unless the benefits are sufficiently reinforcing, or relapse will be a significant problem. The use of new technologies (e.g., Internet, smartphone applications) has the potential to enhance maintenance. Research is needed to develop the most effective and efficient strategies to reduce problems associated with relapse.

KEY REFERENCES

Gatchel, R. J., Peng, Y. B., Peters, M. L., Fuchs, P. N., & Turk, D. C. (2007). The biopsychosocial approach to chronic pain: Scientific advances and future directions. *Psychological Bulletin, 133*, 581–624.

Institute of Medicine. (2011). Relieving pain in America: A blueprint for transforming prevention, care, education, and research. In C. Committee on Advancing Pain Research, and Education (Ed.). Washington DC: NAS Press.

Turk, D. C., Wilson, H. D., & Cahana, A. (2011). Treatment of chronic noncancer pain. *Lancet, 377*, 2226–2235.

Clinician Application

Chronic Pain

Jennifer F. Kelly

COMMENT ON THE EVIDENCE-BASED RECOMMENDATIONS

As noted in the Research Section, pain is a complex disorder that involves physiological, behavioral, and psychosocial aspects. As such, it can be a challenge to treat patients with the condition. It was further noted that the evidence-based cognitive treatment should focus on the role of the patients' thought processes, their attitudes, expectations, and beliefs related to the pain experience. This is basically the standard treatment in working with the population.

CASE EXAMPLE

Subject Information and Brief History

Allison is a 45-year-old African American female who was referred for intervention by her pain management physician for psychological evaluation and treatment. She was receiving both workers' compensation and social security disability benefits. She had been employed as a deputy sheriff for over 20 years and was now disabled from work owing to chronic pain. She is married with two daughters. Her younger daughter is a junior in high school. Her older daughter has three children. She previously helped the daughter to manage the children, but was no longer able to effectively care for them. She was unable to take care of their grooming, could not lift them, and the noise created more stress, and that resulted in an increase in the pain.

Presenting Problem

Allison developed the chronic pain condition of Complex Regional Pain Syndrome or Reflex Sympathetic Dystrophy (RSD) in the right arm following an injury secondary to an injection for immunization for hepatitis B. The immunization was administered by a nurse at the jail, her place of employment. The pain initially occurred in the right arm; however, over time the pain spread to the unaffected extremity. She had originally been treated in another state and when she moved to her new location she began treatment with another physician. When Allison began treatment with the current physician, he indicated that he was concerned about the excess amount of narcotics that she was prescribed. He was specifically concerned about the Oxycontin taken. She noted that she had been taking the narcotics to assist in managing with the pain. However, this medication affected her cognitive functioning and daily living tasks, including grooming and hygiene, as well as her ability to manage within the home as she remained quite sedated. The physician decreased the amount of narcotics taken to what he believed was an appropriate level, that would allow her to be functional enough to take care of her grooming and hygiene; however, she reported a significant increase in the pain and her activity level in the home decreased because of the increase in the pain. For example, she was unable to complete chores around the home such as washing clothes and she no longer prepared meals. She was also taking psychotropic medications, prescribed by the psychiatrist.

Allison was initially seen for a psychological evaluation, which included the clinical interview, mental status examination, and objective test measures including the Minnesota Multiphasic Personality Inventory-2 (MMPI-2). During the initial psychological evaluation, Allison admitted to being depressed and she attributed the depression to the impact of the chronic pain on her functioning. She was more socially isolated and was engaging in her family interactions to a lesser degree. She admitted to feeling more pessimistic about having improvement in the pain and function. She had numerous negative thought processes and these contributed to her disability. For example, she felt that if she could not prepare a full meal each day then she was not a good wife or mother, or if she could not clean the entire home at one time then she should not even attempt to clean one room per day. The psychological evaluation provided confirmation that she was clinically depressed with anxiety. She was diagnosed with Major Depressive Disorder, moderate, recurrent, and Anxiety Disorder, NOS.

Following the evaluation, we discussed treatment goals. The following goals were agreed upon: (a) to have a reduction in the degree of subjective pain sensation; (b) improvement in emotional and behavioral functioning; (c) to be able to monitor her thoughts, emotions, and behaviors, and be able to recognize the relationship between these and the subjective experience of pain; (d) to obtain maximum level of functioning, given limitations imposed by physical impairments; and (e) to have decreased reliance on medications and utilization of the health care system to manage the pain.

Treatment Intervention and Course

The treatment with Allison was cognitive behavioral in nature, and occurred over 20 sessions. There were two components to the treatment: focus on the thought processes and biofeedback training. There was focus on replacing the negative thought processes and beliefs that contributed to prolonged suffering and disability with more adaptive ones. It was felt that the positive changes in her cognitions or thought processes could help her to gain better control over the pain. The first two sessions were spent providing an overview of the cognitive approach to pain management, followed by eight sessions of biofeedback, and then more detailed cognitive behavioral intervention.

The biofeedback and relaxation training occurred over eight sessions. In the first session, the process of biofeedback and relaxation was explained to Allison. During the session she was able to ask questions. Both skin temperature and EMG biofeedback were provided. Sessions 2 to 6 consisted of relaxation-assisted biofeedback training. Allison was instructed in the use of relaxation techniques; progressive muscle relaxation initially, followed by autogenic relaxation in the fourth and fifth sessions. The first 15 minutes of each session was an introductory period during which time was spent discussing her concerns and presenting the goals for the session. She then participated in 30 minutes of relaxation assisted biofeedback training. The last 15 minutes were spent discussing the training session and any problems that might have been encountered. The progressive muscle relaxation involved tensing and relaxing the major muscle groups. The technique was initially implemented to teach general body awareness. This was incorporated with controlled breathing techniques. After she developed mastery over the technique, in three sessions, she progressed to using the autogenic relaxation techniques. It consisted of phrases, such as "I am feeling more relaxed, I can feel the tension dissolving" to elicit the relaxation response. To facilitate generalization outside of the treatment session in the office, Allison was provided with relaxation tapes and she was encouraged to use them at least once daily and whenever she experienced severe levels of pain and tension. The last two sessions focused on further development of skills. She was instructed to use simple phrases, such as "I am feeling more relaxed" to facilitate the relaxation response and for self-regulation. There was focus on incorporating these skills into daily routines, such as using the simple phrases when engaged in daily activities.

The cognitive approach that occurred over 10 sessions focused on the following: (a) dentifying and modifying automatic thoughts about pain; (b) Eliciting and modifying imagery; (c) Identifying and modifying beliefs about pain; (d) Managing medical care; and (e) Assertiveness training. The negative thoughts were not always in Allison's awareness, but a variety of events in her life could trigger the negative thoughts such as having increases in the pain, feeling that she was letting her family down, and stressors, such as financial challenges. As the situations that resulted in negative thought processes were identified, we explored them and their impact on her functioning. There was focus on replacing the negative thoughts with ones that involved solution. For example, she would become upset that she could not clean the entire home and as a result would give up and do nothing. Instead of having this unrealistic goal, she was to replace this with a reasonable goal such as cleaning one room a day, a goal that she could accomplish given the physical limitations. She had the belief that the pain was something that she could not conquer and that it had ruined her life. Instead of seeing herself as suffering, the focus became on seeing the pain as being manageable.

As Allison set and accomplished more realistic goals, she saw the pain as something that she could manage. We addressed the relationship with her pain management physician and the psychiatrist who was prescribing the antidepressant medications. She had been in treatment with both her physicians prior to her referral to me for treatment and was on the current medication regimen. She was prescribed Cymbalta 30 mg three times daily and trazodone 100 mg at bedtime by the psychiatrist. Her pain management physician prescribed Percocet 5/325 mg twice daily as needed, Lyrica 150 mg three times daily, and meloxicam 15 mg once daily. The patient was encouraged to address any concerns regarding her treatment with them. She reported that she did not discuss the concerns with them, and often felt that they were in too much of a hurry when they saw her.

Outcome

By the end of treatment, Allison reported that she was less depressed. She reported improved sleep, felt less agitated and anxious and her appetite had improved. Although she continued to have pain, she reported that she was feeling more confident with her ability to manage with it, especially in dealing with periods of acute pain. She stated she was feeling that she was having more control over the pain and believing that it was something that she could control. She was spending more time with her family. She was pacing herself more in terms of appropriate goal setting. She found herself being more active in the home and getting out of the home more than when treatment had started. She was maintained on the medications that she was prescribed when she was initially seen. However, when she was evaluated she did not believe the dosage was controlling her pain. She was feeling more comfortable with the medications and she no longer requested to have an increase in them.

CHALLENGES IN APPLYING THE EVIDENCE-BASED APPROACH

Chronic pain is a condition that can be a challenge to treat. The physical component of the pain generally does not improve with time and it is something that must be managed. Another challenge is the short-term reinforcing nature of the interventional techniques, such as injections. By the time most of the patients come for psychological intervention, they have had numerous physical interventions that have only provided temporary relief of the pain, if at all. Typically, they are not referred for psychological intervention during the early stages of treatment as would be most appropriate. Instead, the initial focus is on the medical intervention and usually they are only referred for psychological intervention when it is increasingly clear that the interventions will not make a substantial improvement. When patients are seen, they are usually depressed, frustrated, and pessimistic about their condition improving or about having a good quality of life.

Another factor to consider in treatment is that many patients have complicating medical factors that can impact treatment, such as type 2 diabetes, which could be affected by weight gain. Weight gain typically occurs because of the sedentary lifestyle. Another obstacle that they may have to overcome is the dependence on narcotics to manage the pain.

CULTURAL DIVERSITY ISSUES

Allison is an African American female. She requested an African American psychologist as she felt it would be beneficial to have her treatment by someone from a similar cultural background. She reported having challenges in her relationship with the psychiatrist, as she did not believe he was culturally sensitive. She did not feel that the necessary rapport was established and she also did not feel he provided enough time in the session to accurately assess her condition. She did not have the confidence that he provided the accurate treatment for her. She questioned if the lack of adequate time spent was related to her race. I encouraged her to be more assertive and express her concerns with him. Her pain management physician was an African American male.

Research has shown that women generally experience more recurrent pain, more severe pain and longer lasting pain than men. These results held up across a wide variety of diseases and injuries. In addition, women tend to focus on the emotional aspects of pain they experience; men tend to focus on the sensory aspects, for example concentrating on the physical sensations they experience. Women who concentrate on the emotional aspects of their pain may actually experience more pain as a result, possibly because the emotions associated with pain are negative. Studies have also shown that women are more likely to have more negative thoughts about their pain experience or to catastrophize more than men. Interventions designed to reduce catastrophizing, such as cognitive restructuring, may have a greater impact on decreasing pain, pain behavior, and physical disability in women. This was an area of focus with the patient.

FUTURE RESEARCH

Much research continues to be devoted to the area of chronic pain and have shown the interventions that are most effective in treating the condition. It would be beneficial to have more research done in understanding the individual variables, such as the living situation or marital status, in the development and maintenance of pain. More research is needed to evaluate the effectiveness of mindfulness-based therapies in the treatment of chronic pain.

KEY REFERENCES

Thorn, B. E. (2004). *Cognitive therapy for chronic pain: A step-by-step guide*. New York, NY: Guilford Press.

Turk, D. C., & Gatchel, R. (Eds.). (2002). *Psychological approaches to pain management: A practitioner's handbook* (2nd ed.). New York, NY: Guilford Press.

Winterowd, C., Beck, A. T., & Gruener, D. (2007). *Cognitive therapy with chronic pain patients*. New York, NY: Springer Publishing Company.

CHAPTER 44

Heart Disease Interventions

Joel W. Hughes and Carly M. Goldstein

CLINICAL PROBLEM

Individuals with cardiovascular disease can experience a high disease burden characterized by complex medication regimens, frequent medical appointments, expensive bills, and demoralization. About 80% to 90% of deaths from heart disease involve at least one major risk factor influenced by lifestyle. Alcohol/drug abuse, nicotine addiction, anger/hostility, anxiety, depression, chronic stress, cognitive impairment, insomnia, loneliness/social isolation, obesity, and poor patient self-management (i.e., nonadherence to medications, dietary recommendations, exercise prescriptions, and self-care activities) are just a few of the problems health care professionals routinely encounter when treating individuals with heart disease. Many of these behavioral and psychological factors impede treatment, reduce quality of life, and result in referrals to behavioral medicine providers.

Depression may increase risk of developing cardiovascular disease, and cardiovascular disease appears to contribute to the development of depression, suggesting a bidirectional relationship. Depression has been associated with increased risk of death in patients with heart disease in a number of well-controlled investigations. Depression is also associated with smoking and medication nonadherence, which may contribute to poor outcomes. Furthermore, depression can interfere with treatments: one study revealed depressed individuals with heart failure did not benefit from an otherwise effective disease management program. Given the prominence of depression as a mental health correlate of heart disease, a recent science advisory from the American Heart Association (AHA), endorsed by the American Psychiatric Association, recommended routine depression screening of all patients with heart disease.

PREVALENCE

Depression is encountered very frequently in patients with heart disease. It is the leading cause of disability in the modern world and co-occurs with heart disease at rates that exceed chance. After myocardial infarction, 15% to 20% of patients will qualify for a diagnosis of major depressive disorder; another 15% to 20% of hospitalized patients will qualify for "minor depression," which is clinically significant depression symptoms that do not meet full diagnostic criteria. In the Sertraline Antidepressant Heart Attack Randomization Trial (SADHART), 50% of the patients were depressed prior to their heart attacks, suggesting that depression is not merely precipitated by experiencing a major medical event. Moreover, depression often continues posttreatment and after patients recover from the index event.

CULTURAL DIVERSITY ISSUES

Women have a higher prevalence of depression than men, irrespective of whether or not they have heart disease. The risk of mortality conferred by depression in patients with heart disease is about the same for men and women, although treatment response may be different. Specifically, in the Enhancing Recovery in Coronary Heart Disease (ENRICHD) trial, the intervention appeared to be more beneficial for men than for women or minorities. Although the intervention did not reduce depression-related mortality, the trends for subgroups suggested that men benefitted more than women and minorities. Minority women may be at particularly high risk, as they often face a greater socioeconomic disadvantage than other groups.

EVIDENCE-BASED TREATMENTS

The AHA science advisory recommended selective serotonin reuptake inhibitors (SSRIs), cognitive behavioral therapy, and physical activity, such as exercise and cardiac rehabilitation, for depressed patients with heart disease. SSRIs are relatively safe, low cost, and may be associated with better outcomes. However, in SADHART, sertraline only reduced depression symptoms among patients with a history of depression prior to the index heart attack. In the Canadian Cardiac Randomized Evaluation of Antidepressant and Psychotherapy Efficacy (CREATE) trial, citalopram was found to reduce depression symptoms in patients with heart disease.

In the ENRICHD study, cognitive behavioral therapy was shown to reduce depression symptoms and improve perceived social support in patients recovering from a heart attack. In contrast, interpersonal therapy cannot be recommended for depressed cardiac patients at this time as interpersonal therapy was not more effective than medical management of patients in the CREATE trial.

Physical activity is typically recommended for heart disease patients with and without depression, suggesting outpatient cardiac rehabilitation may be an attractive referral choice. Cardiac rehabilitation is a comprehensive multidisciplinary program that includes monitored, supervised exercise, extensive patient education, and counseling regarding smoking cessation, nutrition, weight loss, stress management, adherence to preventive medications, and regular aerobic exercise. In addition to reducing risk of mortality by about 25%, cardiac rehabilitation reduces depression symptoms, and exercise has been shown to have an effect equal to that of antidepressant medication in the health of older adults.

Beyond Depression

Depression is obviously not the only behavioral health concern in patients with heart disease. Many patients struggle with needed behavior changes, such as smoking cessation, exercise, diet, and other health behaviors. One evidence-based, scientifically tested behavioral treatment receiving particular attention in health behavior change research is Motivational Interviewing. Developed by Miller and Rollnick, it has been used and evaluated in relation to alcohol abuse, smoking cessation, weight loss, adherence to treatment and follow-up, increasing physical activity, and treatment of diabetes. Meta-analysis revealed Motivational Interviewing had a significant and clinically relevant effect in approximately three out of four studies, with an equal effect on physiological (72%) and psychological (75%) diseases. Motivational Interviewing in a scientific setting outperforms traditional advice giving in a broad range of behavioral problems and diseases.

FUTURE RESEARCH

Research in the area of depression and heart disease will likely focus on physiological mechanisms, such as inflammatory processes implicated in both heart disease and depression. Understanding mechanisms could aid in the development of more effective interventions. Interventions targeting risk factors, namely for minority women, are necessary to extend effective prevention efforts to everyone at risk. Also, the efficacy of Motivational Interviewing in this specific population should be assessed; as it stands, it appears to be a useful tool, though it has not been examined in individuals with heart disease and depression. Furthermore, the public health effects of the AHA science advisory must be evaluated. That is, whether or not increased screening and referral of depressed cardiac patients for treatment improves outcomes remains an open question. Finally, creative approaches to the treatment of comorbid heart disease and depression must continue to be developed, such as exercise interventions targeting both depression and heart disease, as well as support for patient self-management of their mental and physical health and well-being.

KEY REFERENCES

Blumenthal, J. A., Babyak, M. A., Carney, R. M., Huber, M., Saab, P. G., … Kaufmann, P. G. (2004). Exercise, depression, and mortality after myocardial infarction in the ENRICHD trial. *Medicine and Science in Sports and Exercise, 36*, 746–755.

Glassman, A. H., O'Connor, C. M., Califf, R. M., Swedberg, K., Schwartz, P., … Sertraline Antidepression Heart Attack Randomization Trial (SADHART). (2002). Sertraline treatment of major depression in patients with acute MI or unstable angina. *JAMA: The Journal of the American Medical Association, 288*, 701–709.

Writing Committee for the ENRICHD Investigators. (2003). Effects of treating depression and low perceived social support on clinical events after myocardial Infarction: The Enhancing Recovery in Coronary Heart Disease Patients (ENRICHD) Randomized Trial. *JAMA, 289*, 3106–3116.

Heart Disease Interventions

Erin M. Farrer

COMMENT ON THE EVIDENCE-BASED RECOMMENDATIONS

As the research indicates, individuals who experience cardiovascular-related health problems can have varied behavioral and psychological consequences. Especially challenging is coping with their altered lifestyle after the onset of heart disease or experiencing a cardiac event. Many times, the psychological symptoms can be an intensification of preexisting conditions. That is, those who experience depression or anxiety prior to a cardiac event will find that symptoms of those disorders will increase after the event. Regardless of the onset of symptoms, the presence of anxiety and depression symptoms can greatly interfere with the quality of life after a cardiac event, including increasing the risk for future cardiovascular problems. Patients can be hesitant to follow-through with rehabilitation because of lack of motivation, or in the case example below, an increase in the incidents of panic attacks, which can mimic heart-related symptoms. As one might assume, this can inhibit a person from participating in not only necessary activities for their physical recovery, but also everyday activities that can help them regain a sense of normalcy in their lives.

Cognitive behavioral treatment (CBT) is ideal in the behavioral treatment of heart disease. This approach challenges the maladaptive cognitions associated with the physical symptoms, as well as introducing behavioral activation to increase adherence to treatment and involvement in meaningful activities. In addition, incorporating mindfulness skills can help patients refocus on the desired activities as well as reduce their worries (anxiety) and decrease being stuck in the past (depression). Mindfulness skills incorporate redirecting one's mind to be present in the moment and accept—without judgment—thoughts, feelings, and sensations that occur in that moment. However, there are times when individuals have an existential reaction to the onset of heart disease, in which case, they may be reprioritizing what is important to them. In such a case, I may not begin with CBT, but rather work on values and coping skills. The later application of CBT techniques can then be used to implement some of the value-related goals.

CASE EXAMPLE

Subject Information and Brief History

Harriet was a 42-year-old married female with two young, school-age children. She had no family history of heart disease and had never experienced heart problems before. She reported that she experienced panic attacks in her 30s and changed her lifestyle to avoid future panic attacks. She started to dislike being in crowds and began counseling and pharmacotherapy with escitalopram (Lexapro), a selective serotonin reuptake inhibitor (SSRI). She indicated that neither the counseling nor the medication seemed to be helpful, and she had discontinued both years prior to our work together.

Presenting Problem

Harriet presented for a behavioral health evaluation 4 months after experiencing a cardiac arrest in her home in front of her children. She had participated in cardiac rehabilitation and, at her intake for behavioral health services, had 4 more weeks left of rehab. She reported that since her cardiac arrest, she would experience 10 small panic attacks a day that lasted for 1 to 2 minutes. She also indicated that her heart rate tended to spike to 160 at the end of her rehab exercises, which caused her some alarm about the functioning of her heart. She reported low energy and increased worry about being away from her house for fear that something catastrophic could happen. Her fears were generalized to anything that could lead to death and were not limited to heart problems. She felt guilty for not being able to enjoy time with her family owing to her panic. As is typical, her clinical presentation included symptoms of both depression and anxiety, but for Harriet, anxiety was the predominant presenting problem. She had been prescribed a minimal dose of Xanax—0.25 mg twice a day—by her primary care physician.

Treatment Intervention and Course

At our first weekly therapy session after the intake, Harriet hoped that treatment could help with reducing the amount of panic attacks she experienced. She also reported that that she would like to enjoy time with her family and reduce her worry and panic attacks so that she could stop the medication. She stated that she felt like she was missing out on experiences with her children and husband because she was so worried about what might happen to her physically. She wanted to participate in school activities and family trips without paralyzing fear. We discussed the rationale of CBT. We also discussed common thinking errors, and Harriet identified that she tends to "catastrophize" and use "should" statements. At our second therapy session, Harriet was taught how to use a thought record. She completed an example about her fears for participating in outside activities. For instance, "I cannot spend time outside with my family because if I'm stung by a bee, I will die." Harriet was also introduced to a breathing relaxation exercise to practice twice a day.

At our third session, Harriet began by saying that she worked on several thought records and noted that she only had one instance of a panic attack since our last session. The rest of the session was spent using Socratic questioning to challenge the catastrophizing statements. For instance, Harriet began to use statements such as "I have never had an allergic reaction to bees before." By the fourth session, she was regularly using thought records and creating her own behavioral assignments. She had gone out to dinner with her daughter and enjoyed her time. She also was able to have a picnic outside on her porch. Harriet was hoping to be able to expand her behaviors, but she felt happy that she was able to accomplish what she did. During this session, Harriet was introduced to the concept of mindfulness. This taught her to refocus her attention during specific situations when she noticed her mind was ruminating on the "what ifs."

Outcome

At the time this case example was written, Harriet is still in treatment. She was pleased that her panic attacks had reduced significantly (approximately one or two per week), and she had also reduced the amount of Xanax she was using. Because she had noticed positive results so quickly, Harriet wanted to stay in treatment in order to continue on the trend of adding more enjoyable activities that she had been avoiding.

CHALLENGES IN APPLYING THE EVIDENCE-BASED APPROACH

Perhaps the most difficult challenge in applying CBT is instilling motivation to change behaviors. While patients may understand and desire to change, they are fused to the maladaptive thoughts, whether they are "what ifs" or disappointment that they now have physical limitations. Patients may often *know* that their thinking patterns are maladaptive, but cannot *emotionally* connect to more adaptive thoughts because they still *feel* that their way of thinking is accurate. When this is the case, patients often do not follow-through with their behavioral assignments or with their rehabilitation. Motivational interviewing can be very helpful in this case. If cognitive dissonance can be created in this way, patients can become motivated to at least *try* the homework or the rehab program. Then, success builds on success as their experiments provide feedback that *feels* better than they anticipated.

Patients who do not have experience participating in mental health services may have a hard time recognizing that their symptoms can have a psychological component. Psychoeducation regarding depression and anxiety as they relate to heart disease can be helpful. Also, creating graduated hierarchies of change to be applied with relaxation strategies can help reduce resistance and psychological distress.

CULTURAL DIVERSITY ISSUES

As mentioned in the Research Section, women report a higher incidence of depression, which means they may be more forthcoming of their symptoms and may be more likely to attempt behavioral and psychological interventions than men. However, men benefit from CBT if they are willing to participate in treatment. Certain ethnic groups, such as Hispanics, Native Americans, and Asian Americans, may also be more hesitant to participate in or delay treatment or may report more physical symptoms that could, in fact, be psychologically based. Empathy and understanding of cultural explanations of physical symptoms is important.

FUTURE RESEARCH

An expansion of research on heart disease and psychological interventions within different ethnic populations would greatly benefit the application of treatments for groups who may experience psychological distress translated in physical manifestations. Also, much of the literature uses randomized designs that lend themselves to treatment of individual patients, and it would be helpful to determine if group treatment may be more efficient and equally effective. In addition, and as was suggested in the Research Section, motivational interviewing is useful, especially for individuals who are reluctant to either attend behavioral health interventions or to adhere to a rehab program, diet management, exercise routine, etc. More specific research with this intervention as it pertains to heart patients would be beneficial.

KEY REFERENCES

Allan, R., & Fisher, J. (2011). *Heart and mind: The practice of cardiac psychology.* Washington, DC: American Psychological Association.

Dornelas, E. A. (2008). *Psychotherapy with cardiac patients: Behavioral cardiology in practice.* Washington, DC: American Psychological Association.

Molinari, A., Compare, A., & Parati, G. (Eds.). (2006). *Clinical psychology and heart disease.* New York, NY: Springer.

CHAPTER 45

Insomnia in Adults

Daniel J. Taylor and Allison K. Wilkerson

CLINICAL PROBLEM

Chronic insomnia is defined as difficulty falling or staying asleep at least three nights a week for at least three months that results in clinically significant distress or impairment in daytime functioning. People with insomnia often complain of daytime fatigue, difficulty with attention and memory, mood problems, and behavioral issues, all of which could potentially cause disruption in school, work, and social settings.

Chronic insomnia is more often than not comorbid with medical and psychiatric disorders, and those without a comorbid psychiatric disorder are highly likely to develop one within a year. The underlying mechanism of this connection is unclear, but it appears the relationship is reciprocal, where (a) insomnia is precipitated by the comorbid condition, then becomes semi-independent, exacerbating the original disorder, (b) insomnia is a prodrome of the comorbid disorder, (c) insomnia causes the disorder owing to stress, fatigue, helplessness, and hopelessness, or (d) a third variable (e.g., hyperthyroid) is causing both the insomnia and comorbid disorders. In addition, insomnia is a risk factor for worse mental health treatment response and increased relapse to comorbid psychological disorders.

PREVALENCE

The incidence of insomnia symptoms in adult populations is estimated to be approximately 31%, with nearly 16% of the adult population reporting current chronic insomnia. Once someone develops chronic insomnia, the majority (i.e., 80%) show no remission over the course of 1 year.

CULTURAL DIVERSITY ISSUES

Research has repeatedly shown that insomnia increases with age, with older adults reporting sleep problems more frequently and with greater severity than younger adults. However, many attribute this increased insomnia to increased health complications and medication usage, as well as decreased physical and mental activity associated with aging, rather than just growing older. In addition, women have higher incidence rates and lower remission rates than men. It is still unclear why women report more insomnia than men, but it could be that fluctuating hormone levels, higher propensity to ruminate to cope with problems, and higher levels of stress could all contribute. Studies examining differences in race and ethnicity have reported mixed results, potentially owing to confounding factors that could account for sleep disturbance, such as socioeconomic status and other health concerns prevalent in different groups.

EVIDENCE-BASED TREATMENTS

Cognitive and behavioral interventions for insomnia are the preferred treatment and can be used to effectively treat both primary insomnia and insomnia comorbid with other disorders. They are as effective as medications in the short-term and have better long-term outcomes than medication. The single interventions of stimulus control therapy, sleep restriction, and progressive muscle relaxation are all considered empirically validated treatments and are often combined with sleep education, sleep hygiene, and cognitive interventions into the multimodal cognitive behavioral therapy of insomnia.

Stimulus control arose from the theory that insomnia is maintained by the bedroom becoming associated with poor, rather than good, sleep, as well as other activities such as worrying, planning, or recreation. In order to break the maladaptive associations and increase the association between the bed and sleep, patients are encouraged to use the bed only for sleep and sex. Specific stimulus control instructions are typically: (1) go to bed only when sleepy; (2) do not use your bed or bedroom for anything but sleep (or sex); (3) if you do not fall asleep within about 15 minutes, leave the bed and do something in another room and return to bed only when you feel a strong sleep urge; (4) if you do not fall asleep quickly upon returning to bed, repeat instruction 3 as many times as is necessary; (5) use your alarm to awaken at the same time every morning regardless of the amount of sleep obtained; and (6) do not nap during the day. In order to accomplish step 2, patients are often told to remove everything from their room not associated with sleep, such as TVs, desks, computers, and so forth.

Sleep restriction involves reducing participant's time in bed to more accurately reflect the amount of time they spent sleeping on a typical night. Thus, if a subject spends only 5.5 hours of the night asleep (based on baseline sleep diaries), but spends 10 hours in bed per night, then their time in bed (i.e., sleep schedule) is modified so that the patient is not allowed more time in bed than their average total sleep time (i.e., 5.5 hours), although some allow an additional 30 minutes. The idea is to consolidate sleep, thus improving depth, continuity, and consistency. As patient's total sleep time improves with treatment, their time in bed is also increased, typically by 15 minutes per week, to reflect the improvements. The consistent wake-up times used by both stimulus control and sleep restriction likely strengthen circadian rhythms as well.

Relaxation is used because it has been theorized that people with insomnia have elevated levels of physiological and mental arousal that inhibit sleep. Relaxation therapy counteracts this arousal, thus improving nighttime sleep. In progressive muscle relaxation protocols, patients are typically instructed to make themselves comfortable, close their eyes, and tense and relax different muscle groups (e.g., forearm, upper arm) one at a time. Patients often need several weeks to master this skill. They are generally encouraged to practice at least two times daily, once during the day and once at bedtime.

Sleep hygiene is a group of psychoeducational guidelines designed to address a variety of behaviors that may affect sleep, but it is often not relevant in people with chronic insomnia because they are already practicing good sleep hygiene. The following are the most common instructions: (1) avoid exercise within 3 hours of bedtime, (2) create a sleep environment that is cool, dark, quiet, and comfortable, (3) avoid heavy meals within 2 hours of bedtime, (4) avoid excessive fluids in the evenings, (5) avoid caffeine within 6 hours of bedtime, (6) avoid nicotine within 2 hours of bedtime, and (7) avoid alcohol within 2 hours of bedtime. It is important to note that clinicians sometimes confuse sleep hygiene and stimulus control, because the instructions are similar and are often combined.

Cognitive therapy has been introduced to the treatment of insomnia because it has been theorized that individuals' beliefs, attitudes, and interpretations about their insomnia may contribute to their difficulties. For example, ruminating about the consequences of insomnia or forming unrealistic expectations about sleep needs may perpetuate sleep problems. The goal of cognitive restructuring is to elicit the participants' dysfunctional beliefs and attitudes about sleep and subsequently help them develop more adaptive ones.

FUTURE RESEARCH

Although it is clear that the treatments listed above are efficacious for treating primary and comorbid insomnia, there is still a need for effectiveness trials, trials to see if treating insomnia can improve comorbid disorders, and most importantly studies to determine how best to disseminate these effective interventions to practitioners.

KEY REFERENCES

Lichstein, K. L., Durrence, H. H., Riedel, B. W., Taylor, D. J., & Bush, A. J. (2004). *Epidemiology of sleep: Age, gender, and ethnicity*. Mahwah, NJ: Lawrence Erlbaum Associates.

Morgenthaler, T., Kramer, M., Alessi, C., Friedman, L., Boehlecke, B., & Brown, T. (2006). Practice parameters for the psychological and behavioral treatment of insomnia: An update. An American Academy of Sleep Medicine report. *Sleep, 29*, 1415–1419.

Morin, C. M., Bootzin, R. R., Buysse, D. J., Edinger, J. D., Espie, C. A., & Lichstein, K. L. (2006). Psychological and behavioral treatment of insomnia: Update of the recent evidence (1998-2004). *Sleep, 29*, 1398–1414.

Clinician Application

Insomnia in Adults

Michael Scherer

COMMENT ON THE EVIDENCE-BASED TREATMENTS

A comprehensive cognitive behavioral treatment for insomnia (CBT-I) is an effective treatment. The interventions described by the researchers form the foundation for this approach—sleep restriction and stimulus control, in particular, are essential behavioral interventions. Sleep restriction and stimulus control appear to be simple interventions but can be complex to implement. Thus, the clinician should have some knowledge of sleep medicine, and especially circadian and homeostatic processes affecting sleep. Caution should be used in implementing sleep restriction with some psychiatric populations or when individuals are utilizing sleep medications. Patients may also display "morningness" or "eveningness" tendencies and this may affect preferences and ability to comply when implementing sleep restriction. Relaxation techniques address an additional important component, taking into account the role of physiological and cognitive arousal in association with sleep effort. Progressive muscle relaxation is one of many relaxation techniques which can be incorporated into treatment to reduce arousal. Other techniques, such as autogenic relaxation and diaphragmatic breathing are often preferred by patients.

While behavioral interventions alone can be helpful, an approach that incorporates a cognitive restructuring component is usually necessary. Patients with insomnia present with significant sleep-specific anxiety which is fueled by beliefs about sleep and experiences that validate dyscontrol in relation to sleep effort. For enduring and optimal treatment effect, a comprehensive CBT-I should be sure to include all elements, including education about sleep, cognitive components, and address arousal, as well as motivating basic good sleep hygiene.

CASE EXAMPLE

Subject Information and Brief History

Mary is a 55-year-old married mother who works in an administrative capacity for a large corporation. She was referred for a behavioral sleep medicine consultation by her physician. Insomnia emerged about 1½ years ago when her husband had a failed surgery which left him disabled.

Presenting Problem

Mary presented to the sleep medicine practice with the primary complaint of difficulty initiating and maintaining sleep. Sleep difficulties were nightly. A typical night consisted of a bedtime at 10 p.m., with sleep onset between 45 and 90 minutes. Once asleep, she would wake multiple times, remaining awake for 30 to 120 minutes at a time. She would rise at 7 a.m. during the week and as late as 8 a.m. on weekends. Sleep efficiency (e.g., time asleep in relation to time in bed) averaged 55% based on sleep log data. Screening for other physiological sleep disorders was negative: she did not report indications of sleep apnea, restless legs syndrome, or other conditions. Mary described sleep-specific anxiety and worsened mood as a result of her sleep difficulties.

Treatment Intervention and Course

In our first session, Mary and I reviewed CBT-I. I presented her with the behavioral model of insomnia and explored specific behavioral, cognitive, and psychological factors which may have perpetuated her sleep difficulty. These included, for example, sleep-specific anxiety and mental activity, modification of her sleep schedule to accommodate poor nights of sleep, evening arousal, and sleep hygiene factors. I educated Mary about the competing processes affecting sleep: discussing homeostatic sleep drive, circadian factors, and the role of sympathetic nervous system arousal. Mary demonstrated morningness tendencies and revealed that historically, she would rise for the day at 5:30 a.m. This was now a rarity. Mary did not nap or fall asleep inadvertently during the day or evening. We discussed sleep hygiene factors that could be contributing to her difficulty. Overall, her sleep hygiene was good. Mary exercised daily during the day. She did report caffeine consumption as late as 3 p.m. on some days. Days with later caffeine consumption tended to coincide with more stressful meetings at work. She did not drink alcohol. I provided her with a sleep log for her to maintain. As initial interventions, we agreed she would reduce later caffeine consumption and would maintain a consistent wake time to anchor her sleep phase.

At our second session, Mary and I focused on cognitive factors and implemented both sleep restriction and stimulus control. Given Mary's historical sleep schedule and tendency toward an earlier morning wake time, we implemented sleep restriction by having Mary return to her historical rise time. Sleep log data and Mary's subjective estimate of sleep times suggested she was sleeping about 5 to 6 hours a night. I discussed with her the overexpansion of sleep opportunity which had emerged with the sleep difficulties. She was spending up to 10 hours in bed. Mary agreed she would target about 7 hours of sleep opportunity, with a bedtime of 10:30 p.m. or as she became sleepy thereafter.

When unable to sleep, Mary would remain in bed engaging in mental activity, referencing time, and feeling frustration. This mental activity was primarily worry. Mary and I discussed the conditioned nature of time references and how this affected her emotional state, as well as promoted increased arousal. Mary and I also discussed the physiological stress response as she remained in bed, failing at falling asleep. She had in the past tried "to get out of bed when unable to sleep," engaging in various activities from chores and work, to reading and television, none of which she felt was effective. She reported the belief that "resting in bed" was at least some respite. Motivational interviewing and problem-solving techniques were used to elicit information and resolve barriers to behavioral change. She agreed to get out of bed and engage in a relaxing and distracting activity at the first sign of any increased arousal or mentation. I encouraged her to avoid time references.

At our third session 2 weeks later, Mary reported improvement in her sleep. Sleep efficiency was now 83%. Mary consistently complied with the treatment recommendations and found them to be effective, though initially difficult to adhere to. We discussed nights with longer sleep onset and identified exposure to arousal-inducing stimuli and poor stress coping as factors leading to prolonged sleep onsets on three nights. For example, medical and financial issues were being discussed with her husband in the evening. I introduced Mary to three different relaxation techniques, including progressive muscle relaxation. Mary was instructed to practice these before applying them in relation to sleep effort and to choose one which she felt was most helpful, subsequently applying the technique before bed or when waking during the night. In relation to situations which might increase arousal and mental activity, I encouraged her to limit more stressful discussions, increasing mindfulness of the physiological effect of such activities prior to bedtime. She agreed to make changes to her evening routine such that it was progressively less stimulating. We made slight modifications to the sleep restriction protocol.

Outcome

At our fourth session, Mary indicated further improvement in sleep. Her sleep logs demonstrated sleep onsets were now consistently within 20 minutes. She did not awaken on most days and when awakening did occur, it would be to use the bathroom and she was able to reinitiate sleep readily. She reported reduced mental activity and no recent need to implement stimulus control procedures when waking. She found changes to her evening routine to be helpful. She had implemented relaxation techniques sporadically as she felt she did not need them, but identified a visualization technique as the one she found most helpful. Sleep log data suggested sleep efficiency of 92%, well within normal. At this session, we discussed treatment maintenance instructions and also gradual expansion of sleep time. We agreed to expand sleep opportunity to 7.5 hours. Mary was pleased with her progress, reporting reduced anxiety in relation to her sleep, improved mood, and increasing confidence in her ability to sleep well. A final subsequent session 2 months later indicated maintained improvements.

CHALLENGES IN APPLYING THE EVIDENCE-BASED APPROACH

Several primary challenges are likely to present in relation to the patient with a complaint of insomnia. The first is that patients with insomnia are a varied population with multiple factors and problems, including physiological, psychiatric and psychological, medical conditions, and medications that may all contribute to sleep difficulties. The "masquerade of insomnia" is such that a provider treating insomnia must be skilled in evaluation and assessment to identify which patients are most amenable to a cognitive behavioral treatment approach. A second challenge is the reality that many patients presenting for behavioral treatment are on sleep medications. This requires skill in helping patients manage anxiety about getting off of medications, familiarity with medications and their effects, and an ability to closely work with the prescribing provider to determine if tapering is appropriate, and if so, a tapering schedule which incorporates the patient's anxiety about reduction. A third challenge is inoculation. "Sleep hygiene" recommendations are pervasive and most patients will present with some sense of "having done this all before" as the treatment approach is presented. It is important to know how to identify barriers to prior success, differentiate treatment from prior efforts, and motivate the patient to adhere to treatment recommendations. Inoculation often goes hand in hand with partial compliance with treatment recommendations.

CULTURAL DIVERSITY ISSUES

CBT-I is effective across the age span and different cultures; as such cultural diversity issues are primarily associated with sensitivity to cultural differences in sleep behaviors. For example, cosleeping with children may be important to some cultures—and this may contribute to some patients' sleep difficulties. Attention to medication sensitivity—likely to increase with age—and its effects in producing grogginess in the morning can increase risk of falling or prevent patients from adhering to sleep restriction or stimulus control recommendations.

FUTURE RESEARCH

The field would benefit from research assessing the impact of inoculation—the impact of repeated but incomplete prior exposure to one or more aspects of cognitive behavioral treatment—on treatment as many of the more challenging patients are those who have been exposed multiple times to prior incomplete treatment efforts. For these patients, significant effort is required in motivating behavioral change or adherence to recommendations and this may also affect treatment outcome. Little research has also been conducted evaluating the impact of CBT-I on more clearly medically related insomnia, such as during pregnancy or menopause in women, periods where hormonal factors may play a substantial role. While a presumption may be that CBT-I is less effective given the origin of the difficulty, clinical experience suggests CBT-I can be of some benefit in these populations as well. Research elucidating optimally effective medication tapering schedules would also benefit the field.

KEY REFERENCES

Hauri, P. (1991). *Case studies in insomnia*. New York, NY: Plenum Publishing Corporation.

Perlis, M., Aloia, M., & Kuhn, B. (2011). *Behavioral treatment of sleep disorders*. London, UK: Academic Press.

Perlis, M., Jungquist, C., Smith, M., & Posner, D. (2005). *Cognitive behavioral treatment of insomnia*. New York, NY: Spring Science and Business Media Inc.

CHAPTER 46

Insomnia in Children

Michael Gradisar

CLINICAL PROBLEM

Core symptoms of pediatric insomnia include nighttime sleep disturbances (e.g., difficulty falling asleep, staying asleep, waking too early, and/or unrefreshing sleep) and associated daytime deficits (e.g., daytime sleepiness, fatigue/tiredness, attention/concentration/memory problems, feeling moody/irritable, lacking motivation/energy, somatic symptoms). Behavioral symptoms of bedtime resistance and/or problematic sleep-onset associations (e.g., requiring parental assistance to sleep) are common in pediatric insomnia. Thus, pediatric insomnia is suspected when the child experiences at least one nighttime and one daytime symptom, as well as one (or both) of the behavioral symptoms. When experienced for at least 1 month, this gives rise to the most common pediatric insomnia disorder, Behavioral Insomnia of Childhood (BIC). Rarer in children though, is the insomnia disorder Psychophysiological Insomnia (PI), a disorder often diagnosed in adulthood. Although not exclusive to PI, cognitive symptoms may be present in older children (9+ years) including worries about sleep, and catastrophizations or "mind racing" whilst in bed. As BIC is more common and has more emerging evidence than PI in childhood, this chapter focuses on BIC and its symptoms. For simplicity though, the term pediatric insomnia will be used throughout this chapter.

PREVALENCE

Pediatric insomnia is estimated to occur in 10% to 30% of children. Bedtime resistance estimates range between 5% and 30%. Although not diagnostic, nighttime fears are often associated with pediatric insomnia, and peak in middle childhood with up to 3 out of 4 children reporting such fears (e.g., dark, personal security, ghosts, etc.). No significant gender differences have been found in prevalence estimates nor in those school-aged children whose parents seek treatment.

CULTURAL DIVERSITY ISSUES

Despite the common practice of children sleeping independently in Westernized society, most families in the world cosleep. Cosleeping is influenced by cultural practices, housing space, and concerns over safety. Cosleeping may be an acceptable treatment option for Westernized families. However, a distinction is required between bed-sharing and room-sharing, as risks have been identified for bed-sharing with very young children (under 2 years), including parental alcohol/drug use, parent body mass index (BMI), chronic sleep restriction, soft bedding, and premature birth of infant. No empirical evidence exists for racial or ethnic differences in the prevalence of pediatric insomnia.

EVIDENCE-BASED TREATMENTS

For younger children (infants to 7 years), the American Academy of Sleep Medicine (AASM) has recommended various treatment options for bedtime problems and night wakings on the basis of the level of supporting evidence. At the highest level of evidence, the AASM recommends unmodified extinction (i.e., parents put their child to bed at a set bedtime and ignore the child until morning whilst monitoring for child safety and illness) and parent education/prevention (i.e., educating parents about bedtime routines, sleep schedules, and the child acquiring "self-soothing skills"). The next level of evidence includes the treatments of graduated extinction (i.e., parents ignore child's cries for incremental periods of time [e.g., 5 minutes, then 10 minutes]), faded bedtime (i.e., gradually delaying child's bedtime), response cost (i.e., removing the child from bed if he or she cannot sleep and try again when sleepy), and positive bedtime routine (i.e., implementing a series of positive and calming set of activities prior to bedtime). In clinical practice, a combination of these treatments may be implemented in a multicomponent approach, but care must be taken to match treatment components to the developmental needs of the child.

For older children capable of verbalizing nighttime cognitions (7 to 12 years), cognitive behavior therapy (CBT) has been found effective for pediatric insomnia where problematic sleep-onset associations are identified. CBT involves sleep education (i.e., reducing stimulation before bedtime), faded bedtime, cognitive therapy (i.e., challenging and replacing nighttime fears with realistic thinking), graduated exposure (i.e., gradual nighttime separation from the parent tied to rewards for the child), and relaxation. CBT can be performed over 6 sessions. These various treatments for younger and older children have shown consistent clinical improvements lasting for 3 to 6 months after treatment.

Although many of the abovementioned best-practice treatments (e.g., faded bedtime, graduated extinction, etc.) may be used with atypically developing children, the addition of appropriate treatment components may be needed (e.g., social stories, sensory input, pharmacologic management, etc.) to cater for the needs of special populations.

When sleep is a small part of the overall problem in complex cases involving severe family dysfunction, child abuse, and/or severe parental psychopathology (e.g., substance use, bi- and unipolar depression, psychosis, personality disorders), successful treatment of pediatric insomnia may be facilitated by initially targeting underlying contributors to the child's sleep problem.

FUTURE RESEARCH

Little is known about predisposing, precipitating, and maintaining factors contributing to pediatric insomnia. More controlled studies evaluating treatment components for pediatric insomnia are needed (e.g., faded bedtime, cognitive therapy), as well as identifying child and family characteristics best matched to particular treatment components.

KEY REFERENCES

Gordon, J., King, N., Gullone, E., Muris, P., & Ollendick, T. H. (2007). Treatment of children's nighttime fears: The need for a modern randomized controlled trial. *Clinical Psychology Review, 27*, 98–113.

Morgenthaler, T. I., Owens, J., Alessi, C., Boehlecke, B., Brown, T. M., ... American Academy of Sleep Medicine. (2006). Practice parameters for behavioral treatment of bedtime problems and night wakings in infants and young children. *Sleep, 29*, 1277–1281.

Paine, S., & Gradisar, M. (2011). A randomised controlled trial of cognitive-behaviour therapy for Behavioural Insomnia of Childhood in school-aged children. *Behaviour Research and Therapy, 49*, 379–388.

Clinician Application

Insomnia in Children

Joseph Patrick Hill McNamara and Adam Reid

COMMENT ON THE EVIDENCE-BASED RECOMMENDATIONS

As highlighted in the research section, the ideal treatment approach for pediatric insomnia (PI) is dependent on multiple variables, such as patient age, presenting problems, and parent motivation. However, we traditionally approach most PI cases planning to use an age-appropriate version of cognitive behavioral therapy (CBT), while also augmenting this treatment to address other factors that are contributing to the sleep difficulties. As with all manualized treatment, tailoring the treatment approach to each specific patient is imperative. However, we adhere to some general rules for most patients. For example, unless the patient is a teenager, we generally avoid utilizing cognitive strategies that involve challenging maladaptive thoughts about sleep (e.g., if I don't fall asleep right away, I will never fall asleep). These strategies are generally not effective with younger children because they struggle to identify and challenge cognitions. Similarly, we avoid implementing faded bedtimes with children because asking a child to go to bed later and later each night to build a sleep debt (e.g., making them sleep deprived) impairs there functioning substantially in the daytime and can appear to be encouraging staying up late. We believe the most important aspect of this treatment is sleep hygiene (i.e., reducing environmental cues that interfere with sleep onset), as in today's society children and adolescents are surrounded by electronics both in their room or even in their bed (e.g., Nintendo D.S.). Research aligns with our clinical observations that light, especially blue light that emits from these electronics interferes with melatonin release and thus the ability to fall asleep. While parents often feel these entertainment activities reduce conflict about bedtime and facilitates sleep onset, these activities develop dependency and an association of stimulating activities with lying in bed.

In general and in line with the research, we have found CBT to be effective for treating most cases of PI (ages 7–18). For younger children, we adhere to the American Academy of Sleep Medicine recommendations described earlier, with more of a preference for graduated extinction (e.g., slowly reducing parent time with child at bedtime) over unmodified extinction (e.g., completely stopping parent time with child at bedtime) because we have noted parent's comfort is higher for the former. Often, children will present being on a pharmacological agent to improve sleep and we find it imperative to discuss with the parents and the providing physician the importance of holding the medication dosage constant during the implementation of therapy so that the child and parent see that gains during treatment are clearly behaviorally induced. Sedative withdrawal has had success in our experience when conducted after CBT. It should be noted that several sleep medications are not FDA-approved for younger children.

CASE EXAMPLE

Subject Information and Brief History

Mary is a 9-year-old African American whose parents reported that she has had trouble sleeping for 18 months, specifically with sleep onset (on average 45 minutes/ night) and sleeping independently.

Presenting Problem

Mary's parents brought her to treatment out of frustration about "fights" at bedtime where Mary constantly requests a drink or another bedtime story. In addition, once she finally falls asleep she awakens within a few hours, comes to her parents' bedroom, and climbs in bed with them. Initially, the parents did not discourage this behavior but now desire her to stop because the frequency was increasing. They state that they have tried returning Mary to her own bed once she has fallen asleep only to find that she returns to their bed within an hour or so.

Treatment Intervention and Course

We identified Mary as experiencing PI that would be appropriately treated by CBT and ruled out other possible sleep and psychological diagnoses. Alternative sleep-related diagnoses were ruled out by a polysomography sleep test (e.g., overnight sleep study) provided by a local sleep physician. Possible psychological diagnoses that could contribute to delayed sleep onset or desire to sleep with the parents, such as separation anxiety, were ruled out by a comprehensive subjective (i.e., interview) and objective (i.e., the Anxiety Disorders Inventory Schedule for Children) diagnostic symptom assessment. Treatment occurred over 6 weekly sessions. Session 1 focused on psychoeducation conducted with the parent and child about what factors interfere with a child falling asleep. Sleep hygiene (session 2) and stimulus control (session 3) were also discussed and it was identified that Mary's beverage consumption should be reduced before bed (although she was encouraged to hydrate appropriately during the day to reduce thirst at night). She also needed to reduce her nonsleep activities in her room such as not watching TV or reading in bed, and playing with toys in her room. Several lights from electronics in her room were identified as contributing to her PI. In short, sleep hygiene and stimulus control were used to make Mary's bedroom an environment that invites and is associated with sleep. The parents were also encouraged to gradually increase their active ignoring of Mary's requests for activities to delay her bedtime (e.g., choosing not to tell her she cannot have another glass of water).

Sessions 4 to 6 focused on Mary wanting to get into her parents bed at night and it was identified that the antecedent to Mary coming to her parent's bed was when she felt restless regarding her inability to initiate sleep onset. The consequence of this behavior was receiving positive attention from her parents. The parents constructed a contingency plan where Mary was rewarded for meeting her goal of sleeping independently (this was systematically increased each week) and punished for the number of attempts to come to her parent's bed. Rewards and punishments were delivered in the morning by the parents in order to not model nonsleep behavior at night. Examples of rewards included earning points toward extra computer time or a special weekend activity with friends. Examples of punishing behaviors included loss of these reward points or extra chores.

Outcome

By the end of session 6 (6 weeks after starting treatment), Mary's sleep onset latency had decreased to below an average of 10 minutes and she no longer attempted to sleep with her parents. Treatment outcome data were tracked using a daily sleep diary completed by both Mary and her parents.

CHALLENGES IN APPLYING THE EVIDENCE-BASED APPROACH

Several challenges to implementing CBT for PI exist. Most notable is poor child report of sleep habits. We address this challenge by utilizing parent and child sleep reports, as well as objective data from an actigraphy watch (i.e., wrist worn device that uses movement and daylight to capture sleep behaviors). As with most pediatric treatments, parental adherence is another barrier. Often, parents are overwhelmed with several children and struggle to monitor their children's sleep behavior or implement treatment strategies. Often we will use motivational interviewing techniques on top of additional psychoeducation to increase parents' beliefs regarding the importance of improving their child's sleep.

CULTURAL DIVERSITY ISSUES

Empirical evidence indicates that racial or ethnic differences in the prevalence of pediatric insomnia are virtually nonexistent. An important cultural issue that should be considered is cosleeping. Cosleeping occurs when parents and children sleep in the same bed. Cosleeping is less common in Western cultures but is common in other cultures. In recent years, cosleeping has become more common in Western Cultures as well. Cultural beliefs, safety concerns, home size, and many other factors impact cosleeping practices. An important distinction between bed-sharing and room-sharing needs to be made. Numerous risks have been identified for bed-sharing with very young children (under 2 years), including parental alcohol/drug use, parent body mass index (BMI), chronic sleep restriction, soft bedding, and premature birth of infant. We would argue that room sharing would alleviate many of the factors discussed previously while also providing a safer environment for the child.

FUTURE RESEARCH

The most common referral to mental health professionals for *young* children is related to complaints of dysregulation of *sleep*. Knowing this, it is surprising that the research is sparse on behavioral treatments for PI, especially regarding augmentation strategies (i.e., alternative treatment strategies) or ideal treatment planning. A recent movement in the literature has put an emphasis on targeting treatment at the primary symptom and continuing until secondary symptoms interfere with treatment or become primary. This approach is known as Modular Therapy and would involve quantifying when treatment should shift from focusing on one technique to another technique. In Mary's case, shifting from sleep hygiene techniques and active ignoring of bedtime requests (i.e., the techniques that address the primary symptom of delayed sleep onset) to parental administered rewards and punishments for independent sleep (i.e., the techniques that address the secondary symptom of cosleeping). Modular Therapy would also indicate if the delayed sleep onset or cosleeping should have been addressed first. Following this orientation to pediatric sleep therapy, research trials indicating which sleep-related problems, family environment-related difficulties, or psychological comorbidities should be targeted first would help clinicians be more efficient and improve treatment outcomes for pediatric sleep-related problems.

KEY REFERENCES

Kuhn, B. R., & Elliott, A. J. (2003). Treatment efficacy in behavioral pediatric sleep medicine. *Journal of Psychosomatic Research, 54*, 587–597.

Owens, L. J., France, K. J., & Wiggs, L. (1999). Behavioural and cognitive-behavioural interventions for sleep disorders in infants and children: A review. *Sleep Medicine Reviews, 3*(4), 281–302.

Tikotzky, L., & Sadeh, A. (2009). The role of cognitive-behavioral therapy in behavioral childhood insomnia. *Sleep Medicine, 11*(7), 686–691.

CHAPTER 47

Obesity in Adults

Anthony N. Fabricatore

CLINICAL PROBLEM

Obesity, as readers of this volume are aware, is not a mental disorder. It is a disease that is strongly associated with a host of additional physical and emotional health complications. Obesity is defined as the accumulation of excess body fat and is typically assessed and diagnosed using the body mass index (BMI), which is a measure of weight relative to height. A BMI of less than 18.5 kg/m² falls in the underweight range, 18.5 to 24.9 kg/m² in the normal weight range, 25.0 to 29.9 kg/m² in the overweight range, and 30 kg/m² or higher in the obese range. Obesity is further categorized by severity: Class I (mild) obesity is marked by a BMI of 30.0 to 34.9 kg/m²; class II (moderate) obesity is a BMI of 35.0 to 39.9 kg/m²; and class III (severe) obesity is a BMI of 40 kg/m² or greater.

BMI, it should be noted, is an imperfect measure of adiposity. Elite athletes and other very muscular individuals, for example, may have a high BMI with a low percentage of body fat. Typically, however, this misclassification is easily corrected upon simply looking at the individual in question. A more common misclassification—and one with potentially significant health consequences—occurs when a diagnosis of obesity is not made because the patient presents with a BMI in the normal or overweight range, despite fat accumulation associated with significant disease risk (25% or more of body fat in men; 35% or more of body fat in women). A systematic review and meta-analysis found that BMI of 30 kg/m² or more had 97% specificity, but only 42% sensitivity to detect individuals with excess adiposity.

PREVALENCE

Data from the National Health and Nutrition Examination Survey (NHANES) indicate that the prevalence of obesity among U.S. adults doubled between the 1976–1980 and 1999–2002 data collection periods from ~15% to ~30%. The most recent statistics at the time of this writing (i.e., from 2009–2010) estimate that approximately 36% of U.S. adults are obese, with an additional 33% who are overweight. Fully 6% of adults (4% of men and 6% of women) have severe obesity, which represents a doubling in prevalence in just the past 20 to 25 years.

DIVERSITY

The prevalence statistics outlined above mask significant variability among racial/ethnic groups in the United States. Obesity is present in 35% of non-Hispanic White,

38% of Hispanic, and 50% of non-Hispanic Black adults. Within race/ethnicity, there is further heterogeneity by gender. For example, the prevalence of obesity is 39% in non-Hispanic Black men and 59% in non-Hispanic Black women. Across race/ ethnicity by gender categories, the prevalence of severe obesity ranges from 4% in Hispanic men to 18% in non-Hispanic Black women.

In addition to variability in prevalence and well-documented cross-cultural differences in body image ideals, three other sets of research findings must be noted with respect to diversity. First, BMI thresholds for obesity appear to be too high for certain groups. Metabolic risk has been found to increase at a lower BMI for people of Asian descent than for those of European or African descent. Second, some research suggests that African Americans have lower resting metabolic rates than Caucasians of the same sex, age, and weight. This difference in caloric needs may contribute to differences in prevalence, as well as differences in weight loss observed between the two groups in lifestyle modification programs. Third, obesity is negatively associated with socioeconomic status. Excess weight is more common and more difficult to treat in people who live in "food deserts" (i.e., neighborhoods with limited access to healthy food options).

EVIDENCE-BASED TREATMENTS

Lifestyle modification—an intervention that combines a low-calorie diet with increased physical activity and behavior therapy—is recommended for obese individuals, as well as for those who are overweight and have weight-related comorbid conditions (e.g., type 2 diabetes, hypertension, hypercholesterolemia, asthma, osteoarthritis). This treatment can be provided in groups or individually, and is most commonly delivered by a professional with a background in nutrition, psychology, or exercise physiology. Sessions are typically held weekly for 3 to 6 months and twice monthly for at least another 6 months, but the frequency of sessions and duration of the intervention vary widely by protocol.

Self-monitoring of food intake is the core behavioral component of treatment. In addition to the description, amount, and calorie content of foods and beverages consumed, patients may monitor situational factors, such as time, setting, mood, and hunger. These data will help identify specific targets for behavioral strategies (e.g., goal setting, stimulus control, behavioral substitution) or cognitive interventions (e.g., problem solving, cognitive restructuring). Motivational interviewing strategies may also be appropriate when ambivalence, rather than a deficit in knowledge or skills, is an obstacle to progress.

Perhaps the best example of lifestyle modification and its efficacy comes from the Diabetes Prevention Program (DPP). In this trial, over 3,000 individuals with pre-diabetes were randomized to receive metformin, placebo, or a lifestyle intervention designed to reduce weight by 7% via low-fat, low-calorie diet and at least 150 minutes per week of moderate-intensity activity (e.g., brisk walking). On average, lifestyle participants reached the weight loss goal of 7% at 6 months. Even with continued treatment, these participants regained approximately half of their lost weight at 4 years. Despite the modest net weight loss, the cumulative incidence of type 2 diabetes in the lifestyle group was 58% lower than in the placebo group and 31% lower than in the metformin group.

Researchers have altered the diet, exercise, and behavioral components of lifestyle modification in an attempt to improve both short-term and long-term weight loss.

The literature is too rich to review in detail here, but several conclusions emerge. First, varying the macronutrient profile of the diet (e.g., from low-fat to low-carb, etc.) does not reliably produce better outcomes. Dietary adherence is more predictive of weight loss than diet composition. Second, adherence can be enhanced by adding structure, either with detailed meal plans or with portion-controlled foods. Third, there is a dose-response effect of activity on weight loss, but the level of activity that most obese individuals can comfortably and safely engage in is unlikely to induce significant weight loss in the absence of dietary intervention. Fourth, continuing treatment after weight loss ceases can delay and minimize weight regain, but does not appear sufficient to prevent regain altogether.

A second clinical weight management option is pharmacotherapy. Weight loss medications have a checkered history, with efficacy offset by significant safety concerns. Currently, three medications—orlistat, lorcaserin, and the combination of phentermine and topiramate—are approved for long-term use. Placebo corrected weight losses range from approximately 3 kg with orlistat or lorcaserin to approximately 9 kg with phentermine/topiramate. Research with another drug (sibutramine, which was withdrawn from the U.S. market in 2010) suggests that weight loss medications are best used in combination with, rather than in place of, lifestyle modification. The effects of the two therapies were found to be additive.

The most intensive therapy for obesity is bariatric surgery, which is typically reserved for those with severe obesity or who have moderate obesity plus significant comorbidities. The three most common procedures currently performed are gastric bypass, sleeve gastrectomy, and adjustable gastric banding, which have been found to reduce BMI by $9.0 \ kg/m^2$, $10.1 \ kg/m^2$, and $2.4 \ kg/m^2$, respectively, 1 year after surgery. Despite significant regain on average, bariatric surgery remains the most effective long-term intervention for obesity. Studies suggest a significant reduction in all-cause mortality among bariatric surgery patients, compared with BMI-matched controls.

FUTURE RESEARCH

Research on the dissemination of structured lifestyle modification interventions has increased in recent years and remains a key need. The application of effective obesity interventions outside of academic medical centers—for example, in community centers, websites, and primary care clinics—can have a beneficial impact on public health by increasing the availability and reducing the cost of care. In addition, there is a need for more research on weight control interventions (including obesity prevention measures) that include economic and hard medical outcomes, such as health care costs, incidence of weight-related diseases, and associated mortality.

KEY REFERENCES

Appel, L. J., Clark, J. M., Yeh, H. C., Wang, N. Y., Coughlin, J. W., ... Brancati, F. L. (2011). Comparative effectiveness of weight-loss interventions in clinical practice. *New England Journal of Medicine, 365,* 1959–1968.

Butryn, M. L., Webb, V., & Wadden, T. A. (2011). Behavioral treatment of obesity. *Psychiatric Clinics of North America, 34,* 841–859.

Diabetes Prevention Program Research Group. (2002). Reduction in the incidence of type 2 diabetes with lifestyle intervention or metformin. *New England Journal of Medicine, 346,* 393–403.

Obesity in Adults

Kelly C. Allison

COMMENT ON THE EVIDENCE-BASED RECOMMENDATIONS

There is no quick fix for weight loss, no matter how many advertisements boast their magical cures. Behavioral weight management is the gold standard for treatment and is based on the premise of making long-term, incremental lifestyle changes that will result in 1 to 2 pounds of weight loss per week for several months, with a typical response being a 5% to 10% loss from initial body weight (e.g., 10–20 pounds for a 200 pound patient).

As noted in the Research Section by Dr. Fabricatore, the composition of the diet does not seem to matter as much as one's adherence to the recommendations. For any given dietary approach, the bottom line returns to achieving an energy deficit in a sustainable fashion. Literature regarding a lifestyle modification approach (also known as behavioral weight loss) suggests that keeping a food log (self-monitoring) is the single best predictor of weight loss. This finding is important in that it forms the foundation for the treatment and supports aiming for a specific calorie goal as the first-line approach. Typically, patients weighing less than 250 pounds are given a 1,200 to 1,500 daily calorie goal, while patients weighing greater than 250 pounds are given a 1,500 to 1,800 calorie goal. Involving a dietician in the treatment team is encouraged for patients at extreme weights and with special dietary needs owing to medical comorbidities. Working with patients to modify their food environments (stimulus control), increase their activity levels, and change their response to food cravings and emotional eating cues round out the core aspects of treatment (i.e., the behavioral and cognitive aspects of the treatment). Using specific problem-solving techniques, such as a behavioral chain analysis, is essential to break down the smallest, doable steps toward change. Behavioral weight loss manuals, such as the *LEARN Program for Weight Management*, can be helpful in instituting this approach.

CASE EXAMPLE

Subject Information and Brief History

"Jane" is a single, White, professional female. Her family history of weight is mixed. She recalls that her father was thin, as was her mother until her 40s when she reached menopause and gained weight. Jane's brother is overweight and has type 2 diabetes. Jane has struggled with her weight since childhood. She had three previous significant weight loss attempts with losses of 97, 80, and 70 pounds on separate occasions, mainly through Weight Watchers. However, she describes her previous approaches as "all or nothing," either being on or off the diet, and she was unable to sustain these losses.

Presenting Problem

In the previous 2 years, after her most recent weight loss attempt, Jane became the caretaker for her mother who was diagnosed with terminal cancer. With the combination of her heavy workload (working 10–12 hour days) and caring for her mother, she began gaining weight. She also became depressed, eating very little during the day and binge-eating in the evenings after work. She described her evenings as an "eat-a-thon" after arriving home starving after work and feeling anxious about her day. Her mother died a year before she initiated treatment, and during this time, her depression, social isolation, and long work hours continued, along with her binge eating. When she presented for treatment, she weighed 278 pounds at a height of 5'6.5", yielding a body mass index (BMI) of 44.2 kg/m² (class III obesity). Although she was eligible by weight standards, Jane did not want bariatric surgery because she felt it was too invasive and drastic, and sought to lose weight behaviorally, stop her binge episodes, and maintain her weight loss over the long term. She also recognized that her depression and anxiety, which were intertwined with her eating behaviors, needed intervention.

Treatment Intervention and Course

Jane was asked to keep a food log and provided with resources for nutrition information, including a calorie counter book, websites, and applications for her smartphone. We set her calorie goal at 1,500 to 1,800 calories per day and established a regular eating schedule with calorie ranges for each meal and snack. She was encouraged to add her calories throughout the day, but at least before dinner, so she could budget for the remainder of the day accordingly. She was also encouraged to weigh herself once daily at the same time of day. In the first week, we specifically focused on just recording what she ate and eating more regularly during the day. The second week she started recording calories and worked her way toward her goal. Each week we worked on new behaviors to change, including adding lifestyle activity throughout the day, such as increased use of stairs and parking farther from her destination, and formal exercise sessions, such as walking on a treadmill with an initial goal of 10 minutes, five times per week, to be increased incrementally.

Much of our work focused on creating a long-term lifestyle change. Because of her depression, Jane had isolated herself from friends since her mother's death. She was also anxious about going out to eat with friends or colleagues given that previously she would see her diet as a sprint, not wanting to go out for fear of going "off" her diet, and then going back to her old eating habits when the diet was "done." We combined behavioral activation with cognitive restructuring to help her engage in the social interaction needed to improve her mood and functioning, while practicing portion control and making healthy choices when eating with others. For example, she was encouraged to make plans to go hiking with a friend on a Saturday, and out to eat with one or two other friends on Sunday. We would plan for what meals she may choose among when she was out. This effectively increased her flexibility in food choices and helped her make her changes more sustainable over time. This flexibility included the use of meal replacements (such as frozen meals and shakes), particularly when she was at work and at times when her weight plateaued. She also consulted with a nutritionist throughout treatment to help her maintain a healthy variety of foods, which helped her stay motivated.

Outcome

Jane reduced her weight from 278 pounds to 231 pounds in the first 5 months of treatment. Her weight ranged between 235 to 225 pounds for the next several months, but she continued to come to counseling sessions every 3 weeks, with nutrition appointments in-between to keep her weight maintained and help keep her accountability for her eating patterns high. During this time she continued exercising but did not track her intake as regularly. Jane decided to make a renewed effort at losing weight again and chose to use meal replacements as a "kick-start." One year later, she is now approaching 210 pounds. She continues to use the techniques she has learned over the course of treatment and acknowledges that she has changed her way of thinking about weight loss from a "sprint" to a "marathon."

Jane feels increased self-efficacy about her ability to get back to her healthy eating behaviors if she does eat high calorie foods or has an unplanned food event. With this improvement in self-efficacy, she has not had a binge eating episode in several months. Her mood has been generally good, but she is encouraged that even during stressful times at work and depressing periods at home, she has been able to maintain her weight, if not continue losing weight. We continued to use a cognitive approach to address her mood and stress, as these issues were interrelated with her eating; she did not want to take antidepressants. She recognizes that she needs long-term support, particularly during times of stress, to keep her self-efficacy in place and bolster her motivation to keep up with her healthy lifestyle.

CHALLENGES IN APPLYING THE EVIDENCE-BASED APPROACH

We know that acute weight loss can be achieved fairly reliably through behavioral weight loss methods. Along with dissemination of this treatment to primary care offices, community-based programs, and other accessible locations, the challenge remains achieving long-term weight maintenance. While the initial period of weight loss is in keeping with a time-focused treatment, most patients seek larger weight losses than the "typical" outcome brings. In addition, research and clinical experience alike suggest that long-term support of healthy lifestyle changes is essential for keeping patients motivated for long-term success.

Other challenges rest in individual variability that is likely influenced by genetics, comorbid medical and mental health conditions, and neurobiological factors. Some individuals will never achieve a "normal weight" BMI, but certainly, we can help patients achieve a lifestyle that can improve their overall health. In addition, medications can cause weight gain, which can be discouraging to both the patient and the clinician when interventions do not work as well given this biological force. Finally, the body's response to weight loss is to become more efficient, requiring fewer and fewer calories to maintain its essential processes. This leads to a reduction in energy requirements for weight maintenance, one of the contributing factors for weight regain. For example if a woman required 1,900 calories per day to maintain her weight before losing 10% of her initial body weight, she likely would require fewer calories, such as 1,700 calories per day, to maintain her new, lower weight. Given these challenges, behavioral exhaustion (i.e., getting tired of keeping food logs and making healthy choices) often trumps weight loss intentions, leading to weight regain. Switching providers, using a new smartphone app, adding more variety in one's diet, or changing one's exercise program can provide new motivation for continuing with weight maintenance or loss over the longer term.

CULTURAL DIVERSITY ISSUES

As Dr. Fabricatore mentioned in the Research Section, African Americans are more likely to be obese than non-Hispanic Whites. Research has shown that African Americans lose less weight as compared to their Caucasian counterparts in behavioral weight loss trials. This may be due to cultural issues regarding traditional food preparation, access to healthy foods, and/or a metabolic difference (i.e., a slower basal metabolic rate). Some attention has been paid to making programs more culturally relevant, such as addressing beliefs about the health risks of obesity versus the cultural pressures to be a larger size in order to be attractive (for women), and addressing traditional ways of preparing foods such as frying and the use of fats. Listening to what patients are and are not ready to change is important in this interaction so that dietary intake can be modified in a sustainable fashion. Referring patients to a dietician who can help transition the patient to healthier, yet culturally familiar food choices can also be helpful.

FUTURE RESEARCH

Helping patients lose weight in the short term can be achieved through a variety of dietary approaches, most notably with sustainable lifestyle changes. However, helping these same patients keep weight off over time remains a challenge. Improving methods for sustaining motivation for healthy eating is an area in need of further research. In addition, the prevalence of obesity is growing, as is the prevalence of weight-related medical comorbidities, such as type 2 diabetes, hypertension, and obstructive sleep apnea. We need to develop ways to disseminate evidence-based behavioral weight loss treatment so that it is more accessible to those most vulnerable, such as low socioeconomic groups and African Americans.

KEY REFERENCES

Brownell, K. D. (2004). *The LEARN Program for Weight Management*. Dallas, TX: American Health Publishing Co.

Butryn, M. L., Webb, V., & Wadden, T. A. (2011). Behavioral treatment of obesity. *Psychiatric Clinics of North America, 34*, 841–859.

Makris, A., & Foster, G. D. (2011). Dietary approaches to the treatment of obesity. *Psychiatric Clinics of North America, 34*, 813–827.

CHAPTER 48

Obesity in Children and Adolescents

Robyn S. Mehlenbeck and Antonina S. Farmer

CLINICAL PROBLEM

Obesity among children and adolescents has become one of the greatest public health concerns in the United States. Obese children are at greater risk for elevated blood pressure, cholesterol, and lipid concentrations. They are more likely to suffer from diabetes, sleep apnea, and asthma. In addition, they are more likely to experience psychosocial impairment, including having a distorted body image, global negative self-perceptions, and peer interaction difficulties, such as being teased, bullied, and even socially isolated. Pediatric obesity often continues into adulthood, when being overweight has established associations with chronic health problems, such as cardiovascular disease, particular cancers, and increased mortality. Furthermore, adults who were obese as children tend to have a poorer quality of life, with lower income, less education, and even lower rates of marriage. These findings underlie the importance of developing and implementing efficacious interventions for obesity in childhood and adolescence.

PREVALENCE

Despite increasing awareness of the problem and prevention efforts, obesity rates have doubled among preschool children and tripled among older children and adolescents over the past three decades. National health statistics estimate that approximately one third of youth over the age of 2 years are overweight and one out of six children are obese, which is defined as having a body mass index (BMI) at or above the 95th percentile of sex- and age-specific growth charts. According to the National Health and Nutrition Examination Survey, obesity among preschool children aged 2 to 5 years doubled over the last three decades from 5% in 1980 to 10.5% in 2009. The rate tripled among 6 to 11 year olds (from 6.5 to 19.6%) and among adolescents aged 12 to 19 years (from 5 to 18.1%) during the same time period.

CULTURAL DIVERSITY ISSUES

Some ethnic groups have even higher rates of obesity. Overall, Hispanic and African American youth have greater rates of obesity than non-Hispanic White youth. Among boys, Mexican Americans (24.9%) have the highest prevalence of obesity, while non-Hispanic Black individuals have the highest rate among girls (22.7%). Twin studies suggest that nearly 50% of propensity for obesity is inherited genetically, which may contribute to differences in metabolic rates and body composition; however, numerous social, economic, and environmental factors contribute to disparities in prevalence. Specifically, cultural perceptions of a healthy weight, religious and social dietary practices, as well as attitude toward and perceived access to physical activity are important determinants of children's health behaviors. Consequently, interventions may need to be not only targeted at populations with higher prevalence but tailored for their specific needs to be maximally adopted and effective.

EVIDENCE-BASED TREATMENTS

Obesity Treatment With Children

The literature on effective treatment for pediatric obesity in children is still young, but randomized controlled studies have repeatedly supported comprehensive multidimensional family-based behavioral interventions. First, these comprehensive treatments typically include a *nutritional component* involving education and modification of food intake, such as caloric restriction or specialized diets. Recommended dietary strategies include providing specific guidelines for a reduced-energy diet and presenting nutritional goals to children as well as increasing healthy foods. One successful nutritional intervention is the Traffic Light Diet, which assigns colors to foods to support healthy choices (e.g., green for low-energy, high-nutrient foods). Second, most effective interventions involve an *exercise program* to increase physical activity and/or decrease sedentary activity. The American Academy of Pediatrics recommends that children get at least 60 minutes of moderate physical activity per day. In interventions for obesity, targeting the reduction of sedentary activity (e.g., watching television) and an increase in lifestyle activity (e.g., taking the stairs, active play) have been superior in the short- and long-term to prescribing a regimented aerobic exercise program or calisthenics.

Third, successful interventions include *behavioral modification* strategies that support diet and exercise plans. These may include self-monitoring of food intake, goal setting, stimulus control, contingency management, and praise to support healthy decisions. Lastly, most clinicians emphasize the value of *family participation* in supporting the treatment of childhood obesity, but evidence is inconsistent about whether interventions should target children and their parents simultaneously or the parents alone. By learning behavioral reinforcement and parenting skills, parents can increase the child's perceived support, serve as healthy role models, and provide appropriate feedback for their children. In addition, *cognitive strategies* of modifying maladaptive thoughts and learning problem-solving strategies have been successfully implemented, but evidence suggests using these interventions in combination with behavioral strategies. While interventions with these ingredients have short- and long-term empirical support, outperforming education alone and wait-list control conditions, even the most promising interventions help less than one half of participating children reach nonobese status at 10-year follow-up.

Obesity Treatment With Adolescents

Adolescence represents the developmental transition from childhood into adulthood, marked by many physiological and psychological changes that pose obstacles to weight loss. Compared to treatments for young children (under age 12) and adults, there are relatively fewer rigorous studies of obesity treatments for adolescents. Some interventions have included youth of such broad age ranges (e.g., 8 to 17), which makes efficacy interpretation difficult. Adolescents may respond differently to various components of a comprehensive intervention. While this age group may similarly benefit from a low-calorie diet, adolescents tend to regain weight without continuing support being in place. At least one randomized controlled study found adolescents to lose more weight with a low-glycemic index diet as opposed to a traditional low-fat diet. More developed cognitive skills at this age present the opportunity for advanced interventions like live computerized feedback during meals to develop satiety, slow down eating speed, and reduce total intake. Adolescents who participate in individual cognitive behavioral treatments demonstrate lasting improvements in their physical self-worth and global self-esteem.

Given adolescents' greater autonomy, many studies suggest that they may benefit from less parental involvement than younger children. In fact, parental involvement may not be absolutely necessary for adolescents who have been shown to benefit even from self-delivered contingency management techniques. Provided the increased importance of peers for this age group, older adolescents may particularly benefit from interventions that include a peer-based activity or peer modeling component. One-year follow-up data from various adolescent interventions show mixed results, with some interventions having some sustained weight loss, while others demonstrated a rebound in weight. Overall, more research is needed to evaluate the long-term effectiveness of protocols for adolescents, with particular focus on motivation, cultural values, psychosocial well-being outcomes, and BMI.

It should also be noted that treatment of adolescent obesity with bariatric surgery has proven successful in reducing overweight, at least in the short-term. However, lack of randomized control trial evidence and high risk of severe side effects that may require reoperation suggest limiting consideration for surgery. Potential candidates may be those with particularly severe obesity (50 kg/m² and more) or medical complications (e.g., hypertension, diabetes), who have not made gains with behavioral treatments (in 6 months or more) but are physically and emotionally mature (13 years of age or older for girls and 15 or older for boys). Of note, there are no follow-up studies examining long-term outcome with bariatric surgery in youth.

FUTURE RESEARCH

There are now evidence-based treatments for pediatric obesity, namely comprehensive interventions addressing nutrition, physical activity, behavior modification, and parenting skills training. However, these comprehensive protocols still have little evidence for applicability in real world settings in terms of accessibility and feasibility. Furthermore, despite significant health disparities relating to gender, race, and ethnicity, as well as cultural differences surrounding body image and food practices, most studies have been conducted with predominantly Caucasian, middle-class, motivated families in outpatient health settings.

Several culturally specific programs have been implemented in school-based settings (e.g., Planet Health) and after-school centers (e.g., Hip Hop to Health Jr). Preliminary findings from interventions tailored for African American girls, utilizing similar strategies described above, suggest that treatment components (e.g., parental participation) may have different effectiveness for diverse populations. Overall, findings of divergent outcomes depending on gender, ethnicity, and socioeconomic status emphasize the need for not just targeted but culturally tailored interventions.

Finally, there is a dearth of research on the moderating effects of family context (e.g., single-parent homes), cultural values regarding weight and food, peer influences, developmental level, and comorbid conditions on the outcomes of interventions. Children who present with comorbid psychological problems have been previously excluded from the majority of studies, despite evidence that obesity may contribute to the development and/or maintenance of behavioral and emotional problems. Future studies should include and potentially target this group given the improvements in self-esteem, self-efficacy, and physical self-worth often seen following comprehensive weight management interventions.

KEY REFERENCES

Barlow, S. E., & The Expert Committee. (2007). Expert committee recommendations regarding the prevention, assessment, and treatment of child and adolescent overweight and obesity: Summary report. *Pediatrics, 120*, S164–S192. doi: 10.1542/peds.2007-2329C

Jelalian, E., & Steele, R. G. (Eds.). (2008). *Handbook of childhood and adolescent obesity*. New York, NY: Springer.

Zametkin, A. J., Zoon, C. K., Klein, H. W., & Munson, S. (2004). Psychiatric aspects of child and adolescent obesity: A review of the past 10 years. *Journal of the American Academy of Child & Adolescent Psychiatry, 43*(2), 134–150. doi: 10.1097/00004583-200402000-00008

Clinician Application

Obesity in Children and Adolescents

Wendy L. Ward

COMMENT ON THE EVIDENCE-BASED RECOMMENDATIONS

Children or adolescents found to be either overweight (BMI between the 85th and 95th percentiles for age and gender) or obese (BMI in the 95th percentile or higher for age and gender) should be assessed and treated. High rates of sedentary behavior, low rates of physical activity, caloric intake above recommended levels, high intake of sugary drinks, and intake of calorie-dense, non-nutritive food are all very common in obese youth. Complications of obesity can be both medical and psychological, which must be assessed and treated in order to have optimal health and successful weight management. Common medical problems encountered involve the cardiovascular and respiratory system, chronic pain, insulin resistance, and other endocrine disorders. Common psychological disorders include depression, anxiety, and low self-esteem. Binge eating, emotional eating, nighttime eating, and boredom eating are all common maladapative eating behavioral patterns in obese youth. And finally, insufficient quality or quantity of sleep can have an impact on eating and energy levels which worsen obesity.

Evidence-based treatment of overweight and obese children incorporates a family-based, multidisciplinary approach, including medical treatment, nutrition education, physical activity education, family involvement, and behavior modification.

Recommendations from health care providers should address the following areas: medical care, food choices and eating patterns, physical activity choices and patterns, family strengths and challenges (family eating and activity patterns, parenting skills, parent perceptions of weight and health status), personal strengths and challenges (motivation, disordered eating patterns, psychological state), and environmental and community access/support. Individualized goal setting is critical and must take into account all of these factors.

An important aspect of treating pediatric obesity is the potential effects of treatment on growth and development. Good nutrition must be maintained for optimal health and growth. Youth who are still growing will have different goals for their weight than youth who have stopped growing, and careful goal setting and monitoring by a physician are essential. For instance, it is often recommended that youth maintain weight and grow in height over time as an effective way to change body mass index (BMI). In contrast, recommendations for older obese adolescents who have finished growing may include a component of weight loss. These issues must be clearly discussed with parents/youth in clinical settings and clearly understood in analyzing treatment effectiveness studies.

Bariatric surgery is an option in many places across the country. This option is most useful when reserved for those who have been nonresponsive to standard of practice treatment for at least 6 months or more and limited to adolescents who have finished growing. It is sometimes considered useful for those who are medically at immediate risk. However, some of these risks actually enhance surgical risk (e.g., cardiac and respiratory conditions, sleep apnea, etc.) so this is not always the case. In addition, complications can occur and, after surgery, behavioral modifications in the area of eating and physical activity are still necessary. Weight regain can occur if behavioral modifications are not consistently followed. These limitations of this treatment option are not always understood by those who consider the "quick fix" of a surgical procedure.

CASE EXAMPLE

Subject Information and Brief History

The patient, Paul, was a 14-year-old biracial (African American and Caucasian) young man. He consulted with his primary care physician (PCP) owing to his longstanding obesity and emerging medical concerns. His mother worked the night shift (and slept during the day) so most visits were attended with his grandmother. A multidisciplinary treatment clinic (such as is recommended by most leading organizations including the American Academy of Pediatrics for the treatment of pediatric obesity) was not available in their local area so they only had visits with the PCP and psychologist. Relevant family history included a father who died in a drunk driving incident when Paul was 8 after a long history of driving under influence (DUIs) and several years of unsuccessful treatment for alcoholism. Paul was exhibiting depressive symptoms of anhedonia, dysphoria, and low self-esteem. His older teenage sister and mother have intense conflict on a repeated basis, and Paul felt he was lacking when compared with his sister's social status at school, grades, and level of independence. Paul wanted to date but did not feel desirable or attractive. He exhibited social immaturity (poor ability to make friends and sustain friendships with agemates, dependence on relationship with mother for self-esteem stabilization), separation anxiety from his mother, social withdrawal, and academic underachievement.

Presenting Problem

Paul presented with a nutritional intake including a high amount of sugary drinks, high cheese intake, high whole milk intake, large portion sizes, and grazing behaviors throughout the day. Because of the grazing behaviors, he was never "empty" and therefore did not experience actual hunger nor was hunger a trigger for eating when it did occur. He engaged in binge eating triggered by emotions related to key events including peer rejection/isolation, memories of his father and his death, and his mother's work schedule (switched to night shift after father's death) preventing his having time with her. He occasionally had binge eating, when emotionally overwrought and home alone. He was completely sedentary. Paul's weight had been a problem for years. He was 5'9" and weighed 257 lbs, rendering him with a BMI of 37.9. It was not until his medical issues arose in an annual blood work assessment that motivation to change improved in Paul and his mother. Paul had low density lipoprotein (LDL) cholesterol of 279 (normal is less than 150), triglycerides 439 (normal is less than 100), high density lipoprotein (HDL) cholesterol of 30 (normal is over 40). Fortunately, his blood pressure was normal.

Treatment Intervention and Course

Treatment followed the initial assessment and utilized motivational interviewing to gain a collaborative partnership in designing the treatment goals. While investigating what factors were currently motivating Paul to make changes in his life, it was discovered that Paul wanted to build friendships with a few kids at school who all skateboarded. He felt unable to join in as he had never ridden one. With the psychologist's encouragement, Paul's mother obtained low-cost lessons from a local youth center, and when he built up his skills he decided to join the youth at the skating park. During sessions we discussed his eating habits, first adding vegetables (he preferred salads) and educating him on added cheese portions and healthier dressing options. The psychologist educated him on his "grazing" behaviors and discussed spacing out meals and snacks and the need for hunger awareness. The psychologist also provided supportive counseling to discuss the death of his father and the relationship with his mother, and cognitive behavioral techniques to address binge eating. Specifically, Paul learned to identify the antecedent events and how they triggered his emotions and his episodes of overeating. When these events occurred, he learned to engage in alternative and more positive coping strategies with his negative emotions rather than overeating. The physician monitored medical health indicators and provided monthly weigh-ins.

After achieving these goals, he was ready to reduce sugary drink intake and moved whole milk to 2%. Over time he moved further to skim milk. The physical activity began to be self-reinforcing via peer interest/activity and he filled many of his afterschool hours with this peer-based physical activity. He became quite good and competed in city championships. He and his mother had dinner together every night, building their relationship with weekend activities as well (some involving physical activity).

Finally, the psychologist discussed with Paul key ways to maintain his eating behaviors and physical activity behaviors beyond the treatment phase. Upcoming life stressors were discussed such as graduation and moving into employment or community college, and how to avoid maladaptive coping mechanisms like withdrawal, emotional eating, and binge eating.

Outcome

Paul proceeded in 26 months of therapy through these stages. His mood was brighter and he no longer had a depressive diagnosis or mood-based maladaptive coping behaviors such as emotional eating or binge eating. His self-esteem, body image, and relationships with his mother and sister all improved. His LDL went from 279 to 196, triglycerides from 439 to 143, HDL from 30 to 32. While none of these changes were yet in the normal range, they were significant improvements in that direction. His weight reduced while his height increased (257 lbs, 5'9" in May 2006; 205 lbs, 5'11" in February 2007; 208 lbs, 6'1" April 2007; 200 lbs, 6'1" July 2008). His initial BMI was 37.9 (in the Morbidly Obese classification) and his final BMI being 26.1, just above the average range. He was discharged from therapy after a period of maintenance of his targeted behaviors and mood stability (with decreasing frequency of sessions during this maintenance phase).

CHALLENGES IN APPLYING THE EVIDENCE-BASED APPROACH

There are multiple challenges in applying the evidence-based approach. The first barrier to implementing evidence-based treatment with this population is that studies are still determining what the effective elements are in family-based behavioral interventions beyond simply needing nutritional recommendations, physical activity guidelines, and behavioral modification techniques. The research struggles with clear, effective outcomes because the pediatric obesity population is so varied: age/developmental stage, gender, socioeconomic status, sociocultural background, regional differences (e.g., sweet tea in the south), family dynamics and stressors, parental involvement and feeding behaviors, comorbid psychological conditions (e.g., emotional eating), and so forth. Even the most promising interventions are not effective for all youth given this variability. However, practice guidelines are emerging that detail these elements based on empirical evidence and/or expert consensus and provide a more specific guide for treatment. These guidelines incorporate recommended treatments for youth at different ages and emphasize culturally sensitive practices in both assessment and treatment design, and also provide tailored treatment recommendations for those with developmental delays, economic barriers to healthy nutrition and/or physical activity, comorbid psychological conditions, and other factors.

In addition, there are not enough multidisciplinary treatment programs for obese youth and even those that are available struggle with reimbursement for all the disciplines needed to treat obesity effectively (physician, dietician, psychologist, physical therapist/exercise physiologist). When multidisciplinary treatment is not available, patients either see one of these individuals or a few but rarely all. Communication among the various disciplines is typically suboptimal. Achieving clinically significant outcomes are suboptimal as well.

Even when multidisciplinary treatment programs are available, the ability to provide the treatment is hampered. It is not always the primary caregiver who brings the child in, limiting the effectiveness of "family-based" treatment. Most studies do not recruit "unmotivated" parents and youth, yet these are prevalent in clinical settings. Financial barriers, local nutritional "deserts," and few physical activity options often limit the ability to follow through with team recommendations. The moderating effects of divorce, poverty, food insecurity, maternal depression, cultural values on weight and food, developmental disorders, and comorbid emotional or behavioral disorders (many of these factors are excluded from treatment effectiveness studies) hamper positive effects of treatment. Most importantly, the issue of recidivism and a focus on creating positive health habits and maintaining them is often underappreciated leading to regain and discouragement.

CULTURAL DIVERSITY ISSUES

Some racial/ethnic groups have even higher rates of obesity. Most studies are not undertaken with minorities. Genetic risk and/or cultural perceptions of a healthy weight, healthy eating, and the definition of physical activity have an impact on treatment outcomes. Working within the context of cultural definitions and mores to promote education and health-related behavioral change is recommended. Further, language can be a clear barrier to treatment success. Providing educational material and interactions with health care providers who speak the same language as the patients and families is critical. Furthermore, even in English-speaking patient populations, a true understanding of commonly used terms "healthy eating," "healthy cooking practices," and "vigorous activity" must be carefully discussed and defined to avoid misunderstandings and to maximize outcomes. In short, careful communication and culturally tailored interventions are needed.

FURTHER RESEARCH

More outcomes research on tailored treatment to subpopulations of pediatric obesity is warranted; for example, those with socioeconomic limitations/food insecurity, those who are unmotivated to change, those who speak other languages or come from other racial, ethnic, or cultural backgrounds, those with binge eating, depression, or other comorbid psychological issues. Research on longer-term follow-up and maintenance of health-related behavioral change is also warranted. Discovering ways to improve care for subgroups of pediatric obesity patients should be a priority given the medical and psychosocial risks for this population.

KEY REFERENCES

Austin, H., Smith, K. C., & Ward, W. L. (2012). Bariatric surgery in adolescents: What's the rationale? What's rational? *International Review of Psychiatry, 24,* 254–261.

Epstein, L. H., Paluch, R. A., Gordy, C. C., Saelens, B. E., & Ernst, M. M. (2000). Problem solving in the treatment of childhood obesity. *Journal of Consulting and Clinical Psychology, 68,* 717–721.

Ward, W. L., Baughcum, A., Beck, A., Cadieux, A., Dreyer, M., … Shaffer, L. (2012). Expert Guidelines: The role of psychologists in the assessment and treatment of obese youth. www.childrenshospitals.net/obesity

CHAPTER 49

Postpartum Depression

Michael W. O'Hara

CLINICAL PROBLEM

Postpartum depression is major or minor depression that is manifest in the first year after child birth. It is characterized by typical symptoms of major depression including depressive mood, loss of interest, sleep and appetite disturbances, difficulties in concentration and decision making, psychomotor agitation or retardation, excessive guilt, and suicidal ideation. These symptoms may arise any time in the postpartum period or even carry over from pregnancy; however, the first 3 months after delivery appears to be the period of highest risk and greatest salience to mothers and health care professionals. Postpartum depression should be distinguished from the postpartum blues, which refers to a common mild clinical state that is manifest in the first week to 10 days postpartum. The blues are typically transitory but do serve as a known risk factor for postpartum depression. On the opposite end of the severity spectrum is postpartum psychosis, which is a severe disorder characterized by hallucinations and delusions and usually reflects bipolar disorder. Postpartum psychosis is often manifest early in the postpartum period, usually within the first 2 weeks and typically has an acute onset. Treatment usually involves hospitalization. Postpartum psychosis is not considered to be on a continuum with postpartum depression.

Postpartum depression is often comorbid with generalized anxiety disorder and other anxiety disorders. Postpartum depression is particularly consequential because it occurs at a time of the increased demands on a woman associated with infant care. Postpartum women are particularly likely to experience sleep interruptions, withdrawal from the work force, and isolation from friends. For women who are depressed, these stressors can exacerbate negative mood and lead to further impairment in functioning. Of particular concern is the fact that postpartum depression is associated with suboptimal mother–infant interaction as well as negative consequences for the infant in the realms of social, emotional, and cognitive development.

PREVALENCE

Postpartum depression is common with a prevalence rate between 7% (major depression) and 19% (major and minor depression) over the first 3 months after delivery. Rates of depression tend to be higher in women without partners, younger women, and lower socioeconomic status (SES) women. Debate continues as to whether depression is more common during the postpartum period than other times in a woman's life. There have been no large-scale epidemiological studies to address this question.

365

CULTURAL DIVERSITY ISSUES

Race and ethnicity have been inconsistently related to risk for postpartum depression. Studies conducted in Asia, particularly in Japan, often report much lower rates of postpartum depression than in Western countries.

Developing new approaches to treatment delivery are especially important to women who live in difficult financial circumstances and minority women. These women often have had less than optimal encounters with the formal health and mental health systems and are reluctant to report on their depression because of fears of negative consequences such as losing custody of their child. Interventions offered and delivered by trained nonmental health professionals such as nurses or case managers may be more acceptable to these women. This proposition needs to be tested. It is also well known that many of the negative consequences to offspring of depressed mothers are more evident in children of lower SES women. Identifying the best combination of depression and parenting interventions should be a priority for research. Finally, there is good evidence that male partners do experience depression in the postpartum period and that men are especially at risk if their partner is experiencing a postpartum depression. All of this suggests that interventions aimed at the family system may be optimal from a public health perspective.

EVIDENCE-BASED TREATMENTS

Postpartum depression at its core is "depression" and as such empirically supported treatments for depression are efficacious for postpartum depression. A recent meta-analysis of treatments for perinatal depression identified three major approaches that are empirically supported: nondirective counseling (aka Listening Visits), Interpersonal Psychotherapy, and Cognitive Behavioral Therapy (CBT).

Listening Visits were originally developed in the United Kingdom by Jeni Holden as a brief intervention to be implemented by health visitors who have routine contact with new mothers, often in their homes. Health visitors are typically given relatively brief training in basic listening skills and problem solving. This intervention typically takes place in the home with sessions lasting 30 to 45 minutes over six to eight sessions. The health visitor applies basic counseling skills to understand the mother's problems and then works with her to identify solutions. Numerous clinical trials have tested and validated Listening Visits and it is labeled as an empirically supported treatment for postpartum depression by the National Institute for Clinical Excellence in the United Kingdom.

Interpersonal Psychotherapy (IPT) for postpartum depression is a short-term therapy (8–12 sessions) that can be delivered in individual or group contexts. What makes IPT attractive as a treatment for postpartum depression is its focus on disrupted interpersonal relationships, with a particular emphasis on interpersonal disputes (e.g., with partner, family members) and a focus on a woman's difficulty in making role transitions (e.g., taking on the motherhood role). The first major trial was conducted by Michael O'Hara, Scott Stuart, and their colleagues. In this trial, 120 women with postpartum major depression were randomly assigned to 12 sessions of IPT or a waiting list control (WLC). Following treatment, women in the IPT condition showed significantly lower levels of self-reported and clinician-rated depressive symptoms and higher levels of social adjustment than women in the WLC. One of the goals of this study was to improve the mother–infant relationship, which was assessed before and after treatment. Although women in the IPT condition reported significantly less parenting stress than women in the WLC, there were no differences between the two groups with respect to maternal or infant behavior in the home-based observations of mother–infant interaction. A similar finding was obtained by Peter Cooper and Lynne Murray in their evaluation of CBT and Listening Visits for postpartum depression.

CBT has been tested with postpartum depressed women in Canada, Australia, and the United Kingdom and has been found to be efficacious. However, its implementation has been highly variable. For example, in one study, CBT was implemented in a group setting and adapted Lewinsohn's *Coping with Depression Course*. In another study, CBT was aimed at helping depressed mothers manage their infants more effectively and was only loosely based on Beck's CBT principles. In a Canadian study, CBT was implemented on the basis of Beck's CBT principles but was an "add on" to a medication condition.

A unique feature of postpartum depression is that the period of risk (i.e., first 3 months after delivery) is well established and the beginning of this risk period can be identified well in advance. As a consequence, a number of investigators have tested preventive interventions. These interventions have been of two sorts, universal—applied to all pregnant women, and indicated—targeted toward "high risk" women (often on the basis of the presence of mild depressive symptoms). Universal interventions have not been successful; however, there is evidence now that intervening with women who are at risk for postpartum depression can successfully prevent the development of postpartum depression. These interventions are conducted both in group and individual contexts and are based on IPT and CBT principles.

FUTURE RESEARCH

There is a large research agenda relevant to the treatment of postpartum depression. Preventive interventions can reduce overall rates of depression if properly targeted. However, research must improve the risk factor identification, otherwise, many women will unnecessarily receive preventive interventions. There is almost a complete absence of research on interventions that combine acute depression treatment and a parenting intervention. There is good evidence for the efficacy of psychological interventions in the short-term but there are few long-term studies of outcome. There has been no research comparing treatments of different lengths or settings. It is clear that the burdens of caring for a new infant and often other children make it difficult for many women to access traditional mental health services. Brief treatments and treatments that are delivered in convenient locations (home, online) are very desirable if they are shown to be effective.

KEY REFERENCES

O'Hara, M. W., Stuart, S., Gorman, L. L., & Wenzel, A. (2000). Efficacy of Interpersonal Psychotherapy for postpartum depression. *Archives of General Psychiatry, 57*, 1039–1045.

Sockol, L. E., Epperson, C. N., & Barber, J. P. (2011). A meta-analysis of treatments for perinatal depression. *Clinical Psychology Review, 31*, 839–849.

Stuart, S., & O'Hara, M. W. (2005). The use of Interpersonal Psychotherapy for perinatal mood and anxiety disorders. In A. Riecher-Rössler & M. Steiner (Eds.), *Perinatal stress, mood, and anxiety disorders: From bench to bedside* (pp. 150–166). Basel, Germany: Karger, Bibliotheca Psychiatrica, No. 173.

Clinician Application

Postpartum Depression

Amy Wenzel and Karen Kleiman

COMMENT ON THE EVIDENCE-BASED RECOMMENDATIONS

Women with postpartum depression are often resistant to the notion of psychotherapy. It seems costly, time consuming, inconvenient, and quite possibly, the last thing a new mother feels like squeezing into her demanding day. Because of the significant stressors on postpartum women's time, energy, and resources, overwhelmed new mothers often do best with short-term psychotherapy that holds the promise of immediate symptom relief. The three evidence-based approaches described by Dr. O'Hara have great promise for satisfying this need.

We agree that many core components of cognitive behavioral therapy (CBT) are relevant to the treatment of postpartum depression. One main component of CBT, cognitive restructuring, helps postpartum women develop tools for identifying, evaluating, and modifying unhelpful cognitions that keep them entrenched in their emotional distress (e.g., "My kids would be better off without me"). Behavioral activation can be applied when postpartum women are not actively engaged in their environments and especially when they are not engaged in caring for their newborn. Exposure can be used to encourage postpartum women who are avoiding contact with their infants to provide care to their infants in short increments, with the idea that they will build up to a longer duration of contact. Problem solving can be used when postpartum women need to resolve stressors and challenges that they encounter in the transition to parenthood.

We also agree that Interpersonal Psychotherapy (IPT) is a useful treatment for postpartum depression. As Dr. O'Hara noted, this treatment has a great deal of face validity, as problems in interpersonal relationships with the spouse, partner, or extended family, and difficulties in transitioning to the role of being a mother, are paramount in many cases that we see. Dr. O'Hara also mentioned Listening Visits as an evidence-based treatment for postpartum depression. Unfortunately, this approach to treatment has not been disseminated widely, so most psychotherapists who work with postpartum women are unaware that it exists.

CASE EXAMPLE

Subject Information and Brief History

Joelle was a 26-year-old married woman who stayed at home with her children, ages 4, 2½, and 4 months. Her husband had been spending long hours away from the home in order to finish a rigorous professional degree. She reported a history of obsessive compulsive disorder (OCD) and depression and was taking 50 mg of fluvoxamine (Luvox) at the time treatment commenced.

Presenting Problem

Joelle presented for treatment with postpartum depression and an exacerbation of her preexisting OCD. She reported feeling like she "can't stand" being with her three children, especially in the late afternoon when she had been with them all day and when they typically became rowdy. As a result, she fixated on the beliefs that she is a horrible mother and that her husband never should have married her. Not surprisingly, she reported experiencing depressed mood nearly 90% of the time. She also endorsed symptoms of anhedonia, appetite disturbance, and sleep disturbance, both in excess of that which would be expected of a postpartum woman, fatigue, excessive guilt, and concentration difficulties. She denied suicidal ideation, although she admitted that she had fantasies of leaving the house and never returning.

Joelle's obsessive compulsive symptoms manifested in two ways. First, she compulsively did chores around the house and experienced a "not just right" preoccupation with chores remaining unfinished (e.g., doing only one load of laundry rather than all of the laundry; taking the clothes out of the dryer but not folding them). Not surprisingly, she was often interrupted by her children when she attempted to complete household chores, so she experienced persistent distress and preoccupation with the remaining uncompleted tasks. Second, she was preoccupied with her weight and body shape, weighing herself multiple times a day and closely examining parts of her body in the mirror in order to locate flaws. Because she had little time to exercise and eat healthy meals, she was having difficulty losing her baby weight, and she was consumed with intrusive thoughts about imperfections in her appearance.

Treatment Intervention and Course

The acute phase of treatment lasted 12 sessions, held on a weekly basis. Treatment incorporated many strategic interventions that emerged from the conceptualization of Joelle's presenting problems, such as cognitive restructuring to modify and get distance from self-deprecating statements about her parenting ability and appearance, problem-solving tools to identify ways to receive assistance from extended family members in caring for her children, and exposure exercises coupled with response prevention to reduce compulsive cleaning and checking of her weight and perceived bodily flaws. Her husband attended one session in order to develop a schedule of exposures that he could help Joelle implement in the home, and he helped her to identify opportunities for additional exposure that arose during the course of daily living.

As we have observed with other clients, Joelle had difficulty finding the time to do systematic CBT homework, such as recording her thoughts on a worksheet, despite the fact that she saw its value. To overcome this obstacle, she developed "coping cards" that contained the fruits of the important therapeutic work that took place in session, which she could consult quickly in times of distress outside of session. For example, she developed a list of reasons why she is a good mother so that she could be reminded of the evidence that supports this belief in the midst of self-deprecating thoughts and emotional distress.

Outcome

Currently, Joelle is in a maintenance phase of treatment, attending monthly sessions in order to reinforce the application of the cognitive behavioral tools she gained in treatment and to apply them to new stressors and challenges that have arisen (e.g., the onset of a health concern in her middle child). She reports that the frequency of self-deprecating thoughts about her parenting ability has decreased to approximately twice a week when she is frustrated with the children, and she notes that she is quickly able to apply the cognitive restructuring tools to gain relief from these thoughts. She has developed a sense of acceptance that her home will not be as clean as she would like it to be, given that she has three small children. As a result, she has been free of compulsive urges to clean and for order for several weeks. Although she substantially decreased the frequency of weighing herself and examining herself in the mirror, she admits that she has struggled with body image issues throughout her life and has requested that she and her therapist focus on them, and the core beliefs that underlie them, in the maintenance phase of treatment.

CHALLENGES IN APPLYING THE EVIDENCE-BASED APPROACH

As noted in the case description, an obstacle frequently encountered by therapists is the ability and willingness of postpartum women to complete homework in-between sessions. In our practice, we have heard women express protest in various ways—the mere structure of the treatment can be perceived as an imposition; the idea of homework feels like an intrusion of their precious time; the notion of thinking about how they are thinking feels excessive and counterproductive. They are less impressed with CBT's evidence base and more interested in feeling better right now, without investing additional time or energy outside the office. Therefore, if CBT can be modified to take these factors into account and better respond to the specific needs of postpartum women, it is likely that compliance will be greater, and outcomes will be more successful. We also suggest that psychotherapists pay particular attention to developing and enhancing the therapeutic relationship, as doing so might make some of the CBT between-session exercises more palatable for postpartum women who are exhausted and overwhelmed. The postpartum woman's primary experience must be one of unconditional acceptance, absolute patience and, perhaps most importantly, the sense that she will be cared for—a sanctuary of sorts.

CULTURAL DIVERSITY ISSUES

As Dr. O'Hara suggests, developing interventions that are sensitive to postpartum women with financial difficulties, lower socioeconomic status (SES), or other factors that would make these women reluctant to seek treatment is imperative. Rituals, stigmas, expectations, social pressures, and traditions may all play a significant role in the course of the illness, as well as in the treatment and its outcome. Ideally, the clinical course should be guided by the cultural context. To take but one example, the role of extended family in providing assistance and support in the immediate post-partum period varies widely by culture. It is important for clinicians to understand the cultural forces that determine the amount of involvement of extended family members and to negotiate any problems with these relationships in a culturally sensitive manner.

FUTURE RESEARCH

As Dr. O'Hara noted, several large-scale studies evaluating the efficacy of IPT have been conducted, and there is an expanding literature on the efficacy of CBT and Listening Visits for postpartum depression. We agree with Dr. O'Hara that the implementation of CBT has been highly variable, with some approaches focused mostly on cognitive strategies, and other approaches focused mostly on behavioral strategies. We call upon future researchers to develop and evaluate a CBT protocol that is individualized to mothers with postpartum depression, taking care to cre-atively incorporate strategies that facilitate both cognitive and behavioral mecha-nisms of change in a manner that postpartum women can embrace. We also hope that researchers will focus on the dissemination of such a treatment approach, as we often field questions from psychotherapists who inquire about recommendations for CBT treatment manuals for this population.

In addition, it is important to recognize that many psychotherapists who work with postpartum women use supportive therapy, which is a conversation-based intervention that focuses on symptom relief through the provision of support dur-ing the early phases of the postpartum crisis. It is likely that some, but certainly not all, aspects of supportive therapy of this nature are included in Listening Visits. Thus, another important avenue for future research is to operationalize and evalu-ate a supportive therapy approach for the treatment of postpartum depression. Such research would have the potential to bridge the gap between academic research and the actual clinical practice of many psychotherapists. Moreover, such research could clarify the specific aspects of supportive therapy that are associated with the greatest change so that these aspects can be incorporated into and enhance other evidence-based psychotherapies for postpartum depression.

KEY REFERENCES

Kleiman, K. (2008). *Therapy and the postpartum woman: Notes on healing postpartum depression for clinicians and the women who seek their help.* New York, NY: Routledge.

Kleiman, K., & Raskin, V. (1994). *This isn't what I expected: Overcoming postpartum depression.* New York, NY: Bantam Books.

Wiegartz, P., & Gyoerkoe, K. (2009). *The pregnancy and postpartum anxiety workbook: Practical skills to help you over-come anxiety, worry, panic attacks, obsessions, and compulsions.* Oakland, CA: New Harbinger Publications.

CHAPTER 50

Psycho-Oncology

Wolfgang Linden and Katerina Rnic

CLINICAL PROBLEM

Recent developments in cancer are simultaneously encouraging and problematic. On the one hand, cancer is on the verge of becoming the most frequent cause of death. This is largely driven by an increase in absolute cancer incidence, while conversely, relative cancer-related mortality has decreased owing to the impressive growth in treatment options and improved success rates. For example, breast cancer survival rates have now reached up to 89% when studied over 5-year follow-up periods. Greater treatment success also means that the number of survivors is growing and their unique psychological needs (fear of recurrence, depression, pain, fatigue, and sleep problems) call for much greater attention.

PREVALENCE

It is estimated that in 2013 there will be approximately 12 million cancer survivors in North America. Relevant to this chapter is not so much the prevalence of cancer, but the prevalence of psychological distress and physical symptoms in patients with cancer. Research findings can be confusing because most studies are too underpowered to allow separate prevalence estimates for all possible combinations of cancer type, gender, and prognosis. Fine-grained studies of prevalence are, however, necessary given that patients are remarkably heterogeneous in how they respond emotionally to cancer diagnosis and treatment. Person and disease characteristics that can best explain differential levels of emotional distress therefore need to be identified.

Crude estimates of distress prevalence aggregated for all types of cancer have ranged from 0% to 49%. The term "distress" is intentionally broad and taps into both anxiety and depression, which are the most often studied psychological constructs in the early stages of cancer. When focusing only on large studies with representative samples and good quality measures, the picture becomes clearer and more consistent. A clinical diagnosis for anxiety disorder is justified in about 15% to 20% of patients at time of diagnosis and clinical levels of depression are in the range of 10% to 15%. Generally, the lowest prevalence estimates come from studies that used structured diagnostic interviews, the gold standard in assessment. The quoted prevalence rates apply to prevalence of a clinical diagnosis rather than mere symptom reporting. Timing of the measurement is also critical because anxiety tends to decrease even without targeted intervention as patients move through the care trajectory while levels of depressive symptomatology are more stable.

It makes little sense to aggregate prevalence studies for fatigue and pain because these symptoms are much more likely to be present during acute treatment (and may be transient) and during palliation, whereas they are fairly rare in the early stage of the disease. Furthermore, sequelae vary greatly as a function of cancer type.

Although the more trustworthy figures extracted from high quality studies are lower than some early estimates, they still identify a large proportion of the patient cohort that is distressed and in need of professional support. While moderated by cancer type and stage, women generally report more distress than men as do younger patients.

CULTURAL DIVERSITY ISSUES

Issues related to distress and its treatment across various ethnic and cultural groups have rarely been studied in oncological samples. One study found that Hispanic breast cancer patients experience similar levels of distress to non-Hispanic White cancer patients, whereas African American patients experienced less distress. However, unlike non-Hispanic White patients, both minority groups experienced an increase in distress 1 year after surgery. This preliminary finding suggests that minority groups may have a greater need for long-term monitoring of their distress levels, although further research is needed, including research on other tumor sites and ethnic groups.

In addition, the literature suggests that members of minority groups are less likely to self-refer to counseling, support groups, or other psychological treatments. This emphasizes the need for cancer centers to conduct routine distress screening in order to identify and refer patients who may benefit from psychological treatment and may not have sought out the treatment on their own, therefore allowing for equal chances of access to care.

EVIDENCE-BASED TREATMENTS

To understand the literature on psycho-oncological treatments, one needs to be clear that psychotherapists working in primary medical and rehabilitation care settings do not treat cancer per se (or heart disease or diabetes, etc.); they address concomitant problems and sequelae of cancer such as fear of recurrence, depression, fatigue, and pain. Treatments used by psycho-oncologists were largely developed in psychiatric and clinical psychology environments (e.g., using cognitive behavioral treatment (CBT) for depression) and there are some fundamental differences between psychiatric versus primary medical care environments. In a psychiatric context, psychotherapists directly treat the presenting pathology (e.g., agoraphobia or marital problems), whereas in behavioral medicine, clinicians treat sequelae or use a mediational model such that a reduction in distress is hypothesized to improve a facet of health, immune function for example. Although there was initial hope that treating psychological factors could extend life, the great majority of clinical trials have not been able to replicate the results of earlier, promising studies. The primary goal of psycho-oncological treatment is, therefore, to minimize distress, improve quality of life, and restore function.

A key question for treatment planning is which type of treatment is most effective. This requires meaningful and reliable classifications of therapies into larger, nonoverlapping clusters. While this is prone to disagreement, we consider a crude typology of three classes to be useful: (a) psychoeducation (usually delivered in a cost-effective group format, and often taught by nurses rather than trained psychotherapists), with a focus on educating patients and their families about the disease trajectory, treatment, symptom management, common psychological responses and coping strategies, and community resources, (b) CBT approaches directed at problem solving, and (c) supportive-expressive and meditation therapies that focus on the emotional response. Meta-analyses and other systematic reviews concur that all psychological treatment results are consistently positive, but with highly variable outcomes such that the majority of studies report relatively small effects. Given this pronounced variability in reported outcomes, it is critical to study moderators of outcomes. Cancer type, prognosis, gender, type of treatment, treatment exposure, and quality of the trial design are prime candidates for research on moderating variables. Results have been complex and frequently surprising but can still be condensed to these core findings and directions for future research:

1. The quality of randomly controlled trial designs does not greatly affect outcomes, and treatment type has not yet been shown to differentially affect outcomes, although psychoeducation appears to be surprisingly effective in reducing distress given its relatively low cost.
2. Longer treatments produce significantly better outcomes (dosage is correlated $r = 0.63$ with magnitude of distress reduction); unfortunately, the great majority of patients receive a treatment dosage that is clearly insufficient for maximal outcomes.
3. Possibly the most striking finding relates to floor effects that arise when patients are treated for anxiety or depression although they had not been screened for actual elevations in anxiety or depression. Researchers have reported a 3:1 ratio for observed treatment benefits as a function of distress screening versus not screening. If not screened for distress, effects are usually small (ES around $d = 0.2–0.3$) whereas effects are much larger if only screened patients are treated (ES typically around $d = 0.8$). Ignoring floor effects (which unfortunately most clinical trials in psycho-oncology have done) opens the door to widely different conclusions about meta-analytic results and their meaning.

FUTURE RESEARCH

Owing to space constraints we did not deal with more narrow, but cancer-specific, constructs of interest like fear of recurrence or posttraumatic growth although we do also consider them relevant and deserving of researcher attention.

With respect to distress-reducing treatments, broad conclusions are still hampered by an absence of many possible and interesting studies that simply have not yet been conducted. Particularly understudied moderators are gender differences, the uniqueness of palliative samples, and differential treatment results for varying cancer types other than breast cancer, which is the one cancer type that has received most attention.

KEY REFERENCES

Jacobsen, P. B., & Jim, H. S. (2008). Psychosocial Interventions for anxiety and depression in adult cancer patients: Achievements and challenges. *CA: A Cancer Journal for Clinicians, 58*, 214–230.

Linden, W., & Girgis, A. (2011). Psychological treatment outcomes for cancer patients: What do meta-analyses tell us? *Psycho-Oncology, 21*, 343–350.

Moyer, A., Sohl, S. J., Knapp-Oliver, S. K., & Schneider, S. (2009). Characteristics and methodological quality of 25 years of research investigating psychosocial interventions for cancer patients. *Cancer Treatment Reviews, 35*, 475–484.

Clinician Application

Psycho-Oncology

Lynne S. Padgett

COMMENT ON THE EVIDENCE-BASED RECOMMENDATIONS

The Research Section highlights important points in treating cancer-related distress, and two notable points particularly relevant to clinical practice are made. First, the researchers make a clear delineation between practice contexts: psychiatric and behavioral medicine. While both approaches focus on presenting symptoms, in a psychiatric context the focus is the presenting psychopathology, in the behavioral medicine context, symptoms are viewed through the prism of current health problems and treatments. A behavioral medicine focus is essential in successfully working with the unique needs of cancer patients and allows the constellation of symptoms to be examined from the perspective of psychopathology, but also as symptoms of disease or treatment side effects. Second, the authors rightly emphasize the importance of utilizing strict diagnostic criteria in practice with cancer patients to accurately evaluate intervention effectiveness. The importance of utilizing symptom severity, duration, and course to guide treatment cannot be discounted, even in the presence of a cancer diagnosis.

CASE EXAMPLE

Subject Information and Brief History

Brenda was a 32-year-old, married, White female who had recently been diagnosed with a recurrence of breast cancer. Brenda had been diagnosed with breast cancer at age 30, shortly after the birth of her 2-year-old son. Based on her family history and genetic testing, Brenda knew that she carried the *BRCA* gene and was at high risk for breast cancer. Her initial cancer diagnosis was stage II (locally spread) and after having a double-mastectomy, she was enrolled in a clinical trial for chemotherapy. Brenda described the surgeries (e.g., double mastectomy and reconstructive surgery) as tiring, but stated that her chemotherapy treatment had few side effects. After completing her chemotherapy, she showed no evidence of disease and was told her cancer was in remission. After completing treatment, Brenda had chosen not to return to work. There was no reported psychiatric history for Brenda or her husband.

Presenting Problem

Brenda was referred to psychotherapy by a member of her online support community for young breast cancer survivors. A fellow member of her online support community was a professional colleague of mine. This member referred Brenda to see a psychologist for support at the time of her recurrence, given Brenda's expressed distress. Brenda presented with her husband reporting concerns about dying before her child was old enough to remember her, pessimism about the effectiveness of her current chemotherapy, and her inability to continue training for a half-marathon, owing to fatigue. While Brenda reported several symptoms consistent with a diagnosis of depression or adjustment disorder, a formal diagnosis was not given.

Treatment Intervention and Course

Brenda attended the first session, with her husband at her request. She reported the loss of an important coping mechanism (running) and her awareness and fear that her cancer had returned aggressively, had spread to multiple organs, and she was likely to die from her disease, given that no curative treatment options were available. She had restarted her previous chemotherapy regimen, but stated that "it hadn't kept the cancer away, what makes them think it will work?" Brenda reported that she was receiving support through her online community, but reported some depressive symptoms such as hopelessness regarding the potential success of her treatment. Both she and her husband reported strained relationships with their friends since the cancer recurrence. They attributed this to their friends' anxiety about both the recurrence of Brenda's cancer and fears about what would happen to Brenda. Given the importance of understanding Brenda's prognosis and treatment plan and side effects, oncology medical records were requested and reviewed prior to the second visit. Brenda's assessment of the gravity of her prognosis and the lack of optimism regarding the success of the current treatment was consistent with the chart review.

Brenda attended therapy three times over the next 5 weeks, with cancellations due to multiple medical appointments and fatigue. During these sessions, she continued to exhibit intermittent depressive symptoms. However, at no time did she meet criteria for clinical depression. Her stated goal became "figuring out" how she wanted to spend her remaining time. Interventions with Brenda included resource referral (information about palliative care that focused on fatigue and pain management) and cognitive behavior therapy (CBT) approaches to manage both her psychosocial distress and frustration with her inability to continue marathon training. Brenda, based on conversations with her medical team, suspected her cancer was progressing, and reported trying to enjoy the remaining time she had with her son and husband. Both Brenda and her husband declined interest in common practices such as making a video or writing letters for her son prior to her death because they found it "too depressing."

During what was to be our last face-to-face session, Brenda requested her husband attend, and we focused on conflict between her treatment teams (oncology and palliative care). As Brenda's disease burden grew, she was unable to continue face-to-face sessions, and we spoke by phone briefly on two occasions focusing on her growing awareness of her death and the gifts she had chosen to leave her husband and son. As she declined further, she would place her husband on the phone to speak for her and transitioned to receiving psychosocial support from her palliative care team.

Outcome

Brenda died approximately 4 months after our first session. I spoke with her husband twice by phone after her death. He reported that until the last few days before her death, Brenda was sad, but engaged with her family and support group members. He described that receiving in-home palliative and hospice care had allowed Brenda to die at home with little pain. In addition, the palliative care social worker had worked with Brenda to leave a series of letters and books for her son. In addition, the family was able to talk more easily about Brenda's impending death and her wishes. We spoke about his grief and how to discuss death with their son.

CHALLENGES IN APPLYING THE EVIDENCE-BASED APPROACH

Several challenges emerge in applying evidence-based treatment (EBT) to patients with a cancer diagnosis. First, it can be difficult to consistently deliver EBT approaches (CBT, anxiety management training, self-hypnosis) in the context of failing health or decreasing function. Second, while there is a large body of research literature documenting psychosocial distress in cancer patients, there is little focused on treatment in community or outpatient settings, where most cancer patients are treated. EBT interventions are not developed for delivery in the context of multiple competing appointments with oncology treatment team professionals, when patients may prioritize cancer treatment appointments over mental health appointments. In addition, disease progression or burden and treatment side effects often complicate the consistency needed for effective delivery of EBT interventions. Third, delivering treatment within a behavioral medicine context relies on working closely with the oncology team. This is often difficult in the community outpatient setting owing to a lack of consistent communication between treating professionals and poor care coordination.

CULTURAL DIVERSITY ISSUES

While there were no apparent cultural diversity issues in this case, it is important to note that this client, with a supportive family, online support community, insurance, and other resources, struggled with her recurrence and impending death. How much greater might the struggle be for patients from marginalized populations who are less richly resourced? However, two issues emerged over the course of psychotherapy that are not well addressed in the literature and that represent the diversity that results from being an "atypical" cancer patient. Brenda was a young adult with no history of any health problems and experienced a cancer diagnosis, recurrence, and rapid decline over a short period of time. The "typical" breast cancer patient is older (risk increases with age) and the breast cancer is often treated successfully, without recurrence. Because of this profile, many breast cancer support resources are targeted at older women. While Brenda found several online support communities for young women with breast cancer, participants were primarily single women and women without children. Though this group shared her struggle with having cancer as a young adult, she experienced less support for her struggles as a young mother battling her recurrence. In addition, Brenda's husband reported he was "not ready for my wife to die" and there were few, if any, resources targeted to him as the grieving young father and caregiver.

FUTURE RESEARCH

As the researchers discussed, in addition to expanding research in this area beyond breast cancer populations, further research is needed in clarifying the construct of distress and how it differs from depression and other psychiatric diagnoses, both in presentation and response to treatment. Further examination of distress across the trajectory of cancer, from diagnosis to survivorship and end of life, as well as targeting interventions to these stages is also essential. In addition, exploring the course of psychosocial distress throughout the stages of life for both patients and their caregivers is also needed. Lastly, the nature of psychosocial distress within the context of metastatic disease and at the transition from curative to palliative care are areas where further research would benefit clinical practice.

KEY REFERENCES

Adler, N., & Page A. (2008). *National Institute of Medicine Committee on Psychosocial Services to Cancer Patients/ families in a Community Setting. Cancer care for the whole patient: Meeting psychosocial health needs.* Washington DC: National Academies Press.

Holland, J., Andersen, B., Breitbart, W., Compas, B., Dudley, M., ... NCCN Distress Management Panel. (2010). The NCCN Distress Management clinical Practice guidelines in Oncology. *Journal of the National Comprehensive Cancer Network, 8,* 448–485.

Wei, G., Bennett, M., Stark, D., Murray, S., & Higginson, I. (2010). Psychological distress in cancer from survivorship to end of life care: Prevalence, associated factors and clinical implications. *European Journal of Cancer, 46,* 2036–2044.

CHAPTER 51

Smoking Cessation

Nicole S. Marquinez and Thomas H. Brandon

CLINICAL PROBLEM

Tobacco smoking remains one of the leading preventable causes of disease and death in the United States, responsible for over 400,000 deaths per year, primarily from lung cancer and heart disease. Indeed, smokers have nearly a 50% chance of dying prematurely as a consequence of their smoking.

Fortunately, smoking cessation is associated with improved length and quality of life. It slows the progressively increasing risk of lung cancer, and within 10 years it reduces the risk of heart disease by one half. Although the majority of smokers who quit do so without assistance, smoking cessation is a challenge, with over 90% of self-quitting attempts failing to produce long-term tobacco abstinence. Specific challenges include: coping with unpleasant nicotine withdrawal symptoms (e.g., mood disturbance, sleep disturbance, attentional problems, appetite increase); coping with cravings for tobacco; managing weight gain; coping with life stressors without tobacco; living with other smokers; and avoiding full relapse after an initial "slip." Behavioral and pharmacological interventions have been developed to address these challenges. Moreover, smoking cessation interventions are among the most cost-effective life-saving interventions in the entire public health arena.

PREVALENCE

In the United States, 19% of adults are current smokers, including 22% of men and 17% of women. Smoking is increasingly a behavior of the poor and less educated. For example, the prevalence is 29% among adults living below the poverty level, and 45% among those with only a GED diploma.

Nearly one half of all cigarettes are now smoked by individuals with mental illness or other substance use disorders. Although the rates of tobacco use have declined in recent years, approximately 46 million people continue to smoke in the United States, and there is evidence that the shrinking population of smokers is becoming progressively more difficult to treat.

CULTURAL DIVERSITY ISSUES

In terms of race and ethnicity, the highest prevalence is among Native Americans (32%) and the lowest among Asians (10%) and Hispanics (13%).

Although the prevalence of smoking among African Americans is lower than the population as a whole, African Americans appear to become more addicted to tobacco (i.e., they are less likely to quit smoking), and they suffer disproportionately from tobacco-related diseases. Although the causes of these disparities are unknown, attention has focused on targeted marketing of tobacco products to minorities in general, and menthol cigarettes to African Americans in particular. Moreover, studies indicate that smokers who are African American, Hispanic, or from lower income groups are less likely to be asked about their tobacco use by their health care provider, given advice to quit, or given pharmacotherapies to aid cessation.

EVIDENCE-BASED TREATMENTS

Because of education and changes in routine procedures, health care providers are increasingly addressing tobacco smoking with their patients. However, practicing psychologists lag in this regard, primarily because smoking is not usually the presenting problem and because they do not feel qualified to treat smoking. Nevertheless, psychologists and other mental health professionals have some advantages over other health care providers, including ongoing and closer relationships with their patients, and the expertise to facilitate behavior change.

The US Public Health Service has produced the comprehensive *Clinical Practice Guideline for Treating Tobacco Use and Dependence*, which is based on review and/or meta-analysis of over 8,000 studies. It found that the best cessation rates are produced by a combination of behavioral counseling and pharmacotherapy.

Counseling

Interventions as short as 3 minutes long can increase cessation rates. Brief interventions can be targeted to patients who are willing to quit, are not willing to quit, or have already quit smoking. The Guideline recommends that clinicians take 5 steps when providing patients with a brief intervention. These "5As" include: 1) Ask the patient if he or she uses tobacco; 2) Advise him or her to quit smoking; 3) Assess their willingness to quit in the next 30 days; 4) Assist those who are willing to quit by making a quit plan; and 5) Arrange follow-up contacts to prevent relapse. For patients who are not ready to quit, clinicians should use a brief, personally relevant intervention to increase motivation. Although brief interventions can be effective, there is a dose–response relationship between the intensity of the intervention (number and duration of sessions) and the probability of successful long-term cessation. Among the more intensive counseling approaches, the greatest efficacy has been found for cognitive behavioral therapy (CBT) that includes: social support, education about nicotine dependence and nicotine withdrawal symptoms, identifying what triggers tobacco craving, training in cognitive and behavioral coping skills, and relapse-prevention training. The number of sessions may vary between 6 and 12 and could last anywhere from 2 to 12 weeks, and CBT can be delivered in group or individual formats. Aside from this general CBT approach, other behavioral therapies that have shown evidence of efficacy include Scheduled Reduced Smoking (controlled gradual reduction in smoking) and Rapid Smoking (an aversive technique that has fallen out of favor). Note that there is insufficient evidence at this time to recommend either hypnosis or acupuncture for smoking cessation.

Pharmacotherapy

Seven smoking-cessation medications have been approved by the FDA. Five of these are nicotine replacement therapies (NRTs) designed to reduce cravings and nicotine withdrawal symptoms by delivering relatively small dosages of nicotine. These products include nicotine gum, transdermal patch, inhaler, nasal spray, and lozenge. The transdermal patch differs from the others in that it provides a steady dose of nicotine throughout the day, but all of the products deliver nicotine in a slower, and therefore less addicting, manner than actual smoking. Side effects from these products are minor and primarily related to their particular route of administration (e.g., skin rash from patch).

Two non-nicotine medications also have FDA approval. The first, bupropion (Zyban), is also marketed as an antidepressant (Wellbutrin). The second, varenicline (Chantix) is a nicotine receptor partial agonist. That is, it stimulates nicotinic receptors to relieve craving and withdrawal symptoms, but also blocks those receptors, which reduces satisfaction from smoking. Both of these medications include a run-up period of approximately 1 week prior to quitting smoking. Side effects and contraindications are minimal for these medications. However, based on post-marketing reports, the FDA has issued a boxed warning for both bupropion and varenicline with respect to possible neuropsychiatric and other symptoms. Patient monitoring for these symptoms is recommended.

Clinical trials have found that the NRTs and bupropion tend to double cessation rates compared to placebo, whereas research to date suggests that varenicline may triple cessation rates. Recent research suggests that combining a slower delivery medication (e.g., nicotine patch) with a relatively rapid-delivery medication (e.g., nicotine gum) may produce the highest cessation rates. In addition, there is growing evidence that it is beneficial to use any of these medications for 1 week or more prior to quitting smoking.

Relapse Prevention

Because 70% to 95% of smokers typically relapse following any given quit attempt, high quality interventions usually include a relapse-prevention component that trains patients to use coping responses to avoid a lapse, achieve lifestyle balance without cigarettes, and to prevent an initial slip or lapse from progressing to a full relapse. For self-quitters, a recent meta-analysis concluded that written relapse-prevention booklets are effective.

Telephone Quitlines

Every state now has a smoking cessation quitline that typically provides counseling, literature, local referrals when necessary, and sometimes free pharmacotherapy to smokers. Research supports quitlines as an effective intervention, and they can be a convenient referral for clinicians who do not feel qualified to provide cessation counseling to their patients. The national phone number (1-800-QUITNOW) will automatically route calls to the caller's state quitline.

FUTURE RESEARCH

Although there are many areas of needed research, the following are particularly relevant:

1. Methods for motivating the remaining, often "hard core," smokers to attempt cessation
2. Improving counseling strategies that complement the use of improved pharmacotherapies
3. Enhancing dissemination and implementation of smoking cessation treatments across all health care providers, including mental health professionals.

KEY REFERENCES

Fiore, M. C., Jaen, C. R., Baker, T. B., Bailey, W. C., Benowitz, N. L., ... Wewers, M. E. (2008). *Treating tobacco use and dependence. 2008 update.* Clinical Practice Guideline. Rockville, MD: US Department of Health and Human Services, Public Health Service. May, 2008.

Perkins, K. A., Conklin, C. A., & Levine, M. D. (2007). *Cognitive-behavioral therapy for smoking cessation: A practical guidebook to the most effective treatments.* New York, NY: Routledge.

Phillips, K. M., & Brandon, T. H. (2004). Do psychologists adhere to the clinical practice guidelines for tobacco cessation? A survey of practitioners. *Professional Psychology: Research & Practice, 35*, 281–285.

Clinician Application

Smoking Cessation

Andrew M. Gottlieb

COMMENT ON THE EVIDENCE-BASED RECOMMENDATIONS

The conclusions from the evidence-based recommendations are that the best cessation rates result from a combination of behavioral therapy and drug therapy. The major approach to behavioral therapy is cognitive behavioral therapy (CBT). CBT for cigarette cessation involves multiple components including motivational enhancement components, identifying triggers for smoking and learning skills to deal with these triggers, relaxation training and stress management, relapse prevention, and sometimes, behavioral aversive techniques, such as rapid smoking. There is a strong dose–response relationship of behavioral treatments where both session length and number of sessions are highly correlated with smoking cessation success. It should be noted that the aversive technique of rapid smoking, although less used currently, has considerable evidence suggesting that it leads to very high smoking cessation rates.

Pharmacotherapy for smoking cessation includes seven different options: five types of nicotine replacement and two non-nicotine prescription drugs. Although studies suggest that these medications increase abstinence, perhaps doubling or tripling the natural quit rate, the later relapse rate is very high for all drug options. Thus, medication options should be best seen as helping with short-term quitting rather than longer-term abstinence. This is why behavioral approaches, particularly those incorporating relapse prevention training, are so important. As Mark Twain said, "Giving up smoking is the easiest thing in the world. I know because I've done it thousands of times."

CASE EXAMPLE

Subject Information and Brief History

Charles was a 52-year-old, single, Caucasian physician, currently retired. He was smoking 20 to 30 cigarettes per day of an additive-free organic tobacco brand.

He had first started smoking in his 40s, and had quit multiple times. He had started smoking as a result of social influences, as he had become seriously involved in swing dancing. Many of his peers in the dance community were smokers and he began smoking as a result.

Presenting Problem

Charles presented for treatment to stop smoking cigarettes. He had decided he wanted to quit smoking because he had met a woman that he liked who had told him that she would not get involved with a smoker. He was smoking more than one pack per day. This was interspersed throughout the day, but primarily during two sessions, one in the morning, and one in the late evenings, during which he would sit outside on his deck reading and smoking.

Current stressors in his life included his having little structure in his day owing to his retirement, and having considerable responsibility for the caretaking of his elderly mother who was suffering from dementia.

Treatment Intervention and Course

The first step in treating cigarette smoking is assessing motivation and setting a quit agenda. Using the technique of paradoxical agenda setting developed by Dr. David Burns, MD, we explored all the reasons why he might not want to quit smoking cigarettes. These included pleasure from smoking, avoidance of withdrawal symptoms, social connections with other smokers, stress relief from caring for his elderly mother, and the pairing of relaxed reading and cigarette smoking. I challenged him to convince me that in spite of all of these reasons he would want to quit smoking. He argued that he wanted to date this new woman, and also to be able to play soccer without being winded. He felt that both of these activities could greatly enhance his quality of life.

We developed a treatment plan that involved a combination of behavioral techniques and nicotine replacement therapy. (Prescription medication treatment was ruled out because he had a history of depression and there is a black box warning for suicidal ideation on both of the prescription options.) Because he had such strong positive associations between smoking and relaxed pleasure (i.e., reading on his deck), we decided that the first component would be an in vivo aversive conditioning using rapid smoking. We met at his house, on the deck, for three consecutive days and performed rapid smoking using a standard protocol where he was instructed to smoke several cigarettes, one after another, while inhaling every 6 seconds, cued by a digital tape loop. He continued until he was no longer able to smoke without feeling like vomiting or passing out. This usually took about two or three cigarettes. Charles was instructed not to smoke between sessions. Given the extreme nausea due to the aversive smoking, this was not difficult.

At the end of the rapid smoking sessions, Charles began to use a nicotine patch at the highest 21 mg dose. He was also given nicotine gum in the 4 mg dosing. (Both are over-the-counter medications, and he purchased them before starting rapid smoking.) We met weekly to problem-solve challenges to his smoking cessation. During these sessions, Charles was taught meditation and muscle relaxation methods to help cope with stress. He was also encouraged to increase his daily exercise and began to do some light jogging, that he found very helpful in increasing his stamina for playing soccer. This reinforced his nonsmoking behavior.

He began dating his new woman friend and this also reinforced his nonsmoking. He was also instructed to speak with his smoking friends and ask them to avoid offering him cigarettes or smoking in his proximity. At the end of treatment, we spent several sessions doing relapse prevention, during which we identified potential triggers for relapse (e.g., reading late at night outside on his deck, and cooling off outside a dance bar), and rehearsed ways of dealing with them. He removed the chairs from his deck, so that he'd be forced to read inside where he had no smoking cues. He also decided not to cool off with other smokers when attending dance bars, instead standing with nonsmokers.

Outcome

Treatment lasted 6 weeks and he was abstinent at that point. A follow-up at 1 year revealed a small relapse of several days triggered by his mother's worsening medical condition. After this brief setback his abstinence continued. He was still dating his nonsmoking girlfriend and playing a lot of soccer, as well as jogging. He had stopped using the nicotine patch after the first 6 weeks of abstinence, but occasionally still used nicotine gum when he had cravings.

CHALLENGES IN APPLYING THE EVIDENCE-BASED APPROACH

There are two main challenges to evidence-based treatment of cigarette smoking. The first is selection. That is, given the multiplicity of options, how does the clinician choose which components to include? Of all of the medication options, varenicline (Chantix) has the best cessation rates, but also has the most clinical reports of severe psychiatric side effects (e.g., vivid and disturbing dreams, suicidal ideation and attempts, and homicidal ideation and acts), so risk/reward benefits must be considered by the clinician and the prescribing physician. (Also, the government has banned the use of Chantix for commercial pilots and truck drivers, owing to safety concerns.) For heavier smokers, the use of nicotine replacement options, preferably in the higher dose options is optimal. For lighter smokers, the use of the nicotine patch or nicotine gum or lozenges in lower doses can help, but in this population there is less evidence of the efficacy of pharmacotherapy. In all cases, some version of behavioral and cognitive behavioral counseling will potentiate the effects of treatment.

The second challenge is that even the best evidence-based treatments have relapse rates at 1 year of at least 70%, and often as high as 95%. This is probably because cigarette smoking is intensely addictive, owing to its inhaled mode of administration, and dose-dependent variable effects which allow fingertip control of mood, concentration, and energy. Because the probability of relapse is so high, all interventions should include a strong relapse-prevention component.

CULTURAL DIVERSITY ISSUES

There were no major cultural diversity issues in this case as both the therapist and the patient were Caucasian males. The National Institute of Health concluded that there was no evidence of any differential effectiveness for smoking cessation techniques across diverse ethnic and cultural populations. There are a few populations where medication use is contraindicated (pregnant women), and a few in which medication has not been found to be effective (smokeless tobacco users, light smokers, and adolescents, who have powerful social influences on smoking).

FUTURE RESEARCH

Successful development of truly effective smoking cessation treatments could save millions of lives worldwide, which should encourage research and development in this field. Future research is needed to determine the best combinations of treatments. For instance, one could easily imagine a 2×7 research design that compared each of the pharmacotherapy options combined with either cognitive behavioral counseling or a no counseling control group. Also, we need further research into the optimal combination treatments. Which combination treatments result in higher cessation rates? Because relapse rates are so high, future research could also focus on improving relapse-prevention techniques.

It would also be useful to explore the use of electronic cigarettes as a cessation tool. These devices provide nicotine in vaporized inhalable form without carbon monoxide, tars, or other combustion products. They are widely in use by consumers, but virtually no research has been performed on them as smoking cessation options.

KEY REFERENCES

Brownell, K. D., Glynn, T. J., Glasgow, R., Lando, H., Rand, C., ... Pinney, J. M. (1986). Interventions to prevent relapse. *Health Psychology, 5*(Suppl), 53–68.

Marlatt, G. A., & Gordon, J. R., (1985). *Relapse prevention: Maintenance strategies in the treatment of addictive behaviors.* New York, NY: Guildford Press.

Perkins, K. A., Conklin, C. A., & Levine, M. D. (2008) *Cognitive–behavioral therapy for smoking cessation: A practical guidebook to the most effective treatments.* New York, NY: Routledge.

CHAPTER 52

Somatic Disorders

Robert L. Woolfolk and Lesley A. Allen

CLINICAL PROBLEM

Somatoform disorders are characterized by physical symptoms which suggest a medical condition, but which are not fully explained by a medical condition. Patients with somatoform disorders represent a formidable challenge to the health care system. These patients tend to overuse health care services, derive little benefit from treatment, and experience protracted impairment, often lasting many years. Often, patients with somatoform symptoms are dissatisfied with the medical services they receive and repeatedly change physicians. Likewise, physicians of these treatment-resistant patients often feel frustrated by patients' frequent complaints and dissatisfaction with treatment. Because standard medical care has been relatively unsuccessful in treating somatoform disorders, alternative treatments have been developed.

Although medicine has long recognized a group of patients with medically unexplained physical symptoms, excessive health concerns, and abnormal illness behavior, there has been and continues to be disagreement over suitable diagnostic labels and criteria. The diagnostic label, somatization disorder, was introduced in *DSM-III* and was retained with minor revisions in *DSM-III-R* and *DSM-IV*. According to *DSM-IV*, somatization disorder is a chronic disorder characterized by multiple unexplained physical symptoms (at least four unexplained pain symptoms, two unexplained gastrointestinal symptoms, one unexplained sexual symptom, and one pseudoneurological symptom) which result in functional impairment or the seeking of treatment. Patients presenting with medically unexplained physical symptoms that are too few in number, or not diverse enough to qualify for a diagnosis of somatization disorder, but last at least 6 months, are given a *DSM-IV* diagnosis of undifferentiated somatoform disorder. Hypochondriasis is characterized by a preoccupation with fears of having a serious disease based on one's misinterpretation of bodily symptoms. The preoccupation must last at least 6 months and persist despite medical reassurance. Thus, unlike in somatization where the distress and dysfunction experienced is due to the physical symptoms themselves, in hypochondriasis the distress and dysfunction is due to the patient's interpretation of the meaning of his or her symptoms.

DSM-5 has announced a new diagnostic label, somatic symptom disorder, that subsumes most conditions meeting criteria for somatization disorder, undifferentiated somatoform disorder, and hypochondriasis in earlier editions of the *DSM*. Somatic symptom disorder is characterized by one or more somatic symptoms that are distressing and/or disrupt daily life for at least 6 months. Also, patients must have two of the following: (a) health anxiety, (b) excessive concern about the medical seriousness of the symptoms, (c) excessive time and energy devoted to health concerns. Instead of requiring that symptoms be medically unexplained, *DSM-5* somatic symptom disorder requires that they be accompanied by maladaptive thoughts, feelings, and/or behaviors.

PREVALENCE

Although there is no published epidemiological research on the *DSM-5*'s somatic symptom disorder, research on the older diagnostic categories suggests the following: Somatization disorder and hypochondriasis are relatively rare in the general population, with most prevalence estimates below 1%. Both disorders are more common in primary care, specialty medicine, and psychiatric settings than in the community. When assessing for medically unexplained symptoms and/or health anxiety that are distressing but not severe enough to meet the *DSM-IV* criteria for somatization disorder or hypochondriasis, researchers have found as many as 20% of primary care patients to present with these symptoms. These milder forms of somatization and hypochondriasis are also common in psychiatric practices, though they are often not the presenting complaints.

CULTURAL DIVERSITY ISSUES

Gender, ethnicity, race, and education have been associated with somatization, but not with hypochondriasis. Severe and moderately severely disturbed somatization patients are more likely to be female, non-White, and less educated than non-somatizers. The WHO's Cross-National study, conducted in primary care offices across 14 different countries, revealed a higher incidence of moderate to severe levels of somatization in primary care practices in Latin American countries than in the United States, suggesting an association between somatization and ethnicity. Findings have been inconsistent on whether hypochondriasis is related to any demographic factor.

EVIDENCE-BASED TREATMENTS

Several different psychosocial interventions have been used to treat somatization and hypochondriasis. Most approaches have been brief (6–16 sessions) and theoretically grounded in social learning theory. Interventions typically involve identifying and challenging patients' misinterpretations of physical symptoms as well as constructing more realistic interpretations of them. Training in relaxation and/or assertiveness is included in some interventions. Other strategies include behavioral activation and/or direct attempts to alter illness behaviors. Some treatments for health anxiety have employed exposure and response prevention in which patients construct hierarchies of their own hypochondriacal fears and avoidance behavior patterns, such as checking, reassurance seeking, and avoidance of interoceptive and/or external stimuli. Afterward, patients are given assignments of in vivo exposure and response prevention.

As a whole, most psychosocial treatments have been shown to reduce physical discomfort, health anxiety, and functional limitations in these patients. However, there are few data on the impact of treatment on health care utilization, especially when the cost of a psychosocial intervention is factored into the equation. Although even the most severely and chronically disturbed somatization and hypochondriacal patients have benefited from treatment, a majority of the treated patients continued to suffer with significant symptomatology after treatment ended. A meta-analysis of treatments for hypochondriasis found a positive association between length of treatment and outcome, suggesting longer-term treatments may be more potent.

An evaluation of the empirical research on psychosocial treatments for somatization and hypochondriasis suggests that in some respects it mirrors the literature evaluating the efficacy of psychotherapy with generic mental disorders. A number of different focused psychosocial treatments have been shown to be superior to various control conditions, especially waiting list or standard medical treatment. Effect sizes are respectable, relative to other medical or quasi-medical interventions. There is little evidence that one form of treatment is superior to any other. Treatments that are appropriately conceived as forms of cognitive behavioral therapy (CBT) are the most frequently studied, have a creditable record of success, and, by the sheer volume of data, would appear to be the best candidates for designation as empirically supported treatments.

FUTURE RESEARCH

Future research should be directed toward developing treatments that are acceptable and available to all patients with somatization and/or hypochondriacal concerns. Many treatment studies have been conducted in mental health clinics and include only participants who agree to undergo psychotherapy. Future studies should be administered in primary care settings where most of these patients seek treatment. Given that many somatically overfocused patients fail to follow through with mental health referrals, psychotherapy should be integrated into primary care treatment.

KEY REFERENCES

Allen, L. A., Woolfolk, R. L., Escobar, J. I., Gara, M. A., & Hamer, R. M. (2006). Cognitive-behavioral therapy for somatization disorder: A randomized controlled trial. *Archives of Internal Medicine, 166,* 1512–1518.

Taylor, S., & Asmundson, G. J. G. (2004). *Treating health anxiety: A cognitive-behavioral approach.* New York, NY: Guilford Press.

Woolfolk, R. L., & Allen, L. A. (2007). *Treatment of somatization: A cognitive-behavioral approach.* New York, NY: Guilford Press.

Clinician Application

Somatic Disorder

Anthony F. Tasso

COMMENT ON THE EVIDENCE-BASED RECOMMENDATIONS

Research authors Woolfolk and Allen aptly report on the elusory nature of conceptualizing and diagnosing (i.e., *DSM* nosology) somatization or somatoform disorders. In regards to integrating psychological science with clinical practice, this domain of conditions posits a near-herculean task, particularly in determining if the somatic sequelae are psychogenically or constitutionally determined. A specific challenge for researchers and the sine qua non ethos of control is the rapid fluctuations in the symptomatologies of these conditions. A challenge for psychotherapists involves the differential diagnostic process (especially given the breadth of patient profiles with comorbid psychiatric and/or medical pathologies) as well as the considerable frustration both patients and practitioners commonly experience given such individuals' treatment-resistant tendencies (also poignantly noted by Woolfolk and Allen). Although we are only in the embryonic stages of establishing a solid, empirically grounded database identifying etiological factors and interventional effectiveness with somatoform or hypochondriacal patients, the extant scientific and clinical literatures highlight that psychotherapeutic interventions demonstrate, at minimum, a modicum of symptomatic reduction.

CASE EXAMPLE

Subject Information and Brief History

Kevin was a 26-year-old, physically fit single male of mixed Argentinean and Irish descent living at home with his parents and one younger sister. He had some college experience and has been employed in the food and beverage service industry for the past few years.

Presenting Problem

Kevin was referred to psychotherapy by one of his numerous physicians owing to his excessive long-term host of physical ailments and chronic worry about his constitutional well-being. Starting in his early teen years, Kevin reported dealing with a range of both vague and specific physical problems, many of which had an apparently profound impact on his functionality and emotional welfare. For example, he indicated he would sporadically need to take time off from work due to various physical pains, which caused considerable tension with his employer. Kevin also suggested he would experience secondary depression owing to his compromised physical abilities as well as anticipatory anxiety for future physical impairments. For the past 2 years, Kevin stated that his primary physical ailments have been often severe back and neck pain, fluctuating gastrointestinal (GI) problems, and chest discomfort. He had seen numerous traditional medical specialists, chiropractors, as well as non-Western practitioners (e.g., herbalists, acupuncturists). His lengthy stack of medical reports, examinations, and physician notes reveal Kevin to be in excellent physical health and without any identified biomedical etiology accounting for his deluge of somatic symptoms. Rather than being comforted by such feedback, however, Kevin had become increasingly vexed and despondent with the "ineptitude" of his physicians. Medical providers' recommendations for psychological services engendered anger, with Kevin stating such "misguided" suggestions were merely a way for them to protect their professional self-esteem by intimating it is "all in his head." Most recently, Kevin experienced a mild contusion on his forehead and was convinced he was suffering from atypical concussional symptoms. Despite negative medical findings, Kevin was unwavering in his certitude in his diagnosis and also that he was experiencing prodromal amyotrophic lateral sclerosis (ALS) symptoms (his belief based on recent medical investigations suggesting a concussion-ALS link). One of his neurologists again recommended psychological consultation. He reluctantly agreed to see a psychologist, though "only" under the auspice of needing emotional support to cope with his physical limitations and to help him deal with the failures of the medical field.

Treatment Intervention and Course

Psychotherapeutic treatment commenced by gathering detailed information about Kevin's reported host of physical complaints and reviewing his copious reports from different medical providers, all of which ruled out any organic genesis. Following a pithy discussion about the parameters of psychotherapy, mind–body psychoeducation was gently introduced, attempting to disabuse his belief that somatoform conditions are "not real" owing to the fact that mental processes account for a substantial part of the etiological variance. Given Kevin's considerable distress and the fact that it has accelerated over recent months, I recommended twice-weekly sessions. However, Kevin would not concede to more than one session per week. Initially blamed on time constraints, later he confirmed that this was actually owing to his apprehension that receiving "such intense" mental health treatment would be suggestive of an acquiescence that his physical conditions are psychologically caused and thus likely rooted in severe psychopathology.

Psychotherapy began by highlighting Kevin's preoccupation with somatosensory experiences and concomitant anxieties regarding his overall physical health. First, systematic desensitization, exposure, and diaphragmatic breathing strategies were used both within and outside of hypnosis. For example, Kevin was instructed to rank-order his anxiety-provoking somatosensory experiences, beginning with his least fearful (i.e., "simple" aches in "insignificant" areas like his extremities or digits) to moderately fearful (i.e., back and neck pain due to the substantial functional impairment) and finally to his most fear-inducing somatic symptoms (i.e., head, chest, and other visceral pains due to the belief these were suggestive of serious disease of the brain, heart, or other vital organs). Following this step, Kevin was trained to become deeply relaxed and then encouraged to first imagine the somatic ailments that cause the lowest levels of anxiety (e.g., minor hand or foot pain). Once he was able to experience the least fearful with little to no anxiety, we progressed to his more intensely fearful somatosensory discomforts. Such techniques proved to be helpful and resulted in a noticeable decrease in Kevin's symptomatology.

Cognitive restructuring techniques were also successfully employed. Specifically, Kevin's automatic thoughts that any unusual bodily experience is indicative of an underlying biomedical pathology were productively challenged/disputed. These were the predominant interventional techniques used for the first 15 to 18 sessions. Although Kevin experienced an appreciable reduction of his somatic discomfort and proclivities to categorically interpret such somatosensory experiences as indicators of ominous medical problems, his symptoms did not completely nor satisfactorily remit.

The latter phase of treatment consisted of more insight-oriented, psychoanalytic/psychodynamically focused interventions, which aimed to foster awareness into the origins of his health anxieties and inclinations for somatization. What emerged were Kevin's apparent long-standing inabilities to identify and express emotions. Specifically, he mightily struggled to label any type of negative or unpleasant emotional experience beyond calling it "weird" or "annoying." We illuminated that historically his mother was uncomfortable and often dismissive of her children's emotionality, though parenthetically attentive and soothing to physical illnesses and worries circumscribed to the body. Via this delicate psychoanalytic exploration of his earlier developmental experiences, Kevin came to see that in order to get his emotional needs met as a child, he adaptively (and unconsciously) converted distressing emotions into more physical manifestations—something to which his mother was quite focused and dutiful. This latter treatment approach substantially helped Kevin gain insights to how he personally developed somaticizing propensities—providing a personal framework into which our earlier mind–body psychoeducation now fit.

Outcome

Treatment ended following the 28th session owing to Kevin's work promotion to shift-supervisor but at a different restaurant site, which required relocating to a neighboring state. Kevin reported considerable alleviation in his somatic ailments (especially his chronic back and neck pain) and a near complete remission of his attenuated head pain. He stated that although his GI issues persisted, there were more protracted symptom-free intervals and that his GI flare-ups were significantly less debilitating. Furthermore, Kevin reported a marked reduction in his overall health anxiety. He indicated that he was more aware of the inextricable mind–body link and that his penchant for somatosensory preoccupation and elevated health worry is fertile ground for interpreting atypical physical stimulation as denotative of an underlying biomedical disease. Although there was not a complete remission of such anxieties or GI symptoms, both were significantly better than pretreatment levels. Kevin was encouraged to reflect on our work and reassure himself of his clinical gains and that atypical physical sensations do not necessarily equate with disease.

CHALLENGES IN APPLYING THE EVIDENCE-BASED APPROACH

Patients with somatoform conditions frequently present with comorbid diagnoses, including (though not limited to) depression and anxiety as well as characterological and neurological pathologies. Therefore, given that such somatic conditions do not occur in a vacuum, applying "treatment as usual" is not always plausible. When psychiatric or medical conditions are evident, practitioners are tagged with the imperative need to assess the directionality of the somatic symptomatology to determine whether it is a manifestation of an underlying psychiatric disorder, whether it is causing the secondary psychogenic disorder, or whether the conditions are mutually exclusive. Therefore, diagnostic uncertainty and/or overlapping symptoms can stymie the application of scientifically anchored treatment guidelines.

Another obstacle in using the current empirically supported interventions with somatic disorders is when the patient has a "legitimate" identified biomedical condition—something independent of the somatoform symptoms. Such circumstances posit inherent treatment barriers given the likelihood of buttressing patients' probability of looking at their physicality rather than considering psychosocial determinants. This is particularly relevant with more obsessionally organized persons who frequently struggle with emotional expressiveness.

CULTURAL DIVERSITY ISSUES

There is a paucity of empirical data on somatoform and hypochondriacal conditions at-large. Subsequently, there is clearly a need for broad epidemiological data on a range of cultures and geographical demarcations. This would allow clinicians and researchers to craft more ethnoculturally informed therapeutic interventions.

Gender differences are another challenge with somatoform disorders. With the majority of inflicted individuals being women, a thorough examination of the psychological, societal, and/or biochemical differences accounting for gender variations will help elucidate this challenging but treatable condition.

FUTURE RESEARCH

Somaticizing and hypochondriacal patients present with an oft-fierce resistance to treatment that exceeds most psychotherapy scenarios, other than forensic cases. Therefore, concerted systematic research foci via randomized clinical trials (RCTs) and single-case empirical investigations identifying successful clinical techniques to help patients become more receptive to psychotherapeutic treatments would substantially aid in the treatment of somatic conditions given such evidence's ability to preclude premature termination and putatively expedite symptomatic reduction.

An additional area of fruitful research would be on the etiologies of somatoform disorders. Although this is likely on the periphery of treatment, solid programmatic research using multimodal methodologies examining the interplay between biomedical, sociocultural, interpersonal, affective, and cognitive underpinnings of proclivities to somaticize could potentially enhance the effectiveness of early detection and intervention as well as strengthen "later" stages' treatment effectiveness.

KEY REFERENCES

de Greck, M., Scheidt, L., Bolter, A. F., Frommer, J., Ulrich, C., ... Northoff, G. (2011). Multimodal psychodynamic psychotherapy induces normalization of reward related activity in somatoform disorder. *The Word Journal of Biological Psychiatry, 12*(3–4), 296–308.

Moene, F. C., & Roelofs, K. (2008). Hypnosis in the treatment of conversion and somatization disorders. In M. R. Nash & A. Barnier (Eds.), *The Oxford handbook of hypnosis: Theory, research, and practice* (pp. 625–645). Oxford, UK: Oxford University Press.

Stein, D. J., & Muller, J. (2008). Cognitive-affective neuroscience of somatization disorder and functional somatic syndromes: Reconceptualizing the triad of depression-anxiety-somatic symptoms. *CNS Spectrums, 13*(5), 379–384.

CHAPTER 53

Type 1 Diabetes in Youth

Priscilla W. Powell and Clarissa S. Holmes

CLINICAL PROBLEM

A major challenge for families of youth with type 1 diabetes (T1D) is adherence to the complex medical regimen which requires blood glucose monitoring, insulin administration, dietary guidelines, and moderate daily exercise. Adherence to proper diabetes care minimizes daily blood glucose fluctuations and leads to better glycemic control and fewer chronic health complications.

Health care teams are prepared to help families of youth with T1D navigate the medical complexities of diabetes care adherence. However, several psychosocial challenges may emerge that impact adherence such as family conflict, reduced parental involvement in disease care, diabetes-related stress, and difficulties coping with a chronic illness. Such psychosocial challenges are most potent as youth transition into adolescence, a period characterized by independence and autonomy seeking. Diabetes literature demonstrates significant deterioration in disease care adherence during adolescence and a corresponding decline in glycemic control. Given the acute and chronic health consequences, developmentally appropriate intervention strategies that address psychosocial challenges are crucial to help youth prevent deterioration in adherence and glycemic control.

Generally, T1D programs target parent–youth interactions by teaching families skills to improve communication and problem solving, and to reduce diabetes-related family conflict. When translating research-based programs into clinical practice, youths' current diabetes care behaviors may inform selection of the most appropriate treatment approach. The purpose of *prevention* programs is to facilitate adaptive patterns of behavior, relationships, and coping skills to prevent the deterioration of diabetes care, whereas the purpose of *intervention* programs is to modify existing problematic behavioral and psychosocial patterns in disease care.

PREVALENCE

T1D is one of the most common pediatric chronic illnesses, affecting 1 in 400 to 600 youth in the United States. While diabetes adherence and glycemic control are the primary outcomes of existing psychosocial interventions for youth with T1D owing to their significant impact on long-term health, research reports additional clinical issues among this population. Prevalence of depression among youth with T1D is estimated at approximately 15%, nearly twice the rate among general youth, and more common among female adolescents. Further, mothers of youth with T1D, especially those with very young children, report significantly higher levels of depression, anxiety, and parenting stress in comparison to mothers in the general population. Youth with T1D or caregivers with comorbid psychological issues are at risk of decreased adherence to diabetes care and associated declines in glycemic control and potential long-term health consequences.

CULTURAL DIVERSITY ISSUES

Effects of ethnic and socioeconomic diversity are generally unstudied in intervention outcomes. Low cost, low intensity programs (e.g., Family Teamwork, Coping Skills Training) primarily have evaluated Caucasian, upper-middle class, two-parent families, whereas intensive, expensive programs (e.g., Multisystemic Therapy, Behavioral Family Systems Therapy) have evaluated at-risk samples of lower socioeconomic, minority families. Youth from lower social classes and single parent families are at greater risk for poorer diabetes adherence and greater psychosocial problems; consequently, they may derive the most benefit from intensive intervention. Although programs that target high-risk families yield significant treatment effects, these programs are cost intensive and may not be realistic without modification for use in routine clinical care.

EVIDENCE-BASED TREATMENTS

Coping Skills Training (CST) is an evidence-based *prevention* program designed to enhance mastery and competence in diabetes care by helping youth develop positive cognitive and behavioral coping styles. Group-based CST addresses social problem solving, social skills training, cognitive behavioral modification, and conflict resolution. Improved glycemic control is found at 12 months posttreatment along with greater self-efficacy, decreased T1D burden, and increased quality of life in comparison to control groups. While group treatment may reduce cost of delivering care and provide peer support, limitations of typical group treatments are encountered, such as inconsistent participation, scheduling difficulties, and youth who present with a wide range of barriers to diabetes care.

Family Teamwork (FTW) is another *prevention* program that promotes diabetes care adherence by encouraging parental involvement while minimizing parent–youth conflict. FTW yields significant improvements in glycemic control, increased parental involvement, and decreased or stable levels of family conflict up to 24 months posttreatment in comparison to standard care and attention control groups. A second-generation program with integrated components of FTW and CST yields similar effects of stabilized or improved glycemic control and emphasizes the importance of family coping skills to maintain parental involvement while minimizing family conflict. FTW is a brief, low cost, low intensity program that facilitates translation into clinical care. Limitations of FTW include a restricted focus on parent–youth relationships to the relative exclusion of individual youth factors and adherence issues from other systems in a youth's life, such as school or peer-related stressors.

Multisystemic Therapy (MST) is an intensive, community-based *intervention* program that addresses adherence issues on multiple levels including child, family, peer, school, and health systems. MST yields significant increases in blood glucose monitoring in comparison to standard care; however, improvement in adherence is related to better glycemic control only for youth from single-parent families. Over time, MST efficacy also relates to decreased in-patient hospitalization costs among at-risk youth. While MST demonstrates efficacy among at-risk youth, the estimated cost of $6000 per child may be prohibitive for routine clinical care.

Behavioral Family Systems Therapy for Diabetes (BFST-D) is another *intervention* program that targets parent–youth conflict by teaching families to use problem solving, communication skills, cognitive restructuring, and structural family therapy strategies. BFST-D demonstrates efficacy in improving adherence and family conflict among intervention samples of youth in poorer glycemic control. Youth who complete BFST-D maintain improvement in glycemic control longer than youth in educational support or standard care groups. A home-based BFST program for youth in poorer glycemic control also yields significant decreases in diabetes-specific and general family conflict, but no improvement in glycemic control. BFST-D's limitations relate to the feasibility of its implementation in clinical practice. Randomized clinical trials of BFST-D allow scheduling flexibility with home visits and financial compensation for families; routine clinical translation of BFST-D without these accommodations and resources remains to be demonstrated.

Given the importance of parental involvement in youth's diabetes care, most prevention and intervention programs utilize family-based delivery formats. However, limited research suggests Motivational Interviewing (MI) as an emerging individual treatment approach. This patient-centered style of rolling with resistance provides therapists a unique, developmentally appropriate method to work with adolescents who have established patterns of poor adherence. MI intervention yields improvement in glycemic control and psychosocial factors of well-being, quality of life, and personal models of diabetes. However, further research is needed to establish MI as an effective treatment for youth with T1D.

FUTURE RESEARCH

As more funding resources are available for treatment programs that target adherence and glycemic control, general psychological concerns are often not included in intervention studies despite the intertwined nature of psychological issues and adherence to diabetes care. Future intervention trials may address this gap by including youth and parents with psychological disorders in their samples to better inform treatment approaches for a broader population of youth with T1D.

KEY REFERENCES

Anderson, B. J., Brackett, J., Ho, J., & Laffel, M. (1999). An office-based intervention to maintain parent-adolescent teamwork in diabetes management: Impact on parent involvement, family conflict and subsequent glycemic control. *Diabetes Care, 22*, 713–721.

Grey, M., Boland, E. A., Davidson, M., Yu, C., Sullivan-Bolyai, S., & Tamborlane, W. V. (1998). Short-term effects of coping skills training as adjunct to intensive therapy in adolescents. *Diabetes Care, 21*, 902–908.

Wysocki, T., Harris, M. A., Buckloh, L. M., Mertlich, D., Lochrie, A. S., ... White, N. (2006). Effects of behavioral family systems therapy for diabetes on adolescents' family relationships, treatment adherence, and metabolic control. *Journal of Pediatric Psychology, 31*, 928–938.

Type 1 Diabetes in Youth

Kathryn Maher and Melanie K. Bean

COMMENT ON THE EVIDENCE-BASED RECOMMENDATIONS

The evidence-based treatments (EBTs) described by Powell and Holmes outline important strategies to use when intervening with children and adolescents with type 1 diabetes and provide a comprehensive treatment approach for a wide variety of individuals. Importantly, in contrast to the psychological disorders described in this book (i.e., Bulimia, Posttraumatic Stress Disorder [PTSD]), diabetes is a chronic *medical* illness, and, in itself, does not suggest psychopathology. The selection of a specific EBT is thus complicated by the complexity of patients' presenting problems. Specifically, psychologists do not directly treat the illness, but rather the psychological/behavioral disorders or adherence-related difficulties that may arise as a result of or in addition to diabetes. The goals of psychological treatment are thus to improve both psychological functioning and diabetes care.

It is rare for a clinician to have the luxury of implementing a single evidence-based approach in its entirety. Rather, flexibility is needed to address patients' unique presenting problems. Outside of clinical research studies, entire implementation of EBTs is often not possible in the medical setting where mental health professionals are increasingly integrated. In these settings, brief treatment models and consults are often the norm, and current EBTs do not allow for this more acute and brief model of care, although the Family Teamwork approach most closely fits this model. Nevertheless, careful consideration of EBTs when providing clinical care for children and adolescents with type 1 diabetes is critical as they provide the gold standard for effective treatment strategies.

CASE EXAMPLE

Subject Information and Brief History

Sam is a 9-year-old Caucasian female with type 1 diabetes who lives with her parents. The family had recently moved from a different city, representing a change in Sam's school and social network. Sam was referred to the pediatric psychologist by the pediatric endocrinologist in an academic university-based diabetes clinic owing to experiencing abnormal weight loss, decreased glycemic control, and difficulty communicating with her parents about diabetes behaviors.

Presenting Problem

Sam and her mother initiated psychological treatment due to a number of factors. First, Sam was missing insulin doses, with the suspected intent to promote weight loss. In addition, she reported feeling lonely and isolated with her family's recent move to a new city. Sam and her mother began experiencing increased communication problems, including Sam being dishonest about her blood glucose numbers and whether or not she administered her insulin. These difficulties were negatively impacting both her diabetes care and her quality of life. Sam and her mother were interested in addressing both of these factors in treatment.

Treatment Intervention and Course

Sam and her mother attended eight psychotherapy sessions over a 6½-month period. Sessions were divided between Sam individually, and with Sam and her mother together. Treatment predominantly focused on addressing body image concerns, anxiety around diabetes management, improving coping and management of diabetes, increasing family teamwork, and consequently decreasing diabetes conflict (e.g., arguments related to completion of diabetes-related behaviors). EBTs implemented included portions of Coping Skills Training (problem solving and communication) and Family Teamwork (decreasing family conflict and promoting teamwork). In addition, the clinician used Motivational Interviewing throughout treatment to elicit and strengthen Sam's motivation for change. Evidence-based approaches that addressed anxiety and disordered eating concerns were also integrated (e.g., cognitive behavioral therapy) into her treatment. However, none of these approaches was used in their entirety.

Owing to the family's concerns with Sam's weight loss and the suspected eating pathology, the first two treatment sessions addressed Sam's negative body image cognitions and concerns and focused on building her diabetes self-efficacy. These were initially helpful. However, it quickly became apparent that her presenting problem was not disordered eating, but rather generalized anxiety with specific anxiety surrounding diabetes care. This anxiety had contributed to mismanagement of her diabetes, resulting in unintentional weight loss. Further, the family was experiencing parent–child conflict around diabetes management.

Toward that end, the next phase of treatment involved primarily cognitive behavioral therapy, assisting Sam in identifying her maladaptive thinking patterns and ineffective behaviors contributing to her anxiety. Sam was taught appropriate coping skills such as relaxation and problem solving, as well as cognitive restructuring focused on her maladaptive thought patterns regarding her diabetes management. Reducing her anxiety through use of these techniques facilitated Sam's ability to execute diabetes tasks with greater ease.

In addition to continuing to treat Sam's anxiety, the remaining sessions included teaching Sam coping skills to promote adherence to diabetes behaviors, decreasing family conflict, and increasing the transition of developmentally appropriate diabetes responsibilities to Sam. For example, by teaching positive communication, techniques to avoid arguments, and problem-solving skills, Sam and her family learned how to effectively address Sam's dishonesty about her blood glucose numbers. These strategies led to decreased family conflict and increased blood glucose monitoring, both important outcomes related to better diabetes management and quality of life.

Outcome

Sam demonstrated improved adherence to diabetes care with the developmentally appropriate gain of diabetes responsibilities (e.g., cleaning out her meter case, using alcohol swabs, and changing lancets). On occasion, her family continued to exhibit poor communication around diabetes management, which was associated with the patient's dishonesty about high blood glucose levels in order to avoid a negative reaction from her mother. Overall, however, both Sam and her mother reported a significant decrease in dishonesty and an increased ability to engage in problem-solving techniques to address diabetes care challenges. Sam exhibited continued minor generalized worries in several life domains. However she was no longer as "occupied" by cognitions and worries at treatment termination, reflecting Sam's increased control of thoughts and feelings related to anxiety. In addition, Sam's metabolic control, or hemoglobin A1c (HbA1c; the marker of diabetes control), improved. Specifically, Sam's HbA1c was 10.3 at the onset of psychological intervention and decreased to 7.1 at termination. This decline represents a significant and clinically meaningful improvement that may decrease diabetes complications as the Diabetes Control and Complications trial found the risk of long-term disease complications decreases with as little as 1% decrease in HbA1c. Through continued use of strategies learned in the course of psychological treatment, it is expected that Sam's glycemic control will continue to improve.

CHALLENGES IN APPLYING THE EVIDENCE-BASED APPROACH

One challenge in applying the current treatment was addressing both diabetes-related behavioral concerns and Sam's anxiety. As noted in Powell and Holmes, there is a lack of research for adolescents with diabetes and comorbid psychological concerns. Adolescents with psychological disorders such as anxiety may not benefit solely from the diabetes-specific EBTs described. Instead, EBTs for specific psychopathologies (i.e., cognitive behavioral therapy for anxiety) may be more appropriate as adjunctive treatments. As evidenced in Sam's case, treatment may need to initially (or concurrently) focus on the patient's acute psychological problems prior to addressing diabetes-specific issues.

A second challenge worth noting is how to developmentally tailor treatments. Diabetes can occur at any age or developmental period, thus developmental factors must be considered when implementing an EBT. In Sam's case, she was in the preadolescent stage of development and treatment goals were appropriate for her age and level: promoting some independence while maintaining significant family involvement in her diabetes management. However, strategies would differ at other developmental stages. For example, as adolescents transition to young adulthood, most should become independent in their diabetes care. Treatment would thus focus on ensuring patients have the skills and abilities to transition to the adult model of care.

A challenge that clinicians must face with all patients is integrating a transdisciplinary patient care model. Owing to the transdisciplinary nature of diabetes clinics (i.e., diabetes educators, registered dietitians, psychologists, pediatric endocrinologists, and nursing), it is important to collaborate with the treatment team on goals which may result in deviation from a sole evidence-based approach. It is crucial to build on goals set by the rest of the treatment team (i.e., physician) and adapt and reinforce these goals in psychological treatment sessions.

CULTURAL DIVERSITY ISSUES

As mentioned in Powell and Holmes, cultural diversity issues are relatively unstudied in intervention outcomes. Clinically, there are numerous cultural diversity issues to consider with patients with type 1 diabetes. Various factors such as access to health care, knowledge about availability of services, healthy lifestyle options in their neighborhood, and patient–provider communication style are shown to differ between cultural groups (i.e., ethnic and socioeconomic groups) and may impact diabetes care. For example, despite the fact that an intensive insulin regimen is largely recommended by physicians, research indicates that Caucasians are more likely to use an intensive insulin regimen than African Americans and Mexican Americans. In addition, cultural factors may also impact the patient's beliefs about participating in psychological treatment. Cultural factors must, therefore, be assessed and addressed in treatment to ensure engagement and progress. However, it is also important not to generalize patients on the basis of ethnic or cultural factors. Rather, taking a strength-based approach to effectively integrate patient strengths into a treatment plan is essential to providing appropriate care.

FUTURE RESEARCH

Future clinical research examining children and adolescents with diabetes and comorbid psychological concerns is needed. Specifically, studies should examine how to best integrate treatment of common psychopathologies into already established EBTs for type 1 diabetes. In addition, there is a paucity of research examining implementation of EBTs among "emerging adults" with diabetes (i.e., late adolescent/young adult patients transitioning from pediatric to adult providers). These vulnerable patients face unique shifts in health care, relationships, emotions, finances, and living situations that are often not well-addressed in the clinical setting. Owing to a lack of evidence to support strategies for successful transition of emerging adults to adult care, EBTs that address these gaps are needed. Although the quality of EBTs and clinical care has advanced rapidly in recent years, additional research is needed to provide more comprehensive and effective treatments for children and adolescents with type 1 diabetes.

KEY REFERENCES

Barnard, K. D., & Lloyd, C. E. (2012). *Psychology and diabetes care: A practical guide.* New York, NY: Springer.

Leichter, S. B., Dreelin, E., & Moore, S. (2004). Integration of clinical psychology in the comprehensive diabetes team. *Clinical Diabetes, 22,* 129–231.

Snoek, F. J., & Skinner, T. C. (2002). *Psychology in diabetes care* (2nd ed.). West Sussex, UK: Wiley Press.

SECTION IV: SEXUALITY AND RELATIONSHIPS

CHAPTER 54

Dating Anxiety in Adolescents

Rachel L. Grover, Kate M. Esterline, and Douglas W. Nangle

CLINICAL PROBLEM

Dating anxiety refers to anxiety and behavioral inhibition specific to dating situations or to social interactions with potential dating partners. Dating anxiety has cognitive (e.g., worries about rejection from a potential dating partner), physiological (e.g., increased heart rate, sweatiness), and behavioral (e.g., avoidance of dating situations) components. More circumscribed than social anxiety, which refers to anxiety across a range of social situations, dating anxiety is focused specifically on dating situations. Although dating anxiety can occur at all dating-eligible ages, it is particularly relevant during the adolescent years.

The onset of dating represents a key developmental milestone in the lives of adolescents. Their social worlds are rapidly evolving from near same-sex exclusivity in early adolescence to increasingly mixed-sex interactions that are predominant in late adolescence. Increased interaction with the other sex creates the opportunity for the formation of romantic relationships and by mid-adolescence dating is common social practice. Romantic relationships in adolescence serve important developmental functions including opportunities for intimacy, identity development, increase in social standing, experimentation with sex-role behaviors, and sexual activity. Seminal developmental theorists view the successful establishment of romantic relationships as critical to long-term adjustment. In fact, minimal dating and/or dating anxiety are associated with low self-esteem, loneliness, and poorer quality best-friendships.

PREVALENCE

Dating anxiety is common among adolescents with anywhere from 12% to 30% of late adolescents reporting high levels. Studies are mostly confined to college-age adolescents, and some show slightly higher rates in men than in women, but findings are not always separated by gender, or indicative of gender differences. In contrast, a recent study found that college-age women were more likely to report dating anxiety than college-age men.

CULTURAL DIVERSITY ISSUES

Research on dating anxiety to date has most often involved college-age, White, heterosexual men and has focused solely on date initiation behaviors. Studies including women and ethnic and sexual minorities are rare, although there is ongoing discussion about the need for different measures of anxiety that are not specific to heterosexuals, age, or culture. A recent study that compared levels of dating anxiety across gender and ethnicity found that women and ethnic minorities were more likely to report dating anxiety. Research supports that there are cultural differences in the timing of dating onset and the patterns of dating involvement (e.g., how much time is spent in mixed-sex peer groups); therefore, it is possible that prevalence, form, and associated effects of dating anxiety may differ across cultures.

EVIDENCE-BASED TREATMENTS

Treatment of dating anxiety should be preceded by a thorough assessment to aid in identification and differential diagnosis, as well as to help guide and monitor the effectiveness of intervention. The central goal of assessment is to ascertain the severity of the anxiety (i.e., level of distress and avoidance) and the specific situations that engender anxiety (so that they may be the focus of treatment). Measures directly related to adolescent dating anxiety include the Dating Anxiety Scale for Adolescents and the Survey of Heterosexual Interactions (SHI), which assesses anxiety in date initiation situations. As social competence is related to social anxiety, it is also wise to assess competence in dating situations. The Measure of Adolescent Heterosocial Competence (MAHC) assesses competence in a broad range of social situations with other-sex peers and includes several items specific to dating.

Research on treatment of dating anxiety peaked in the 1970s with few articles on the topic published after 1980. The existing literature provides support that anxiety that is specific to date initiation situations can be successfully reduced through therapeutic intervention. Treatments with the most empirical support include systematic desensitization and/or social skills training. In a seminal study, Twentyman and McFall randomly assigned 31 males identified as "shy" based on both self-report and the SHI into a behavioral training group or an assessment-only control group. Behavioral training included modeling and rehearsal with feedback over three training sessions, starting with responses to women's voices over an intercom, and graduating to actual face-to-face interactions with female assistants. Participants were assessed using self-reported anxiety, behavioral diary of interactions with women, pulse rate at designated points in the assessments, incidence of avoidance, and the observations of two raters positioned behind a one-way mirror in the assessment room. Postintervention, participants in the behavioral training group rated themselves and were rated by outside raters as significantly less anxious than the control group. In addition, participants in the behavioral training group reported an increase in interactions with women.

More recent interventions also show promising results, although the samples remain almost exclusively male. Grossman, McNamara, and Dudley found that a self-help manual comprised of relaxation techniques, cognitive reframing, and exposure by way of self-initiated practice dates significantly increased dating frequency and decreased anxiety in heterosexual social situations in a group of dating anxious males. In addition, treatment gains were maintained over 8 months. Foster, Krumboltz, and Ford designed and tested a cognitive behavioral workshop that consisted of normalizing anxiety in dating situations, teaching anxiety reduction techniques, teaching behaviors associated with highly competent daters, and practice of date initiation behaviors. Those in the workshop intervention group obtained higher ratings of social competence at a staged singles function than participants in a practice dating or control group. In addition, workshop participants reported significantly increased social self-efficacy and dating frequency when compared to the control group.

FUTURE RESEARCH

The existing research on the treatment of dating anxiety serves as a strong foundation for future research. As the potential variations in dating practices and anxiety are currently unknown, basic qualitative work with different cultures, ages, and sexual orientations is critical. Second, dating anxiety intervention research needs to include women and ethnic and sexual minority youth. Research with more diverse samples will yield important information on the effectiveness of current interventions as well as aid in the identification of moderators of existing treatments. Third, our current dating anxiety assessments should be normed by gender, culture, and sexual orientation to allow clinicians to make empirically informed decisions on if, when, and how to effectively intervene. Finally, "dating" involves much more than just asking for a date or starting a conversation. Indeed, a focus group study of adolescents revealed that teens reported several challenging situations within a dating relationship (e.g., handling jealousy, discussing commitment, negotiating a sexual relationship) that presumably would also be affected by anxiety. Future research should include measures of dating anxiety in dating situations including and beyond date initiation situations.

KEY REFERENCES

Allen, M., Bourhis, J., Emmers-Sommer, T., & Sahlstein, E. (1998). Reducing dating anxiety: A meta-analysis. *Communication Reports, 11*, 49–55.

Foster, S. L., Krumboltz, J. D., & Ford, M. E. (1997). Teaching social skills to shy single men. *The Family Journal: Counseling and Therapy for Couples and Families, 5*, 37–48. doi: 10.1177/1066480797051005

Twentyman, C. T., & McFall, R. M. (1975). Behavioral training of social skills in shy males. *Journal of Consulting and Clinical Psychology, 43*, 384–395. doi: 10.1037/h0076743

Dating Anxiety in Adolescents

David J. Palmiter, Jr.

COMMENT ON THE EVIDENCE-BASED RECOMMENDATIONS

I find the evidence-based recommendations by Grover, Esterline, and Nangle to be both well grounded in the scientific literature and well conceived and articulated. While some clinicians may need to learn more before deciding that psychometrics designed exclusively for this problem are commonly necessary in order to sufficiently resolve the presenting problems, the Research Section recommends treatment strategies that are both cost-effective and well tolerated by teens and their parents.

CASE EXAMPLE

Subject Information and Brief History

Brandon was a 17-year-old, Caucasian, heterosexual, high-school junior. His parents brought him in for an evaluation because of mounting distress over his academic responsibilities. However, the evaluation determined that Brandon's most salient psychological issues was that he was petrified to approach a girl in pursuit of romance and that he had never done so.

Presenting Problem

Brandon worried excessively throughout the day about a myriad of issues. His parents were concerned that these worries could compromise his performance on his SATs. The evaluation, which consisted of a family interview, an individual interview, behavior rating scales, and a review of school records, suggested a primary diagnosis of Generalized Anxiety Disorder.

An intelligent kid, Brandon had a few good friends and engaged in a couple of extracurricular activities with success. While he experienced anxiety in many social situations, he could usually successfully engage others. The one exception pertained to his dating. Brandon had never engaged in even remote approaches (e.g., using social networking sites) to dating. Brandon's stated reason was a fear of rejection. Though he seemed to have a fair appraisal of his slightly better than average looks and generally pleasing personality, he imagined his odds of rejection to be high.

Treatment Intervention and Course

Cognitive behavioral therapy (CBT) was chosen as the preferred treatment approach with Brandon. The first phase was skill building, with parent consultation. I typically teach between 6 and 10 standard CBT skills in individual sessions (e.g., externalizing the problem, physiological calming, behavioral tracking, behavioral activation, coping thoughts, distraction strategies, thought testing, problem solving, techniques for combating insomnia, mindfulness strategies) sometimes integrating interventions from positive psychology (e.g., gratitude letters, acts of kindness, gratitude lists). Parents are then typically apprised of the techniques in family sessions during the skill-building phase. The second phase was gradated exposure (i.e., making a fear hierarchy and exposing the client to fears in a manner that both is doable and challenging). Treatment plan goals were as follows: worrying no more than 15% of his waking day (estimated to be 95% at intake), asking at least six girls out on a date, or have a girlfriend (whichever came first) and six times intentionally giving the wrong answer in class without fretting about it afterward (the latter is a common exposure I do for kids whose academic perfectionism is a source of discomfort). My default is to review goal progress every 10 sessions, deciding together if we are on track toward meaningful goals, stuck and in need of revision to the approach, somewhat on track but in need of revision to some of the goals, or some combination thereof. It is also natural to review the goals when we transition from the skill building to the exposure phase of the work. Once the goals have been met, we are typically finished, though sometimes, a client will ask me to consider helping him or her with some new goals. The average range for the skill-building phase is 6 to 12 visits. The number of modules I deliver depends upon the motivation of the client and how much I estimate that additional modules would be helpful to him or her. I then take another 6 to 12 visits to complete the exposure phase. Of course, the work can take much longer when the client's motivation is compromised, the symptoms are severe, or there are other complicating factors (e.g., substance abuse).

The first step for Brandon was to "externalize the problem." I introduced this module by quoting Stephen King's line from the introduction to *The Shining*: "The truth is that monsters are real, ghosts are real too. They live inside us, and sometimes they win." Brandon named his internal enemy (the anxiety), "the black mamba." The next step was to introduce a collection of "weapons" for defeating the black mamba. These included progressive muscle relaxation and diaphragmatic breathing, coping thoughts, behavioral activation (because Brandon's lifestyle was morphing into all work and no play), thought testing (i.e., collecting factual evidence that both support and disconfirm the truth of a painful thought, with the former coming first) and problem solving. I also used the emWave biofeedback system to track his ability to calm himself on demand. (This system assesses the state of a person's relaxation by measuring her or his heart rhythm pattern. I find clients engage well with the visual displays and games that are available.) Brandon's parents joined him in a couple of counseling sessions in order to be coached on how to support Brandon's use of the CBT weapons and to not enable the black mamba (e.g., reinforcing or supporting histrionics or avoidance strategies). The parents were also encouraged to do a weekly "special time" exercise to strengthen their bond with Brandon and I shared with them a family-level method for problem solving. Brandon did most of the in-between session work, as did his parents, which facilitated a resolution of his chronic worrying.

Next came the exposure phase. I said something like this: "Okay, the black mamba has mostly stopped attacking you. But, now we need to go where it lives, knock on its door, and call it out for an ass kicking." This served as a prelude for establishing a fear hierarchy that included the other two treatment plan goals and a variety of other situations that Brandon indicated would evoke a black mamba attack (e.g., introducing himself to someone at a party, changing his order at a restaurant). Several things helped to support the exposure of asking out a girl on a date. Brandon was coached in the art of the risk-free flirt, including in-session role-plays (e.g., creating a pretense for a phone call) and in-between session gradated exposures, some of which were done electronically. His father was encouraged to share stories of his own flounderings with female creatures, which I did as well, to normalize Brandon's experience. He was also coached on how to create a date experience that would put less pressure on him (e.g., a group movie date). Physiological calming (i.e., muscle relaxation and diaphragmatic breathing), coping thoughts and thought testing were all used to make Brandon more comfortable with this sequence of exposures (a little bit of problem solving as well when he tried playing the "I have no time to date" card). Several sessions into this phase of the treatment, we worked on finding a suitable candidate for him to ask out. Once a candidate was nominated and a plan formed, I said something like this to him: "Brandon, I really hope Susan will say 'yes.' But, for the purposes of our black mamba work, it would almost be better if she, and the next five girls you ask out, would say 'no' so that you could more quickly realize that a 'no' ain't no thing, that everyone goes through it, that there are a countless number of girls lined up right behind Susan and that the black mamba is a lying liar that tries to make you think that a 'no' is some big mamba drama."

Outcome

He asked out three girls before one accepted his invitation; the first two rejections were handled with equanimity after some thought testing. At the next two booster sessions (6 months apart) he was still enjoying dating the girl who first went out with him. From the intake to the booster phase took 21 visits.

CHALLENGES IN APPLYING THE EVIDENCE-BASED APPROACH

The toughest routine clinical challenge I've encountered with this population is when the teen has not sufficiently developed the psychological muscles for doing things when he or she doesn't feel like it (i.e., employing task persistence when no immediate external reinforcements are available). Sometimes this is attached to a diagnosis (e.g., Oppositional Defiant Disorder [ODD]), but it almost always exists in a family system where parents have not done the difficult work of developing these skills in their child. In these instances, I find adjunctive behaviorally oriented family therapy (and sometimes individual therapy for the parents) is necessary in order to establish sufficient incentives for the teen to do the in-between session work and to cooperate with the exposure sequence. On a different note, I also find that many parents need coaching in age-appropriate monitoring techniques and that many teens need sex education, especially in regards to the significant risk of contracting a sexually transmitted disease. On the latter score, I wish every teen would read the first chapter of Jill Grimes' book (*Seductive Delusions: How Everyday People Catch STDs*) on this topic.

CULTURAL DIVERSITY ISSUES

The most challenging cultural diversity issue I've seen in my practice regards teens with an LGBT orientation. Large portions of our culture still equate less common sexual interest with dysfunction and/or are made anxious by such. Hence, there are issues with educating parents (which is complicated when their religious attitudes conflict with a less conventional sexual orientation) and helping the teen to realize that when we discuss how to be prudent in regard to public displays, that this is not that same thing as implying that her or his interests are troubled.

FUTURE RESEARCH

I would most benefit from research that articulates those family level behavioral interventions that are most successful in augmenting CBT with resistant teens. It would also be helpful to develop evidence-based strategies for teen dating anxiety when it is comorbid with a chronic underlying developmental problem such as Asperger's disorder or compromised intellectual functioning.

KEY REFERENCES

Grimes, J. (2008). *Seductive delusions: How everyday people catch STDs*. Baltimore, MD: The John Hopkins University Press.

Kendall, P. C., Choudhury, M., Hudson, J., & Webb, A. (2002). *"The C.A.T. Project" Workbook for the cognitive behavioral treatment of anxious adolescents*. Ardmore, PA: Workbook Publishing.

Palmiter, D. J. (2007). Child clinician's corner: Externalizing the problem. *The Independent Practitioner, 27,* 142–143.

CHAPTER 55

Hypersexual Disorder

Rory C. Reid and Sheila Garos

CLINICAL PROBLEM

The proposed diagnostic criteria for Hypersexual Disorder (HD) that was considered for the *DSM-5* characterized the phenomenon as a repetitive and intense preoccupation with sexual fantasies, urges, and behaviors, leading to adverse consequences and clinically significant distress or impairment in social, occupational, or other important areas of functioning. Patients seeking help for HD typically experience multiple unsuccessful attempts to control or diminish the amount of time spent engaging in sexual fantasies, urges, and behaviors in response to dysphoric mood states or stressful life events.

Individuals seeking help for HD present with high levels of comorbid psychopathology including mood, anxiety, attention-deficit, and substance-related disorders. Personality characteristics such as boredom proneness, impulsivity and shame, interpersonal sensitivity, alexithymia, loneliness, and low self-esteem have also been observed in association with hypersexual behavior. Although some have suggested that HD may emerge as an attempt to compensate for developmental attachment ruptures or childhood trauma, studies have failed to provide convincing support for this hypothesis.

HD has received increased attention among mental health professionals and researchers in an effort to understand more clearly the etiology, consequences, and associated features of HD, including possible health risks associated with sexually transmitted diseases. In addition to the shame and guilt associated with the disorder, higher rates of divorce exist among couples whose marriages have been adversely affected by a partner's hypersexual behavior.

PREVALENCE

Researchers estimate that 3% to 6% of the general population in the United States suffer from HD; however, no published studies have been cited to support this figure. Like other forms of sexual behavior (e.g., rape, paraphilias), obtaining true estimates of the prevalence of HD is a difficult task owing to underreporting. Moreover, until recently, many allied health professionals were reluctant to classify uncontrolled sexual behavior as a "disorder," and debated about how such behavior should be classified. Nonetheless, existent accounts of HD suggest that although most pronounced in adulthood, a significant portion of adult patients began experiencing problematic sexual behavior during adolescence. Approximately one half of patients seeking help for HD report a chronic and persistent pattern of sexual activity, while the other half report an episodic or cyclical pattern of sexual acting out.

CULTURAL DIVERSITY ISSUES

Studies suggest that men are more likely to develop HD than women. This is particularly true for men who report a homosexual preference. Although studies frequently indicate the majority of individuals who engage in hypersexual behavior are Caucasian heterosexual and homosexual men. However, comparisons of hypersexual men, many of whom are "straight" or bisexual, who have sex with other men reflect more similarities than differences across racial and ethnic groups. It has been hypothesized that gay and bisexual men may be at a greater risk for developing HD given reports of higher levels of lifetime sex partners compared to other social groups. Moreover, gay and bisexual hypersexual men tend to frequent a greater variety of sexual outlets such as bathhouses or sex parties. Among the paucity of studies about HD in adult women, some evidence suggests that childhood sex abuse is more common in hypersexual women than in samples of hypersexual men. Thus, childhood sexual abuse may be a predisposing risk factor in the development of HD in women.

A Swedish study reported prevalence rates of hypersexual behavior in 11.8% of men ($n = 1,279$) and 6.8% of women ($n = 1,171$) on the basis of the frequency of engagement in masturbation, pornography consumption, and sexual infidelity. A nonclinical sample of men ($n = 474$) and women ($n = 466$) in New Zealand were asked to report "out of control" sexual fantasies and urges over a 12-month period. Although 12.7% of men and 6.7% of women reported having uncontrolled sexual fantasies and urges, these rates dropped to only 0.8% and 0.6%, respectively, when actual sexual *behavior* that disrupted daily life was analyzed. Finally, an online study of men ($n = 5,834$) and women ($n = 7,251$) designed to help the researchers investigate differences between sexually dysregulated behavior and high levels of sexual desire found that 1.83% of men and 0.95% of women had significantly elevated scores on the Sexual Compulsivity Scale *and* a history of having sought treatment for sexual compulsivity, addiction, or impulsivity.

EVIDENCE-BASED TREATMENTS

There are numerous self-help materials and workbooks containing anecdotal suggestions for change that have been published to help hypersexual patients. However, the number of rigorous outcome studies assessing the efficacy or effectiveness of treatment interventions in this population is scant. Case studies and nonrandomized open clinical trials have reported successful treatment of hypersexual patients with pharmacotherapeutic interventions such as selective serotonin reuptake inhibitors (SSRIs) or opiate agonists such as naltrexone. Nonmedication strategies suggest a vast array of interventions including cognitive behavior therapy, gestalt therapy, acceptance and commitment therapy, and 12-step programs. It should be pointed out that there is limited empirical support for these approaches at this time. Currently, the preferred treatment appears to include a cognitive behavioral or experiential approach, group psychotherapy, and attendance at a 12-step support meeting, such as Sex Addict Anonymous or Sex and Love Addicts Anonymous. Concurrent pharmacotherapeutic interventions are often introduced to address both comorbid psychopathology and because the sexual side effects produced with many SSRIs (e.g., reduced desire) can be a helpful deterrent to acting out. Recent work suggests that participation in an 8-week Mindfulness Based Stress Reduction program can also help to attenuate symptoms of hypersexuality. Collectively, the goal of these treatments is to arrest hypersexuality and address underlying issues that precipitate or perpetuate problematic sexual behaviors.

FUTURE RESEARCH

Understanding the etiology, prevalence, treatment, and associated characteristics of HD is in its infancy. Important questions about the neurobiological mechanisms underlying HD remain unanswered at the present time. Debates continue as to which theoretical conceptualizations of HD might offer the best explanation (e.g., addiction, compulsivity, impulse-control models, etc.). Findings from the UCLA *DSM-5* Field Trial for HD suggested the proposed criteria can be reliably diagnosed and exhibit some validity with other measures of similar constructs. While the proposed criteria for HD were not included in the *DSM-5* publication, the criteria have the potential to provide a more unified consensus on hypersexual behavior to a fragmented field. As advances continue to be made, investigators might benefit from assessing the body of literature about other nonsubstance related dysfunctional behaviors such as eating disorders or pathological gambling in order to generate hypothesis to guide future research endeavors.

KEY REFERENCES

Carnes, P. J., & Adams, K. M. (2002). *The clinical management of sex addiction*. New York, NY: Brunner-Routledge.

Edwards, W. M. (2011). *Living a life I love: Healing sexual compulsivity, sexual addiction, sexual avoidance, and other sexual concerns* (2nd ed.). CreateSpace.

Maltz, W., & Maltz, L. (2010). *The porn trap. The essential guide to overcoming problems caused by pornography*. New York, NY: Haper Collins.

Clinician Application

Hypersexual Disorder

Joshua N. Hook and Jan Paul Hook

COMMENT ON THE EVIDENCE-BASED RECOMMENDATIONS

Overall, we are encouraged by the increased focus on research examining Hypersexual Disorder (HD). We see the potential for the term Hypersexual Disorder to unite the field, because it can accommodate different theoretical perspectives. We think having specific criteria for HD may clear up some of the misconceptions about the disorder (i.e., it is a way to control or limit a person's sexuality, it is an excuse for men to use who cheat on their spouses, etc.). HD appears to be increasing in prevalence over the last several years, and it is important that it is acknowledged as a disorder.

The research discussing the correlates and disorders comorbid with HD is important. Many clients with HD present with other types of addictions (e.g., alcohol, drugs, food, work, etc.). Many of these clients have been in recovery from alcohol or drugs. Many have been able to achieve sobriety from drugs or alcohol, but continue to struggle with HD. Perhaps part of this disconnect is that the goals for treatment of drug addiction and HD are somewhat different. For drug addiction, often the goal of treatment is complete sobriety. However, for HD, often the goal of treatment is not complete cessation of sexual activity, but rather, attaining a healthy sexuality. We have found it to be common that HD is found in clients who have experienced developmental attachment ruptures or trauma. Clients often struggle to experience intimacy with others, and many of these clients have experienced past traumas. In addition to experiencing traumas such as sexual abuse, many clients were also introduced to sex at a young age (7 or 8), through exposure to pornography.

We agreed with many of the recommendations for treatment. Psychopharmacological treatments are often helpful, especially for clients who also are also depressed or have ADHD. In our experience, group treatment has been the most helpful modality (sometimes clients will attend group and individual treatment concurrently). Group therapy allows clients to work with other individuals to manage problematic sexual behaviors, explore their addictive process, and develop healthy intimacy. We also encourage clients to be involved in 12-step groups. HD needs to be something that clients work on every day.

CASE EXAMPLE

Subject Information and Brief History

Jeff was a 55-year-old, married, White male who had two adult children. He had been married for 30 years. He worked in upper management at a successful business and was currently in the middle of an extramarital affair. Jeff had a history of marital infidelity. After being caught in an extramarital affair 2 years ago, he vowed never to cheat on his wife again. Unfortunately, despite his efforts, Jeff was unable to control his sexual impulses and began another affair soon after the first one had ended. Jeff continued this pattern of affairs until his wife discovered a sexually explicit e-mail on the home computer and confronted him.

Presenting Problem

Jeff presented to counseling at the request of his wife, who had threatened to leave the marriage after discovering this last extramarital affair. Jeff did not want to lose his marriage, so he contacted me (JPH) to set up an appointment. Jeff felt that he was unable to control his sexual urges, fantasies, and behaviors. Especially when he felt down or stressed about his work or family, Jeff would seek out sexual encounters with women to feel better and improve his mood.

Treatment Intervention and Course

Jeff began to attend my interpersonal HD group. The group consisted of eight men, all of who were struggling with HD. The first part of therapy involved Jeff identifying his goals for treatment, and allowing the group to hold him accountable for his target behaviors. Then, in the context of the group, Jeff began to hear other men's stories, and realize that he was not alone in this work. Other men had similar stories. Jeff began to have hope that he might be able to overcome his problems with HD. He began to identify specific events and contexts in his life that triggered his acting out. With the help of the group, he began to identify alternative ways of acting and behaving when these difficult times surfaced. As the group focused on feelings and underlying needs, Jeff also began to identify those underlying issues that were driving him to act out sexually. For Jeff, these needs focused on validation and love, neither of which he received in his family of origin. Jeff was able to get some of these needs of validation and love met by the other men in the group. For example, as he shared his need to be validated, men in the group would validate him (e.g., note the courage it took to share). The group became a laboratory where he could get his needs met and try out new behaviors.

Outcome

Jeff was able to use what he learned in group to help him relate with his wife. He was increasingly able, for example, to share his feelings, identify his needs, and ask for his needs to be met through his marriage. As he began to get these needs met in healthy ways, he was able to decrease and eventually stop his sexual acting out. Over the course of treatment, Jeff did have some "slips" that came in the form of internet pornography and masturbation although he did not have another affair. When he did slip, Jeff informed both the group and his wife. Telling the truth and not hiding was an important factor for his wife's ability to forgive him. Although these slips were not deal-breakers for her, his wife, if Jeff had continued to lie and hide his sexual behaviors, would likely have left the marriage.

CHALLENGES IN APPLYING THE EVIDENCE-BASED APPROACH

One challenge about treating clients with HD is that they often struggle to own and take responsibility for their problem. Clients typically do not come to treatment on their own accord. Rather, they seek treatment because they were caught acting out sexually, and they present to treatment in order to save their marriage or job. One key to effective treatment is helping clients get to the place where they want to change for themselves, irrespective of whether their relationship succeeds or fails. Often clients have to "hit bottom" before they decide to change for themselves. At this point, sometimes their situation or circumstances can be very difficult. A second challenge is that healing often requires reaching out, or being in healthy relationship with others. Often, clients present to treatment having very little experience with healthy attachments in relationships. They may have spent a lifetime attaching to objects such as pornography or other people whom they have treated as objects, rather than attaching to people.

CULTURAL DIVERSITY ISSUES

Most of our clinical experience has been with men who struggle with HD. It does seem that HD is much more common in men than women, although it seems that more women are seeking treatment than in previous years. We see HD in both straight and gay men. Also, some men in our groups identify as straight, but may act out sexually with other men. One aspect of diversity that may play a role in HD is religion. At times, religion can be a protective or helpful factor in recovery from HD, as it provides support and ways to cope with stress. However, some versions of religion can also set up rigid ways of thinking and behaving in clients, which may exacerbate the addictive cycle when clients are unable to maintain their unrealistically high standards for behavior. Because HD often involves a high degree of shame, individuals from cultures who are more shame-based may have more difficulty sharing problems with HD with psychotherapists or with groups.

FUTURE RESEARCH

One area of future research that is pertinent to clinicians is to identify the most effective treatments for HD. Are certain treatments better for treating HD than others? Are certain treatments more or less effective for certain types of clients? Is it helpful to employ 12-step groups as an adjunct to psychotherapy? Questions such as these remain mostly unanswered. We think that perhaps researchers and clinicians could collaborate to design high-quality treatment studies of HD. Finally, most research has focused on the experiences of men. More research must be conducted examining how women experience HD.

KEY REFERENCES

Hook, J. N., Hook, J. P., & Hines, S. (2008). Reach out or act out: Long-term group therapy for sexual addiction. *Sexual Addiction and Compulsivity, 15,* 217–232.

Kafka, M. P. (2010). Hypersexual disorder: A proposed diagnosis for *DSM-V*. *Archives of Sexual Behavior, 39,* 377–400.

Kaplan, M. S., & Krueger, R. B. (2010). Diagnosis, assessment, and treatment of hypersexuality. *Journal of Sex Research, 47,* 181–198.

CHAPTER 56

Infidelity

Donald H. Baucom and Douglas K. Snyder

CLINICAL PROBLEM

Infidelity is the most frequently cited cause of divorce. As such, affairs contribute to the overall effects of relationship breakups, including negative psychological and health effects on partners, as well as increases in psychological difficulties for children. Affairs can be viewed as major relationship betrayals that significantly disrupt spouses' basic beliefs about their relationships, their partners, and themselves. Because affairs violate individuals' basic assumptions about how their relationship and their partner operate, they frequently result in emotional and behavioral symptoms consistent with posttraumatic stress reactions. Based on these clinical observations, conceptualizing affairs as an interpersonally traumatic event provides useful implications for planning effective therapy. Surveys of couple therapists indicate that they regard extramarital affairs as among the most difficult conflicts to treat.

PREVALENCE

Representative community surveys indicate a lifetime prevalence of sexual infidelity of approximately 21% among men and 11% among women. Broadening infidelity to encompass emotional as well as sexual affairs increases these rates among men and women to 44% and 25%, respectively. Approximately 40% of divorced individuals report at least one extramarital sexual contact during their marriage.

CULTURAL DIVERSITY ISSUES

The prevalence rates of infidelity across cultures and subcultures are not clear. More importantly, little is known about differential effects of infidelity across cultures and subcultures. Because affairs appear to have devastating effects by disrupting an individual's assumptions about relationships and their partners, it is important to understand relationship assumptions of a given culture or subculture. Thus, a given subculture might assume that males will have affairs but holds to the standards that females must not. If a woman subscribes to these beliefs, she might not be as severely impacted if her husband has an affair compared to the effects of her having an affair. In most Western cultures, affairs are deemed to be unacceptable for both genders; however, in working clinically with a given couple, it is essential to understand that particular couple's assumptions and standards for fidelity in order to understand the impact of infidelity.

EVIDENCE-BASED TREATMENTS

The authors have developed an integrative approach to working with couples struggling to recover from an extramarital affair. This approach draws on the theoretical and empirical literature regarding traumatic response as well as interpersonal forgiveness. It incorporates empirically supported interventions from both cognitive behavioral and insight-oriented approaches to treating couple distress. This affair-specific intervention is the *only* couple-based intervention designed specifically to address both individual and relationship consequences of infidelity to have been empirically supported in clinical research. The model includes three major stages that parallel the stages involved in the traumatic response. These include: (a) absorbing and addressing the traumatic impact of the affair, (b) constructing meaning for why the affair occurred, and (c) moving forward with one's life within the context of this new understanding.

Stage 1: Addressing the Impact of an Affair

Following disclosure or discovery of an affair, one or both partners may report inability to complete the most basic daily tasks of caring for themselves or their children and may be unable to function effectively outside the home. Intervening effectively with affair couples requires that the therapist establish and maintain an atmosphere of safety and trust by limiting partners' aggressive exchanges within sessions in an empathic but firm way. Stage 1 requires that the therapist implements specific interventions targeting difficulties commonly experienced by partners during the initial recovery phase. These include (a) setting clear and strong boundaries or limits on how partners interact with each other and with persons outside their relationship; (b) promoting essential self-care attending to physical well-being as well as both social and spiritual support; (c) teaching time-out and venting techniques as a way of regulating difficult negative emotions; (d) facilitating emotional expressiveness and empathic listening regarding the impact of the affair, along with offering a rationale for the importance of this process; and (e) helping both partners to recognize and cope with "flashback" phenomenon including intense feelings, images, or recollections of the affair.

Stage 2: Examining Context and Finding Meaning

After addressing the initial impact of the affair in stage 1, the second stage of treatment focuses on helping the couple explore and understand the context of the affair. Specific components comprising stage 2 interventions are designed to promote partners' shared comprehensive understanding or formulation of how the affair came about. This process includes guiding the partners in examining aspects of their relationship, stresses from outside the marriage, and issues specific to each of the partners for their potential role as predisposing or precipitating influences leading up to the affair, factors that influenced the maintenance of the affair and eventual discovery or disclosure, and influences bearing on partners' subsequent responses or recovery.

After examining potential contributing factors across diverse domains, the therapist helps the couple to integrate the disparate pieces of information they have gleaned into a coherent narrative explaining how the affair came about. Achieving a shared understanding of why the affair occurred is central to partners' developing a new set of assumptions about themselves, each other, and their relationship. Upon constructing a shared narrative of the affair, the couple can then examine what aspects of their relationship may need additional attention and how this can be accomplished in order to help them avoid future betrayals.

Stage 3: Moving On

In order to move forward, the couple needs to achieve three goals by the end of this third stage: (a) develop a realistic and balanced view of their relationship, (b) experience a release from being dominated by negative affect about the event, and for the injured partner to relinquish voluntarily one's right to punish the participating partner, and (c) carefully evaluate their relationship and reach healthy decisions about moving on separately or together. Treatment strategies in stage 3 initially emphasize helping partners examine their personal beliefs about forgiveness and how these relate to their efforts to move on from the affair. Additional interventions facilitate partners' integration of what they have learned about themselves and their relationship—well beyond the affair—to reach an informed decision about whether to continue in their relationship or move on separately. For couples deciding to move on together, interventions emphasize changes partners will need to undertake either individually or conjointly to strengthen their relationship and reduce the risk of future affairs. If either partner decides to end the relationship, the couple will need assistance to help them implement that decision in ways that are least hurtful to themselves and others they love—including other family members and friends.

Preliminary evidence for the efficacy of this treatment approach rests upon a replicated case study of couples recovering from infidelity. The majority of injured partners entering this treatment initially showed significantly elevated levels of depression and symptoms consistent with a Posttraumatic Stress Disorder. Concern with emotional regulation and struggles to understand their betrayal dominated. Relationship distress was severe; feelings of commitment, trust, and empathy were low. By termination, injured partners demonstrated gains in each of these areas. Treatment effect sizes were moderate to large and approached average effect sizes for efficacious couple therapies not specifically targeting couples struggling from an affair. When describing the impact of treatment, participating partners expressed that treatment was critical to (a) understanding their own affair behavior in a manner that reduced likely recurrence, (b) tolerating their injured partners' negativity, (c) collaborating with their partners in an uncomfortable process of examining factors contributing to the affair, and (d) deferring their own needs for immediate forgiveness until a more comprehensive process had been completed.

FUTURE RESEARCH

While the initial findings from this open trial are encouraging, additional treatment studies including a randomized controlled trial will be important, perhaps comparing the current intervention with a broad-based couple therapy that is not targeted to infidelity itself. Likewise, understanding the efficacy of the intervention across cultures and with various groups who have different standards for fidelity will be essential.

KEY REFERENCES

Baucom, D. H., Snyder, D. K., & Gordon, K. C. (2009). *Helping couples get past the affair*. New York, NY: Guilford Press.

Gordon, K. C., Baucom, D. H., & Snyder, D. K. (2004). An integrative intervention for promoting recovery from extramarital affairs. *Journal of Marital and Family Therapy, 30*, 213–231.

Snyder, D. K., Baucom, D. H., & Gordon, K. C. (2008). Treating infidelity: An integrative approach to resolving trauma and promoting forgiveness. In P. R. Peluso (Ed.), *In love's debris: A practitioner's guide to addressing infidelity in couples therapy* (pp. 95–125). New York, NY: Routledge.

Clinician Application

Infidelity

Brian V. Abbott

COMMENT ON THE EVIDENCE-BASED RECOMMENDATIONS

Although there is a growing literature regarding theoretical and conceptual processes inherent to forgiveness and infidelity, the approach offered by Baucom and Snyder in this book represents a unique contribution to the literature in that it offers a specific roadmap for treatment. Affairs have the effect of unearthing every painful issue that a couple has previously laid to rest in their relationship as well as resurrecting raw emotions associated with attachment injuries in previous relationships. Consequently, affair couples often present with a dizzying array of emotions and complaints that can be overwhelming to both the clinician and the couple. Having a clear structure for the treatment of infidelity not only reassures the couple in crisis, but also calms the clinician and bolsters his or her confidence. Clinicians will find that the utility of this approach lies in understanding what types of issues are most likely to be successfully resolved during each phase of treatment. Affair couples readily grasp the rationale underlying the approach and thus are typically willing to invest in a more thorough and systematic healing process. Clinicians interested in utilizing this approach should consult *Helping Couples Get Past the Affair*. It contains a wealth of useful information about each stage of treatment and a more nuanced discussion about different types of affairs.

CASE EXAMPLE

Subject Information and Brief History

Sarah and Jim, both in their early 30s, had been married for 8 years. After 2 years of unsuccessful fertility treatments, the couple was considering adoption as an alternative. In describing their courtship, Sarah reported that she was attracted to Jim's easygoing affable manner. In contrast to the abuse she experienced as a child, Jim made her feel extremely safe. Jim reported that he was attracted to Sarah's outgoing personality, her drive, and her quick wit. The couple also shared a strong bond through their spiritual and religious beliefs.

Presenting Problem

Sarah was devastated when Jim unexpectedly confessed that he had been carrying on an affair with one of their mutual friends for 3 months. He was deeply remorseful and said that he could not live with a guilty conscience any longer. He explained that the infidelity began when they invited their friend, Katie, to stay with them over the Labor Day weekend. Katie was going through a difficult divorce at the time and Jim had intended to provide a sympathetic ear. Instead, their conversations became very personal and Jim disclosed some thoughts, feelings, and needs that he had never discussed with anyone before. Although they did not have intercourse, he admitted to having several brief sexual encounters with Katie. Even during this short period of time, Jim's feelings for Katie became so compelling that he briefly considered leaving his marriage in order to be with her. Despite his strong feelings for Katie, he recognized that Sarah had always been committed to him and he did not feel ready to give up on his marriage.

Sarah was stunned. It was the last thing she expected—two of her closest friends having an affair. How could either one of them betray her in this manner? She had always trusted Jim explicitly; he was the one person who would never hurt her. Sarah was overwhelmed and confused by the torrent of conflicting emotions that ensued. One minute she never wanted to see Jim again and next minute they were having the best sex of their marriage. She longed for reassurance from Jim, but felt angry with herself if she allowed him to get too close. Sometimes she felt numb, but more often she felt anxious. She found herself doubting basic assumptions about life, relationships, and people. Simultaneously, Jim was trying to make sense of his own feelings and behavior. He was genuinely confused about how he could do something that was so contrary to his espoused beliefs. Although he had ended the relationship with Katie, he felt ashamed that he continued to have lingering feelings of affection for her.

Treatment Intervention and Course

Treatment proceeded consistent with the three stages of treatment described by Baucom and Snyder: (a) absorbing and addressing the traumatic impact of the affair, (b) constructing meaning for why the affair occurred, and (c) moving forward with one's life within the context of this new understanding. Because the couple was experiencing a high level of acute distress, therapy initially focused on helping them get through each day without doing unnecessary damage to their relationship. Both partners were unsure how to respond to Sarah's overwhelming and constantly fluctuating emotions. It seemed like her every waking thought was consumed with the affair. She wanted to talk about it constantly, but usually felt worse when she did. The couple found it enormously helpful to understand that Sarah was experiencing many Posttraumatic Stress Disorder (PTSD)-like symptoms (e.g., repetitive intrusive thoughts about the affair, efforts to avoid affair-related stimuli, emotionally numbing, and arousal symptoms such as irritability and difficulty sleeping) that are frequently experienced in the aftermath of an affair. Normalizing her experience enabled her to be less reactive to any particular emotion that she might be experiencing. She was encouraged to attend to her emotions and label her experience without allowing any particular emotion to define the relationship, herself, or her partner. For instance, Sarah could talk about "hating Jim," while at the same time recognizing that such feelings do not define or accurately reflect the entirety of their 8-year relationship. Understanding the depth of Sarah's traumatization helped Jim to be less reactive and more empathic toward Sarah. The couple elected to reserve in-depth discussion of the affair for therapy sessions. These early interventions enabled the couple to resume some of their daily routines and opened the door for them to spend more positive time together. Another source of considerable stress during the initial phase of treatment was how the couple should communicate with their close friends and family about what was happening. Ultimately, the couple opted to take a more private stance in relation to their larger social system, choosing to share limited information with loved ones.

As the couple regained a sense of order and predictability in their relationship, they began to explore contextual factors that may have made their relationship more vulnerable to an affair. Jim made this exploration more palatable by accepting full responsibility for his hurtful behavior. During this phase of therapy it became clear that Jim had lived his entire life avoiding conflict at all costs. As a child he learned how to tell people what they wanted to hear as a way to avoid punishment, even if this meant suppressing his own thoughts and feelings. He gradually became disconnected from his own emotions. The pattern continued into adulthood. Although he rarely had conflict in his relationships and was typically well liked by others, he did not feel close to people. He realized that he had been doing the same thing with his wife. Sarah explained that she never felt "good enough" in her family of origin. Her family environment was chaotic and unpredictable. She felt "invisible" to her parents.

The couple identified a pattern within their marriage in which Sarah experienced Jim's silence and tendency to acquiesce as an indication that she was not "good enough" for him either, that he did not love her as much as she loved him. She tried to be the "perfect wife" so that he would love her more. However, when her efforts were not recognized, she would become sarcastic and critical, prompting Jim to become even more passive and withdrawn, resulting in a vicious cycle. They agreed that they were unintentionally recreating many of the painful emotions they had experienced as children. Ongoing fertility treatments and several unsuccessful pregnancies had further strained the couple's interactions. The couple's shared formulation about how the affair occurred was transformative. Not only did it help the couple to begin to move past the affair, but it fundamentally altered the way that each partner perceived themselves and each other in the relationship, triggering a cascade of behavioral changes pertaining to communication, expression of emotion, and conflict resolution.

Outcome

The final stage of treatment (moving on) did not happen overnight, but came as a natural extension of the couple's fresh understanding of their relationship. Trust returned gradually. As Sarah observed Jim's efforts to be more emotionally present and invested in their relationship, her confidence grew. She responded with more acceptance and less criticism, prompting Jim to be even more self-disclosing. The focus of therapy naturally shifted from the affair to current processes in the relationship. With a more balanced view of their relationship, the couple began to seriously consider their future together. Initially, the couple opted to stay together largely out of anxiety and uncertainty. However, during the final stage of therapy, the couple's willingness to commit to their relationship, even with an understanding of its limitations, became a sign of their deep love for each other. Sometimes, Sarah would still feel the pain of the affair, but instead of attacking Jim she would seek his comfort and he would provide the desired reassurance.

CHALLENGES IN APPLYING THE EVIDENCE-BASED APPROACH

Each stage of the treatment model presents unique challenges. In the immediate aftermath of an affair, there can be a strong push for partners to justify their behavior, to make binding decisions about the relationship, and to "forgive" before they are prepared to do so. Consequently, the primary challenge during the first stage of treatment is to help the couple to commit to a longer-term therapeutic process that will ultimately provide them more of the answers they are seeking. The second stage of treatment is focused on developing a coherent narrative explaining how the affair occurred. Balancing the need to hold the participating partner accountable for their behavior while at the same time not ignoring key contextual variables can be complicated. It is therefore essential that the psychotherapist remain attuned to the injured partner's feelings in this regard, to discuss ruptures in the therapeutic relationship as soon as they occur, and to validate each partner's experience. The primary challenge during the third stage of treatment is overcoming problematic or unrealistic beliefs surrounding the concept of forgiveness (e.g., that one must forget to forgive, that one should not continue to feel anger if one has forgiven, that forgiveness is the same as excusing hurtful behavior, that one must continue the relationship if one forgives, and that forgiving makes a person weak).

CULTURAL DIVERSITY ISSUES

The emotional trauma produced by an affair is the result of a complex interplay between the nature of the actual offense and the context in which it occurs. Psychotherapists who fail to attend to issues of culture and diversity will be prone to overestimating or underestimating the traumatic impact of infidelity. It is essential that clinicians spend the time necessary to educate themselves regarding issues of religion, ethnic background, gender roles, and sexual orientation with the couple acting as their guide. Men and women may view various types of infidelity (e.g., emotional, sexual, online) quite differently. It is equally important that clinicians maintain awareness of how their own cultural background may be influencing their understanding of each case.

FUTURE RESEARCH

There are far more questions than answers when it comes to our understanding of infidelity. The following represent just a few important questions that could be addressed by future research: Which relationship/personality variables are most predictive of subsequent affairs? Are there certain types of affairs that are more or less traumatic? What are the most crucial "active ingredients" of effective treatments (e.g., crisis containment, exploring contextual variables, or forgiveness)?

KEY REFERENCES

Baucom, D. H., Snyder, D. K., & Gordon, K. C. (2009). *Helping couples get past the affair*. New York, NY: Guilford Press.

Snyder, D. K., Baucom, D. H., & Gordon, K. C. (2007). *Getting past the affair: A program to help you cope, heal, and move on – together or apart*. New York, NY: Guilford Press.

Spring, J. A. (1997). *After the affair: Healing the pain and rebuilding trust when a partner has been unfaithful*. New York, NY: HarperCollins.

CHAPTER 57

Inhibited Sexual Desire in Women

Andrea Bradford

CLINICAL PROBLEM

Hypoactive Sexual Desire Disorder (HSDD), formerly termed inhibited sexual desire, is defined by a chronic low level or absence of sexual thoughts, sexual fantasies, or desires for sexual activity causing marked distress or interpersonal difficulty. This latter aspect of the definition is important, as the prevalence of HSDD is inflated dramatically when distress is not taken into account.

In both sexes, sexual desire tends to decline through middle and older age, although this is not necessarily accompanied by distress. HSDD is frequently acquired but may be lifelong, in which case it is important to differentiate from a sexual aversion disorder or an asexual orientation. The disorder may be primary, or it may be secondary to another sexual dysfunction, a mood or anxiety disorder, the effects of substances, or a general medical condition.

PREVALENCE

Low sexual desire and HSDD represent the most common type of sexual complaint in women. Although prevalence estimates vary considerably, recent studies suggest that the prevalence of HSDD is approximately 10% to 20% in women and appears to peak in midlife. Prevalence estimates for male HSDD are more variable, although studies suggest this figure to be in the single digits.

CULTURAL DIVERSITY ISSUES

Cultural practices and mores have a strong, if not paramount, influence on sexual expression. Cultural, social, and religious characteristics of particular interest include patriarchal value systems, reproductive health policies and customs, and population histories of oppression and marginalization. For any given individual, these and other characteristics intersect to influence one's sexual attitudes and identity. However, some broad patterns are worthy of mention. Not surprisingly, gender differences in sexual attitudes and behaviors are smaller in nations that are characterized as having greater gender equality, and this is often a function of more permissive attitudes and behaviors among women. There appear to be ethnic differences in the prevalence of low sexual desire and HSDD, with relatively high rates among women who identify ethnically as East Asian. While some studies suggest no greater prevalence of low sexual desire among women in same-sex partnerships, others identify internalized homophobia as a risk factor unique to lesbians and bisexual women.

EVIDENCE-BASED TREATMENTS

Research on psychological interventions for HSDD is limited and focused almost exclusively on women. The limited data available suggest that treatment outcomes tend to be poorer in men with HSDD than in women. Male HSDD is thought to be an underrecognized yet distinct clinical entity that is not necessarily a reaction to erectile dysfunction, mood disturbance, or hypogonadism. Thus, although the psychological treatment approaches described in this chapter may generalize to men, they should be interpreted in light of these knowledge gaps.

Interventions for HSDD are generally oriented toward the acquired/situational type and focus on modifying precipitating or contributing circumstances or behaviors. Sex therapy, cognitive behavioral therapy (CBT), and relationship/marital therapy are the major treatment approaches represented in the empirical literature. However, the nonempirical literature contains rich descriptions of other treatment philosophies. Although the past decade has seen a surge of interest in pharmacologic treatment of HSDD in women, the current evidence does not support pharmacologic management as a first-line treatment.

Sex Therapy

Traditional sex therapy is a behavioral treatment that aims to facilitate the client's engagement in erotic experiences while reducing anxiety and concern about sexual performance. Masters and Johnson's original sex therapy program was delivered by opposite-sex cotherapists to couples in a brief but intensive format. Their methods have since been adapted to more conventional formats (e.g., individual, group, and self-help). Important treatment components include sexuality education, partner communication skills training, and sensate focus. Sensate focus is a core component of behavioral sex therapy and consists of a progressive series of exercises between partners (assigned as homework) to enhance partners' awareness of pleasurable experiences and their own preferences for sexual touch while reducing anxiety through graded exposure. Sex therapy is modestly effective in treating clients with low sexual desire and compliance with behavioral exercises appears to be an important mediator of treatment outcome in this population.

Cognitive Behavioral Therapy

Sex therapy has been increasingly conceptualized within broader theoretical frameworks, most notably CBT. Cognitive-behavioral sex therapy incorporates behavioral sex therapy components but places greater emphasis on modifying thought patterns or beliefs that undermine intimacy and sexual enjoyment. For example, common maladaptive beliefs include exaggerated fears of abandonment, cultural myths about "normal" sex, and negative comparisons of one's own sexual attributes to those of others. These beliefs are modifiable with the use of cognitive restructuring. In one study, 12 sessions of group CBT significantly improved sexual function in women with HSDD, with 74% of participants no longer meeting criteria for HSDD posttreatment; 64% remaining improved at 1 year posttreatment. However, another trial of CBT, delivered largely in an individual format, failed to resolve low sexual desire for most participants. Another study found that CBT enhanced with sexual skills training focused on improving orgasmic function resulted in significant improvement in sexual desire in women with HSDD, particularly when delivered to couples. More recently, "third wave" CBT components, such as mindfulness training, have shown some efficacy in improving sexual dysfunction in women, though not specifically those with HSDD.

Relationship Therapy

Marital/couple therapy is indicated when assessment reveals evidence of clinically significant interpersonal conflict. Relational distress may be an important etiologic factor in reduced sexual desire or a consequence thereof. Prefacing sex therapy with marital therapy appears to improve outcomes. Marital therapy alone has limited efficacy for improving sexual desire and, at present, should be considered adjunctive to the sex therapy approaches described. Sex therapies informed by systems conceptualizations have gained prominence in the clinical literature but as yet have had little empirical examination.

FUTURE RESEARCH

HSDD represents a persistent and distressing extreme of typical variations in sexual desire over the course of the life span. Although this is a relatively common presenting problem, there are few high quality empirical studies to inform best practices in the treatment of HSDD. Furthermore, treatment outcome studies represent relatively few men with HSDD and overwhelmingly represent White, heterosexual, middle-class clients. At present, most experts advocate for an integrative approach to treatment. Future research should focus on identifying effective treatment components of existing interventions, evaluating the efficacy of systemic therapy approaches, tailoring therapies to the needs of men, ethnic minority, and sexual minority clients, and disseminating best practices to a broader range of clinicians.

KEY REFERENCES

Basson, R., Brotto, L. A., Laan, E., Redmond, G., & Utian, W. H. (2005). Assessment and management of women's sexual dysfunctions: Problematic desire and arousal. *Journal of Sexual Medicine, 2*, 291–300.
Leiblum, S. R. (Ed.). (2010). *Treating sexual desire disorders: A clinical casebook.* New York, NY: Guilford Press.
Masters, W. H., & Johnson, V. E. (1970). *Human sexual inadequacy.* Boston, MA: Little, Brown.

Inhibited Sexual Desire in Women

Lori Schwartz

COMMENT ON THE EVIDENCE-BASED RECOMMENDATIONS

Desire problems among men and women are the most common reason for referral in sex therapy. This is the case compared to other sexual complaints such as pain disorders, anorgasmia, premature orgasm, and erectile dysfunction. Specifically, desire problems are experienced by clinicians as difficult to treat owing to the lack of clarity in definition. Agreement on the frequency of sex, the pattern of sexual behaviors, and the difference between subjective and objective arousal desire are difficult to define. The different etiologies and the lack of sound outcome studies also make desire problems challenging to treat. Sex therapy patients can benefit from identification of the change process and validation of their experience. Helping patients to perceive self-efficaciousness in their change process is critical and focusing on their competencies is impactful in the process of change. Similar to other therapies, relationship factors between the clinician and the patient are critical in promoting behavior change. Small, identifiable treatment goals, which the patient perceives as desirable and attainable, can influence behavioral change. Improving and highlighting aspects of personal control, such as internal locus of control, is another salient task in the treatment of Hypoactive Sexual Desire Disorder (HSDD).

CASE EXAMPLE

Subject Information and Brief History

Susan is a 30-year-old married, Caucasian female who is employed as a nurse at a hospital in a Midwestern city. She presents with a history of sexual desire concerns that began early in her marriage. The desire symptoms presented initially about 2 years after the marriage. She has sought treatment along with her husband in an effort to address these concerns.

Presenting Problem

Susan and her husband Jeremy presented at the initial interview because her husband complained that their sex life was unsatisfactory. He indicated Susan seemed disinterested in having intercourse with him. Both Susan and Jeremy perceived that

Susan had become increasingly sexually distant from him in their marriage of 5 years and this had become more apparent since having two young children in the last 3 years. More recently, he noticed a decrease in affection or physical contact and she admitted to this distance because this could "send him the wrong signal." Susan admitted that she would feel comfortable avoiding intercourse altogether in the future but feels guilty to admit this and she reported feeling no desire to be sexual either in partnered or masturbatory experiences. However, once she and Jeremy have intercourse, they both find the experience satisfactory. She exhibits occasional situational orgasms with vibrator stimulation, but notes that Jeremy feels distressed about this and she believes he would rather her not use her vibrator. Susan indicates that her onset of sexual desire problems began following her marriage, and reports there was a sporadically active sexual activity level during her courtship with Jeremy.

Treatment Intervention and Course

Initially, data were gathered from both partners regarding their sexual histories. Interventions such as cognitive framing were initiated relating to the cognitive distortions exhibited by both Susan and Jeremy. For example, Jeremy held the belief that most women if they were aroused properly would be able to orgasm through penetration. Susan did not exhibit multiple orgasms prior to marriage but Jeremy believed this would change for Susan with "practice." This had been his earlier sexual experience with other partners and he believed his prior partners to have had multiple orgasms primarily through penetration. In addition, Jeremy believed that Susan was behaving in this fashion because she found him unattractive. Susan believed that intercourse should be a pinnacle experience of intimacy involving emotional connection and bonding. She felt Jeremy was only interested in his own orgasm although she had always felt pressure to have an orgasm each time they had intercourse. She also felt that she couldn't "live up" to Jeremy's expectations and experience with past partners but felt responsible for providing him a "sexual outlet." She believed that men in general needed "a release."

Consistent with models on sex therapy, the first several sessions were used to provide information about normal male and female sexual functioning. Data about female orgasm frequency and its relationship to penetrative intercourse were discussed. Moreover, in the next sessions a discussion regarding the role of responsibility for pleasure was undertaken. Also, at that time, a referral was made for Susan to participate in a medical examination with her gynecologist in an effort to rule out a biological basis for her low desire. Data were gathered to discover any substance use or medications which could be contributory factors to the couple's problems. Neither Susan nor Jeremy used any medications and Susan had not resumed using oral contraceptives since the birth of their last child, 2 years ago. Instead, the couple was using condoms because Susan wondered if her oral contraceptives contributed to her low desire.

During the next session, the couple was instructed on the concepts of nondemand sensate focus exercises to learn more about sensual touch. A plan was constructed to begin these exercises with Susan initiating the touching role and Jeremy initiating with the role of being touched. After completion of this exercise, they were instructed to reverse touching roles. Instructions included avoidance of genitals. Repeated instructions were suggested for the couple to practice on the goal of learning about their partner's body and a reminder that the goal is not to arouse or stimulate the person being touched. The person being touched was instructed to maintain a quiet stance unless he or she was experiencing physical pain and then they would be allowed to redirect their partner to alter the touch with a simple directive. The process of sensate focus exercises was graduated across the course of 12 sessions to eventually include touching of breasts and chest areas and ultimately genitals, with the continued focus on the experience of the person engaging in the touching. Throughout the course of treatment, continued psychoeducational techniques were employed, such as clarifying patterns of female orgasm, optimizing communication techniques, and exploring methods to increase pleasure.

Outcome

After 12 sessions, Susan and Jeremy reported improvements in several areas of functioning. These areas included improved understanding of the sexual pleasure options, and they reported having learned about their desired sexual patterns. They also reformulated some of their perceptions about the role of responsibility in pleasure and were able to more effectively communicate. Negotiation patterns improved, even if Susan remained less interested in intercourse than Jeremy.

CHALLENGES IN APPLYING THE EVIDENCE-BASED APPROACH

Several keys challenges exist to evidence-based treatment approaches for low desire. Although the higher desire partner may be motivated to effect a change in the relationship, the lower desire partner may desire only to prevent the disruption of the relationship or to prevent what he or she believes will be an onset of infidelity in the partner. The question to be addressed is what is the motivation for change in the patterns of sexual desire? In addition, both parties may fear a change in patterns. Even though the couple, particularly the high desire partner, states a desire for change, both parties may harbor covert fears about change. Examples of these fears are a change in familiar patterns as well as fears about the change in desire impacting identity. Moreover, some patients struggle with allowing for heightened desire because it could produce a change in self-perception. Higher desire partners may sustain covert fears that heightened desire in their once low desire partners may prompt infidelity or a change in the power dynamic in the couple. Higher desire partners at times can exhibit demanding or critical patterns, while lower desire partners can exhibit passive negativity. Changes in these dynamics can produce novel challenges for the couple.

In addition, another challenge to treatment is that underlying problems can be present that manifest as symptoms of low desire. This could include problems related to attraction between partners, past secrets replete with guilt or shame, or sexual orientation dynamics. Other diagnostic concerns, such as depression, anxiety disorders, or posttraumatic stress disorder can present obstacles to the treatment of HSDD in women and should be assessed as possible contributory factors.

CULTURAL DIVERSITY ISSUES

Hypoactive desire disorder is more common in women, and particularly younger women compared to men. For men, the prevalence increases with age. In reports by clinicians in the practice of sex therapy, men with HSDD are seen nearly as equally as women, but because of cultural, social, and gender role expectations for male sexual prowess, male HSDD may be underreported. In addition, women living with men with HSDD are more complacent with a problem they may find embarrassing or confusing, and therefore therapy is often not pursued. Particular populations have a higher incidence of HSDD such as those diagnosed with HIV. Individuals with a history of orthodox religious beliefs, individuals struggling with infertility, and individuals with a history of multiple incidents of sexual abuse also are at risk for low desire.

FUTURE RESEARCH

The most salient aspect for future research involves the definition of desire disorder. There are varied definitions and theoretical models which inhibit the prospect of developing adequate assessment measures. Understanding how hypoactive desire disorders are unique from other sexual dysfunctions will be an important direction.

Specific techniques to enhance interest in sex have not been fully investigated. A critical area of research includes the role of biological and hormonal influences on desire. The role of these agents for women are particularly complex and, at this time, no pharmacological agents exist for the treatment of desire, although they do exist for the treatment of male arousal disorder. In addition, the role of promising, alternative therapies such as bibliotherapy should be investigated. These combined efforts would assist in defining and treating HSDD in women.

KEY REFERENCES

Beck, J. G. (1995). Hypoactive sexual desire disorder: An overview. *Journal of Counseling and Clinical Psychology, 63*, 919–927.

Donahey, K. M., & Miller, S. D. (2001). "What works" in sex therapy: A common factor alternatives. In P. J. Kleinplatz (Ed.), *New directions in sex therapy innovations and alternatives* (pp. 210–232). Philadelphia, PA: Brunner Routledge.

Pridal, C. G., & LoPiccolo, J. (2000). Multielement treatment of desire disorders: Integration of cognitive, behavioral, and systemic therapy. In S. R. Leiblum & R. C. Rosen (Eds.), *Principles and practice of sex therapy* (pp. 57–81). New York, NY: Guilford Press.

CHAPTER 58

Sexual Dysfunction in Males

Donald S. Strassberg and Michael A. Perelman

CLINICAL PROBLEM

Male sexual dysfunctions (MSD) is a generic term describing a variety of different conditions, which impair motivation and/or capacity to achieve sexual satisfaction. MSDs are challenging to the clinicians who treat them, and by definition are distressing to the men experiencing them and/or their partners. These all too common disorders can be best understood as disruptions of the desire, arousal, and orgasm phases of the male sexual response cycle. There are numerous medical/biological and psychosocial/behavioral factors that are frequently implicated in the etiology of these disorders, and awareness of them improves treatment planning.

MSDs may manifest differently both between and within given individuals. The sexual difficulty may be lifelong (primary) or acquired (secondary) after a period of normal functioning. They can occur in every sexual encounter with every partner (generalized), or they may be intermittent or situational. MSDs may also vary as a function of the specific sexual activity, for example, difficulty during intercourse, but not with masturbation. MSDs severity can be characterized as mild to severe, but clinically this may vary for a given man as a result of dynamic changes in any medical/biological and/or psychosocial/behavioral or cultural vectors. Medical/biological factors that can cause, maintain, or exacerbate an MSD are numerous and varied. Reliable and satisfying sex depends on adequate functioning of the anatomical, neurological, hormonal, and cardiovascular systems. Therefore, any medical condition (e.g., multiple sclerosis, diabetes, atherosclerosis, etc.), treatment (e.g., prostatectomy, dialysis, etc.), or drug (e.g., antidepressants, anxiolytics, alcohol, etc.) that compromises the functioning of any of these systems could, in principle, interfere with adequate sexual functioning. In addition, a wide variety of psychosocial/behavioral factors can also underlie any of the MSDs. This includes a range of *DSM* disorders (e.g., depression, anxiety disorders), sexual performance and relationship issues (e.g., anger, loss of sexual interest in partner, partner sexual dysfunction), and other variables (e.g., abuse history or religious orthodoxy, etc.).

Increasingly, clinicians recognize that effective evaluation and treatment of MSDs requires identifying and impacting the specific physical and psychosocial factors that underlie each man's disorder. The Sexual Tipping Point (STP)® model offers a particularly useful perspective for illustrating the interactive role of medical and psychosocial factors in conceptualizing both the etiology and treatment of MSD. The treatment of an MSD might differ both within and between individuals, secondary to an assessment of the dynamic and interacting medical and psychosocial factors determining its etiology. For the previous 40 years, mental health professionals

(MHP) typically employed sex therapy (short term, problem focused), couples counseling, and individual psychotherapy, all of which can be effective in treating some cases of MSD. However, during the last decade, sexual pharmaceuticals typically prescribed by primary care physicians (PCP) have become the standard treatment for many MSDs, as these clinicians are often the first professionals men consult. This is especially true in the United States, owing to the ubiquitous presence of direct-to-the-consumer pharmaceutical advertising for these disorders. This has triggered, along with a multiplicity of other factors concerning female sexual disorders, significant debate about the medicalization and pharmaceuticalization of treatment. These drugs are often initially successful, however, noncompliance is common and recidivism typically occurs when the drugs are discontinued. The aforementioned debate and greater appreciation of the simultaneous importance of psychosocial factors have resulted in increased use of combination treatment (CT). In such cases, medication and sexual counseling are both utilized with evidence building that, for many MDS, this model yields better outcomes than either approach alone.

PREVALENCE

The National Health and Social Life Survey included interviews with over 1,500 men (age 18–51) throughout the United States, and reported a prevalence rate for all male sexual disorders of 31%. In terms of Sexual Desire Disorder, 16% of men surveyed acknowledged that during the previous 12 months there had been a period of at least several months when they "lacked interest in having sex." Male sexual arousal disorder, also known as erectile dysfunction, has a prevalence rate in the general population of approximately 20%. The prevalence of ED increases significantly after age 40, and erectile quality generally deteriorates progressively for men after age 60. While all agree that Premature Ejaculation (PE) is exceedingly common, the NHSLS highly publicized estimate supporting 30% prevalence for U.S. men has been questioned by other experts who quote an approximate 16% rate. Reported prevalence rates for delayed ejaculation (DE) are generally quite low, rarely exceeding 3%.

CULTURAL DIVERSITY ISSUES

Culture can have a profound influence on every aspect of sexuality, including the nature, etiology, and treatment of virtually any form of sexual problem. For example, a culture's (or even a subculture's) perspective on the "appropriate" roles of men and women can dramatically impact the sexual expectations of the members of that group. Such expectations can, in turn, become sources of performance anxiety as members of the culture come to hold themselves and their partners to the demands of those mandated/preferred sexual scripts.

Research by health professionals, anthropologists, and other social scientists has identified meaningful differences across cultures in a number of phenomena associated with sexual dysfunctions. For example, the overall prevalence of erectile dysfunction among men age 40 and above has been found to vary by ethnicity with African Americans showing a relatively high rate (24.4%), followed by Caucasians (21.9%) and Hispanics (19.95). Other observed cultural differences related to sexual dysfunctions include the value of traditional (e.g., herbal) and ethnic remedies (alone or in combination with Western medicine); who, if anyone, is seen as appropriate for treatment as a function of both age and gender; time to orgasm in men and women; beliefs (including "myths") about male and female sexual functioning (normal and dysfunctional); and the effects of culturally specific attitudes and experiences on sexual functioning.

It is now well understood that clinicians assessing and treating any biopsychosocial problem should have an appreciation for the many roles culture can play in the expression of symptoms generally, and sexual concerns specifically. Therefore, cultural sensitivity and intelligence is required for proper assessment and treatment of MSDs.

EVIDENCE-BASED TREATMENTS

Sexual Desire Disorder

How intrinsically interested one is in sex varies considerably from one man to another. Some men prefer partnered sex daily, while others might be quite content with experiencing it a couple of times a month, or less. Because of this great variability, it is not easy to evaluate how much interest is "normal," or what minimal level of interest would meet the *DSM* criterion of, "Persistently or recurrently deficient (or absent) sexual/erotic thoughts or fantasies and desire for sexual activity."

Almost any of the psychological, interpersonal, or biological causes of MSDs (or their combination) described earlier in this chapter can underlie a clinically significant lack of sexual desire in a man. In addition, everyday stress (work, family, money) or any prolonged debilitating (especially painful) physical illness may also cause diminished desire. Desire problems generally (and "primary" desire disorders, in particular) can be quite difficult to treat, with long-term results often being less successful than therapy for other MSDs. Many psychotherapeutic and pharmacological treatment approaches have been tried, with no single approach proving routinely superior. In general, therapists seek to identify and address the likely cause(s) of a man's desire problem (e.g., sex negative messages growing up, anger at his partner, sexual orientation conflict, low testosterone), before any traditional sex therapy techniques might be implemented. The many possible etiologies for a desire problem make identification and treatment of this problem challenging, with treatment being typically longer than for other dysfunctions, and prognosis more guarded.

Sexual desire discrepancy is a related issue that, while not a true sexual dysfunction, can cause much couple distress. Here, one person's level of interest is significantly lower than that of their partner, although he (or she) does not have a clinically significant desire disorder (e.g., one prefers sex four times a week, the other once a week). Most MHPs will utilize a cognitive behavioral approach to assist such a relational conflict. Typically, some form of compromise between the individuals' preferred desired frequency for sex is sought, as would be the case in attempting to orchestrate couple differences in any area of their relationship. However, be forewarned that a discrepancy in desire preference can be as recalcitrant to resolve (even in the absence of significant individual or relationship pathology) as a true desire disorder.

Sexual Arousal Disorder

Male sexual arousal disorder, also known as erectile dysfunction (ED), is the most common sexual complaint for which men seek treatment. ED is a condition in which the man is unable to obtain or to maintain a penile erection sufficient for intercourse. It can vary in severity (e.g., the man may get partial erections or no erection at all) and frequency (he may experience ED every time, or only occasionally). Like other MSDs, ED can result from any wide variety of anatomic, neurologic, hormonal, and/or cardiovascular conditions, many common medications, and/or psychosocial problems (both individual and dyadic), and many related endothelial diseases are comorbid with ED. Importantly, once a man has experienced an episode of ED, no matter its cause (e.g., being too tired, having too much alcohol), he can quite easily become sufficiently concerned about his erectile ability that the resulting performance anxiety alone may be sufficient to continue interfering with his sexual functioning for some time.

The past decade's introduction of safe and effective oral medications in the form of phosphodiasterase type 5 inhibitors (sildenafil, vardenafil, tadalafil) have revolutionized the treatment of ED. However, despite the efficacy of these drugs (i.e., able to help as many as two thirds of men with ED) and millions of prescriptions being written, there appears to be a nonrenewal rate of over 50%, causing a reexamination of what would constitute optimal care. While PCPs will typically refer to urologists for more intrusive medical and surgical approaches (e.g., intracavernosal injections, penile implants), it is the PCPs who'll often be the ones prescribing the ED oral medications. Whatever the medical intervention, increasingly, sexual counseling is also being provided adjunctively, or by the physicians themselves. This combination treatment approach may improve the long-term satisfaction with ED medications and the other medical treatments. Such counseling/therapy typically focuses on: (a) each member of the couple's sexual beliefs, desires, expectations, and fears/anxieties, and (b) the couple's communication patterns, both regarding sexual and nonsexual matters. In many cases, brief considerations of these areas may be sufficient to optimize the efficacy of the ED medications. When this is not the case, longer-term sex therapy with an appropriately trained clinician will be necessary.

Premature Ejaculation

Premature (or rapid) ejaculation is a type of Male Orgasmic Disorder (MOD) and is probably the most common MSD. Unlike ED, it is not usually associated with other comorbid conditions. A man with PE is characterized by the International Society for Sexual Medicine definition as distressed at his inability to delay his ejaculation, "…which always or nearly always occurs prior to or within about one minute of vaginal penetration." This definition is controversial and there are a number of learned papers debating the relative merits of phenomenological versus temporal definitions. Nonetheless, there are clearly millions of men suffering from a lifelong (primary) PE, or less frequently, an acquired one. Importantly, some men do develop an acquired PE later in life secondary to hyperstimulation in their attempt to ward off an incipient ED. A variety of theories have been offered regarding the etiology of PE, including intrapsychic (e.g., performance anxiety), behavioral (e.g., too little sex), and interpersonal (passive aggressive anger) explanations, none having yet to garner substantial empirical support. Most experts believe there is a strong biological component to the disorder, whereby the amount of physical genital stimulation in men triggering an orgasm is primarily physiologically predetermined, that is, most men with PE (particularly those with lifelong PE) are simply born with an especially low orgasmic threshold.

Two behavioral techniques ("squeeze" and "stop-start") used by sex therapists are often helpful in treating PE. Over the last 20 years, a number of antidepressant medications (e.g., selective serotonin reuptake inhibitors [SSRIs], tricyclics) known to delay orgasm (via a presumed serotonergic mechanism of action) have been used "off-label" and demonstrated efficacy in treating PE. In addition, many clinicians will recommend a variety of anesthetic products. Yet, with these as well as other compounds mentioned earlier, once medication is withdrawn the symptom actually returns. Similar to ED, that result has prompted more practitioners to consider a combination treatment approach, and the ISSM has recently offered such guidelines.

Delayed Ejaculation

MOD should be reserved as an overarching nomenclature category for the wide spectrum of ejaculatory disorders. In the *DSM-5* "delayed ejaculation" (DE) names the specific condition. DE is one of the least common, least studied, and least understood of the MSDs. It is defined currently as the "persistent or recurrent delay in, or absence of, orgasm after a normal sexual excitement phase during sexual activity." Orgasm/ejaculation is a reflex, one triggered when a threshold of sexual arousal has been reached. For most men, 6 to 10 minutes of heterosexual intercourse provides sufficient stimulation to reach this threshold, while for men with DE, 20 minutes or more of such partnered stimulation may still not reliably result in orgasm. These men do not typically report difficulty in obtaining or maintaining an erection. Over time, their partners frequently become distressed (like with ED) and will often wonder if the man's difficulty in reaching orgasm is the result of his no longer finding them attractive or sexually desirable,

A number of biological elements have been implicated in the development of DE; for example, any disruption of neurologic functioning in the genital region (e.g., multiple sclerosis, diabetes, SSRIs) could affect ejaculatory/orgasmic function. Yet there are also many psychosocial/behavioral reasons for DE, including, but not limited to, inadequate sexual arousal, loss of sexual interest in the partner, sexual performance anxiety, religious orthodoxy, partner sexual dysfunction, and an idiosyncratic masturbatory style and/or frequency. Treatment for DE is usually targeted at the medical or psychosocial elements suspected of being etiologically significant in each case. For example, if a man's difficulty in reaching orgasm appears to be secondary to his partner's lack of sexual arousal, her dysfunction would likely be the first target of treatment which, if successfully resolved, should increase his chances of becoming orgasmic. Similarly, if his orgasmic difficulties seem to be a consequence of his anger at his partner, this relationship issue would be a logical first target of treatment.

FUTURE RESEARCH

Much of the future research around MSDs will likely be pharmacological in nature; for example, the identification of non-testosterone-based medications to help in treatment of men with low sexual desire, especially those already androgen replete. There are new drugs already in the pipeline for the treatment of PE and for ED. More research is certainly also warranted in developing individual or couples' psychotherapy for all of the MSDs. Unfortunately, while drug companies are motivated to invest the millions of dollars necessary to develop a new medication for treating a common sexual problem (especially after the success of the ED drugs), government funding agencies are quite reluctant to fund comparable research on psychotherapeutic approaches to their treatment.

KEY REFERENCES

Laumann, E., Gagnon, J., Michael, R., & Michaels, S. (1994). *The social organization of sexuality: Sexual practices in the United States*. Chicago, IL: University of Chicago Press.

Montorsi, F., Basson, R., Adaikan, G., Becher, E., Clayton, A., ... Sharlip, I. (2010). Sexual medicine: Sexual dysfunctions in men. *Journal of Sexual Medicine, 7,* 3572–3588.

Perelman, M. (2005). Psychosocial evaluation and combination treatment of men with erectile dysfunction. *Urologic Clinics of North America, 32,* 431–445, vi. doi: 10.1016/j.ucl.2005.08.010

Clinician Application

Sexual Dysfunction in Males

Daniel N. Watter

COMMENT ON THE EVIDENCE-BASED RECOMMENDATIONS

As noted in Strassberg and Perelman's excellent research section, the assessment and treatment of male sexual dysfunction (MSD) has undergone a significant transformation in the past decade. With the advent of sildenafil citrate (Viagra), and other pharmaceuticals, the first line of treatment has shifted from a primarily psychological conceptualization to a more medicalized view of understanding and addressing these concerns. This has set off an oftentimes heated debate in sexual medicine circles as to the most appropriate and clinically effective means of treatment for MSDs. Given the high rate of patient noncompliance and recidivism identified by Strassberg and Perelman, an increased emphasis on combined (psychological and medical) treatments has become the standard of care for much of sex therapy.

Unfortunately, the identification of evidence-based treatments in the treatment of MSDs has been complicated by the many nuances and complexities in the presentation of such disorders. Given the multiplicity of personal and relational dynamics involved in human sexual expression, it is frequently difficult to apply treatment approaches on the basis of symptom manifestation alone. For this reason, psychological and medical treatments must be viewed in concert if those suffering with MSDs are to be treated efficaciously. If medications are to be utilized in the treatment of these matters, it would appear that psychological interventions are required as well in order to assure positive treatment outcomes.

CASE EXAMPLE

Subject Information and Brief History

Steve was a 47-year-old married male who had been experiencing erectile dysfunction (ED) for approximately 2 years. He initially consulted his urologist who prescribed a trial of Viagra. Steve reported that he had used the medication as prescribed, and had little difficulty achieving penile erection. However, he would continue to lose his erection just prior to the initiation of penile–vaginal intercourse. After an increase in the dose of the medication did little to alleviate the situation, Steve's urologist referred him for sex therapy.

Presenting Problem

Steve presented for psychological evaluation following a 2-year bout with ED that did not resolve with trial of oral medication. An otherwise healthy male, Steve presented as anxious, mildly depressed, and frustrated. His mental status examination was essentially unremarkable, and Steve believed that most of his symptoms were the result of his erectile difficulties.

Treatment Intervention and Course

During session 1, Steve described the history of his erectile difficulties and attempts at resolution. When pressed as to the circumstances surrounding the onset of his symptomology, he reported that his wife had just discovered his long-term extramarital affair. She was, understandably, angry and hurt and was threatening divorce. Despite a year of couple's therapy, the marriage had not improved. Steve's wife was unable to forgive him, and was taking his erectile failures personally. She interpreted them as an indication that he was not attracted to her and did not love her anymore. She was telling him that if he did not get his sexual difficulties resolved, she was unwilling to stay in the marriage. As a result, Steve was highly anxious about sexual functioning, and the potential loss of his marriage.

Subsequent sessions focused on the reasons for Steve's affair, as well as strategies for approaching sex with his wife in a less anxious manner. However, this, along with the medication, still did not produce much improvement in the situation. A deeper probing into Steve's background and family of origin revealed the untimely death of his mother when Steve was just a young boy. Since that time, Steve had been preoccupied with death and loss. The likelihood that he would lose his wife (whom he loved and depended on) brought these concerns to the forefront, even though Steve did not recognize this at the outset of therapy.

As the focus of the treatment shifted to Steve's unresolved grief and fears of additional loss, his sexual functioning began to improve. Viagra was utilized as an aid for building erectile confidence and was gradually withdrawn over a 4-month period as erectile functioning improved.

Outcome

Steve has been in therapy for approximately 1 year, and is doing quite well, although the marriage is still in a precarious phase. Couple's therapy, with another psychotherapist, appears to be helpful for them.

CHALLENGES IN APPLYING THE EVIDENCE-BASED APPROACH

This case is an excellent illustration of the difficulties and limitations of using evidence-based treatments for MSD. While the general proposition that medical/pharmaceutical interventions should be used in combination with psychotherapy/sex therapy is sound, it is challenging to provide more specific indications. In large part, this is due to what has been noted above; namely that human sexual functioning is so individual and dynamic. Kleinplatz has noted, "… multifactorial, multideter-mined problems require commensurately complex clinical strategies—not simple treatment algorithms." This has led some in the sex therapy field to lament that the emphasis on evidence-based, or empirically validated treatments, leads to a mechanistic, reductionistic view of human sexuality. The practicing clinician who is treating MSDs must always be mindful of the limitations of research that attempts to simplify sexual dysfunction into a single-issue phenomenon. Clinical practice is often much less "clean" than the research studies that inform the protocols for evidence-based practice. For the clinician interpreting the research, caution is the byword.

CULTURAL DIVERSITY ISSUES

Researchers have pointed out that much of what we know about human sexuality and human sexual functioning has been learned from the study of Western societ-ies. As a result, we know little about what sexual issues are most important to those across cultures and the treatments that would be most helpful for them. Most psy-chotherapeutic interventions have been designed by Westerners and are evaluated with White, middle-class, heterosexual clients. As clinicians, these issues must be considered when attempting to treat those from poorly researched populations and cultures.

FUTURE RESEARCH

Future research should certainly keep in mind the cultural diversity issues noted above. In addition, when treating MSDs, it would be especially helpful to have more information regarding the needs and experiences of nonheterosexual patients. There is a dearth of research data that are useful in guiding the clinician when working with sexual minorities. Finally, it would be valuable to strive for a fuller understanding of the myriad variables that contribute to the successful resolution of MSDs.

KEY REFERENCES

Kleinplatz, P. J. (Ed.). (2012). *New directions in sex therapy: Innovations and alternatives* (2nd ed.). New York, NY: Routledge.
Leiblum, S. R. (Ed.). (2007). *Principles and practice of sex therapy* (4th ed.). New York, NY: The Guilford Press.
Levine, S. B., Risen, C. B., & Althof, S. E. (2010). *Handbook of clinical sexuality for mental health professionals* (2nd ed.). New York, NY: Routledge.

SECTION V: VIOLENCE AND TRAUMA

CHAPTER 59

Intimate Partner Violence Perpetrators

Christopher I. Eckhardt and Joel G. Sprunger

CLINICAL PROBLEM

Intimate partner violence (IPV) is defined as any behavior enacted with the primary proximal goal of causing physical or psychological harm to a romantic partner who is motivated to avoid being harmed. A variety of actions fall under the rubric of IPV. In addition to acts of partner-directed physical aggression, IPV also includes insulting, demeaning, and verbally abusive comments; actions and statements designed to coerce, intimidate, and otherwise produce fear in the partner; acts of sexual aggression and coercion; and behaviors enacted to impinge on a partner's freedoms (e.g., isolating a partner from friends and family; restricted access to finances).

Individuals experiencing physical IPV report more physical injuries, and both male and female IPV victim-survivors report a wide range of negative consequences. Relative to those who have not experienced IPV, victim-survivors of IPV are at substantially higher risk for depression, suicide, posttraumatic stress disorder, alcohol/drug abuse or dependence, and poor physical health. The financial toll on victim-survivors is substantial as well, as the broad financial costs associated with IPV exceed 5.8 billion dollars each year. In addition, children who witness parental IPV are at higher risk for developing externalizing disorders and a variety of social and academic problems.

Despite the prevalence of IPV and the wealth of negative physical and psychological consequences associated with IPV victimization, it is often difficult to identify the perpetrators of such crimes and get them into effective treatment programs. For example, many victim-survivors of IPV are reluctant to notify police, seek social services, or make use of shelters because they are intimidated by (and fearful of) their current or former abusive partners, overcome by the complexity of accessing these services, and/or experience shame or denial given the many stigmas associated with being in an abusive relationship. As a result, only about 10% to 20% of IPV occurrences are actually reported to police. Given that most IPV perpetrators who receive treatment are those mandated to receive it by the criminal justice system, police involvement in IPV incidents is often a necessary first step in the treatment process. In addition, many IPV perpetrators do not regard their abusive actions as harmful, deviant, or fear inducing. Instead, perpetrators are likely to minimize or deny such behaviors, or insist that they were necessary punishments for partner transgressions. Still, others perpetrate acts of IPV during episodes of heavy substance use or in the context of serious symptoms of mental illness. Not surprisingly, therefore, only a very small percentage of IPV perpetrators seek treatment voluntarily, and models of behavior change applied to IPV perpetrators must reflect the coercive nature of their referral to treatment.

PREVALENCE

Surveys of adults conducted in the United States and abroad indicate that IPV occurs at an alarmingly high frequency. According to the most recent survey of U.S. adults, almost 7 million women and 5.5 million men experience physical violence, stalking, or rape from an intimate partner each year. The lifetime prevalence rate of physical IPV victimization is over 35% for women and 28% for men. Rates of psychological aggression are somewhat normative in most community and clinical samples, with 75% of males and 80% of females reporting psychological aggression perpetration. Large-scale surveys, longitudinal studies, and several meta-analytic reviews indicate that rates of physical and psychological IPV perpetration are roughly similar between males and females, with a trend toward showing higher perpetration rates among females (especially young adults). This finding has been quite controversial in branches of the IPV field that have traditionally assumed IPV to be solely defined as male-to-female abuse. In general, rates of IPV are higher in clinical samples, with perpetration prevalence rates ranging from 35% to 50% for male-to-female IPV and 37% to 57% for female-to-male IPV. Also, the frequency with which IPV is perpetrated is not the only matter of concern, as severe acts of IPV resulted in the deaths of 1,640 women and 740 men in the United States in 2007.

CULTURAL DIVERSITY ISSUES

IPV occurs across a multitude of age groups and at high rates among individuals of all ethnic, racial, and cultural backgrounds. Nevertheless, recent data have suggested that cultural factors may be associated with issues related to interventions for IPV perpetrators. Researchers have reported that individuals' attitudes toward close relationships and approval of violence within their relationships are heavily influenced by information learned via implicit and explicit mechanisms within community and cultural subgroups. In general, African American couples engage in higher rates of unidirectional as well as bidirectional IPV relative to Latino/Hispanic and European American couples. Within the criminal justice system, African American males comprise about half of those on probation for IPV-related offenses and are thus overrepresented relative to other racial/ethnic groups. In addition, rates of treatment dropout and IPV recidivism are higher among African American men relative to men of other races/ethnicities attending similar intervention programs. These data have led to speculation that current programs for IPV perpetrators may not be meeting the needs of minority clients, and African American males in particular. While more research is needed in this area, a recent randomized trial comparing a culturally focused counseling group for African American males to a standard mixed-race group intervention and an all-African American standard intervention failed to find group differences in treatment outcomes. Regardless, it is crucial for the therapist working with an IPV offender to focus the case formulation on risk and protective factors that may affect the current likelihood of IPV, as well as attending to attitudinal factors stemming from early socialization experiences based on shared attitudes toward IPV within one's cultural and community subgroups.

EVIDENCE-BASED TREATMENTS

Programs for perpetrators of IPV, often labeled "Batterer Intervention Programs" (BIPs), have been a topic of empirical investigation for a relatively short period of time. While such programs share the broad goals of reducing levels of IPV and promoting victim safety, there is considerable variability in the ways in which programs aim to achieve these goals. Most programs employ an open admissions group format, with one to two counselors facilitating group discussion and activities. Clients are predominantly referred by the criminal justice system, and program length varies widely depending on individual states' BIP standards (e.g., from 8–52 weeks). Despite a legal mandate to attend, individuals drop out of BIPs at a very high rate (40%–60% attrition is typical), with dropouts having higher rates of recidivism than completers.

There are three broad types of BIPs: (a) the traditional feminist-informed psychoeducational model, (b) the therapeutic cognitive behavioral therapy (CBT) approach, and (c) alternative programs. The feminist BIP model is based upon the long-standing notion that IPV is an outgrowth of normal male behavior and patriarchal socialization. BIPs based on this model, such as the Domestic Abuse Intervention Program (more commonly known as the "Duluth Model"), rely on a gender reeducation approach that presumes that violence reduction is best achieved by exposing offenders' patriarchal/misogynistic attitudes, educating offenders about the effects of IPV on women and children, encouraging accountability and personal responsibility for coercive tactics in relationships, and promoting gender-egalitarian attitudes and behaviors. These programs tend not to support causal analyses of IPV that rely on the offender's personality/psychopathology, substance use, interactional processes, or related factors that would imply causes outside the realm of personal accountability. Most existing intervention programs and state laws or guidelines that regulate IPV intervention espouse key aspects of the feminist perspective on IPV etiology and BIP content.

A second approach to BIP is a hybrid integration of feminist theory and CBT that has emerged over the last 25 years. This therapeutically oriented CBT framework retains the focus on perpetrators' cognitive distortions and faulty attitudes/beliefs. It also expands the range of treatment targets to beyond misogynistic beliefs to include additional factors empirically associated with IPV, such as emotion dysregulation and relationship skills deficits. These approaches are based on cognitive therapies for psychopathology that achieve the goal of behavior change through a collaborative therapeutic relationship, exposure and disputation of distorted cognitions, problem solving, relationship skills training, and emotion regulation. The approach follows a more traditional CBT group format, and considers perpetrators as clients seeking change rather than offenders needing to be reeducated.

A final category of BIPs reflect recent efforts to move beyond the two "traditional" approaches to IPV reduction in favor of alternate behavior change models that focus on: (a) clients' readiness to change; (b) interaction processes in close relationships; and (c) coexisting substance abuse problems. Interventions that have incorporated the readiness to change approach have typically done so in two ways. First, usage of motivational enhancement techniques during the intake and initial sessions of BIP have been shown to enhance attendance and reduce rates of reoffending during the course of treatment. Second, a general integration of core motivational interviewing techniques (such as those commonly used in substance abuse treatment) into BIP programming has proven to be more effective at reducing recidivism than traditional gender-themed groups. Another alternative approach to traditional BIP groups is couples-based treatment. This approach has received much attention, with strong effectiveness data in support of its implementation, especially with bidirectionally violent couples who plan on staying together. However, it is also a controversial approach in some branches of the IPV field, as some feel it may lead to increased safety concerns for partners. Finally, intervention approaches that address substance problems and IPV in an integrative manner may be superior to the traditional approach of sequentially treating each problem as a separate entity.

Is there evidence that BIPs are indeed effective at reducing rates of IPV? This turns out to be a frustratingly difficult question to answer. It is important to note that only six randomized clinical trials of standard IPV perpetrator interventions have been published. The majority of BIP evaluation research has been nonexperimental or quasi-experimental in nature. Prior reviews have noted difficulties in arriving at unequivocal conclusions regarding BIP effectiveness due to widespread shortcomings in research design, inconsistencies in definition and monitoring of the active components of interventions evaluated, limitations in the breadth and methods of the clinical outcomes being assessed, difficulties associated with high attrition rates from BIPs, and little attention paid to factors that may mediate treatment success and/or failure. These methodological shortcomings make it difficult to determine meaningful inferences regarding treatment effectiveness.

In terms of *traditional intervention programs* for IPV offenders based on either gender-themed or therapeutically oriented CBT orientations, the effects are very small. About one half of studies show that BIPs are more effective than a no treatment control condition in preventing new episodes of IPV. In other words, CBT-oriented BIP programming will perform better as often as it performs "no better" than a no treatment control group at preventing IPV. Studies also indicate that there is little effectiveness evidence that would favor one type of traditional CBT-oriented intervention over another. For example, results of a randomized trial suggested that having IPV perpetrators meet with, and be monitored by, probation officers (without attending a BIP) was as effective in preventing new instances of IPV as having perpetrators attend 26 weeks of court-mandated feminist-psychoeducational BIP. However, it is worth noting once again that there have been precious few randomized trials conducted regarding BIP effectiveness and it would be inappropriate to offer generalizations based upon a single trial. Finally, there is guarded enthusiasm for BIPs with nontraditional, "alternative" content. Researchers suggest that IPV-related outcomes are improved after incorporating motivational enhancement techniques, and that, in some cases, outcomes following a couples-based treatment of IPV is as effective as traditional CBT approaches.

Overall, the small volume of research investigating BIP effectiveness is fraught with methodological problems that limit broad generalizations about clinical effectiveness. Perhaps the most reasonable conclusion that one can make concerning the effectiveness of intervention programs for IPV perpetrators is that the small number of unbiased studies with adequate evidence of internal and external validity simply do not allow for unambiguous conclusions about clinical effectiveness.

FUTURE RESEARCH

Future research in this area will involve an expansion of treatment models and formats for IPV offenders. Specifically, there is a critical need to move beyond the traditional feminist-informed, group-based intervention model, about which there is insufficient evidence of effectiveness to justify their widespread application. Interventions that are more strongly focused on empirically supported risk factors for IPV and that incorporate evidence-based methods of behavior change should be a primary focus of future research. Similarly, interventions must be developed that better take into account the high degree of overlapping areas of dysfunction present among IPV perpetrators. It is more common than not for clients to have issues pertaining to substance abuse and psychopathology, and traditional BIP models are ill-equipped to address these comorbidity concerns. In addition, given the coercive nature of how individuals are referred to BIPs, it will be important for researchers and clinicians to continue to apply motivational enhancement techniques to foster a positive, change-focused approach to treatment. Lastly, additional research is needed to develop intervention methods that are culturally and/or ethnically sensitive to the backgrounds of IPV perpetrators. Given that most interventions presume that nonviolent change is mediated by changes in perpetrator attitudes and beliefs about the acceptability of IPV, it is essential for treatments to be matched to clients' unique perspectives and culturally informed ideologies, rather than simply one-size-fits-all (or most) approaches.

KEY REFERENCES

Eckhardt, C. I., Murphy, C. M., Whitaker, D. J., Sprunger, J., Dykstra, R., & Woodin, E. (2013). #17 The effectiveness of intervention programs for perpetrators and victims of intimate partner violence. *Partner Abuse*, 4(2), 1–26. doi: 10.1891/1946-6560.4.2.e17

Murphy, C., & Eckhardt, C. (2005). *Treating the abusive partner: An individualized cognitive behavioral approach.* New York, NY: Guilford Press.

O'Leary, K. D., & Woodin, E. (2009). *Psychological and physical aggression in couples: Causes and interventions.* Washington, DC: American Psychological Association.

Clinician Application

Intimate Partner Violence Perpetrators

John Hamel

COMMENT ON THE EVIDENCE-BASED RECOMMENDATIONS

The empirical research evidence presented by Eckhardt and Sprunger presents a mixed picture regarding the effectiveness of clinical interventions in cases of intimate partner abuse, particularly with respect to clients mandated to complete a court-approved batterer intervention program (BIP). However, their findings would seem promising for clinicians who favor a client-centered approach that takes into account a client's individual needs and characteristics (including resistance to change), emphasizes a strong client–facilitator alliance, and is open to working outside the traditional group model to include the formats of couples and family therapy.

Methodologically sound research on BIPs is indeed in its infancy; nonetheless, BIPs are expected to help clients cease their violence and keep victims safe, and cannot wait on results of control-group experiments before choosing a particular treatment plan. As a practical matter, in our group practice we have had to accept a broader definition of what is "evidence based," to include known risk factors. For example, contrary to prevailing stereotypes about dominant male batterers, it has been established that most partner violence is bi-directional, involving negative reciprocal and repetitive interaction sequences, negative emotionality (impulsivity, problems with anger), and high levels of relationship conflict. Although California PC 1203.097 restricts much of our work to the group format, we incorporate such findings in our intervention efforts to help clients correctly identify and overcome their abusive and dysfunctional interaction patterns. We teach our clients prosocial skills (anger management, communication and conflict resolution techniques), encourage them to dispute their irrational and proviolent beliefs, and take more responsibility for their lives. This is done within a broad motivational interviewing approach that validates client experiences and assists them to arrive at their own solutions.

CASE EXAMPLE

Subject Information and Brief History

Susan L., a White 20-year-old retail clerk, was arrested on a misdemeanor domestic violence charge after she punched her boyfriend, Bill, and kicked in the side of his car after he spurned her sexual advances. She was subsequently ordered to complete a 52-week batterer intervention group. Although this was her first arrest, she admitted in her assessment interview that she had physically assaulted Bill on three previous occasions. Although she grew up in a comfortable, middle-class home, Susan had witnessed more often than she cared to remember her parents swearing at one another, or her mother throwing things at her father, typically over his philandering. Susan found herself dropping out of community college because of excessive partying with friends, and reported on an assessment questionnaire that she had been drinking during approximately half of her verbal or physical fights with Bill, including the incident for which she was arrested.

Presenting Problem

Susan initially stated that she had sought treatment because it was mandated by the courts, but later in her intake interview added that she also wished to learn ways to calm down when angry.

Treatment Intervention and Course

Our assessment protocol includes a few paper-and-pencil questionnaires, some of which are then readministered upon program completion. One of these is the Safe at Home Questionnaire, a validated instrument based on the Stages of Change model. In this model, individuals enter therapy at varying levels of motivation, from Pre-contemplation (not at all motivated, not thinking about taking responsibility) to Contemplation, Action and Maintenance and treatment providers can use this information to help clients overcome initial resistance. Susan scored somewhere between the Pre-contemplation and Contemplation stages, indicating a low-to-moderate level of motivation to take responsibility for her behavior. She gave herself low scores on the Relationship Functioning Self-Assessment (a relationship skills measure based on early research with couples in a Navy domestic violence program) conceding to having "anger issues" but she also blamed much of her violence on Bill's verbal put-downs and tendency to emotionally withdraw, as well as her use of alcohol. She scored about average (compared to other women in BIPs) on the Controlling and Abusive Tactics Questionnaire (CAT), a measure of psychological abuse and control, and rated Bill as well above average on this scale

Mindful of this client's low level of motivation, the group facilitator was careful in the first few weeks of the program to validate Susan's version of her relationship problems and to show genuine concern about her welfare. Rather than assign blame on Susan for her violence, the facilitator instead encouraged her to complete her assigned progress logs, part of our program's cognitive behavioral component. A useful tool for gauging attachment issues is the Experiences in Close Relationships questionnaire (ECR-R), a commonly used instrument and a standard part of our assessment protocol that includes questions on a client's psychosocial history with a focus on issues of anger, aggression, and relationship conflict. On the ECR-R Susan scored higher than average on the Anxiety over Abandonment scale. The group facilitator gave her feedback from this questionnaire. Together with input from the other groups members and what she learned from her logs, she was able to discover for herself how her aggression, rather than help her "stand up" for herself against Bill's verbal abuse, only served to reinforce his tendency to avoid her. At the facilitator's urging, Susan attended meetings of Alcoholics Anonymous for 3 months, and even though she did not identify as an alcoholic, she voluntarily stopped drinking. By the midpoint of the 52 group sessions, Susan was sober, reporting a complete cessation of her physical abuse, and a significant reduction in her use of controlling and possessive behaviors (e.g., no longer calling him so frequently at work to check on him).

Unfortunately, while Susan dutifully practiced emotion regulation and conflict containment, she reported that Bill continued to verbally abuse her, remaining resentful about the way she had previously treated him, and continually resistant to any meaningful discussion of their relationship problems. Aware that there is no better way for a couple to work out relationship issues than to meet with a third party who is able to observe and comment directly on their interactions, the group facilitator invited Bill to meet in a one-on-one session. Presented to Bill as an opportunity to "consult" on Susan's progress, the session also provided the facilitator an opportunity to determine Bill's commitment to Susan and to overcoming his own anger and abuse issues, and to gauge the couple's suitability for conjoint sessions. Although skeptical, Bill grudgingly agreed to conjoint therapy (at another agency, and concurrent with, rather than in lieu of, her mandated group sessions, as dictated by California law).

Outcome

By the time Susan had finished her group sessions, she had reported (and the couples therapist had confirmed) a breakthrough in Bill's ability to engage in intimate conversation. On the Safe at Home Questionnaire, she had moved well into the Action stage, and her CAT exit scores indicated a substantial reduction in her and Bill's use of psychological abuse and control, and the Relationship Functioning Self-Assessment reflected a substantial increase in her ability to manage anger, cope with stress, and resolve interpersonal conflicts. At a 1-year follow-up, conducted over the telephone, Susan reported that she and Bill briefly separated but were now back together and engaged to be married, doing so well that they were now meeting with their couples therapist only twice a month. More importantly, Susan reported to feeling in control of her life, like she never had before.

CHALLENGES IN APPLYING THE EVIDENCE-BASED APPROACH

The challenges in applying an evidence-based approach are much more pronounced in work with court-mandated partner violence perpetrators in comparison to individuals who seek treatment voluntarily, or referred without a criminal case. In many states, including California, treatment providers are prohibited from treating court-ordered clients in the modalities of couples or family counseling, and are only permitted to see these clients in individual therapy in special cases (e.g., the client has serious mental health issues) and with the approval of the local probation department or the referring criminal court. Otherwise, the treatment provider is limited to the same-sex group format, and to a specific number of sessions (52 in California), irrespective of a client's actual treatment needs. In many states, such as Oregon, providers must work within a feminist-based psychoeducational approach in which the root causes of partner violence are presumed to stem from patriarchal social structures and other, more empirically based explanations (e.g., poor impulse control, substance abuse) are expressly prohibited.

CULTURAL DIVERSITY ISSUES

Recent research indicates that risk factors for partner abuse are quite similar across ethnic minority groups, and similar between heterosexual and LGBT populations. Clear differences do exist, however, in the way that clients from various cultural backgrounds approach the criminal justice system as well as mental health counselors. Many African Americans and Latinos, for example, are suspicious about cooperating with any agency, however well intended, that is in any way connected to a legal system which has not always treated them fairly. White counselors and group facilitators also need to be careful to not buy into common stereotypes, such as Latino men as always being "hot tempered" or necessarily "macho" and hostile to women. At times, the streetwise conversational style of some young African Americans may be wrongly interpreted as aggressive, or indicating resistance to change. Asian and Latino men may be reluctant to disclose personal information to an outsider. Because of the greater symmetry in size and strength among LGBT couples, abuse between them may be mistakenly assumed to always be reciprocal rather than caused at times by a dominant aggressor. When facilitated by someone who is familiar with the cultural characteristics of his or her clients and is willing to have them learn at their own pace, a psychoeducational group format may be a safe and effective way to impart important interpersonal skills and to challenge proviolent attitudes.

FUTURE RESEARCH

One of the major limitations of current BIPs are their "one-size-fits-all" approaches to partner violence. There is therefore a need for research on improving assessment protocols, and on differential treatment for different clients based on personality, cultural background, and known risk factors. Further studies will need to be conducted on Motivational Interviewing and other promising treatment approaches to determine if their findings can be replicated. Finally, more research is needed on programs for female offenders.

KEY REFERENCES

Dutton, D. (2006). *Domestic violence reexamined*. Vancouver, Canada: University of British Columbia Press.

Hamel, J. (2005). *Gender-inclusive treatment of intimate partner abuse: A comprehensive approach*. New York, NY: Springer.

Hamel, J. (2012). "But she's violent, too!": Holding domestic violence offenders accountable within a systemic approach to batterer intervention. *Journal of Aggression, Conflict and Peace Research, 4*, 124–135.

CHAPTER 60

Men Sexually Abused as Children

Elisa Romano and Rayleen V. De Luca

CLINICAL PROBLEM

Researchers and clinicians alike are becoming increasingly aware of the reality that male childhood sexual abuse occurs and that effective treatment must be made available to address abuse-related needs in this population. Childhood sexual abuse in men has been found to be associated with a range of mental health impairments, including mood, anxiety, and substance use disorders, as well as problems in sexual and interpersonal functioning. Because childhood sexual abuse is not a clinical problem per se but rather a traumatic experience that can influence various domains of functioning, psychological interventions can vary widely in terms of their identified treatment targets and objectives. Not surprisingly, childhood sexual abuse has most often been considered within the context of Posttraumatic Stress Disorder (PTSD). One prospective study found that, as adults, the most frequent diagnoses for men were anxiety and acute stress disorders (including PTSD). There also is evidence that sexually abused adult males exhibit just as many posttraumatic symptoms as females.

PREVALENCE

Research in this area is fraught with challenges. Studies on the prevalence of childhood sexual abuse in men show considerable variability, with estimates of 4.8% to 28% among university students, 2.8% to 16% among community-based men, and 3% to 23% among clinical samples. In general, a well-accepted statistic is that approximately one in six men experiences sexual abuse during childhood. Note, however, that rates are higher still when one considers that there are roughly three to four times as many cases of sexual abuse than are actually disclosed or reported. Moreover, underreporting of male sexual abuse is especially significant because of such issues as gender stereotypes and abuse characteristics (e.g., fears of being labeled homosexual if the perpetrator was also male).

CULTURAL DIVERSITY ISSUES

Interventions for abuse-related PTSD have been developed primarily in Western society, so the extent to which their effectiveness would generalize to non-Western cultures remains an open question. However, it appears that across different societies and cultures, PTSD is a universal response to trauma. Having said this, there is no research, to our knowledge, that has specifically addressed diversity issues as they pertain to culture and race among men who have experienced childhood sexual abuse. The primary diversity issue relates to gender and the powerful messages that exist around what it means to be a man. For example, there are messages about masculinity (e.g., men are not victims and should protect themselves against aggressors), sexuality (e.g., men will be labeled homosexual if the perpetrator was also male, sexual activity with an older female is not abuse), and feelings (e.g., men should not express feelings of vulnerability such as sadness, fear, or confusion), to name a few. Such messages can make it difficult for men to disclose childhood sexual abuse and to seek psychological services. Once in treatment, it is important to address these messages as there is likely to be much self-blame and shame among men who, for example, were not able to "fight off" their perpetrator, or who have a homosexual orientation, or who felt very scared during the sexually abusive experiences.

EVIDENCE-BASED TREATMENTS

A number of evidence-based treatments for abuse-related PTSD have been identified. A systematic review of randomized controlled trials of psychological interventions for adults with PTSD located 33 studies. Of note is that most of the included studies focused on adult females who experienced assault (primarily sexual). While there were a number of studies that included individuals with various traumas, the specific sample composition in terms of number of males/females and type of trauma often was not specified. Undoubtedly, several of these mixed-sex studies included sexually abused adult men but the bottom line is that there were no empirically rigorous studies that evaluated treatment effects specifically for this population that could be identified for purposes of inclusion in the systematic review. Results identified trauma-focused cognitive behavioral therapy (TF-CBT) and eye movement desensitization and reprocessing as most efficacious in terms of improving clinician-reported PTSD symptoms. There also was support, albeit more limited, for the efficacy of stress management and group cognitive behavioral therapy. It is interesting to note that certain medications, specifically antidepressants, such as selective serotonin reuptake inhibitors (SSRIs) and serotonin-norepinephrine reuptake inhibitors (SNRIs), have also been found to be effective for PTSD treatment, although they are not as effective when compared to cognitive behavioral interventions.

Turning to TF-CBT, exposure appears to be a particularly effective intervention in reducing PTSD symptoms. Typically, it involves both imaginal exposure to the trauma memory (creation of a detailed trauma narrative that is audiotaped and repeatedly listened to by the individual) and in vivo exposure to feared or avoided trauma reminders. Another effective TF-CBT intervention is cognitive therapy which, in brief, involves teaching individuals to identify, challenge, and replace inaccurate or unhelpful abuse-related thoughts, which are often related to themes of safety/danger, responsibility, mistrust, self-esteem, and intimacy. Finally, stress inoculation training is a multicomponent behaviorally based program that teaches individuals a number of anxiety management strategies, such as muscle relaxation, breathing retraining, and guided self-dialogue. While the empirical support for these interventions comes primarily from studies on females, there is, nonetheless, preliminary research supporting their use for males.

Within the general TF-CBT framework, there most certainly will be issues that are of particular relevance for sexually abused adult men, as previously mentioned.

One common issue stems from the rigid and narrow gender messages that dominate our culture (especially North American) and to which males are socialized from birth. These messages that "real" men are dominant, physically strong, and powerful often make it very difficult for men to accept that their masculinity has not been compromised by childhood sexual abuse, which by its nature is an experience of extreme vulnerability and lack of power. As such, men often experience a deep sense of failure and self-blame as well as associated struggles (e.g., excessive sexual activity to prove one's masculinity, sexual identity confusion, fear of or intolerance of homosexuality). One evaluation of a treatment program for sexually abused adult men attested to the predominance of self-blame in this population as well as to the efficacy of CBT interventions (e.g., cognitive restructuring) to decrease these feelings.

Another issue of particular relevance for men is that of effectively identifying and communicating one's feelings. Men often have difficulty accessing the full range of feelings that they experience with regard to their sexual abuse experience, instead often focusing on anger which can become an all-encompassing emotion that masks other underlying feelings. This difficulty again is undoubtedly linked to strong socialization influences about acceptable male behavior and about the meaning of certain feelings (e.g., fear, sadness, and confusion are linked with vulnerability while anger is linked with power). Evaluation studies also underline anger as being an important issue that requires interventions which allow men to explore their anger, to tap into other abuse-related feelings, and to develop strategies for effectively managing these various feelings.

Finally, it would seem that substance use problems may be overrepresented in men who have experienced sexual abuse as children. Relying on alcohol and drugs to manage abuse-related memories and distress is often a helpful short-term coping strategy, but it is not effective in the long term. In response to the frequent cooccurrence of substance abuse and PTSD (often found among individuals who have experienced childhood sexual abuse), "Seeking Safety," an evidence- and CBT-based treatment program that addresses these comorbid conditions by way of an integrated, present-focused coping skills model, has been developed. The program can be administered at an individual or group level, and data attesting to its effectiveness have been collected on males.

FUTURE RESEARCH

In light of the existing literature, there are two important and interrelated research avenues that require attention. First, as previously discussed, childhood sexual abuse is a traumatic experience that often results in trauma-related stress if not full-blown PTSD. There are evidence-based interventions for adult PTSD, and these should be consulted when working therapeutically with sexually abused adult males. While these interventions have a wealth of empirical evidence, much of the research on males is based on noninterpersonally based traumas, most notably combat-related PTSD. As such, it is imperative to assess the efficacy of these PTSD interventions, specifically for men who have experienced childhood sexual abuse. Such data would allow for firmer conclusions about the generalizability of these interventions for sexually abused adult males and would help in delineating any special considerations in the treatment of this particular population. The second related point is that there exists much information on treatment considerations for sexually abused adult males that is easily accessible through books, journal publications, and reputable web-based organizations (e.g., 1in6.org; www.malesur vivor.org). Most of this information, while representing years of clinical experience working in the field, has not undergone rigorous empirical testing. Therefore, it is imperative for these clinicians and organizations to subject their treatment protocol to scientific testing as a way to validate their interventions and advance the field of male sexual abuse treatment. Along these lines, a recent evaluation of a group treatment developed specifically for men who experienced childhood sexual abuse (i.e., Men & Healing program) indicated significant improvements in self-reported posttraumatic and depressive symptoms. Such endeavors are encouraging and particularly timely given the growing emphasis on evidence-based interventions.

KEY REFERENCES

Cloitre, M., Cohen, L. R., & Koenen, K. C. (2006). *Treating survivors of childhood abuse: Psychotherapy for the inter-rupted life.* New York, NY: Guilford Press.

Foa, E. B., Keane, T. M., Friedman, M. J., & Cohen, J. A. (Eds.). (2009). *Effective treatments for PTSD: Practice guidelines from the International Society for Traumatic Stress Studies.* New York, NY: Guilford Press.

Lew, M. (2004). *Victims no longer: The classic guide for men recovering from sexual child abuse* (2nd ed.). New York, NY: Harper.

Clinician Application

Men Sexually Abused as Children

Rick Goodwin

COMMENT ON THE EVIDENCE-BASED RECOMMENDATIONS

What the authors have said in the Research Section are absolutely correct: the knowl-edge gap concerning issues of male sexual victimization[1] needs to be addressed hand in hand with the development of specialized treatment[2] strategies for male survivors.[3] Despite significant progress in the field, the sexual abuse of boys and

---

[1] Our treatment services address adult male survivors of childhood sexual abuse. "Male sexual assault" is the term generally used to describe sexual violence against an adult male. The needs of sexually assaulted men are not addressed in this section.

[2] The terms "counselling," "psychotherapy," and "treatment" are used interchangeably in this section.

[3] A "survivor" is the term that is generally used to refer to those who have been sexually victim-ized, and is seen as the preferred term for both male and female abuse victims.

male youth is still common, underreported, underrecognized, and undertreated. Working in one of the few centers in North America dedicated to serving male survivors and their families, we recognize that clinicians need both conceptual and practical direction in order to assist male survivors in their recovery.

The past generation of feminist research and advocacy has informed us that childhood sexual victimization creates a myriad of lifelong consequences for female survivors. Our understanding of and intervention with male survivors has benefited significantly from this pioneering work. That being said, research on men's experience of sexual trauma has trailed feminist research—possibly by an entire generation. The acknowledgment that boys and men can be victims of such experiences has only recently been recognized; the psychosocial impact of sexual trauma on males is not well understood, and clinical services for male survivors are vastly underdeveloped.

This emerging sector badly requires evidence-based treatment. What is out there is limited. While some cognitive behavior therapy (CBT)-informed approaches have been studied in terms of outcome, their application is useful but not sufficient. Two nuggets from Bessel van der Kolk help inform us to go further in our interventions: "The body keeps score" and as well, "Experiential therapy is the treatment of choice for trauma survivors." Both quotes suggest to us as practitioners to move beyond the cognition and the rational to other life domains to help our clients find relief. While traumatic sequelae is universal, much of the injury of sexual abuse victims results in wounds to their gender identity and meaning. To put it another way, if the code word for masculine identity is "invulnerability," than male victims cannot identify, let alone address, their victimization. Richard Gartner suggests that male survivors need to experience a form of psychological death of their masculine identity for a new self-definition (and thus therapy) to take place. As the authors of the Research Section noted, gender is critical to comprehending the impact of male sexual trauma. What is lacking, however, is an evidence base for cohesive male-centered treatment.

Group engagement as an intervention is another area where trauma theory meets practice. Not only does group therapy allow male cultural conditioning to be decoded in a circle of peers, it also provides, by its very form, a conduit to engage and eradicate shame. It is recognized that group therapy is studied less than individual treatment. It requires a different skill set by the clinician, and demands greater commitment for programming by the mental health service. Despite these challenges, group work (combined with individual therapy) possibly provides the greatest wealth to the clients served.

CASE EXAMPLE

Subject Information and Brief History

Jim is a 45-year-old male who came to us for treatment for issues relating to his childhood sexual abuse issues. He first became aware of his need for psychotherapy after being arrested for domestic violence. While the courts directed him to attend an abuse education service, he was able to source much of his rage to his experience of sexual victimization by an older brother. The sexual abuse he experienced was violent, involved other offenders, and other child victims as well.

Presenting Problem

Jim described an array of posttraumatic stress behaviors upon assessment. Polarized cognition, mood swings, bouts of rage, and patterns of isolation plagued his marriage. Despite being a 20-year veteran of Alcoholics Anonymous, his pattern within relationships and distrust of authority figures prevented him from any stable pattern of employment. His children were fearful of him.

Treatment Intervention and Course

Jim took well to the first phase of our intervention program and actively engaged in its curriculum. This consisted of 10 group sessions of highly structured psychoeducation concerning trauma, its impacts in terms of life domains, presentations on masculinity, and special focus on three "shame pathways"—alcohol and drug use, rage and violence, and sexual dysregulated behavior.

After graduating from phase I, he entered phase II (a process-oriented group therapy program that can last up to 100 weeks of treatment) and this elicited considerable anxiety at first. Being in a circle of men, knowing that this was now the time to divulge much of his internal pain, brought with it a lot of self-doubt. Within the first couple of sessions, Jim started making connections to other men in the program and the similar stories that they shared. Jim gained insight into the profound shame that led him into the restricted life he had been living. Utilizing notions from ego state therapy, he not only became acquainted with his victim state but also understood the role his persecutory state played when he acted out of this pain.

Through his conviction of finding emotional integrity—one of the central tenets of our male-centered approach—he soon deepened his commitment to personal change as he embraced the program's goals. Like others in group therapy, he first was able to demonstrate compassion with the other men in the circle before he found compassion in terms of his own life story. Rather than hiding vulnerable emotions, he learned to speak through a shaky voice and tears when he felt pain. Equally as profound, he found that he could give other men strength through complimenting and supporting them on their courage to self-disclose. In essence, he found that by giving to others, he was able to give to himself.

Outcome

By week 40 of the program, Jim completed his testimony—a semistructured verbal narrative in front of the group of his past abuse and the trials it put him through over the years. Part of the testimony process is to reflect on not only the negative things that have happened to the individual, but the self-discovery and strengths gained from dealing with adversity. He included in his testimony the most shaming element of his story—that he was forced by his perpetrator to "recruit" other children for abuse. One of these childhood friends had since committed suicide—an incredible weight that was his last "secret" to the abuse.

Jim has since finished the program with pride and confidence. He received his graduating diploma and the well wishes of his "brothers" (his language) in the circle. He now states that he has "found" himself—something he has never experienced in his life. While he maintains his sobriety and his commitment to nonviolence, he finds he receives strength by being of service to others—now volunteering at a homeless shelter and engaging with men there who are struggling with addictions and violence. He is proud that he is rebuilding connections with his ex-wife and children, and expresses appreciation of his life now.

CHALLENGES IN APPLYING THE EVIDENCE-BASED APPROACH

Suffice to say, evidence-based approaches that engage men in male-centered trauma treatment are few and far between. Given how gendered child sexual abuse is, clinicians should be hesitant to apply female-focused research on male clients, or expect that "the gender injury" can be addressed in treatment strategies that avoid this issue altogether. Cognitive-based strategies, even trauma-informed cognitive therapies, are best applied to front-end service engagement. In phased programming (somewhat of a gold standard in community-based services), cognitive approaches constitute phase I intervention. Again, they are seen as useful, but not sufficient. The men in our service are repeatedly told in phase I that they are in the shallow end, and they need to demonstrate competence before engaging in the process-oriented deep-end trauma therapy of phase II.

While providing essential conceptual knowledge and a working language for the men, the cognitive approach takes the back seat in phase II. This is when emotionally focused and deeper processing work takes dominance. Here, the integration of memory, mourning of the loss, and providing an overarching narrative to the trauma and subsequent recovery are all key elements of this stage of engagement. It is unfortunate that there is little in the way of evidence-based treatment to help carve out this phase of service; however, the recent evaluation of our services is promising.

Following Judith Herman's three stages of recovery, the men's final steps are to work toward reconnection with their lives. Subsequent phase II activities no longer require a "survivor" lens to their work, as they are encouraged to take steps in becoming better fathers, partners, and community members. Again, this end stage of intervention is essentially unchartered territory.

CULTURAL DIVERSITY ISSUES

There is very little material on cultural diversity on male survivor treatment issues, assuming that one does not think of gender as culture. That being said, there are a number of subpopulations of male survivors that warrant particular focus, both in terms of understanding and potential intervention. We identify them as gay and bisexual men, Aboriginal men, men with histories of marginalization, men with physical and/or intellectual impairments, male psychiatric patients, men who attended residential institutions (including clergy abuse victims), and newcomer men (both immigrants as well as refugees).

FUTURE RESEARCH

Part of the challenges for all of us, both researchers and clinicians alike, is that there are so few treatment centers for men. How can more comprehensive research occur in such a vacuum? It is incumbent to us all to build these resources for men, all the while we conduct research in terms of treatment. Such services need to be "laboratories" to help inform us all.

While it needs to be said that cognitive studies do have their use, it is problematic that there is so much focus on research stays with this domain. This overreliance, well based in psychological research (at least here in North America), provides little to direct the clinician to find deeper, and hopefully more profound means of change for clients. Of course, cognitive work is our primary default in applying psychology to clinical services—it's so much easier to consider research in this domain as well—but I don't think this is what most trauma therapists need. What we fundamentally need in the field is the research findings on working through issues of trauma on an emotional, physiological, and spiritual plains of engagement.

The same can be said for male-centered approaches to treatment. Despite the fact that trauma is universal, our engagement styles with men versus women should not be. This relatively new domain of the psychology of men has yet to make the quantum leap to trauma therapy considerations—particularly sexual trauma. The question remains: How can we speak effectively to men who are struggling with recovery? What aspects of their masculine selves remains the entry point to their healing? We are just beginning to tackle one of the last legacies of masculine prerogative—the invisibility of male victimization.

KEY REFERENCES

Gartner, R. B. (1999). *Betrayed as boys: Psychodynamic treatment of sexually abused men*. New York, NY: Guilford Press.

Herman, J. L. (1997). *Trauma and recovery*. New York, NY: Basic Books.

Van der Kolk, B. A. (1996). The body keeps the score: Approaches to the psychobiology of posttraumatic stress disorder. In B. A. van der Kolk, A. C. McFarlane, & L. Weisaeth (Eds.), *Traumatic stress: The effects of overwhelming experience on mind, body, and society*. New York, NY: Guilford Press.

CHAPTER 61

Rape Victims

Michelle J. Bovin, Stephanie Y. Wells, and Patricia A. Resick

CLINICAL PROBLEM

Rape is a violent crime that can lead to devastating consequences. In the aftermath of a rape, survivors tend to experience increases in negative emotions (e.g., fear, guilt) as well as psychological symptoms (e.g., anxiety and depression, acute stress disorder). For many rape survivors, these symptoms will naturally remit within 3 to 4 months of the event. However, there are still large numbers of rape survivors who will not recover and will experience psychopathology that disrupts functioning for months or years.

PREVALENCE

Research has found that Posttraumatic Stress Disorder (PTSD) and Major Depressive Disorder (MDD) are the two most common disorders that develop as a result of rape. Rape survivors compose the single largest group of people with PTSD, and epidemiological studies have found rape to be the trauma that is most likely to lead to PTSD. For example, one study that examined a sample of female rape survivors who were an average of 17 years post-rape found that 57% of rape victims met lifetime diagnostic criteria for PTSD, and 16.5% met criteria for current PTSD. Regarding MDD, one study compared women who had been raped at least one year before to a nonvictim control group. Results indicated that the rape survivors (19%) were significantly more depressed than the control group (8%).

CULTURAL DIVERSITY ISSUES

Although both genders can be victims of rape, women tend to be overrepresented as victims of this crime. Epidemiological studies indicate that approximately one in seven women report having experienced a completed rape. The occurrence of rape is likely more prevalent than these estimates suggest, because rape is often under-reported. This may be particularly true for male rape victims. Studies have also found that although White and non-White women appear to be at equal risk for rape, group differences in risk emerge when only minority women are considered. In one study that examined minority women, Native American women were the most likely to report having been raped, whereas Hispanic women were the least likely to report this having occurred. Studies examining rates of rape by socioeconomic status (SES) have been somewhat equivocal; however, women of low SES tend to report more rapes than women of high SES. Finally, there is some evidence that rates of rape may vary by world region, with Southern Africa, Oceania, and North America reporting the most rapes, and Asia reporting the fewest. However, it remains unclear if these prevalence rates are a result of differential risk or under-reporting by group.

EVIDENCE-BASED TREATMENTS

Three treatment packages have demonstrated the most treatment of rape-related psychopathology: Stress Inoculation Training (SIT), Prolonged Exposure (PE), and Cognitive Processing Therapy (CPT). SIT was one of the earliest treatment packages to be used with rape survivors, and has strong empirical support. For example, two randomized studies found that a modified version SIT was superior to both a waitlist control and supportive counseling in decreasing symptoms of PTSD and depression.

SIT consists of three phases: an initial phase, a skill-building phase, and an application phase. In the initial phase, patients are provided with psychoeducation that serves to normalize their reactions to the rape by explaining the relationship between fear cues, automatic fear reactions, intrusive thoughts, and avoidance behaviors. In addition, this phase is used to present the rationale for the treatment. In the skill-building phase, patients are trained in six distinct skills: muscle relaxation, breath control, covert modeling, thought stopping, role playing, and guided self-dialogue. Finally, in the application phase of the treatment, patients use their newly acquired skills in anxiety-provoking situations in which fear cues are matched with coping skills.

PE is an exposure-based therapy which is used to treat PTSD and other trauma sequelae. The goal of PE is to activate a proposed fear network and provide corrective information so that emotional processing can occur. PE has received a high level of empirical support across studies. Five randomized studies conducted with survivors of assault (predominantly rape) found that PE was successful in reducing PTSD and other rape-related psychopathology. One of these studies compared PE to a modified version of SIT; the authors found that whereas SIT was the most effective treatment in reducing PTSD symptoms immediately after treatment, women who had been treated with PE demonstrated significantly more PTSD decreases 3½ months after treatment. The authors concluded that of these two therapies, whereas SIT may be most effective in the short term, PE is the most effective in the long term.

PE is delivered in an individual format, and typically consists of 9 to 12 90-minute sessions, each of which is audiotaped. It includes four components: psychoeducation about trauma and PTSD, breathing retraining, in vivo exposure (i.e., confrontation of low-risk situations that patients have been avoiding because of their association with the trauma), and imaginal exposure (confrontation of trauma memories). At the end of each session, the clinician and patients process the thoughts and feelings that the patients have experienced during the session. Patients are then assigned to listen to the tape and engage in 45 minutes of in vivo exposure each day.

Unlike SIT or PE, CPT is a cognitive therapy and is rooted in cognitive theory. It was developed for the purposes of treating rape-related PTSD, but has since been expanded to treat other populations as well (e.g., combat veterans). CPT has demonstrated strong empirical support when used with female sexual and physical assault survivors as well as with adult female survivors of childhood sexual abuse. Research comparing CPT and PE has found that the two therapies were equally effective in reducing symptoms of PTSD and depression, and that there is very little relapse in rape victims treated with either treatment 5 to 10 years later. However, CPT was found to be superior to PE in reducing feelings of guilt on two out of four subscales, health-related concerns, and hopelessness.

CPT has three therapy goals. The first goal is to target emotions that commonly occur as a product of the trauma of rape, including anger, humiliation, shame, guilt, and sadness. In this way, CPT is unique because it moves beyond the view that rape-related symptoms are only associated with fear. The second goal of CPT is to examine the meaning of the traumatic memory to the victim. The third goal, related to the second, is to help the client develop more balanced and fact-based beliefs than previously held beliefs. CPT strives to help patients appropriately accommodate the rape into their existing memory and beliefs. This is accomplished by first helping patients to challenge any distorted beliefs ("It's my fault") that are maintained in order to preserve patients' old beliefs about themselves and the world, particularly those associated with justice and fairness. The protocol then focuses on challenging patients' overgeneralized beliefs about the rape that are maintained at the expense of previously held beliefs, particularly those associated with safety, trust, power/control, esteem, and intimacy. CPT was designed to be a 12-week program, administered in weekly, 50- to 60-minute sessions.

FUTURE RESEARCH

The three therapy protocols described here each demonstrate strong empirical support for the treatment of rape-related symptoms. However, additional research is still needed to assist clinicians in determining which treatment is most effective for their individual patient's needs, as well as to examine whether these treatments are effective with other populations (e.g., male rape victims). Further, applied research will help clarify mediators and moderators of change in the therapeutic process. Together with current knowledge, these advances provide clinicians and patients with hope for addressing the damaging consequences associated with this trauma.

KEY REFERENCES

Foa, E. B., & Rothbaum, B. O. (1998). *Treating the trauma of rape: Cognitive-behavioral therapy for PTSD*. New York, NY: Guilford Press.

Resick, P. A., & Schnicke, M. K. (1993). *Cognitive processing therapy for rape victims: A treatment manual*. Newbury Park, CA: Sage Publications, Inc.

Veronen, L. J., & Kilpatrick, D. G. (1983). Stress management for rape victims. In D. Meichenbaum & M. Jaremko (Eds.), *Stress prevention and management* (pp. 341–374). New York, NY: Plenum.

Rape Victims

Emily Malcoun, Megan Kearns, and Barbara Olasov Rothbaum

COMMENT ON THE EVIDENCE-BASED RECOMMENDATIONS

We agree with Drs. Bovin, Wells, and Resick that there is hope for rape victims with several effective treatments available. There are several evidence-based treatments that have been shown to be effective for PTSD in general, and rape victims in particular, particularly prolonged exposure therapy and cognitive processing therapy.

CASE EXAMPLE

Subject Information and Brief History

This case was part of a larger ongoing investigation of an early psychological intervention in the immediate aftermath of a trauma to prevent development of PTSD. The patient, "Anna," was a 19-year-old African American female and a full-time college student residing at a local homeless shelter. She had a history of several prior acquaintance rapes.

Presenting Problem

Anna presented to the emergency department (ED) at a large southeastern United States metropolitan Level I trauma center immediately following sexual assault by a male acquaintance with whom she sought temporary shelter. As a Level I trauma center, this ED provides the highest level of surgical care to trauma patients and therefore receives the highest volume of trauma patients, including rape victims, in the region. She initially presented as tearful and extremely angry toward the perpetrator. Anna awoke during the night to the perpetrator vaginally penetrating her. When he threatened her, she feared for her life and narrowly escaped his residence. She enlisted assistance from police officers at a public transit station, who drove her to the perpetrator's residence to identify him before taking her to the ED.

Treatment Intervention and Course

Anna's initial assessment and first treatment session occurred 6 to 8 hours post trauma. She received a total of three 60-minute weekly sessions of modified prolonged exposure therapy delivered in the ED. Session 1 included an introduction to the intervention and treatment rationale, psychoeducation about normal reactions to trauma, and 30 minutes of prolonged imaginal exposure to the assault (repeated recounting of the trauma narrative). Themes identified during imaginal exposure were processed with the psychotherapist, and behavioral exposures to safe, but avoided reminders of the assault (e.g., interacting with trusted male peers, taking public transportation) and self-care tasks (e.g., listening to soothing music and eating three meals a day) were identified. Anna was also taught breathing retraining, a technique that slows down breathing and deactivates the fight/flight response overfunctioning in trauma survivors. She was assigned daily homework that included listening to a recording of her trauma narrative, practicing breathing retraining, enlisting helpful self-statements, and engaging in behavioral tasks to combat avoidance and promote self-care. Sessions 2 and 3 followed the same protocol, and included homework review. Themes processed in session 1 included feelings of self-blame, betrayal, and anger toward the accused, whom she considered a friend and had confided in about previous assaults. Anna identified spending time in public with safe male friends as a useful exposure to counteract her feeling that men are generally dangerous and untrustworthy and should be avoided. Treating herself to a meal outside the shelter, listening to music, and reminding herself of her goal to complete college were identified as helpful self-care tasks and statements to practice during the first week. Given Anna's pattern of being assaulted during overnight stays with male friends, the psychotherapist worked with her to establish safety rules around men. The theme of learning from the traumatic event without being responsible for the crime committed against her was highlighted.

In session 2, Anna complied with homework but reported difficulty listening to the imaginal exposure. A new theme of helplessness emerged and was reframed in processing as a sense of triumph for escaping from a dangerous situation. Homework remained the same with the addition of reminding herself that she exited the situation and assisted police officers to identify the assailant.

In session 3, Anna again complied with homework and noted that her feeling of repulsion around safe male friends as decreasing. Imaginal exposure focused on two "hot spots" (points in the trauma narrative soliciting the greatest distress), including awakening to sexual penetration by the perpetrator and returning to his residence with police investigators. Following imaginal exposure, Anna identified "it's not my fault" and "I am strong" as statements that would help her move forward from the traumatic event.

Outcome

Anna was assessed for PTSD and depressive symptoms 4 and 12 weeks following the intervention using the clinician administered PTSD Symptom Scale (PSS-I). PTSD was not assessed at presentation to the ED as it was within hours of the assault and would not have been valid at that point. Her PSS-I decreased by 9% from a total of 23 at week 4 to 21 at week 12. She did not meet the *DSM* criteria for a diagnosis of PTSD as a result of this assault at either assessment. Her Beck Depression Inventory (BDI) scores were 30 (beginning of Severe Depression) in the ED and 6 (Minimal Depression) 4 weeks later (depression was not assessed at week 12). This intervention was effective in preventing the development of PTSD, a common sequela found in women who have been sexually assaulted.

CHALLENGES IN APPLYING THE EVIDENCE-BASED APPROACH

There are several challenges to applying this treatment approach to recent survivors of rape. First, some trauma survivors may not be ready to discuss the trauma immediately following the event and feelings of numbness and dissociation may interfere with emotional processing of the trauma memory. Patients should therefore be thoroughly assessed to determine whether imaginal exposure in the immediate aftermath of an assault is appropriate. Second, applying this treatment in an ED setting incurred a number of challenges, including coordinating delivery of the intervention with the medical team, locating and securing a private room in which to deliver treatment, and working around survivors' urge to avoid the ED when it is associated with the trauma. Lastly, delivering this treatment to individuals residing in a homeless shelter presents unique challenges of securing privacy to practice the imaginal exposure between sessions, risks to the patient's physical safety at the shelter, and difficulties with transportation to and from treatment. Careful planning and coordination of treatment with ED and shelter staff, with the patient's permission, and psychoeducation around the importance of regular session attendance and facing, rather than avoiding, anxiety-provoking stimuli can assist in managing these challenges.

CULTURAL DIVERSITY ISSUES

The results of this case suggest that evidence-based, early intervention designed to prevent PTSD among at-risk populations can be effective and may particularly benefit rape victims, women, and minorities. There is substantial data supporting the generalizability of prolonged exposure (PE) across cultural groups within the United States (e.g., African Americans) and abroad, including Israel, Japan and China. For some trauma survivors, cultural variables of the psychotherapist may be avoided trauma reminders and therefore impede the client's ability to work with a particular psychotherapist. For example, an African American female whose assailant was a White male may not be willing or able to work with a Caucasian male psychotherapist. This challenge is particularly relevant when the client has survived a racially motivated trauma. The psychotherapist is encouraged to address and problem solve this issue collaboratively with the client. Working with the psychotherapist can function as a corrective in vivo exposure facilitating recovery from the trauma. In some cases, however, the client may need to work with a member of a cultural group she identifies as safe, and work toward incorporating behavioral exposures to members of the avoided cultural group.

FURTHER RESEARCH

Future research should focus on identifying predictors for developing PTSD that can be assessed in the immediate aftermath of trauma exposure, and then early interventions for those at risk to thwart the development of PTSD. We certainly need to continue to improve our treatments for chronic PTSD to be more effective for more sufferers, but if we can prevent the development of PTSD in the first place, we have eliminated so much suffering.

DISCLOSURES AND ACKNOWLEDGMENTS

This chapter was supported by National Institute of Mental Health Grant No. R34 MH083078, "Effects of Early Psychological Intervention to Prevent PTSD," and the Emory Center for Injury Control, Center for Disease Control Grant No. 5R49CE001494.

KEY REFERENCES

Foa, E., Hembree, E., & Rothbaum, B. O. (2007). *Prolonged exposure therapy for PTSD: Emotional processing of traumatic experiences (therapist guide)*. New York, NY: Oxford University Press.

Rothbaum, B. O., Kearns, M. C., Price, M., Malcoun, E., Davis, M., … Houry, D. (2012). Early intervention may prevent the development of PTSD: A pilot civilian study with modified prolonged exposure. *Biological Psychiatry, 72*, 957–963.

Zoellner, L. A., Feeny, N. C., Fitzgibbons, L. E., & Foa, E. B. (1999). Response of African-American and Caucasian women to cognitive behavioral therapy for PTSD. *Behavior Therapy, 30*(4), 581–595.

CHAPTER 62

Road Rage

Tara E. Galovski

CLINICAL PROBLEM

The problem of aggressive driving or, in its most severe form, *road rage*, has most likely been around as long as there have been automobiles. Since the advent of the automobile and the subsequent proliferation of roadways and traffic congestion, efforts have been made to quantify both the phenomenon of aggressive driving as well as the resultant societal cost. Definitions must differentiate aggressive driving from lapses in judgment or driver error by including the important element of *intent* by the perpetrator to threaten, harm, punish, or frighten another individual or his or her property. Specific driving behaviors included in the domain of aggressive driving include slow driving with the intent to block another's passage, tailgating, illegal passing on the shoulder, cutting drivers off after passing, failing to keep right, horn-honking, flashing high beams, failing to signal properly and personal attacks on other drivers (obscene gestures, verbal insults, throwing objects, waving firearms, and vehicular assault).

Aggressive driving has further been identified as a risk factor for motor vehicle accident morbidity and mortality at a rate equal to that of drunk driving with both victims and perpetrators experiencing a significantly greater risk of collision.

With the accumulation of evidence indicating the enormity of the societal risks and implications of aggressive driving, researchers have developed studies to understand exactly *who* is driving aggressively and *how* to treat the problem. Elevations in anger, hostility and aggression, and significant incidence of psychiatric comorbidity including intermittent explosive disorder, alcohol and substance disorders, attention deficit/hyperactivity disorder, antisocial personality disorder, and trends for anxiety and mood disorders have been observed in aggressive driving samples when compared to controls. Stress, traffic congestion, time urgency, young age, and male gender may also play a role in aggressive driving.

It is difficult to typify the aggressive driver as no single profile has emerged. In his pioneering work, Larson developed a typology of aggressive drivers including the Speeder, the Competitor, the Passive-Aggressor, the Narcissist, and the Vigilante. The titles alone convey the substantial range of the "type" of person who might engage in aggressive driving behaviors as well as their motivating factors. More recently, Lennon and Watson conducted a qualitative review of aggressive driver interviews and identified a "theme" suggesting that the aggressive drivers were attempting to correct or influence perceived infractions of their fellow drivers. Two subthemes included "teaching other drivers a lesson" or "justified retaliation" in which the aggressor perceived intent on the part of the other driver and retaliated in kind.

PREVALENCE

Estimating the prevalence and scope of aggressive driving is challenging given the myriad of driving behaviors and range of severity levels across definitions. The AAA Foundation for Traffic Safety data were used in a landmark study by Mizell who estimated that approximately 1,500 people died annually between 1990 and 1996 as a result of acts of aggression on the roadways.

CULTURAL DIVERSITY ISSUES

There are no significant cultural diversity factors related to the incidence and treatment of road rage. Men are more likely than women to experience this problem behavior than women.

EVIDENCE-BASED TREATMENTS

Larson's pioneering one-day program included psychoeducation about anger as well as self-identification with the five driver categories developed by Larson. The goal of the intervention was to aid the driver in challenging negative beliefs and behaviors associated with aggressive driving. The results were described as impressive.

Deffenbacher's original trial offered an improvement on Larson's work by comparing a self-management relaxation coping skills intervention to relaxation plus cognitive restructuring of faulty thinking in driving situations. Both treatment conditions (conducted in group format in 1-hour sessions over 8 weeks) were superior to an assessment only control, with few differences between active interventions. A second trial increased the latitude of the cognitive component in the relaxation plus cognitive condition. The positive results of the first trial were replicated with enhanced success in the relaxation plus cognitive therapy condition. Overall, both trials resulted in significant reductions in driving anger and aggressive driving when compared to the no-treatment controls. Treatment benefits were maintained at the 1-month follow-up.

The Albany program tested a cognitive behavioral intervention with a community sample of both court-mandated and self-referred aggressive drivers. The treatment was conducted in group format and included four weekly sessions of 2 hours' duration. The cognitive behavioral intervention included psychoeducation, self-identification as an aggressive driver, progressive muscle relaxation, the identification and challenging of driving-related cognitive distortions, and behaviorally oriented anger management techniques. The entire treatment protocol is published in Galovski, Malta, and Blanchard's work. Results showed significant improvements in individual aggressive driving behaviors, driving anger, and driver stress. Interestingly, the benefits of treatment appeared to generalize to related dimensions of psychological distress including anger and anxiety.

FUTURE RESEARCH

There is little doubt that aggressive driving is a significant contributor to motor vehicle accident risk, morbidity, and mortality. The level of psychological distress and significant psychopathology within the aggressive driving population has also been reported. Several studies have now demonstrated the success of cognitive behavioral interventions in high-risk college samples and both self-referred and court-mandated community samples. Future research should incorporate translation strategies (across law enforcement, traffic safety, social and clinical psychology) in an effort to more efficiently identify aggressive drivers and systemically offer opportunities (similar to driver education and drunk driving) in these types of treatment programs to aid these drivers in remediating these behaviors.

KEY REFERENCES

Deffenbacher, J. L., White, G. S., & Lynch, R. S. (2004). Evaluation of two new scales assessing driver anger: The Driving Anger Expression Inventory and the Driver's Angry Thoughts Questionnaire. *Journal of Psychopathology and Behavioral Assessment*, 26, 87–99.

Galovski, T. E., Malta, L. S., & Blanchard, E. B. (2006). *Road rage: Assessment and treatment of the angry, aggressive driver.* Washington DC: APA Books.

Hennessy, D. A., & Wiesenthal, D. L. (Eds.). (2005). *Contemporary issues in traffic research and road user safety.* New York, NY: Nova Science Publishers, Inc.

Clinician Application

Road Rage

Jerry L. Deffenbacher

COMMENT ON THE EVIDENCE-BASED RECOMMENDATIONS

There is empirical support, including studies cited in the Research Section, for relaxation (six studies), cognitive (two studies), behavioral (two studies), cognitive-relaxation (three studies), and cognitive behavioral (one study) interventions for angry, aggressive drivers. However, there is little or no replicated differential outcome between interventions. That is, there is no gold standard to guide choice of intervention. It is suggested that practitioners use the empirically supported literature to map interventions onto the defining characteristics of the client's anger while driving (e.g., relaxation for heightened emotional and physiological arousal, cognitive for anger-engendering cognitions, and behavioral for dysfunctional forms of anger expression).

CASE EXAMPLE

Subject Information and Brief History

The client was a single, White, 27-year-old college-educated male living in a large city, commuting over 30 minutes each morning and evening, and driving over 400 miles a week. He had a 10-year history of highly angry, aggressive driving, was one ticket away from losing his driver's license, had been warned by police officers that his conduct with them was unacceptable, and experienced interpersonal problems with his friends (e.g., teasing) and female partner (e.g., she did not want to ride with him) because of his angry, aggressive driving.

Presenting Problem

He reported frequent, lengthy driving anger episodes marked by high emotional and physiological arousal; cognitive distortions such as demanding (e.g.,"shoulds" for drivers and driving conditions), catastrophes (e.g., how awful and unbearable impedance was), hostile attributions (e.g., others purposefully doing things to anger or slow him), and inflammatory labeling (e.g., denigrating, inventively obscene labels for others); verbal (e.g., yelling at others, telling others off), physical (e.g., shaking fist, making obscene gestures), and vehicular (e.g., flashing lights, cutting drivers off) aggression; and risky behavior (e.g., rapidly cutting in and out of traffic, excessive speeding).

Treatment Intervention and Course

Psychotherapy consisted of seven 2-hour sessions every other week owing to the distance to the psychotherapist's office and combined cognitive, relaxation, and behavioral approaches. Between sessions, homework was emailed and reviewed in a 15-minute phone call.

Psychotherapy initially had a behavioral and relaxation focus with half of the sessions devoted to each modality. The behavioral component targeted dysfunctional anger expression. Social skills interventions employed with many anger problems did not map well onto driving anger, because of communication barriers and interpersonal distance involved in driving. Socratic questions and behavioral information collection (i.e., asking friends how they handled situations like being late, being stuck in traffic, or being the recipient of an obscene gesture) identified anger-reducing behaviors of: (a) *calming/distracting behaviors* (e.g., listening to music, planning for a meeting); (b) *avoiding anger triggers* (e.g., adding a time buffer to prevent being late); (c) *problem solving* (e.g., calling ahead if late); (d) *focusing on safe driving* (e.g., slowing down, letting another driver into his lane); (e) *disengaging/time out* (e.g., slowing and slowly moving away from an offending driver, pulling into a parking lot for a time out), and (f) *aggression-incompatible behaviors* (e.g., keeping hands at the 10 and 2 o'clock positions to interfere with angry gestures or keeping his tongue against the roof of his mouth to prevent yelling or cursing). He prepared cards clearly describing these behaviors, visualized using each once per day, and employed them in vivo with feedback and revision in subsequent sessions.

The relaxation component focused on progressive relaxation training and the development of specific relaxation coping skills (i.e., relaxation without tension, cue-controlled relaxation, deep breathing cued relaxation, and relaxation imagery). Relaxation coping skills were then employed to lower anger elicited by visualizing driving-related anger scenes. The client visualized a driving scene (e.g., being cut off by another driver), experienced emotional and physiological arousal, and then relaxed away experienced arousal. Initially, the psychotherapist provided considerable assistance in relaxation retrieval, and anger arousal was moderate. Over sessions, the psychotherapist's assistance was faded, and anger-arousing capacity of the scene increased, such that in the last session, the client self-induced relaxation for anger aroused by his most angering driving situations. Relaxation coping skills were applied in vivo and in contracted exposure, such as purposefully driving in heavy traffic or being late. In later sessions, attention shifted to maintenance and application to other sources of anger (e.g., anger when criticized).

Cognitive change began in the third session. Exploration of a situation in which the client was not highly angry revealed that he had accepted that he could not change poor drivers and turned on the radio and planned for a meeting (behaviors identified in the behavioral portion of treatment).The psychotherapist reinforced behavioral interventions, summarized thoughts and feelings, and asked him what he usually thought of, which identified high anger and several inflammatory labels, demands, catastrophes, and hostile attributions. The psychotherapist noted that the situation did not change over time, contrasted the feelings recorded with those typically experienced, and asked the client why there was such a difference. He indicated it was due to a change in his perspective. A cognitive rationale was introduced, and cognitive restructuring the following began: (a) *catastrophes* (e.g., "This is awful. I can't stand it." versus "This is frustrating, but not the end of the world. Just get in line and take your turn."); (b) *demanding* (e.g., "He should pull over." versus "I wish he would pull over and let me by, but sometimes you just get a poor or inattentive driver. Live with it."); (c) *inflammatory, derogatory labeling* (e.g., "Stupid ass!!" versus "Another poor driver, but stupid ass? Concretely define your terms. If he is a 'retarded burro' (picturing the image), now that is pretty funny and might explain his driving."); (d) *hostile appraisals/attributions* (e.g., "He did that on purpose." versus "Poor behavior for sure, but I do not know why. Maybe he didn't see the sign. Maybe he thinks the speed limit is different. Maybe he is distracted. Maybe he is sick. Maybe, maybe, maybe... I will focus on being a safe driver and let this go."); and (e) *accepting/tolerating/realistic expectations* (e.g., "I am stuck in traffic. I don't like it and may be late, but it happens from time to time. Basically, I have two choices. I can be stuck and furious or I can be stuck and fairly calm. Either way, I am stuck, but the choice of how angry I am is mine."). Cognitive responses were added to relaxation for in-session rehearsals and in vivo applications.

Maintenance strategies were also introduced to the client. These included client visualization and rehearsal of relaxation, cognitive and behavioral coping skills to two anger scenes five times per week, in vivo application with weekly psychotherapist email review and feedback, and three monthly booster sessions.

Outcome

After seven sessions, diary data showed roughly the pretreatment frequency of anger, but with much lower intensities and durations, and low rates of aggressive and risky behavior. On psychometric instruments, the client decreased from above the 90th percentile to the 45th percentile on driving anger (Driving Anger Scale) and from over the 80th percentile on measures of hostile cognitions (Driver's Angry Thoughts Questionnaire) and verbal, physical, and vehicular aggressive anger expression (Driving Anger Expression Inventory) to at or near the mean on these measures. Adaptive/constructive anger expression (Driving Anger Expression Inventory) moved from below the mean to the 75th percentile.

CHALLENGES IN APPLYING THE EVIDENCE-BASED APPROACH

For this clinician, the single biggest challenge is the issue of readiness for action-oriented therapy. Some individuals are highly angry drivers, but deny, minimize, normalize, justify, or blame others for their anger. For example, research has found that high-anger samples that turned down psychotherapy when it was free and accessible were demonstrably at risk and greater in numbers than angry drivers who entered psychotherapy. Readiness may be an even greater issue in groups who are legally or otherwise mandated into psychotherapy. Angry, aggressive drivers, as the transtheoretical or general stages of change literature suggests, are not ready for or good candidates for change-oriented interventions. They are at precontemplative (not thinking they have a problem) or contemplative (thinking they might have a problem, but not yet accepting and owning that they have a problem) stages of change, not the action-oriented stage for which interventions described in this chapter are appropriate. If interventions do not match the client's stage of change, they are likely to be ineffective. As such it is important to assess readiness and not immediately jump to change-oriented psychotherapies when the client is not ready for and accepting of them. Moving to action-oriented interventions when clients are not ready disrespects clients and increases resistance, impasse, and potentially premature termination.

CULTURAL DIVERSITY ISSUES

Outcome research has not studied diversity factors as potential mediators or moderators of psychotherapy. Correlational research offers some suggestions. Studies comparing urban and rural samples and White non-Hispanic and Mexican American samples show no differences. Gender differences tend not to be found in level of driving anger. Small to moderate gender effects are found for hostile/aggressive thinking and driving anger expression. However, these differences sometimes do not replicate. Age is a consistent factor. Younger drivers report more driving anger, more hostile thinking, aggressive and risky behavior, and less constructive anger expression. However, relationships among variables are of the same magnitude across age, suggesting that older "hotheads" tend to think and behave in similar ways, but to a lesser extent than their younger peers. These findings suggest gender, ethnicity, and urban/rural status may not influence individual or group psychotherapy composition, although age might be considered in group therapy composition (e.g., groups might be constructed for those under and those over 25 so that levels of anger and forms of thinking and expression might be more similar for group members). In summary, there is little research to guide how diversity factors might influence treatment. Practitioners need to be sensitive to cultural and religious practices which prohibit certain forms of meditation and relaxation practices and thereby make some relaxation interventions unacceptable. This requires that the clinician identify other culturally congruent relaxation interventions.

FUTURE RESEARCH

Outcome research with angry, aggressive drivers is still new. Future research should address the following issues: (a) Alternative interventions should be developed and evaluated with groups who differ by age, gender, occupational status (e.g., bus or truck drivers, police officers), ethnic background, and mandated status (e.g., self-identified volunteers vs. court mandated). This research will identify effective interventions, and mediation and moderation analyses will help identify other variables which may influence intervention. (b) Initial studies suggest long-term maintenance of effects, but long-term follow-up is needed. (c) Matching of client characteristics to interventions, as suggested earlier in this chapter, should be studied to assess if it improves outcome. (d) Individual psychotherapy should be compared to group interventions. Most research has been with small psychotherapy groups. Individual psychotherapy, however, provides for greater individualization of treatment which might improve outcomes. Relative efficacy and cost-to-benefit data can only be collected in such research. (e) Readiness for action- or change-oriented interventions needs attention. Researchers need to develop and evaluate interventions to see if readiness can be changed and individuals moved toward action-oriented forms of therapy. For example, motivational interviewing or a nonjudgmental exploration of driving anger consequences and whether driving anger is getting the individual what he or she wants could be explored.

KEY REFERENCES

Deffenbacher, J. L. (2013). Cognitive behavioral therapy for angry drivers. In E. Fernandez (Ed.), *Treatment for anger in specific populations: Theory, applications, and outcome* (Chap. 2). New York, NY: Oxford University Press.

Deffenbacher, J. L., Filetti, L. B., Lynch, R. S., Dahlen, E. R., & Oetting, E. R. (2002). Cognitive-behavioral treatment of high anger drivers. *Behaviour Research and Therapy, 40,* 895–910.

Galovski, T. E., Malta, L. S., & Blanchard, E. B. (2006). *Road rage: Assessment and treatment of the angry, aggressive driver.* Washington, DC: APA Books.

CHAPTER 63

Sex Offender Treatment

Mark E. Olver and Stephen C. P. Wong

CLINICAL PROBLEM

The sexual victimization of children and adults is a serious social concern with severe mental health and emotional sequelae. Victims of sexual assault are at risk for developing severe depression and anxiety, difficulties in sexual functioning and intimate relationships, substance abuse, and suicidal ideation among other concerns. Child victims of sexual abuse are at marked risk for developing similar mental health symptoms following the abuse and this can extend into their adult years. As such, it is important to develop effective assessment and treatment interventions to address these offenders.

Static and Dynamic Predictors of Sexual Recidivism

Empirical research has identified several risk markers predictive of sexual recidivism including both static (i.e., historical or unchangeable) variables, which generally cluster into indicators of length or severity of offending history (e.g., prior sex offenses), victim characteristics (e.g., male victim, unrelated), and offender characteristics (e.g., young age) as well as dynamic or potentially changeable or treatable variables such as sexually deviant interests or preoccupation, general lifestyle criminality, intimacy deficits, and offense supportive attitudes/cognitions.

Assessment of Sexual Offending Risk

There is a large range of actuarial tools developed; some use primarily static predictors, such as the Sex Offender Risk Appraisal Guide and Static 99/Static 99-R , while others incorporate dynamic predictors such as the Stable 2007, Sexual Violence Risk-20, and the Violence Risk Scale-Sexual Offender version. Meta-analytic research has demonstrated that no single tool has superior predictive accuracy for sexual violence. The choice of a tool should depend on the task at hand, for example, to assess risk of recidivism or to assess risk and to guide treatment. In practice, ideally, it is recommended that clinicians utilize multiple assessment measures and methods, assessing multiple domains of functioning, and using multiple information sources. Assessment is intended to appraise the probability of future sexual violence, identify areas to intervene therapeutically, and to inform supervision/risk management to reduce sexual violence.

Phallometric assessment entails measuring an individual's erectile responses to deviant and nondeviant visual or auditory stimuli. It is commonly used to assess the presence of deviant sexual interests/preferences and is frequently incorporated into risk assessments. Phallometric testing has demonstrated acceptable reliability, ability to differentiate among sex offender types, and sensitivity for detecting victim age and gender preferences. Although phallometric measurements of certain deviant interests (e.g., children) have demonstrated predictive accuracy for sexual recidivism, the procedure should not be used as a standalone tool for predicting recidivism. The technology can also be expensive, controversy exists regarding the stimuli used, and concerns have been raised regarding a lack of standardization in procedures.

Comorbidity Issues

Sex offenders frequently present with comorbid mental health concerns with prevalent conditions including paraphilias, substance abuse, personality disorders (e.g., antisocial personality disorder), and mood disorders. The presence of psychopathy or psychopathic personality is a particular concern as psychopathic sex offenders are more likely to drop out of treatment, are at higher risk to sexually and violently reoffend, and the combined presence of psychopathy and sexual deviance has been found to interact to increase risk.

PREVALENCE

According to the most recent U.S. National Crime Victimization Survey in 2009, an estimated 125,910 rapes/sexual assaults occurred against individuals age 12 and over. Sexual victimization rates were more than four times higher for females. The estimated prevalence rates of sexual abuse vary among sources, although national U.S. surveys suggest approximately 1 to 5 children out of 1,000 have been victims of sexual abuse in recent years and that approximately 9% to 32% of women and 5% to 10% of men report having experienced sexual abuse or assault in childhood. North American victimization surveys repeatedly demonstrate that more than half of self-reported sexual assaults are not reported to the police. International estimates also suggest the vast majority (95%) of sexual assault perpetrators are male, while less than 5% are female. Thus, service providers face an important challenge to assess, treat, and supervise sexual offenders to prevent/reduce recidivism. Preventative detention (e.g., sexually violent predator) laws intended to protect the public from dangerous individuals also highlight the importance of accurate assessment and effective treatment.

Rates of Sexual Recidivism

A Canadian follow-up study of 4,724 offenders documented recidivism rates of 14% after 5 years, 20% after 10 years, and 24% after 15 years. It also reported that sexual recidivism rates decline substantially with age: base rates were cut roughly in half for those over age 50 at release compared to those under 50, across all follow-ups. Debate continues about how best to account for age-related risk changes: by differentially weighing age-related predictors versus using age corrected risk adjustments for older offenders.

CULTURAL DIVERSITY ISSUES

In Canada, for instance, Aboriginal people comprise only 3% of the general Canadian population but approximately 20% of its federal inmate population. Accordingly, sex offender programs designed for aboriginal offenders use a blend of cognitive behavioral and traditional healing approaches. For instance, through employing aboriginal Elders or program facilitators who are fully familiar with indigenous culture and language and who can use traditional healing methods (e.g., sweat lodge, smudging) or teachings to maximize therapeutic engagement and gain. Similarly New Zealand's Te Piriti and Kia Marama Programs for child sexual abusers have integrated indigenous treatment approaches from Maori culture to maximize client engagement and benefit. Finally, although Latinos account for approximately 20% of the incarcerated population in the United States, very little has been written on assessment and treatment issues with Latino sex offenders. Available guidelines underscore the importance of delivering sex offender treatment services in Spanish to clients for whom their primary or preferred language is Spanish, sensitivity to issues of acculturation, and an awareness of cultural differences (e.g., regarding gender roles, sexual behavior, etc.) that may impact response to treatment.

EVIDENCE-BASED TREATMENTS

Models of Sex Offender Treatment

Two prominent models of offender treatment are the Risk-Need-Responsivity (RNR) and the Good Lives Model (GLM). Central to the RNR model, which has extensive empirical support, are the principles of Risk (treatment intensity should be matched to the client's level of risk), Need (dynamic risk factors linked to sexual or nonsexual violence should be prioritized for treatment), and Responsivity (using cognitive behavioral interventions, referred to as *general responsivity*), and tailoring the content and delivery of treatment to the individual client characteristics such as motivation, learning style, or cultural heritage, referred to as *specific responsivity*. Some emphases of the GLM include utilizing and building upon client strengths and resiliencies and helping the client develop skills to achieve "common goods," in addition to addressing criminogenic needs. The RNR model also takes into account client strengths and the attainment of prosocial goals, while prioritizing targeting of criminogenic needs.

Cognitive Behavioral Treatment/Relapse Prevention

A comprehensive survey of sex offender treatment programs in North America found the majority to be cognitive behavioral in orientation, address a comprehensive range of needs, and employ a group treatment format frequently augmented with individual psychotherapy. Although the structure, organization, setting, and delivery of treatment programs vary, common treatment foci include intimacy and relationships skills, restructuring attitudes and cognitions supportive of sexual offending, victim empathy training, managing sexually deviant interests and arousal, emotional regulation, overcoming denial and minimization and accepting responsibility, problem-solving skills, and social skills training. Frequently, programs will also employ relapse prevention (RP) techniques and principles, culminating in an individuals RP plan that enables offenders to manage high risk situations, utilizing existing or acquired coping strategies to prevent relapse. Some programs, in fact, have adopted RP as a primary therapeutic framework for treatment, although in recent years this has decreased possibly owing to declining support for this approach as a primary focus in treatment.

The importance of the community setting and supports in sex offender treatment and reintegration cannot be understated. Personal and family supports are paramount, although in cases where this may be insufficient or nonexistent, support services, such as Circles of Support & Accountability (CoSA) provide community reintegration support for offenders released at the end of their sentences and are available in several major cities across North America and the United Kingdom. The therapeutic process can also extend to healing communities that have been impacted by sexual abuse as seen in some Aboriginal community initiatives in Central and Western Canada. Although the foci and content of the programs vary, a common thread is the role of the community in providing support and oversight in the treatment and reintegration of the offender, the healing of the victims and families impacted by the abuse, and the incorporation of traditional Aboriginal philosophies.

Issues in Sex Offender Treatment: Denial and Treatment Noncompletion

Some common treatment domains, such as denial and empathy, bear weak relationships to sexual recidivism, although denial can be a specific responsivity issue given that it can impede therapeutic progress and high levels of denial have been linked to dropout. Successful efforts to help offenders overcome denial have been documented, although doubts have recently been expressed about the necessity of having offenders fully disclose all details of their offending given this has not been linked to improved treatment outcomes. Recommendations have been advanced to employ motivational engagement strategies such as motivational interviewing with resistant clientele regardless of their level of denial. The importance of retaining sex offender clientele in treatment is underscored by meta-analytic research demonstrating that high risk offenders are more likely to drop out of treatment and that sex offender treatment noncompleters demonstrate higher rates of sexual and violent recidivism.

Biomedical Treatments

The use of antiandrogens and selective serotonin reuptake inhibitors for sex offenders are common biomedical interventions which serve to reduce sex drive and the frequency and intensity of sexual fantasy and arousal. Although research has demonstrated the efficacy of antiandrogen therapy to reduce sexual recidivism, it is recommended that biomedical interventions should be used in conjunction with psychological interventions and not as a standalone treatment.

Efficacy of Treatment Programs

Evaluating "what works" in the treatment of sex offenders can be organized into three paradigms: (a) pre–postprogram evaluations of within treatment change, (b) single treatment outcome designs, and (c) meta-analysis of treatment outcome studies. Pre–post evaluations have provided some support that sex offenders can make changes in relevant treatment domains (e.g., intimacy deficits, attitudes/ cognitions, negative emotional states). Such designs, however, seldom include control groups and few evaluations have examined whether such changes translate into reductions in postprogram recidivism, although two studies have found this to be the case.

Single treatment outcome studies vary in methodological quality, size, scope, and treatment foci with the vast majority having been nonrandomized quasi-experimental evaluations. Importantly, these designs directly address the question as to whether treatment reduces recidivism. There have been very few randomized controlled trials in this field, with the most prominent, the RP-based Sex Offender Treatment Evaluation Project (SOTEP), finding few differences between treated and matched untreated offenders. Over the past 15 years, there have been at least five meta-analyses of this literature. The most inclusive of these examined 69 studies and found that treated offenders had about a 6% point reduction in sexual recidivism (11.1 vs. 17.5, a 37% relative difference) with cognitive behavioral therapy (CBT), behavioral, and biomedical approaches showing the largest reductions. The most recent review included only those studies that met minimum methodological standards and found an 8% point difference (10.9 vs. 19.2, a 43% relative difference) between treatment and comparison groups across 22 studies; programs adhering to the RNR principles tended to have larger effects. In short, the available literature would indicate a robust effect of sex offender treatment for reducing sexual violence with evidence-informed programs demonstrating the most substantive reductions.

FUTURE RESEARCH

There are many important avenues of pure and applied sex offender research that could improve release decision making, the effectiveness of sex offender assessment and treatment, and community risk management. For one, there is a need to examine what contributes to treatment efficacy by using, for example, more powerful evaluation methodologies such as randomized controlled trials. An additional fruitful avenue is continued research using new technologies (e.g., fMRI) on the etiologic mechanisms underpinning deviant sexual interests and behavior, which may inform risk management and intervention strategies. Finally, in our view, the field may benefit from continued examination of therapeutic change mechanisms and processes among sexual offenders; that is, to what extent service providers can obtain valid and reliable measures of risk change and incorporate this information into posttreatment risk estimates and management strategies to prevent sexual violence.

KEY REFERENCES

Andrews, D. A., & Bonta, J. (2010). *The psychology of criminal conduct* (5th ed.). New Providence, NJ: LexisNexis.
Laws, D. R., & O'Donohue, W. T. (2008). *Sexual deviance: Theory, assessment, and treatment* (2nd ed.). New York, NY: Guilford Press.
Marshall, W. L., Marshall, L. E., Serran, G. A., & O'Brien, M. D. (2011). *Rehabilitating sexual offenders: A strength based approach.* Washington, DC: American Psychological Association.

Sex Offender Treatment

Lawrence Ellerby

COMMENT ON THE EVIDENCE-BASED RECOMMENDATIONS

Cognitive behavioral therapy (CBT) has been identified as the most frequent psychotherapeutic approach in North American sex offender treatment programs and has been found to be effective in treating this population. Although CBT is important, most clinicians integrate additional approaches that tend not to be identified or empirically investigated, given the emphasis on CBT (e.g., humanistic therapy, narrative therapy, integrative or holistic therapy). For many years, Relapse Prevention (RP) has been a central component of most sex offender programs. The primary construct of RP is the identification of the factors that contributed to the offending behavior and have the potential to place the individual at future risk for offending behavior and the development of strategies to avoid and/or manage these risk factors. Despite recent challenges to RP in the literature, it continues to be present and important in clinical practice. There has been growing interest in the use of the Good Lives Model (GLM), which promotes a positive, strength-based approach to risk management by attending to key need areas defined as "primary goods" (e.g., healthy living and functioning, knowledge, hobbies and recreational pursuits, mastery experiences, autonomy and self-directedness, relationships, inner-peace, a sense of community and spirituality). This model is appealing for many psychotherapists. However, practitioners are still learning to translate the model into practice and the GLM is in the early stages of empirical validation. The Risk-Need Responsivity (RNR) model is a cornerstone in our practice. RNR guides the psychotherapist in matching the intensity of the intervention to the level of risk and need presented by the client, directs treatment to target areas most relevant to risk management (e.g., antisocial personality pattern, procriminal attitudes and values, negative peer group, family, and/or marital relationship problems, substance abuse, deficits in education, employment, and/or healthy recreation) and highlights the importance of interventions being delivered in ways that consider and will optimize client engagement and the impact of the intervention (e.g., client age, gender, cultural background, level of cognitive functioning, trauma history, presence of a mental disorder, experience of anxiety, depression). Despite the importance of this model, in a survey of North American sex offender treatment programs, few programs identified RNR as a central part of their program.

CASE EXAMPLE

Subject Information and Brief History

Joe is a 38-year-old Canadian Aboriginal man with a history of committing sexual offences against children. He was raised by alcoholic parents, witnessed and experienced violence in the home, observed inappropriate sexual behavior, and had been sexually abused by a male relative. He did poorly academically and socially, had limited employment skills, and was first incarcerated at age 18 for sexually abusing three of his prepubescent female cousins. Following his release from prison at age 37 after serving an 8-year sentence for sexually assaulting a pubescent boy, he was referred for treatment by his parole officer. He was mandated to attend treatment as part of his release conditions.

Presenting Problem

Typical of this population, Joe presented with a multitude of problem areas. He was referred because of his offending behavior and continued sexual interest in children. In addition, he had a history of alcohol abuse and aggressive behavior, presented with emotional regulation issues, had poor social and interpersonal skills, and had been diagnosed with Depression and Antisocial Personality Disorder. All of these served as areas of vulnerability and contributing factors to his offending behavior. In addition, owing to the amount of his life spent incarcerated, issues of institutionalization were present (e.g., dependent on a high level of structure and direction, a heightened level of anxiety being in public, adherence to the prison subculture value system/code of conduct, lack of knowledge and ability related to common life skills—use of common technology, public transportation, money management, appropriate social and problem-solving skills).

Treatment Intervention and Course

Joe's treatment consisted of individual psychotherapy, group therapy, as well as adjunct interventions including working with a community support worker (a Community Integration Manager–CIM) as well as with Aboriginal Elders/Spiritual Helpers. The initial treatment goal with Joe was establishing a therapeutic rapport. Given he was a mandated client and presented with significant trust and attachment issues, it was essential to create a safe and collaborative psychotherapeutic relationship for positive outcome. Initial interventions focused on addressing a host of practical concerns (e.g., generalized distrust; off putting style of dress and deportment; absence of personal identification; unattended medical needs) and basic coping skills to support successful community adjustment (e.g., managing anxiety on the bus; challenging distorted, paranoid, and negative thinking while walking on the street). A host of strategies such as relaxation techniques, cognitive restructuring, role playing, behavioral rehearsal, and modeling were used to support these treatment goals. As Joe reported actively struggling with inappropriate sexual thoughts of children, treatment focused on a range of CBT and behavioral strategies to help him address these thoughts. This included teaching him to use thought-stopping techniques, reminding himself of the inappropriate nature of these thoughts and how they can contribute to moving closer to offending, focusing on the consequences of sexualizing and sexually abusing children (impact on the child, the child's family, himself, his family, the larger community), personalizing the child (thinking of them as a child versus a sexual object), thinking about the positive things in their life (e.g., their freedom), and future goals. We also developed a plan to avoid placing himself in high-risk situations and to manage high-risk situations he might encounter. For example, basic behavioral interventions were discussed to manage situations where an arousal trigger was present such as engaging in distracting activities (e.g., on the bus having something to read, puzzles to do, and/or music to listen to if there were children present) or removing himself from the situation. Simultaneously, sessions focused on helping Joe alter his masturbation practices in an attempt to reduce his focus on age-inappropriate sexual arousal. In this regard, strategies were used to help him interrupt and reduce interest in and reinforcement of inappropriate sexual arousal and to enhance focus on and reinforcement of age-appropriate consenting images for fantasy and masturbation (masturbatory satiation, orgasmic reconditioning, covert sensitization). It is important to note that these strategies are not required for all individuals who have committed a sexual offence. They should be targeted for those who demonstrate a sexual interest in children versus those offenders who offend primarily as a result of emotionally based reasons versus arousal-based motivation (e.g., incest type offenders). As well, these techniques are most effective for individuals who also reported being able to experience arousal to adults. They are less effective with individuals whose sexual interest is exclusive to children. Individual and group intervention also focused on helping Joe enhance his level of self-disclosure and accountability related to his sexual offending behavior. This allowed for addressing his defenses (e.g., defensive avoidance), challenging distorted perceptions (e.g., his belief that his victims did not resist so they must have been willing participants, minimizing the harm done to his victims, maintaining that since he was hurt as a child others should be made to feel the same way) and identifying factors that contributed to his offending (e.g., disruptions in attachment, trauma symptomatology, substance abuse, marked feelings of insecurity and fear of rejection, anger/rage, a sense of entitlement, egocentricity, a tendency toward personalization and negative framing of his perceptions and experiences, an absence of trust, empathy deficits, underdeveloped interpersonal skills, intimacy deficits, and limited knowledge about healthy sexuality), and the need areas relevant to this (e.g., seeking in distorted ways, a sense of competency and mastery, power, and control and sense of attachment and connection). Individual psychotherapy and group treatment then systematically addressed each of the identified areas of vulnerability/risk. In an effort to consolidate and integrate his treatment gains, Joe developed a wellness plan highlighting what he was learning in therapy and about himself and his risk in regards to the things he needed to avoid (e.g., attending places where children were likely to congregate, being alone with a child, unhealthy peers, situations where alcohol was prominent) and/or manage (e.g., his tendency to personalize, revenge based thinking, sexualizing children), and what he needed to be proactively doing in order to live a healthy and offence-free life (e.g., perception checks, positive self-talk, maintaining healthy relationships and a feeling of connectedness, proactive problem solving, engaging in activities that fostered a sense of competency, satisfaction, and enjoyment). This plan was reviewed with the other key supports in his life (his parole officer, family members) so they could be informed support people who could assist him in managing his risk and living a healthy lifestyle.

Outcome

After about 5 months of weekly individual and group therapy, Joe incrementally became more comfortable and confident living in the community, built a good psychotherapeutic working relationship, and developed a strong support system (of professionals and nonprofessionals). After a year of individual and group treatment, Joe has remained in the community offence free. He reports appropriately managing his sexual thoughts and behavior and being fairly consistent in challenging and replacing distorted, negative, and antisocial thinking (e.g., a reduced frequency of personalizing, more other oriented thinking, and attentive to how his mood and behavior impact others). He also reports feeling more competent and capable and has demonstrated improvements in his social skills and interpersonal relationships, use of approach-oriented coping styles (e.g., seeking out supports, enhanced personal disclosure, being assertive, engaging in active problem solving), and improved emotional regulation (much improved anger management, less emotionally fragile and fearful of rejection, and better able to identify, experience, and express a range of emotions). He remains on medication to assist him with his depression and has developed a strong support group consisting of other men in treatment who are doing well, reestablished relationships with family members, faith-based support people, and his professional supports.

CHALLENGES IN APPLYING THE EVIDENCE-BASED APPROACH

At times, research findings are not consistent with clinical wisdom (e.g., treating low-risk offenders makes them worse, accountability and empathy are not relevant treatment goals to support risk reduction). Such findings are often purported to be definitive when they may reflect methodological issues, particularly in regards to attempting to measure difficult constructs. For example, the need to take absolute full accountability is not required to produce treatment gains and manage risk; however, enhanced disclosure allows for better identification and targeting of offence precursors and for addressing what are often generalized defense mechanisms (e.g., denial, minimization, suppression, repression, projection of responsibility) and processing often present issues of shame and a negative sense of self. These are complex issues to separate out, to operationally define, and to measure. Similarly, attention to victim empathy issues in treatment, not as a punitive therapeutic component to shame but to facilitate an appreciation of the impact of one's behavior on others, the harm caused by sexual acting out, to facilitate moral and ethical development, to explore blocks to empathy and to enhance the ability for emotional connection, are important treatment goals. Empirical findings that suggest this not be a part of treatment are problematic given the current ability to empirically define and assess empathy and the limited scope of how empathy has been investigated with this population. As well, at times research has yet to to establish what clinical experience identifies as relevant and important treatment goals. For example, many offenders come from histories of trauma, which significantly impacts their emotional development and coping styles. Clinical experience suggests that addressing trauma is central to positive outcome. Empirical investigation into the role of trauma in understanding vulnerability to engage in sexual offending behavior and as a dynamic risk factor requiring therapeutic intervention could help guide clinical intervention.

CULTURAL DIVERSITY ISSUES

As Joe was interested in his Aboriginal culture and traditional healing, we worked collaboratively with Aboriginal Spiritual Helpers so he had the opportunity to participate in psychotherapy as well as traditional healing practices (e.g., sharing circles, Sweat Lodge Ceremonies, spiritual teachings). This approach was to ensure the interventions being provided were meaningful, engaging, and would facilitate positive treatment outcome. Attending to cultural diversity issues is a responsivity factor from the RNR model. It is important to determine, and as necessary, attend to responsivity factors in the treatment of all individuals who engage in sexual offending behavior (e.g., age, gender, and racial and religious backgrounds).

FUTURE RESEARCH

Research that could help guide clinical practice could include further investigation into responsivity factors, understanding the impact of addressing specific dynamic risk factors, and exploring the role trauma plays in contributing to offending behavior.

KEY REFERENCES

Andrews, D. A., & Bonta, J. (2010). *The psychology of criminal conduct* (5th ed.). Cincinnati, OH: Anderson.

Association for the Treatment of Sexual Abusers (ATSA). (2001). *Practice standards and guidelines for members of the Association for the Treatment of Sexual Abusers*. Beaverton, OR: Author.

Hanson, R. K., Bourgon, G., Helmus, L., & Hodgson, S. (2009). *A meta-analysis of the effectiveness of treatment for sexual offenders: Risk, need, and responsivity*. Ottawa, Ontario: Public Safety Canada.

CHAPTER 64

Sexually Abused Children

Michele Many and Phillip Stepka

CLINICAL PROBLEM

Cases of alleged child sexual abuse (CSA) often are regarded by clinicians with caution. This reflects a number of problems that CSA presents. These include the lack of a standardized definition of CSA, difficulties in accurately measuring the incidence and prevalence of CSA, the low rate of substantiated cases versus reported cases, the low rate of contemporaneous disclosure overall, and the persistence of recantation. Unlike other forms of abuse, CSA often lacks physical findings and thus is less likely to be substantiated by Child Protective Services or law enforcement. Thus the treating clinician may lack clarity about whether abuse has occurred or not. Also, CSA is seldom an isolated trauma, often presenting as physical and emotional abuse, nested within other adverse events such as neglect, domestic violence, and/or substance abuse in the household. Children who present with a history of CSA may exhibit a range of symptoms or no symptoms at all. Symptomatology is related to the frequency and duration of the abuse, relationship to the abuser, what form the abuse took (i.e., fondling vs. penetration), the child's perception of threat, and whether there are concurrent environmental and interpersonal stressors. The most common symptoms are those consistent with any trauma: loss of developmental milestones, hypervigiliance, numbing, and reexperiencing. In young children, reexperiencing can present as repetitive, joyless play themes replicating the traumatic event without resolution. Children may also present with symptoms of hyperarousal including irritability, clinginess, aggression, and emotional dysregulation. Sexualized behavior problems may be present as well, but is also found in nonsexually abused children exposed to physical abuse, neglect, domestic violence, and/or substandard parenting practices. No symptom picture is thought to be diagnostic of CSA, but the presence of trauma symptoms along with precocious sexual knowledge may indicate that CSA has occurred.

PREVALENCE

Current research indicates that there has been a marked decline in the incidence of CSA over the past 20 years. The National Child Abuse and Neglect Data System (NCANDS) report released in December 2011 documented a decline of substantiated sexual abuse rates of 62% between 1990 and 2010. Between 2009 and 2010 alone the rate dropped 3%, to an estimated rate of 8.6 per 10,000 substantiated cases. Concerns raised initially that economic pressures and/or changes in reporting policies or statistical procedures might have impacted the dramatic decline in substantiated cases were eased when the Fourth National Incidence Study of Child Abuse and Neglect (which was less susceptible to such issues) indicated similar declines. Some possible reasons were offered for the decline including improved staffing of child protection and law enforcement agencies and more public awareness of CSA, more effective mental health treatment of victims of CSA, and improvements in the prosecution of offenders.

Prevalence statistics prove more elusive. Different studies use varied definitions of sexual abuse. Some focused on contact sexual abuse, although state statutes include other kinds of offending such as exposure to sexually explicit media. Different methodologies (face to face interviews, questionnaires, telephone interviews) can impact subject responses due to embarrassment, lack of privacy, or poor rapport between interviewer and subject. In addition, it is well documented that survivors of CSA often delay disclosure of or may never disclose their abuse. Many respondents across multiple studies denied ever having disclosed their abuse to anyone but the interviewer. In one review of the literature of retrospective surveys of adults, of those respondents who endorsed a history of CSA, only one third reported having ever disclosed the abuse prior to the current interview. The same study reported that only 10% to 18% of these cases were reported to the authorities. This would lead us to estimate that the most widely reported prevalence rates of 25% to 40% of women and 8% to 16% of men may significantly underrepresent the actual prevalence of CSA.

CULTURAL DIVERSITY ISSUES

CSA occurs across the cultural, ethnic, and socioeconomic spectrum. Some studies indicate that culture may impact disclosure, how families respond to the occurrence of abuse, and if and to whom families and survivors will reach out for help. It is beyond the scope of this chapter to explore the ways diversity impacts CSA disclosure and treatment. Nevertheless, Fontes and Plummer urge us to educate ourselves about how culture and ethnicity may impact family responses to CSA, while also avoiding harmful generalizations and stereotypes.

EVIDENCE-BASED TREATMENTS

As discussed, the experience of CSA is associated with a wide range of outcomes that are multi-determined and vary in severity across individual children. While there are many negative outcomes associated with CSA, several of which are more or less consistent with different ages and abuse experiences, it is important to note that abuse by itself does not qualify someone with a diagnosable disorder. As is discussed subsequently, treatment should be tailored to the individual context and presenting issues of the child and should not be informed by unconfirmed stereotypes or overgeneralized treatment approaches.

Currently, the treatment of sexually abused children is informed by many theoretical models and has been attempted using a wide variety of techniques. Abuse-focused cognitive behavioral therapies (CBT) have undergone the most frequent and rigorous examination regarding the treatment of sexually abused children. However, there is emerging evidence to suggest that these approaches not only can be improved by integrating non-CBT approaches, but other approaches can be more helpful with various sequella of sexual abuse. In recent meta-analyses of various therapeutic modalities used in treating sexually abused children, it was discovered that various treatments were differentially effective in treating the secondary presenting problems associated with CSA. Specifically, play therapy was found to improve social functioning over other approaches. CBT and supportive approaches were similarly best suited for improving behavioral problems. CBT and family therapy were most effective in relieving psychological distress associated with CSA. Finally, CBT and group therapies were most effective in improving self-esteem. Furthermore, with children demonstrating sexual and disruptive behavior problems (frequently secondary to sexual abuse), caregiver involvement in treatment is more influential than specific treatment modality (e.g., CBT, Relapse Prevention, Psychoeducation) and that interventions which were adapted from adult sex offender treatments/theories were not significant predictors of therapeutic change.

Regarding findings guiding best practices in treating sexually abused children, overall treatment effect sizes are maximized across global outcome measures, sexualized behaviors, and general behavior problems when abuse-focused CBTs are combined with supportive, psychodynamic, experiential, and/or play-based approaches. This is in line with examinations of the developmental appropriateness of cognitive and language-loaded interventions with children. Capacities such as self-reflection, perspective taking, understanding causality, logical reasoning, and proficient receptive and expressive language skills are necessary prerequisites for many CBT interventions. Unfortunately, these abilities are generally absent or insufficiently developed in children under 7 years (particularly in clinical populations) and the treatment effects of cognitive interventions are often found to be inconsistent in children younger than 11 years of age. Taking these developmental limitations into account for preadolescent children, it stands to reason that supplementing more traditional CBT approaches with alternative treatment modalities is likely to make them more developmentally appropriate and increase their overall effectiveness.

These findings strongly argue against a generic "sexual abuse treatment" approach and emphasize the importance of tailoring treatment to the most salient presenting problems of sexually abused children and highlight the benefits of supplementing/integrating cognitive behavioral approaches with supportive, expressive, experiential, and caregiver-involved approaches.

FUTURE RESEARCH

Considering the differential efficacy of various treatment modalities, paired with support for tailoring treatments to specific presenting difficulties, future research would benefit from conducting component analyses of prevailing treatments to further distill the aspects of various treatments which are most efficacious with differing presenting problems. Once a better understanding of the beneficial components of various approaches is achieved, modular approaches to the treatment of childhood sexual abuse could be developed and tested. Such modular approaches could be a promising option that would help retain the integrity of evidence-based interventions while encouraging integrative approaches to the treatment of sexually abused children and adolescents. However, in order for such approaches to be most effective, further development and exploration of comprehensive theories of sexual abuse effects and attendant case conceptualization must be conducted. Current findings argue that the treatment of the whole family/caregiving system and the individual child are necessary for the most therapeutic change. Therefore, treatments that are guided by conceptualizations that address both symptoms and underlying emotional, relational, and cognitive influences are necessary to offer the best chances for the recovery and growth of sexually abused children.

KEY REFERENCES

Blaustein, M. E., & Kinniburgh, K. M. (2010). *Treating traumatic stress in children and adolescents: How to foster resilience through attachment, self-regulation, and competency.* New York, NY: Guilford Press.

Cohen, J., Mannarino, A., & Deblinger, E. (2006). *Treating trauma and traumatic grief in children and adolescents.* New York, NY: Guilford Press.

Gil, E. (2006). *Helping abused and traumatized children: Integrating directive and nondirective approaches.* New York, NY: Guilford Press.

Clinician Application

Sexually Abused Children

Marianne Celano, Marissa N. Petersen-Coleman, and Lindsay Pate

COMMENT ON THE EVIDENCE-BASED RECOMMENDATIONS

As noted in the Research Section, child sexual abuse has a broad and variable impact on a range of developmental outcomes for the victim. Consequently, treatment should begin with a comprehensive assessment guided by an ecological, systemic perspective, in which the child's functioning is shaped by complex, transactional processes at the levels of the individual child, the family, and the community. The assessment should include screening for exposure to an array of specific traumatic events, including domestic violence, along with evaluation of trauma-related symptoms. In addition, the clinician must assess the risk for harm in the child's environment; ensure safety in collaboration with other involved systems of care; identify the parents' perceptions and feelings about the alleged abuse; and consider culturally influenced values, beliefs, and practices related to the abuse experience.

An important point made in the Research Section is that treatment should be tailored to the most salient presenting problems of the sexually abused child. Given the heterogeneous symptom picture associated with child sexual abuse, no one evidence-based approach is likely to be appropriate or efficacious for all sexually abused children. However, there is considerable consensus in the clinical and research literature that abused children presenting with trauma-related symptoms benefit from evidence-based, trauma-focused psychotherapy delivered to the child victim and his or her nonoffending caregiver. Of these evidence-based models, Trauma-Focused Cognitive Behavioral Therapy (TF-CBT) has the strongest empirical support. TF-CBT is a components-based, hybrid treatment approach that integrates trauma-specific interventions (including gradual exposure and cognitive restructuring), cognitive behavioral principles, and family interventions. Sessions are structured to include both the child and parent throughout treatment. Randomized clinical trials have demonstrated the superiority of TF-CBT over child-centered, standard community care in reducing posttraumatic stress disorder (PTSD) symptoms among children who have experienced sexual abuse, with treatment gains maintained at 1-year follow up. Developed for children ages 3 to 21, this model includes the following sequential components: (a) psychoeducation about abuse/trauma and parenting, (b) relaxation skills, (c) affective regulation, (c) cognitive coping, (d) trauma narrative and processing, (e) in vivo mastery of trauma reminders, (e) conjoint parent–child sessions, and (f) enhancing safety. Treatment structure and content can be tailored to the child's developmental level; for example, very young children may need a parent present during most of the sessions.

CASE EXAMPLE

Subject Information and Brief History

Melba[1] is a 16-year-old Latina female referred for treatment at a child advocacy center (CAC) following her disclosure of sexual abuse by her uncle. Melba lives with her mother, father, and five older sisters. Her parents moved to the United States when she was a toddler, and she remained in Mexico with her maternal grandmother and sisters. When Melba was 8 years old, she and her oldest sister joined her parents in the United States.

Melba presented with a history of academic difficulties due, in part, to English language barriers. Currently, she is repeating the eighth grade. However, she attended school only in August and September, refusing to return for the past several months. Melba reported that teachers spoke negatively about her to her peers. She also indicated a history of social anxiety and current sleep problems.

Presenting Problem

During a meeting with the school counselor to discuss her truancy, Melba reported suicidal ideation with a plan to overdose with pills. Upon further questioning, she disclosed that her uncle had been sexually abusing her. The counselor informed the parents and the statutory child protection agency about the disclosure, and Melba was referred to the local hospital emergency room for further evaluation of her suicidal ideation. She was subsequently admitted to a psychiatric hospital for 5 days. Upon discharge, Melba was referred to a psychiatrist for follow-up pharmacological treatment for depression. During a forensic interview at the local CAC, Melba provided details about the abuse; the first incident happened a year ago when she awoke to find her jeans undone and her uncle's fingers in her vagina. Over time, the abuse reportedly escalated to include penile–vaginal intercourse. Reportedly none of her sisters had been sexually abused. The forensic team referred Melba to a bilingual CAC psychologist.

---

[1] Name changed to protect confidentiality.

Treatment Intervention and Course

At the time of assessment, Melba denied suicidal ideation and was able to create a safety plan in case she again became suicidal. Based on her responses to the UCLA PTSD Index, Melba met diagnostic criteria for PTSD related to the alleged sexual abuse. She also had endorsed other traumatic events, including witnessing a man shooting another man during her migration to the United States. Melba's parents believed her allegations and expressed outrage toward the alleged perpetrator, who had reportedly fled the country following her disclosure. TF-CBT was recommended to reduce PTSD symptoms, strengthen the parent–child relationship, and assist the parents in managing Melba's depressive symptoms and academic difficulties.

Melba's treatment began with psychoeducation, which focused on normalizing her exposure and reactions to traumatic events, presenting information about sexual abuse, and discussing how trauma affects the brain and the body. Sessions with the parents focused on similar content as well as recommended ways to reinforce school attendance and implement appropriate consequences for truancy.

Melba progressed through the early components of TF-CBT at a slow pace due to multiple treatment barriers including transportation challenges and her refusal to attend school, which required treatment to prioritize a focus on truancy. She indicated that it was difficult for her to practice relaxation skills in their crowded two bedroom apartment, as doing so would have drawn attention to her "problems." To garner more family support for her healing process, Melba's parents and sisters were asked to share their personal *"cuentos"* (stories) of trauma and overcoming adversity during a family session.

TF-CBT resumed with a focus on feelings identification and emotional regulation. Melba identified the various feelings she experienced when asked to discuss her abuse. She used a pictorial thermometer to illustrate a range of distress from zero (no distress) to ten (most distressing). In parallel sessions, her parents discussed their emotional reactions to the abuse and their perception of Melba's difficulties expressing her feelings. Subsequent sessions introduced the cognitive triangle in which feelings, thoughts, and behaviors were differentiated. Melba readily acknowledged that thoughts could be challenged and she engaged in discussions of how unhelpful thoughts can lead to negative thoughts and behaviors. For example, Melba identified that the belief her teachers were talking about her had led to feelings of loneliness and school avoidance.

The trauma narrative was created over four sessions. Parent sessions reviewed relevant aspects of the narrative with the goal of increasing their understanding of Melba's abuse experiences. Although the parents knew that the abuse included vaginal penetration, they were unaware of the frequency. They had difficulty understanding why their daughter did not tell them about the abuse following the first incident. As the narrative unfolded, it became clear that fear of harm to herself and deportation of her (undocumented) family halted Melba's disclosure.

Melba used an emotional thermometer to communicate her level of distress throughout the narrative construction. She initially dictated the narrative in English without much affect or reported distress. When she switched to Spanish, she became more emotionally engaged in the process. Melba's narrative included several cognitive distortions (e.g., "I should have known he was going to do it") and negative core beliefs (e.g., "All adult men will hurt me"). These distortions were gently challenged and replaced by more helpful cognitions (e.g., "nobody can tell someone is an abuser just by looking at them"). Melba shared her narrative in conjoint parent–child sessions by reading it aloud to her mother. Her mother's prior preparation enabled her to respond in a supportive manner and to reinforce her daughter's helpful cognitions (e.g., some men *can* be trusted). The remaining sessions of TF-CBT addressed steps that Melba and her family could take to reduce the future risk of victimization.

Outcome

By the end of 20 sessions, Melba's scores on the UCLA PTSD Index indicated that she no longer met criteria for PTSD. She endorsed decreased depressive symptoms, communicated constructively with family members, and slept through the night. Halfway through treatment, Melba began to attend school regularly. As Melba continued to experience some social anxiety with peers, the family elected to continue medication management with the psychiatrist after ending TF-CBT.

CHALLENGES IN APPLYING THE EVIDENCE-BASED APPROACH

Although TF-CBT is a well-supported, efficacious treatment for child sexual abuse victims and their families, several factors impede its widespread adoption. First, training in TF-CBT requires 2 days of in-person workshops and at least 6 months of twice monthly consultation calls with an approved trainer. These can be time consuming and expensive. In addition, the model works best in the context of strong organizational support and a trauma-informed system of care for children, which is not always readily available. Second, TF-CBT is intended for children whose primary behavioral reactions are related to a trauma; children with significant or preexisting disruptive behavior problems should receive treatment that stabilizes this negative behavior before beginning TF-CBT. Third, the family interventions in TF-CBT may present challenges to psychotherapists who traditionally have conducted individual interventions with child victims. Although TF-CBT has been modified for use in residential treatment settings, foster care, and school, the involvement of a supportive adult caregiver remains a core feature of the model. Parents may experience distress as a result of their child's sexual abuse experience, and TF-CBT assists parents in managing this distress so that it doesn't interfere with optimal parenting. In addition, parents in TF-CBT help the child practice coping skills, supportively respond to his or her trauma narrative, and counter abuse-related cognitive distortions.

CULTURAL DIVERSITY ISSUES

TF-CBT has yielded positive outcomes for Caucasian, African American, and Latino populations in the United States as well as European, Australian, and African youth. The treatment model has been used successfully with families with diverse socioeconomic backgrounds and religions from rural, urban, and suburban regions. Given its components-based approach, TF-CBT offers flexibility in how the modules are presented to individual families. As the case example illustrates, the model format and content can be tailored to individual family beliefs, values, and preferences. The model is equally effective for males and females, and for different cultural and ethnic groups.

FUTURE RESEARCH

Future research examining treatment outcomes for victims of child sexual abuse should explore mechanisms of change, especially the role of parental involvement and the exposure component in the form of the written trauma narrative. For example, TF-CBT research findings suggest that an exposure component is important to optimize outcomes, yet it is unclear if a written trauma narrative is necessary for recovery among all child victims. It is also imperative that researchers carry out effectiveness studies to study the implementation of TF-CBT and similar evidence-based models in a range of community settings, including home-based treatment and telemedicine applications. Finally, comparison effectiveness trials are needed to help clinicians determine how TF-CBT stacks up against alternative active, evidence-based interventions for trauma-related symptoms associated with sexual abuse.

KEY REFERENCES

Cohen, J. A., Mannarino, A. P., & Deblinger, E. (2006). *Treating trauma and traumatic grief in children and adolescents*. New York, NY: Guilford Press.

Cohen, J. A., Mannarino, A. P., & Deblinter, E. (2012). *Trauma-focused CBT for children and adolescents: Treatment applications*. New York, NY: Guilford Press.

Saunders, B. E., Berliner, L., & Hanson, R. F. (Eds.). (2004). *Child physical and sexual abuse: Guidelines for treatment*. Charleston, SC: National Crime Victims Research and Treatment Center.

CHAPTER 65

Women Sexually Abused as Children

Joanne E. Taylor and Shane T. Harvey

CLINICAL PROBLEM

Child sexual abuse (CSA) is a serious international public health problem, broadly defined as the use of a child for sexual stimulation by an adult or another child who, by either age or development, is in a position of trust or power. CSA is an adverse experience, not a disorder, disease, or diagnosis. It is diverse in terms of its characteristics (e.g., intra- and extra-familial abuse, contact and non-contact activities) and tends to involve particular interpersonal features that can impact on development in distinct ways compared with other types of child maltreatment (e.g., sexual trauma, boundary violations, betrayal, secrecy).

Although CSA does not always result in clinically significant negative outcomes, there is consistent evidence of a wide range of adverse but relatively non-specific mental health effects in childhood that may extend into adulthood. This is even after taking into account sociodemographic variables, subsequent interpersonal victimization, and childhood physical abuse. Efforts to identify causal links between CSA and psychopathology have been hampered by the quality and inconsistency of studies in the area, making it difficult for professionals to make sense of and be clearly guided by the literature. However, the complexity of the abuse experience is extraordinarily difficult to capture in research. The effects of CSA usually constitute a dynamic sequence of interrelated consequences that are influenced by both pre- and post-abuse circumstances as well as characteristics of the abuse itself. For example, the negative family environments experienced by many CSA survivors can themselves significantly influence the development of later psychopathology. Research has started to examine the complex relationships between CSA, contextual factors, and adult mental health.

PREVALENCE

Prevalence data vary depending on the way CSA is operationally defined, the characteristics of the sample studied, and differences in research methodology. However, a recent meta-analysis of the prevalence of CSA in adults using 65 articles from 22 countries reported that 19.7% of women had experienced sexual abuse prior to the age of 18. Life course following CSA can include effects that can be continuous, solitary, and/or a combination of outcomes. Children as well as adults can experience temporary, discontinuous, or "sleeper" effects that remain undetected but emerge at key times in a person's life or in new situations.

CULTURAL DIVERSITY ISSUES

As noted earlier, both the experience and effects of CSA are inherently diverse, making for a wide and complex range of adverse outcomes that can have major implications for treatment. A history of CSA is more prevalent in women, and some research indicates that it is associated with higher rates of psychopathology in women. CSA is one of the most common manifestations of violence around the world. While CSA does not discriminate by ethnicity, culture, age, disability, sexual orientation, or spiritual background, these factors can influence the expression of CSA sequelae (e.g., religious beliefs, cultural norms and practices) and, by implication, decisions regarding appropriate treatment.

EVIDENCE-BASED TREATMENTS

Although psychotherapy outcome research for adult survivors of CSA has been conducted for more than 25 years, no treatments have been identified as empirically supported. This is probably at least in part due to the fact that many studies treat survivors of CSA, with all of the complex effects and pathways to and from abuse that that entails, while relatively few focus their treatment efforts at specific effects, such as posttraumatic stress disorder (PTSD). However, psychological treatments are effective in reducing symptoms and improving outcomes for adults who were sexually abused as children. Group, couple, and individually focused treatments have been studied, with the vast majority of research on group approaches. Treatment modalities have ranged from single-theory focused treatments (e.g., cognitive behavioral therapy, eye movement desensitization reprocessing, emotion-focused therapy, cognitive processing therapy), to multidisciplinary, insight and/or experiential, combination, or eclectic treatments.

Most attempts to synthesize the outcome research using meta-analysis have been limited to single approaches, used flawed methodology, or not considered the multitude of factors that might account for the variability in treatment outcome. Our recent meta-analysis addressed these issues. Overall treatment effects, regardless of approach used, were moderate for PTSD/trauma symptoms ($g = 0.72$–0.77), internalizing symptoms ($g = 0.68$–0.72), externalizing symptoms ($g = 0.41$–0.53), self-esteem ($g = 0.56$–0.58), and global functioning ($g = 0.57$–0.60), and inconsistent for interpersonal functioning. Effects were largely maintained at follow-up, although few studies provided follow-up data.

However, different characteristics of therapy moderated the effectiveness of treatments depending on the symptom domain or outcome being measured, and some of these variables were based on stronger evidence than others. The degree of effectiveness differed according to clinician variables (e.g., experience, discipline), the nature of treatment (e.g., structure, modality, treatment approach, length of treatment), client variables (e.g., presenting condition, nature of abuse), and contextual factors (e.g., inpatient/outpatient, inclusion of out-of-session work). For PTSD/trauma symptoms, individual therapy approaches were associated with better outcomes ($g = 1.04$–1.17) than group-based approaches ($g = 0.37$–0.61). More studies have since been published, some more rigorous than others, showing beneficial effects of group therapy for trauma symptoms following CSA. Additional studies supporting individual and combined approaches (e.g., dialectical behavior therapy) for trauma symptoms have also been reported. Trauma outcomes improved when therapy included out-of-session work. Alternatively, the treatment of issues related to self-esteem responded well to semistructured interventions delivered by experienced practitioners. No clear moderating differences were found when treating externalizing symptoms, interpersonal functioning, or global symptoms. Furthermore, no differences were found between therapeutic approaches for the different outcome domains, with the exception of cognitive behavioral therapies having better outcomes for internalizing symptoms such as anxiety and depression.

FUTURE RESEARCH

Characteristics of each woman and her abuse experience are likely to also function as moderators of treatment outcome, but clearer analysis of these influences in meta-analysis will not be possible until researchers report this information systematically. Furthermore, women with CSA histories more often than not experience a constellation of abuse-related effects as opposed to isolated outcomes, and more advanced meta-analytic techniques are needed to evaluate outcomes for various abuse and effect profiles. This is particularly important considering the multifaceted etiology of the effects of child sexual abuse.

KEY REFERENCES

Maniglio, R. (2009). The impact of child sexual abuse on health: A systematic review of reviews. *Clinical Psychology Review, 29*, 647–657.

Peleikis, D. E., & Dahl, A. A. (2005). A systematic review of empirical studies of psychotherapy with women who were sexually abused as children. *Psychotherapy Research, 15*, 304–315.

Taylor, J. E., & Harvey, S. T. (2010). A meta-analysis of the effects of psychotherapy with adults sexually abused in childhood. *Clinical Psychology Review, 30*(6), 749–767.

Clinician Application

Women Sexually Abused as Children

Christine A. Courtois

COMMENT ON THE EVIDENCE-BASED RECOMMENDATIONS

The reviewers offer a good and inclusive definition of sexual abuse; however, two dimensions are in need of emphasis: (a) most sexual abuse is incestuous, perpetrated by parents/primary caretakers, relatives or others in close relationship to the child (as clergy, teacher, coach, mentor, therapist—who have fiduciary duties to the child that are abandoned when they engage in abuse). This relationship dimension compounds a trauma that is already complex in terms of its intrusiveness and its occurrence out of the normal sequence of psychosexual development and without consent; (b) although this review focuses exclusively on girls and women (and gender is a significant diversity factor that renders them especially vulnerable), sexual abuse is also a significant problem for boys and men, but at a lesser prevalence. So far, the treatment that has been developed for adult women sexually abused as children has general applicability when the abuse is incestuous (although specialized information and approaches are recommended) and when applied to sexually abused men.

Both the diversity and variability of sexual abuse and its outcomes that are stressed in the review are important considerations for clinicians working with adult survivors. A wide range of developmental outcomes and symptoms beyond those required for the diagnosis of posttraumatic stress disorder (PTSD; classic symptoms) have been identified. They have been organized into the diagnostic formulation of Complex PTSD (an associated feature of PTSD in the *DSM-IV* and *DSM-5*). This formulation gives clinicians a comprehensive picture of the range of mental health, relational, and medical aftereffects (and their expression in developmental age/stage ways) beyond the classic symptoms of PTSD that are normative sequelae of repeated incest/child sexual abuse. It also assists clinicians in assessing the objective aspects of the pre- and postabuse circumstances (including attachment security with primary caregivers and other family factors that impact the child's vulnerability to sexual and other forms of abuse and the response or intervention that is received or not), the child's temperament and resilience in the face of the abuse and other relevant family and contextual factors, and the impact initially and in the short and longer term.

CASE EXAMPLE

Subject Information and Brief History

Ginger, a 23-year-old Caucasian woman, first sought treatment at a local rape crisis center where she attempted to join a specialized group for sexual abuse survivors. She had been abused multiple times over the course of her childhood by her brother, alone and later with some of his friends. She was assessed by the rape crisis staff as too emotionally fragile and too symptomatic (with major symptoms of depression, anxiety, and PTSD) for a group and was referred for individual therapy.

Presenting Problem

Ginger's presenting problem was that she was continuously jumpy, especially when she was around boys and men (especially her father and brother), and was quite depressed/hopeless and "rudderless" in her life. She was unable to see a clear future for herself and she was in despair. Her stated intention in joining a group was to meet others who had had experiences of abuse similar to hers so she "wouldn't feel like such a freak."

Treatment Intervention and Course

Ginger was quite fearful of treatment that would require her to talk about her life—including the sexual abuse—with the therapist, who she viewed as an authority figure/parent substitute. Treatment began slowly. Over time, it emerged that Ginger was deeply shamed by the fact that she had been repeatedly abused by her older brother starting at age 5. Over the course of the abuse, her brother had become more forceful and violent, more sexually intrusive, and voyeuristic. On a number of occasions, he invited several of his friends to abuse her while he watched. Ginger was unable to say the word "incest" when she began treatment and instead referred to her sexual abuse as fitting the "i" word. She was keenly aware of not wanting to get her brother in trouble and of his status in the family. She felt that her parents would never believe her and, if they did, they would blame her rather than him. They had consistently favored her brother while ignoring his controlling and cruel behavior toward his siblings and toward the family pets. This lack of intervention and resultant lack of safety was but one example of a family with a great deal of dysfunction. Ginger described her parents as having been unhappily married, constantly at odds with one another, and as commonly presenting their children with diametrically opposite values and behaviors (e.g., her father, a career military man, was described as rigid, verbally and physically abusive, and sexually repressive; her mother, a passive and depressed woman who was unsuccessful in standing up to her husband was also a "free spirit" and naturalist who only wore clothing when her husband was at home—otherwise, she spent her days in the nude, grossly overstimulating her children (especially her sons) in the process. This was one of the more startling discrepancies that Ginger described as common in her family and not as something that she had considered to be problematic before discussing them with the therapist.

Ginger settled into treatment gradually and with great guardedness; however, she never missed a session and showed diligence in learning about trauma (and abuse such as hers as traumatic) and understanding its resultant developmental impact and symptoms and on learning new skills in a number of life domains (i.e., personal safety, emotion regulation, self-esteem, assertiveness, boundary management, life stabilization, career decision making). At the start of treatment, she was profoundly depressed (sad affect, physical lethargy, sleep disturbance, difficulty concentrating) and had posttraumatic symptoms (hypervigilance, hyperarousal/startle response, day and night terrors). She reluctantly agreed to the recommendation for a medication evaluation; once started on an antidepressant, improvement in her mood and energy level was immediate. This, in turn, provided her a more solid emotional foundation from which to tackle issues pertaining to her sexual abuse and associated family problems.

The treatment was applied in sequence, as recommended and outlined in Courtois and Ford and Herman, involving a hierarchy of tasks organized into three main stages. The early stage of treatment—which lasted approximately 12 months—included attention to the tasks of education about trauma and posttraumatic reactions and symptoms, safety planning, life stabilization, skill development, and building the therapeutic alliance. During this stage, Ginger was encouraged to begin to face rather than avoid her experiences through graduated cognitive exposure (beginning to talk about the abuse and her family) in the context of the therapist's active attunement, support, and empathy. During the middle stage of treatment, once it was determined that Ginger had sufficient emotion regulation capacity and life safety and stability and with her informed consent, more formal graduated exposure strategies for the sexual trauma were implemented. She was asked to focus on particularly traumatic abuse experiences and to experience the emotions associated with them, again with the therapist providing support while gently challenging Ginger's misconceptions, including erroneous beliefs and cognitions (i.e., that she deserved the abuse and that her brother had a right to use her sexually). After approximately 18 months of treatment, she had a different and more realistic set of beliefs and cognitions about her abuse. She was able to discuss it in more detail and with more emotional congruence and her symptoms of PTSD and depression began to remit. The third and last phase of treatment (directed toward addressing current life issues and improving relationships post-resolution of the trauma symptoms) had several main foci, including the application of learning derived from the trauma processing and behavioral changes. Ginger became more assertive at work and was given a promotion and a raise. Although she had previously had anxiety to the point of being phobic about developing a romantic relationship with a man, at this point in treatment Ginger began dating. She also decided to disclose the incest to her mother and to confront her brother. To her surprise, her mother responded very supportively and told her she had always worried that her brother might have hurt her. Her mother also took responsibility for her share of the chaos in their family (parents divorced when Ginger was 20). When she confronted her brother about the abuse and its extent and impact, he minimized it and was dismissive toward her. In response (and based on the education that she had received about the dynamics of older brother–younger sister incest), she made the decision to cut off contact with him after informing his wife of the past abuse, in the hopes of preventing his sexual abuse of his own children.

Outcome

Ginger completed treatment after several years and moved out of state for a job promotion. Subsequently over the next several years, she routinely contacted the psychotherapist to inform her of her various successes as they occurred. For example, being able to have a satisfying sexual relationship, getting married, testifying against her brother when he was arrested for sexually abusing his daughter, and getting another promotion at work.

CHALLENGES IN APPLYING THE EVIDENCE-BASED APPROACH

Treatment challenges have to do with the multiple or co-occurring symptoms and what can be daunting challenges in helping clients to stabilize their lives and regulate their emotions. Even developing a therapeutic relationship may create challenges due to the client's mistrust, low self-esteem, suspicion of others and their motives, and insecure attachment style (most often avoidant/fearful but also disoriented/dissociated) in clients whose caregivers' ability to adequately respond was impaired in some way. Thus, it often takes more time and effort on the therapist's part to gain a modicum of trust and to begin to work against what has often been a lifetime of symptoms, personal disruptions, and patterns of avoidance and suppression used by the client to cope in the absence of assistance or intervention at the time of the abuse and later.

Empirically supported treatments for Complex PTSD have developed more slowly than those developed for "classic" PTSD, but several are now available. The wholesale applicability of some empirically supported treatments for symptoms of PTSD, notably Prolonged Exposure (PE), has been questioned. Among other issues, reservations have been expressed about the validity of the studies on which the recommendations were based as most excluded subjects with complex symptom presentations. Moreover, because complex trauma survivors often have pronounced deficits in the ability to identify and regulate emotions, some leave exposure-based treatment prematurely. Despite these reservations, when Prolonged Exposure is applied, it is recommended as a middle-stage intervention to be used after the client has developed needed skills in emotional regulation.

CULTURAL DIVERSITY ISSUES

Ginger's family was rigidly organized on gender lines and had many characteristics and risk factors for abuse to occur between members. The boys were more favored, had more education and career encouragement, and were less disciplined ("boys will be boys"). In the case of Ginger and her sisters, this left her unprotected with regard to her brother who had been taught he "could get away with anything." In contrast, the girls in the family were expected to be role compliant, polite, caretaking of others, and to marry soon after high school, with no expectations for furthering their education or developing a career. Ginger's mother was a superficially compliant woman who outwardly met gender expectations but was in constant conflict with her husband and his restrictions. Ginger's family appeared to be middle class but was constantly in the throes of economic chaos, the result of her parent's joint financial mismanagement. Although certainly not the only precipitants, ongoing stress and economic and power disparities between spouses and partners are often implicated in domestic violence of all sorts, including the abuse of children.

When treatment began, Ginger was morbidly obese, dressed in frumpy and unattractive clothing designed to deflect the attention of others, and presented as less intelligent than she actually was. She was underemployed and had a low socioeconomic status (SES) as a result, with few resources for treatment. She was given a sliding scale and, as she was quite motivated after her initial fears of the therapist dissipated, she was very responsible regarding payment. It was important not to stereotype her on the basis of gender expectations, SES, social class, work status, intelligence, obesity, and general self-presentation, all of which improved considerably by the end of treatment. Additional research is needed regarding the role played by diversity issues in both the occurrence and treatment of incest/child sexual abuse.

FUTURE RESEARCH

Future research must address the treatment of symptoms beyond those of classic PTSD and the use of multiple modalities that are applied concurrently or sequentially to treat the multiple and co-occurring symptoms. The pool of subjects in research studies must be expanded to include those who have a more complex and comorbid presentations and resulting developmental deficits. At the present time, treatment outcome studies for complex trauma are underway and their findings will determine the sequenced applicability of established techniques for the symptoms of Complex PTSD with or without additional modalities.

KEY REFERENCES

Courtois, C. A. (1988, 2010). *Healing the incest wound: Adult survivors in therapy* (2nd ed.). New York: W. W. Norton & Co.

Courtois, C. A., & Ford, J. D. (Eds.). (2009). *Treating complex traumatic stress disorders: An evidence-based guide.* New York, NY: Guilford Press.

Herman, J. L. (1997). *Trauma and recovery: The aftermath of violence-from domestic to political terror* (2nd ed.). New York, NY: Basic Books.

References

CHAPTER 1

Research

Afifi, T. D., & McManus, T. (2010). Divorce disclosures and adolescents' physical and mental health and parental relationship quality. *Journal of Divorce & Remarriage, 5*, 83–107.

Afifi, T. D., & Schrodt, P. (2003). 'Feeling caught' as a mediator of adolescents' and young adults' avoidance and satisfaction with their parents in divorced and non-divorced households. *Communication Monographs, 70*, 142–173.

Amato, P. R. (2000). The consequences of divorce for adults and children. *Journal of Marriage & the Family, 62*, 1269–1287.

Amato, P. R., & Afifi, T. D. (2006). Feeling caught between parents: Adult children's relations with parents and subjective well-being. *Journal of Marriage and Family, 68*, 222–235.

Amato, P. R., & Keith, B. (1991). Parental divorce and the well-being of children: A meta analysis. *Psychological Bulletin, 110*, 26–46.

Bing, N. M., Nelson III, W. M., & Wesolowski, K. L. (2009). Comparing the effects of amount of conflict on children's adjustment following parental divorce. *Journal of Divorce & Remarriage, 50*, 159–171.

Burt, S. A., Barnes, A. R., McGue, M., & Iacono, W. G. (2008). Parental divorce and adolescent delinquency: Ruling out the impact of common genes. *Developmental Psychology, 44*, 1668–1677.

Chase-Lansdale, P., & Hetherington, E. M. (1990). The impact of divorce on life-span development: Short and long term effects. In R. M. Lerner (Ed.), *Life-span development and behavior* (Vol. 10, pp. 105–150). Hillsdale, NJ: Lawrence Erlbaum Associates, Inc.

Ehrenberg, M. F., & Regev, R. (2010). Siblings relationships in divorcing families. In J. Caspi (Ed.), *Sibling development: Implications for mental health practitioners.* New York, NY: Springer Publishing Company.

Fosco, G. M., & Grych, J. H. (2008). Emotional, cognitive, and family systems mediators of children's adjustment to interparental conflict. *Journal of Family Psychology, 22*, 843–854.

Franck, K. L., & Buehler, C. (2007). A family process model of marital hostility, parental depressive affect, and early adolescent problem behavior: The roles of triangulation and parental warmth. *Journal of Family Psychology, 21*, 614–625.

Grall, T. S. (2007). *Custodial mothers and fathers and their child support: 2005.* Washington, DC: U.S. Bureau of the Census.

Henderson, C. E., Hayslip, B., Jr., Sanders, L. M., & Louden, L. (2009). Grandmother-grandchild relationship quality predicts psychological adjustment among youth from divorced families. *Journal of Family Issues, 30*, 1245–1264.

Hetherington, E. M., Stanley-Hagan, M., & Anderson, E. R. (1989). Marital transitions: A child's perspective. *American Psychologist, 44*, 303–312.

Lansford, J. E., Malone, P. S., Castellino, D. R., Dodge, K. A., Pettit, G. S., & Bates, J. E. (2006). Trajecories of internalizing, externalizing, and grades for children who have and have not experienced their parents' divorce. *Journal of Family Psychology, 20*, 292–301.

Luedemann, M. B., Ehrenberg, M. F., & McFarlane, J. (2004). Understanding parentification of children in divorcing families: Research and practice implications. *The BC Counsellor, 26*, 53–64.

Maccoby, E. E., & Mnookin, R. H. (1992). *Dividing the child: Social and legal dilemmas of custody.* Cambridge, MA: Harvard University Press.

McIntosh, J. E., Wells, Y. D., Smyth, B. M., & Long, C. M. (2008). Child-focuses and child-inclusive divorce mediation: Comparative outcomes from a prospective study of post-separation. *Family Court Review, 46*, 105–124.

National Center for Health Statistics. (2002). Cohabitation, marriage, divorce, and remarriage in the United States Series (Report 23, No. 22). Retrieved July 26, 2011 from http://www.cdc.gov/nchs/data/series /sr_23/sr23_022.pdf

Pedro-Carroll, J. (2005). Fostering resilience in the aftermath of divorce: The role of evidence based programs for children. *Family Court Review, 43*, 52–64.

Pedro-Carroll, J., Nakhnikian, E., & Montes, G. (2001). Assisting children through transition—Helping parents protect their children from the toxic effects of ongoing conflict in the aftermath of divorce. *Family Court Review, 39*, 377–392.

Potter, D. (2010) Psychosocial well-being and the relationship between divorce and children's academic achievement. *Journal of Marriage and Family, 72*, 933–946.

Regev, R., & Ehrenberg, M. F. (2012). A pilot study of a support group for children in divorcing famlies: Aiding community program development and marking pathways to resilience. *Journal of Divorce and Remarriage, 53*, 220–230.

Short, J. L. (2002). The effects of parental divorce during childhood on college student. *Journal of Divorce & Remarriage, 38*, 143–156.

Tejada-Vera, B., Sutton, P. D. (2010). Births, marriages, divorces, and deaths: Provisional data for 2009. In *National vital statistics reports* (Vol. 58, no. 25). Hyattsville, MD: National Center for Health Statistics.

Tillman, K. H. (2007). Family structure pathways and academic disadvantage among adolescents in stepfamilies. *Sociological Inquiry, 77*, 383–424.

U.S. Census Bureau. (2003, October). Marital status: 2000, Census 2000 brief. Retrieved July 26, 2011, from http://www.census.gov/prod/2003pubs/c2kbr-30.pdf

Vanier Institute of the Family. (2009). Child and family Canada: Contemporary trends. *Divorce facts, figures and consequences.* http://www.vanierinstitute.ca/include/get.php?nodeid=190

Walker (Nicholson), T. R., & Ehrenberg, M. F. (1998). Perceived reasons for parental divorce: Influence on young adults' attachment styles. *Journal of Adolescent Research, 13*, 320–342.

Wallerstein, J., & Lewis, J. M. (2007). Disparate parenting and step-parenting with siblings in the post-divorce family: Report from a 10-year longitudinal study. *Journal of Family Studies, 13*, 224–235.

Wallerstein, J. S., Lewis, J. M., & Blakeslee, S. (2000). *The unexpected legacy of divorce: A 25 year landmark study.* New York, NY: Hyperion

Zuberbuhler, J. (2001). Early intervention mediation: The use of court-ordered mediation in the initial stages of divorce litigation to resolve parenting issues. *Family Court Review, 39*, 203–206.

Clinician Application

Izzo, E., & Carpel Miller, V. (2011). *Second-hand shock: Surviving & overcoming vicarious trauma.* San Diego, CA: High Conflict Institute Press.

CHAPTER 2

Research

American Psychiatric Association. (2000). *Diagnostic and statistical manual of mental disorders* (4th ed., text rev.). Washington, DC: Author.

Archer, J. (2004). Sex differences in aggression in real world settings: A meta-analytic review. *Review of General Psychology, 8*, 291–322.

Beck, R., & Fernandez, E. (1998a). Cognitive-behavioral therapy in the treatment of anger: A meta-analysis. *Cognitive Therapy and Research, 22*, 63–74.

Beck, R., & Fernandez, E. (1998b). Cognitive-behavioral self-regulation of anger. *Journal of Psychopathology and Behavioral Assessment, 20*, 217–229.

Biaggio, M. K. (1980). Assessment of anger arousal. *Journal of Personality Assessment, 44*, 289–298.

Biaggio, M. K., & Maiuro, R. D. (1985). Recent advances in anger assessment. In C. D. Spielberger & J. N. Butcher (Eds.), *Advances in personality assessment* (Vol. 5, pp. 71–111). Hillsdale, NJ: Erlbaum.

Blumstein, A., Farrington, D. P., & Moitra, S. D. (1985). Delinquency careers: Innocents, desisters, and persisters. In M. Tonry & N. Morris (Eds.), *Crime and justice: An annual review of research* (Vol. 6, pp. 137–168). Chicago, IL: The University of Chicago Press.

Brunner, T. M. (2010). Comprehensive assessment of an attention-based learning problem: Capturing the relevance of "psychological vital signs". In N. Mather & L. E. Jaffe (Eds.), *Comprehensive evaluations: Case reports for psychologists, diagnosticians, and special educators.* New York, NY: John Wiley & Sons.

Campbell, A., & Muncer, S. (2008). Intent to harm or injure? Gender and the expression of anger. *Aggressive Behavior, 34*, 282–293.

Campbell, A., Muncer, S., & Coyle, E. (1992). Social representation of aggression as an explanation of gender differences. *Aggressive Behavior, 18*, 95–108.

Cox, D. L., Stabb, S. D., & Hulgus, J. F. (2000). Anger and depression in girls and boys: A study of gender differences. *Psychology of Women Quarterly, 24*, 110–112.

Dahlberg, L. L. (1998). Youth violence in the United States: Major trends, risk factors, and prevention approaches. *American Journal of Preventive Medicine, 14*, 259–272.

Dahlen, E. R., & Deffenbacher, J. L. (2000). A partial component analysis of Beck's cognitive therapy for the treatment of general anger. *Journal of Cognitive Psychotherapy, 14*, 77–95.

Dahlen, E. R., & Deffenbacher, J. L. (2001). Anger management. In W. J. Lyddon & J. V. Jones (Eds.), *Empirically supported cognitive therapies: Current status and future applications* (pp. 163–181). New York, NY: Springer.

Darwin, C. (1965). *The expression of the emotions in man and animals*. Chicago, IL: University of Chicago Press.

Deffenbacher, J. L. (1999). Cognitive-behavioral conceptualization and treatment of anger. *Journal of Clinical Psychology, 55*, 295–309.

Deffenbacher, J. L., Dahlen, E. R., Lynch, R. S., Morris, C. D., & Gowensmith, W. N. (2000). An application of Beck's cognitive therapy to general anger reduction. *Cognitive Therapy and Research, 24*, 689–697.

Deffenbacher, J. L., & Swaim, R. C. (January 01, 1999). Anger expression in Mexican American and White non-Hispanic adolescents. *Journal of Counseling Psychology, 46*(1), 61–69.

Del Barrio, V., Aluja, A., & Spielberger, C.D. (2003). Anger assessment with the STAXI-CA: Psychometric properties of a new instrument for children and adolescents. *Personality & Individual Differences, 37*, 227–244.

Feindler, E. L. (1990). Adolescent anger control: Review and critique. In M. Hersen, R. Eisler, & R. Miller (Eds.), *Progress in behavior modification* (Vol. 26, pp. 11–59). Thousand Oaks, CA: Sage.

Feindler, E. L. (1991). Capitalizing on the power of the peer group: The challenge of adolescent group psychotherapy [Review of the book *Adolescent group psychotherapy* edited by F. J. Cramer-Azima & L. H. Richmond]. *Contemporary Psychology, 36*, 315–316.

Feindler, E. L., Adler, N., Brooks, D., & Bhumitra, E., (1993). Children's Anger Response Checklist (CARC). In L. VandeCreek, S. Knapp, & T. L. Jackson, (Eds.), *Innovations in clinical practice: A source book* (Vol. 12, pp. 337–362). Sarasota, FL: Professional Resource Press.

Feindler, E. L. & Guttman, J. (1994). Cognitive-behavioral anger control training: A treatment manual. In C. W. LeCroy (Ed.), *Handbook of child and adolescent treatment manuals*. New York, NY: Lexington Books.

Kerr, M. A., & Schneider, B. H. (2008). Anger expression in children and adolescents: A review of the empirical literature. *Clinical Psychology Review, 28*, 559–577.

Koop, C., & Lundberg, G. D. (1992). Violence in America: A public health emergency. Time to bite the bullet back. *JAMA, 267*(22), 3075–3076.

Lochman, J. E., Curry, J. F., Dane, H., & Ellis, M. (2001, January 01). The anger coping program: An empirically-supported treatment for aggressive children. *Residential Treatment for Children & Youth, 18*, 63–74.

Nickel, M., Luley, J., Krawczyk, J., Nickel, C., Widermann, C., … Loew, T. (2006). Bullying girls— changes after brief strategic family therapy: A randomized, prospective, controlled trial with one-year follow-up. *Psychotherapy and Psychosomatics, 75*(1), 47–55.

Nickel, M., Mühlbacher, M., Egger, C., Buschmann, W., Rother, N., … Nickel, C. (2007, February 01). Influence of family therapy on bullying behavior, cortisol secretion, anger, and quality of life in bullying male adolescents: A randomized, prospective, controlled study. *Ppmp - Psychotherapie · Psychosomatik · Medizinische Psychologie, 57*, 2.

Nickel, M. K., Krawczyk, J., Nickel, C., Forthuber, P., Kettler, C., … Loew, T. H. (2005). Anger, interpersonal relationships, and health-related quality of life in bullying boys who are treated with outpatient family therapy: A randomized, perspective, controlled trial with 1 year of follow-up. *Pediatrics, 116*(2), e247–e254.

Ono, Y., & Pumariega, A. J. (2008, January 01). Violence in youth. *International Review of Psychiatry (Abingdon, England), 20*(3), 305–316.

Pinheiro, P. S. (2006). *World report on violence against children*. Geneva, Switzerland: ATAR Roto Presse SA.

Spielberger, C. D. (1988). *State-Trait Anger Expression Inventory (STAXI) professional manual*. Lutz, FL: Psychological Assessment Resources.

Spielberger, C. D. (1999). *State-Trait Anger Expression Inventory–2 (STAXI-2) professional manual*. Lutz, FL: Psychological Assessment Resources.

Spielberger, C. D., Johnson, E. G., Russell, S. F., Crane, R. S., Jacobs, G. A., & Worden, T. J. (1985). The experience and expression of anger: Construction and validation of an anger expression scale. In M. A. Chesney & R. H. Rosenman (Eds.), *Anger and hostility in cardiovascular and behavioral disorders* (pp. 5–30). New York, NY: Hemisphere/McGraw-Hill.

Spielberger, C. D., Reheiser, E., & Sydeman, S. J. (1995). Measuring the experience, expression and control of anger. In H. Kassinove (Ed.), *Anger disorders: Definition, diagnosis, and treatment. Series in clinical and community psychology* (pp. 49–67). Washington, DC: Taylor & Francis.

Sukhodolsky, D. G., Kassinove, H., & Gorman, B. S. (2004). Cognitive-behavioral therapy for anger in children and adolescents: A meta-analysis. *Aggression and Violent Behavior, 9*(3), 247–269.

U.S. Bureau of Justice Statistics. (1993). *Criminal victimization in the United States, 1991*. Washington DC: U.S. Department of Justice, Office of Justice Programs.

U.S. Department of Health and Human Services, Office of the Surgeon General. (2001). *Youth violence: A report of the Surgeon General*. Washington, DC: U.S. Government Printing Office.

Yarcheski, A., Mahon, N. E., & Yarcheski, T. J. (2002, January 01). Anger in early adolescent boys and girls with health manifestations. *Nursing Research New York, 51*, 229–236.

CHAPTER 3

Research

Anderson, E. R., & Mayes, L. C. (2010). Race/ethnicity and internalizing disorders in youth: A review. *Clinical Psychology Review, 30*, 338–348.

Aschenbrand, S. G., Kendall, P. C., Webb, A., Safford, S. M., & Flannery-Schroeder, E. (2003). Is childhood separation anxiety disorder a predictor of adult panic disorder and agoraphobia? A seven-year longitudinal study. *Journal of the American Academy of Child and Adolescent Psychiatry, 42*, 1478–1485.

Barrett, P., Dadds, M., & Rapee, R. (1996). Family treatment of child anxiety: A controlled trial. *Journal of Consulting and Clinical Psychology, 64*, 333–342.

Beidel, D. C., Turner, S. M., & Morris, T. L. (2000). Behavioral treatment of childhood social phobia. *Journal of Consulting and Clinical Psychology, 68*, 1072–1080.

Beidel, D. C., Turner, S. M., Young, B., & Paulson, A. (2005). Social effectiveness training for children: Three-year follow-up. *Journal of Consulting and Clinical Psychology, 73*, 721–725.

Beidas, R. S., Suarez, L., Simpson, D., Read, K., Wei, C., … Kendall, P. (2012). Contextual factors and anxiety in minority and European American youth presenting for treatment across two urban university clinics. *Journal of Anxiety Disorders, 26*, 544–554.

Bouchard, S., Mendlowitz, S. L., Coles, M. E., & Franklin, M. (2004). Considerations in the use of exposure with children. *Cognitive and Behavioral Practice, 11*, 56–65.

Canino, G. (2004). Are somatic symptoms and related distress more prevalent in Hispanic/Latino youth? Some methodological considerations. *Journal of Clinical Child and Adolescent Psychology, 33*, 272–275.

Chavira, D. A., Stein, M. B., Bailey, K., & Stein, M. T. (2004). Child anxiety in primary care: Prevalent but untreated. *Depression and Anxiety, 20*, 155–164.

Cohen, J. A., Mannarino, A. P., Perel, J. M., & Staron, V. (2007). A pilot randomized controlled trial of combined Trauma-Focused CBT and Sertraline for childhood PTSD symptoms. *Journal of the American Academy of Child and Adolescent Psychiatry, 46*, 811–819.

Costello, E. J., Mustillo, S., Keeler, G., & Angold, A. (2004). Prevalence of psychiatric disorders in childhood and adolescence. In B. L. Levin & J. Petrila (Eds.), *Mental health services: A public health perspective* (pp. 111–128). New York, NY: Oxford University Press.

Ehrenreich-May, J., Southam-Gerow, M. A., Hourigan, S. E., Wright, L. R., Pincus, D. B., & Weisz, J. R. (2011). Characteristics of anxious and depressed youth seen in two different clinical contexts. *Administration and Policy in Mental Health and Mental Health Services Research, 38*, 398–411.

Gee, C. B. (2004). Assessment of anxiety and depression in Asian American youth. *Journal of Clinical Child and Adolescent Psychology, 33*, 269–271.

Gordon-Hollingsworth, A. T., Ginsburg, G. S., & the CAMS Team. (2012). *Anxiety disorders in Caucasian and African American children: A comparison of clinical characteristics, treatment process variables, and treatment outcomes in the CAMS sample*. Manuscript in preparation.

Greco, L., & Morris, T. (2005). Factors influencing the link between social anxiety and peer acceptance: Contributions of social skills and close friendships during middle childhood. *Behavior Therapy, 36*, 197–205.

Gudino, O. G., & Lau, A. S. (2010). Parental cultural orientation, shyness, and anxiety in Hispanic children: An exploratory study. *Journal of Applied Developmental Psychology, 31*, 202–210.

Howard, B., Chu, B. C., Krain, A. L., Marrs-Garcia, M. A., & Kendall, P. C. (2000). *Cognitive-behavioral family therapy for anxious children: Therapist manual* (2nd ed.). Ardmore, PA: Workbook Publishing. www.WorkbookPublishing.com

Kazdin, A. E., & Weisz, J. R. (1998). Identifying and developing empirically supported child and adolescent treatments. *Journal of Consulting and Clinical Psychology, 66*, 19–36.

Kendall, P. C. (1994). Treating anxiety disorders in children: Results of a randomized clinical trial. *Journal of Consulting and Clinical Psychology, 62*, 100–110.

Kendall, P. C., & Beidas, R. S. (2007). Smoothing the trail for dissemination of evidence-based practices for youth: Flexibility within fidelity. *Professional Psychology: Research and Practice, 38*, 13–19.

Kendall, P. C., Choudhury, M., Hudson, J., & Webb, A. (2002). *The C.A.T. project therapist manual*. Ardmore, PA: Workbook Publishing. www.WorkbookPublishing.com

Kendall, P. C., Compton, S. N., Walkup, J. T., Birmaher, B., Albano, A. M., … Piacentini, J. (2010). Clinical characteristics of anxiety disordered youth. *Journal of Anxiety Disorder, 24*, 360–365.

Kendall, P. C., Flannery-Schroeder, E., Panichelli-Mindel, S., Southam-Gerow, M., Henin, A., & Warman, M. (1997). Therapy for youth with anxiety disorders: A second randomized clinical trial. *Journal of Consulting and Clinical Psychology, 65*, 366–380.

Kendall, P. C., & Hedtke, K. (2006a). *Cognitive-behavioral therapy for anxious children: Therapist manual* (3rd ed.). Ardmore, PA: Workbook Publishing. www.WorkbookPublishing.com

Kendall, P. C., & Hedtke, K. (2006b). *Coping Cat workbook* (2nd ed.). Ardmore, PA: Workbook Publishing. www .WorkbookPublishing.com

Kendall, P. C., Hudson, J. L., Gosch, E., Flannery-Schroeder, E., & Suveg, C. (2008). Cognitive-behavioral therapy for anxiety disordered youth: A randomized clinical trial evaluation child and family modalities. *Journal of Consulting and Clinical Psychology, 76*, 282–297.

Kendall, P. C., & Khanna, M. S. (2008). Camp Cope-A-Lot. [DVD] Ardmore, PA: Workbook Publishing. www .WorkbookPublishing.com.

Kendall, P. C., Safford, S., Flannery-Schroeder, E., & Webb, A. (2004). Child anxiety treatment: Outcomes in adolescence and impact on substance use and depression at 7.4-year follow-up. *Journal of Consulting and Clinical Psychology, 72*, 276–287.

Kendall, P. C., & Southam-Gerow, M. A. (1996). Long-term follow-up of a cognitive-behavior therapy for anxiety-disordered youth. *Journal of Consulting and Clinical Psychology, 64*, 724–730.

Khanna, M. S., & Kendall, P. C. (2010). Computer-assisted cognitive-behavioral therapy for child anxiety: Results of a randomized clinical trial. *Journal of Consulting and Clinical Psychology, 78*, 737–745.

Lambert, S. F., Cooley, M. R., Campbell, K. D., Benoit, M. Z., & Stansbury, R. (2004). Assessing anxiety sensitivity in inner-city African American children: Psychometric properties of the childhood anxiety sensitivity index. *Journal of Clinical Child and Adolescent Psychology, 33*, 248–259.

March, J. S., & Mulle, K. (1998). *OCD in children and adolescents: A cognitive behavioral treatment manual.* New York, NY: Guilford Press.

Masi, G., Mucci, M., Favilla, L., Romano, R., & Poli, P. (1999). Symptomatology and comorbidity of generalized anxiety disorder in children and adolescents. *Comprehensive Psychiatry, 40*, 210–215.

Mychailyszyn, M., Cohen, J., Edmunds, J., Crawley, S., & Kendall, P. C. (2010). Treating social anxiety in youth. In K. Rubin & R. Coplan (Eds.), *The development of shyness and social withdrawal.* New York, NY: Guilford Press.

Mychailyszyn, M., Domingues, J., Treadwell, K., & Kendall, P. C. (2010). Separation anxiety. In V. S. Ramachandran (Ed.), *Encyclopedia of human behavior* (2nd ed.). Kidlington, UK: Elsevier.

Nepon, J., Belik, S., Bolton, J., & Sareen, J. (2010). The relationship between anxiety disorders and suicide attempts: Findings from the national epidemiologic survey on alcohol and related conditions. *Depression and Anxiety, 27*, 791–798.

Ollendick, T. H., & King, N. J. (2012). Evidence-based treatments for children and adolescents: Issues and commentary. In P. C. Kendall (Ed.), *Child and adolescent therapy: Cognitive-behavioral procedures* (4th ed.). New York, NY: Guilford Press.

Piacentini, J., Gitow, A., Jaffer, M., Graae, F., & Whitaker, A. (1994). Outpatient behavioral treatment of child and adolescent obsessive compulsive disorder. *Journal of Anxiety Disorders, 8*, 277–289.

Pina, A. A., & Silverman, W. K. (2004). Clinical phenomenology, somatic symptoms, and distress in Hispanic/ Latino and European American youths with anxiety disorders. *Journal of Clinical Child and Adolescent Psychology, 33*, 227–236.

Rapee, R. M., & Spence, S. H. (2004). The etiology of social phobia: Empirical evidence and an initial model. *Clinical Psychology Review, 24*, 737–767.

Robin, J., Puliafico, A., Creed, T., Comer, J., Hofflich, S., … Kendall, P. C. (2006). Generalized anxiety disorder. In M. Hersen & J. Thomas (Eds.), *Child psychopathology.* New York, NY: Wiley.

Rudd, D., Joiner, T., & Rumzek, H. (2004). Childhood diagnoses and later risk for multiple suicide attempts. *Suicide and Life-Threatening Behavior, 34*, 113–125.

Spence, S. H., Donovan, C., & Brechman-Toussaint, M. (2000). The treatment of childhood social phobia: The effectiveness of a social skills training-based, cognitive-behavioral intervention, with and without parental involvement. *Journal of Child Psychology and Psychiatry, 41*, 713–726.

Van Amerigen, M., Manicini, C., & Farvolden, P. (2003). The impact of anxiety disorders on educational achievement. *Journal of Anxiety Disorders, 17*, 561–571.

Varela, R. E., Vernberg, E. M., Sanchez-Soz, J. J., Riveros, A., Mitchell, M., & Mashunkashey, J. (2004). Anxiety reporting and culturally associated interpretation biases and cognitive schemas: A comparison of Mexican, Mexican American, and European American families. *Journal of Clinical Child and Adolescent Psychology, 33*, 237–247.

Verduin, T. L., & Kendall, P. C. (2003). Differential occurrence of comorbidity within childhood anxiety disorders. *Journal of Clinical Child and Adolescent Psychology, 32*, 290–295.

Verduin, T. L., & Kendall, P. C. (2008). Peer perceptions and liking of children with anxiety disorders. *Journal of Abnormal Child Psychology, 36,* 459–469.

Woodward, L. J., & Fergusson, D. M. (2001). Life course outcomes of young people with anxiety disorders in adolescence. *Journal of the American Academy of Child and Adolescent Psychiatry, 40,* 1086–1093.

CHAPTER 4

Research

American Academy of Pediatrics. (2000). Clinical practice guidelines: Diagnosis and evaluation of the child with attention-deficit/hyperactivity disorder. *Pediatrics, 105,* 1158–1170.

American Academy of Pediatrics. (2001). Clinical practice guideline: Treatment of the school-aged child with attention-deficit/hyperactivity disorder. *Pediatrics, 108,* 1033–1043.

Barkley, R. A. (2002). The international consensus statement on ADHD. *Clinical Child and Family Psychology Review, 5,* 89–111.

Biederman, J., Faraone, S., Milberger, S., Curtis, S., Chen, L., ... Spencer, T. (1996). Predictors of persistence and remission of ADHD into adolescence: Results from a four-year prospective follow-up study. *Journal of the American Academy of Child and Adolescent Psychiatry, 35,* 343–351.

DuPaul, G. J., & Stoner, G. (2003). *ADHD in the schools* (2nd ed.). New York, NY: Guilford Press.

Faraone, S. V., Perlis, R. H., Doyle, A. E., Smoller, J. W., Goralnick, J. J., ... Sklar, P. (2005). Molecular genetics of attention-deficit/hyperactivity disorder. *Biological Psychiatry, 57,* 1313–1323.

Milich, R., Ballentine, A. C., & Lynam, D. (2001). ADHD Combined Type and ADHD Predominantly Inattentive Type are distinct and unrelated disorders. *Clinical Psychology: Science and Practice, 8,* 463–488.

Nigg, J. (2006). *What Causes ADHD? Understanding what goes wrong and why.* New York, NY: Guilford Press.

Pliszka, S. R. (2009). *Treating ADHD and comorbid disorders: Psychosocial and psychopharmacological interventions.* New York, NY: Guilford Press.

Polanczyk, G., de Lima, M. S., Horta, B. L., Biederman, J., & Rohde, L. A. (2007). The worldwide prevalence of ADHD: A systematic review and metaregression analysis. *American Journal of Psychiatry, 164,* 942–948.

Sonuga-Barke, E. J., & Sergeant, J. (2005). The neuroscience of ADHD: Multidisciplinary perspectives on a complex developmental disorder. *Developmental Science, 8,* 103–104.

Clinician Application

Langberg, J. M. (2011). *Homework, organization, and planning skills (HOPS) interventions: A treatment manual.* Bethesda, MD: National Association of School Psychologists.

McBurnett, K., & Pfiffner, L. J. (2008). *Attention deficit hyperactivity disorder: Concepts, controversies, new directions.* New York, NY: Informa Healthcare. Free book download available from: http://ebookee.org/Attention-Deficit-Hyperactivity-Disorder-Concepts-Controversies-New-Directions_269920.html

Pfiffner, L. J. (2011). *All about ADHD: The complete practical guide for classroom teachers* (2nd ed.). New York, NY: Scholastic.

Wolraich, M. L., Wibbelsman, C. J., Brown, T. E., Evans, S. W., Gotlieb, E. M., ... Wilens, T. (2005). Attention deficit hyperactivity disorder among adolescents: A review of the diagnosis, treatment, and clinical implications. *Pediatrics, 115,* 1734–1746. http://www.pediatrics.org/cgi/content/full/115/6/1734

CHAPTER 5

Research

Fristad, M. A., & Goldberg Arnold, J. S. (2004). *Raising a moody child.* New York, NY: Guilford Press.

Geller, B., & DelBello, M. P. (Eds.). (2008). *Treatment of bipolar disorder in children and adolescents.* New York, NY: Guilford Press.

Kowatch, R. A., Fristad, M., Birmaher, B., Wagner, K. D., Findling, R. L., & Hellander, M. (2005). Treatment guidelines for children and adolescents with bipolar disorder. *Journal of the American Academy of Child and Adolescent Psychiatry, 44,* 213–235.

Kowatch, R. A., Strawn, J. R., & Sorter, M. T. (2009). Clinical trials support new algorithm for treating pediatric bipolar mania. *Current Psychiatry, 8,* 19–34.

McClellan, J., Kowatch, R., Findling, R. L., & The Work Group on Quality Issues. (2007). Practice parameter for the assessment and treatment of children and adolescents with bipolar disorder. *Journal of the American Academy of Child and Adolescent Psychiatry, 46*, 107–125.

Miklowitz, D. J., & Cicchetti, D. (Eds.). (2010). *Understanding bipolar disorder: A developmental psychopathology perspective*. New York, NY: Guilford Press.

Miklowitz, D. J., & George, E. L. (2007). *The bipolar teen: What you can do to help your child and your family*. New York, NY: Guilford Press.

Nandagopal, J. J., & DelBello, M. P. (2010). Pharmacotherapy for pediatric bipolar disorder. *Psychiatric Annals, 40*, 221–230.

Pavuluri, M. (2008). *What works for bipolar kids: Help and hope for parents*. New York, NY: Guilford Press.

Pfeifer, J. C., Kowatch, R. A., & DelBello, M. P. (2010). Pharmacotherapy of bipolar disorder in children and adolescents. *CNS Drugs, 24*, 575–593.

West, A. E., & Pavuluri, M. N. (2009). Psychosocial treatments for childhood and adolescent bipolar disorder. *Child and Adolescent Psychiatric Clinics of North America, 18*, 471–482.

Young, M. E., & Fristad, M. A. (2007). Evidence based treatments for bipolar disorder in children and adolescents. *Journal of Contemporary Psychotherapy, 37*, 157–164.

CHAPTER 6

Research

American Psychiatric Association. (2000). *Diagnostic and statistical manual of mental disorders* (4th ed., text rev.). Washington, DC: Author.

Berkout, O. V., Young, J. N., & Gross, A. M. (2011). Mean girls and bad boys: Recent research on gender differences in conduct disorder. *Aggression and Violent Behavior, 16*, 503–511. doi: 10.1016/j.avb.2011.06.001

Drug Strategies. (2005). *Bridging the gap: A guide to drug treatment in the juvenile justice system*. Washington, DC: Author.

Henderson, C. E., Dakof, G. A., Greenbaum, P. E., & Liddle, H. A. (2010). Effectiveness of multidimensional family therapy with higher severity substance-abusing adolescents: Report from two randomized controlled trials. *Journal of Consulting and Clinical Psychology, 78*, 885–897. doi: 10.1037/a0020620

Henderson, C. E., Young, D. W., Jainchill, N., Hawke, J., Farkas, S., & Davis, R. (2007). Program use of effective drug abuse treatment practices for juvenile offenders. *Journal of Substance Abuse Treatment, 32*, 279–290. doi: 10.1016/j.jsat.2006.12.021

Hogue, A., Dauber, S., Stambaugh, L., Cecero, J., & Liddle, H. (2006). Early therapeutic alliance and treatment outcome in individual and family therapy for adolescent behavior problems. *Journal of Consulting and Clinical Psychology, 74*, 121–129.

Kazdin, A. E. (1995). Conduct disorder. In F. C. Verhulst, H. M. Koot, F. C. Verhulst, H. M. Koot (Eds.), *The epidemiology of child and adolescent psychopathology* (pp. 258–290). New York, NY: Oxford University Press.

Keenan, K., Wroblewski, K., Hipwell, A., Loeber, R., & Stouthamer-Loeber, M. (2010). Age of onset, symptom threshold, and expansion of the nosology of conduct disorder for girls. *Journal of Abnormal Psychology, 119*, 689–698. doi: 10.1037/a0019346

Kessler, R. C., Avenoli, S., Costello, J. E., Georgiades, K., Green, J. G., ... Merikangas, K. R. (2012). Prevalence, persistence, and sociodemographic correlates of *DSM-IV* disorders in the national comorbidity survey replication adolescent supplement. *Archives of General Psychiatry*, E1-E9. *69*, 372–380. doi: 10.1001/archgenpsychiatry.2011.160

Kim-Cohen, J., Caspi, A., Moffitt, T. E., Harrington, H., Milne, B. J., & Poulton, R. (2003). Prior juvenile diagnoses in adults with mental disorder: Developmental follow-back of a prospective-longitudinal cohort. *Archives of General Psychiatry, 60*, 709–717. doi: 10.1001/archpsyc.60.7.709

Lambert, E. W., Wahler, R. G., Andrade, A. R., & Bickman, L. (2001). Looking for the disorder in conduct disorder. *Journal of Abnormal Psychology, 110*, 110–123.

Liddle, H. A., Rowe, C. L., Dakof, G. A., Henderson, C. E., & Greenbaum, P. E. (2009). Multidimensional family therapy for young adolescent substance abuse: Twelve-month outcomes of a randomized controlled trial. *Journal of Consulting and Clinical Psychology, 77*, 12–25.

Lyons, J. S., Baerger, D., Quigley, P., Erlich, J., & Griffin, E. (2001). Mental health service needs of juvenile offenders: A comparison of detention, incarceration, and treatment settings. *Children's Services: Social Policy, Research, & Practice, 4*, 69–85. doi: 10.1207/S15326918CS0402_2

Merikangas, K., He, J., Burstein, M., Swanson, S. A., Avenevoli, S., ... Swendsen, J. (2010). Lifetime prevalence of mental disorders in U.S. adolescents: Results from the National Comorbidity Survey Replication-Adolescent Supplement (NCS-A). *Journal of the American Academy of Child & Adolescent Psychiatry, 49,* 980–989.

Nissen, L. (2006). Effective adolescent substance abuse treatment in juvenile justice settings: Practice and policy recommendations. *Child & Adolescent Social Work Journal, 23,* 298–315.

Nock, M. K., Kazdin, A. E., Hiripi, E., & Kessler, R. C. (2006). Prevalence, subtypes, and correlates of *DSM-IV* conduct disorder in the National Comorbidity Survey Replication. *Psychological Medicine: A Journal of Research in Psychiatry and the Allied Sciences, 36,* 699–710. doi: 10.1017/S0033291706007082

North, L., & Henderson, C. *The effectiveness of adolescent psychosocial substance abuse treatments on comorbid conduct problems.* Manuscript submitted for publication.

Rawal, P., Romansky, J., Jenuwine, M., & Lyons, J. S. (2004). Racial differences in the mental health needs and service utilization of youth in the juvenile justice system. *The Journal of Behavioral Health Services & Research, 31,* 242–254. doi: 10.1097/00075484-200407000-00002

Ridenour, T. A., Cottler, L. B., Robins, L. N., Campton, W. M., Spitznagel, E. L., & Cunningham-Williams, R. M. (2002). Test of the plausibility of adolescent substance use playing a causal role in developing adulthood antisocial behavior. *Journal of Abnormal Psychology, 111,* 144–155. doi: 10.1037/0021-843X.111.1.144

Rowe, C., Liddle, H., Greenbaum, P., & Henderson, C. (2004). Impact of psychiatric comorbidity on treatment of adolescent drug abusers. *Journal of Substance Abuse Treatment, 26,* 129–140.

Sawyer, A. M., & Borduin, C. M. (2011). Effects of multisystemic therapy through midlife: A 21.9-year follow-up to a randomized clinical trial with serious and violent juvenile offenders. *Journal of Consulting and Clinical Psychology, 79,* 643–652.

Wise, E. A. (2011). Statistical significance testing and clinical effectiveness studies. *Psychotherapy, 48,* 225–228. doi: 10.1037/a0022701

Young, D. W., Dembo, R., & Henderson, C. E. (2007). A national survey of substance abuse treatment for juvenile offenders. *Journal of Substance Abuse Treatment, 32,* 255–266. doi: 10.1016/j.jsat.2006.12.018

Clinician Application

Algoe, S. B., & Haidt, J. (2009). Witnessing excellence in action: The "other-praising" emotions of elevation, gratitude, and admiration. *Journal of Positive Psychology, 4,* 105–127.

Aron, A., Norman, C. C., Aron, E. N., McKenna, C., & Heyman, R. E. (2000). Couples' shared participation in novel and arousing activities and experienced relationship quality. *Journal of Personality & Social Psychology, 78,* 273–284.

Elliot, A. J. (2006). The hierarchical model of approach-avoidance motivation. *Motivation and Emotion, 30,* 111–116.

Fleurides, C., Nelson, T. S., & Rosenthal, D. M. (1986). The evolution of circular questions: Training family therapists. *Journal of Marital and Family Therapy, 12,* 113–127.

Gable, S. L., & Reis, H. T. (2010). Good news! Capitalizing on positive events in an interpersonal context. In M. P. Zanna (Ed.), *Advances in experimental social psychology* (Vol. 42, pp. 195–257). San Diego, CA: Elsevier.

Kornfield, J. (2008). *The art of forgiveness, loving kindness, and peace.* New York, NY: Bantam.

Lambert, N. M., Fincham, F. D., Gwinn, A. M., & Ajayi, C. A. (2011). Positive relationship science: A new frontier for Positive Psychology? In K. M. Sheldon, T. B. Kashden, & M. F. Steger (Eds.), *Designing positive psychology: Taking stock and moving forward.* (pp. 280–294). New York, NY: Oxford University Press.

Liddle, H. A. (1992). A multidimensional model for treating the adolescent who is abusing alcohol and other drugs. In W. Snyder & T. Ooms (Eds.), *Empowering families, helping adolescents: Family-centered treatment of adolescents with alcohol, drug abuse, and mental health problems* (pp. 91–100). Rockville, MD: U.S. Government Printing Office.

Liddle, H. A. (2002). *Multidimensional Family Therapy Treatment (MDFT) for adolescent cannabis users: Vol. 5 Cannabis Youth Treatment (CYT) manual series.* Rockville, MD: Center for Substance Abuse Treatment, Substance Abuse and Mental Health Services Administration.

Mehl, M. R., Holleran, S. E., Clark, C. S., & Vazire, S. (2010). Eavesdropping on happiness: Well-being is related to having less small talk and more substantive conversations. *Psychological Science, 21,* 539–541.

Rusbult, C. E., Kumashiro, M., Stocker, S. L., & Wolf, S. T. (2005). The Michelangelo phenomenon in close relationships. In A. Tesser, J. Wood, & D. A. Stapel (Eds.), *On building, defending, and regulating the self: A psychological perspective* (pp. 1–29). New York, NY: Psychology Press.

Sherman, C. (2010, December). *Multidimensional Family Therapy for adolescent drug abuse offers broad, lasting benefits.* NIDA Notes, Vol. 23, No. 3. Retrieved June 10, 2012 from http://med.miami.edu/ctrada/documents/MDFTEpacket/MDFTNIDANotesVol23No3ResearchFindings.pdf

Tomm, K. (1988). Interventive interviewing: Part III: Intending to ask lineal, circular, strategic, or reflexive questions? *Family Process, 27,* 1–15.

CHAPTER 7

Research

Adler, R., Nunn, R., Northam, E., Lebnan, V., & Ross, R. (1994). Secondary prevention in childhood firesetting. *Journal of the American Academy of Child and Adolescent Psychiatry, 33*, 1194–1202.

Arson Prevention Bureau. (2003). *Arson—Key Facts.* Retrieved 03 July, 2009 from http://kb.keepbritaintidy .org/criminaldamage/publications/arson.pdf

Barreto, S. J., Boekamp, J. R., Armstrong, L. M., & Gillen, P. (2004). Community-based interventions for juvenile firestarters: A brief family-centered model. *Psychological Services, 1*, 158–168.

Becker, K. D., Stuewig, J., Herrera, V. M., & McCloskey, L. A. (2004). A study of firesetting and animal cruelty in children: Family influences and adolescent outcomes. *Journal of the American Academy of Child and Adolescent Psychiatry, 43*, 905–912.

Bumpass, E. R., Brix, R. J., & Preston, D. (1985). A community-based program for juvenile firesetters. *Hospital and Community Psychiatry, 36*, 529–530.

Bumpass, E. R., Fagelman, F. D., & Brix, R. J. (1983) Intervention with children who set fires. *American Journal of Psychotherapy, 37*, 328–345.

Chen, Y., Arria A. M., & Anthony, J. C. (2003). Firesetting in adolescence and being aggressive, shy and rejected by peers: New epidemiologic evidence from a national sample survey. *Journal of the American Academy of Psychiatry and the Law, 31*, 44–52.

Dadds, M. R., & Fraser, J. A. (2006). Fire interest, fire setting and psychopathology in Australian Children: A normative study. *Australian and New Zealand Journal of Psychiatry, 40*, 581–586.

Del Bove, G., Caprara, G. V., Pastorelli, C., & Paciello, M. (2008). Juvenile firesetting in Italy: Relationship to aggression, psychopathology, personality, self-efficacy, and school functioning. *European Child and Adolescent Psychology, 17*, 235–244.

Del Bove, G., & Mackay, S. (2011). An empirically derived classification system for juvenile firesetters. *Criminal Justice and Behaviour, 38*, 796–817. doi: 10.1177/0093854811406224

Fineman, K. R. (1995). A model for the qualitative analysis of child and adult fire deviant behaviour. *American Journal of Forensic Psychology, 13*, 31–60.

Franklin, G. A., Pucci, P. S., Arbabi, S., Brandt, M., Wahl, W. L., & Taheri, P. A. (2002). Decreased juvenile arson and firesetting recidivism after implementation of a multidisciplinary prevention program. *The Journal of Trauma, 53*, 260–264.

Hall, J. R. (2007). *Intentional fires and arson.* Quincey, MA: National Fire Protection Association.

Hickle, K. E., & Roe-Sepowitz, D. E. (2010). Female juvenile arsonists: An exploratory look at characteristics and solo and group arson offences. *Legal and Criminological Psychology, 15*, 385–399.

Kolko, D. J. (2001). Efficacy of cognitive-behavioral treatment and fire safety education for children who set fires: Initial and follow-up outcomes. *Journal of Child Psychology and Psychiatry, 42*, 359–369.

Kolko, D. J. (Ed.). (2002). *Handbook on firesetting in children and youth.* San Diego, CA: Academic Press.

Kolko, D. J., Day, B. T., Bridge, J. A., & Kazdin, A. E. (2001). Two-year prediction of children's firesetting in clinically referred and nonreferred samples. *Journal of Child Psychology and Psychiatry, 42*, 371–380.

Kolko, D. J., Herschell, A. D., & Scharf, D. M. (2006). Education and treatment for boys who set fires: specificity, moderators and predictors of recidivism. *Journal of Emotional and Behavioral Disorders, 14*, 227–239.

Kolko, D. J., & Kazdin, A. E. (1990). Matchplay and firesetting in children: Relationship to parent, marital & family dysfunction. *Journal of Clinical Child Psychology, 19*, 229–238.

Kolko, D. J., & Kazdin A. E. (1991). Aggression and psychopathology in matchplaying and firesetting children: A replication & extension. *Journal of Clinical Child Psychology, 20*, 191–201.

Kolko, D. J., & Kazdin, A. E. (1992). The emergence and recurrence of child firesetting: A one-year prospective study. *Journal of Abnormal Child Psychology, 20*, 17–37.

Kolko, D. J., Watson, S., & Faust, J. (1991). Fire safety/prevention skills training to reduce involvement with fire in young psychiatric inpatients: Preliminary findings. *Behaviour Therapy, 22*, 269–284.

Lambie, I., & Randell, I. (2011). Creating a firestorm: A review of children who deliberately light fires. *Clinical Psychology Review, 31*, 307–327.

MacKay, S., Henderson, J., Del Bove, G., Marton, P., Warling, D., & Root, C. (2006). Fire interest and antisociality as risk factors in the severity and persistence of juvenile firesetting. *Journal of the American Academy of Child and Adolescent Psychiatry, 45*, 1077–1084.

MacKay, S., Paglia-Boak, A., Henderson, J., Marton, P., & Adlaf, E. (2009). Epidemiology of firesetting in adolescents: Mental health and substance use correlates. *Journal of Child Psychology and Psychiatry, 50*, 1282–1290.

Martin, G., Bergen, H., Richardson, A. S., Roegar, L., & Allison, S. (2004). Correlates of firesetting in a community sample of young adolescents. *Australian and New Zealand Journal of Psychiatry, 38*, 148–154.

McCardle, S., Lambie, I., & Barker-Collo, S. (2004). *Adolescent firesetting: A NZ case-controlled study of risk factors for adolescent firesetters*. New Zealand Fire Service Commission. Retrieved 03 July, 2009 from http://www .fire.org.nz/Research/Published-Reports/Documents/85ef271de5e12e5d7e143d153ea1fc39.pdf

Palmer, E. J., Caufield, L. S., & Hollin, C. R. (2007). Interventions with arsonists and young firesetters: A survey of the national picture in England and Wales. *The British Psychological Society, 12*, 101–116.

Root, C., MacKay, S., Henderson, J., Del Bove, G., & Warling, D. (2008). The link between maltreatment and juvenile firesetting: Correlates and underlying mechanisms. *Child Abuse & Neglect, 32*, 161–176.

Sakheim, G. A., & Osborn, E. (1999). Severe vs. nonsevere firesetters revisited. *Child Welfare, 78*, 411–434.

Stadolnik, R. F. (2000). *Drawn to the flame: Assessment & treatment of juvenile firesetting behaviour*. Sarasota, FL: Professional Resource Press.

Statistics New Zealand. (2008). Calendar year apprehension statistics. Retrieved from http://wdmzpub01 .stats.govt.nz/wds/TableViewer/tableView.aspx

U.S. Department of Justice—Federal Bureau of Justice. (2010). Crime in the United States, 2009. Table 36—Current year over previous year arrest trends. Retrieved from http://www2.fbi.gov/ucr/cius2009/data/table_36.html

Clinician Application

Childress, C. A., Fineman, K. R., & Patterson, B. L. (2004a). Initial fire evaluation survey, Version 1.0, in firefriends.org, Department of Justice, United States of America.

Childress, C. A., Fineman, K. R., & Patterson, B. L. (2004b). Fire F.R.I.E.N.D.S. behavioral health evaluation interview-juvenile, Version 2.0, in firefriends.org, Department of Justice, United States of America.

Fineman, K. R. (1976). Some psychological aspects of child caused fires. *The California Fireman, 1*, 47–50.

Fineman, K. R. (1980). Firesetting in children and adolescents. In B. J. Blinder (Ed.), *Psychiatric clinics of North America, Vol. 3. Child psychiatry: Contributions to diagnosis, treatment, and research* (pp. 483–500). Philadelphia/London/Toronto: W. B. Saunders.

Fineman, K. R. (1985). Forensic evaluation of child and adult arsonists. Invited paper presented at the Convention of the American College of Forensic Psychology, Newport Beach, California.

Fineman, K. R. (1988). Child, adolescent, and family interview forms. In J. Gaynor & C. Kartchmer, *Adolescent firesetter handbook: Ages 14–18*. Washington, DC: Federal Emergency Management.

Fineman, K. R. (1997). Comprehensive FireRisk Assessment. In C. Poage, M. Doctor, J. B. Day, K. Rester, C. Velasquez, … L. Marshburn (Eds.), *Juvenile firesetter prevention program: Training seminar* (Vol. I, pp. 1–25), Denver, CO: Colorado Division of Fire Safety.

Fineman, K. R. (2002). Juvenile and family interview forms. In J. Gaynor (Ed.), *Juvenile firesetter intervention handbook*: Washington, D.C.: U.S. Fire Administration and U.S. Government Printing Office.

Fineman, K. R. (2004a). Comprehensive firerisk assessment (Fire Service Professional, Version 3.0). United States Fire Administration, Federal Emergency Management Agency.

Fineman, K. R. (2004b). Basic treatment issues, video with transcript, in firefriends.org. Department of Justice, United States of America.

Fineman, K. R., Baizerman, M., Mieszala, P., Day, J. B., Emshoff, B., & Bookbinder, L. (1988). *Juvenile firesetter handbook: Dealing with children 7-13*. Washington, DC: Federal Emergency Management Agency.

Kolko, D. J. (Ed.). (2002). *Handbook on firesetting in children and youth*. New York, NY: Kluwer/Academic Press.

Kolko, D. J., Scharf, D. M., Herschell, A. D., Wilcox, D., Okuluitch, J., & Pinsonnealt, I. (2008). A survey of juvenile firesetter intervention programs in North America: Overall description and comparison of independent vs coalition-based programs. *American Journal of Forensic Psychology, 26*(4), 41–66.

Lambie, I., & Randell, I. (2011). Creating a firestorm: A review of children who deliberately light fires. *Clinical Psychology Review, 31*, 307–327.

Schwartzman, P., Fineman, K., Slavkin, M., Mieszala, P., Thomas, J., … Baer, M. (2000). *Juvenile firesetter mental health intervention: A comprehensive discussion of treatment, service delivery, and training of providers* (pp. 1–87). The Office of Juvenile and Delinquency Prevention, National Association of State Fire Marshalls Juvenile Firesetter Intervention Project.

Steadolnik, R. F. (2000). *Drawn to the flame: Assessment & treatment of juvenile firesetting behaviour*. Sarasota, FL: Professional Resources Press.

CHAPTER 8

Research

American Psychiatric Association. (2000). *Diagnostic and statistical manual of mental disorders* (4th ed., text rev.). Washington, DC: American Psychiatric Association.

American Psychological Association. (2002). Ethical principles of psychologists and code of conduct. *American Psychologist, 57*, 1060–1073.

Angold, A., Costello, J., & Erkanli, A. (1999). Comorbidity. *Journal of Child Psychology and Psychiatry, 40*, 57–87.

Antshel, K., Faraone, S., Maglione, K., Doyle, A., Fried, R., … Biederman, J. (2008). Temporal stability of ADHD in the high-IQ population: Results from the MGH longitudinal family studies of ADHD. *Journal of the American Academy of Child & Adolescent Psychiatry, 47*, 817–825.

Antshel, K., Farone, S., Stallone, K., Nave, A., Kaufmann, F., … Biederman, J. (2007). Is attention deficit hyperactivity disorder a valid diagnosis in the presence of high IQ? Results from the MGH longitudinal family studies of ADHD. *Journal of Child Psychology and Psychiatry, 48*, 687–694.

Assouline, S. G., Foley Nicpon, M., & Whiteman, C. S. (2011). Cognitive and psychosocial characteristics of gifted students with written language disability: A reply to Lovett's response. *Gifted Child Quarterly, 55*, 152–157.

Bachelor, A., & Horwath, A. (1999). The therapeutic relationship. In M. A. Hubble, B. L. Duncan & S. D. Miller (Eds.), *The heart and soul of change: What works in therapy* (pp. 133–178). Washington, DC: American Psychological Association.

Baker, J. A. (1995). Depression and suicidal ideation among academically talented adolescents. *Gifted Child Quarterly, 39*, 218–223.

Baum, S., Olenchak, F., & Owens, S. (1998). Gifted students with attention deficits: Fact and/or fiction? Or, can we see the forest from the trees? *Gifted Child Quarterly, 42*, 96–104.

Baum, S., & Owen, S. V. (2004). *To be gifted and learning disabled*. Mansfield, CT: Creative Learning Press.

Betts, G. T. (1986). Development of the emotional and social needs of gifted individuals. *Journal of Counseling and Development, 64*, 587–589.

Betts, G. T., & Neihart, M. F. (1986). Eight affective activities to enhance the emotional and social development of the gifted and talented. *Roeper Review, 8*, 18–23.

Bordin, E. S. (1979). The generalizability of the psychoanalytic concept of the working alliance. *Psychotherapy: Theory, Research, and Practice, 16*, 252–260.

Brody, L. E., & Mills, C. J. (1997). Gifted children with learning disabilities: A review of the issues. *Journal of Learning Disabilities, 30*, 282–296.

Castellanos, F. X., Glaser, P. E., & Gehardt, G. A. (2006). Towards a neuroscience of ADHD: Fractionating the phenotype. *Journal of Neuroscience Methods, 151*, 1–4.

Ceci, S. J., & Papierno, P. B. (2005). The rhetoric and reality of gap closing: When the "have-nots" gain but he "haves" gain even more. *American Psychologist, 60*, 149–160.

Ceci, S. J., & Williams, W. M. (1997). Schooling, intelligence, and income. *American Psychologist, 52*, 1051.

Ceci, S. J., Williams, W. M., & Barnett, S. M. (2009). Women's underrepresentation in science: Sociocultural and biological considerations. *Psychological Bulletin, 135*, 218–261.

Colangelo, N., & Zaffrann, R. T. (1979). *New voices in counseling the gifted*. Dubuque, IA: Kendall Hunt.

Cross, T. L. (2008). Suicide. In J. A. Plucker & C. M. Callahan (Eds.), *Critical issues and practices in gifted education: What the research says* (pp. 629–639). Waco, TX: Prufrock Press.

Cross, T. L. (2011). *On the social and emotional lives of gifted children* (4th ed.). Waco, TX: Prufrock Press.

Cross, T. L., Cassady, J. C., & Miller, K. A. (2006). Suicide ideation and personality characteristics among gifted adolescents. *Gifted Child Quarterly, 50*, 295–358.

Daniels, S., & Piechowski, M. M. (2009). *Living with intensity: Understanding the sensitivity, excitability, and emotional development of gifted children, adolescents, and adults*. Scottsdale, AZ: Great Potential Press.

Delisle, J. R. (1992). *Guiding the social and emotional development of gifted youth: A practical guide for educators and counselors*. New York, NY: Longman.

Eliason, M. M. (2011). Introduction to special issue on suicide, mental health, and youth development. *Journal of Homosexuality, 58*, 4–9.

Feldhusen, J. F. (2005). Giftedness, talent, expertise, and creative achievement. In R. J. Sternberg & J. E. Davidson (Eds.), *Conceptions of giftedness* (2nd ed., pp. 64–79). New York, NY: Cambridge University Press.

Foley Nicpon, M., Allmon, A., Sieck, B., & Stinson, R. D. (2011). Empirical investigation of twice-exceptionality: Where have we been and where are we going? *Gifted Child Quarterly, 55*, 3–17.

Foley Nicpon, M., & Pfeiffer, S. I. (2011). High ability students: New ways to conceptualize giftedness and provide psychological services in the schools. *Journal of Applied School Psychology, 27*, 293–305.

Frost, R., Marten, P., Lahart, C., & Rosenblate, R. (1990). The dimensions of perfectionism. *Cognitive Therapy and Research, 14*, 449–468.

Gagné, F. (2005). From gifts to talents: The DMGT as a developmental model. In R. J. Sternberg & J. E. Davidson (Eds.), *Conceptions of giftedness* (2nd ed., pp. 98–120). Cambridge, UK: Cambridge University Press.

Gallagher, J. J. (2008). Psychology, psychologists, and gifted students. In S. I. Pfeiffer (Ed.), *Handbook of giftedness in children* (pp. 1–11). New York, NY: Springer.

Gardner, H. (1983). *Frames of mind*. New York, NY: Basic Books.

Gardner, H. (1993). *Multiple intelligences: The theory in practice*. New York, NY: Basic Books.

Goertzel, V., Goertzel, M., Goertzel, T., & Hansen, A. (2004). *Cradles of eminence: Childhoods of more than 700 famous men and women* (2nd ed.). Tucson, AZ: Great Potential Press.

Gottfredson, L. S. (1998). The general intelligence factor. *Scientific American, 9*, 24–30.

Gross, M. U. M. (1994). Radical acceleration: Responding to academic and social needs of extremely gifted adolescents. *Journal of Secondary Gifted Education, 5*, 27–34.

Hamachek, D. E. (1978). Psychodynamics of normal and neurotic perfectionism. *Psychology, 15*, 27–33.

Hollingsworth, L. S. (1926). *Gifted children: Their nature and nurture*. New York, NY: Macmillan.

Horowitz, F. D., Subotnik, R. F., & Matthews, D. J. (Eds.). (2009). *The development of giftedness and talent across the life span*. Washington, DC: American Psychological Association.

Individuals With Disabilities Education Improvement Act of 2004, 20 U.S.C. § 1400 et seq. (2004).

Kendall, P. C. (2006). Guiding theory for therapy with children and adolescents. In P. C. Kendall (Ed.), *Child and adolescent therapy: Cognitive-behavioral procedures* (pp. 3–30). New York, NY: Guilford Press.

Kennedy-Moore, E., & Lowenthal, M. S. (2011). *Smart parenting for smart kids*. New York, NY: Jossey-Bass.

Kitano, M. K. (1990). Intellectual abilities and psychological intensities in young children: Implications for the gifted. *Roeper Review, 13*, 5–10.

Kratochwill, T. R., & Stoiber, K. C. (2002). Evidence-based interventions in school psychology: Conceptual foundations of the Procedural and Coding Manual of Division 16 and the Society for the Study of School Psychology Task Force. *School Psychology Quarterly, 17*, 341–389.

Landrum, M. S., Callahan, C. M., & Shaklee, B. D. (Eds.). (2001). *Aiming for excellence: Gifted program standards*. Waco, TX: Prufrock Press.

Lazarus, A. A. (1993). Tailoring the therapeutic relationship, or being an authentic chameleon. *Psychotherapy, 30*, 404–407.

Lee, S. Y., & Olszewski-Kubilius, P. (2006). Comparison between talent search students qualifying via scores on standardized tests via parent nomination. *Roeper Review, 28*, 157–166.

Lind, S. (2001). Overexcitability and the gifted. *SENG Newsletter, 1*, 3–6. Retrieved from http://www. sengifted .org/archives/articles/overexcita-bility-and-the-gifted

Lovett, B. J. (2011). On the diagnosis of learning disabilities in gifted students: Reply to Assouline et al. (2010). *Gifted Child Quarterly, 55*, 149–151.

Lovett, B. J., & Lewandowski, L. J. (2006). Gifted students with learning disabilities: Who are they? *Journal or Learning Disabilities, 39*, 515–527.

Marland, S. P. (1972). *Education of the gifted and talented* (2 Vols.). Report to congress of the United States Commissioner of Education. Washington, DC: Government Printing Office.

Martin, D. J., Garske, J. P., & Davis, M. K. (2000). Relation of the therapeutic alliance with outcome and other variables: A meta-analytic review. *Journal of Consulting and Clinical Psychology, 38*, 438–450.

Martin, L. T., Burns, R. M., & Schonlau, M. (2010). Mental disorders among gifted and nongifted youth: A selected review of the epidemiologic literature. *Gifted Child Quarterly, 54*, 31–41.

Mayer, R. E. (2005). The scientific study of giftedness. In R. J. Sternberg & J. E. Davidson (Eds.), *Conceptions of giftedness* (2nd ed., pp. 437–447). New York, NY: Cambridge University Press.

McClain, M. C., & Pfeiffer, S. I. (2012). Identification of gifted students in the U.S. today: A look at state definitions, policies, and practices. *Journal of Applied School Psychology, 28*, 59–88.

McCoach, D. B., & Siegle, D. (2008). Underachievers. In J. A. Plucker & C. M. Callahan (Eds.), *Critical issues and practices in gifted education: What the research says* (pp. 721–734). Waco, TX: Prufrock Press.

Mendaglio, S., & Peterson, J. S. (Eds.). (2007). *Models of counseling gifted children, adolescents, and young adults*. Waco, TX: Prufrock Press.

Moon, S. M. (2002a). Counseling needs and strategies. In M. Neihart, S. M. Reis, N. M. Robinson, & S. M. Moon (Eds.), *The social and emotional development of gifted children. What do we know?* (pp. 213–222). Waco, TX: Prufrock Press.

Moon, S. M. (2002b). Gifted children with Attention-Deficit/Hyperactivity Disorder. In M. Neihart, S. M. Reis, N. M. Robinson, & S. M. Moon (Eds.), *The social and emotional development of gifted children. What do we know?* (pp. 193–201). Waco, TX: Prufrock Press.

National Association for Gifted Children. (2009). *2008-2009 state of states in gifted education: National policy and practice data*. Washington, DC: Author.

National Center for Education Statistics (NCES). (2000). Number and percentage of gifted and talented students in public elementary and secondary schools by sex and state: 2000. Retrieved December 1, 2008, from http://nces.ed.gov/programs/digest/d04/tables/dt04_055.asp

National Commission on Excellence in Education. (1983, April). A nation at risk: The imperative for educational reform. Retrieved June 30, 2006, from http://data-center.spps.org/uploads/sotw_a_nation _at_risk_1983.pdf

National Education Association. (2006). *The twice-exceptional dilemma.* Washington, DC: Author.

National Research Council. (2002). *Minority students in special and gifted education* (Committee on Minority Representation in Special Education, M. S. Donovan & C. T. Cross (Eds.), Division of Behavioral and Social Sciences and Education). Washington, DC: National Academy Press.

Neihart, M. (1999). The impact of giftedness on psychological well-being: What does the empirical literature say? *Roeper Review, 22,* 10–17.

Neihart, M. (2008). Identifying and providing services to twice exceptional children. In S. I. Pfeiffer (Ed.), *Handbook of giftedness in children* (pp. 115–137). New York, NY: Springer

Neihart, M., Reis, S., Robinson, N., & Moon, S. (Eds.). (2002). *The social and emotional development of gifted children.* Waco, TX: Prufrock Press.

Neisser, U., Boodoo, G., Bouchard, T. J., Boykin, A. W., Brody, N., … Urbina, S. (1996). Intelligence: Knowns and unknowns. *American Psychologist, 51,* 77–101.

Nisbett, R. E. (2009). *Intelligence and how to get it.* New York, NY: Norton.

Norcross, J. C. (Ed.). (2002). *Psychotherapy relationships that work: Therapists contributions and responsiveness to patients.* New York, NY: Oxford University Press.

Norcross, J. C., Beutler, L. E., & Levant, R. F. (Eds.). (2006). *Evidence-based practices in mental health: Debate and dialogue on the fundamental questions.* Washington, DC: American Psychological Association.

Norcross, J. C., Hogan, T. P., & Koocher, G. P. (2008). *Clinician's guide to evidence-based practice.* New York, NY: Oxford University Press.

Olenchak, F. R., & Reis, S. M. (2002). Gifted students with learning disabilities. In M. Neihart, S. M. Reis, N. M. Robinson, & S. M. Moon (Eds.), *The social and emotional development of gifted children. What do we know?* (pp. 177–191). Waco, TX: Prufrock Press.

Olszewski-Kubilius, P. (2008). The role of the family in talent development. In S. I. Pfeiffer (Ed.), *Handbook of giftedness in children* (pp. 53–70). New York, NY: Springer.

Peterson, J. S., & Moon, S. M. (2008). Counseling the gifted. In S. I. Pfeiffer (Ed.), *Handbook of giftedness in children* (pp. 223–245). New York, NY: Springer.

Peterson, J. S., & Ray, K. E. (2006). Bullying and the gifted: Victims, perpetrators, prevalence, and effects. *Gifted Child Quarterly, 50,* 252–268.

Pfeiffer, S. I. (2001). Professional psychology and the gifted: Emerging practice opportunities. *Professional Psychology: Research and Practice, 32,* 175–180.

Pfeiffer, S. I. (2003a). Challenges and opportunities for students who are gifted: What the experts say. *Gifted Child Quarterly, 47,* 161–169.

Pfeiffer, S. I. (2003b). Psychological considerations in raising a healthy gifted child. In P. Olszewski-Kubilius, L. Limburg-Weber, & S. I. Pfeiffer (Eds.), *Early gifts: Recognizing and nurturing children's talents* (pp. 173–185). Waco, TX: Prufrock Press.

Pfeiffer, S. I. (2012). *Serving the gifted: Clinical and psychoeducational practices.* New York, NY: Routledge.

Pfeiffer, S. I. (In press). Lessons learned from working with high-ability students. *Gifted Education International.*

Pfeiffer, S. I., & Stocking, V. (2000). Vulnerabilities of academically gifted students. *Journal of Applied School Psychology, 16,* 83–93.

Reis, S. M., & McCoach, D. B. (2002). Underachievement in gifted students. In M. Neihart, S. M. Reis, N. M. Robinson, & S. M. Moon (Eds.), *The social and emotional development of gifted children* (pp. 81–91). Waco, TX: Prufrock Press.

Reis, S. M., & Hébert, T. P. (2008). Gender and giftedness. In S. I. Pfeiffer (Ed.), *Handbook of giftedness in children* (pp. 271–291). New York, NY: Springer.

Rimm, S. B. (2008). Underachievement syndrome: A psychological defensive pattern. In S. I. Pfeiffer (Ed.), *Handbook of giftedness in children* (pp. 139–160). New York, NY: Springer.

Robinson, A., & Clinkenbeard, P. R. (2008). History of giftedness: Perspectives from the past presage modern scholarship. In S. I. Pfeiffer (Ed.), *Handbook of giftedness in children* (pp. 13–31). New York, NY: Springer.

Robinson, N. M. (2008). The social world of gifted children and youth. In S. I. Pfeiffer (Ed.), *Handbook of giftedness in children* (pp. 33–51). New York, NY: Springer.

Ross, P. O. (1993). National excellence: A case for developing America's talent. Washington, DC: U.S. Government Printing Office. Retrieved February 14, 2005, from https://www.ocps.net/cs/ese/programs/gifted/Documents/National%20Excellence_%20A%20Case%20for%20Developing%20America's%20Talent_%20Introduction.pdf

Silverman, L. K. (1993). *Counseling the gifted and talented.* Denver, CO: Love.

Silverman, L. K., & Golon, A. S. (2008). Clinical practice with gifted families. In S. I. Pfeiffer (Ed.), *Handbook of giftedness in children* (pp. 199–222). New York, NY: Springer.

Sternberg, R. J., & Davidson, J. E. (Eds.). (2005). *Conceptions of giftedness* (2nd ed.). New York, NY: Cambridge University Press.

Sternberg, R. J., Jarvin, L., & Grigorenko. E. L. (2011). *Explorations in giftedness*. New York, NY: Cambridge University Press.

Subotnik, R. F. (2003). A developmental view of giftedness: From being to doing. *Roeper Review, 26*, 14–15.

Tannenbaum, A. J. (1983). *Gifted children: Psychological and educational perspectives*. New York, NY: Macmillan.

Terman, L. M., & Oden, M. H. (1951). The Stanford studies of the gifted. In P. Witty (Ed.), *The gifted child*. Boston, MA: D. C. Heath.

Thompson, K. C., & Morris, R. J. (2008). Ethical and professional practice issues in the provision of educational services to gifted students. In S. I. Pfeiffer (Ed.), *Handbook of giftedness in children* (pp. 309–326). New York, NY: Springer.

Webb, J. T., Amend, E. R., Webb, N. E., Goerss, J., Beljan, P., & Olenchak, F. R. (2005). *Misdiagnosis and dual diagnoses of gifted children and adults: ADHD, bipolar, OCD, Asperger's, depression and other disorders*. Scottsdale, AZ: Great Potential Press.

Whitmore, J. R. (1981). Gifted children with handicapping conditions: A new frontier. *Exceptional Children, 48*, 106–114.

Wood, S. (2010). Best practices in counseling the gifted in schools: What's really happening? *Gifted Child Quarterly, 54*, 42–58.

Ziv, A. (1977). *Counseling the intellectually gifted child*. Toronto, Ontario: Guidance Centre University of Toronto.

Clinician Application

Baker, J. A. (1995). Depression and suicidal ideation among academically gifted adolescents. *Gifted Child Quarterly, 39*, 218–223.

Cassady, J. C., & Cross, T. L. (2006). A factorial representation of suicidal ideation among academically gifted adolescents. *Journal for the Education of the Gifted, 29*, 290–304.

Cross, T. L., Cassady, J. C., & Miller, K. A. (2006). Suicide ideation and personality characteristics among gifted adolescents. *Gifted Child Quarterly, 50*, 295–306.

Day-Vines, N. L., Patton, J. M., Quck, C. G., & Wood, S. (2009). Addressing social-emotional and curricular needs of gifted African-American adolescents. In J. L. VanTassel-Baska, T. L. Cross, & F. R. Olenchak (Eds.), *Social-emotional curriculum with gifted and talented students* (pp. 152–192). Waco, TX: Prufrock Press.

Delisle, J. R. (1986). Death with honors: Suicide among gifted adolescents. *Journal of Counseling and Development, 64*, 558–560.

Diaz, E. I. (1998). Perceived factors influencing the academic underachievement of talented students of Puerto Rican descent. *Gifted Child Quarterly, 42*, 105–122.

Ellsworth, J. (1998). Adolescence and gifted: Addressing existential dread. Retrieved from http://www.sengifted .org/articles_counseling/Ellsworth_AdolescenceAndGiftedAddressingExistentialDread.shtml

Evans, K. M. (1993). Multicultural counseling. In L. K. Silverman (Ed.), *Counseling the gifted and talented* (pp. 277–290). Denver, CO: Love Publishing Company.

Exum, H. A. (1983). Key issues in family counseling with gifted and talented Black students. *Roeper Review, 5*(3), 28–31.

Fahlman, S. A. (2004). Perceptions of giftedness among gifted females in emerging adulthood. *Qualitative Research in Psychology, 1*, 285–306.

Ford, D. Y., Harris, J. J. III, & Schuerger, J. M. (1993). Racial identity development among gifted Black students: Counseling issues and concerns. *Journal of Counseling and Development, 71*, 409–417.

Graham, S. (2009). Giftedness in adolescence: African-American gifted youth and their challenges from a motivational perspective. In F. D. Horowitz, R. F. Subotnik, & D. J. Matthews (Eds.), *The development of giftedness and talent across the life span* (pp. 109–130). Washington, DC: American Psychological Association.

Grobman, J. (2006). Underachievement in exceptionally gifted adolescents and young adults: A psychiatrist's view. *Journal of Secondary Gifted Education, 17*, 199–210.

Hazell, C. G. (1999). The experience of emptiness and the use of Dabrowski's theory in counseling gifted clients: Clinical case examples. *Advanced Development Journal, 8*, 31–46.

Jackson, P. S. (1998). Bright star—black sky: A phenomenological study of depression as a window into the psyche of the gifted adolescent. *Roeper Review, 20*, 215–221.

Jackson, P. S. (2003). Depressive disorder in highly gifted adolescents. *Journal of Secondary Gifted Education, 14*, 175–186. *Roeper Review, 20*, 215–211.

Kwan, K-L. K., & Hilson, W. J., Jr. (2009). Counseling gifted students from non-White racial groups: Conceptual perspectives and practical suggestions. In J. L. VanTassel-Baska, T. L. Cross, & F. R. Olenchak (Eds.), *Social-emotional curriculum with gifted and talented students* (pp. 133–151). Waco, TX: Prufrock Press.

Levy, J. J., & Plucker, J. A. (2003). Assessing the psychological presentation of gifted and talented clients: A multicultural perspective. *Counselling Psychology Quarterly, 16*, 229–247.

Lindstrom, R. R., & Van Sant, S. (1986). Special issues in working with gifted minority adolescents. *Journal of Counseling and Development, 64*, 583–586.

Lovecky, D. V. (1986). Can you hear the flowers singing? Issues for gifted adults. *Journal of Counseling and Development, 64*, 572–575.

Lovecky, D. V. (1990). Warts and rainbows: Issues in the psychotherapy of the gifted. *Advanced Development, 2*, 65–83.

McMann, N., & Oliver, R. (1988). Problems in families with gifted children: Implications for counselors. *Journal of Counseling and Development, 66*, 275–278.

Neihart, M. (2002). Gifted children and depression. In M. Neihart, S. M. Reis, N. M. Robinson, & S. M. Moon (Eds.), *The social and emotional development of gifted children: What do we know?* (pp. 93–101). Waco, TX: Prufrock Press.

Noble, K. D. (1989). Counseling gifted women: Becoming the heroes of our own stories. *Journal for the Education of the Gifted, 12*, 131–141.

Perrone, K. M., Webb, L. K., Wright, S. L., Jackson, Z. V., & Ksiazak T. M. (2006). Relationship of spirituality to work and family roles and life satisfaction among gifted adults. *Journal of Mental Health Counseling, 28*, 253–268.

Robbins, R. (1991). American Indian gifted and talented students: Their problems and proposed solutions. *Journal of American Indian Education, 31*, 15–24.

Robbins, R., Tonemah, S., & Robbins, S. (2002). Project Eagle: Techniques for multi-family psycho-educational group therapy with gifted American Indian adolescents and their parents. *American Indian and Alaska Native Mental Health Research, 10*, 56–74.

Rocamora, M. (1992). Counseling issues with recognized and unrecognized creatively gifted adults. *Advanced Development Journal, 4*, 75–89.

Yermish, A. (2010b). Provisional clinical guidelines for therapists working with gifted clients [PDF document]. Retrieved from http://www.davincilearning.org/sketchbook/clinical_guidelines.pdf

CHAPTER 9

Research

American Psychiatric Association. (2000). *Diagnostic and statistical manual of mental disorders* (4th ed.). Arlington, VA: Author.

Barrett, P. M., & Healy, L. J. (2003). An examination of the cognitive processes involved in childhood obsessive-compulsive disorder. *Behaviour Research and Therapy, 41*, 285–299.

Foa E. B., Kozak, M. J., Goodman W. K., Hollander, E., Jenike, M. A., & Rasmussen, S. A. (1995). *DSM-IV* field trial: Obsessive-compulsive disorder. *American Journal of Psychiatry, 152*, 90–96.

Foa, E. B., Steketee, G., Grayson, J. B., Turner, R. M., & Latimer, P. (1984). Deliberate exposure and blocking of obsessive-compulsive rituals: Immediate and long-term effects. *Behavior Therapy, 15*, 450–472.

Fontenelle, L. F., Mendlowicz, M. V., Marques, C., & Versiani, M. (2004). Trans-cultural aspects of obsessive-compulsive disorder: A description of a Brazilian sample and a systematic review of international clinical studies. *Journal of Psychiatric Research, 38*, 403–411.

Franklin, M. E, & Foa, E. B. (2007). Obsessive-compulsive disorder. In D. H. Barlow (Ed.), *Clinical handbook of psychological disorders* (4th ed., pp. 164–215). New York, NY: Guilford Press.

Greenberg, D. (1994). Cultural aspects of obsessive compulsive disorder. In E. Hollander (Ed.), *Current insights in obsessive compulsive disorder* (pp. 11–21). New York, NY: Wiley.

Lack, C. W., & Storch, E. A. (2008). The use of computers in the assessment and treatment of obsessive-compulsive disorder. *Computers in Human Behavior, 24*, 917–929.

Lack, C. W., Storch, E. A., Keely, M., Geffken, G. R., Ricketts, E., ... Goodman, W. K. (2009). Quality of life in children and adolescents with obsessive-compulsive disorder. *Social Psychiatry and Psychiatric Epidemiology, 44*, 935–942.

Lack, C. W., Storch, E. A., & Murphy, T. K. (2006). More than just monsters under the bed: Assessing and treating pediatric OCD. *Psychiatric Times, 23*(3), 54–57.

Lemelson, R. (2003). Obsessive-compulsive disorder in Bali: The cultural shaping of a neuropsychiatric disorder. *Transcultural Psychiatry, 40*, 377–408.

Lewin, A., Storch, E., Merlo, L., Adkins, J., Murphy, T., & Geffken, G. (2005). Intensive cognitive behavioral therapy for pediatric obsessive-compulsive disorder: A treatment protocol for mental health providers. *Psychological Services, 2*, 91–104.

Mancuso, E., Faro, A., Joshi, G., & Geller, D. A. (2010). Treatment of pediatric obsessive-compulsive disorder: A review. *Journal of Child and Adolescent Psychopharmacology, 20*, 299–308.

Matsunaga, H., Maebayashi, K., Hayashida, K., Okino, K., Matsui, T., ... Stein, D. J. (2008). Symptom structure in Japanese patients with obsessive-compulsive disorder. *American Journal of Psychiatry, 165,* 251–253.

Mowrer, O. H. (1960). *Learning theory and behavior.* New York, NY: Wiley.

Murphy, T. K., Kurlan, R., & Leckman, J. (2010). The immunobiology of Tourette's disorder, pediatric autoimmune neuropsychiatric disorders associated with Streptococcus, and related disorders: A way forward. *Journal of Child and Adolescent Psychopharmacology, 20,* 317–331.

Storch, E. A., Geffken, G. R., Merlo, L. J., Mann, G., Duke, D., ... Goodman, W. K. (2007). Family-based cognitive-behavioral therapy for pediatric obsessive-compulsive disorder: Comparison of intensive and weekly approaches. *Journal of the American Academy of Child and Adolescent Psychiatry, 46,* 469–478.

Storch, E. A., Merlo, L., Larson, M., Geffken, G. R., Lehmkuhl, H. D., ... Goodman, W. K. (2008). Impact of comorbidity on cognitive-behavioral therapy response in pediatric obsessive-compulsive disorder. *Journal of the American Academy of Child and Adolescent Psychiatry, 47,* 583–592.

Storch, E. A., Murphy, T. K., Goodman, W. K., Geffken, G. R., Lewin, A. B., ... Geller, D. A. (2010). A preliminary study of d-cycloserine augmentation of cognitive-behavioral therapy in pediatric obsessive-compulsive disorder. *Biological Psychiatry, 68,* 1073–1076.

Swedo, S. E., Rapoport, J. L., Leonard, H., Lenane, M., & Cheslow, D. (1989). Obsessive-compulsive disorder in children and adolescents: Clinical phenomenology of 70 consecutive cases. *Archives of General Psychiatry, 46,* 335–341.

Zohar, A. H. (1999). The epidemiology of obsessive-compulsive disorder in children and adolescents. *Child and Adolescent Psychiatric Clinics of North America, 8,* 445–460.

CHAPTER 10

Research

Alisic, E., Jongmans, M. J., van Wesel, F., & Kleber, R. J. (2011). Building child trauma theory from longitudinal studies: A meta-analysis. *Clinical Psychology Review, 31,* 736–747. doi: 10.1016/j.cpr.2011.03.001

Breslau, N., Davis, G. C., Andreski, P., & Peterson, E. (1991). Traumatic events and Posttraumatic Stress Disorder in an urban population of young adults. *Archives of General Psychiatry, 48,* 216–222. doi: 10.1001/archpsyc.1991.01810270028003

Carrion, V. G., Weems, C. F., Ray, R., & Reiss, A. L. (2002). Toward an empirical definition of pediatric PTSD: The phenomenology of PTSD symptoms in youth. *Journal of the American Academy of Child & Adolescent Psychiatry, 41,* 166–173.

Carrion, V. G., Weems, C. F., & Reiss, A. L. (2007). Stress predicts brain changes in children: A pilot longitudinal study on youth stress, posttraumatic stress disorder, and the hippocampus. *Pediatrics, 119,* 509–516.

Chemtob, C. M., Nakashima, J. P., & Hamada, R. S. (2002). Psychosocial intervention for postdisaster trauma symptoms in elementary school children: A controlled community field study. *Archives of Pediatrics and Adolescent Medicine, 156,* 211–216.

Cohen, J. A., Deblinger, E., Mannarino, A. P., & Steer, R. A. (2004). A multisite, randomized controlled trial for children with sexual abuse–related PTSD symptoms. *Journal of the American Academy of Child and Adolescent Psychiatry, 43,* 393–402. doi: 10.1097/00004583-200404000-00005

Cohen, J. A., Mannarino, A. P., & Deblinger, E. (2006). *Treating trauma and traumatic grief in children and adolescents.* New York, NY: Guilford Press.

De Arellano, M. A., Waldrop, A. E., Deblinger, E., Cohen, J. A., Danielson, C. K., & Mannarino, A. R. (2005). Community outreach program for child victims of traumatic events. *Behavior Modification, 29,* 130–155. doi: 10.1177/0145445504270878

Deblinger, E., Lippmann, J., & Steer, R. (1996). Sexually abused children suffering posttraumatic stress symptoms: Initial treatment outcome findings. *Child Maltreatment, 1,* 310–321. doi: 10.1177/1077559596001004003

De Young, A. C., Kenardy, J. A., & Cobham, V. E. (2011). Diagnosis of Posttraumatic Stress Disorder in preschool children. *Journal of Clinical Child & Adolescent Psychology, 40,* 375–384. doi: 10.1080/15374416.2011.563474

De Young, A. C., Kenardy, J. A., Cobham, V. E., & Kimble, R. (2012). Prevalence, comorbidity and course of trauma reactions in young burn-injured children. *Journal of Child Psychology and Psychiatry, 53,* 56–63. doi: 10.1111/j.1469-7610.2011.02431.x

Egger, H. L., & Angold, A. (2006). Common emotional and behavioral disorders in preschool children: Presentation, nosology, and epidemiology. *Journal of Child Psychology and Psychiatry, 47,* 313–337.

Ehlers, A., & Clark, D. M. (2000). A cognitive model of posttraumatic stress disorder. *Behaviour Research and Therapy, 38,* 319–345. doi: 10.1016/s0005-7967(99)00123-0

Essau, C. A., Conradt, J., & Petermann, F. (2000). Frequency, comorbidity, and psychosocial impairment of anxiety disorders in German adolescents. *Journal of Anxiety Disorders, 14,* 263–279. doi: 10.1016 /s0887-6185(99)00039-0

Feeny, N. C., Foa, E. B., Treadwell, K. R. H., & March, J. (2004). Posttraumatic Stress Disorder in youth: A critical review of the cognitive and behavioral treatment outcome literature. *Professional Psychology: Research and Practice, 35,* 466–476. doi: 10.1037/0735-7028.35.5.466

Felitti, V. J., Anda, R. F., Nordenberg, D., Williamson, D. F., Spitz, A. M., ... Marks, J. S. (1998). Relationship of childhood abuse and household dysfunction to many of the leading causes of death in adults: The Adverse Childhood Experiences (ACE) Study. *American Journal of Preventive Medicine, 14,* 245–258.

Gilboa-Schechtman, E., Foa, E. B., Shafran, N., Aderka, I. M., Powers, M. B., ... Apter, A. (2010). Prolonged exposure versus dynamic therapy for adolescent PTSD: A pilot randomized controlled trial. *Journal of the American Academy of Child and Adolescent Psychiatry, 49,* 1034–1042.

Green, J. G., McLaughlin, K. A., Berglund, P. A., Gruber, M. J., Sampson, N. A., ... Kessler, R. C. (2010). Childhood adversities and adult psychiatric disorders in the national comorbidity survey replication I: Associations with first onset of *DSM-IV* disorders. *Archives of General Psychiatry, 67,* 113–123.

Jaycox, L. H., Cohen, J. A., Mannarino, A. P., Walker, D. W., Langley, A. K., ... Schonlau, M. (2010). Children's mental health care following Hurricane Katrina: A field trial of trauma-focused psychotherapies. *Journal of Traumatic Stress, 23,* 223–231. doi: 10.1002/jts.20518

Kataoka, S. H., Stein, B. D., Jaycox, L. H., Wong, M., Escudero, P. I. A., ... Fink, A. (2003). A school-based mental health program for traumatized Latino immigrant children. *Journal of the American Academy of Child and Adolescent Psychiatry, 42,* 311–318. doi: 10.1097/00004583-200303000-00011

Kazak, A. E., Alderfer, M. A., Streisand, R., Simms, S., Rourke, M. T., ... Cnaan, A. (2004). Treatment of posttraumatic stress symptoms in adolescent survivors of childhood cancer and their families: A randomized clinical trial. *Journal of Family Psychology, 18,* 493–504. doi: 10.1037/0893-3200.18.3.493

King, N. J., Tonge, B. J., Mullen, P., Myerson, N., Heyne, D., ... Ollendick, T. H. (2000). Treating sexually abused children with posttraumatic stress symptoms: A randomized clinical trial. *Journal of the American Academy of Child and Adolescent Psychiatry, 39,* 1347–1355. doi: 10.1097/00004583-200011000-00008

Langeland, W., & Olff, M. (2008). Psychobiology of posttraumatic stress disorder in pediatric injury patients: A review of the literature. *Neuroscience & Biobehavioral Reviews, 32,* 161–174.

Le Brocque, R. M., Hendrikz, J., & Kenardy, J. A. (2010a). The course of posttraumatic stress in children: Examination of recovery trajectories following traumatic injury. *Journal of Pediatric Psychology, 35,* 637–645.

Le Brocque, R. M., Hendrikz, J., & Kenardy, J. A. (2010b). Parental response to child injury: Examination of parental posttraumatic stress symptom trajectories following child accidental injury. *Journal of Pediatric Psychology, 35,* 646–655.

Lieberman, A. F., & Van Horn, P. (2008). *Psychotherapy with infants and young children: Repairing the effects of stress and trauma on early attachment.* New York, NY: Guilford Press.

Lieberman, A. F., Van Horn, P., & Ippen, C. G. (2005). Toward evidence-based treatment: Child-parent psychotherapy with preschoolers exposed to marital violence. *Journal of the American Academy of Child and Adolescent Psychiatry, 44,* 1241–1248. doi: 10.1097/01.chi.0000181047.59702.58

Meiser-Stedman, R., Yule, W., Dalgleish, T., Smith, P., & Glucksman, E. (2006). The role of the family in child and adolescent posttraumatic stress following attendance at an emergency department. *Journal of Pediatric Psychology, 31,* 397–402.

Perry, B. D., Pollard, R. A., Blakley, T. L., Baker, W. L., & Vigilante, D. (1995). Childhood trauma, the neurobiology of adaptation, and "use-dependent" development of the brain: How "states" become "traits". *Infant Mental Health Journal, 16,* 271–291.

Rolfsnes, E. S., & Idsoe, T. (2011). School-based intervention programs for PTSD symptoms: A review and meta-analysis. *Journal of Traumatic Stress, 24,* 155–165. doi: 10.1002/jts.20622

Scheeringa, M. S., Weems, C. F., Cohen, J. A., Amaya-Jackson, L., & Guthrie, D. (2010). Trauma-focused cognitive-behavioral therapy for posttraumatic stress disorder in three through six year-old children: A randomized clinical trial. *Journal of Child Psychology and Psychiatry, 52,* 853–860. doi: 10.1111/j.1469-7610.2010.02354.x

Scheeringa, M. S., Zeanah, C. H., & Cohen, J. A. (2010). PTSD in children and adolescents: Toward an empirically based algorithm. *Depression and Anxiety, 28,* 1–13. doi: 10.1002/da.20736

Scheeringa, M. S., Zeanah, C. H., Myers, L., & Putnam, F. W. (2005). Predictive validity in a prospective follow-up of PTSD in preschool children. *Journal of the American Academy of Child & Adolescent Psychiatry, 44,* 899–906.

Smith, P., Yule, W., Perrin, S., Tranah, T., Dalgleish, T., & Clark, D. M. (2007). Cognitive-behavioral therapy for PTSD in children and adolescents: A preliminary randomized controlled trial. *Journal of the American Academy of Child & Adolescent Psychiatry, 46,* 1051–1061.

Stein, B. D., Jaycox, L. H., Kataoka, S. H., Wong, M., Tu, W., … Fink, A. (2003). A mental health intervention for schoolchildren exposed to violence. *JAMA: The Journal of the American Medical Association, 290,* 603–611. doi: 10.1001/jama.290.5.603

Trickey, D., Siddaway, A. P., Meiser-Stedman, R., Serpell, L., & Field, A. P. (2012). A meta-analysis of risk factors for post-traumatic stress disorder in children and adolescents. *Clinical Psychology Review, 32,* 122–138. doi: 10.1016/j.cpr.2011.12.001

Trowell, J., Kolvin, I., Weeramanthri, T., Sadowski, H., Berelowitz, M., … Leitch, I. (2002). Psychotherapy for sexually abused girls: Psychopathological outcome findings and patterns of change. *The British Journal of Psychiatry, 180,* 234–247. doi: 10.1192/bjp.180.3.234

Clinician Application

Blaustein, M. E., & Kinniburgh, K. M. (2010). *Treating traumatic stress in children and adolescents: How to foster resilience through attachment, self-regulation, and competency.* New York, NY: The Guilford Press.

Crisci, G., lay, M., & Lowenstein, L. (1998). *Paper dolls and paper airplanes: Therapeutic exercises for sexually traumatized children.* Indianapolis, IN: KIDSRIGHTS.

Goodyear-Brown, P. (2012). *Handbook of child sexual abuse: Identification, assessment, and treatment.* Hoboken, NJ: John Wiley and Sons.

Holmes, M. M. (2000). *A terrible thing happened: A story for children who have witnessed violence or trauma.* Washington, DC: Magination.

Kagan, R., (2004). *Rebuilding attachments with traumatized children.* Binghamton, NY: The Haworth Press, Inc.

Kagan, R. (2006). *Real life heroes.* Binghamton, NY: The Haworth Press.

Lieberman, A. F., & Van Horn, P. (2008). *Psychotherapy with infants and young children: Repairing the effects of stress and trauma on early attachment.* New York, NY: Guilford Press.

Ottenweller, J. (1991). *Please tell!: A child's story about sexual abuse.* Hazeldon Foundation.

Silovsky, J. (2009). *Taking action: support for families of children with sexual behavior problems.* Brandon, VT: Safer Society Press.

Stauffer, L., & Deblinger, E. (2004). *Let's talk about taking care of you: An educational book about body safety.* Hatfield, PA: Hope for Families, Inc.

van der Kolk, B. A. (2005). Developmental trauma disorder. *Psychiatric Annals, 35,* 401–408.

CHAPTER 11

Research

Bridgeland, J. M., Dilulio, J. J., & Morison, K. B. (2006). *The silent epidemic: Perspectives of high school dropouts.* Seattle, WA: Bill and Melinda Gates Foundation.

Christenson, S. L., & Thurlow, M. L. (2004). School dropouts: Prevention considerations, interventions, and challenges. *Current Directions in Psychological Science, 13,* 36–39. doi: 10.1111/j.0963-7214.2004.01301010.x

Dube, S. R., & Orpinas, P. (2009). Understanding excessive school absenteeism as school refusal behavior. *Children and Schools, 31,* 87–95. doi: 10.1093/cs/31.2.87

Egger, H. L., Costello, E. J., & Angold, A. (2003). School refusal and psychiatric disorders: A community study. *Journal of the American Academy of Child and Adolescent Psychiatry, 42,* 797–807. doi: 10.1097/01. CHI.0000046865.56865.79

EPE Research Center. (2008). *Closing the graduation gap: Educational and economic conditions in America's largest cities.* Bethesda, MD: Editorial Projects in Education.

Freudenberg, N., & Ruglis, J. (2007). Reframing school dropout as a public health issue. *Preventing Chronic Disease, 4,* 1–11.

Graeff-Martins, A. S., Dmitrieva, T., El Din, A. S., Caffo, E., Flament, M. F., … Rohde, L. A. (2007). School dropout: A systematic worldwide review concerning risk factors and preventive interventions. In H. Remschmidt, B. Nurcombe, M. L. Belfer, N. Sartorius, & A. Okasha (Eds.), *The mental health of children and adolescents: An area of global neglect* (pp. 165–178). Hoboken, NJ: Wiley.

Guare, R. E., & Cooper, B. S. (2003). *Truancy revisited: Students as school consumers.* Lanham, MD: Scarecrow.

Haight, C., Kearney, C. A., Hendron, M., & Schafer, R. (2011). Confirmatory analyses of the School Refusal Assessment Scale-Revised: Replication and extension to a truancy sample. *Journal of Psychopathology and Behavioral Assessment, 33,* 196–204. doi: 10.1007/s10862-011-9218-9

Henry, K. L. (2007). Who's skipping school: Characteristics of truants in 8th and 10th grade. *Journal of School Health, 77,* 29–35. doi: 10.1111/j.1746-1561.2007.00159.x

Henry, K. L., & Huizinga, D. H. (2007). Truancy's effect on the onset of drug use among urban adolescents placed at risk. *Journal of Adolescent Health, 40,* 358.e9–358.e17. doi: 10.1016/j.jadohealth.2006.11.138

Heyne, D., King, N. J., Tonge, B. J., Rollings, S., Young, D., ... Ollendick, T. H. (2002). Evaluation of child therapy and caregiver training in the treatment of school refusal. *Journal of the American Academy of Child and Adolescent Psychiatry, 41*, 687–695. doi: 10.1097/00004583-200206000-00008

Heyne, D., Sauter, F. M., Van Widenfelt, B. M., Vermeiren, R., & Westenberg, P. M. (2011). School refusal and anxiety in adolescence: Non-randomized trial of a developmentally sensitive cognitive behavioral therapy. *Journal of Anxiety Disorders, 25*, 870–878. doi: 10.1016/j.janxdis.2011.04.006

Hibbett, A., & Fogelman, K. (1990). Future lives of truants: Family formation and health-related behaviour. *British Journal of Educational Psychology, 60*, 171–179. doi: 10.1111/j.2044-8279.1990.tb00934.x

Hibbett, A., Fogelman, K., & Manor, O. (1990). Occupational outcomes of truancy. *British Journal of Educational Psychology, 60*, 23–36. doi: 10.1111/j.2044-8279.1990.tb00919.x

Ingul, J. M., Klockner, C. A., Silverman, W. K., & Nordahl, H. M. (2012). Adolescent school absenteeism: Modelling social and individual risk factors. *Child and Adolescent Mental Health, 17*, 93–100. doi: 10.1111/j.1475-3588.2011.00615.x

Jimerson, S., Egeland, B., Sroufe, L. A., & Carlson, B. (2000). A prospective longitudinal study of high school dropouts examining multiple predictors across development. *Journal of School Psychology, 38*, 525–549. doi: 10.1016/S0022-4405(00)00051-0

Kearney, C. A. (2003). Bridging the gap among professionals who address youth with school absenteeism: Overview and suggestions for consensus. *Professional Psychology: Research and Practice, 34*, 57–65. doi: 10.1037/0735-7028.34.1.57

Kearney, C. A. (2007). Forms and functions of school refusal behavior in youth: An empirical analysis of absenteeism severity. *Journal of Child Psychology and Psychiatry, 48*, 53–61. doi: 10.1111/j.1469-7610.2006.01634.x

Kearney, C. A. (2008a). School absenteeism and school refusal behavior in youth: A contemporary review. *Clinical Psychology Review, 28*, 451–471. doi: 10.1016/j.cpr.2007.07.012

Kearney, C. A. (2008b). An interdisciplinary model of school absenteeism in youth to inform professional practice and public policy. *Educational Psychology Review, 20*, 257–282. doi: 10.1007/s10648-008-9078-3

Kearney, C. A., & Albano, A. M. (2004). The functional profiles of school refusal behavior: Diagnostic aspects. *Behavior Modification, 28*, 147–161. doi: 10.1177/0145445503259263

Kearney, C. A., & Albano, A. M. (2007). *When children refuse school: A cognitive-behavioral therapy approach: Therapist guide* (2nd ed.). New York, NY: Oxford.

Kearney, C. A., & Silverman, W. K. (1999). Functionally-based prescriptive and nonprescriptive treatment for children and adolescents with school refusal behavior. *Behavior Therapy, 30*, 673–695. doi: 10.1016/S0005-7894(99)80032-X

King, N. J., Tonge, B. J., Heyne, D., Pritchard, M., Rollings, S., ... Ollendick, T. H. (1998). Cognitive-behavioral treatment of school-refusing children: A controlled evaluation. *Journal of the American Academy of Child and Adolescent Psychiatry, 37*, 395–403. doi: 10.1097/00004583-199804000-00017

Last, C. G., Hansen, C., & Franco, N. (1998). Cognitive-behavioral treatment of school phobia. Journal of the *American Academy of Child and Adolescent Psychiatry, 37*, 404–411. doi: 10.1097/00004583-199804000-00018

Layne, A. E., Bernstein, G. A., Egan, E. A., & Kushner, M. G. (2003). Predictors of treatment response in anxious-depressed adolescents with school refusal. *Journal of the American Academy of Child and Adolescent Psychiatry, 42*, 319–326. doi: 10.1097/00004583-200303000-00012

Lyon, A. R., & Cotler, S. (2009). Multi-systemic intervention for school refusal behavior: Integrating approaches across disciplines. *Advances in School Mental Health Promotion, 2*, 20–34.

Mac Iver, M. A., & Mac Iver, D. J. (2010). How do we ensure that everyone graduates? An integrated prevention and tiered intervention model for schools and districts. *New Directions for Youth Development, 127*, 25–35. doi: 10.1002/yd.360

McShane, G., Walter, G., & Rey, J. M. (2001). Characteristics of adolescents with school refusal. *Australian and New Zealand Journal of Psychiatry, 35*, 822–826.

National Center for Education Statistics. (2006). *The condition of education 2006*. Washington, DC: US Department of Education.

Pina, A. A., Zerr, A. A., Gonzales, N. A., & Ortiz, C. D. (2009). Psychosocial interventions for school refusal behavior in children and adolescents. *Child Development Perspectives, 3*, 11–20. doi: 10.1111/j.1750-8606.2008.00070.x

Redmond, S. M., & Hosp, J. L. (2008). Absenteeism rates in students receiving services for CDs, LDs, and EDs: A macroscopic view of the consequences of disability. *Language, Speech, and Hearing Services in Schools, 39*, 97–103. doi: 10.1044/0161-1461(2008/010)

Reid, K. (2005). The causes, views and traits of school absenteeism and truancy: An analytical review. *Research in Education, 74*, 59–82.

Sutphen, R. D., Ford, J. P., & Flaherty, C. (2010). Truancy interventions: A review of the research literature. *Research on Social Work Practice, 20*, 161–171. doi: 10.1177/1049731509347861

Suveg, C., Aschenbrand, S. G., & Kendall, P. C. (2005). Separation anxiety disorder, panic disorder, and school refusal. *Child and Adolescent Psychiatric Clinics of North America, 14*, 773–795. doi: 10.1016/j.chc.2005.05.005

Tolin, D. F., Whiting, S., Maltby, N., Diefenbach, G. J., Lothstein, M. A., ... Gray, K. (2009). Intensive (daily) behavior therapy for school refusal: A multiple baseline case series. *Cognitive and Behavioral Practice, 16*, 332–344. doi: 10.1016/j.cbpra.2009.02.003

US Census Bureau. (2005). *Educational attainment in the United States: 2004.* Washington DC: Author.

Zhang, D., Katsiyannis, A., Barrett, D. E., & Willson, V. (2007). Truancy offenders in the juvenile justice system: Examinations of first and second referrals. *Remedial and Special Education, 28*, 244–256.

Clinician Application

Heyne, D., King, N. J., Tonge, B. J., & Cooper, H. (2001). School refusal: Epidemiology and management. *Pediatric Drugs, 10*, 719–732.

CHAPTER 12

Research

Albano, A. M. (1995). Treatment of social anxiety in adolescents. *Cognitive and Behavioral Practice, 2*, 271–298.

Alfano, C., Beidel, D. C., & Turner, S. M. (2002). Cognition in childhood anxiety: Conceptual, methodological, and developmental issues. *Clinical Psychology Review, 22*, 1209–1238.

American Psychiatric Association. (2000). *Diagnostic and statistical manual of mental disorders* (Rev. 4th ed.). Washington, DC: Author.

Barrett, P. M., Dadds, M. R., & Rapee, R. M. (1996). Family treatment of childhood anxiety: A controlled trial. *Journal of Consulting and Clinical Psychology, 64*, 333–342.

Beidel, D. C., & Turner, S. M. (1988). Comorbidity of test anxiety and other anxiety disorders in children. *Journal of Abnormal Child Psychology, 16*, 275–287.

Beidel, D. C., Turner, S. M., & Morris, T. L. (1999). Psychopathology of childhood social phobia. *Journal for the American Academy of Child and Adolescent Psychiatry, 36*(5), 643–650.

Beidel, D. C., Turner, S. M., & Morris, T. L. (2000). Behavioral treatment of childhood social phobia. *Journal of Consulting and Clinical Psychology, 68*, 1072–1080.

Beidel, D. C., Turner, S. M., & Morris, T. L. (2004). *Social effectiveness therapy for children and adolescents (SET-C).* Toronto, ON: Multi-Health Systems, Inc.

Beidel, D. C., Turner, S. M., Sallee, F. R., Ammerman, R. T., Crosby, L. A., & Pathak, S. (2007). SET-C versus fluoxetine in the treatment of childhood social phobia. *American Academy of Child and Adolescent Psychiatry, 46*(12), 1622–1632.

Beidel, D. C., Turner, S. M., & Young, B. J. (2006). Social effectiveness therapy for children: Five years later. *Behavior Therapy, 37*, 416–425.

Beidel, D. C., Turner, S. M., Young, B., & Paulson, A. (2005). Social effectiveness therapy for children: Three-year follow-up. *Journal of Consulting and Clinical Psychology, 73*, 721–725.

Clark, D. B. (1993). Assessment of social anxiety in adolescents. Paper presented at the Anxiety Disorders Association of America Annual Convention, Charleston, SC, March 19–21.

Costello, E. J., Egger, H. L., & Angold, A. (2004). Developmental epidemiology of anxiety disorders. In: Ollendick, T. H., March, J. S. (Eds.), *Phobic and anxiety disorders in children and adolescents: A clinician's guide to effective psychosocial and pharmacological Interventions* (pp. 61–91). New York, NY: Oxford.

Costello, J., Egger, H., & Angold, M. R. (2005). 10-year research update review: The epidemiology of child and adolescent psychiatric disorders: I. Methods and public health burden. *Journal American Child Adolescent Psychiatry, 44*(10), 972–986.

Costello, E. J., Mustillo, S., Erkanli, A., Keeler, G., & Angold, A. (2003). Prevalence and development of psychiatric disorders in childhood and adolescence. *Archives of General Psychiatry, 60*, 837–844.

DeWit, D. J., Ogborne, A., Offord, D. R., & MacDonald, K. (1999). Antecedents of the risk of recovery from *DSM-III-R* social phobia. *Psychological Medicine, 29*, 569–582.

Dinnel, D. L., Kleinknecht, R. A., & Tanaka-Matsumi, J. (2002). A cross-cultural comparison of social phobia symptoms. *Journal of Psychopathology and Behavioral Assessment, 24*, 75–84.

Ferrell, C. B., Beidel, D. C., & Turner, S. M. (2004). Assessment and treatment of socially phobic children: A cross cultural comparison. *Journal of Clinical Child and Adolescent Psychopathology, 33*(2), 260–268.

Flannery-Schroeder, E. C., & Kendall, P. C. (2000). Group and individual cognitive-behavioral treatments for youth with anxiety disorders: A randomized clinical trial. *Cognitive Therapy and Research, 24*, 251–278.

Ginsburg, G., Kendall, P.C., Sakolsky, D., Compton, S. N., Piacentini, J., ... March, J. (2011). Remission after acute treatment in children and adolescents with anxiety disorders: Findings from the CAMS. *Journal of Consulting and Clinical Psychology, 79*, 806–813.

Ginsburg, G. S., Riddle, M. A., & Davies, M. (2006). Somatic symptoms in children and adolescents with anxiety disorders. *Journal for the American Academy of Child and Adolescent Psychiatry, 45*(10), 1179–1187.

Hayward, C., Varady, S., Albano, A. M., Thienemann, M., Henderson, L., & Schatzberg, A. F. (2000). Cognitive-behavioral group therapy for social phobia in female adolescents: Results of a pilot study. *Journal of the American Academy of Child and Adolescent Psychiatry, 39*, 721–726.

Heimberg, R. G., Stein, M. B., Hiripi, E., & Kessler, R. C. (2000). Trends in the prevalence of social phobia in the United States: A synthetic cohort analysis of changes over four decades. *European Psychiatry, 15*(1), 29–37.

Juster, H. R., Brown, E. J., & Heimberg, R. G. (1996). Social phobia. In J. Margraf (Ed.), *Textbook of behavior therapy* (pp. 43–59). Berlin, Germany: Springer-Verlag.

Kendall, P. C. (1994). Treating anxiety disorders in children: Results of a randomized clinical trial. *Journal of Consulting and Clinical Psychology, 62*, 200–210.

Kendall, P. C., Flannery-Schroeder, E., Panichelli-Mindel, S. M., Southam-Gerow, M., Henin, A., & Warman, M. (1997). Therapy for youth with anxiety disorders: A second randomized clinical trial. *Journal of Consulting and Clinical Psychology, 65*, 366–380.

Kendall, P. C., Hudson, J. L., Gosch, E., Flannery-Schroeder, E., & Suveg, C. (2008). Cognitive-behavioral therapy for anxiety disordered youth: A randomized clinical trial evaluating child and family modalities. *Journal of Consulting and Clinical Psychology, 76*(2), 282–297.

Kerig, P. K., & Wenar, C. (2006). *Developmental psychopathology*. New York, NY: McGraw-Hill.

Kessler, R. C. (2003). The impairments caused by social phobia in the general population: Implications for intervention. *Acta Psychiatry Scand, 108*, 19–27.

Lau, A. S., Fung, J., Wang, S., & Kang, S. (2009). Explaining elevated social anxiety among Asian Americans: Emotional attunement and a cultural double blind. *Cultural Diversity & Ethnic Minority Psychology, 15*, 77–85.

Lecrubier, Y. (1998). Comorbidity in social anxiety disorder: Impact on disease burden and management. *Journal of Clinical Psychiatry, 59*, 33–37.

Masia-Warner, C., Fisher, P. H., Shrout, P. E., Rathor, S., & Klein, R. G. (2007). Treating adolescents with social anxiety disorder in school: An attention control trial. *Journal of Child Psychology and Psychiatry, 48*(7), 676–686.

Masia-Warner, C., Klein, R. G., Dent, H. C., Fisher, P. G., Alvir, J., ... Guardino, M. (2005). School-based intervention for adolescents with social anxiety disorder: Results of a controlled study. *Journal of Abnormal Child Psychology, 33*(6), 707–722.

Schneier, F. R., Johnson, J., Hornic, C. D., Liebowitz, M. R., & Weissman, M. M. (1992). Social phobia: Comorbidity and morbidity in an epidemiologic sample, *Archives of General Psychiatry, 49*, 282–288.

Shortt, A. L., Barrett, P. M., & Fox, T. L. (2001). Evaluating the FRIENDS program: A cognitive-behavioral group treatment for anxious children and their parents. *Journal of Clinical Child and Adolescent Psychology, 30*, 525–535.

Silverman, W. K., Kurtines, W. M., Ginsburg, G. S., Weems, C. F., Rabian, B., & Serafini, L. T. (1999). Contingency management, self-control, and education support in the treatment of childhood phobic disorders: A randomized clinical trial. *Journal of Consulting and Clinical Psychology, 67*(5), 675–687.

Silverman, W. K., Pina, A. A., & Viswesvaran, C. (2008). Evidence-based psychosocial treatments for phobic and anxiety disorders in children and adolescents. *Journal of Clinical Child & Adolescent Psychology, 37*(1), 105–130.

Spence, S. H., Donovan, C., & Brechman-Toussaint, M. (2000). The treatment of childhood social phobia: The effectiveness of social skills training-based, cognitive-behavioural intervention, with and without parental involvement. *Journal of Child Psychology & Psychiatry, 41*, 713–726.

Spence, S., Donovan, C., & Toussaint, M. B. (1999). Social skills, social outcomes, and cognitive features of childhood social phobia. *Journal of Abnormal Psychology, 108*(2), 211–221.

Stein, M., Chavira, D., & Jang, K. (2001). Bringing up bashful baby developmental pathways to social phobia. *Psychiatric Clinics of North America, 24*(4), 661–675.

Turk, C. L., Heimberg, R. G., Orsillo, S. M., Holt, C. S. Gitow, A., ... Liebowitz, M. R. (1998). An investigation of gender differences in social phobia. *Journal of Anxiety Disorders, 12*(3), 209–223.

Walkup, J. T., Albano, A. M., Piacentini, J., Birmaher, B., Compton, S. N., ... Kendall, P. C. (2008). Cognitive behavioral therapy, sertraline, or a combination in childhood anxiety. *The New England Journal of Medicine, 326*(26), 2753–2766.

Weiss, D. D., & Last, C. G. (2001). Developmental variations in the prevalence and manifestation of anxiety disorders. In M. W. Vasey & M. R. Dadds (Eds.), *The developmental psychopathology of anxiety* (pp. 27–43). New York, NY: Oxford University Press.

Wittchen, H. U., Stein, M. B., & Kessler, R. C. (1999). Social fears and social phobia in a community sample of adolescents and young adults: Prevalence, risk factors and co-morbidity. *Psychological Medicine, 29*, 309–323.

Clinician Application

Alfano, C. A., Beidel, D. C., & Turner, S. M. (2002). Cognition in childhood anxiety: Conceptual, methodological, and developmental issues. *Clinical Psychology Review, 22,* 1209–1238.

Alfano, C. A., Pina, A. A., Villalta, I. K., Beidel, D. C., Ammerman, R. T., & Crosby, L. E. (2009). Mediators and moderators of outcome in the behavioral treatment of childhood social phobia. *Journal of the American Academy of Child and Adolescent Psychiatry, 48,* 945–953.

Alvord, M. K., & O'Leary, K. D. (1985). Teaching children to share through stories. *Psychology in the Schools, 22,* 323–330.

Alvord, M. K., & Rich, B. A. (2012). Resilience builder program: Practice and research in a private clinical setting. *Independent Practitioner, 32,* 18–20.

Alvord, M. K., Zucker, B., & Alvord, B. (2011). *Relaxation and self-regulation techniques for children and teens: Mastering the mind-body connection* [Audio CD]. Champaign, IL: Research Press.

Antony, M., & Swinson, R. (2008). *Shyness and social anxiety workbook: Proven step-by-step techniques for overcoming your fear* (2nd ed.). Oakland, CA: New Harbinger Publications.

Barrett, P. M., Dadds, M. R., & Rapee, R. M. (1996). Family treatment of childhood anxiety: A controlled trial. *Journal of Consulting and Clinical Psychology, 64,* 333–342.

Beidel, D. C., & Alfano, C. A. (2011). *Child anxiety disorders: A guide to research and treatment* (2nd ed.). New York, NY: Routledge.

Beidel, D. C., Turner, S. M., & Morris, T. L. (2000). Behavioral treatment of childhood social phobia. *Journal of Consulting and Clinical Psychology, 68,* 1072–1080.

Beidel, D. C., Turner, S. M., & Morris, T. L. (2004). *Social effectiveness therapy for children and adolescents (SET-C).* Toronto, Ontario: Multi-Health Systems.

Beidel, D. C., Turner, S. M., & Young, B. J. (2006). Social effectiveness therapy for children: Five years later. *Behavior Therapy, 37,* 416–425.

Chavira, D. A., & Stein, M. B. (2005). Childhood social anxiety disorder: From understanding to treatment. *Child and Adolescent Psychiatric Clinics of North America, 14,* 797–818.

Davis, T. E., May, A., & Whiting, S. E. (2011). Evidence-based treatment of anxiety and phobia in children and adolescents: Current status and effects on the emotional response. *Clinical Psychology Review, 31,* 592–602.

Ferrell, C. B., Beidel, D. C., & Turner, S. M. (2004). Assessment and treatment of socially phobic children: A cross-cultural comparison. *Journal of Clinical Child and Adolescent Psychology, 33,* 260–268.

Flannery-Schroeder, E. C., & Kendall, P. C. (2000). Group and individual cognitive-behavioral treatment for youth with anxiety disorders: A randomized clinical trial. *Cognitive Therapy and Research, 24,* 251–278.

Friedberg, R. D., McClure, J. M., & Garcia, J. H. (2009). *Cognitive therapy techniques for children and adolescents: Tools for enhancing practice.* New York, NY: Guilford Press.

Gallagher, H., Rabian, B., & McCloskey, M. (2004). A brief cognitive-behavioral intervention for social phobia in childhood. *Journal of Anxiety Disorders, 18,* 459–479.

Hodson, K. J., McManus, F. V., Clark, D. M., & Doll, H. (2008). Can Clark and Wells' (1995) cognitive model of social phobia be applied to young people? *Behavioural and Cognitive Psychotherapy, 36,* 449–461.

Kendall, P. C., Flannery-Schroeder, E., Panichelli-Mindel, S. M., Southam-Gerow, M., Henin, A., & Warman, M. (1997). Therapy for youth with anxiety disorders: A second randomized clinical trial. *Journal of Consulting and Clinical Psychology, 65,* 366–380.

Kendall, P. C., & Hedtke, K. A. (2006). *Cognitive-behavioral therapy for anxious children: Therapist manual* (3rd ed.). Ardmore, PA: Workbook Publishing.

Kendall, P. C., Khanna, M. S., Edson, A., Cummings, C., & Harris, M. S. (2011). Computers and psychosocial treatment for child anxiety: Recent advances and ongoing efforts. *Depression and Anxiety, 28,* 58–66.

King, N. J. (1994). Physiological assessment. In T. H. Ollendick, N. J. King, & W. Yule (Eds.), *International handbook of phobic and anxiety disorders in children and adolescents* (pp. 365–379). New York, NY: Plenum Press.

Kley, H., Heinrichs, N., Bender, C., & Tuschen-Caffier, B. (2012). Predictors of outcome in a cognitive-behavioral group program for children and adolescents with social anxiety disorder. *Journal of Anxiety Disorders, 26,* 79–87.

Melfsen, S., Kuhnemund, M., Schwieger, J., Warnke, A., Stadler, C., … Stangier, U. (2011). Cognitive behavioral therapy of socially phobic children focusing on cognition: A randomized wait-list control study. *Child and Adolescent Psychiatry and Mental Health, 5,* 1–12.

Mendalowitz, S. L., Manassis, K., Bradley, S., Scapillato, D., Miezitis, S., & Shaw, B. F. (1999). Cognitive-behavioral group treatments in childhood anxiety disorders: The role of parental involvement. *Journal of the American Academy of Child and Adolescent Psychiatry, 38,* 1223–1229.

Morris, T. L., & Ale, C. M. (2011). Social Anxiety. In D. McKay & E. A. Storch (Eds.), *Handbook of child and adolescent anxiety disorders* (pp. 289–301). New York, NY: Springer.

Muris, P., Merckelbach, H., & Damsma, E. (2000). Threat perception bias in non-referred, socially anxious children. *Journal of Clinical Child Psychology, 29,* 348–359.

Pina, A. A., Silverman, W. K., Fuentes, R. M., Kurtines, W. M., & Weems, C. F. (2003). Exposure-based cognitive-behavioral treatment for phobic and anxiety disorders: Treatment effects and maintenance for Hispanic/Latino relative to European-American youths. *Journal of the American Academy of Child and Adolescent Psychiatry, 42*, 1179–1187.

Schniering, C. A., & Rapee, R. M. (2002). Development and validation of a measure of children's automatic thoughts: The children's automatic thoughts scale. *Behaviour Research and Therapy, 40*, 1091–1109.

Segool, N. K., & Carlson, J. S. (2008). Efficacy of cognitive-behavioral and pharmacological treatments for children with social anxiety. *Depression and Anxiety, 25*, 620–631.

Shannon, J. (2012). *The shyness and social anxiety workbook for teens: CBT and ACT skills to help you build social confidence.* Oakland, CA: New Harbinger Publications.

Silverman, W. K., Pina, A. A., & Viswesvaran, C. (2008). Evidence-based psychosocial treatments for phobic and anxiety disorders in children and adolescents. *Journal of Clinical Child and Adolescent Psychology, 37*, 105–130.

Spence, S. H. (1995). *Social skills training: Enhancing social competence with children and adolescents.* Windsor, UK: NFER-Nelson.

Spence, S. H., Donovan, C., & Brechman-Toussaint, M. (1999). Social skills, social outcomes, and cognitive features of childhood social phobia. *Journal of Abnormal Psychology, 108*, 211–221.

Spence, S. H., Donovan, C., & Brechman-Toussaint, M. (2000). The treatment of childhood social phobia: The effectiveness of a social skills training-based, cognitive-behavioural intervention, with and without parental involvement. *Journal of Child Psychology and Psychiatry and Allied Disciplines, 41*, 713–726.

Walkup, J., Albano, A. M., Piacentini, J., Birmaher, B., Compton, S. N., … Kendall, P. C. (2008). Cognitive behavioral therapy, sertraline, or a combination in childhood anxiety. *The New England Journal of Medicine, 359*, 2753–2766.

Whiteside, S. P., & Abramowitz, J. (2012). Mayo Clinic Anxiety Coach (Version 1.0) [Mobile application software]. Retrieved from http://itunes.apple.com

CHAPTER 13

Research

American Psychiatric Association. (2000). *Diagnostic and statistical manual of mental disorders - Text revision* (4th ed.). Washington, DC: Author.

Burrow-Sanchez, J. J., Jenson, W. R., & Clark, E. (2009). School-based interventions for students with substance abuse. *Psychology in the Schools, 46*, 238–245. doi: 10.1002/pits.20368

Johnston, L. D., O'Malley, P. M., Bachman, J. G., & Schulenberg, J. E. (2011). *Monitoring the Future national results on adolescent drug use: Overview of key findings, 2010.* Ann Arbor, MI: Institute for Social Research, The University of Michigan. http://www.monitoringthefuture.org

Kaminer, Y. (2005). Challenges and opportunities of group therapy for adolescent substance abuse: A critical review. *Addictive Behaviors, 30*, 1765–1774. doi: 10.1016/j.addbeh.2005.07.002

Liddle, H. A. (2010). Treating adolescent substance abuse using multidimensional family therapy. In J. R. Weisz & A. E. Kazdin (Eds.), *Evidence-based psychotherapies for children and adolescents* (2nd ed., pp. 416–432). New York, NY: Guilford Press.

Monti, P. M., Abrams, D. B., Kadden, R. M., & Cooney, N. L. (1989). *Treating alcohol dependence: A coping skills training guide.* New York, NY: Guilford Press.

O'Leary-Tevyaw, T., & Monti, P. M. (2004). Motivational enhancement and other brief interventions for adolescent substance abuse: Foundations, applications and evaluations. *Addiction, 99*(Suppl 2), 63–75. doi: 10.1111/j.1360-0443.2004.00855.x

Waldron, H. B., & Brody, J. L. (2010). Functional family therapy for adolescent substance use disorders. In J. R. Weisz & A. E. Kazdin (Eds.), *Evidence-based psychotherapies for children and adolescents* (2nd ed., pp. 401–415). New York, NY: Guilford Press.

Waldron, H. B., & Kaminer, Y. (2004). On the learning curve: The emerging evidence supporting cognitive-behavioral therapies for adolescent substance abuse. *Addiction, 99*, 93–105.

Winters, K. C. (2001). Assessing adolescent substance use problems and other areas of functioning: State of the art. In P. M. Monti, S. M. Colby & T. A. O'Leary (Eds.), *Adolescents, alcohol, and substance abuse: Reaching teens through brief interventions* (pp. 80–108). New York, NY: Guilford Press.

Clinician Application

Center for Substance Abuse Treatment. (2008). The adolescent community reinforcement approach for adolescent cannabis users. Rockville (MD): Substance Abuse and Mental Health Services Administration (US). (Cannabis Youth Treatment (CYT) Series, Vol. 4.)

Kadden, R., Carroll, K. M., Donovan, D., Cooney, N., Monti, P., ... Hester, R. (1994). *Cognitive-behavioral coping skills therapy manual: A clinical research guide for therapists treating individuals with alcohol abuse and dependence.* Project MATCH Monograph Series, Vol. 3. DHHS Publication No. 94-3724. Rockville, MD: NIAAA.

Miller, W., Zweben, A., DiClementi, C., & Ryctarik, R. (1995). *Motivational enhancement therapy manual.* NIH Publication No. 94-3723. Retrieved from http://casaa.unm.edu/manuals/met.pdf

Waldron, H. B., & Turner, C. W. (2008). Evidence-based psychosocial treatments for adolescent substance abuse. *Journal of Clinical Child & Adolescent Psychology, 37,* 238–261.

CHAPTER 14

Research

American Psychiatric Association (2013). *Diagnostic and statistical manual of mental disorders* (5th ed.). Washington, DC: Author.

Azrin, N. H., & Nunn, R. G. (1973). Habit-reversal: A method of eliminating nervous habits and tics. *Behaviour Research and Therapy, 11,* 619–628. doi: 10.1016/0005-7967(73)90119-8

Bloch, M. H., & Leckman, J. F. (2009). Clinical course of Tourette syndrome. *Journal of Psychosomatic Research, 67,* 497–501. doi: 10.1016/j.jpsychores.2009.09.002

Evers, R. A. F., & van de Wetering, B. J. M. (1994). A treatment model for motor tics based on specific tension-reduction technique. *Journal of Behavior Therapy and Experimental Psychiatry, 25,* 255–260. doi: 10.1016/0005-7916(94)90026-4

Gilbert, D. (2006). Treatment of children and adolescents with tics and Tourette syndrome. *Journal of Child Neurology, 21,* 690–700. doi: 10.1177/08830738060210080401

Himle, M. B., & Woods, D. W. (2005). An experimental evaluation of tic suppression and the tic rebound effect. *Behaviour Research and Therapy, 43,* 1443–1451. doi: 10.1016/j.brat.2004.11.002

Himle, M. B., Woods, D. W., Conelea, C. A., Bauer, C. C., & Rice, K. A. (2007). Investigating the effects of tic suppression on premonitory urge ratings in children and adolescents with Tourette's syndrome. *Behaviour Research & Therapy, 45,* 2964–2976. doi: 10.1016/j.brat.2007.08.007

Himle, M. B., Woods, D. W., Piacentini, J., & Walkup, J. (2006). A brief review of habit reversal training for Tourette syndrome. *Journal of Child Neurology, 21,* 719–725. doi: 10.1177/08830738060210080101

Kadesjo, B., & Gillberg, C. (2000). Tourette's disorder: Epidemiology and comorbidity in primary school children. *Journal of the American Academy of Child and Adolescent Psychiatry, 39,* 548–555. doi: 10.1097/00004583-200005000-00007

Kwak, C., Vuong, K. D., & Jankovic, J. (2003). Premonitory sensory phenomenon in Tourette's syndrome. *Movement Disorders, 18,* 1530–1533. doi: 10.1002/mds.10618

Leckman, J. F., King, R. A., & Cohen, D. J. (1999). Tics and tic disorders. In J. F. Leckman & D. J. Cohen (Eds.), *Tourette's syndrome-tics, obsessions, compulsions: Developmental psychopathology and clinical care* (pp. 23–42). New York, NY: John Wiley & Sons.

Leckman, J. F., Riddle, M. A., Hardin, M. T., & Ort, S. I. (1989). The Yale Global Tic Severity Scale: Initial testing of a clinician-rated scale of tic severity. *Journal of the American Academy of Child & Adolescent Psychiatry, 28,* 566–573. doi: 10.1097/00004583-198907000-00015

Leckman, J. F., Walker, D. E., & Cohen, D. J. (1993). Premonitory urges in Tourette's syndrome. *American Journal of Psychiatry, 150,* 98–102. Retrieved from http://ajp.psychiatryonline.org

Leckman, J. F., Zhang, H., Vitale, A., Lahnin, F., Lynch, K., ... Peterson, B. S. (1998). Course of tic severity in Tourette syndrome: The first two decades. *Pediatrics, 102,* 14–19. doi: 10.1542/peds.102.1.14

Piacentini, J. C., Woods, D. W., Scahill, L. D., Wilhelm, S., Peterson, A., ... Walkup, J. T. (2010). Behavior therapy for children with Tourette Syndrome: A randomized controlled trial. *Journal of the American Medical Association, 303,* 1929–1937. doi: 10.1001/jama.2010.607

Robertson, M. M. (2008). The prevalence and epidemiology of Gilles de la Tourette syndrome Part 1: The epidemiological and prevalence studies. *Journal of Psychosomatic Research, 65,* 461–472.

Silva, R. R., Munoz, D. M., Barickman, J., & Friedhoff, A. J. (1995). Environmental factors and related fluctuation of symptoms in children and adolescents with Tourette's disorder. *Journal of Child Psychology and Psychiatry, 36,* 305–312. doi: 10.1111/j.1469-7610.1995.tb01826.x

Wilhelm, S., Peterson, A.L., Piacentini, J., Woods, D.W., Deckersbach, T., ... Scahill, L. (2012). Randomized trial of behavior therapy for adults with Tourette syndrome. *Archives of General Psychiatry, 69,* 795–803.

Woods, D. W., Conelea, C. A., & Walther, M. R. (2007). Barriers to dissemination: Exploring the criticisms of behavior therapy for tics. *Clinical Psychology: Science and Practice, 14,* 279–282. doi: 10.1111/j.1468-2850.2007.00088.x

Woods, D. W., Himle, M. B., Miltenberger, R. G., Carr, J. E., Osmon, D. C., ... Bosch, A. (2008). Durability, negative impact, and neuropsychological predictors of tic suppression in children with chronic tic disorder. *Journal of Abnormal Child Psychology, 36,* 237–245. doi: 10.1007/s10802-007-9173-9

Woods, D. W., Miltenberger, R. G., & Lumley, V. A. (1996). Sequential application of major habit reversal components to treat motor tics in children. *Journal of Applied Behavior Analysis, 29*, 483–493. doi: 10.1901/jaba.1996.29-483

Woods, D. W., Twohig, M. P., Flessner, C. A., & Roloff, T. A. (2003). Treatment of vocal tics in children with Tourette syndrome: Investigating the efficacy of habit reversal. *Journal of Applied Behavior Analysis, 36*, 109–112. doi: 10.1901/jaba.2003.36-109

Woods, D. W., Watson, T. S., Wolfe, E., Twohig, M. P., & Friman, P. C. (2001). Analyzing the influence of tic-related talk on vocal and motor tics in children with Tourette's syndrome. *Journal of Applied Behavior Analysis, 34*, 353–356. doi: 10.1901/jaba.2001.34-353

Wright, K., & Miltenberger, R. (1987). Awareness training in the treatment of head and facial tics. *Journal of Behavior Therapy and Experimental Psychiatry, 18*, 269–274. doi: 10.1016/0005-7916(87)90010-3

CHAPTER 15

Research

American Psychiatric Association. (2000). *Diagnostic and statistical manual of mental disorders* (4th ed., text rev.). Washington, DC: Author.

Barkley, R. A. (2011). *Barkley deficits in executive functioning scale (BDEFS)*. New York, NY: Guilford.

Barkley, R. A., Murphy, K. R., & Fischer, M. (2008). *ADHD in adults: What the science says*. New York, NY: Guilford.

Biederman, J., Faraone, S. V., Spencer, T. J., Mick, E., Monuteaux, M. C., & Aleardi, M. (2006). Functional impairments in adults with self-reports of diagnosed ADHD: A controlled study of 1001 adults in the community. *Journal of Clinical Psychiatry, 67*, 524–540.

Connor, D. F. (2006). Stimulants. In R. A. Barkley (Ed.), *Attention-deficit hyperactivity disorder: A handbook for diagnosis and treatment* (pp. 608–647). New York, NY: Guilford.

DuPaul, G. J., Schaughency, E. A., Weyandt, L. L., Tripp, G., Kiesner, J., ... Stanish, H. (2001). Self-report of ADHD symptoms in university students: Cross-gender and cross-national prevalence. *Journal of Learning Disabilities, 34*, 370–379.

Faraone, S. V., Biederman, J., & Mick, E. (2006). The age-dependent decline of attention deficit hyperactivity disorder: A meta-analysis of follow-up studies. *Psychological Medicine, 36*, 159–165.

Fayyad, J., DeGraaf, R., Kessler, R., Alonso, J., Angermeyer, M., ... Jin, R. (2007). Cross-national prevalence and correlates of adult attention-deficit hyperactivity disorder. *British Journal of Psychiatry, 190*, 402–409.

Kessler, R. C., Adler, L. A., Barkley, R. A., Biederman, J., Conners, C. K., ... Zaslavsky, A. M. (2005). Patterns and predictors of attention-deficit/hyperactivity disorder persistence into adulthood: Results from the national comorbidity survey replication. *Biological Psychiatry, 57*, 1442–1451.

Kessler, R. C., Adler, L. A., Barkley, R. A., Biederman, J., Conners, C. K., ... Zaslavsky, A. M. (2006). The prevalence and correlates of adult ADHD in the United States: Results from the national comorbidity survey replication. *American Journal of Psychiatry, 163*, 716–723.

Kessler, R. C., Green, J. G., Adler, L. A., Barkley, R. A., Chatterji, S., ... Van Brunt, D. L. (2010). Structure and diagnosis of adult attention-deficit/hyperactivity disorder: Analysis of expanded symptom criteria from the Adult ADHD Clinical Diagnostic Scale. *Archives of General Psychiatry, 67*, 1168–1178.

Mahomedy, Z., van der Westhuizen, D., van der Linde, M. J., & Coetsee, J. (2007). Persistence of attention deficit/hyperactivity disorder into adulthood: A study conducted on parents of children diagnosed with attention deficit/hyperactivity disorder. *South African Psychiatry Review, 10*, 93–98.

Montes, L. G. A., Garcia, A. O. H., & Ricardo-Garcell, J. (2007). ADHD prevalence in adult outpatients with nonpsychotic psychiatric illnesses. *Journal of Attention Disorders, 11*, 150–156. doi: 10.1177/1087054707304428

Norvilitis, J. M., Ingersoll, T., Zhang, J., & Jia, S. (2008). Self-reported symptoms of ADHD among college students in China and the United States. *Journal of Attention Disorders, 11*, 558–567. doi: 10.1177/1087054707308496

Polanczyk, G., Silva de Lima, M., Horta, B. L., Biederman, J., & Rohde, L. A. (2007). The worldwide prevalence of ADHD: A systematic review and metaregression analysis. *American Journal of Psychiatry, 164*, 942–948.

Prince, J. B., Wilens, T. E., Spencer, T. J., & Biederman, J. (2006). Pharmacotherapy of ADHD in adults. In R. A. Barkley (Ed.), *Attention-deficit hyperactivity disorder: A handbook for diagnosis and treatment* (pp. 704–736). New York, NY: Guilford.

Ramsay, J. R. (2010). *Nonmedication treatments for adult ADHD: Evaluating impact on daily functioning and well-being*. Washington, DC: American Psychological Association.

Ramsay, J. R., & Rostain, A. L. (2008). *Cognitive behavioral therapy for adult ADHD: An integrative psychosocial and medical approach*. New York, NY: Routledge.

Ramsay, J. R., & Rostain, A. L. (2011). CBT without medications for adult ADHD: An open pilot study of five patients. *Journal of Cognitive Psychotherapy: An International Quarterly, 25,* 277–286. doi: 10.1891/0889-8391.25.4.277

Safren, S. A., Perlman, C. A., Sprich, S., & Otto, M. W. (2005). *Mastering your adult ADHD: A cognitive-behavioral treatment program – Therapist guide.* Oxford, UK: Oxford University Press.

Safren, S. A., Sprich, S., Mimiaga, M. J., Surman, C., Knouse, L., … Otto, M. W. (2010). Cognitive behavioral therapy vs relaxation with educational support for medication-treated adults with ADHD and persistent symptoms: A randomized controlled trial. *Journal of the American Medical Association, 304,* 875–880.

Solanto, M. V. (2011). *Cognitive behavioral therapy for adult ADHD: Targeting executive functions.* New York, NY: Guilford.

Solanto, M. V., Marks, D. J., Wasserstein, J., Mitchell, K. J., Abikoff, H., … Kofman, M. D. (2010). Efficacy of meta-cognitive therapy for adult ADHD. *American Journal of Psychiatry, 167,* 958–968. doi: 10.1176/appi.ajp.2009.09081123

Waite, R., & Ramsay, J. R. (2010). Adults with ADHD: Who are we missing? *Issues in Mental Health Nursing, 31,* 670–678. doi: 10.3109/01612840.2010.496137

Weiss, N. (2011). Assessment and treatment of ADHD in adults. *Psychiatric Annals, 41,* 23–31. doi: 10.3928/00485713-20101221-05

Young, S. J., Adamou, M., Bolea, B., Gudjonsson, G., Müller, U., … Asherson, P. (2011). The identification and management of ADHD offenders within the criminal justice system: A consensus statement from the UK Adult ADHD Network and criminal justice agencies. *BMC Psychiatry, 11,* 32. doi: 10.1186/1471-244X-11-32

Clinician Application

Barkley, R. A. (2010). *Taking charge of adult ADHD.* New York, NY: Guilford.

Bertin, M. (2011). *The family ADHD solution: A scientific approach to maximizing your child's attention and minimizing parental stress.* New York, NY: Palgrave Macmillan.

Orlov, M. (2010). *The ADHD effect on marriage: Understand and rebuild your relationship in six steps.* Plantation, FL: Specialty Press.

Pera, G. (2008). *Is it you, me, or adult A.D.D.? Stopping the roller coaster when someone you love has attention deficit disorder.* San Francisco, CA: 1201 Alarm Press.

Roggli, L. (2011). *Confessions of an ADDiva: Midlife in a non-linear lane.* Durham, NC: Passionate Possibility Press.

Sarkis, S. (2008). *Making the grade with ADD: A student's guide to succeeding in college with attention deficit disorder.* Oakland, CA: New Harbinger.

Sarkis, S. (2011a). *Adult ADD: A guide for the newly diagnosed.* Oakland, CA: New Harbinger.

Sarkis, S. (2011b). *10 simple solutions to adult ADD: How to overcome chronic distraction & accomplish your goals* (2nd ed.). Oakland, CA: New Harbinger.

Sarkis, S., & Klein, K. (2009). *ADD and your money: A guide to personal finance for adults with attention-deficit disorder.* Oakland, CA: New Harbinger.

Tschudi, S. (2012). *Loving someone with attention deficit disorder: A practical guide to understanding your partner, improving your communication, and strengthening your relationship.* Oakland, CA: New Harbinger.

Tuckman, A. (2009). *More attention, less deficit: Success strategies for adults with ADHD.* Plantation, FL: Specialty Press.

Tuckman, A. (2012). *Understand your brain, get more done: The ADHD executive functions workbook.* Plantation, FL: Specialty Press.

Zylowska, L. (2012) *The mindfulness prescription for adult ADHD: An 8-step program for strengthening attention, managing emotions, and achieving your goals.* Boston, MA: Trumpeter.

CHAPTER 16

Research

American Psychiatric Association. (2000). *Diagnostic and statistical manual of mental disorders* (4th ed., text rev.). Washington, DC: American Psychiatric Association.

Grant, B. F., Dawson, D. A., Stinson, F. S., Chou, P., Dufour, M. C., & Pickering, R. P. (2004). The 12-month prevalence and trends in DSM-IV alcohol abuse and dependence: United States, 1991–1992 and 2001–2002. *Drug and Alcohol Dependence, 74,* 223–234.

Kelly, J. F. (2003). Self-help for substance use disorders: History, effectiveness, knowledge gaps, and research opportunities. *Clinical Psychology Review, 23,* 639–663.

Lash, S. J., Stephens, R. S., Burden, J. L., Grambow, S. C., DeMarce, J. M., … Horner, R. D. (2007). Contracting, prompting, and reinforcing substance use disorder continuing care: A randomized clinical trial. *Psychology of Addictive Behaviors, 21,* 387–397.

McKay, J. R. (2009). Continuing care research: What we have learned and where we are going. *Journal of Substance Abuse Treatment, 36,* 131–145.

Miller, W. R., & Sanchez, V. C. (1993). Motivating young adults for treatment and lifestyle change. In G. Howard & P. E. Nathan (Eds.), *Issues in alcohol use and misuse by young adults.* Notre Dame, IN: University of Notre Dame Press.

Schaefer, J., Harris A. H., Cronkite, R. C., & Turrubiartes, P. (2008). Treatment staff's continuity of care practices, patients' engagement in continuing care, and abstinence following outpatient substance-use disorder treatment. *Journal of Studies on Alcohol and Drugs, 69,* 747–756.

Substance Abuse and Mental Health Services Administration (SAMHSA). (2012). Results from the 2010 National Survey on Drug Use and Health: Mental Health Findings. NSDUH Series H-42, HHS Publication No. (SMA) 11-4667. Rockville, MD: Substance Abuse and Mental Health Services Administration.

Clinician Application

Alcoholics Anonymous World Services. (1975). *Living sober.* New York, NY: Author.

Daley, D. C., & Marlatt, G. A. (2006). *Overcoming your alcohol or drug problem: Effective recovery strategies: Therapist guide* (2nd ed.). New York, NY: Oxford University Press.

Klein, A. A., Slaymaker, V. J., Dugosh, K. L., & McKay, J. R. (2012). Computerized continuing care support for alcohol and drug dependence: A preliminary analysis of usage and outcomes. *Journal of Substance Abuse Treatment, 42,* 25–34. doi: 10.1016/j.jsat.2011.07.002

Maisto, S. A., Connors, G. J., & Dearing, R. L. (2007). *Alcohol use disorders.* Cambridge, MA: Hogrefe & Huber.

McCrady, B. S., Haaga, D. A. F., & Lebow, J. (2006). Integration of therapeutic factors in treating substance use disorders. In L. G. Castonguay & L. E. Beutler (Eds.), *Principles of therapeutic change that work* (pp. 341–349). New York, NY: Oxford.

Moore, B. A., Fazzino, T., Garnet, B., Cutter, C. J., & Barry, D. T. (2011). Computer-based interventions for drug use disorders: A systematic review. *Journal of Substance Abuse Treatment, 40,* 215–223. doi: 10.1016/j.jsat.2010.11.002

National Institute of Alcohol Abuse and Alcoholism. http://www.niaaa.nih.gov

O'Farrell, T. J., & Fals-Stewart, W. (2006). *Behavioral couples therapy for alcoholism and drug abuse.* New York, NY: Guilford.

Sellman, D. (2010). The 10 most important things known about addiction. *Addiction, 105,* 6–13. doi: 10.1111/j.1360-0443.2009.02673.x

Smith, J. E., & Meyers, R. J. (2004). *Motivating substance abusers to enter treatment: Working with family members.* New York, NY: Guilford.

CHAPTER 17

Research

Archer, J. (2000). Sex differences in aggression between heterosexual partners: A meta-analytic review. *Psychological Bulletin, 126,* 651–680.

Averill, J. R. (1982). *Anger and aggression: An essay on emotion.* New York, NY: Springer-Verlag.

Blanchard-Fields, F., & Coats, A. H. (2008). The experience of anger and sadness in everyday problems impacts age differences in emotion regulation. *Developmental Psychology, 44*(6), 1547–1556.

Campbell, A., & Muncer, S. (2008). Intent to harm or injure? Gender and the expression of anger. *Aggressive Behavior, 34,* 282–293.

Deffenbacher, J. L., & McKay, M. (2000). *Overcoming situational and general anger: A protocol for the treatment of anger based on relaxation, cognitive restructuring, and coping skills training.* Oakland, CA: New Harbinger Publications.

Deffenbacher, J. L., & Swaim, R. C. (1999). Anger expression in Mexican American and White non-Hispanic adolescents. *Journal of Counseling Psychology, 46*(1), 61–69.

Ellis, A., & Tafrate, R. C. (1997). *How to control your anger before it controls you.* New York, NY: Citadel Press.

Exline, J. L., Park, C. L., Smyth, J. M., & Carey, M. P. (2011). Anger toward God: Social-cognitive predictors, prevalence, and links with adjustment to bereavement and cancer. *Journal of Personality and Social Psychology, 100*(1), 129–148.

Feindler, E. L. (2006). *Anger related disorders: A practitioner's guide to comparative treatments.* New York, NY: Springer.

Fischer, A. H., & Evers, C. (2010). Anger in the context of gender. In M. Potegal, G. Stemmler, & C. Spielberger (Eds.), *International handbook of anger* (pp. 349–360). New York, NY: Springer.

Hayamizu, T., Kino, K., & Takagi, K. (2007). Effects of age and competence type on the emotions: Focusing on sadness and anger. *Japanese Psychological Research, 49*(3), 211–221.

Kassinove, H. (2007). Finding a useful model for the treatment of anger and aggression: Comments on Novaco's "Anger Dysregulation: Its Assessment and Treatment" and DiGiuseppe, Cannela and Kelter's "Effective anger treatments require a functional analysis of the anger response." In T. Cavell & K. T. Malcolm (Eds.), *Anger, aggression, and interventions for interpersonal violence.* New York, NY: Erlbaum.

Kassinove, H. (2009). Anger. In D. McKay, J. Abramowitz, & S. Taylor (Eds.), *The expanded scope of cognitive behavior therapy. Lessons learned from refractory cases.* Washington, DC: APA Press.

Kassinove, H., & Tafrate, R. C. (2002). *Anger management: The complete treatment guidebook for practitioners.* Atascadero, CA: Impact Publishers.

Kassinove, H., & Tafrate, R. (2005). Disruptive anger. In A. Freeman (Ed.), *Encyclopedia of cognitive behavior therapy.* New York, NY: Kluwer/Springer.

Kassinove, H., & Tafrate, R. (2006). Anger related disorders: Basic issues, models, and diagnostic considerations. In E. Feindler (Ed.), *Comparative treatments of anger disorders* (pp. 1–27). New York, NY: Springer.

Kassinove, H., & Tafrate, R. C. (2010). Application of a flexible, clinically driven approach for anger reduction in the case of Mr. P. *Cognitive and Behavioral Practice, 10,* 222–234.

Kim, I. J., & Zane, N. W. S. (2004). Ethnic and cultural variations in anger regulation and attachment patterns among Korean American and European American male batterers. *Cultural Diversity and Ethnic Minority Psychology, 10*(2), 151–168.

Magdol, L., Moffitt, T. E., Avshalom, C., Newman, D. L., Fagan, J., & Silva, P. A. (1997). Gender differences in partner violence in a birth cohort of 21-year-olds: Bridging the gap between clinical and epidemiological approaches. *Journal of Consulting and Clinical Psychology, 65,* 68–78.

Maier, K. J., Goble, L. A., Neumann, S. A., Giggey, P. P., Suarez, E. C., & Waldstein, S. R. (2009). Dimensions across measures of dispositional hostility, expressive style, and depression show some variation by race/ethnicity and gender in young adults. *Journal of Social and Clinical Psychology, 28*(10), 1199–1225.

Miller, W. R., & Rollnick, S. (2002). *Motivational interviewing.* New York, NY: Guilford.

Novaco, R. W. (2007). Anger dysregulation. In T. Cavell & K. Malcolm (Eds.), Anger, aggression, and interventions for interpersonal violence (pp. 3–54). Mahwah, NJ: Erlbaum.

Novaco, R. W., & Taylor, J. L. (2006). Anger. In A. Carr & M. McNulty. *The handbook of adult clinical psychology: An evidence-based practice approach* (pp. 978–1009). New York, NY: Routledge.

Saini, M. (2009). A meta-analysis of psychological treatment of anger: Developing guidelines for evidence based practice. *Journal of the American Academy of Psychiatry and the Law, 37*(4), 438–441.

Sukhodolsky, D. G., Kassinove, H., & Gorman, B. S. (2004). Cognitive behavioral therapy for anger in children and adolescents: A meta-analysis. *Aggression and Violent Behavior, 9*(3), 247–269.

Tafrate, R. C., & Kassinove, H. (2004). Cognitive behavior therapy with anger disordered patients: Strategies of the beginning phase of treatment. In R. Leahy (Ed.), *Overcoming roadblocks in cognitive behavior therapy.* New York, NY: Guilford.

Tafrate, R. C., & Kassinove, H. (2006). Cognitive behavioral treatment for the case of Anthony. In E. Feindler (Ed.), *Comparative treatments of anger disorders* (pp. 115–137). New York, NY: Springer.

Tafrate, R. C., & Kassinove, H. (2009). *Anger management for everyone: Seven proven methods to control anger.* Atascadero, CA: Impact Publishers.

Tafrate, R., Kassinove, H., & Dundin, L. (2002). Anger episodes in high and low trait anger community adults. *Journal of Clinical Psychology, 58,* 1573–1590.

Wolpe, J. (1969). *The practice of behavior therapy.* New York, NY: Pergamon Press.

CHAPTER 18

Research

Boelen, P. A., de Keijser, J., van den Hout, M., & van den Bout, J. (2007). Treatment of complicated grief: A comparison between cognitive-behavioral therapy and supportive counseling. *Journal of Clinical and Consulting Psychology, 75,* 277–284.

Bonanno, G. A., Neria, Y., Mancini, A., Coifman, K., Litz, B., & Insel, B. (2007). Is there more to complicated grief than depression and posttraumatic stress disorder? A test of incremental validity. *Journal of Abnormal Psychology, 116,* 342–351.

Bowlby, J. (1980). *Attachment and loss: Loss, sadness and depression* (Vol. 3). New York, NY: Basic.

Burke, L. A., Neimeyer, R. A., McDevitt-Murphy, M. E., Ippolito, M., & Roberts, J. M. (2011). Faith in the wake of homicide: Religious coping and bereavement distress in an African American sample. *International Journal for the Psychology of Religion, 21*, 289–307.

Currier, J. M., Holland, J., & Neimeyer, R. A. (2006). Sense making, grief and the experience of violent loss: Toward a mediational model. *Death Studies, 30*, 403–428.

Currier, J. M., Neimeyer, R. A., & Berman, J. S. (2008). The effectiveness of psychotherapeutic interventions for the bereaved: A comprehensive quantitative review. *Psychological Bulletin, 134*, 648–661.

Holland, J. M., Neimeyer, R. A., Boelen, P. A., & Prigerson, H. G. (2009). The underlying structure of grief: A taxometric investigation of prolonged and normal reactions to loss. *Journal of Psychopathology and Behavioral Assessment, 31*, 190–201.

Jordan, J. R., & McIntosh, J. L. (Eds.). (2010). *Grief after suicide*. New York, NY: Routledge.

Kissane, D. W., McKenzie, M., Block, S., Moskowitz, C., McKenzie, D. P., & O'Neill, I. (2006). Family Focused Grief Therapy: A randomized, controlled trial in palliative care and bereavement. *American Journal of Psychiatry, 163*, 1208–1218.

Lichtenthal, W. G., Burke, L. A., & Neimeyer, R. A. (2011). Religious coping and meaning-making following the loss of a loved one. *Counseling and Spirituality, 30*, 113–136.

Lichtenthal, W. G., & Cruess, D. G. (2010). Effects of directed written disclosure on grief and distress symptoms among bereaved individuals. *Death Studies, 34*, 475–499.

McDevitt-Murphy, M. E., Neimeyer, R. A., Burke, L. A., Williams, J. L., & Lawson, K. (2012). The toll of traumatic loss in African Americans bereaved by homicide. *Psychological Trauma: Theory, Research, Practice, and Policy, 4*, 303–311.

Neimeyer, R. A. (2011). Reconstructing meaning in bereavement. In W. Watson & D. Kissane (Eds.), *Handbook of psychotherapies in cancer care*. New York, NY: Wiley.

Neimeyer, R. A. (2012). Reconstructing the self in the wake of loss: A dialogical contribution. In H. Hermans & T. Gieser (Eds.), *Handbook on the dialogical self*. Cambridge, UK: Cambridge University Press.

Neimeyer, R. A., & Currier, J. M. (2009). Grief therapy: Evidence of efficacy and emerging directions. *Current Directions in Psychological Science, 18*, 252–256.

Prigerson, H. G., Horowitz, M. J., Jacobs, S. C., Parkes, C. M., Aslan, M., ... Maciejewski, P. K. (2009, August). Prolonged Grief Disorder: Psychometric validation of criteria proposed for DSM-V and ICD-11. *PLoS Medicine, 6*(8), 1–12.

Rubin, S. S., Malkinson, R., & Witztum, E. (2011). *Working with the bereaved*. New York, NY: Routledge.

Shear, M. K., Simon, N., Wall, M., Zisook, S., Neimeyer, R., ... Keshaviah, A. (2011). Complicated grief and related bereavement issues for DSM-5. *Depression and Anxiety, 28*, 103–117.

Shear, K., Frank, E., Houch, P. R., & Reynolds, C. F. (2005). Treatment of complicated grief: A randomized controlled trial. *Journal of the American Medical Association, 293*, 2601–2608.

Clinician Application

Kosminsky, P. (2007). *Getting back to life when grief won't heal*. New York, NY: McGraw-Hill.

Lichtenthal, W. (2010). Effects of directed written disclosure on grief and distress symptoms among bereaved individuals. *Death Studies, 34*, 475–499.

Parkes, C. M. (2006). *Love and loss: The roots of grief and its complications*. New York: Routledge.

Zech, E., & Arnold, C. (2011). Attachment and coping with bereavement: Implications for therapeutic interventions with the insecurely attached. In R. Neimeyer, D. Harris, H. Winokur, & G. Thornton (Eds.), *Grief and bereavement in contemporary society: Bridging research and practice* (pp. 23–36). New York, NY: Routledge.

CHAPTER 19

Research

Castle, D. J., Berk, L., Lauder, S., Berk, M., & Murray, G. (2009). Psychosocial interventions for bipolar disorder. *Acta Neuropsychiatrica, 21*, 275–284.

Cuellar, A. K., Johnson, S. L., & Winters, R. (2005). Distinctions between bipolar and unipolar depression. *Clinical Psychology Review, 25*, 307–339.

Johnson, S. L. (2005a). Life events in bipolar disorder: Towards more specific models. *Clinical Psychology Review, 25*, 1008–1027.

Johnson, S. L. (2005b). Mania and dysregulation in goal pursuit: A review. *Clinical Psychology Review, 25*, 241–262.

Miklowitz, D. J., & Johnson, S. L. (2006). The psychopathology and treatment of bipolar disorder. *Annual Review of Clinical Psychology, 2,* 199–235.

Mitchell, P. B., Goodwin, G. M., Johnson, G. F., & Hirschfeld, R. M. (2008). Diagnostic guidelines for bipolar depression: A probabilistic approach. *Bipolar Disorders, 10*(1 Pt 2), 144–152.

Murray, G., Goldstone, E., & Cunningham, E. (2007). Personality and the predisposition(s) to bipolar disorder: Heuristic benefits of a two-dimensional model. *Bipolar Disorders, 9,* 453–461.

Murray, G., & Harvey, A. (2010). Circadian rhythms and sleep in bipolar disorder. *Bipolar Disorders, 12,* 459–472.

Murray, G., & Johnson, S. (2010). The clinical significance of creativity in bipolar disorder. *Clinical Psychology Review, 30,* 721–732.

Murray, G., & Michalak, E. (2007). Quality of life in patients with bipolar disorder: Defining and measuring goals. *Psychiatric Times, XXIV,* 24–26.

Suto, M., Murray, G., Hale, S., Amari, E., & Michalak, E. E. (2010). What works for people with bipolar disorder? Tips from the experts. *Journal of Affective Disorders, 124,* 76–84.

Clinician Application

Frank, E., & Swartz, H. (2004). Interpersonal and social rhythm. In S. L. Johnson & R. L. Leahy (Eds.), *Psychological treatment of bipolar disorder.* New York, NY: The Guilford Press.

Jamison, K. R. (1995). *An unquiet mind.* New York, NY: Alfred A. Knopf.

McManamy, J. (2006). *Living well with depression and bipolar disorder.* New York, NY: HarperCollins.

Miklowitz, D. J. (2004). Family therapy. In S. L. Johnson & R. L. Leahy (Eds.), *Psychological treatment of bipolar disorder.* New York, NY: The Guilford Press.

Russell, S. (2008). Role of a 'stay well' approach in the management of bipolar disorder. *The Royal Australian and New Zealand Journal of Psychiatry, 42,* 551–554.

Scott, J. (2006). Psychotherapy for bipolar disorders—efficacy and effectiveness. *Journal of Psychopharmacology, 20,* 346.

CHAPTER 20

Research

Allen, A., Hadley, S. J., Kaplan, A., Simeon, D., Friedberg, J., … Hollander, E. (2008). An open-label trial of venlafaxine in body dysmorphic disorder. *CNS Spectrums, 13,* 138–144.

American Psychiatric Association. (2000). *Diagnostic and statistical manual of mental disorders* (4th ed., Text Revision). Washington DC: American Psychiatric Association.

Aouizerate, B., Pujol, H., Grabot, D., Faytout, M., Suire, K., … Tignol, J. (2003). Body dysmorphic disorder in a sample of cosmetic surgery applicants. *European Psychiatry, 18,* 365–368.

Ashraf, H. (2000). Surgery offers little help for patients with body dysmorphic disorder. *The Lancet, 355,* 2055.

Bartsch, D. (2007). Prevalence of body dysmorphic disorder symptoms and associated clinical features among Australian university students. *Clinical Psychologist, 11,* 16–23.

Bohne, A., Keuthen, N. J., Wilhelm, S., Deckersback, T., & Jenike, M. A. (2002). Prevalence of symptoms of body dysmorphic disorder and its correlates: A cross-cultural comparison. *Psychosomatics, 43,* 486–490.

Bohne, A., Wilhelm, S., Keuthen, N. J., Florin, I., Baer, L., & Jenike, M. A. (2002). Prevalence of body dysmorphic disorder in a German college student sample. *Psychiatry Research, 109,* 101–104.

Boroughs, M. S., Krawczyk, R., & Thompson, J. K. (2010). Body dysmorphic disorder among diverse racial/ethnic and sexual orientation groups: Prevalence estimates and associated factors. *Sex Roles, 63,* 725–737.

Campisi, T. A. (1996). Exposure and response prevention in the treatment of Body Dysmorphic Disorder. *Dissertation Abstracts International: Section B: The Sciences and Engineering, 56,* 7036.

Cansever, A., Uzun, Ö., Dönmez, E., & Ozsahin, A. (2003). The prevalence and clinical features of body dysmorphic disorder in college students: A study in a Turkish sample. *Comprehensive Psychiatry, 44,* 60–64.

Conroy, M., Menard, W., Fleming-Ives, K., Modha, P., Cerullo, H., & Phillips, K. A. (2007). Prevalence and clinical characteristics of body dysmorphic disorder in an adult inpatient setting. *General Hospital Psychiatry, 30,* 67–72.

Cotterill, J. A. (1996). Body dysmorphic disorder. *Dermatology Clinic, 14,* 457–463.

Crerand, C. E., Phillips, K. A., Menard, W., & Fay, C. (2005). Nonpsychiatric medical treatment of body dysmorphic disorder. *Psychosomatics, 46,* 549–555.

Geremia, G., & Neziroglu, F. (2001). Cognitive therapy in the treatment of body dysmorphic disorder. *Clinical Psychology Psychotherapy, 8,* 241–251.

Gunstad, J., & Phillips, K. A. (2003). Axis I comorbidity in body dysmorphic disorder. *Comprehensive Psychiatry, 44,* 270–276.

Ishigooka, J., Iwao, M., Suzuki, M., Fukuyama, Y., Murasaki, M., & Miura S. (1998). Demographic features of patients seeking cosmetic surgery. *Psychiatry Clinical Neuroscience, 52,* 283–287.

Koran, L. M., Abujaoude, E., Large, M. D., & Serpe, R. T. (2008). The prevalence of body dysmorphic disorder in the United States adult population. *CNS Spectrums, 13,* 316–322.

McKay, D., Todaro, J., Neziroglu, F., & Campisi, T. (1997). Body dysmorphic disorder: A preliminary evaluation of treatment and maintenance using exposure with response prevention. *Behavioral Research Therapy, 35,* 67–70.

Neziroglu, F., McKay, D., Todaro, J., & Yaryura-Tobias, J. A. (1996). Effect of cognitive behavior therapy on persons with body dysmorphic disorder and comorbid Axis II diagnosis. *Behavioral Therapy, 27,* 67–77.

Otto, M. W., Wilhelm, S., Cohen, L. S., & Harlow, B. L. (2001). Prevalence of body dysmorphic disorder in a community sample of women. *American Journal of Psychiatry, 158,* 2061–2063.

Pearson, A. N., Heffner, M., & Follette, V. (2010). *Acceptance & Commitment Therapy for body image dissatisfaction: A practitioners guide to using mindfulness, acceptance & values based behavior change strategies.* Oakland, CA: New Harbinger Publications, Inc.

Perugi, G., Akiskal, H. S., Giannotti, D., Frare, F., Di Vaio, S., & Cassano, G. B. (1997). Gender-related differences in body dysmorphic disorder (dysmorphophobia). *Journal of Nervous and Mental Disease, 185,* 578–582.

Perugi, G., Giannotti, D., Di Vaio, S., Valori, E., Maggi, L., ... Akiskal, H. P. (1997). Prevalence, phenomenology and co-morbidity of dysmorphophobia (body dysmorphic disorder) in a clinical population. *International Journal of Psychiatry in Clinical Practice, 1,* 77–82.

Phillips, K. A. (1991). Body dysmorphic disorders: The distress of imagined ugliness. *American Journal of Psychiatry, 148,* 1138–1149.

Phillips, K. A. (1996). *The broken mirror: Understanding and treating Body Dysmorphic Disorder.* New York, NY: Oxford University Press.

Phillips, K. A., & Diaz, S. F. (1997). Gender differences in body dysmorphic disorder. *Journal of Nervous and Mental Disease, 185,* 570–577.

Phillips, K. A., Grant, J., Siniscalchi, J., & Albertini, R. S. (2001). Surgical and nonpsychiatric medical treatment of patients with body dysmorphic disorder. *Psychosomatics, 42,* 504–510.

Phillips, K. A., & Hollander, E. (2008). Treating body dysmorphic disorder with medication: Evidence, misconceptions, and a suggested approach. *Body Image, 5,* 13–27.

Phillips, K. A., McElroy, S. L., Kecik, P. E., Jr., Pope, H. G., Jr., & Hudson, J. I. (1993). Body dysmorphic disorder: 30 cases of imagined ugliness. *American Journal of Psychiatry, 150,* 302–308.

Phillips, K. A., & Menard, W. (2009). A prospective pilot study of levetiracetam for body dysmorphic disorder. *CNS Spectrums, 14,* 252–260.

Phillips, K. A., Menard, W., & Fay, C. (2006). Gender similarities and differences in 200 individuals with body dysmorphic disorder. *Comprehensive Psychiatry, 47,* 77–87.

Phillips, K. A., Menard, W., Fay, C., & Pagano, M. E. (2005). Psychosocial functioning and quality of life in body dysmorphic disorder. *Comprehensive Psychiatry, 46,* 254–260.

Phillips, K. A., Menard, W., Fay, C., & Weisberg, R. (2005). Demographic characteristics, phenomenology, comorbidity, and family history in 200 individuals with body dysmorphic disorder. *Psychosomatics, 46,* 317–325.

Rief, W., Buhlmann, U., Wilhelm, S., Borkenhagen, A., & Braehler, E. (2006). The prevalence of body dysmorphic disorder: A population-based survey. *Psychological Medicine, 36,* 877–885.

Rosen, J. C., Reiter, J., & Orosan, P. (1995). Cognitive-behavioral body image therapy for body dysmorphic disorder. *Journal of Consulting and Clinical Psychology, 63,* 263–269.

Sarwer, D. B., Wadden, T. A., Pertschuk, M. J., & Whitaker, L. A. (1998). Body image dissatisfaction and body dysmorphic disorder in 100 cosmetic surgery patients. *Plastic Reconstructive Surgery, 101,* 1644–1649.

Sarwer, D. B., Whitaker, L. A., Pertschuk, M. J., & Wadden, T. A. (1998). Body image concerns of reconstructive surgery patients: An underrecognized problem. *Annals of Plastic Surgery, 40,* 403–407.

Veale, D., Boocok, A., Gournay, K., Dryden, W., Shah, F., ... Walburn, J. (1996). Body dysmorphic disorder: A survey of fifty cases. *British Journal of Psychiatry, 169,* 196–201.

Veale, D., Gournay, K., Dryden, W., Boocock, A., Shah, F., ... Walburn, J. (1996). Body dysmorphic disorder: A cognitive behavioural model and pilot randomised controlled trial. *Behavioral Research Therapy, 34,* 717–729.

Wilhelm, S., Phillips, K. A., Steketee, G., Didie, E., Fama, J., & Buhlmann, U. (2009). A randomized controlled trial of CBT for Body Dysmorphic Disorder. Paper presented at the 43rd Annual Association for Behavioral and Cognitive Therapies Conference.

CHAPTER 21

Research

American Psychological Association. (2000). *Diagnostic and statistical manual of mental disorders* (4th ed., Text Revision). Washington, DC: Author.

Barley, W., Buie, S., & Peterson, E., Hollingsworth, A., Griva, M., ... Bailey, B. (1993). Development of an inpatient cognitive-behavioral treatment program for borderline personality disorder. *Journal of Personality Disorders, 7*, 232–240.

Bateman, A., & Fonagy, P. (1999). Effectiveness of partial hospitalization in the treatment of borderline personality disorder: A randomized controlled trial. *American Journal of Psychiatry, 156*, 1563–1569.

Bateman, A., & Fonagy, P. (2001). Treatment of borderline personality disorder with psychoanalytically oriented partial hospitalization: An 18-month follow-up. *American Journal of Psychiatry, 158*, 36–42.

Bateman, A., & Fonagy, P. (2008). Eight year follow-up of patients treated for borderline personality disorder: Mentalization-based treatment versus treatment as usual. *American Journal of Psychiatry, 165*, 631–638.

Bateman, A., & Fonagy, P. (2009). Randomized controlled trial of outpatient mentalization-based treatment versus structured management for borderline personality disorder. *American Journal of Psychiatry, 166*, 1355–1364.

Blum, N., Pfohl, B., St. John, D., Monahan, P., & Black, D. (2002). STEPPS: A cognitive-behavioral systems-based group treatment for outpatients with borderline personality disorder—a preliminary report. *Comprehensive Psychiatry, 43*, 301–310.

Blum, N., St. John, D., Pfohl, S., Stuart, S., McCormick, B., ... Black, D. (2008). STEPPS: Systems training for emotional predictability and problem solving (STEPPS) for outpatients with borderline personality disorder: A randomized controlled trial and 1-year follow-up. *Comprehensive Psychiatry, 1*, 1–11.

Bogenschutz, M., & Nurnberg, H. (2004). Olanzapine versus placebo in the treatment of borderline personality disorder. *Journal of Clinical Psychiatry, 65*, 104–109.

Bohus, M., Haaf, B., Simms, T., Limberger, M., Schmahl, C., ... Linehan, M. (2004). Effectiveness of inpatient dialectical behavioral therapy for borderline personality disorder: A controlled trial. *Behaviour Research and Therapy, 42*, 487–499.

Bohus, M., Haaf, B., Stiglmayr, C., Pohl, U., Böhme, R., & Linehan, M. (2000). Evaluation of inpatient dialectical behavioral therapy for borderline personality disorder: A prospective study. *Behaviour Research and Therapy, 38*, 875–887.

Bradley, R., Zittel Conklin, C., & Westen, D. (2005). The borderline personality diagnosis in adolescents: Gender differences and subtypes. *Journal of Child Psychology and Psychiatry and Allied Disciplines, 46*(9), 1006–1019.

Chen, E., Matthews, L., & Allen, C., Kuo, J., & Linehan M. (2008). Dialectical behavior therapy for clients with binge-eating disorder or bulimia nervosa and borderline personality disorder. *International Journal of Eating Disorders, 41*(6), 505–512.

Chen, K., Banducci, A., Guller, L., Macatee, R., & Lavelle, A. (In Press). An examination of mental health comorbidities within a residential substance use treatment program. *Drug and Alcohol Dependence.*

Clarkin, J., Levy, K., Lenzenweger, M., & Kernberg, O. (2007). Evaluating three treatments for borderline personality disorder: A multiwave study. *American Journal of Psychiatry, 164*, 922–928.

Comtois, K., Elwood, L., & Holdcraft, L., Smith, W., & Simpson, T. (2007). Effectiveness of dialectical behavior therapy in a community mental health center. *Cognitive and Behavioral Practice, 14*, 406–414.

Cottraux, J., Note, I., & Boutitie, F., Milliery, M., Genouihlac, V., ... Gueyffier, F. (2009). Cognitive therapy versus Rogerian supportive therapy in borderline personality disorder: Two-year follow-up of a controlled pilot study. *Psychotherapy and Psychosomatics, 78*, 307–316.

Davidson, K., Norrie, J., & Tyrer, P., Gumley, A., Tata, P., ... Palmer, S. (2006). The effectiveness of cognitive behavior therapy for borderline personality disorder: Results from the borderline personality disorder study of cognitive therapy (BOSCOT) trial. *Journal of Personality Disorders, 20*, 450–465.

De la Fuente, J., & Lotstra, F. (1994). A trial of carbamazepine in borderline personality disorder. *European Neuropsychopharmacology, 4*, 479–486.

Dimeff, L., & Linehan, M. (2008). Dialectical behavior therapy for substance abusers. *Addiction Science & Clinical Practice, 4*, 39–47.

Doering, S., Horz, S., Rentrop, M., Fischer-Kern, M., Schuster, P., ... Buchheim, P. (2010). Transference-focused psychotherapy v. treatment by community psychotherapists for borderline personality disorder: Randomized controlled trial. *British Journal of Psychiatry, 196*, 389–395.

EliLilly. (2007a). Efficacy and safety of olanzapine in patients with borderline personality disorder: A randomized, flexible-dose, double-blind comparison with placebo (summary 6253, Clinical Study Summary: Study F1D-MC-HGKK).

EliLilly. (2007b). Efficacy and safety of olanzapine in patients with borderline personality disorder: A random-ized, flexible-dose, double-blind comparison with placebo (Summary ID 6257. Clinical Study Summary: Study F1D-MC-HGKL).

Farrell, J., Shaw, I., & Webber, M. (2009). A schema-focused approach to group psychotherapy for outpa-tients with borderline personality disorder: A randomized controlled trial. *Journal of Behavior Therapy and Experimental Psychiatry, 40*, 317–328.

Frankenburg, F., & Zanarini, M. (2002). Divalproex sodium treatment of women with borderline personal-ity disorder and bipolar II disorder: A double-blind placebo-controlled pilot study. *Journal of Clinical Psychiatry, 63*, 442–446.

Giesen-Bloo, J., van Dyck, R., & Spinhoven, P., et al. (2006). Outpatient psychotherapy for borderline per-sonality disorder: Randomized trial of schema-focused therapy vs transference-focused psychotherapy. *Archives of General Psychiatry, 63*, 649–658.

Goldberg, S., Schulz, S., Schulz, P., Resnick, R., Hamer, R., & Friedel, R. (1986). Borderline and schizotypal personality disorders treated with low-dose thiothixene vs placebo. *Archives of General Psychiatry, 43*, 680–686.

Golomb, M., Fava, M., Abraham, M., & Rosenbaum, J. F. (1995). Gender differences in personality disorders. *American Journal of Psychiatry, 152*, 579–582.

Grant, B., Chou, S., Goldstein, R., Huang, B., & Stinson, F., … Ruan, W. (2008). Prevalence, correlates, disability and comorbidity of DSM-IV borderline personality disorder: Results from the wave 2 national epidemio-logic survey on alcohol and related conditions. *Journal of Clinical Psychiatry, 69*, 533–545.

Gratz, K., & Gunderson, J. (2006). Preliminary data on acceptance-based emotion regulation group interven-tion for deliberate self-harm among women with borderline personality disorder. *Behavior Therapy, 37*, 25–35.

Grilo, C. M., Becker, D. F., Fehon, D. C., Walker, M. L., Edell, W. S., & McGlashan, T. H. (1996). Gender differ-ences in personality disorders in psychiatrically hospitalized adolescents. *American Journal of Psychiatry, 153*, 1089–1091.

Hallahan, B., Hibbeln, J., Davis, J., & Garland, M. (2007). Omega-3 fatty acid supplementation in patients with recurrent self-harm: Single-centre double-blind randomized controlled trial. *British Journal of Psychiatry, 190*, 118–122.

Harned, M., & Linehan, M. (2008). Integrating dialectical behavior therapy and prolonged exposure to treat co-occurring borderline personality disorder and PTSD: Two case studies. *Cognitive and Behavioral Practice, 15*, 263–276.

Hollander, E., Allen, A., Lopez, R., Bienstock, C., Grossman, R., … Stein, D. (2001). A preliminary double-blind, placebo-controlled trial of divalproex sodium in borderline personality disorder. *Journal of Clinical Psychiatry, 62*, 199–203.

Ingenhoven, T., & Duivenvoorden, H. (2011). Differential effectiveness of antipsychotics in borderline person-ality disorder: Meta-analysis of placebo-controlled randomized clinical trials on symptomatic outcomes. *Journal of Clinical Psychopharmacology, 31*, 489–496.

Johnson, D. M., Shea, M. T., Yen, S., Battle, C. L., Zlotnick, C., … Zanarini, M. C. (2003). Gender differences in borderline personality disorder: Findings from the collaborative longitudinal personality disorders study. *Comprehensive Psychiatry, 44*, 284–292.

Koons, C., Robins, C., & Tweed, J., Lynch, T., Gonzalez, A., … Bastian, L. (2001). Efficacy of dialectical behavior therapy in women veterans with borderline personality disorder. *Behavior Therapy, 32*, 371–390.

Leone, N. (1982). Response of borderline patients to loxapine and chlorpromazine. *Journal of Clinical Psychiatry, 43*, 148–150.

Levy, K. N., Becker, D. F., Grilo, C. M., Mattanah, J. J. F, Garnet, K. E., … McGlashan, T. H. (1999). Concurrent and predictive validity of the personality disorder diagnosis in adolescent inpatients. *American Journal of Psychiatry, 156*, 1522–1528.

Lieb, K., Vollm, B., Rucker, G., Timmer, A., & Stoffers, J. (2010). Pharmacotherapy for borderline personality disorder: Cochrane systematic review for randomized trials. *British Journal of Psychiatry, 196*, 4–12.

Linehan, M. (1993). *Cognitive behavioral treatment of borderline personality disorder*. New York, NY: Guilford Press.

Linehan, M., Armstrong, H., Suarez, A., Allmon, D., & Heard, H. (1991). Cognitive-behavioral treatment of chronically parasuicidal borderline patients. *Archives of General Psychiatry, 48*, 1060–1064.

Linehan, M., Comtois, K., Murray, A., Brown, M., Gallop, R., … Lindenboim, N. (2006). Two-year randomized controlled trial and follow-up of dialectical behavior therapy vs. therapy by experts for suicidal behaviors and borderline personality disorder. *Archives of General Psychiatry, 63*, 757–766.

Linehan, M., Dimeff, L., Reynolds, S., Comtois, K., & Welch, S. (2002). Dialectical behavior therapy versus comprehensive validation therapy plus 12-step for the treatment of opioid dependent women meeting criteria for borderline personality disorder. *Drug and Alcohol Dependence, 67*, 13–26.

Linehan, M., Heard, H., & Armstrong, H. (1993). Naturalistic follow-up of a behavioral treatment for chronically parasuicidal borderline patients. *Archives of General Psychiatry, 50,* 971–974.

Linehan, M., McDavid, J., Brown, M., Sayrs, J., & Gallop, R. (2008). Olanzapine plus dialectical behavior therapy for women with high irritability who meet criteria for borderline personality disorder: A double-blind, placebo-controlled pilot study. *Journal of Clinical Psychiatry, 69,* 999–1005.

Linehan, M. M., Schmidt, H., Dimeff, L., Craft, J., Kanter, J., & Comtois, K. (1999). Dialectical behavior therapy for patients with borderline personality disorder and drug dependence. *American Journal on Addictions, 8,* 279–292.

Linehan, M., Tutek, D., Heard, H., & Armstrong, H. (1994). Interpersonal outcome of cognitive behavioral treatment for chronically suicidal borderline patients. *American Journal of Psychiatry, 151,* 1771–1776.

Loew, T., Nickel, M., Muehlbacher, M., Kaplan, P., Nickel, C., ... Egger, C. (2006). Topiramate treatment for women with borderline personality disorder: A double-blind, placebo-controlled study. *Journal of Clinical Psychopharmacology, 26,* 61–66.

Mattanah, J. J. F., Becker, D. F., Levy, K. N., Edell, W. S. & McGlashan, T. H. (1995). Diagnostic stability in adolescents followed up 2 years after hospitalization. *American Journal of Psychiatry, 152,* 889–894.

McMain, S., Links, S., Gnam, W., Guimond, T., Cardish, R., ... Streiner, D. (2009). A randomized trial of dialectical behavior therapy versus general psychiatric management for borderline personality disorder. *American Journal of Psychiatry, 166,* 1365–1375.

Montgomery, D., Roy, D., & Montgomery, S. (1981). Mianserin in the prophylaxis of suicidal behaviour: A double-blind placebo controlled trial. 10th International Congress of Suicide Prevention and Crisis Intervention (pp. 786–790). Pergamon.

Montgomery, S., Montgomery, D., Janyanthi, R., Roy, D., Shaw, P., & McAuley, R. (1979). Maintenance therapy in repeat suicidal behaviour: A placebo controlled trial. 10th International Congress of Suicide Prevention and Crisis Intervention: International Association for Suicide Prevention.

Nickel, M., Muehlbacher, M., Nickel, C., Kettler, C., Pedrosa, G., ... Kaplan, P. (2006b). Aripiprazole in the treatment of patients with borderline personality disorder: A double-blind, placebo-controlled study. *British Journal of Psychiatry, 163,* 833–838.

Nickel, M., Nickel, C., Mitterlehner, F., Tritt, K., Lahmann, C., ... Loew, T. (2004). Topiramate treatment of aggression in female borderline personality disorder patients: A double-blind, placebo-controlled study. *Journal of Clinical Psychiatry, 65,* 1515–1509.

Nickel, M. K., Nickel, C., Kaplan, P., Lahmann, C., Muhlbacher, M., ... Loew, T. (2005). Treatment of aggression with topiramate in male borderline patients: A double-blind, placebo-controlled study. *Biological Psychiatry, 57,* 495–499.

Palmer, R., Birchall, H., Damani, S., Gatward, N., McGrain, L., & Parker, L. (2003). A dialectical behavior therapy program for people with an eating disorder and borderline personality disorder: Description and outcome. *International Journal of Eating Disorders, 33,* 281.

Paris, J. (2005). The development of impulsivity and suicidality in borderline personality disorder. *Development and Psychopathology, 17,* 1091–1104.

Pascual, J., Soler, J., Puigdemont, D., Perez-Egea, R., Tiana, T., ...Perez, V. (2008). Ziprasidone in the treatment of borderline personality disorder: A doubleblind, placebo-controlled, randomized study. *Journal of Clinical Psychiatry, 69,* 603–608.

Rinne, T., van den Brink, W., Wouter, L., & van Dyck, R. (2002). SSRI treatment of borderline personality disorder: A randomized, placebo-controlled clinical trial for female patients with borderline personality disorder. *American Journal of Psychiatry, 159,* 2048–2054.

Safer, D., Telch, C. F., & Agras, W. (2001). Dialectical behavior therapy for bulimia nervosa. *American Journal of Psychiatry, 158,* 632–634.

Salzman, C., Wolfson, A., Schatzberg, A., Looper, J., Henke, R., ... Miyawaki, E. (1995). Effect of fluoxetine on anger in symptomatic volunteers with borderline personality disorder. *Journal of Clinical Psychopharmacology, 15,* 23–29.

Shafti, S., & Shahveisi, B. (2011). Olanzapine versus haloperidol in the management of borderline personality disorder: A randomized double-blind trial. *Journal of Clinical Psychopharmacology, 30,* 44–47.

Simpson, E., Yen, S., Costello, E., Rosen, K., Begin, A., ... Pearlstein, T. (2004). Combined dialectical behavior therapy and fluoxetine in the treatment of borderline personality disorder. *Journal of Clinical Psychiatry, 65,* 379–385.

Skodol, A., Oldham, J., Hyler, S. E., Stein, D. J., Hollander, E., ... Lopez, A. E. (1995). Patterns of anxiety and personality disorder comorbidity. *Journal of Psychiatric Research, 29,* 361–374.

Skodol, A. E., Gunderson, J. G., Pfohl, B., Widiger, T. A., Livesley, W. J., & Siever, L. J. (2002). The borderline diagnosis I: Psychopathology comorbidity, and personality structure. *Biological Psychiatry, 51,* 936–950.

Skodol, M., Johnson, J., Cohen, P., Sneed, J., & Crawford, T. (2007). Personality disorder and impaired functioning from adolescence to adulthood. *British Journal of Psychiatry, 190,* 415–420.

Soler, J., Pascual, J., Campins, J., Barrachina, J., Puigdemont, D., ... Perez, V. (2005). Double-blind, placebo-controlled study of dialectical behavior therapy plus olanzapine for borderline personality disorder. *American Journal of Psychiatry, 162*, 1221–1224.

Soloff, P., Cornelius, J., George, A., Nathan, S., Perel, J., & Ulrich, R. (1993). Efficacy of phenelzine and haloperidol in borderline personality disorder. *Archives of General Psychiatry, 50*, 377–385.

Soloff, P., George, A., Nathan, S., Schulz, P., Cornelius, J., ... Perel, J. (1989). Amitriptyline versus haloperidol in borderlines: Final outcomes and predictors of response. *Journal of Clinical Psychopharmacology, 9*, 238–246.

Telch, C., Agras, W., & Linehan, M. (2001). Dialectical behavior therapy for binge eating disorder. *Journal of Consulting and Clinical Psychology, 69*, 1061–1065.

Torgersen, S., Kringlen, E., & Cramer, V. (2001). The prevalence of personality disorders in a community sample. *Archives of General Psychiatry, 58*, 590–596.

Tritt, K., Nickel, C., Lahmann, C., Leiberich, P., Rother, W., ... Nickel, M. (2005). Lamotrigine treatment of aggression in female borderline-patients: A randomized, double-blind, placebo-controlled study. *Journal of Psychopharmacology, 19*, 287–291.

Turner, R. M. (2000). Naturalistic evaluation of dialectical behavior therapy-oriented treatment for borderline personality disorder. *Cognitive Behavioral Practice, 7*, 413–419.

van den Bosch, L., Koeter, M., Stijnen, T., Verheul, R., & van den Brink, W. (2005). Sustained efficacy of dialectical behavior therapy for borderline personality disorder. *Behaviour Research and Therapy, 43*, 1231–1241.

van den Bosch, L., Verheul, R., Schippers, G., & van den brink, W. (2002). Dialectical behavior therapy of borderline patients with and without substance use problems: Implementation and long-term effects. *Addictive Behaviors, 27*, 911–923.

Verheul, R., van den Bosch, L., Koeter, M., De Ridder, M. A., Stijnen, T., & Van Den Brink, W. (2003). Dialectical behaviour therapy for women with borderline personality disorder: Twelve month, randomized clinical trial in The Netherlands. *British Journal of Psychiatry, 182*, 135–140.

Weinberg, I., Gunderson, J., & Hennen, J., & Cutter, C. J., Jr. (2006). Manual assisted cognitive treatment for deliberate self-harm in borderline personality disorder. *Journal of Personality Disorders, 20*, 482–492.

Widiger, T., & Weissman, M. (1991). Epidemiology of borderline personality disorder. *Psychiatric Services, 42*, 1015–1021.

Zanarini, M., Frankenburg, F., Khera, G., & Bleichmar, J. (2001). Treatment histories of borderline inpatients. *Comprehensive Psychiatry, 42*, 144–150.

Zanarini, M., Frankenburg, F., & Parachini, E. (2004). A preliminary, randomized trial of fluoxetine, olanzapine, and the olanzapine-fluoxetine combination in women with borderline personality disorder. *Journal of Clinical Psychiatry, 65*, 903–907.

CHAPTER 22

Research

American Psychological Association. (2003). Guidelines on multicultural education, training, research, practice and organizational change for psychologists. *American Psychologist, 58*, 377–402.

Cooper, L. A., Gonzales, J. J., Gallo, J. J., Rost, K. M., Meredith, L. S., ... Ford, D. E. (2003). The acceptability of treatment for depression among African-American, Hispanic, and white primary care patients. *Medical Care, 41*(4), 479–489.

DeRubeis, R. J., Hollon, S. D., Amsterdam J. D., Shelton, R. C., Young, P. R., ... Gallop, R. (2005). Cognitive therapy vs. medications in the treatment of moderate to severe depression. *Archives of General Psychiatry, 62*, 409–416.

Dimidjian, S., Hollon, S. D., Dobson, K. S., Schmaling, K. B., Kohlenberg, R. J., ... Jacobson, N. S. (2006). Randomized trial of behavioral activation, cognitive therapy, and antidepressant medication in the acute treatment of major depression. *Journal of Consulting and Clinical Psychology, 74*, 658–670.

George, M. S., Rush, A. J., Marangell, L. B., Sackeim, H. A., Brannan, S. K., ... Goodnick, P. (2005). A one-year comparison of vagus nerve stimulation with treatment as usual for treatment-resistant depression. *Biological Psychiatry, 58*(5), 364–373.

Gitlan, M. J. (2009). Pharmacotherapy and other somatic treatments for depression. In I. H. Gotlib & C. L. Hammen (Eds.), *Handbook of depression* (2nd ed.). New York, NY: Guilford Press.

Hollon, S. D., & Dimidjian, S. (2009). Cognitive and behavioral treatment of depression. In I. H. Gotlib & C. L. Hammen (Eds.), *Handbook of depression* (2nd ed.). New York, NY: Guilford Press.

Imel, Z. E., Malterer, M. B., McKay, K. M., & Wompold, B. E. (2008). A meta-analysis of psychotherapy and medication in unipolar depression and dysthymia. *Journal of Affective Disorders, 110*(3), 197–206.

Kessler, R. C., Berglund, P., Demler, O., Jin, R., Koretz, D., ... Wang, P. S. (2003). The epidemiology of major depressive disorder: Results from the National Comorbidity Survey Replication (NCS-R). *Journal of the American Medical Association, 289*, 3095–3105.

Kessler, R. C., Berglund, P., Demler, O., Jin, R., Merikangas, K. R., & Walters, E. E. (2005). Lifetime prevalence and age-of-onset distributions of DSM-IV disorders in the National Comorbidity Survey Replication. *Archives of General Psychiatry, 62*, 593–602.

Kessler, R. C., McGonagle, K. A., Zhao, S., Nelson, C. B., Hughes, M., ... Kendler, K. S. (1994). Lifetime and 12-month prevalence of DSM-III-R psychiatric disorders in the United States: Results from the National Comorbidity Survey. *Archives of General Psychiatry, 51*, 8–19.

Kessler, R. C., Mickelson, K. D., Barber, C., & Wang, P. (2001). The association between chronic medical conditions and work impairment. In A. S. Rossi (Ed.), *Caring and doing for others: Social responsibility in the domains of family, work, and community* (pp. 403–426). Chicago, IL: University of Chicago Press.

Lawrence, V., Banerjee, S., Bhugra, D., Sangha, K. J., Turner, S., & Murray, J. (2006). Coping with depression in later life: A qualitative study of help-seeking in three ethnic groups. *Psychological Medicine, 36*, 1375–1383.

Linde, K., Berner, M., Egger, M., & Mulrow, C. (2005). St John's wort for depression: Meta-analysis of randomized controlled trials. *British Journal of Psychiatry, 18*, 99–107.

Merikangas, K. R., & Angst, J. (1995). The challenge of depressive disorders in adolescence. In M. Rutter (Ed.), *Psychosocial disturbances in young people: Challenges for prevention* (pp. 131–165). Cambridge, UK: Cambridge University Press.

Murray, C. J. L., & Lopez, A. D. (1997). Global mortality, disability, and the contribution of risk factors: Global Burden of Disease Study. *Lancet, 349*, 1436–1442.

U.S. Department of Health Human Services. (2001). *Mental health: Culture, race, and ethnicity. A supplement to mental health: A report of the surgeon general*. Rockville, MD: U.S. Department of Health and Human Services.

Wells, K. B., Steward, A., Hays, R. D., Burnam, A., Rogers, W., ... Ware, J. (1989). The functioning and well-being of depressed patients: Results from the medical outcomes study. *Journal of the American Medical Association, 262*, 914–919.

Clinician Application

Barlow, D. H. (2008). *Clinical handbook of psychological disorders, Fourth Edition: A step by step treatment manual*. New York, NY: Guilford

Beck, A. T., Rush, A. J., Shaw, B. F., & Emory, G. (1979). *Cognitive therapy of depression*. New York, NY: Guilford.

Bower, S., & Bower, G. (1991). *Asserting yourself*. Cambridge, MA: Perseus Books.

Keisler, D. J. (1982). Confronting the client-therapist relationship in psychotherapy. In J. C. Anchin & D. J. Keisler (Eds.), *Handbook of interpersonal psychotherapy* (pp. 274–295). Elmsford, NY: Pergamon Press.

Ramirez-Basco, M., Wright, J. H., & Thase, M. E. (2006). *Learning cognitive therapy: An illustrated guide*. Arlington, VA: American Psychiatric Publishing Incorporated.

Webb, C. A., DeRubeis, R. J., Amsterdam, J. D., Shelton, R. C., Hollon, S. D., & Dimidjian, S. (2011). Two aspects of the therapeutic alliance: Differential relations with depressive symptom change. *Journal of Consulting and Clinical Psychology, 79*, 279–283. doi: 10.1037/a0023252

CHAPTER 23

Research

Baars, E. W., van der Hart, O., Nijuenhuis, E. R. S., Chu, J. A., Glas, G., & Draijer, N. (2011). Predicting stabilizing treatment outcomes for complex posttraumatic stress disorder and dissociative identity disorder: An expertise-based prognostic model. *Journal of Trauma & Dissociation, 12*, 67–87.

Brand, B. L., Lanius, R. Loewenstein, R. J., Vermetten, E., & Spiegel, D. (2012). Where are we going? An update on assessment, treatment, and neurobiological research in dissociative disorders as we move towards the DSM-5. *Journal of Trauma & Dissociation, 13*, 9–31. doi: 10.1080/15299732.2011.620687

Brand, B. L., Myrick, A. C., Loewenstein, R. J., Classen, C., Lanius, R...Putnam, F. W. (2012). A survey of practices and recommended treatment interventions among expert therapists treating patients with dissociative identity disorder and dissociative disorder not otherwise specified. *Psychological Trauma: Theory, Research, Practice, and Policy, 4*, 490–500.

Coons, P. M, Bowman, E. S., & Milstein, V. (1988). Multiple personality disorder: A clinical investigation of 50 cases. *Journal of Nervous and Mental Disease, 176*, 519–527.

Dell, P. F. (2009). The long struggle to diagnose multiple personality disorder (MPD): MPD. In P. F. Dell & J. A. O'Neil (Eds.), *Dissociation and the dissociative disorders: DSM-V and beyond* (pp. 383–402). New York, NY: Routledge.

Kluft, R. P. (2009). A clinician's understanding of dissociation: Fragments of an acquaintance. In P. F. Dell & J. A. O'Neil (Eds.), *Dissociation and the dissociative disorders: DSM-V and beyond* (pp. 599–624). New York, NY: Routledge.

Putnam, F. W. (1997). *Dissociation in children and adolescents: A developmental perspective.* New York, NY: Guilford Press.

Steele, K., Boon, S., & van der Hart, O. (2011). *Coping with trauma-related dissociation: Skills training for patients and therapists.* New York, NY: Norton.

CHAPTER 24

Research

American Psychiatric Association. (2013). *Diagnostic and statistical manual of mental health disorders: DSM-5* (5th ed.). Washington, DC: American Psychiatric Publishing.

Blaszczynski, A., & Nower, L. (2002). A pathways model of problem and pathological gambling. *Addiction, 97,* 487–499.

Bowden-Jones, H., & Smith, N. (2012). The medical management of problem gamblers. [Editorial]. *British Medical Journal, 344,* e1559. doi: 10.1136/bmj.e1559

Chou, K. L., & Afifi, T. O. (2011). Disordered (pathologic or problem) gambling and axis I psychiatric disorders: Results from the National Epidemiologic Survey on Alcohol and Related Conditions. *American Journal of Epidemiology, 173,* 1289–1297.

Faregh, N., & Leth-Steensen, C. (2009). Reflections on the voluntary self-exclusion of gamblers and the lawsuits against Ontario Lottery and Gaming Corporation. *Journal of Gambling Studies, 25,* 131–138.

Ferguson, C. J., Coulson, M., & Barnett, J. (2011). A meta-analysis of pathological gaming prevalence and comorbidity with mental health, academic and social problems. *Journal of Psychiatric Research, 45,* 1573–1578.

Ferris, J., & Wynne, H. (2001). *The Canadian Problem Gambling Index.* Ottawa, Canada: Canadian Centre on Substance Abuse.

Jackson, A. C., Wynne, H., Dowling, N. A., Tomnay, J., & Thomas, S. A. (2009). Using the CPGI to determine Problem Gambling prevalence in Australia: Measurement issues. *International Journal of Mental Health Addiction, 8,* 570–582.

Lorains, F. K., Cowlishaw, S., & Thomas, S. A. (2011). Prevalence of comorbid disorders in problem and pathological gambling: Systematic review and meta-analysis of population surveys. *Addiction, 106,* 490–498. doi: 10.1111/j.1360-0443.2010.03300.x

Papineau, E., & Leblond, J. (2011). The stakes of online gambling in Canada: A public health analysis. *Canadian Journal of Public Health, 102,* 417–420.

Problem Gambling Research and Treatment Centre. (2011). *Guideline for screening, assessment and treatment in problem gambling.* Clayton, Australia: Monash University.

Raisamo, S., Halme, J., Murto, A., & Lintonen, T. (2013). Gambling-related harms among adolescents: A population-based study. *Journal of Gambling Studies, 29,* 151–159. doi: 10.1007/s10899-012-9298-9

Shaffer, H. J., & Korn, D. A. (2002). Gambling and related mental disorders: A public health analysis. *Annual Review of Public Health, 23,* 171–212.

Slutske, W. S. (2006). Natural recovery and treatment-seeking in pathological gambling: Results of two U.S. national surveys. *American Journal of Psychiatry, 163,* 297–302.

Thomas, S. A., Merkouris, S. S., Radermacher, H. L., Dowling, N. A., Misso, M. L., ... Jackson, A. C. (2011). Australian guideline for treatment of problem gambling: An abridged outline. *Medical Journal of Australia, 195,* 664–665.

Thomas, S. A., Piterman, L., & Jackson, A. C. (2008). Problem gambling: What do general practitioners need to know and do about it? *Medical Journal of Australia, 189,* 135–136.

Volberg, R. A. (1994). The prevalence and demographics of pathological gamblers: Implications for public health. *American Journal of Public Health, 84,* 237–241.

Clinician Application

Burns, D. (1980). *Feeling good: The new mood therapy.* New York, NY: Harper Collins.

McKay, M., & Fanning, P. (1992). *Self-esteem: A proven program of cognitive techniques for assessing, improving, and maintaining your self-esteem.* Oakland, CA: New Harbinger.

CHAPTER 25

Research

American Psychiatric Association. (2000). *Diagnostic and statistical manual of mental disorders* (4th ed.). Washington, DC: American Psychiatric Association.

Angst, J., Gamma, A., Ajdacic, V., Rossler, W., & Regier, D. A. (2010). *Diagnostic issues in depression and generalized anxiety disorder: Refining the research agenda for DSM-V*. Washington, DC: American Psychiatric Association.

Asmal, L., & Stein, D. J. (2009). Anxiety and culture. In M. Anthony & M. Stein (Eds.), *Oxford handbook of anxiety and related disorders* (pp. 657–664). New York, NY: Oxford University Press.

Barrera, T. L., & Norton, P. J. (2009). Quality of life impairment in generalized anxiety disorder, social phobia, and panic disorder. *Journal of Anxiety Disorders, 23*(8), 1086–1090. doi: 10.1016/j.janxdis.2009.07.011

Borkovec, T. D., & Ruscio, A. M. (2001). Psychotherapy for generalized anxiety disorder. *Journal of Clinical Psychiatry, 62*(Suppl. 11), 37–45.

Borkovec, T. D., & Sharpless, B. (2004). Generalized anxiety disorder: Bringing cognitive-behavioral therapy into the valued present. In S. C. Hayes, V. M. Follette, & M. M. Linehan (Eds.), *Mindfulness and acceptance: Expanding the cognitive-behavioral tradition* (pp. 209–242). New York, NY: Guilford Press.

Campbell-Sills, L., & Brown, T. A. (2010). Generalized anxiety disorder. In M. M. Antony & D. H. Barlow (Eds.), *Handbook of assessment and treatment planning for psychological disorders* (2nd ed., pp. 224–266). New York, NY: Guilford Press.

Fisher, P. L., & Wells, A. (2011). Conceptual models of generalized anxiety disorder. *Psychiatric Annals, 41*(2), 127–132.

Francis, K., & Dugas, M. J. (2004). Assessing positive beliefs about worry: Validation of a structured interview. *Personality and Individual Differences, 37*(2), 405–415. doi: 10.1016/j.paid.2003.09.012

Helsley, J. D. (2008). Generalized anxiety disorder. In J. R. Vanin & J. D. Helsley (Eds.), *Anxiety disorders: A pocket guide for primary care.*(pp. 183–193). Totowa, NJ: Humana Press. doi: 10.1007/978-1-59745-263-2_12

Hettema, J. M. (2008). The nosologic relationship between generalized anxiety disorder and major depression. *Depression and Anxiety, 25*(4), 300–316. doi: 10.1002/da.20491

Hoyer, J. R., van der Heiden, C., & Portman, M. E. (2011). Psychotherapy for generalized anxiety disorder. *Psychiatric Annals, 41*(2), 87–94.

Katzman, M. A. (2009). Current considerations in the treatment of generalized anxiety disorder. *CNS Drugs, 23*(2), 103–120. doi: 10.2165/00023210-200923020-00002

Kessler, R. C., Berglund, P., Demler, O., Jin, R., Merikangas, K. R., & Walters, E. E. (2005). Lifetime prevalence and age-of-onset distributions of *DSM-IV* disorders in the National Comorbidity Survey Replication. *Archives of General Psychiatry, 62*(6), 593–602. doi: 10.1001/archpsyc.62.6.593

Kessler, R. C., Chiu, W. T., Demler, O., Merikangas, K. R., & Walters, E. E. (2005). Prevalence, severity, and comorbidity of 12-month *DSM-IV* disorders in the National Comorbidity Survey Replication. *Archives of General Psychiatry, 62*(6), 617–627. doi: 10.1001/archpsyc.62.6.617

Kessler, R. C., Gruber, M., Hettema, J. M., Hwang, I., Sampson, N., … Regier, D. A. (2010). Major depression and generalized anxiety disorder in the National Comorbidity Survey follow-up survey. In D. Goldberg, K. Kendler, P. Sirovatka, & D. Regier (Eds.), *Diagnostic issues in depression and generalized anxiety disorder: Refining the research agenda for DSM-V* (pp. 139–170). Arlington, VA: American Psychiatric Publishing.

Lewis-Fernandez, R., Hinton, D. E., Laria, A. J., Patterson, E. H., Hofmann, S. G., … Liao, B. (2010). Culture and the anxiety disorders: Recommendations for *DSM-V. Depression and Anxiety, 27*(2), 212–229. doi: 10.1002/da.20647

Newman, M. G., Castonguay, L. G., Borkovec, T. D., Fisher, A. J., Boswell, J. F., … Nordberg, S. S. (2011). A randomized controlled trial of cognitive-behavioral therapy for generalized anxiety disorder with integrated techniques from emotion-focused and interpersonal therapies. *Journal of Consulting and Clinical Psychology, 79*(2), 171–181. doi: 10.1037/a0022489

Newman, M. G., Castonguay, L. G., Borkovec, T. D., Fisher, A. J., & Nordberg, S. S. (2008). An open trial of integrative therapy for generalized anxiety disorder. *Psychotherapy, 45*(2), 135–147. doi: 10.1037/0033-3204.45.2.135

Newman, M. G., & Llera, S. J. (2011). A novel theory of experiential avoidance in generalized anxiety disorder: A review and synthesis of research supporting a contrast avoidance model of worry. *Clinical Psychology Review, 31*(3), 371–382. doi: 10.1016/j.cpr.2011.01.008

Newman, M. G., Przeworski, A., Fisher, A. J., & Borkovec, T. D. (2010). Diagnostic comorbidity in adults with generalized anxiety disorder: impact of comorbidity on psychotherapy outcome and impact of psychotherapy on comorbid diagnoses. *Behavior Therapy, 41*(1), 59–72. doi: 10.1016/j.beth.2008.12.005

Portman, M. E., Starcevic, V., & Beck, A. T. (2011). Challenges in assessment and diagnosis of generalized anxiety disorder. *Psychiatric Annals, 41*(2), 79–85.

Provencher, M. D., Ladouceur, R., & Dugas, M. J. (2006). Comorbidity in generalized anxiety disorder: Prevalence and course after cognitive-behavioural therapy. *Canadian Journal of Psychiatry, 51*(2), 91–99.

Przeworski, A., Newman, M. G., Pincus, A. L., Kasoff, M. B., Yamasaki, A. S., … Berlin, K. S. (2011). Interpersonal pathoplasticity in individuals with generalized anxiety disorder. *Journal of Abnormal Psychology, 120*(2), 286–298. doi: 10.1037/a0023334

Rapgay, L., Bystritsky, A., Dafter, R., & Spearman, M. (2011). New strategies for combining mindfulness with integrative cognitive behavioral therapy for the treatment of generalized anxiety disorder. *Journal of Rational-Emotive & Cognitive-Behavior Therapy, 29*(2), 92–119. doi: 10.1007/s10942-009-0095-z

Torpy, J. M., Burke, A. E., & Golub, R. M. (2011). JAMA patient page. Generalized anxiety disorder. *JAMA, 305*(5), 522. doi: 10.1001/jama.305.5.522

Treanor, M., Erisman, S. M., Salters-Pedneault, K., Roemer, L., & Orsillo, S. M. (2011). Acceptance-based behavioral therapy for GAD: Effects on outcomes from three theoretical models. *Depression and Anxiety, 28*(2), 127–136. doi: 10.1002/da.20766

Turk, C. L., & Mennin, D. S. (2011). Phenomenology of generalized anxiety disorder. *Psychiatric Annals, 41*(2), 72–78.

Vesga-Lopez, O., Schneier, F. R., Wang, S., Heimberg, R. G., Liu, S. M., … Blanco, C. (2008). Gender differences in generalized anxiety disorder: Results from the national epidemiologic survey on alcohol and related conditions (NESARC). *Journal of Clinical Psychiatry, 69*, 1606–1616.

Weisberg, R. B. (2009). Overview of generalized anxiety disorder: Epidemiology, presentation, and course. *Journal of Clinical Psychiatry, 70*(Suppl. 2), 4–9.

Weisberg, R. B., Beard, C., Pagano, M. E., Maki, K. M., Culpepper, L., & Keller, M. B. (2010). Impairment and functioning in a sample of primary care patients with generalized anxiety disorder: Results from the primary care anxiety project. *Primary Care Companion Journal of Clinical Psychiatry, 12*(5). doi: 10.4088/PCC.09m00890blu

Clinician Application

Benjamin, L. S. (draft). *Interpersonal reconstructive therapy for anger, anxiety, depression and more: It's about broken hearts, not broken brains.* Washington, DC: American Psychological Association.

Kabat-Zinn, J. K. (1990). *Full catastrophe living.* New York, NY: Delacorte.

Miller, W. R., & Rollnick, S. (2012). *Motivational interviewing, Third Edition: Helping people change.* New York, NY: Guilford Press.

Molnar, C. (2010, June). Mindfulness training changes the brain and builds neuropsychological resources. *Pennsylvania Psychologist, 8*, 8, 11.

Newman, M. G., Castonguay, L. G., Borkovec, T. D., & Molnar, C. (2004). Integrative psychotherapy. In R. G. Heimberg, C. L. Turk, & D. S. Mennin (Eds.), *Generalized anxiety disorder: Advances in researchand practice* (pp. 320–350). New York, NY: Guilford Press.

Nolen-Hoeksema, S., Wisco, B., & Lyubomirsky, S. (2008). Rethinking rumination. *Perspectives on Psychological Science, 3*, 400–424.

Segal, Z. V., Williams, J. M. G., & Teasdale, J. D. (2012). *Mindfulness-based cognitive therapy for depression* (2nd ed.). New York, NY: Guilford Press.

CHAPTER 26

Research

Alexopoulos, G., Raue, P., & Arean, P. (2003). Problem-solving therapy versus supportive therapy in geriatric major depression with executive dysfunction. *American Journal of Geriatric Psychiatry, 11*, 46–52.

Areán, P. A., Perri, M. G., Nezu, A. M., Schein, R. L., Christopher, F., & Joseph, T. X. (1993). Comparative effectiveness of social problem-solving therapy and reminiscence therapy as treatments for depression in older adults. *Journal of Consulting and Clinical Psychology, 61*, 1003–1010.

Beck, A. T., Rush, A. J., Shaw, B. F., & Emery, G. (1979). *Cognitive therapy of depression.* New York, NY: Guilford.

Birren, J. E., & Deutchman, D. E. (1991). *Guiding autobiography groups for older adults.* Baltimore, MD: Johns Hopkins University Press.

Birrer, R. B., & Vemuri, S. P. (2004). Depression in later life: A diagnostic and therapeutic challenge. *American Family Physician, 69*, 2375–2382.

Blazer, D. G. (2003). Depression in late life: Review and commentary. *Journal of Gerontology: Medical Sciences, 58A,* 249–265.

Boswell, E. B., & Stoudemire, A. (1996). Major depression in the primary care setting. *The American Journal of Medicine, 101*(6A), 3S–9S.

Burns, D. (1980). *Feeling good.* New York, NY: Signet.

Chiriboga, D. A., Yee, B. W. K., & Jang, Y. (2005). Minority and cultural issues in late-life depression. *Clinical Psychology: Science and Practice, 12*(3), 358–363.

Floyd, M., Scogin, F., McKendree-Smith, N. L., Floyd, D. L., & Rokke, P. D. (2004). Cognitive therapy for depression: A comparison of individual psychotherapy and bibliotherapy for depressed older adults. *Behavior Modification, 28,* 297–318.

Gallagher, D. E., & Thompson, L. W. (1981). *Depression in the elderly: A behavioral treatment manual.* Los Angeles, CA: University of Southern California Press.

Gallagher-Thompson, D. E., & Steffen, A. M. (1994). Comparative effects of cognitive-behavioral and brief psychodynamic psychotherapies for depressed family caregivers. *Journal of Consulting and Clinical Psychology, 62,* 543–549.

Gottfries, C. G. (1998). Is there a difference between elderly and younger patients with regard to the symptomatology and aetiology of depression? *International Clinical Psychopharmacology, 13*(Suppl. 5), S13–S18.

Horowitz, M., & Kaltreider, N. (1979). Brief therapy of the stress response syndrome. *Psychiatric Clinics of North America, 2,* 365–377.

Katon, W., & Ciechanowski, P. (2002). Impact of major depression on chronic medical illness. *Journal of Psychosomatic Research, 53,* 859–863.

Knifton, L., Gervais, M., Newbigging, K., Mirza, N., Quinn, N., ... Hunkins-Hutchison, E. (2010). Community conversation: Addressing mental health stigma with ethnic minority communities. *Social Psychiatry and Psychiatric Epidemiology, 45,* 497–504.

Laidlaw, K., Davidson, K., Toner, H., Jackson, G., Clark, S., ... Cross, S. (2008). A randomized controlled trial of cognitive behavior therapy vs treatment as usual in the treatment of mild to moderate late life depression. *International Journal of Geriatric Psychiatry, 23,* 843–850.

Lewinsohn, P. (1974). A behavioral approach to depression. In R. Friedman & M. Katz (Eds.), *The psychology of depression: Contemporary theory and research* (pp. 157–176). New York, NY: Wiley.

Lewinsohn, P., Biglan, A., & Zeiss, A. (1976). Behavioral treatment of depression. In P. Davidson (Ed.), *Behavioral management of anxiety, depression, and pain.* New York, NY: Brunner/Mazel.

Lichtenberg, P. A., Kimbarow, M. L., Morris, P., & Vangel, S. J. (1996). Behavioral treatment of depression in predominately African-American medical patients. *Clinical Gerontologist, 17,* 15–33.

Nezu, A. M., Nezu, C. M., & Perri, M. G. (1989). *Problem-solving therapy for depression: Theory, research, and clinical guidelines.* Oxford, UK: Wiley.

Rose, J., & DelMaestro, S. (1990). Separation-individuation conflict as a model for understanding distressed caregivers: Psychodynamic and cognitive case studies. *The Gerontologist, 30,* 693–697.

Scogin, F., Hamblin, D., & Beutler, L. (1987). Bibliotherapy for depressed older adults: A self-help alternative. *The Gerontologist, 27,* 383–387.

Thompson, L. W., Gallagher, D., & Breckenridge, J. S. (1987). Comparative effectiveness of psychotherapies for depressed elders. *Journal of Consulting and Clinical Psychology, 55,* 385–390.

Wang, J. (2005). The effects of reminiscence on depressive symptoms and mood status of older institutionalized adults in Taiwan. *International Journal of Geriatric Psychiatry, 20,* 57–62.

CHAPTER 27

Research

Ayers, C. R., Saxena, S., Golshan, S., & Wetherell, J. L. (2009). Age of onset and clinical features of late life compulsive hoarding. *Geriatric Psychiatry, 25*(2), 142–149.

Bratiotis, C., Sorrentino Schmalisch, C., & Steketee, G. (2011). *The hoarding handbook: A guide for human service professionals.* New York, NY: Oxford University Press.

Frost, R. O., & Hartl, T. L. (1996). A cognitive-behavioral model of compulsive hoarding. *Behaviour Research and Therapy, 34,* 341–350.

Frost, R. O., & Pekareva-Kochergina, A. (submitted). The effectiveness of a biblio-based self-help program for hoarding disorder.

Frost, R. O., Steketee, G., & Tolin, D. (submitted). Comorbidity in hoarding disorder.

Frost, R. O., Steketee, G., & Williams, L. (2000). Hoarding: A community health problem. *Health & Social Care in the Community, 8,* 229–234.

Iervolino, A. C., Perroud, N., Fullana, M. A., Guipponi, M., Cherkas,L., ... Mataix-Cols, D. (2009). Prevalence and heritability of compulsive hoarding: A twin study. *American Journal of Psychiatry, 166*, 1156–1161.

Mueller, A., Mitchell, J. E., Crosby, R. D., Glaesmer, H., & deZwaan, M. (2009). The prevalence of compulsive hoarding and its association with compulsive buying in a German population based sample. *Behaviour Research and Therapy, 47*, 705–709. doi: 10.1016/j.brat.2009.04.005

Muroff, J., Steketee, G., Rasmussen, J., Gibson, A., Bratiotis, C., & Sorrentino, C. (2009). Group cognitive and behavioral treatment for compulsive hoarding: a preliminary trial. *Depression and Anxiety, 26*(7), 634–640. doi: 10.1002/da.20591

Pertusa, A., Frost, R., Fullana, M., Samuels, J., Steketee, G., ... Mataix-Cols, D. (2010). Refining the diagnostic boundaries of compulsive hoarding: A critical review. *Clinical Psychology Review, 30*, 371–386.

Samuels, J., Bienvenu, O. J., Grados, M. A., Cullen, B., Riddle, M.A., ... Nestadt, G. (2008). Prevalence and correlates of hoarding behavior in a community-based sample. *Behaviour Research and Therapy, 46*, 836–844.

Saxena, S., Brody, A. L., Maidment, K. M., & Baxter, L. R. (2007). Paroxetine treatment of compulsive hoarding. *Journal of Psychiatric Research, 41*, 481–487.

Steketee, G., & Frost, R. (2003). Compulsive hoarding: Current status of the research. *Clinical Psychology Review, 23*, 905–927.

Steketee, G., Frost, R. O., & Kyrios, M. (2003). Cognitive aspects of compulsive hoarding. *Cognitive Therapy and Research, 27*, 463–479.

Tolin, D. F., Frost, R. O., & Steketee, G. (2007). An open trial of cognitive-behavioral therapy for compulsive hoarding. *Behaviour Research and Therapy, 45*, 1461–1470.

Tolin, D., Frost, R., & Steketee, G. (2010). A brief interview for assessing compulsive hoarding: The Hoarding Rating Scale. *Psychiatry Research, 178*, 147–152.

Turner, K., Steketee, G., & Nauth, L. (2010). Treating elders with compulsive hoarding: A pilot program. *Cognitive and Behavioral Practice, 17*, 449–457.

Clinician Application

Ayers, C., Saxena, S., Golshan, S., & Wetherell, J. (2010). Age at onset and clinical features of late-life compulsive hoarding. *International Journal of Geriatric Psychiatry, 25*, 142–149.

Bratiotis, C., & Flowers, K. (2010). Home-based intervention for elderly hoarders: What really works? *Journal of Geriatric Care Management, 20*, 15–20.

Frost, R. O., & Hartl, T. L. (1996). A cognitive-behavioral model of compulsive hoarding. *Behaviour Research and Therapy, 34*, 341–350.

CHAPTER 28

Research

American Academy of Sleep Medicine. (2001). *The International Classification of Sleep Disorders* (revised). Westchester, IL: Author.

Breslau, N., Roth, T., Rosenthal, L., & Andreski, P. (1996). Sleep disturbance and psychiatric disorders: A longitudinal epidemiological study of young adults. *Biological Psychiatry, 39*, 411–418.

Calhoun, P. S., Wiley, M., Dennis, M. F., Means, M. K., Edinger, J. D, & Beckham, J. C. (2007). Objective evidence of sleep disturbance in women with posttraumatic stress disorder. *Journal of Traumatic Stress, 20*, 1009–1018.

Cukrowicz, K. C., Otamendi, A., Pinto, J. V., & Bernert, R. A. (2006). The impact of insomnia and sleep disturbances on depression and suicidality. *Dreaming, 16*, 1–10.

Davis, J. L., Byrd, P., Rhudy, J. L., & Wright, D. C. (2007). Characteristics of chronic nightmares in a trauma exposed clinical sample. *Dreaming, 17*, 187–198.

Davis, J. L., Rhudy, J. L., Pruiksma, K. E., Byrd, P., Williams, A. E., ... Bartley, E. J. (2011). Physiological predictors of response to Exposure, Relaxation, and Rescripting Therapy for chronic nightmares in a randomized clinical trial. *Journal of Clinical Sleep Medicine, 7*, 622–631.

Davis, J. L., & Wright, D. C. (2005). Case series utilizing Exposure, Relaxation, and Rescripting Therapy: Impact on nightmares, sleep quality, and psychological distress. *Behavioral Sleep Medicine, 3*, 151–157.

Davis, J. L., & Wright, D. C. (2007). Randomized clinical trial for treatment of chronic nightmares in trauma-exposed adults. *Journal of Traumatic Stress, 20*, 123–133.

Forbes, D., Phelps, A. J., & McHugh, T. (2001). Treatment of combat-related nightmares using imagery rehearsal: A pilot study. *Journal of Traumatic Stress, 14*, 433–442.

Forbes, D., Phelps, A. J., McHugh, A. F., Debenham, P., Hopwood, M., & Creamer, M. (2003). Imagery rehearsal in the treatment of posttraumatic nightmares in Australian veterans with chronic combat-related PTSD: 12-month follow-up data. *Journal of Traumatic Stress, 16*, 509–513.

Foulkes, W. D. (1962). Dream reports from different stages of sleep. *Journal of Abnormal and Social Psychology, 65*, 14–25.

Frank, M. G. (2006). The function of sleep. In Lee-Chiong (Ed.), *Sleep: A comprehensive handbook* (pp. 3–9). Hoboken, NJ: John Wiley & Sons.

Geer, J. H., & Silverman, I. (1967). Treatment of a recurrent nightmare by behavior-modification procedures: A case study. *Journal of Abnormal Psychology, 72*, 188–190.

Germain, A., Shear, M. K., Hall, M., & Buysse, D. J. (2007). Effects of a brief behavioral treatment for PTSD-related sleep disturbances: A pilot study. *Behaviour Research and Therapy, 45*, 627–632.

Hetta, J. A., Agren, H., Hambert, G., Liljenberg, G. B., & Roos, B. E. (1985). Prevalence of sleep disturbances and related symptoms in a middle-aged Swedish population. In W. Koella, E. Ruther, & H. Schultz (Eds.), *Sleep '84: Proceedings of the 7th European Congress of Sleep Research* (pp. 373–376). Stuttgart, Germany: Gustaf Fischer-Verlag.

Hinton, D. E., Pich, V., Chhean, D., Pollack, M. H., & McNally, R. J. (2005). Sleep paralysis among Cambodian refugees: Association with PTSD diagnosis and severity. *Depression and Anxiety, 22*, 47–51.

Kellner, R., Neidhardt, J., Krakow, B., & Pathak, D. (1992). Changes in chronic nightmares after one session of desensitization or rehearsal instructions. *The American Journal of Psychiatry, 149*, 659–663.

Kobayashi, I., Boarts, J. M., & Delahanty, D. L. (2007). Polysomnographically measured sleep abnormalities in PTSD: A meta-analytic review. *Psychophysiology, 44*, 660–669.

Krakow, B., Artar, A., Warner, T. D., Melendrez, D., Johnston, L., … Koss, M. (2000). Sleep disorder, depression, and suicidality in female sexual assault survivors. *Crisis, 21*, 163–170.

Krakow, B., Johnston, L., Melendrez, D., Hollifield, M., Warner, T. D., … Herlan, M. J. (2001). An open-label trial of evidence-based cognitive behavior therapy for nightmares and insomnia in crime victims with PTSD. *American Journal of Psychiatry, 158*, 2043–2047.

Krakow, B., Kellner, R., Neidhardt, J., Pathak, D., & Lambert, L. (1993). Imagery rehearsal treatment of chronic nightmares: With a thirty month follow-up. *Journal of Behavioral Therapy & Experimental Psychiatry, 24*, 325–330.

Krakow, B., Melendrez, D., Pedersen, B., Johnston, L., Hollifield, M., … Schrader, R. (2002). Complex insomnia: Insomnia and sleep-disordered breathing in a consecutive series of crime victims with nightmares and post-traumatic stress disorder. *Biological Psychiatry, 49*, 948–953.

Krakow, B., & Zadra, A. (2006). Clinical management of chronic nightmares: Imagery rehearsal therapy. *Behavioral Sleep Medicine, 4*, 45–70.

Lancee, J., Spoormaker, V. I., Krakow, B., & van den Bout, J. (2008). A systematic review of cognitive-behavioral treatment for nightmares: Toward a well-established treatment. *Journal of Clinical Sleep Medicine, 4*, 475–480.

Long, M. E., Hammons, M. E., Davis, J. L., Frueh, B. C., Khan, M. M., … Teng, E. J. (2011). Imagery rescripting and exposure group treatment of posttraumatic nightmares in veterans. *Journal of Anxiety Disorders, 25*, 531–535.

Lu, M., Wagner, A., Male, L. V., Whitehead, A., & Boehnlein, J. (2009). Imagery rehearsal therapy for posttraumatic nightmares in U.S. veterans. *Journal of Traumatic Stress, 22*, 236–239.

Mellman, T. A., Aigbogun, N., Graves, R. E., Lawson, W. B., & Alim, T. N. (2008). Sleep paralysis and trauma, psychiatric symptoms and disorders in an adult African American population attending primary medical care. *Depression and Anxiety, 25*, 435–440.

Mellman, T. A., Pigeon, W. R., Nowell, P. D., & Nolan, B. (2007). Relationships between REM sleep findings and PTSD symptoms during the early aftermath of trauma. *Journal of Traumatic Stress, 20*, 893–901.

Miller, W. R., & DiPilato, M. (1983). Treatment of nightmares via relaxation and desensitization: A controlled evaluation. *Journal of Consulting and Clinical Psychology, 51*, 870–877.

Moore, B., & Krakow, B. (2007). Imagery rehearsal therapy for acute posttraumatic nightmares among combat soldiers in Iraq. *American Journal of Psychiatry, 164*, 683–684.

Nappi, C. M., Drummond, S. P., Thorp, S. R., & McQuaid, J. R. (2010). Effectiveness of imagery rehearsal therapy for the treatment of combat-related nightmares in veterans. *Behavioral Therapy, 41*, 237–244.

Neidhardt, E. J., Krakow, B., Kellner, R., & Pathak, D. (1992). The beneficial effects of one treatment session and recording of nightmares on chronic nightmare sufferers. *Sleep, 15*, 470–473.

Nielsen, T. A., & Zadra, A. (2005). Nightmares and other common dream disturbances. In N. Kryger, N. Roth, & W. C. Dement. (Eds.), *Principles and practice of sleep medicine* (4th ed, pp. 926–935). Philadelphia, PA: Elsevier Saunders.

Ohayon, M. M., & Shapiro, C. M. (2000). Sleep disturbances and psychiatric disorders associated with post-traumatic stress disorder in the general population. *Comprehensive Psychiatry, 41*, 469–478.

Rhudy, J. L., Davis, J. L., Williams, A. E., McCabe, K. M., Bartley, E. J., … Pruiksma, K. E. (2010). Cognitive-behavioral treatment for chronic nightmares in trauma-exposed persons: Assessing physiological reaction to nightmare-related fear. *Journal of Clinical Psychology, 66*, 365–382.

Rhudy, J. L., Davis, J. L., Williams, A. E., McCabe, K. M., & Byrd, P. M. (2008). Physiological-emotional reactivity to nightmare-related imagery in trauma-exposed persons with chronic nightmares. *Behavioral Sleep Medicine, 6*, 158–177.

Ross, R. J., Ball, W. A., Sullivan, K. A., & Caroff, S. N. (1989). Sleep disturbance as the hallmark of posttraumatic stress disorder. *American Journal of Psychiatry, 146*, 697–707.

Schreuder, B. J., Kleijn, W. C., & Rooijmans, H. G. (2000). Nocturnal re-experiencing more than forty years after war trauma. *Journal of Traumatic Stress, 13*, 453–463.

Spoormaker, V. I., & Montgomery, P. (2008). Disturbed sleep in post-traumatic stress disorder: Secondary symptom or core feature? *Sleep Medicine Reviews, 12*, 169–184.

Swanson, L. M., Favorite, T. K., Horin, E., & Arnedt, J. T. (2009). A combined group treatment for nightmares and insomnia in combat veterans: A pilot study. *Journal of Traumatic Stress, 22*, 639–642.

Tanskanen, A., Tuomilehto, J., Viinamaki, H., Vartiainen, E., Lehtonen, J., & Puska, P. (2001). Nightmares as predictors of suicide. *Sleep, 24*, 845–848.

Wanner, J., Long, M. E., & Teng, E. J. (2010). Multi-component treatment for posttraumatic nightmares in Vietnam veterans: Two case studies. *Journal of Psychiatric Practice, 16*, 243–249.

Clinician Application

Davis, J. L., Byrd, P., Rhudy, J. L., & Wright, D. C. (2007). Characteristics of chronic nightmares in a trauma exposed clinical sample. *Dreaming, 17*, 187–198.

Krakow, B., Artar, A., Warner, T. D., Melendrez, D., Johnston, L., … Koss, M. (2000). Sleep disorder, depression, and suicidality in female sexual assault survivors. *Crisis, 21*, 163–170.

Krakow, B., & Zadra, A. (2006). Clinical management of chronic nightmares: Imagery rehearsal therapy. *Behavioral Sleep Medicine, 4*, 45–70.

Lancee, J., Spoormaker, V. I., Krakow, B., & van den Bout, J. (2008). A systematic review of cognitive-behavioral treatment for nightmares: Toward a well-established treatment. *Journal of Clinical Sleep Medicine, 4*, 475–480.

Moore, B., & Krakow, B. (2007). Imagery rehearsal therapy for acute posttraumatic nightmares among combat soldiers in Iraq. *American Journal of Psychiatry, 164*, 683–684.

Nappi, C. M., Drummond, S. P., Thorp, S. R., & McQuaid, J. R. (2010). Effectiveness of imagery rehearsal therapy for the treatment of combat-related nightmares in veterans. *Behavioral Therapy, 41*, 237–244.

CHAPTER 29

Research

American Psychiatric Association. (2000). *Diagnostic and statistical manual of mental disorders* (4th ed., text revision). Washington, DC: Author.

Andover, M. S., & Gibb, B. E. (2010). Non-suicidal self-injury, attempted suicide, and suicidal intent among psychiatric inpatients. *Psychiatry Research, 178*, 101–105. doi: 10.1016/j.psychres.2010.03.019

Andover, M. S., Pepper, C. M., & Gibb, B. E. (2007). Self-mutilation and coping strategies in a college sample. *Suicide & Life Threatening Behaviors, 37*, 238–243. doi: 10.1521/suli.2007.37.2.238

Andover, M. S., Pepper, C. M., Ryabchenko, K. A., Orrico, E. G., & Gibb, B. E. (2005). Self-mutilation and symptoms of depression, anxiety, and borderline personality disorder. *Suicide & Life-Threatening Behavior, 35*, 581–591. doi: 10.1521/suli.2005.35.5.581

Andover, M. S., Primack, J. M., Gibb, B. E., & Pepper, C. M. (2010). An examination of non-suicidal self-injury in men: Do men differ from women in basic NSSI characteristics? *Archives of Suicide Research, 14*, 1–10. doi: 10.1080/13811110903479086

Arensman, E., Townsend, E., Hawton, K., Bremner, S., Feldman E., … Träskman-Bendz, L. (2001). Psychosocial and pharmacological treatment of patients following deliberate self-harm: The methodological issues involved in evaluating effectiveness. *Suicide and Life-Threatening Behavior, 31*, 169–180. doi: 10.1521/suli.31.2.169.21516

Barrocas, A. L., Hankin, B. L., Young, J. F., & Abela, J. R. Z. (2012). Rates of nonsuicidal self-injury in youth: Age, sex, and behavioral methods in a community sample. *Pediatrics, 130*, 39–45. doi: 10.1542/peds.2011-2094

Bohus, M., Haaf, B., Simms, T., Limberger, M. F., Schmahl, C., … Linehan, M. M. (2004). Effectiveness of inpatient dialectical behavioral therapy for borderline personality disorder: A controlled trial. *Behaviour Research and Therapy, 42*, 487–499. doi: 10.1016/S0005-7967(03)00174-8

Briere, J., & Gil, E. (1998). Self-mutilation in clinical and general population samples: Prevalence, correlates, and functions. *American Journal of Orthopsychiatry, 68*, 609–620. doi: 10.1037/h0080369

Chambless, D. L., & Hollon, S. D. (1998). Defining empirically supported therapies. *Journal of Consulting and Clinical Psychology, 66*, 7–18. doi: 10.1037/0022-006X.66.1.7

Claes, L., Vandereycken, W., & Vertommen, H. (2001). Self-injurious behaviors in eating-disordered patients. *Eating Behaviors, 2*, 263–272. doi: 10.1016/S1471-0153(01)00033-2

Comtois, K. A., & Linehan, M. M. (2006). Psychosocial treatments of suicidal behaviors: A practice-friendly review. *Journal of Clinical Psychology, 62*, 161–170. doi: 10.1002/jclp.20220

Deliberto, T. L., & Nock, M. K. (2008). An exploratory study of correlates, onset, and offset of non-suicidal self-injury. *Archives of Suicide Research, 12*, 219–231. doi: 10.1080/13811110802101096

Evans, K., Tyrer, P., Catalan, J., Schmidt, U., Davidson, K., … Thompson, S. (1999). Manual-assisted cognitive-behaviour therapy (MACT): A randomized controlled trial of a brief intervention with bibliotherapy in the treatment of recurrent deliberate self-harm. *Psychological Medicine, 29*, 19–25. doi: 10.1017/S003329179800765X

Gratz, K. L. (2003). Risk factors for and functions of deliberate self-harm: An empirical and conceptual review. *Clinical Psychology: Science and Practice, 10*, 192–205. doi: 10.1093/clipsy/bpg022

Gratz, K. L. (2007). Targeting emotion dysregulation in the treatment of self-injury. *Journal of Clinical Psychology, 63*, 1091–1103. doi: 10.1002/jclp.20417

Gratz, K. L., & Gunderson, J. G. (2006). Preliminary data on an acceptance-based emotion regulation group intervention for deliberate self-harm among women with borderline personality disorder. *Behavior Therapy, 37*, 25–35. doi: 10.1016/j.beth.2005.03.002

Gratz, K. L., & Tull, M. T. (2011). Extending research on the utility of an adjunctive emotion regulation group therapy for deliberate self-harm among women with borderline personality pathology. *Personality Disorders: Theory, Research, and Treatment, 2*, 316–326. doi: 10.1037/a0022144

Hawton, K., Arensman, E., Townsend, E., Bremner S., Feldman, E., … Träskman-Bendz, L. (1998). Deliberate self harm: Systematic review of efficacy of psychosocial and pharmacological treatments in preventing repetition. *British Medical Journal, 317*, 441–447. doi: 10.1136/bmj.317.7156.441

Hilt, L. M., Nock, M. K., Lloyd-Richardson, E. E., & Prinstein, M. J. (2008). Longitudinal study of nonsuicidal self-injury among adolescents: Rates, correlates, and preliminary test of an interpersonal model. *Journal of Early Adolescence, 28*, 455–469. doi: 10.1177/0272431608316604

Jacobson, C. M., & Gould, M. (2007). The epidemiology and phenomenology of non-suicidal self-injurious behavior among adolescents: A critical review of the literature. *Archives of Suicide Research, 11*, 129–147. doi: 10.1080/13811110701247602

Jacobson, C. M., Muehlenkamp, J. J., Miller, A. L., & Turner, J. B. (2008). Psychiatric impairment among adolescents engaging in different types of deliberate self-harm. *Journal of Clinical Child and Adolescent Psychology, 37*, 363–375. doi: 10.1080/15374410801955771

Klonsky, E. D. (2011). Non-suicidal self-injury in United States adults: Prevalence, sociodemographics, topography, and functions. *Psychological Medicine, 41*, 1981–1986. doi: 10.1017/S0033291710002497

Klonsky, E. D., & Muehlenkamp, J. J. (2007). Self-injury: A research review for the practitioner. *Journal of Clinical Psychology, 63*, 1045–1056. doi: 10.1002/jclp.20412

Klonsky, E. D., & Olino, T. M. (2008). Identifying clinically distinct subgroups of self-injurers among young adults: A latent class analysis. *Journal of Consulting and Clinical Psychology, 76*, 22–27. doi: 10.1037/0022-006X.76.1.22

Klonsky, E. D., Oltmanns, T. F., & Turkheimer, E. (2003). Deliberate self-harm in a nonclinical population: Prevalence and psychological correlates. *American Journal of Psychiatry, 160*, 1501–1508. doi: 10.1176/appi.ajp.160.8.1501

Langbehn, D. R., & Pfohl, B. (1993). Clinical correlates of self-mutilation among psychiatric inpatients. *Annals of Clinical Psychiatry, 5*, 45–51. doi: 10.3109/10401239309148923

Linehan, M. M. (1993). *Cognitive-behavioral treatment of borderline personality disorder*. New York, NY: Guilford Press.

Miller, A. L., Rathus, J. H., & Linehan, M. M. (2007). *Dialectical behavior therapy with suicidal adolescents*. New York, NY: Guilford Press.

Muehlenkamp, J. J. (2005). Self-injurious behavior as a separate clinical syndrome. *American Journal of Orthopsychiatry, 75*, 324–333. doi: 10.1037/0002-9432.75.2.324

Muehlenkamp, J. J. (2006). Empirically supported treatments and general therapy guidelines for non-suicidal self-injury. *Journal of Mental Health Counseling, 28*, 166–185.

Nafisi, N., & Stanley, B. (2007). Developing and maintaining the therapeutic alliance with self-injuring patients. *Journal of Clinical Psychology: In Session, 63*, 1069–1079. doi: 10.1002/jclp.20414

Nijman, H. L., Dautzenberg, M., Merckelbach, H. L., Jung, P., Wessel, I., & del Campo, J. A. (1999). Self-mutilating behaviour of psychiatric inpatients. *European Psychiatry, 14,* 4–10. doi: 10.1016/S0924-9338(99)80709-3

Nock, M. K., Holmberg, E. B., Photos, V. I., & Michel, B. D. (2007). Self-Injurious Thoughts and Behaviors Interview: Development, reliability, and validity in an adolescent sample. *Psychological Assessment, 19,* 309–317. doi: 10.1037/1040-3590.19.3.309

Nock, M. K., Joiner, T. E., Gordon, K. H., Lloyd-Richardson, E., & Prinstein, M. J. (2006). Non-suicidal self-injury among adolescents: Diagnostic correlates and relation to suicide attempts. *Psychiatry Research, 144,* 65–72. doi: 10.1016/j.psychres.2006.05.010

Nock, M. K., Teper, R., & Hollander, M. (2007). Psychological treatment of self-injury among adolescents. *Journal of Clinical Psychology: In Session, 63,* 1081–1089. doi: 10.1002/jclp.20415

Rodham, K., & Hawton, K. (2009). Epidemiology and phenomenology of nonsuicidal self-injury. In M. K. Nock (Ed.), *Understanding nonsuicidal self-injury: Origins, assessment, and treatment* (pp. 37–62). Washington, DC: American Psychological Association.

Salkovskis, P. M., Atha, C., & Storer, D. (1990). Cognitive-behavioural problem solving in the treatment of patients who repeatedly attempt suicide: A controlled trial. *British Journal of Psychiatry, 157,* 871–876. doi: 10.1192/bjp.157.6.871

Serras, A., Saules, K. K., Cranford, J. A., & Eisenberg, D. (2010). Self-injury, substance use, and associated risk factors in a multi-campus probability sample of college students. *Psychology of Addictive Behaviors, 24,* 119–128. doi: 10.1037/a0017210

Slee, N., Spinhoven, P., Garnefski, N., & Arensman, E. (2008). Emotion regulation as mediator of treatment outcome in therapy for deliberate self-harm. *Clinical Psychology and Psychotherapy, 15,* 205–216. doi: 10.1002/cpp.577

Stanley, B., Brodsky, B., Nelson, J. D., & Dulit, R. (2007). Brief dialectical behavior therapy (DBT-B) for suicidal behavior and non-suicidal self-injury. *Archives of Suicide Research, 11,* 337–341. doi: 10.1080/13811110701542069

Suyemoto, K. L. (1998). The functions of self-mutilation. *Clinical Psychology Review, 18,* 531–554. doi: 10.1016/S0272-7358(97)00105-0

Tyrer, P., Thompson, S., Schmidt, U., Jones, V., Knapp, M., ... Wessely, S. (2003). Randomized controlled trial of brief cognitive behavior therapy versus treatment as usual in recurrent deliberate self-harm: The POPMACT study. *Psychological Medicine, 33,* 969–976. doi: 10.1017/S0033291703008171

van den Bosch, L. M. C., Koeter, M. W. J., Stijnen, T., Verheul, R., & van den Brink, W. (2005). Sustained efficacy of dialectical behavior therapy for borderline personality disorder. *Behaviour Research and Therapy, 43,* 1231–1241. doi: 10.1016/j.brat.2004.09.008

Verheul, R., van den Bosch, L. M. C., Koeter, M. W. J., de Ridder, M. A. J., Stijnen, T., & van den Brink, W. (2003). Dialectical behaviour therapy for women with borderline personality disorder: 12-month, randomized clinical trial in the Netherlands. *British Journal of Psychiatry, 182,* 135–140.

Weinberg, I., Gunderson, J. G., Hennen, J., & Cutter, C. J. (2006). Manual assisted cognitive treatment for deliberate self-harm in borderline personality disorder patients. *Journal of Personality Disorders, 20,* 482–492. doi: 10.1521/pedi.2006.20.5.482

Whitlock, J., & Knox, K.L. (2007). The relationship between self-injurious behavior and suicide in a young adult population. *Archives of Pediatrics and Adolescent Medicine, 161,* 634–640.

Whitlock, J., Muehlenkamp, J., & Eckenrode, J. (2008). Variation in nonsuicidal self-injury: Identification and features of latent classes in a college population of emerging adults. *Journal of Clinical Child & Adolescent Psychology, 37,* 725–735. doi: 10.1080/15374410802359734

Wilhelm, S., Keuthen, N. J., Deckersbach, T., Engelhard, I. M., Forker, A. E., ... Jenike, M. A. (1999). Self-injurious skin picking: Clinical characteristics and comorbidity. *Journal of Clinical Psychiatry, 60,* 454–459.

Wilkinson, P., Kelvin, R., Roberts, C., Dubicka, B., & Goodyer, I. (2011). Clinical and psychosocial predictors of suicide attempts and nonsuicidal self-injury in the Adolescent Depression Antidepressants and Psychotherapy Trial (ADAPT). *American Journal of Psychiatry, 168,* 495–501. doi: 10.1176/appi.ajp.2010.10050718

Zlotnick, C., Mattia, J. I., & Zimmerman, M. (1999). Clinical correlates of self-mutilation in a sample of general psychiatric patients. *Journal of Nervous and Mental Disease, 187,* 296–301.

Clinician Application

Asarnow, J. R., Porta, G., Spirito, A., Emslie, G., Clarke, G., ... Brent, D. A. (2011). Suicide attempts and nonsuicidal self-injury in the treatment of resistant depression in adolescents: Findings from the TORDIA study. *Journal of the American Academy of Child and Adolescent Psychiatry, 50,* 772–781.

Brent, D., Emslie, G., Clarke, G., Wagner, K. D., Asarnow, J. R., ... Zelazny, J. (2008). Switching to another SSRI or to Venlafaxine with or without cognitive behavioral therapy for adolescents with SSRI-resistant depression: The TORDIA randomized controlled trial. *Journal of the American Medical Association, 299,* 901–913.

Crowell, S. E., Beauchaine, T. P., Hsiao, R. C., Vasilev, C. A., Yaptangco, M., ... McCauley, E. (2012). Differentiating adolescent self-injury from adolescent depression: Possible implications for borderline personality development. *Journal of Abnormal Child Psychology, 40,* 45–57. doi: 10.1007/s10802-011-9578-3

D'zurilla, T. J., & Nezu, A. M. (2010). Problem-solving therapy. In K. S. Dobson (Ed.), *Handbook of cognitive-behavioral therapies* (3rd ed., pp. 197–225). New York, NY: Guilford Press.

Evans, K., Tyrer, P., Catalan, J., Schmidt, U., Davidson, K., ... Thompson, S. (1999). Manual-assisted cognitive-behaviour therapy (MACT): A randomized controlled trial of a brief intervention with bibliotherapy in the treatment of recurrent deliberate self-harm. *Psychological Medicine, 29,* 19–25.

Fleischhaker, C., Böhme, R., Sixt, B., Brück, C., Schneider, C., & Schulz, E. (2011). Dialectical behavioral therapy for adolescents (DBT-A): A clinical trial for patients with suicidal and self-injurious behavior and borderline symptoms with a one-year follow-up. *Child and Adolescent Psychiatry and Mental Health, 5,* 3.

Glenn, C. R., & Klonsky, E. D. (2011). Prospective prediction of nonsuicidal self-injury: A 1-year longitudinal study in young adults. *Behavior Therapy, 42,* 751–762. doi: 10.1016/j.beth.2011.04.005

Gratz, K. L. (2007). Targeting emotion dysregulation in the treatment of self-injury. *Journal of Clinical Psychology, 63,* 1091–1103.

Gratz, K. L., & Tull, M. T. (2011). Extending research on the utility of an adjunctive emotion regulation group therapy for deliberate self-harm among women with borderline personality pathology. *Personality Disorders: Theory, Research, and Treatment, 2,* 316–326.

Hooley, J. M., Hoa, D. T., Slatera, J., & Lockshina, A. (2010). Pain perception and nonsuicidal self-injury: A laboratory investigation. *Personality Disorders: Theory, Research, and Treatment, 1,* 170–179.

Klein, D. A., & Miller, A. L. (2011). Dialectical behavior therapy for suicidal adolescents with borderline personality disorder. *Child and Adolescent Psychiatric Clinics of North America, 20,* 205–216.

Klonsky, E. D. (2011). Non-suicidal self-injury in United States adults: Prevalence, sociodemographics, topography and functions. *Psychological Medicine, 41,* 1981–1986. doi: 10.1017/S0033291710002497

Levy, K. N., Yeomans, F. E., & Diamond, D. (2007). Psychodynamic treatments of self-injury. *Journal of Clinical Psychology, 63,* 1105–1120. doi: 10.1002/jclp.20418

Linehan, M. M. (1993). *Cognitive-behavioral treatment of personality disorder.* New York, NY: Guilford Press.

Linehan, M. M., Comtois, K. A., Murray, A. M., Brown, M. Z., Gallop, R. J., ... Lindenboim, N. (2006). Two-year randomized controlled trial and follow-up of dialectical behavior therapy vs therapy by experts for suicidal behaviors and borderline personality disorder. *Archives of General Psychiatry, 63,* 757–766. doi: 10.1001/archpsyc.63.7.757

Linehan, M. M., Heard, H. L., & Armstrong, H. E. (1993). Naturalistic follow-up of a behavioral treatment for chronically parasuicidal borderline patients. *Archives of General Psychiatry, 50,* 971–974.

Miller, A., Rathus, J., & Linehan, M. (2007). *Dialectical behavior therapy with suicidal adolescents.* New York, NY: Guilford

Moreau, D., Mufson, L., Weissman, M. M., & Klerman, G. L. (1991). Interpersonal psychotherapy for adolescent depression: Description of modification and preliminary application. *Journal of the American Academy of Child and Adolescent Psychiatry, 30,* 642–651. doi: 10.1097/00004583-199107000-00018

Muehlenkamp, J. J. (2006). Empirically supported treatments and general therapy guidelines for non-suicidal self-injury. *Journal of Mental Health Counseling, 28,* 166–185.

Shaffer, D., & Jacobson, C. (2010). *Proposal to the DSM-V childhood disorder and mood disorder work groups to include non-suicidal self-injury (NSSI) as a DSM-V disorder.* Washington, DC: American Psychiatric Association.

Tyrer, P., Thompson, S., Schmidt, U., Jones, V., Knapp, M., ... Wessely, S. (2003). Randomized controlled trial of brief cognitive behaviour therapy versus treatment as usual in recurrent deliberate self-harm: The POPMACT study. *Psychological Medicine, 33,* 969–976.

Washburn, J. J., Gebhardt, M., Styer, K. R., Juzwin, K. R., & Gottlieb, L. (2012). Co-occurring disorders in the treatment of non-suicidal self-injury: An evidence-informed approach. *Journal of Cognitive Psychotherapy, 26,* 348–364.

Washburn, J. J., Richardt, S., Styer, D. M., Gebhardt, M., Juzwin, K. R., Yourek, A., & Aldridge, A. (2012). Psychotherapeutic approaches to non-suicidal self-injury in adolescents. *Child and Adolescent Psychiatry and Mental Health, 6,* 14. doi: 10.1186/1753-2000-6-14

Wilkinson, P., & Goodyer, I. (2011). Non-suicidal self-injury. *European Child and Adolescent Psychiatry, 20,* 103–108.

Wood, A., Trainor, G., Rothwell, J., Moore, A., & Harrington, R. (2001). Randomized trial of group therapy for repeated deliberate self-harm in adolescents. *Journal of the American Academy of Child and Adolescent Psychiatry, 40,* 1246–1253. doi: 10.1097/00004583-200111000-00003

CHAPTER 30

Research

Abramowitz, J. S. (1996). Variants of exposure and response prevention in the treatment of obsessive compulsive disorder: A meta-analysis. *Behavior Therapy, 27*, 583–600.

Abramowitz, J. S., Foa, E. B., & Franklin, M. E. (2003). Exposure and ritual prevention for obsessive compulsive disorder: Effects of intensive versus twice-weekly sessions. *Journal of Consulting & Clinical Psychology, 71*, 394–398.

American Psychiatric Association. (2000). *Diagnostic and statistical manual of mental disorders* (4th ed., Text Revised). Washington, DC: Author.

Clomipramine Collaborative Study Group. (1991). Clomipramine in the treatment of patients with obsessive compulsive disorder. *Archives of General Psychiatry, 48*, 730–738.

Dougherty, D. D., Rauch, S. L., & Jenike, M. A. (2002). Pharmacological treatments for obsessive compulsive disorder. In P. E. Nathan & J. M. Gorman (Eds.), *A guide to treatments that work* (2nd ed., pp. 387–410). London, UK: Oxford University Press.

Foa, E. B., Franklin, M. E., & Moser, J. (2002). Context in the clinic: How well do CBT and medications work in combination? *Biological Psychiatry, 51*, 989–997.

Foa, E. B., & Kozak, M. J. (1985). Treatment of anxiety disorders: Implications for psychopathology. In A. H. Tuma & J. D. Maser (Eds.), *Anxiety and the anxiety disorders*. Hillsdale, NJ: Erlbaum.

Foa, E. B., Kozak, M. J., Goodman, W. K., Hollander, E., Jenike, M. A., & Rasmussen, S. (1995). DSM-IV field trial: Obsessive compulsive disorder. *American Journal of Psychiatry, 152*, 90–96.

Foa, E. B., Liebowitz, M. R., Kozak, M. J., Davies, S., Campeas, R., ... Tu, X. (2005). Randomized, placebo-controlled trial of exposure and ritual prevention, clomipramine, and their combination in the treatment of obsessive-compulsive disorder. *American Journal of Psychiatry, 162*, 151–161.

Foa, E. B., Steketee, G., Grayson, J. B., Turner, R. M., & Latimer, P. (1984). Deliberate exposure and blocking of obsessive-compulsive rituals: Immediate and long-term effects. *Behavior Therapy, 15*, 450–472.

Franklin, M. E., Abramowitz, J. S., Kozak, M. J., Levitt, J., & Foa, E. B. (2000). Effectiveness of exposure and ritual prevention for obsessive compulsive disorder: Randomized compared with non-randomized samples. *Journal of Consulting and Clinical Psychology, 68*, 594–602.

Goodman, W. K., Price, L. H., Rasmussen, S. A., Mazure, C., Delgado, P., ... Charney, D. S. (1989). The Yale-Brown obsessive-compulsive scale. II. Validity. *Archives of General Psychiatry, 46*, 1012–1016.

Goodman, W. K., Price, L. H., Rasmussen, S. A., Mazure, C., Fleischmann, R. L., ... Charney, D. S. (1989). The Yale-Brown obsessive-compulsive scale. I. Development, use, and reliability. *Archives of General Psychiatry, 46*, 1006–1011.

Greist, J. H., Jefferson, J. W., Kobak, K. A., Katzelnick, D. J., & Serlin, R. C. (1995). Efficacy and tolerability of serotonin reuptake inhibitors in obsessive compulsive disorder: A meta-analysis. *Archives of General Psychiatry, 46*, 53–60.

Huppert, J. D., Simpson, H. B., Nissenson, K. J., Liebowitz, M. R., & Foa, E. B. (2009). Quality of life and functional impairment in obsessive-compulsive disorder: A comparison of patients with and without comorbidity, patients in remission, and healthy controls. *Depression and Anxiety, 26*, 39–45.

Huppert, J. D., Walther, M. R., Hajcak, G., Yadin, E., Foa, E. B., ... Liebowitz, M. R. (2009). The OCI-R: Validation of the subscales in a clinical sample. *Journal of Anxiety Disorders, 21*, 394–406.

Kessler, R. C., Berglund, P., Demler, O., Jin, R., Merikangas, K. R., & Walters, E. E. (2005). Lifetime prevalence and age-of-onset distributions of DSM-IV disorders in the National Comorbidity Survey Replication. *Archives of General Psychiatry, 62*, 593–602.

Kessler, R. C., Chiu, W. T., Demler, O., Merikangas, K. R., & Walters, E. E. (2005). Prevalence, severity, and comorbidity of 12-month DSM-IV disorders in the National Comorbidity Survey Replication. *Archives of General Psychiatry, 62*, 617–627.

Koran, L. M., Thienenmann, L. L., & Davenport, R. (1996). Qualtity of life for patients with obesessive-compulsive disorder. *American Journal of Psychiatry, 153*, 783–788.

March, J. S., Frances, A., Carpenter, D., & Kahn, D. (1997). The Expert Consensus Guideline Series: Treatment of obsessive compulsive disorder. *Journal of Clinical Psychiatry, 58*(Suppl 4), 1–72.

Meyer, V. (1966). Modification of expectations in cases with obsessional rituals. *Behaviour Research and Therapy, 4*, 273–280.

Pato, M. T., Zohar-Kadouch, R., Zohar, J., & Murphy, D. L (1988). Return of symptoms after discontinuation of clomipramine in patients with obsessive-compulsive disorder. *American Journal of Psychiatry, 145*, 1521–1525.

Rasmussen, S. A., & Eisen, J. L. (1990). Epidemiology of obsessive-compulsive disorder. *Journal of Clinical Psychiatry, 51,* 10–14.

Simpson, H. B., Foa, E. B., Liebowitz, M. R., Ledley, D. R., Huppert, J. D., ... Petkova, E. (2008). A randomized, controlled trial of cognitive-behavioral therapy for augmenting pharmacotherapy in obsessive-compulsive disorder. *The American Journal of Psychiatry, 165,* 621–630.

Simpson, H. B., Liebowitz, M. R., Foa, E. B., Kozak, M. J., Schmidt, A. B., ... Campeas, R. (2004). Post-treatment effects of exposure therapy and clomipramine in obsessive-compulsive disorder. *Depression and Anxiety, 19,* 225–233.

Yadin, E., Foa, E. B., & Lichner, T. K. (2012). *Treating your OCD with exposure and response prevention therapy patient workbook.* London, UK: Oxford University Press.

Zohar, J., Judge, R., & OCD-Paroxetine-Study-Investigators. (1996). Paroxetine versus clomipramine in the treatment of obsessive-compulsive disorder. *British Journal of Psychiatry, 169,* 468–474.

CHAPTER 31

Research

Antony, M. M., Purdon, C. L., Huta, V., & Swinson, R. P. (1998). Dimensions of perfectionism across the anxiety disorders. *Behaviour Research and Therapy, 36,* 1143–1154.

Arpin-Cribbie, C. A., Irvine, J., Ritvo, P., Cribbie, R. A., Flett, G. L., & Hewitt, P. L. (2008). Perfectionism and psychological distress: A modeling approach to understanding their therapeutic relationship. *Journal of Rational-Emotive and Cognitive-Behavior Therapy, 26,* 151–167.

Ashbaugh, A., Antony, M. M., Liss, A., Summerfeldt, L. J., McCabe, R. E., & Swinson, R. P. (2007). Changes in perfectionism following cognitive-behavioral treatment for social phobia. *Depression and Anxiety, 24,* 169–177.

Baldwin, S. A., Wampold, B. E., & Imel, Z. E. (2007). Untangling the alliance-outcome correlation: Exploring the relative importance of therapist and patient variability in the alliance. *Journal of Consulting and Clinical Psychology, 75,* 842–852.

Bardone-Cone, A. M. (2007). Self-oriented and socially prescribed perfectionism dimensions and their associations with disordered eating. *Behaviour Research and Therapy, 45,* 1977–1986

Bieling, P. J., Israeli, A. L., & Antony, M. M. (2004). Is perfectionism good, bad, or both? Examining models of the perfectionism construct. *Personality and Individual Differences, 36,* 1373–1385.

Bizuel, C., Sadowsky, N., & Riguad, D. (2001). The prognostic value of EDI scores in anorexia nervosa patients: A prospective follow-up study of 5–10 years. *European Psychiatry, 16,* 232–238.

Blankstein, K. R., & Dunkley, D. M. (2002). Evaluative concerns, self-critical, and personal standards perfectionism: A structural equation modeling. In G. L. Flett & P. L. Hewitt (Eds.), *Perfectionism: Theory, research, and treatment* (pp. 285–316). Washington, DC: American Psychological Association.

Blatt, S. J., Quinlan, D. M., Pilkonis, P. A., & Shea, M. T. (1995). Impact of perfectionism and need for approval on the brief treatment of depression: The National Institute of Mental Health Treatment of Depression Collaborative Research program revisited. *Journal of Consulting and Clinical Psychology, 63,* 125–132.

Blatt, S. J., & Zuroff, D. C. (2005). Empirical evaluation of the assumptions in identifying evidence based treatments in mental health. *Clinical Psychology Review, 25,* 459–486.

Blatt, S. J., Zuroff, D. C., Hawley, L. L., & Auerbach, J. S. (2010). The impact of the two-configurations model of personality development and psychopathology on psychotherapy research: Rejoiner to Beutler and Wolf. *Psychotherapy Research, 20,* 65–70.

Burns, J. L., Lee, R. M., & Brown, L. J. (2011). The effect of meditation on self-reported measures of stress, anxiety, depression, and perfectionism in a college population. *Journal of College Student Psychotherapy, 25,* 132–144.

Castro, J. R., & Rice, K. G. (2003). Perfectionism and ethnicity: Implications for depressive symptoms and self-reported academic achievement. *Cultural Diversity and Ethnic Minority Psychology, 9,* 64–78.

Chang, E. C. (Ed.). (2007). *Self-criticism and self-enhancement: Theory, research, and clinical implications.* Washington, DC: American Psychological Association.

Chang, E. C., & Asakawa, K. (2003). Cultural variation on optimistic and pessimistic bias for self versus a sibling: Is there evidence for self-enhancement in the West and for self-criticism in the East when the referent group is specified? *Journal of Personality and Social Psychology, 84,* 569–581.

Dunkley, D. M., Blankstein, K. R., Halsall, J., Williams, M., & Winkworth, G. (2000). The relation between perfectionism and distress: Hassles, coping, and perceived social support as mediators and moderators. *Journal of Counseling Psychology, 47,* 437–453.

Dunkley, D. M., Zuroff, D. C., & Blankstein, K. R. (2006). Self-critical perfectionism and daily affect: Dispositional and situational influences on stress and coping. *Journal of Personality and Social Psychology, 84,* 234–252.

Egan, S. J., Wade, T. D., & Sharfran, R. (2011). Perfectionism as a transdiagnostic process: A clinical review. *Clinical Psychology Review, 31*, 203–212.

Flett, G. L., & Hewitt, P. L. (2008). Treatment interventions for perfectionism. A cognitive perspective: Introduction to the special issue. *Journal of Rational-Emotive and Cognitive-Behavior Therapy, 26*, 127–133

Frost, R. O., Heimberg, R. G., Holt, C. S., Mattia, J. I., & Neubauer, A. L. (1993). A comparison of two measures of perfectionism. *Personality and Individual Differences, 14*, 119–126.

Frost, R. O., Marten, P., Lahart, C., & Rosenblate, R. (1990). The dimensions of perfectionism. *Cognitive Therapy and Research, 14*, 449–468.

Gilbert, P. (Ed.). (2005). *Compassion: Conceptualisations, research, and use in psychotherapy.* London, UK: Routledge.

Gilbert, P. (2009). Moving beyond cognitive behaviour therapy. *The Psychologist, 22*, 400–403.

Gilbert, P., Durrant, R., & McEwan, K. (2006). Investigating the relationship between perfectionism, forms and functions of self-criticism and sensitivity to put-down. *Personality and Individual Differences, 41*, 1299–1308.

Glover, D. S., Brown, G. P., Fairburn, C. G., & Shafran, R. (2007). A preliminary evaluation of cognitive-behaviour therapy for clinical perfectionism: A case series. *British Journal of Clinical Psychology, 46*, 85–94.

Halmi, K. A., Tozzi, F., Thornton, L. M., Crow, S., Fichter, M. M., … Bulik, C. M. (2005). The relation among perfectionism, obsessive–compulsive personality disorder and obsessive-compulsive disorder in individuals with eating disorders. *International Journal of Eating Disorders, 38*, 371–374.

Harpaz-Rotem, I., & Blatt, S. J. (2009). A pathway to therapeutic change: Changes in self-representation in the treatment of adolescents and young adults. *Psychiatry, 72*, 32–49.

Hawley, L., Ho, M. R., Zuroff, D. C., & Blatt, S. J. (2006). The relationship of perfectionism, depression, and therapeutic alliance during treatment for depression: Latent difference score analysis. *Journal of Consulting and Clinical Psychology, 74*, 930–942.

Herman, K. C., Trotter, R., Reinke, W. M., & Ialongo, N. (2011). Developmental origins of perfectionism among African American youth. *Journal of Counseling Psychology, 58*, 321–334.

Hewitt, P. L., & Flett, G. L. (1991). Dimensions of perfectionism in unipolar depression. *Journal of Abnormal Psychology, 100*, 98–101.

Kelly, A. C., Zuroff, D. C., Foa, C. L., & Gilbert, P. (2010). Who benefits from training in self-compassionate self-regulation? A study of smoking reduction. *Journal of Social and Clinical Psychology, 29*, 727–755.

Lo, C., Helwig, C. C., Chen, S. X., Ohashi, M. M., & Cheng, C. M. (2011). The psychology of strengths and weaknesses: Assessing self-enhancing and self-critical tendencies in Eastern and Western cultures. *Self and Identity, 10*, 203–212.

Lundh, L. G., & Ost, L. G. (2001). Attentional bias, self-consciousness and perfectionism in social phobia before and after cognitive-behaviour therapy. *Scandinavian Journal of Behaviour Therapy, 30*, 4–16.

Neff, K. D. (2003). Self-compassion: An alternative conceptualization of a healthy attitude toward oneself. *Self and Identity, 2*, 85–102.

Pleva, J., & Wade, T. D. (2007). Guided self-help versus pure self-help for perfectionism: A randomised controlled trial. *Behaviour Research and Therapy, 45*, 849–861.

Powers, T. A., Koestner, R., Zuroff, D. C., Milyavskaya, M., & Gorin, A. (2011). The effects of self-criticism and self-oriented perfectionism on goal pursuit. *Personality and Social Psychology Bulletin, 37*, 964–975.

Rector, N. A., Bagby, R. M., Segal, Z. V., Joffe, R. T., & Levitt, A. (2000). Self-criticism and dependency in depressed patients treated with cognitive therapy or pharmacotherapy. *Cognitive Therapy and Research, 24*, 571–584.

Rice, K. G., & Ashby, J. S. (2007). An efficient method for classifying perfectionists. *Journal of Counseling Psychology, 54*, 72–85.

Rice, K. G., Gilman, R., & Ashby, J. S. (2011). Classifying adolescent perfectionists. *Psychological Assessment, 23*, 563–577.

Sassaroli, S., Lauro, L. J. R., Ruggiero, G. M., Mauri, M. C., Vinai, P., & Frost, R. (2008). Perfectionism in depression, obsessive–compulsive disorder and eating disorders. *Behaviour Research and Therapy, 46*, 757–765.

Shahar, G., Blatt, S. J., Zuroff, D. C., Krupnick, J., & Sotsky, S. M. (2004). Perfectionism impedes social relations and response to brief treatment for depression. *Journal of Social and Clinical Psychology, 23*, 140–154.

Shapiro, S. L., Brown, K. W., & Biegel, G. M. (2007). Teaching self-care to caregivers: Effects of mindfulness-based stress reduction on the mental health of therapists in training. *Training and Education in Professional Psychology, 1*, 105–115.

Slaney, R., Chadha, N., Mobley, M., & Kennedy, S. (2000). Perfectionism in Asian Indians: Exploring the meaning of the construct in India. *The Counseling Psychologist, 28*, 10–31.

Steele, A., & Wade, T. D. (2008). A randomised trial investigating guided self-help to reduce perfectionism and its impact on bulimia nervosa: A pilot study. *Behaviour Research and Therapy, 46*, 1316–1323.

Stoeber, J., & Otto, K. (2006). Positive conceptions of perfectionism: Approaches, evidence, challenges. *Personality and Social Psychology Review, 10*, 295–319.

Van Yperen, N., Verbraak, M., & Spoor, E. (2011). Perfectionism and clinical disorders among employees. *Personality and Individual Differences, 50*, 1126–1130.

Wampold, B. E. (2001). *The great psychotherapy debate: Models, methods, and findings*. Mahwah, NJ: Erlbaum.

Wang, K., Yuen, M., & Slaney, R. (2009). Perfectionism, depression, loneliness, and life satisfaction: A study of high school students in Hong Kong. *The Counseling Psychologist, 37*, 249–274.

Wang, K. T., Slaney, R. B., & Rice, K. G. (2007). Perfectionism in Chinese university students from Taiwan: A study of psychological well-being and achievement motivation. *Personality and Individual Differences, 42*(7), 1279–1290.

Whelton, W. J., & Greenberg, L. S. (2005). Emotion in self-criticism. *Personality and Individual Differences, 38*, 1583–1595.

Zuroff, D. C., & Blatt, S. J. (2002). Interpersonal relatedness and self-definition: Two prototypes for depression. *Clinical Psychology Review, 12*, 527–562.

Zuroff, D. C., Blatt, S. J., Sanislow, C. A., Bondi, C. M., & Pilkonis, P. A. (1999). Vulnerability to depression: Reexamining state dependence and relative stability. *Journal of Abnormal Psychology, 108*, 76–89.

Zuroff, D. C., Blatt, S. J., Sotsky, S. M., Krupnick, J. L., Martin, D. J., & Simmens, S. (2000). Relation of therapeutic alliance and perfectionism to outcome in brief outpatient treatment of depression. *Journal of Consulting and Clinical Psychology, 68*, 114–124.

Zuroff, D. C., Koestner, R., Moskowitz, D. S., McBride, C., & Bagby, R. M. (2011). Therapist's autonomy support and patient's self-criticism predict motivation during brief treatments for depression. *Journal of Social and Clinical Psychology, 31*, 903–932.

Clinician Application

Joiner, T. E. Jr., Walker, R. L., Rudd, M. D., & Jobes, D. A. (1999). Scientizing and routinizing the assessment of suicidality in outpatient practice. *Professional Psychology: Research & Practice, 30*, 447–453.

Shahar, G., Blatt, S. J., Zuroff, D. C., Krupnick, J., & Sotsky, S. M. (2004). Perfectionism impedes social relations and response to brief treatment for depression. *Journal of Social and Clinical Psychology, 23*, 140–154.

CHAPTER 32

Research

Cohen, J., & Ferrari, J. R. (2010). Take some time to think this over: The relation between rumination, indecision, and creativity. *Creativity Research Journal, 22*, 68–73.

Diaz-Morales, J. F., Cohen, J., & Ferrari, J. R. (2008). An integrated view of personality styles related to avoidant procrastination. *Personality and Individual Differences, 45*, 554–558.

Diaz-Morales, J. F., Ferrari, J. R., Diaz, K., & Argumendo, D. (2006). Factor structure of three procrastination scales with a Spanish adult population. *European Journal of Personality Assessment, 22*, 132-137.

Ferrari, J. R. (1991a). A preference for a favorable public impression by procrastination: Selecting among cognitive and social tasks. *Personality and Individual Differences, 12*, 1233–1237.

Ferrari, J. R. (1991b). Self-handicapping by procrastinators: Protecting social-esteem, self-esteem, or both? *Journal of Research in Personality, 25*, 245–261.

Ferrari, J. R. (1992a). Procrastination and perfect behavior: An exploratory factor analysis of self-presentational, self-awareness, and self-handicapping components. *Journal of Research in Personality, 26*, 75–84.

Ferrari, J. R. (1992b). Procrastination in the workplace: Attributions for failure among individuals with similar behavioral tendencies. *Personality and Individual Differences, 13*, 315–319.

Ferrari, J. R. (1992c). Psychometric validation of two procrastination inventories for adults: Arousal and avoidance measures. *Journal of Psychopathology and Behavioral Assessment, 14*, 97–110.

Ferrari, J. R. (1993). Christmas and procrastination: Explaining lack of diligence at a "real-world" task deadline. *Personality and Individual Differences, 14*, 25–33.

Ferrari, J. R. (1994). Dysfunctional procrastination and its relationship with self-esteem, interpersonal dependency, and self-defeating behaviors. *Personality and Individual Differences, 15*, 673–679.

Ferrari, J. R. (2000). Procrastination and attention: Factor analysis of attention deficit, boredomness, intelligence, self-esteem and task delay frequencies. *Journal of Social Behavior and Personality, 15*, 185–196.

Ferrari, J. R. (2001). Procrastination as self-regulation failure of performance: Effects of cognitive load, self-awareness, and time limits on "working best under pressure." *European Journal of Personality, 15*, 391–406.

Ferrari, J. R., Barnes, K. L., & Steel, P. (2009). Life regrets by avoidant and arousal procrastinators: Why put off today what you will regret tomorrow? *Journal of Individual Differences, 30*, 163–168.

Ferrari, J. R., & Diaz-Morales J. F. (2007). Procrastination: Different time perspectives predict different motives. *Journal of Research in Personality, 41*, 707–714.

Ferrari, J. R., Diaz-Morales, J. F., O'Callaghan, J., Diaz, K., & Argumendo, D. (2007). Frequent behavioral delay tendencies by adults: International prevalence rates of chronic procrastination. *Journal of Cross-Cultural Psychology, 38*, 458–464.

Ferrari, J. R., & Dovidio, J. F. (2000). Examining behavioral processes in indecision: Decisional procrastination and decision-making style. *Journal of Research in Personality, 34*, 127–137.

Ferrari, J. R., & Dovidio, J. F. (2001). Behavioral decision making strategies by indecisives. *Personality and Individual Differences, 30*, 1113–1123.

Ferrari, J. R., Driscoll, M., & Diaz-Morales, J. F. (2007). Examining the self of chronic procrastinators: Actual, ought, and undesired attributes. *Individual Differences Research, 5*, 115–128.

Ferrari, J. R., & Emmons, R. A. (1994). Procrastination as revenge: Do people report using delays as strategy for vengeance? *Personality and Individual Differences, 15*, 539–544.

Ferrari, J. R., & Emmons, R. A. (1995). Methods of procrastination and their relation to self-control and self-reinforcement: An empirical study. *Journal of Social Behavior and Personality, 10*, 135–142.

Ferrari, J. R., Harriott, J., & Zimmerman, M. (1999). The social support networks of procrastinators: Friends or family in times of trouble? *Personality and Individual Differences, 26*, 321–334.

Ferrari, J. R., & McCrown, W. (1994). Procrastination tendencies among obsessive-compulsives and their relatives. *Journal of Clinical Psychology, 50*, 162–167.

Ferrari, J. R. & Patel, T. (2004). Social comparisons by procrastinators: Rating peers with similar and dissimilar delay tendencies. *Personality and Individual Differences, 37*, 1493–1501.

Ferrari, J. R., & Pychyl, T. A. (2007). Regulating speed, accuracy, and judgments by indecisives: Effects of frequent choices on self-regulation failure. *Personality and Individual Differences, 42*, 777–787.

Ferrari, J. R., & Olivette, M. J. (1994). Parental authority influences on the development of female dysfunctional procrastination. *Journal of Research in Personality, 28*, 87–100.

Ferrari, J. R., Özer, B. U., & Demir, A. (2009). Chronic procrastination among Turkish adults: Exploring decisional, avoidant, and arousal styles. *Journal of Social Psychology, 149*, 302–307.

Ferrari, J. R., & Tice, D. M. (2000). Procrastination as a self-handicap for men and women: A task avoidance strategy in a laboratory setting. *Journal of Research in Personality, 34*, 73–83.

Gropel, P., & Steel, P. (2008). A mega-trial investigation of goal setting, interest enhancement, and energy on procrastination. *Personality and Individual Differences, 45*, 406–411.

Harriott, J., Ferrari, J. R., & Dovidio, J. F. (1996). Distractibility, daydreaming, and self-critical cognitions as determinants of indecision. *Journal of Social Behavior and Personality, 11*, 337–344.

Klassen, R., Ang, R. P., Chong, W. H., Krawchuk, L. L., Huan, V. S., … Yeo, L. S. (2009). A cross-cultural study of adolescent procrastination. *Journal of Research on Adolescence, 19*, 799–811.

Neenam, M. (2008). Tackling procrastination: An REBT perspective for coaches. *Journal of Rational-Emotive & Cognitive Behavior Therapy, 26*, 53–62.

Rabin, L. A., Fogel, J., & Nutter-Upham, K. E. (2011). Academic procrastination in college students: The role of self-reported executive function. *Journal of Clinical and Experimental Neuropsychology, 33*, 344–357.

Sirois, F. M. (2007). I'll look after my health, later: A replication and extension of the procrastination-health model with community-dwelling adults. *Personality and Individual Differences, 43*, 15–26.

Stead, R., Shanahan, M. J., & Neufeld, R. W. (2010). I'll go to therapy, eventually: Procrastination, stress and mental health. *Personality and Individual Differences, 49*, 175–180.

Clinician Application

Fiore, N. (2007). *The Now Habit.* New York, NY: Tarcher.

Sapadin, L. (2006). Overcoming resistance: What's stopping you? In D. Ricklin (Ed.), *101 great ways to improve your life* (Vol. 2, pp. 285–288). Marlboro, NJ: Self-Growth Publishing.

Sapadin, L. (2004). *Master your fears: How to triumph over your worries and get on with your life.* Hoboken, NJ: Wiley & Sons.

Sapadin, L. (2012). Why all the enlightenment, empowerment and opportunity embedded in this book may mean nothing to you. In C. Stout (Ed.), *Getting better at private practice* (pp. 379–383). Hoboken, NJ: Wiley & Sons.

Sapadin, L. (2013). *Procrastination busting strategies for perfectionists.* Long Beach, NY: PsychWisdom Publishing.

Yuen, L., & Burka, J. (2008). *Procrastination: Why you do it, what to do about it.* Boston, MA: Da Capo.

CHAPTER 33

Research

American Psychiatric Association. (2013). *Diagnostic and statistical manual of mental disorders* (5th ed). Washington, DC: Author.

Becker, C. B., Zayfert, C., & Anderson, E. (2004). A survey of psychologists' attitudes towards and utilization of exposure therapy for PTSD. *Behaviour Research and Therapy, 42*, 277–292.

Blanchard, E. B., Hickling, E. J., Barton, K. A., Taylor, A. E., Loos, W. R., & Jones-Alexander, J. (1996). One-year prospective follow-up of motor vehicle accident victims. *Behaviour Research and Therapy, 34*, 775–786.

Brewin, C. R., Andrews, B., & Valentine, J. D. (2000). Meta-analysis of risk factors for posttraumatic stress disorder in trauma-exposed adults. *Journal of Consulting and Clinical Psychology, 68*, 748-766.

Chapman, C., Mills, K., Slade, T., McFarlane, A. C., Bryant, R. A., ... Teeson, M. (2012). Remission from post-traumatic stress disorder in the general population. *Psychological Medicine, 42*, 1695–1703.

Cougle, J. R., Keough M. E., Riccardi, C. J., & Sachs-Ericsson, N. (2009). Anxiety disorders and suicidality in the National Comorbidity Survey-Replication. *Journal of Psychiatric Research, 43*, 825–829.

Foa, E. B., Dancu, C. V., Hembree, E. A., Jaycox, L. H., Meadows, E. A., & Street, G. P. (1999). A comparison of exposure therapy, stress inoculation training, and their combination for reducing posttraumatic stress disorder in female assault victims. *Journal of Consulting and Clinical Psychology, 67*, 194-200.

Foa, E. B., Hembree, E. A., Cahill, S. P., Rauch, S. A. M., Riggs, D. S., ... Yadin, E. (2005). Randomized trial of prolonged exposure for posttraumatic stress disorder with and without cognitive restructuring: Outcome at academic and community clinics. *Journal of Consulting and Clinical Psychology, 73*, 953-964.

Greenberg, P. E., Sisitsky, T., Kessler, R. C., Finkelstein, S. N., Berndt, E. R., ... Fyer, A. J. (1999). The economic burden of anxiety disorders in the 1990s. *Journal of Clinical Psychiatry, 60*, 427-435.

Hembree, E. A., Foa, E. B., Dorfan, N. M., Street, G. P., Kowalski, J., & Tu, X. (2003). Do patients drop out prematurely from exposure therapy for PTSD? *Journal of Traumatic Stress, 16*, 555–562.

Keane, T. M., & Barlow, D. H. (2002). Posttraumatic stress disorder. In D.H. Barlow (Ed.), *Anxiety and its disorders* (pp. 418–453). New York, NY: The Guildford Press.

Litz, B. T., Gray, M. T., Bryant, M. J., & Adler, A. B. (2002). Early intervention for trauma: Current status and future directions. *Clinical Psychology: Science and Practice, 9*, 112–134.

Pietrzak, R. H., Goldstein, R. B., Southwick, S. M., & Grant, B. F. (2011). Prevalence and Axis I comorbidity of full and partial posttraumatic stress disorder in the United States: Results from Wave 2 of the National Epidemiologic Survey on Alcohol and Related Conditions. *Journal of Anxiety Disorders, 25*, 456–465.

Powers, M. B., Halpern, J. M., Ferenschak, M. P., Gillihan, S. J., & Foa, E. B. (2010). A meta-analytic review of prolonged exposure for posttraumatic stress disorder. *Clinical Psychology Review, 30*, 635–641.

Ramchand, R., Schell, T., Karney, B., Osilla, K., Burns, R., & Caldarone, L. (2010). Disparate prevalence estimates of PTSD among service members who served in Iraq and Afghanistan: Possible explanations. *Journal of Traumatic Stress, 23*, 59–68.

Roberts, A. L., Gilman, S. E., Breslau, J., Breslau, N., & Koenen, K. C. (2011). Race/ethnic differences in exposure to traumatic events, development of post-traumatic stress disorder, and treatment-seeking for post-traumatic stress disorder in the United States. *Psychological Medicine, 41*, 71–83.

CHAPTER 34

Research

American Psychological Association. (2000). *Diagnostic and statistical manual of mental disorders* (4th ed., Text revision). Washington, DC: American Psychiatric Publishing, Inc.

Amir, N., Weber, G., Beard, C., Bomyea, J., & Taylor, C. T. (2008). The effect of a single-session attention modification program on response to a public-speaking challenge in socially anxious individuals. *Journal of Abnormal Psychology, 117*(4), 860–868. doi: 10.1037/a0013445

Anderson, P. L., Price, M., Edwards, S. M., Obasaju, M. A., Schmertz, S. K., Zimand, E., & Calamaras, M. R. (in press). Virtual reality exposure therapy for social phobia: A randomized controlled trial. *Journal of Consulting and Clinical Psychology*.

Antony, M. M. (1997). Assessment and treatment of social phobia. *Canadian Journal of Psychiatry, 42*, 826–834.

Barlow, D. (2002). *Anxiety and its disorders: The nature and treatment of anxiety and panic* (2nd ed.). New York, NY: The Guilford Press.

Blöte, A. W., Kint, M. J. W., Miers, A. C., & Westenberg, P. M. (2009). The relation between public speaking anxiety and social anxiety: A review. *Journal of Anxiety Disorders, 23*(3), 305–313. doi: 10.1016/j.janxdis.2008.11.007

Cho, Y., Smits, J. A. J., & Telch, M. J. (2004). The Speech Anxiety Thoughts Inventory: Scale development and preliminary psychometric data. *Behaviour Research and Therapy, 42*(1), 13–25. doi: 10.1016/s0005-7967(03)00067-6

Cho, Y., & Wan, H. (1997). Cognitive assessment of social anxiety: A study on the development and validation of the social interaction self-efficacy scale. *Issues in Psychological Reseasrch, 4*, 397–434.

Davidson, R. J., Marshall, J. R., Tomarken, A. J., & Henriques, J. B. (2000). While a phobic waits: Regional brain electrical and autonomic activity in social phobics during anticipation of public speaking. *Biological Psychiatry, 47*, 85–95.

Ferguson, B. A., & Anderson, P. L. (2008). Caucasians and 'other': A review of race/ethnicity in treatment outcome studies for social anxiety. Poster presented at the Association for Behavioral and Cognitive Therapies' (ABCT) 42nd Annual Convention, Orlando, FL.

Foa, E. B., & Kozak, M. J. (1986). Emotional processing of fear: Exposure to corrective information. *Psychological Bulletin, 99*(1), 20–35. doi: 10.1037/0033-2909.99.1.20

Hart, T. A., & Heimberg, R. G. (2001). Presenting problems among treatment-seeking gay, lesbian, and bisexual youth. *Journal of Clinical Psychology, 57*(5), 615–627. doi: 10.1002/jclp.1032

Heinrichs, N., Hoffman, E. C., & Hofmann, S. G. (2001). Cognitive-behavioral treatment for social phobia in Parkinson's disease: A single-case study. *Cognitive and Behavioral Practice, 8*(4), 328–335. doi: 10.1016/s1077-7229(01)80005-5

Meyer, I. H. (2003). Prejudice, social stress, and mental health in lesbian, gay, and bisexual populations: Conceptual issues and research evidence. *Psychological Bulletin, 129*(5), 674–697. doi: 10.1037/0033-2909.129.5.674

Pollard, C. A., & Henderson, J. F. (1988). Four types of social phobia in a community sample. *Journal of Nervous and Mental Disease, 176*, 440–445.

Rodebaugh, T. L., Holaway, R. M., & Heimberg, R. G. (2004). The treatment of social anxiety disorder. *Clinical Psychology Review, 24*(7), 883–908. doi: 10.1016/j.cpr.2004.07.007

Ruscio, A. M., Brown, T. A., Chiu, W. T., Sareen, J., Stein, M. B., & Kessler, R. C. (2008). Social fears and social phobia in the USA: Results from the National Comorbidity Survey Replication. *Psychological Medicine: A Journal of Research in Psychiatry and the Allied Sciences, 38*(1), 15–28. doi: 10.1017/s0033291707001699

Schneier, F. R., Johnson, J., Hornig, C. D., & Liebowitz, M. R. (1992). Social phobia: Comorbidity and morbidity in an epidemiologic sample. *Archives of General Psychiatry, 49*, 282–288.

Stein, M. B. (1996). How shy is too shy? *Lancet, 347*, 1131–1132.

Stein, M. B., Heuser, I. J., Juncos, J. L., & Uhde, T. W. (1990). Anxiety disorders in patients with Parkinson's disease. *The American Journal of Psychiatry, 147*(2), 217–220.

Stein, M. B., & Kean, Y. M. (2000). Disability and quality of life in social phobia: Epidemiologic findings. *The American Journal of Psychiatry, 157*, 1606–1613.

Stein, M. B., Walter, J. R., & Forde, D. R. (1996). Public speaking fears in a community sample: Prevalence, impact on functioning, and diagnostic classification. *Archives of General Psychiatry, 53*, 169–174.

Stein, M. B., Watker, J. R., & Forde, D. R. (1994). Setting diagnostic thresholds for social phobia: Considerations from a community survey of social anxiety. *American Journal of Psychiatry, 151*, 408–412.

Wallach, H. S., Safir, M. P., & Bar-Zvi, M. (2009). Virtual reality cognitive behavior therapy for public speaking anxiety: A randomized clinical trial. *Behavior Modification, 33*(3), 314–338. doi: 10.1177/0145445509331926

Wiederhold, B. K., & Wiederhold, M. D. (2005). *Virtual reality therapy for anxiety disorders: Advances in evaluation and treatment.* Washington, DC: American Psychological Association.

CHAPTER 35

Research

Blazer, D. G., Kessler, R. C., & Schwartz, M. S. (1998). Epidemiology of recurrent major and minor depression with a seasonal pattern: The National Comorbidity Survey. *British Journal of Psychiatry, 172*, 164–167.

Booker, J. M., & Hellekson, C. J. (1992). Prevalence of seasonal affective disorder in Alaska. *American Journal of Psychiatry, 149*, 1176–1182.

Eastman, C. I., Gallo, L. C., Lahmeyer, H. W., & Fogg, L. F. (1993). The circadian rhythm of temperature during light treatment for winter depression. *Biological Psychiatry, 34*, 210–220.

Golden, R. N., Gaynes, B. N., Ekstrom, R. D., Hamer, R. M., Jacobsen, F. M., … Nemeroff, C. B. (2005). The efficacy of light therapy in the treatment of mood disorders: A meta-analysis of the evidence. *American Journal of Psychiatry, 162*, 656–662.

Guzman, A., Rohan, K. J., Yousufi, S. M., Soriano, J. J., & Postolache, T. T. (2007). Seasonality of mood in African college students in Washington, D.C. *The Scientific World Journal: Child Health and Human Development, 7*, 584–591.

Hebert, M., Dumont, M., & Lachapelle, P. (2002). Electrophysiological evidence suggesting a seasonal modulation of retinal sensitivity in subsyndromal winter depression. *Journal of Affective Disorders, 68*, 191–202.

Jang, K. L., Lam, R. W., Livesley, W. J., & Vernon, P. A. (1997). Gender differences in the heritability of seasonal mood change. *Psychiatry Research, 70*, 145–154.

Kasper, S., Rogers, S. L. B., Yancey, A., Schultz, P. M., Skwerer, R. G., & Rosenthal, N. E. (1989). Phototherapy in individuals with and without subsyndromal seasonal affective disorder. *Archives of General Psychiatry, 46*, 837–844.

Lam, R. W., Levitt, A. J., Levitan, R. D., Enns, M., Morehouse, R. L., ... Tam, E. M. (2006). The CAN-SAD study: A randomized controlled study of light therapy and fluoxetine in patients with winter seasonal affective disorder. *American Journal of Psychiatry, 163,* 805–812.

Lambert, G. W., Reid, C., Kaye, D. M., Jennings, G. L., & Esler, M. D. (2002). Effect of sunlight and season on serotonin turnover in the brain. *Lancet, 360,* 1840–1842.

Levitt, A. J., Joffe, R. T., Brecher D., & MacDonald, C. (1993). Anxiety disorders and anxiety symptoms in a clinic sample of seasonal and non-seasonal depressives. *Journal of Affective Disorders, 28,* 51–56.

Lewy, A. J., Lefler, B. J., Emens, J. S., & Bauer, V. K. (2006). The circadian basis of winter depression. *PNAS Proceedings of the National Academy of Sciences of the United States of America, 103,* 7414–7419.

Madden, P. A., Heath, A. C., Rosenthal, N. E., & Martin, N. G. (1996). Seasonal changes in mood and behavior. The role of genetic factors. *Archives of General Psychiatry, 53,* 47–55.

Magnusson, A. (2000). An overview of epidemiological studies on seasonal affective disorder. *Acta Psychiatrica Scandinavica, 101,* 176–184.

Magnusson, A., & Partonen, T. (2005). The diagnosis, symptomatology, and epidemiology of seasonal affective disorder. *CNS Spectrums, 10,* 625–634.

Mersch, P. P., Middendorp, H. M., Bouhuys, A. L., Beersma, D. G. M., & van den Hoofdakker, R. H. (1999). Seasonal affective disorder and latitude: A review of the literature. *Journal of Affective Disorders, 53,* 35–48.

Modell, J. G., Rosenthal, N. E., Harriett, A. E., Krishen, A., Asgharian, A., ... Wrightman, D. S. (2005). Seasonal affective disorder and its prevention by anticipatory treatment with Buproprion XL. *Biological Psychiatry, 58,* 658–667.

Rohan, K. J. (2008). *Coping with the seasons: A cognitive-behavioral approach to seasonal affective disorder. Therapist guide.* In the Treatments that Work™ Series. New York, NY: Oxford University Press.

Rohan, K. J., & Nillni, Y. I. (2008). Thinking outside of the light box: Applications of cognitive-behavioral theory and therapy to seasonal affective disorder. *International Journal of Child Health and Human Development, 1,* 155–164.

Rohan, K. J., Roecklein, K. A., Lacy, T. J., & Vacek, P. M. (2009). Winter depression recurrence one year after cognitive-behavioral therapy, light therapy, or combination treatment. *Behavior Therapy, 40,* 225–238.

Rohan, K. J., Sigmon, S. T., Dorhofer, D. M. (2003). Cognitive-behavioral factors in seasonal affective disorder. *Journal of Consulting and Clinical Psychology, 71,* 22–30.

Rosen, L. N., Targum, S. D., Terman, M., Bryant, M. J., Hoffman, H., ... Rosenthal, N. E. (1990). Prevalence of seasonal affective disorder at four latitudes. *Psychiatry Research, 31,* 131–144.

Rosenthal, N. E., Sack, D. A., Gillin, J. C., Lewy, A. J., Goodwin, F. K., ... Wehr, T. A. (1984). Seasonal affective disorder: A description of the syndrome and preliminary findings with light therapy. *Archives of General Psychiatry, 41,* 72–80.

Sigmon, S. T., Pells, J. J., Schartel, J. G., Hermann, B. A., Edenfield, T. M., ... Whitcomb-Smith, S. R. (2007). Stress reactivity and coping in seasonal and nonseasonal depression. *Behaviour Research and Therapy, 45,* 965–975.

Sohn, C.-H., & Lam, R. W. (2005). Update on the biology of seasonal affective disorder. *CNS Spectrums, 10,* 635–646.

Terman, M., Terman, J. S., Quitkin, F., McGrath, P., Stewart, J., & Rafferty, B. (1989). Light therapy for seasonal affective disorder: A review of efficacy. *Neuropsychopharmacology, 2,* 1–22.

Wehr, T. A., Duncan, W. C., Jr., Sher, L., Aeschbach, D., Schwartz, P. J., ... Rosenthal, N. E. (2001). A circadian signal of change of season in patients with seasonal affective disorder. *Archives of General Psychiatry, 58,* 1108–1114.

Westrin, A., & Lam, R. W. (2007). Seasonal affective disorder: A clinical update. *Annals of Clinical Psychiatry, 19*(4), 239–246.

Clinician Application

Berson, D. M., Dunn, F. A. & Takao, M. (2002). Phototransduction by retinal ganglion cells that set the circadian clock. *Science, 295,* 1070–1073.

Booker, J. M., & Helleckson, C. J. (1992). Prevalence of seasonal affective disorder in Alaska. *American Journal of Psychiatry, 149,* 1176–1182.

Hattar, S., Liao, H. -W., Takao, M., Berson, D. M., & Yau. K. -W. (2002). Melanopsin-containing retinal ganglion cells: Architecture, projections and intrinsic photosensitivity. *Science, 295,* 1065–1070.

Lam, R. W., & Levitt, A. J. (1999). *Clinical guidelines for the treatment of seasonal affective disorder.* Vancouver, Canada: Clinical & Academic Publishing.

Rosenthal, N. E., Sack, D. A., Gillin, J. C., Lewy, A. J., Goodwin, F. K., ... Wehr, T. A. (1984). Seasonal affective disorder: A description of the syndrome and preliminary findings with light therapy. *Archives of General Psychiatry, 41,* 72–80.

CHAPTER 36

Research

American Psychiatric Association. (2000). *Diagnostic and statistical manual of mental disorders* (4th ed., Text Revision). Washington, DC: American Psychiatric Association.

Baumeister, R. F., Campbell, J. D., Krueger, J. I., & Vohs, K. D. (2003). Does high self-esteem cause better performance, interpersonal success, happiness, or healthier lifestyles? *Psychological Science in the Public Interest, 4*, 1–44.

Beck, A. T. (1967). *Depression: Clinical, experimental, and theoretical aspects*. New York, NY: Harper & Row.

Beck, J. S. (1995). *Cognitive therapy: Basics and beyond*. New York, NY: Guilford Press.

Bednar, R., & Peterson, S. (1995). *Self-esteem: Paradoxes and innovations in clinical theory and practice* (2nd ed.). Washington, DC: American Psychological Association.

Blankertz, L. (2001). Cognitive components of self-esteem for individuals with severe mental illness. *American Journal of Orthopsychiatry, 71*, 457–465.

Brown, J. D., & Marshall, M. A. (2006). The three faces of self-esteem. In M. H. Kernis (Ed.), *Self-esteem issues and answers: A source book of current perspectives* (pp. 4–9). New York, NY: Psychology Press.

California Task Force to Promote Self-Esteem and Personal and Social Responsibility. (1990). *Toward a state of self-esteem*. Sacramento, CA: California State Department of Education.

Campbell, J. D., & Lavallee, L. F. (1993). Who am I? The role of self-concept confusion in understanding the behavior of people with low self-esteem. In R. F. Baumeister (Ed.), *Self-esteem: The puzzle of low self-regard* (pp. 3–20). New York, NY: Plenum Press.

Frey, D., & Carlock, C. J. (1989). *Enhancing self-esteem* (2nd ed.). Muncie, IN: Accelerated Development.

Gentile, B., Twenge, J. M., & Campbell, W. K. (2010). Birth cohort differences in self-esteem, 1988-2008: Cross-temporal meta-analysis. *Review of General Psychology, 14*, 261–268.

Hakim-Larson, J., & Mruk, C. (1997). Enhancing self-esteem in a community mental health setting. American Journal of Orthopsychiatry, 67, 655–659.

Haney, P., & Durlak, J. A. (1998). Changing self-esteem in children and adolescents: A meta-analytic review. *Journal of Clinical Child Psychology, 27*, 423–433.

James, W. (1890). *The principles of psychology* (Vol. 1). New York, NY: Holt.

Kernis, M. H. (2003). Toward a conceptualization of optimal self-esteem. *Psychological Inquiry, 14*, 1–26.

McKay, M., & Fanning, P. (1992). *Self-esteem*. Oakland, CA: New Harbinger.

Mruk, C. (2006). *Self-esteem: Research, theory, and practice* (3rd ed.). New York, NY: Springer.

Newns, K., Bell, L., & Thomas, S. (2003). The impact of a self-esteem group for people with eating disorders: An uncontrolled study. *Clinical Psychology and Psychotherapy, 10*, 64–68.

O'Brien, E. J., Bartoletti, M., & Leitzel, J. D. (2006). Self-esteem, psychopathology, and psychotherapy. In M. H. Kernis (Ed.), *Self-esteem issues and answers: A sourcebook of current perspectives* (pp. 306–315). New York, NY: Psychology Press.

Orth, U., Robins, R. W., & Roberts, B. W. (2008). Low self-esteem prospectively predicts depression in adolescence and young adulthood. *Journal of Personality and Social Psychology, 95*, 695–708.

Pope, A., McHale, S., & Craighead, E. (1988). *Self-esteem enhancement with children and adolescents*. New York, NY: Pergamon Press.

Roberts, J. E. (2006). Self-esteem from a clinical perspective. In M. H. Kernis (Ed.), *Self-esteem issues and answers: A sourcebook of current perspectives* (pp. 298–305). New York, NY: Psychology Press.

Rogers, C. R. (1959). A theory of therapy, personality, and interpersonal relationships, as developed in the client-centered framework. In S. Koch (Ed.), *Psychology: A study of science* (Vol. 3, pp. 184–256). New York, NY: McGraw-Hill.

Smith, M. L., Glass, G. V., & Miller, T. I. (1980). *The benefits of psychotherapy*. Baltimore, MD: Johns Hopkins University Press.

Swann, W. B., Chang-Schneider, C., & Larsen McClarty, K. (2007). Do people's self-views matter? Self-concept and self-esteem in everyday life. *American Psychologist, 62*, 84–94.

Trzesniewski, K. H., & Donnellan, M. B. (2009). Reevaluating the evidence for increasingly positive self-views among high school students: More evidence for consistency across generations (1976-2006). *Psychological Science, 20*, 920–922.

Trzesniewski, K. H., & Donnellan, M. B. (2010). Rethinking 'Generation Me': A study of cohort effects from 1976-2006. *Perspectives on Psychological Science, 5*, 58–75.

Trzesniewski, K. H., Donnellan, M. B., Moffitt, T. E., Robins, R. W., Poulton, R., & Caspi, A. (2006). Low self-esteem during adolescence predicts poor health, criminal behavior, and limited economic prospects during adulthood. *Developmental Psychology, 42*, 381–390.

Twenge, J. M., & Campbell, W. K. (2001). Age and birth cohort differences in self-esteem: A cross-temporal meta-analysis. *Personality and Social Psychology Review, 5*, 321–344.

Twenge, J. M., & Campbell, W. K. (2010). Birth cohort differences in the monitoring the future dataset and elsewhere: Further evidence for Generation Me – Commentary on Trzesniewski & Donnellan (2010). *Perspectives on Psychological Science, 5,* 81–88.

Vitousek, K., Watson, S., & Wilson, G. T. (1998). Enhancing motivation for change in treatment-resistant eating disorders. *Clinical Psychology Review, 18,* 391–420.

Young, J. E., Weinberger, A. D., & Beck, A. T. (2001). Cognitive therapy for depression. In D. H. Barlow (Ed.), *Clinical handbook of psychological disorders: A step-by-step treatment manual* (3rd ed., pp. 264–308). New York, NY: Guilford Press.

Zeigler-Hill, V. (2011). The connections between self-esteem and psychopathology. *Journal of Contemporary Psychotherapy, 41,* 157–164.

Clinician Application

Mruk, C. (1999). *Self-esteem: Research, theory, and practice* (2nd ed.). New York, NY: Springer Books.

CHAPTER 37

Research

American Psychiatric Association. (2000). *Diagnostic and statistical manual of mental disorders* (4th ed., text revision). Washington DC: Author.

Beidel, D. C., Turner, S. M., & Dancu, C. V. (1985). Physiological, cognitive and behavioral aspects of social anxiety. *Behaviour Research and Therapy, 23,* 109–117. doi: 10.1016/0005-7967(85)90019-1

Blanco, C., Heimberg, R. G., Schneier, F. R., Fresco, D. M., Chen, H., ... Liebowitz, M. R. (2010). A placebo-controlled trial of phenelzine, cognitive behavioral group therapy, and their combination for social anxiety disorder. *Archives of General Psychiatry, 67,* 286–295. doi: 10.1001/archgenpsychiatry.2010.11

Block, J. A., & Wulfert, E. (2000). Acceptance and change: Treating socially anxious college students with ACT or CBGT. *Behavior Analyst Today, 1,* 3–10.

Borge, F. -M., Hoffart, A., Sexton, H., Clark, D. M., Markowitz, J. C., & McManus, F. (2008). Residential cognitive therapy versus residential interpersonal therapy for social phobia: A randomized clinical trial. *Journal of Anxiety Disorders, 22,* 991–1010. doi: 10.1016/j.janxdis.2007.10.002

Chapman, T. F., Mannuzza, S., & Fyer, A. J. (1995). Epidemiology and family studies of social phobia. In R. G. Heimberg, M. R. Liebowitz, D. A. Hope, & F. R. Schneier (Eds.), *Social phobia: Diagnosis, assessment, and treatment* (pp. 21–40). New York, NY: Guilford Press.

Choy, Y., Schneier, F. R., Heimberg, R. G., Oh, K. -S., & Liebowitz, M. R. (2008). Features of the offensive subtype of *Taijin-Kyofu-Sho* in U.S. and Korean patients with DSM-IV social anxiety disorder. *Depression and Anxiety, 25,* 230–240. doi: 10.1002/da.20295

Clark, D. M., Ehlers, A., McManus, F., Hackmann, A., Fennell, M., ... Louis, B. (2003). Cognitive therapy versus fluoxetine in generalized social phobia: A randomized placebo-controlled trial. *Journal of Consulting and Clinical Psychology, 71,* 1058–1067. doi: 10.1037/0022-006X.71.6.1058

Clark, D. M., & Wells, A. (1995). A cognitive model of social phobia. In R. Heimberg, M. Liebowitz, D. Hope & F. Schneier (Eds.), *Social phobia: Diagnosis, assessment, and treatment* (pp. 69–93). New York, London: The Guilford Press.

Dalrymple, K. L., & Herbert, J. D. (2007). Acceptance and Commitment Therapy for generalized social anxiety disorder. *Behavior Modification, 31,* 543–568. doi: 10.1177/0145445507302037

Davidson, J. R., Hughes, D. L., George, L. K., & Blazer, D. G. (1993). The epidemiology of social phobia: Findings from the Duke Epidemiological Catchment Area Study. *Psychological Medicine, 23,* 709–718. doi:10.1017/S0033291700025484

Davidson, J. R., Potts, N., Richichi, E., Krishnan, R., Ford, S. M., ... Wilson, W.H. (1993). Treatment of social phobia with clonazepam and placebo. *Journal of Clinical Psychopharmacology, 13,* 423–428. doi: 10.1097/00004714-199312000-00008

Foa, E. B., Franklin, M. E., & Moser, J. (2002). Context in the clinic: How well do cognitive-behavioral therapies and medications work in combination? *Biological Psychiatry, 52,* 987–997. doi: 10.1016/S0006-3223(02)01552-4

Heimberg, R. G., & Becker, R. E. (2002). *Cognitive- behavioral group therapy for social phobia: Basic mechanisms and clinical strategies.* New York, NY: The Guildford Press.

Heimberg, R. G., Brozovich, F. A., & Rapee, R. M. (2010). A cognitive behavioral model of social anxiety disorder: Update and extension. In S. G. Hofmann & P. M. Dibartolo (Eds.), *Social anxiety: Clinical, developmental, and social perspectives* (2nd ed., pp. 395–422). Amsterdam, The Netherlands: Elsevier. doi: 10.1016/B978-0-12-375096-9.00015-8

Heimberg, R. G., Dodge, C. S., Hope, D. A., Kennedy, C. R., Zollo, L. J., & Becker, R. E. (1990). Cognitive behavioral group therapy for social phobia: Comparison with a credible placebo control. *Cognitive Therapy and Research, 14*, 1–23. doi: 10.1007/BF01173521

Heimberg, R. G., Holt, C. S., Schneier, F. R., Spitzer, R. L., & Liebowitz, M. R. (1993). The issue of subtypes in the diagnosis of social phobia. *Journal of Anxiety Disorders, 7*, 249–269. doi: 10.1016/0887-6185(93)90006-7

Heimberg, R. G., Liebowitz, M. R., Hope, D. A., Schneier, F. R., Holt, C. S., ... Klein, D. F. (1998). Cognitive behavioral group therapy vs phenelzine therapy for social phobia: 12-week outcome. *Archives of General Psychiatry, 55*, 1133–1141. doi: 10.1001/archpsyc.55.12.1133

Heimberg, R. G., Salzman, D. G., Holt, C. S., & Blendell, K. A. (1993). Cognitive-behavioral group treatment for social phobia: Effectiveness at five-year followup. *Cognitive Therapy and Research, 17*, 325–339. doi: 10.1007/BF01177658

Hofmann, S. G., Meuret, A. E., Smits, J. A. J., Simon, N. M., Pollack, M. H., ... Otto, M.W. (2006). Augmentation of exposure therapy with D-cycloserine for social anxiety disorder. *Archives of General Psychiatry, 63*, 298–304. doi: 10.1001/archpsyc.63.3.298

Hope, D. A., Heimberg, R. G., & Turk, C. L. (2010a). *Managing social anxiety: A cognitive-behavioral therapy approach (client workbook)* (2nd ed.). New York, NY: Oxford University Press.

Hope, D. A., Heimberg, R. G., & Turk, C. L. (2010b). *Managing social anxiety: A cognitive-behavioral therapy approach (therapist guide)* (2nd ed.). New York, NY: Oxford University Press.

Katzelnick, D. J., & Greist, J. H. (2001). Social anxiety disorder: An unrecognized problem in primary care. *Journal of Clinical Psychiatry, 62*(Suppl. 1), 11–15.

Kessler, R. C., Berglund, P., Demler, O., Jin, R., Merikangas, K. R., & Walters, E. E. (2005). Lifetime prevalence and age-of-onset distributions of DSM-IV disorders in the National Comorbidity Survey Replication. *Archives of General Psychiatry, 62*, 593–768. doi: 10.1001/archpsyc.62.6.593

Kessler, R. C., Chiu, W. T., Demler, O., Merikangas, K., & Walters, E. E. (2005). Prevalence, severity, and comorbidity of 12-month DSM-IV disorders in the National Comorbidity Survey Replication. *Archives of General Psychiatry, 62*, 617–627. doi: 10.1001/archpsyc.62.6.617

Kocovski, N. L., Fleming, J. E., & Rector, N. A. (2009). Mindfulness and acceptance-based group therapy for social anxiety disorder: An open trial. *Cognitive and Behavioral Practice, 16*, 276–289. doi: 10.1016/j.cbpra.2008.12.004

Ledley, D. R., Heimberg, R. G., Hope, D. A., Hayes, S. A., Zaider, T. I., ... Fresco, D. M. (2009). Efficacy of a manualized and workbook-driven individual treatment for social anxiety disorder. *Behavior Therapy, 40*, 414–424. doi: 10.1016/j.beth.2008.12.001

Liebowitz, M. R., Heimberg, R. G., Schneier, F. R., Hope, D. A., Davies, S., ... Klein, D. F. (1999). Cognitive-behavioral group therapy versus phenelzine in social phobia: Long-term outcome. *Depression and Anxiety, 10*, 89–98. doi: 10.1002/(SICI)1520-6394(1999)10:3<89::AID-DA1>3.0.CO;2-5

Lipsitz, J. D., Gur, M., Vermes, D., Petkova, E., Cheng, J., ... Fyer, A. (2008). A randomized trial of interpersonal therapy versus supportive therapy for social anxiety disorder. *Depression and Anxiety, 25*, 542–553. doi: 10.1002/da.20364

Magee, W. J., Eaton, W. W., Wittchen, H. -U., McGonagle, K. A., & Kessler, R. C. (1996). Agoraphobia, simple phobia, and social phobia in the National Comorbidity Survey. *Archives of General Psychiatry, 53*, 159–168.

Otto, M. W., Pollack, M. H., Gould, R. A., Worthington, J. J., McArdle, E. T., ... Heimberg, R. G. (2000). A comparison of the efficacy of clonazepam and cognitive-behavioral group therapy for the treatment of social phobia. *Journal of Anxiety Disorders, 14*, 345–358. doi: 10.1016/S0887-6185(00)00027-X

Pontoski, K. E., & Heimberg, R. G. (2010). The myth of the superiority of concurrent combined treatments for anxiety disorders. *Clinical Psychology: Science and Practice, 17*, 107–111. doi: 10.1111/j.1468-2850.2010.01200.x

Powers, M. B., & Sigmarsson, S. R., & Emmelkamp, P. M. G. (2008). A meta-analytic review of psychological treatments for social anxiety disorder. *International Journal of Cognitive Therapy, 1*, 94–113. doi: 10.1521/ijct.2008.1.2.94

Rapee, R. M. (1995). Descriptive psychopathology of social phobia. In R. Heimberg, M. Liebowitz, D. Hope & F. Schneier (Eds.), *Social Phobia: Diagnosis, assessment, and treatment* (pp. 41–68). New York, NY: Guildford Press.

Rapee, R. M., & Heimberg, R. G. (1997). A cognitive-behavioral model of anxiety in social phobia. *Behaviour Research and Therapy, 35*, 741–756. doi: 10.1016/S0005-7967(97)00022-3

Rodebaugh, T. L. (2009). Social phobia and perceived friendship quality. *Journal of Anxiety Disorders, 23*, 872–878. doi: 10.1016/j.janxdis.2009.05.001

Sakurai, A., Nagata, T., Harai, H., Yamada, H., Mohri, I., ...Furukawa, T. A. (2005). Is "relationship fear" unique to Japan? Symptom factors and patient clusters of social anxiety disorder among the Japanese clinical population. *Journal of Affective Disorders, 87*, 131–137. doi: 10.1016/j.jad.2005.03.003

Schneier, F. R., Heckelman, L. R., Garfinkel, R. C., Campeas, R., Fallon, B. A., . Liebowitz, M. R. (1994). Functional impairment in social phobia. *Journal of Clinical Psychiatry, 55*, 322–331.

Takahashi, T. (1989). Social phobia syndrome in Japan. *Comprehensive Psychiatry, 30*, 45–52. doi: 10.1016/0010-440X(89)90117-X

Taylor, S. T. (1996). Meta-analysis of cognitive-behavioral treatments for social phobia. *Journal of Behavior Therapy and Experimental Psychiatry, 27*, 1–9. doi: 10.1016/0005-7916(95)00058-5

Torgrud, L. J., Walker, J. R., Murray, L., Cox, B. J., Chartier, M., & Kjernisted, K. D. (2004). Deficits in perceived social support associated with generalized social phobia. *Cognitive Behaviour Therapy, 33*, 87–96. doi: 10.1080/16506070410029577

Weeks, J. W., Heimberg, R. G., Rodebaugh, T. L., & Norton, P. J. (2008). Exploring the relationship between fear of positive evaluation and social anxiety. *Journal of Anxiety Disorders, 22*, 386–400. doi: 10.1016/j.janxdis.2007.04.009

Weinstock, L. S. (1999). Gender differences in the presentation and management of social anxiety disorder. *Journal of Clinical Psychiatry, 60*, 9–13.

Whisman, M. A. (2007). Marital distress and DSM-IV psychiatric disorders in a population-based national survey. *Journal of Abnormal Psychology, 116*, 638–643. doi: 10.1037/0021-843X.116.3.638

Wittchen, H.-U., & Fehm, L. (2001). Epidemiology, patterns of comorbidity, and associated disabilities of social phobia. *Psychiatric Clinics of North America, 24*, 617–641. doi: 10.1016/S0193-953X(05)70254-9

Clinician Application

Bruch, M. A., & Heimberg, R. G. (1994). Differences in perceptions of parental and personal characteristics between generalized and nongeneralized social phobics. *Journal of Anxiety Disorders, 8*, 155–168.

Bruch, M. A., Heimberg, R. G., Berger, P., & Collins, T. M. (1989). Social phobia and perceptions of early parental and personal characteristics. *Anxiety Research, 2*, 57–63.

Dalrymple K. L., & Herbert J. D. (2007). Acceptance and commitment therapy for generalized social anxiety disorder. *Behavior Modification, 31*, 543–568.

Engfer, A. (1993). Antecedents and consequences of shyness in boys and girls: A 6-year longitudinal study. In K. H. Rubin & J. B. Asendorpf (Eds.), *Social withdrawal, inhibition, and shyness in childhood* (pp. 49–79). Hillsdale, NJ: Erlbaum.

Hofmann, S. G., Asnaani, A., & Hinton, D. E. (2010). Cultural aspects in social anxiety and social anxiety disorder. *Depression and Anxiety, 27*, 1117–1127.

Juster, H. R., Heimberg, R. G., Frost, R. O., & Holt, C. S. (1996). Social phobia and perfectionism. *Personality and Individual Differences, 21*, 403–410.

Koszycki D., Benger M., Shlik J., & Bradwejn J. (2007). Randomized trial of a meditation-based stress reduction program and cognitive behavior therapy in generalized social anxiety disorder. *Behaviour Research and Therapy, 45*, 2518–2526.

Leung, A. W., Heimberg, R. G., Holt, C. S., & Bruch, M. A. (1994). Social anxiety and perceptions of early parenting among American, Chinese American, and social phobic samples. *Anxiety, 1*, 80–89.

Ossman, W. A., Wilson, K. G., Storaasli, R. D., & McNeill, J. W. (2006) A preliminary investigation of the use of acceptance and commitment therapy in a group treatment for social phobia. *International Journal of Psychology and Psychological Therapy, 6*, 397–416.

Roemer, L., & Orsillo, S. M. (2007). An open trial of acceptance-based behavior therapy for generalized anxiety disorder. *Behavior Therapy, 38*, 72–85.

Spokas, M. E., & Heimberg, R. G. (2009). Overprotective parenting, social anxiety, and external locus of control: Cross-sectional and longitudinal relationships. *Cognitive Therapy and Research, 33*, 543–551.

Westra, H. A., & Dozois, D. J. A. (2006). Preparing clients for cognitive behavioural therapy: A randomized pilot study of motivational interviewing for anxiety. *Cognitive Therapy and Research, 30*, 481–498.

CHAPTER 38

Research

American Psychiatric Association. (2013). *Diagnostic and statistical manual of mental disorders* (5th ed.). Washington, DC: American Psychiatric Association.

Azrin, N. H., & Nunn, R. G. (1973). Habit-reversal: A method of eliminating nervous habits and tics. *Behaviour Research and Therapy, 11*(4), 619–628. doi: 10.1016/0005-7967(73)90119-8

Bloch, M. H. (2009). Trichotillomania across the life span. *Journal of the American Academy of Child and Adolescent Psychiatry, 48*, 879–883. doi: 10.1097/CHI.0b013e3181ae09f3

Chamberlain, S. R., Odlaug, B. L., Boulougouris, V., Finberg, N. A., & Grant, J. E. (2009). Trichotillomania: Neurobiology and treatment. *Neuroscience and Biobehavioral Reviews, 33,* 831–842. doi: 10.1016/j.neubiorev.2009.02.002

Christenson, G. A., Pyle, R. L., & Mitchell, J. E. (1991). Estimated lifetime prevalence of trichotillomania in college students. *Journal of Clinical Psychology, 52,* 415–417.

Diefenbach, G. J., Tolin, D. F., Hannan, S., Crocetto, J., & Worhunsky, P. (2005). Trichotillomania: Impact on psychosocial functioning and quality of life. *Behaviour Research and Therapy, 43,* 869–884. doi: 10.1016/j.brat.2004.06.010

Diefenbach, G. J., Tolin, D. R., Hannan, S., Maltby, N., & Crocetto, J. (2006). Group treatment for trichotillomania: Behavior therapy versus supportive therapy. *Behavior Therapy, 37,* 353–363. doi: 10.1016/j.beth.2006.01.006

Flessner, C. A., Woods, D. W., Franklin, M. E., Keuthen, N. J., & Piacentini, J. (2009). Cross-sectional study of women with trichotillomania: A preliminary examination of pulling styles, severity, phenomenology, and functional impact. *Child Psychiatry and Human Development, 40,* 153–167. doi: 10.1007/s10578-008-0118-5

Flessner, C. A., Woods, D. W., Franklin, M. E., Keuthen, N. J., Piacentini, J. P., & Trichotillomania Learning Center Scientific Advisory Board. (2008). Styles of pulling in youths with trichotillomania: Exploring differences in symptom severity, phenomenology, and comorbid psychiatric symptoms. *Behaviour Research & Therapy, 46,* 1055–1061. doi: 10.1016/j.brat.2008.06.006

Franklin, M. E., Edson, A. L., Ledley, D. A., & Cahill, S. P. (2011). Behavior therapy for pediatric trichotillomania: A randomized controlled trial. *Journal of the American Academy of Child & Adolescent Psychiatry, 50,* 763–771. doi: 10.1016/j.jaac.2011.05.009

Franklin, M. E., Flessner, C. A., Woods, D. W., Keuthen, N. J., Piacentini, J. C., ... Stein, D. J. (2008). The Child and Adolescent Trichotillomania Impact Project: Descriptive psychopathology, comorbidity, functional impairment, and treatment utilization. *Journal of Developmental and Behavioral Pediatrics, 29,* 493–500. doi: 10.1097/DBP.0b013e31818d4328

Keijsers, G. P. J., van Minnen, A., Hoogduin, C. A. L., Klassen, B. N. W., Hendriks, M. J., & Tanis-Jacobs, J. (2006). Behavioural treatment of trichotillomania: Two year follow-up results. *Behaviour Research & Therapy, 44,* 359–370. doi: 10.1016/j.brat.2005.03.004

Keuthen, N. J., Fraim, C., Deckersbach, T., Dougherty, D. D., Baer, L., & Jenike, M. A. (2001). Longitudinal follow-up of naturalistic treatment outcome in patients with trichotillomania. *Journal of Clinical Psychiatry, 62,* 101–107. doi: 10.4088/JCP.v62n0205

Keuthen, N. J., Rothbaum, B. O., Welch, S. S., Taylor, C., Falkenstein, M., ... Jenike, M.A. (2010). Pilot trial of dialectical behavior therapy-enhanced habit reversal for trichotillomania. *Depression & Anxiety, 27,* 953–959. doi 10.1002/da.20732

Lerner, J., Franklin, M. E., Meadows, E. A., Hembree, E., & Foa, E. B. (1998). Effectiveness of a cognitive behavioral treatment program for trichotillomania: An uncontrolled evaluation. *Behavior Therapy, 29,* 157–171. doi: 10.1016/S0005-7894(98)80036-1

Lewin, A. B., Piacentini, J. P., Flessner, C. A., Woods, D. W., Franklin, M. E., ... the Trichotillomania Learning Center Scientific Advisory Board. (2009). Depression, anxiety, and functional impairment in children with trichotillomania. *Depression and Anxiety, 26,* 521–527.

Lochner, C., Seedat, S., & Stein, D. J. (2010). Chronic hair-pulling: Phenomenology-based subtypes. *Journal of Anxiety Disorders, 24,* 196–202. doi: 10.1016/j.janxdis.2009.10.008

Mansueto, C. S., Golomb, R. G., McCombs-Thomas, A., & Townsley-Stemberger, R. M. (1999). A comprehensive model for behavioral treatment of trichotillomania. *Cognitive and Behavioral Practice, 6,* 23–43. doi: 10.1016/S1077-7229(99)80038-8

Mansueto, C. S., Townsley-Stemberger, R. M., McCombs-Thomas, A., & Goldfinger-Golomb, R. (1997). Trichotillomania: A comprehensive behavioral model. *Clinical Psychology Review, 17,* 567–577. doi: 10.1016/S0272-7358(97)00028-7

Meunier, S. A., Tolin, D. F., & Franklin, M. E. (2009). Affective and sensory correlates of hair pulling in pediatric trichotillomania. *Behavior Modification, 33,* 396–407. doi: 10.1177/0145445508326260

Moore, P. S., Franklin, M. E., Keuthen, N. J., Flessner, C. A., Woods, D. W., ... Trichotillomania Learning Center Scientific Advisory Board. (2009). Family functioning in pediatric trichotillomania. *Child & Family Behavior Therapy, 31,* 255–269. doi: 10.1080/07317100903311000

Stein, D. J., Christenson, G. A., & Hollander, E. (1991). *Trichotillomania.* Washington, DC: American Psychiatric Press.

Woods, D. W., Flessner, C. A., Franklin, M. E., Keuthen, N. J., Goodwin, R., ... Trichotillomania Learning Center Scientific Advisory Board. (2006). The Trichotillomania Impact Project (TIP): Exploring phenomenology, functional impairment, and treatment utilization. *Journal of Clinical Psychiatry, 67,* 1877–1888. doi: 10.4088/JCP.v67n1207

Woods, D. W., & Twohig, M. P. (2008). *Trichotillomania: An ACT-enhanced Behavior Therapy Approach–Therapy Guide.* Oxford University Press.

Woods, D. W., Wetterneck, C. T., & Flessner, C. A. (2006). A controlled evaluation of acceptance and commitment therapy plus habit reversal for the treatment of trichotillomania. *Behaviour Research & Therapy, 44*, 639–656. doi: 10.1016/j.brat.2005.05.006

Clinician Application

Azrin, N. H., & Nunn, R. G. (1973). Habit-reversal: A method of eliminating nervous habits and tics. *Behaviour Research and Therapy, 11*, 619–628.

Keuthen, N. J., Rothbaum, B. O., Welch, S. S., Taylor, C., Falkenstein, M., ... Jenike, M.A. (2010). Pilot trial of dialectical behavior therapy-enhanced habit reversal for trichotillomania. *Depression & Anxiety, 27*, 953–959.

Neal-Barnett, A., Flessner, C., Franklin, M., Woods, D., Keuthen, N., & Stein, D. (2010). Ethnic differences in trichotillomania: Phenomenology, interference, impairment, and treatment efficacy. *Journal of Anxiety Disorders, 24*, 553–558.

Woods, D. W., & Twohig, M. P. (2008). *Trichotillomania: An ACT-enhanced behavior therapy approach–therapy guide.* New York, NY: Oxford University Press.

CHAPTER 39

Research

Bender, B. G., & Rand, C. (2004). Medication non-adherence and asthma treatment cost. *Current Opinion in Allergy and Clinical Immunology, 4*, 191–195.

European Community Respiratory Health Survey (ECRHS). (1996). Variations in the prevalence of respiratory symptoms, self-reported asthma attacks, and use of asthma medication in the European Community Respiratory Health Survey (ECRHS). *European Respiratory Journal, 9*, 687–695.

Fritz, G. K., McQuaid, E. L., Kopel, S. J., Seifer, R., Klein, R. B., ... Canino, G. (2010). Ethnic differences in perception of lung function: A factor in pediatric asthma disparities? *American Journal of Respiratory and Critical Care Medicine, 182*, 12–18.

Gillissen, A. (2004). Managing asthma in the real world. *International Journal of Clinical Practice, 58*, 592–603.

Global Initiative for Asthma (GINA). (2010). Global Strategy for Asthma Management and Prevention. Available from: http://www.ginasthma.org

Griffiths, C., Kaur, G., Gantley, M., Feder, G., Hillier, S., ... Packe, G. (2001). Influences on hospital admission for asthma in south Asian and white adults: qualitative interview study. *BMJ, 323*, 962.

Hasler, G., Gergen, P. J., Kleinbaum, D. G., Ajdacic, V., Gamma, A., ... Angst, J. (2005). Asthma and panic in young adults: A 20-year prospective community study. *American Journal of Respiratory and Critical Care Medicine, 171*, 1224–1230.

Horne, R., & Weinman, J. (2002). Self-regulation and self-management in asthma: Exploring the role of illness perceptions and treatment beliefs in explaining non-adherence to preventer medication. *Psychology and Health, 17*, 17–32.

Janson, C., Chinn, S., Jarvis, D., & Burney, P. (1997). Physician-diagnosed asthma and drug utilization in the European Community Respiratory Health Survey. *European Respiratory Journal, 10*, 1795–1802.

Janssens, T., Verleden, G., De Peuter, S., Van Diest, I., & Van den Bergh, O. (2009). Inaccurate perception of asthma symptoms: A cognitive-affective framework and implications for asthma treatment. *Clinical Psychology Review, 8*, 211–219.

Kopel, S. J., Walders-Abramson, N., McQuaid, E. L., Seifer, R., Koinis-Mitchell, D., ... Fritz, G. K. (2010). Asthma symptom perception and obesity in children. *Biological Psychology, 84*, 135–141.

Kotses, H., & Creer, T. L. (2010). Asthma self-management. In A. Harver & H. Kotses (Eds.), *Asthma, health and society* (pp. 117–139). New York, NY: Springer.

Lavoie, K. L., Bacon, S. L., Barone, S., Cartier, A., Ditto, B., & Labrecque, M. (2006). What is worse for asthma control and quality of life. *Chest, 130*, 1039–1047.

Lavoie, K. L., Boudreau, M., Plourde, A., Campbell, T. S., & Bacon, S. L. (2011). Association between Generalized Anxiety Disorder and asthma morbidity. *Psychosomatic Medicine, 73*, 504–513.

Lehrer, P. M., Feldman, J., Giardino, N., Song, H. S., & Schmaling, K. (2002). Psychological aspects of asthma. *Journal of Consulting and Clinical Psychology, 70*, 691–711.

Lehrer, P. M., Karavidas, M. K., Lu, S. E., Feldman, J., Kranitz, L., ... Reynolds, R. (2008). Psychological treatment of comorbid asthma and panic disorder: A pilot study. *Journal of Anxiety Disorders, 22*, 671–683.

Marin, T. J., Chen, E., Munch, J. A., & Miller, G. E. (2009). Double-exposure to acute stress and chronic family stress is associated with immune changes in children with asthma. *Psychosomatic Medicine, 71*, 378–384.

Meuret, A. E., & Ritz, T. (2010). Hyperventilation in panic disorder and asthma: Empirical evidence and clinical strategies. *International Journal of Psychophysiology, 78,* 68–79.

Pachter, L. M., Weller, S. C., Baer, R. D., de Alba Garcia, J. E., Trotter, R. T., ... Klein, R. (2002). Variation in asthma beliefs and practices among mainland Puerto Ricans, Mexican-Americans, Mexicans, and Guatemalans. *Journal of Asthma, 39,* 119–134.

Peters, S. P., Jones, C. A., Haselkorn, T., Mink, D. R., Valacer, D. J., & Weiss, S. T. (2007). Real-world evaluation of asthma control and treatment (REACT): Findings from a national web-based survey. *Journal of Allergy and Clinical Immunology, 119,* 1454–1461.

Put, C., Van den Bergh, O., Lemaigre, V., Demedts, M., & Verleden, G. (2003). Evaluation of an individualised asthma programme directed at behavioural change. *European Respiratory Journal, 21,* 109–115.

Ritz, T., Ayala, E. S., Trueba, A. F., Vance, C. D., & Auchus, R. J. (2011). Acute stress-induced increases in exhaled nitric oxide in asthma and their association with endogenous cortisol. *American Journal of Respiratory and Critical Care Medicine, 183,* 26–30.

Ritz, T., Dahme, B., & Roth, W. T. (2004). Behavioral interventions in asthma: Biofeedback techniques. *Journal of Psychosomatic Research, 56,* 711–720.

Sandberg, S., Paton, J. Y., Ahola, S., McCann, D. C., McGuinness, D., ... Oja, H. (2000). The role of acute and chronic stress in asthma attacks in children. *The Lancet, 356,* 982–987.

Thomas, M., McKinley, R. K., Mellor, S., Watkin, G., Holloway, E., ... Pavord, I. (2009). Breathing exercises for asthma: A randomised controlled trial. *Thorax, 64,* 55–61.

Vandenplas, O., Dramaix, M., Joos, G., Louis, R., Michils, A., ... Bachert, C. (2010). The impact of concomitant rhinitis on asthma-related quality of life and asthma control. *Allergy, 65,* 1290–1297.

Vollmer, W. M., Markson, L. E., O'Connor, E., Sanocki, L. L., Fitterman, L., ... Buist, A. S. (1999). Association of asthma control with health care utilization and quality of life. *American Journal of Respiratory and Critical Care Medicine, 160,* 1647–1652.

Weiser, E. (2007). The prevalence of anxiety disorders among adults with asthma: A meta-analytic review. *Journal of Clinical Psychology in Medical Settings, 14,* 297–307.

Yorke, J., Fleming, S. L., & Shuldham, C. (2007). Psychological interventions for adults with asthma: A systematic review. *Respiratory Medicine, 101,* 1–14.

CHAPTER 40

Research

American Psychiatric Association. (2000). *Diagnostic and statistical manual of mental disorders* (4th ed. text revision) (DSM-IV TR). Washington, DC: American Psychiatric Press.

Ayala, E. S., Meuret, A. E., & Ritz, T. (2010). Confrontation with blood and disgust stimuli precipitates respiratory dysregulation in blood-injury-injection phobia. *Biological Psychology, 84,* 88–97.

Barlow, D.H. (2002). *Anxiety and its disorders: The nature and treatment of anxiety and panic* (2nd ed.). New York, NY: Guildford Press.

Bienvenu, O. J., & Eaton, W. W. (1998). The epidemiology of blood-injection-injury phobia. *Psychological Medicine, 28,* 1129–1136.

Chapman, L. K., Kertz, S. J., Zurlage, M. M., & Woodruff-Borden, J. (2008). A confirmatory factor analysis of specific phobia domains in African American and Caucasian American young adults. *Journal of Anxiety Disorders, 22,* 763–771.

Cisler, J. M., Olatunji, B. O., & Lohr, J. M. (2009). Disgust, fear, and the anxiety disorders: A critical review. *Clinical Psychology Review, 29,* 34–46.

Engel, G. L. (1978). Psychological stress, vasodepressor (vasovagal) syncope, and sudden death. *Annals of Internal Medicine, 89,* 403–412.

Hellström, K., Fellenius, J., & Öst, L. G. (1996). One versus five sessions of applied tension in the treatment of blood phobia. *Behaviour Research and Therapy, 34,* 101–112.

Hirai, M., & Vernon, L. (2011). The role of disgust propensity in blood-injection-injury phobia: Comparisons between Asian Americans and Caucasian Americans. *Cognition and Emotion, 25,* 1500–1509.

Kleinknecht, R. A., Lenz, J., Ford, G., & DeBerard, S. (1990). Types and correlates of blood/injury-related vasovagal syncope. *Behaviour Research and Therapy, 28,* 289–295.

Meltzer, H., Vostanis, P., Dogra, N., Doos, L., Ford, T., & Goodman, R. (2009). Children's specific fears. *Child: Care, Health and Development, 35,* 781–789.

Olatunji, B. O., Etzel, E. N., & Ciesielski, B. G. (2010). Vasovagal syncope and blood donor return: Examination of the role of experience and affective expectancies. *Behavior Modification, 34,* 164–174.

Olatunji, B. O., Smits, J. A., Connolly, K., Willems, J., & Lohr, J. M. (2007). Examination of the decline in fear and disgust during exposure to threat-relevant stimuli in blood-injection-injury phobia. *Journal of Anxiety Disorders, 21,* 445–455.

Öst, L. G. (1987). A maintenance program for behavioral treatment of anxiety disorders. *Behaviour Research and Therapy, 27*, 123–130.

Öst, L. G., Fellenius, J., & Sterner, U. (1991). Applied tension, exposure in vivo, and tension only in the treatment of blood phobia. *Behaviour Research and Therapy, 29*, 561–574.

Öst, L. G., Sterner, U., & Fellenius, J. (1989). Applied tension, applied relaxation, and the combination in the treatment of blood phobia. *Behaviour Research and Therapy, 27*, 109–121.

Ritz, T., Meuret, A. E., & Ayala, E. S. (2010). The psychophysiology of blood-injection-injury phobia: Looking beyond the diphasic response paradigm. *International Journal of Psychophysiology, 78*, 50–67.

Ritz, T., Wilhelm, F. H., Kullowatz, A., Gerlach, A., & Roth, W. T. (2005). End-tidal PCO2-levels in blood phobia during viewing of emotional and disease-relevant films. *Psychosomatic Medicine, 67*, 661–668.

Tolin, D. F., Lohr, J. M., Sawchuk, C. N., & Lee, T. C. (1997). Disgust and disgust sensitivity in blood-injection-injury and spider phobia. *Behaviour Research and Therapy, 35*, 949–953.

Clinician Application

Alvord, M. K., Zucker, B., & Alvord, B. (2011). *Relaxation and self-regulation techniques for children and teens.* Champaign, IL: Research Press. Individual breathing scripts available for download.

Olatunji, B. O., Ciesielski, B. G., Wolitzky-Taylor, K. B., Wentworth, B. J., & Viar, M. A. (2012). Effects of experienced disgust on habituation during repeated exposure to threat-relevant stimuli in blood-injection-injury phobia. *Behavior Therapy, 43*, 132–141.

van Overveld, M., de Jong, P. J., & Peters, M. L. (2011). The Multi-Dimensional Blood/Injury Phobia Inventory: Its psychometric properties and relationship with disgust propensity and disgust sensitivity. *Journal of Anxiety Disorders, 25*, 319–325.

Wolitzky-Taylor, K. B, Horowitz, J. D., Powers, M. P., & Telch, M. J. (2008). Psychological approaches in the treatment of specific phobias: A meta-analysis. *Clinical Psychology Review, 28*, 1021–1037.

CHAPTER 41

Research

Agras, W. S. Crow, S. J., Halmi, K. A., Mitchell, J. E., Wilson, G. T., & Kraemer, H. C. (2000). Outcome predictors for the cognitive behavior therapy treatment of bulimia nervosa: Data from a multisite study. *American Journal of Psychiatry, 157*, 1302–1308.

Agras, W. S., Rossiter, E. M., Arnow, B., Schneider, J. A., Telch, C. F., & Raeburn, S. D. (1992). Pharmacologic and cognitive-behavioral treatment for bulimia nervosa: A controlled comparison. *The American Journal of Psychiatry, 149*, 82–87.

Agras, W. S., Walsh, B. T., Fairburn, C. G., Wilson, G. T., & Kraemer, H. C. (2000). A multicenter comparison of cognitive-behavioral therapy and interpersonal psychotherapy for bulimia nervosa. *Archives of General Psychiatry, 57*, 459–466.

Alegria, M., Woo, M., Cao, Z., Torres, M., Meng, X., & Striegel-Moore, R. (2007). Prevalence and correlates of eating disorders in Latinos in the United States. *International Journal of Eating Disorders, 40*, S15–S21.

Arnold, L. M., McElroy, S. L., Hudson, J. I., Welge, J. A., Bennett, A. J. & Keck, P. E. (2002). A placebo-controlled, randomized trial of fluoxetine in the treatment of binge-eating disorder. *Journal of Clinical Psychiatry, 63*, 1028–1033.

Devlin, M. J., Goldfein, J. A., Petkova, E., Jiang, H., Raizman, P.S., … Walsh, B. T. (2005). Cognitive behavioral therapy and fluoxetine as adjuncts to group behavioral therapy for binge eating disorder. *Obesity Research, 13*, 1077–1088.

Eddy, K. T., Dorer, D. J., Franko, D. L., Tahilani, K., Thompson-Brenner, H., & Herzog, D. B. (2008). Diagnostic crossover in anorexia nervosa and bulimia nervosa: Implications for DSM-V. *The American Journal of Psychiatry, 165*, 245–250.

Eisler, I., Dare, C., Hodes, M., Russell, G., Dodge, E., & Le Grange, D. (2000). Family therapy for adolescent anorexia nervosa: The results of a controlled comparison of two family interventions. *Journal of Child Psychology and Psychiatry and Allied Disciplines, 41*, 727–736.

Eisler, I., Dare, C., Russell, G. F. M., Szmukler, G. I., Le Grange, D., & Dodge, E. (1997). Family and individual therapy in anorexia nervosa: A 5-year follow-up. *Archives of General Psychiatry, 54*, 1025–1030.

Fairburn, C. G. (1997). Interpersonal psychotherapy for bulimia nervosa. In D. M. Garner & P. E. Garfinkel (Eds.), *Handbook of treatment for eating disorders* (pp. 278–294). New York, NY: The Guilford Press.

Fairburn, C. G. (2008). *Cognitive behavior therapy and eating disorders.* New York, NY: The Guilford Press.

Fairburn, C. G., Cooper, Z., Bohn, K., O'Connor, M. E., Doll, H. A., & Palmer R. L. (2007). The severity and status of eating disorder NOS: Implications for DSM-V. *Behaviour Research and Therapy, 45*, 1705–1715.

Fairburn, C. G., Cooper, Z., Doll, H. A., O'Connor, M. E., Bohn, K., ... Palmer, R. L. (2009). Transdiagnostic cognitive-behavioral therapy for patients with eating disorders: A two-site trial with 60-week follow-up. *American Journal of Psychiatry, 166*, 311–319.

Fairburn, C. G., Cooper, Z., & Shafran, R. (2003). Cognitive behaviour therapy for eating disorders: A "transdiagnostic" theory and treatment. *Behaviour Research and Therapy, 41*, 509–529.

Fairburn, C. G., Jones, R., Peveler, R. C., Hope, R. A., & O'Connor, M. (1993). Psychotherapy and bulimia nervosa: The longer-term effects of interpersonal psychotherapy, behaviour therapy, and cognitive behaviour therapy. *Archives of General Psychiatry, 50*, 419–428.

Fairburn, C. G., Marcus, M. D., & Wilson, G. T. (1993). Cognitive behaviour therapy for binge eating and bulimia nervosa: A comprehensive treatment manual. In C. G. Fairburn & G. T. Wilson (Eds.), *Binge eating: Nature, assessment and treatment* (pp. 361–404). New York, NY: The Guilford Press.

Fluoxetine Bulimia Nervosa Collaborative Study Group. (1992). Fluoxetine in the treatment of bulimia nervosa: A multicenter, placebo-controlled, double-blind trial. *Archives of General Psychiatry, 49*, 139–147.

Grilo, C. M., Masheb, R. M., & Wilson, G. T. (2005). Efficacy of cognitive behavioral therapy and fluoxetine for the treatment of binge eating disorder: A randomized double-blind placebo controlled comparison. *Biological Psychiatry, 57*, 301–309.

Hudson, J. I., Hiripi, E., Pope, H. G., & Kessler, R. C. (2007). The prevalence and correlates of eating disorders in the National Comorbidity Survey Replication. *Biological Psychiatry, 61*, 348–358.

Hudson, J. I., McElroy, S. L., Raymond, N. C., Crow, S., Keck, P. E., ... Jonas, J. M. (1998). Fluvoxamine in the treatment of binge-eating disorder: A multicenter placebo-controlled, double-blind trial. *The American Journal of Psychiatry, 155*, 1756–1762.

Keel, P. K., & Haedt, A. (2008). Evidence-based psychosocial treatments for eating problems and eating disorders. *Journal of Clinical Child & Adolescent Psychology, 37*, 39–61.

Le Grange, D., Crosby, R. D., Rathouz, P. J., & Levinthal, B. L. (2007). A randomized controlled comparison of family-based treatment and supportive psychotherapy for adolescent bulimia nervosa. *Archives of General Psychiatry, 64*, 1049–1056.

Le Grange, D., & Lock, J. (2007). *Treating bulimia in adolescents: A family-based approach*. New York, NY: The Guilford Press.

Linehan, M. M. (1993). *Cognitive-behavioral treatment of borderline personality disorder*. New York, NY: Guilford Press.

Lock, J., Agras, W. S., Bryson, S., & Kraemer, H. C. (2005). A comparison of short- and long-term family therapy for adolescent anorexia nervosa. *Journal of the American Academy of Child & Adolescent Psychiatry, 44*, 632–639.

Lock, J., Le Grange, D., Agras, W. S., & Dare, C. (2001). *Treatment manual for anorexia nervosa: A family-based approach*. New York, NY: The Guilford Press.

Lock, J., Le Grange, D., Agras, W. S., Moye, A., Bryson, S. W., & Jo, B. (2010). Randomized clinical trial comparing family-based treatment with adolescent-focused individual therapy for adolescents with anorexia nervosa. *Archives of General Psychiatry, 67*(10), 1025–1032.

Marcus, M. D. (1997). Adapting treatment for patients with binge eating disorder. In D. M. Garner & P. E. Garfinkel (Eds.), *Handbook of treatment for eating disorders* (pp. 484–493). New York, NY: The Guilford Press.

Milos, G., Spindler, A., Schnyder, U., & Fairburn, C. G. (2005). Instability of eating disorder diagnoses: Prospective study. *British Journal of Psychiatry, 187*, 573–578.

Mitchell, J. E., Devlin, M. J., deZwaan, M., Crow, S. J., & Peterson, C. B. (2008). *Binge eating disorder: Clinical foundation and treatment*. New York, NY: Guilford Press.

Mitchell, J. E., Hatsukami, D., Pyle, R. L., & Eckert, E. D. (1987). Late onset bulimia. *Comprehensive Psychiatry, 28*, 323–328.

Mussell, M. P., Crosby, R. D., Crow, S. J., Knope, A. J., Peterson, C. B., ... Mitchell, J. E. (2000). Utilization of empirically supported psychotherapy treatments for individuals with eating disorders: A survey of psychologists. *International Journal of Eating Disorders, 27*, 230–237.

Nauta, H., Hospers, H., Kok, G., & Jansen, A. (2000). A comparison between a cognitive and a behavioral treatment for obese binge eaters and obese non-binge eaters. *Behavior Therapy, 21*, 441–461.

Neumark-Sztainer, D., Croll, J., Story, M., Hannan, P. J., French, S. A., & Perry, C. (2002). Ethnic/racial differences in weight-related concerns and behaviors among adolescent girls and boys: Findings from Project EAT. *Journal of Psychosomatic Research, 53*, 963–974.

Nicdao, E. G., Hong, S., & Takeuchi, D. T. (2007). Prevalence and correlates of eating disorders among Asian Americans: Results from the national Latinos and Asian American study. *International Journal of Eating Disorders, 40*, S22–S26.

Ricca, V., Mannucci, E., Mezzani, B., Moretti, S., DiBernardo, M., ... Faravelli, C. (2001). Fluoxetine and fluvoxamine combined with individual cognitive-behavior therapy in binge eating disorder: A one-year follow-up study. *Psychotherapy and Psychosomatics, 70*, 298–306.

Russell, G. F. M., Szmukler, G. I., Dare, C., & Eisler, I. (1987). An evaluation of family therapy in anorexia nervosa and bulimia nervosa. *Archives of General Psychiatry, 44*, 1047–1056.

Safer, D. L., Robinson, A. H., & Jo, B. (2010). Outcome from a randomized controlled trial of group therapy for binge eating disorder: Comparing dialectical behavior therapy adapted for binge eating to an active comparison group therapy. *Behavior Therapy, 41*, 106–120.

Safer, D. L., Telch, C. F., & Agras, W. S. (2001). Dialectical behavior therapy for bulimia nervosa. *American Journal of Psychiatry, 158*, 632–634.

Stefano, S. C., Bacaltchuk, J., Blay, S. L., & Hay, P. (2006). Self-help treatments for disorders of recurrent binge eating: A systematic review. *Acta Psychiatrica Scandinavica, 113*, 452–459.

Sysko, R., & Walsh, B. T. (2008). A critical evaluation of the efficacy of self-help interventions for the treatment of bulimia nervosa and binge-eating disorder. *International Journal of Eating Disorders, 41*, 97–112.

Tanofsky-Kraff, M., & Wilfley, D. E. (2010). Interpersonal psychotherapy for bulimia nervosa and binge eating disorder. In C. M. Grilo & J. E. Mitchell (Eds.), *The treatment of eating disorders: A clinical handbook.* New York, NY: The Guilford Press.

Taylor, J. Y., Caldwell, C. H., Baser, R. E., Faison, N., & Jackson, J. S. (2007). Prevalence of eating disorders among blacks in the national survey of American life. *International Journal of Eating Disorders, 40*, S10–S14.

Telch, C. F., Agras, W. S., & Linehan, M. M. (2001). Dialectical Behavioral Therapy for binge eating disorder. *Journal of Consulting and Clinical Psychology, 69*, 1061–1065.

Telch, C. F., Agras, W. S., Rossiter, E. M., Wilfley, D. E., & Kenardy, J. (1990). Group cognitive-behavioral treatment for the nonpurging bulimic: An initial evaluation. *Journal of Consulting and Clinical Psychology, 58*, 629–635.

Thomas, J. J., Vartanian, L. R., & Brownell, K. D. (2009). The relationship between eating disorder not otherwise specified (EDNOS) and officially recognized eating disorders: Meta-analysis and implications for DSM. *Psychological Bulletin, 135*, 407–433.

Turner, H., & Bryant-Waugh, R. (2004). Eating disorder not otherwise specified (EDNOS): Profiles of clients presenting at a community eating disorder service. *European Eating Disorders Review, 12*, 18–26.

von Ranson, K. M., & Robinson, K. E. (2006). Who is providing what type of psychotherapy to eating disorder clients? A survey. *International Journal of Eating Disorders, 39*, 27–34.

Wade, T. D., Bergin, J. L., Martin, N. G., Gillespie, N. A., & Fairburn, C. G. (2006). A transdiagnostic approach to understanding eating disorders. *Journal of Nervous and Mental Disease, 194*, 510–517.

Wilfley, D. E., Agras, W. S., Telch, C. F., Rossiter, E. M., Schneider, J. A., ... Raeburn, S. D. (1993). Group cognitive-behavioral therapy and group interpersonal psychotherapy for the nonpurging bulimic individual: A controlled comparison. *Journal of Consulting and Clinical Psychology, 61*, 296–305.

Wilfley, D. E., Welch, R. R., Stein, R. I., Spurrell, E. B., Cohen, L. R., ... Matt, G. E. (2002). A randomized comparison of group cognitive-behavioral therapy and group interpersonal psychotherapy for the treatment of overweight individuals with binge-eating disorder. *Archives of General Psychiatry, 59*, 713–721.

Wilson, G. T., & Fairburn, C. G. (2000). The treatment of binge eating disorder. *European Eating Disorders Review, 8*, 351–354.

Wilson, G. T., Fairburn, C. G., & Agras, W. S. (1997). Cognitive-behavioral therapy for bulimia nervosa. In D. M. Garner & P. E. Garfinkel (Eds.), *Handbook of treatment for eating disorders* (pp. 67–93). New York, NY: The Guilford Press.

Wilson, G. T., Grilo, C. M., & Vitousek, K. M. (2007). Psychological treatment of eating disorders. *American Psychologist, 62*, 199–216.

Wilson, G. T., & Shafran, R. (2005). Eating disorders guidelines from NICE. *The Lancet, 365*, 79–81.

Wonderlich, S. A., Engel, S. G., Peterson, C. B., Robinson, M. D., Crosby, R. D., ... Simonich, H. K. (2008). Examining the conceptual model of integrative cognitive-affective therapy for BN: Two assessment studies. *International Journal of Eating Disorders, 41*, 748–754.

Clinician Application

Crow, S. J., Frisch, M. J., Peterson, C. J., Croll, J., Raatz, S. K., & Nyman J. A. (2009). Monetary costs associated with bulimia. *International Journal of Eating Disorders, 42*, 81–83.

Keel, P. (2007). Purging disorder: Subthreshold variant or full-threshold eating disorder? *International Journal of Eating Disorders, 40*, S89–S94.

Lock, J., & le Grange, D. (2005). *Help your teenager beat an eating disorder.* New York, NY: Guilford Press.

Pratt, E. M., Niego, S. H., & Agras, S. W. (1998). Does the size of a binge matter? *International Journal of Eating Disorders, 24*, 307–312.

CHAPTER 42

Research

Antoni, M. H., Carrico, A. W., Duran, R. E., Spitzer, S., Penedo, F., ... Schneiderman, N. (2006). Randomized clinical trial of cognitive behavioral stress management on human immunodeficiency virus viral load in gay men treated with highly active antiretroviral therapy. *Psychosomatic Medicine, 68,* 143–151.

Bazelmans, E., Prins, J., & Bleijenberg, G. (2006). Cognitive behavior therapy for relatively active and for passive chronic fatigue syndrome patients. *Cognitive and Behavioral Practice, 13,* 157–166.

Buchwald, D., Pearlman, T., Umali, J., Schmaling, K., & Katon, W. (1996). Functional status in patients with chronic fatigue syndrome, other fatiguing illnesses, and healthy individuals. *The American Journal of Medicine, 101,* 364–370.

Cairns, R., & Hotopf, M. (2005). A systematic review describing the prognosis of chronic fatigue syndrome. *Occupational Medicine, 55,* 20–31.

Chambers, D., Bagnall, A. M., Hempel, S., & Forbes, C. (2006). Interventions for the treatment, management and rehabilitation of patients with chronic fatigue syndrome/myalgic encephalomyelitis: An updated systematic review. *Journal of the Royal Society of Medicine, 99,* 506–520.

Cooper, L. (2001). Report of survey members of local ME groups. *Perspectives.* Retrieved from http://www .afme.org.uk/res/img/resources/Group%20Survey%20Lesley%20Cooper.pdf

Fukuda, K., Straus, S. E., Hickie, I., Sharpe, M. C., Dobbins, J. G., & Komaroff, A. (1994). The chronic fatigue syndrome: A comprehensive approach to its definition and study. *Annals of Internal Medicine, 121,* 953–959.

Jason, L., Benton, M., Torres-Harding, S., & Muldowney, K. (2009). The impact of energy modulation on physical functioning and fatigue severity among patients with ME/CFS. Patient Education and Counseling, 77, 237–241.

Jason, L. A., Muldowney, K., & Torres-Harding, S. (2008). The energy envelope theory and myalgic encephalomyelitis/chronic fatigue syndrome. AAOHN Journal, 56, 189–195.

Jason, L. A., Najar, N., Porter, N., & Reh, C. (2009). Evaluating the Centers for Disease Control's empirical chronic fatigue syndrome case definition. *Journal of Disability Policy Studies, 20,* 93–100.

Jason, L. A., Richman, J. A., Rademaker, A. W., Jordan, K. M., Plioplys, A. V., ... Plioplys, S. (1999). A community-based study of chronic fatigue syndrome. *Archives of Internal Medicine, 159,* 2129–2137.

Jones, J. F., Nisenbaum, R., & Reeves, W. C. (2003). Medication use by persons with chronic fatigue syndrome: Results of a randomized telephone survey in Wichita, Kansas. *Health and Quality of Life Outcomes, 1,* 74. doi: 10.1186/1477-7525-1-74

Komaroff, A., Fagioli, L. R., Doolittle, T. H., Gandek, B., Gleit, M. A., ... Bates, D. W. (1996). Health status in patients with chronic fatigue syndrome and in general population and disease comparison groups. *The American Journal of Medicine, 101,* 281–290.

Lerner, A. M., Beqaj, S., Fitzgerald, J. T., Gill, K., Gill, C., & Edington, J. (2010). Subset-directed antiviral treatment of 142 herpesvirus patients with chronic fatigue syndrome. *Virus Adaptation and Treatment, 2,* 47–57.

Malouff, J. M., Thorsteinsson, E. B., Rooke, S. E., Bhullar, N., & Schutte, N. S. (2008). Efficacy of cognitive behavioral therapy for chronic fatigue syndrome: A meta-analysis. *Clinical Psychology Review, 28,* 736–745.

Porter, N., Jason, L. A., Boulton, A., Bothne, N., & Coleman, B. (2010). Alternative medical interventions used in the treatment and management of myalgic encephalomyelitis/chronic fatigue syndrome and fibromyalgia. *Journal of Alternative and Complementary Medicine, 16,* 235–249.

Redinbaugh, E. M., Creola, D., Arnold, J., & Baum, A. (2004). Behavioral medicine approaches to assessing and treating cancer pain. *The Journal of Psychological Practice, 10,* 45–59.

Reeves, W. C., Jones, J. J., Maloney, E., Heim, C., Hoaglin, D. C., ... Devlin, R. (2007). New study on the prevalence of CFS in metro, urban and rural Georgia populations. *Population Health Metrics 2007, 5,* 5. doi: 10.1186/1478-7954-5-5

Whiting, P., Bagnall, A. M., Snowden, A. J., Cornell, J. E., Mulrow, C. D., & Ramirez, G. (2001). Interventions for the treatment and management of chronic fatigue syndrome. A systematic review. *Journal of the American Medical Association, 286,* 1360–1368.

CHAPTER 43

Research

Buhrman, M., Faltenhag, S., Strom, L., & Andersson, G. (2004). Controlled trial of Internet-based treatment with telephone support for chronic back pain. *Pain, 111,* 368–377.

Burns, J. W., Kubilus, A., Bruehl, S., Harden, R. N., & Lofland, K. (2003). Do changes in cognitive factors influence outcome following multidisciplinary treatment for chronic pain? A cross-lagged panel analysis. *Journal of Consulting and Clinical Psychology, 71*, 81–91.

CDC. (2005). Racial/ethnic differences in the prevalence and impact of doctor-diagnosed arthritis: United States. *MMWR, 54*, 119–123.

CDC. (2010). Summary health statistics for US adults: National Health Interview Survey 2009. In U. D. o. H. a. H. Services (Ed.) (Vol. 10). Hyattsville, MD: DHHS Publication.

Chiesa, A., & Serretti, A. (2009). Mindfulness-based interventions for chronic pain: A systematic review of the evidence. *Journal of Alternative Complemental Medicine, 17*, 83–93.

Eccleston, C., Williams, A. C., & Morley, S. (2009). Psychological therapies for the management of chronic pain (excluding headache) in adults. *Cochrane Database Syst Rev, (2)*, CD007407.

Guzman, J., Esmail, R., Karjalainen, K., Malmivaara, A., Irvin, E., & Bombardier, C. (2002). Multidisciplinary bio-psycho-social rehabilitation for chronic low back pain. *Cochrane Database Syst Rev (1)*, CD000963.

Hoffman, B. M., Papas, R. K., Chatkoff, D. K., & Kerns, R. D. (2007). Meta-analysis of psychological interventions for chronic low back pain. *Health Psycholology, 26*, 1–9.

International Association for the Study of Pain. (1986). Classification of chronic pain. Descriptions of chronic pain syndromes and definitions of pain terms. *Pain, 3*, S1–S226.

Karjalainen, K., Malmivaara, A., van Tulder, M., Roine, R., Jauhiainen, … Koes, B. (2001). Multidisciplinary biopsychosocial rehabilitation for subacute low back pain in working-age adults: A systematic review within the framework of the Cochrane Collaboration Back Review Group. *Spine, 26*, 262–269.

Macea, D. D., Gajos, K., Daglia Calil, Y. A., & Fregni, F. (2010). The efficacy of Web-based cognitive behavioral interventions for chronic pain: A systematic review and meta-analysis. *Journal of Pain, 11*, 917–929.

McCracken, L. M., & Turk, D. C. (2002). Behavioral and cognitive-behavioral treatment for chronic pain: Outcome, predictors of outcome, and treatment process. *Spine (Phila Pa 1976), 27*, 2564–2573.

Okifuji, A., & Turk, D. C. (In press). The influence of the psychosocial environment in pain comorbidities. In M. A. Giamberadino & T. S. Jensen (Eds.), *Pain comorbidities: Understanding and treating the complex patient.* Seattle, WA: IASP Press.

Portenoy, R. K., Ugarte, C., Fuller, I., & Haas, G. (2004). Population-based survey of pain in the United States: Differences among white, African American, and Hispanic subjects. *Journal of Pain, 5*, 317–328.

Ratcliffe, G. E., Enns, M. W., Belik, S. L., & Sareen, J. (2008). Chronic pain conditions and suicidal ideation and suicide attempts: An epidemiologic perspective. *Clinical Journal of Pain, 24*, 204–210.

Reyes-Gibby, C. C., Aday, L. A., Todd, K. H., Cleeland, C. S., & Anderson, K. O. (2007). Pain in aging community-dwelling adults in the United States: Non-Hispanic whites, non-Hispanic blacks, and Hispanics. *Journal of Pain, 8*, 75–84.

Sawyer, P., Bodner, E. V., Ritchie, C. S., & Allman, R. M. (2006). Pain and pain medication use in community-dwelling older adults. *American Journal of Geriatric Pharmacotherapy, 4*, 316–324.

Schmidt, S., Grossman, P., Schwarzer, B., Jena, S., Naumann, J., & Walach, H. (2011). Treating fibromyalgia with mindfulness-based stress reduction: Results from a 3 armed randomized controlled trial. *Pain, 152*, 361–369.

Stewart, W. F., Ricci, J. A., Chee, E., Morganstein, D., & Lipton, R. (2003). Lost productive time and cost due to common pain conditions in the US workforce. *Journal of the American Medical Association, 290*, 2443–2454.

Thomsen, A. B., Sorensen, J., Sjogren, P., & Eriksen, J. (2002). Chronic non-malignant pain patients and health economic consequences. *European Journal of Pain, 6*, 341–352.

Thorn, B. E., Day, M. A., Burns, J., Kuhajda, M. C., Gaskins, S. W., … Cabbil, C. (2011). Randomized trial of group cognitive behavioral therapy compared with a pain education control for low-literacy rural people with chronic pain. *Pain, 152*, 2710–2720.

Turk, D. C., Meichenbaum, D., & Genest, M. (1983). *Pain and behavioral medicine: A cognitive-behavioral perspective.* New York, NY: Guilford.

Turk, D. C., & Okifuji, A. (1998). Psychological approaches in pain management: What works? *Current Opinions in Anaesthesiology, 11*, 547–552.

Turk, D. C., & Okifuji, A. (2009). Pain terms and taxonomies of pain. In S. B. Fishman, J. C. Ballantyne, & J. P. Rathmell (Eds.), *Bonica's management of pain* (4th ed., pp. 13–23). New York, NY: Lippincott Williams & Wilkins.

Turk, D. C., Okifuji, A., Sinclair, J. D., & Starz, T. W. (1998). Differential responses by psychosocial subgroups of fibromyalgia syndrome patients to an interdisciplinary treatment. *Arthritis Care Research, 11*, 397–404.

Unruh, A. M. (1996). Gender variations in clinical pain experience. *Pain, 65*, 123–167.

Clinician Application

Cassisi, J. E., Umeda, M., Deisinger, J. A., Sheffer, C., Lofland, K. R., & Jackson, C. (2004). Patterns of pain descriptor usage in African-Americans and European-Americans with chronic pain. *Cultural Diversity and Ethnic Minority Psychology, 10*, 81–89.

Disorbio, J. M., Bruns, D., & Barolat, G. (2006, March). Assessment and treatment of chronic pain: A physician's guide to a biopsychosocial approach. Retrieved August 8, 2007, from http://www.pearsonassessments .com/NR/rdonlyres/C28A90B8-78A5-4E3B-B446-C6EEDD986BF2/0/bruns306reprint.pdf

Greenspan, J. D., Craft, R. M., LeResche, L., Arendt-Nielsen, L., Berkley, K. J., ... Traub, R. J. (2007). Studying sex and gender differences in pain and analgesia: A consensus report. *Pain, 132,* S26–S45.

Johnson, L. M., Zatura, A. J., & Davis, M.C. (2006). The role of illness uncertainty on coping with fibromyalgia symptoms. *Health Psychology, 25,* 696–703.

Keefe, F. J., Lefebvre, J. C., Egert, J. R., Affleck, G., Sullivan, M. J., & Caldwell, D. S. (2000). The relationship of gender to pain, pain behavior, and disability in osteoarthritis patients: The role of catastrophizing. *Pain, 87,* 325–334.

Keogh, E., & Herdenfeldt, M. (2002). Gender, coping and the perception of pain. *Pain, 97,* 195–201.

Kerns, R. D., Sellinger, J., & Goodin, B. R. (2011). Psychological treatment of chronic pain. *Annual Review of Clinical Psychology, 7,* 411–434. doi: 10.1146/annurev-clinpsy-090310-120430

Tait, R. C., & Chinball, J. T. (2005). Racial and ethnic disparities in the evaluation and treatment of pain: Psychological perspectives. *Professional Psychology: Research and Practice, 36,* 595–601.

Tennen, H., Affleck, G., & Zatura, A. (2006). Depression history and coping with chronic pain: A daily process analysis. *Health Psychology, 25,* 370–379.

Turk, D. C., & Burwinkle, T. M. (2005). Assessment of chronic pain in rehabilitation: Outcome measures in clinical trials and clinical practice. *Rehabilitation Psychology, 50,* 56–64.

Turk, D. C., Swanson, K. S., & Tunks, E. R. (2008). Psychological approaches in the treatment of chronic pain patients—When pills, scalpels, and needles are not enough. *The Canadian Journal of Psychiatry / La Revue canadienne de psychiatrie, 53,* 213–223.

CHAPTER 44

Research

American Psychiatric Association. (2000). *Diagnostic and statistical manual of mental disorders* (4th ed., Text Rev. ed.). Washington, DC: Author.

Barth, J., Schumacher, M., & Herrmann-Lingen, C. (2004). Depression as a risk factor for mortality in patients with coronary heart disease: A meta-analysis. *Psychosomatic Medicine, 66,* 802–813.

Carney, R. M., Freedland, K. E. (2003). Depression, mortality, and medical morbidity in patients with coronary heart disease. *Biological Psychiatry, 54,* 241–247.

Carney, R. M., Freedland, K. E., Eisen, S. A., Rich, M. W., & Jaffe, A. S. (1995). Major depression and medication adherence in elderly patients with coronary artery disease. *Health Psychology, 14,* 88–90.

Carney, R. M., Rich, M. W., teVelde, A., Saini, J., Clark, K., & Freedland, K. E. (1988). The relationship between heart rate, heart rate variability and depression in patients with coronary artery disease. *Journal of Psychosomatic Research, 32,* 159–164.

Egede, L. E. (2007). Major depression in individuals with chronic medical disorders: Prevalence, correlates and association with health resource utilization, lost productivity and functional disability. *General Hospital Psychiatry, 29,* 409–416.

Frasure-Smith, N., & Lesperance, F. (2005). Reflections on depression as a cardiac risk factor. *Psychosomatic Medicine, 67,* S19–S25.

Frasure-Smith, N., & Lesperance, F. (2006). Recent evidence linking coronary heart disease and depression. *Canadian Journal of Psychiatry Revue canadienne de psychiatrie, 51,* 730–737.

Freedland, K. E., Carney, R. M., Lustman, P. J., Rich, M. W., & Jaffe, A. S. (1992). Major depression in coronary artery disease patients with vs. without a prior history of depression. *Psychosomatic Medicine, 54,* 416–421.

Glassman, A. H., Helzer, J. E., Covey, L. S., Cottler, L. B., Stetner, F., ... Johnson, J. (1990). Smoking, smoking cessation, and major depression. *JAMA: The Journal of the American Medical Association, 264,* 1546–1549.

Glassman, A. H., O'Connor, C. M., Califf, R. M., Swedberg, K., Schwartz, P., ... Sertraline Antidepression Heart Attack Randomization Trial (SADHART). (2002). Sertraline treatment of major depression in patients with acute MI or unstable angina. *JAMA: The Journal of the American Medical Association, 288,* 701–709.

Jaarsma, T., Lesman-Leegte, I., Hillege, H. L., Veeger, N. J., Sanderman, R., & van Veldhuisen, D. J. (2009). Depression and the usefulness of a disease management program in heart failure: Insights from the COACH (Coordinating study evaluating Outcomes of Advising and Counseling in Heart failure) Study. *Journal of the American College of Cardiology, 55,* 1837–1843.

King, M. L. (2009). Improving the quality of care following an acute cardiac event—The role of cardiac reha-bilitation in the care continuum. *US Cardiology, 6*, 79–82.

Lichtman, J. H., Bigger, J. T., Jr., Blumenthal, J. A., Frasure-Smith, N., Kaufmann, P. G., ... American Psychiatric Association. (2008). Depression and coronary heart disease: Recommendations for screening, referral, and treatment: A science advisory from the American Heart Association Prevention Committee of the Council on Cardiovascular Nursing, Council on Clinical Cardiology, Council on Epidemiology and Prevention, and Interdisciplinary Council on Quality of Care and Outcomes Research: Endorsed by the American Psychiatric Association. *Circulation, 118*, 1768–1775.

McGee, H. M., Doyle, F., Conroy, R. M., De La Harpe, D., & Shelley, E. (2006). Impact of briefly-assessed depression on secondary prevention outcomes after acute coronary syndrome: A one-year longitudinal survey. *BMC health services research, 6*, 9.

Miller, W. R., & Rollnick, S. (1991). *Motivational Interviewing, preparing people to change addictive behavior.* New York, NY: The Guildford Press.

Rieckmann, N., Gerin, W., Kronish, I. M., Burg, M. M., Chaplin, W. F., ... Davidson, K. W. (2006). Course of depressive symptoms and medication adherence after acute coronary syndromes: An electronic medica-tion monitoring study. *Journal of the American College of Cardiology, 48*, 2218–2222.

Rozanski, A., Blumenthal, J. A., Davidson, K. W., Saab, P. G., & Kubzansky, L. (2005). The epidemiology, pathophysiology, and management of psychosocial risk factors in cardiac practice: the emerging field of behavioral cardiology. *Journal of the American College of Cardiology, 45*, 637–651.

Rubak, S., Sandbaek, A., Lauritzen, T., & Christensen, B. (2005). Motivational Interviewing: A systematic review and meta-analysis. *British Journal of General Practice, 55*, 305–312.

Van Melle, J. P., De Jonge, P., Spijkerman, T. A., Tijssen, J. G. P., Ormel, J., ... van den Berg, M. P. (2004). Prognostic association of depression following myocardial infarction with mortality and cardiovascular events: A meta-analysis. *Psychosomatic Medicine, 66*, 814–822.

World Health Organization. (2002). *The World Health Report 2002* (Rep. No. 58). Geneva, Switzerland: World Health Organization.

CHAPTER 45

Research

American Psychiatric Association. (2013). *Diagnostic and statistical manual of mental disorders* (5th ed.) Washington, DC: American Psychiatric Association.

Bootzin, R. R. (1972). A stimulus control treatment for insomnia. Paper presented at the American Psychological Association.

Durrence, H. H., & Lichstein, K. L. (2006). The sleep of African Americans: A comparative review. *Behavioral Sleep Medicine, 4*, 29–44.

Jacobs, G. D., Pace-Schott, E. F., Stickgold, R., & Otto, M. W. (2004). Cognitive behavior therapy and pharmaco-therapy for insomnia: A randomized controlled trial and direct comparison. *Archives of Internal Medicine, 164*, 1888–1896.

McGrath, E., Keita, G. P., Strickland, B. R., & Russo, N. F. (1990). *Women and depression: Risk factors and treatment issues: Final report of the American Psychological Association's National Task Force on Women and Depression.* Washington, DC: American Psychological Association.

Morin, C. M. (1993). *Insomnia: Psychological assessment and management.* New York, NY: The Guilford Press.

Morin, C. M., Colecchi, C., Stone, J., Sood, R., & Brink, D. (1999). Behavioral and pharmacological therapies for late-life insomnia: A randomized controlled trial. *JAMA: The Journal of the American Medical Association, 281*(11), 991–999.

Ohayon, M. M. (1997). Prevalence of DSM-IV diagnostic criteria of insomnia: Distinguishing insomnia related to mental disorders from sleep disorders. *Journal of Psychiatric Research, 31*, 333–346.

Ohayon, M. M., & Roth, T. (2003). Place of chronic insomnia in the course of depressive and anxiety disorders. *Journal of Psychiatric Research, 37*, 9–15.

Ohayon, M. M., Zulley, J., Guilleminault, C., Smirne, S., & Priest, R. G. (2001). How age and daytime activities are related to insomnia in the general population: Consequences for older people. *Journal of the American Geriatric Society, 49*, 360–366.

Sateia, M. J., Doghramji, K., Hauri, P. J., & Morin, C. M. (2000). Evaluation of chronic insomnia. *Sleep, 23*, 243–305.

Sivertsen, B., Omvik, S., Pallesen, S., Bjorvatn, B., Havik, O. E., & Kvale, G. (2006). Cognitive behavioral ther-apy vs zopiclone for treatment of chronic primary insomnia in older adults: A randomized controlled trial. *Journal of the American Medical Association, 295*, 2851–2858.

Stepanski, E. J., & Rybarczyk, B. (2006). Emerging research on the treatment and etiology of secondary or comorbid insomnia. *Sleep Medicine Reviews, 10,* 7–18.

Taylor, D. J., Lichstein, K. L., & Durrence, H. H. (2003). Insomnia as a health risk factor. *Behavioral Sleep Medicine, 1,* 227.

Taylor, D. J., Lichstein, K. L., Durrence, H. H., Riedel, B. W., & Bush, A. J. (2005). Epidemiology of insomnia, depression, and anxiety. *Sleep, 28,* 1457–1464.

Taylor, D. J., Mallory, L. J., Lichstein, K. L., Durrence, H. H., Riedel, B. W., & Bush, A. J. (2007). Comorbidity of chronic insomnia with medical problems. *Sleep, 30,* 213–218.

Vitiello, M. V., Moe, K. E., & Prinz, P. N. (2002). Sleep complaints cosegregate with illness in older adults: Clinical research informed by and informing epidemiological studies of sleep. *Journal of Psychosomatic Research, 53,* 555–559.

CHAPTER 46

Research

American Academy of Sleep Medicine. (2005). *The International Classification of Sleep Disorders: Diagnostic and coding manual* (2nd ed.). Westchester, IL: American Academy of Sleep Medicine.

Gregory, A., Noone, D. M., Eley, T. C., Harvey, A. G., & The STEPS Team. (2010). Catastrophizing and symptoms of sleep disturbance in children. *Journal of Sleep Research, 19,* 175–182.

Mindell, J. A., Emslie, G., Blumer, J., Genel, M., Glaze, D., ... Banas, B. (2006). Pharmacologic management of insomnia in children and adolescents: Consensus statement. *Pediatrics, 117,* e1223–e1232.

Mindell, J. A., Kuhn, B., Lewin, D. S., Meltzer, L., & Sadeh, A. (2006). Behavioral treatment of bedtime problems and night wakings in infants and young children. *Sleep, 29,* 1263–1276.

Office of the State Coroner. (2010). Finding of inquest (Inquest Number 25/2009). Adelaide, South Australia: Author. Retrieved September 6, 2011, from http://www.courts.sa.gov.au/CoronersFindings/Lists/Coroners%20Findings/Attachments/423/Infant%20Co-Sleeping.pdf

Richdale, A., & Wiggs, L. (2005). Behavioral approaches to the treatment of sleep problems in children with developmental disorders: What is the state of the art? *International Journal of Behavioral and Consultation Therapy, 1,* 165–190.

Clinician Application

Devera, M. V. (1997). Sleep disturbances. In H. Steiner (Ed.), *Treating preschool children* (pp. 61–82). San Francisco, CA: Jossey-Bass.

Foley, L. S., Maddison, R., Jiang, Y., Marsh, S., Olds, T., & Ridley, K. (2013). Presleep activities and time of sleep onset in children. *Pediatrics, 131,* 276–282.

Pelayo, R., & Dubik, M. (2008). Pediatric sleep pharmacology. *Seminars in Pediatric Neurology, 15,* 79–90.

Weisz, J. R., Chorpita, B. F., Palinkas, L. A., Schoenwald, S. K., Miranda, J., ... Research Network on Youth Mental Health. (2012). Testing standard and modular designs for psychotherapy treating depression, anxiety, and conduct problems in youth: A randomized effectiveness trial. *Archives of General Psychiatry, 69,* 274–282.

CHAPTER 47

Research

Adams, T. D., Gress, R. E., Smith, S. C., Halverson, R. C., Simper, S. C., ... Hunt, S. C. (2007). Long-term mortality after gastric bypass surgery. *New England Journal of Medicine, 357,* 753–761.

Amundson, H. A., Butcher, M. K., Gohdes, D., Hall, T. O., Harwell, T. S., ... Vanderwood, K. K. (2009). Translating the Diabetes Prevention Program into practice in the general community: Findings from the Montana Cardiovascular Disease and Diabetes Prevention Program. *Diabetes Educator, 35,* 209–220.

Cash, T. F., & Henry, P. E. (1995). Women's body images: The results of a national survey in the U.S.A. *Sex Roles, 33,* 19–28.

Dansinger, M. L., Gleason, J. A., Griffith, J. L., Selker, H. P., & Schaefer, E. J. (2005). Comparison of the Atkins, Ornish, Weight Watchers, and Zone diets for weight loss and heart disease risk reduction: A randomized trial. *Journal of the American Medical Association, 293,* 43–53.

Fabricatore, A. N. (2007). Behavior therapy and cognitive-behavioral therapy of obesity: Is there a difference? *Journal of the American Dietetic Association, 107*, 92–99.

Flegal, K. M., Carroll, M. D., Kit, B. K., & Ogden, C. L. (2012). Prevalence of obesity and trends in the distribution of body mass index among US adults, 1999-2010. *Journal of the American Medical Association, 307*, 491–497.

Flegal, K. M., Carroll, M. D., Ogden, C. L., & Curtin, L. R. (2010). Prevalence and trends of obesity among US adults, 1999-2008. *Journal of the American Medical Association, 303*, 235–241.

Fleming, J. W., McClendon, K. S., & Riche, D. M. (2013). New obesity agents: lorcaserin and phentermine/topiramate. *Annals of Pharmacotherapy, 47*, 1007–16.

Gardner, C. D., Kiazand, A., Alhassan, S., Kim, S., Stafford, R. S., ... King, A. C. (2007). Comparison of the Atkins, Zone, Ornish, and LEARN diets for change in weight and related risk factors among overweight premenopausal women: The A to Z Weight Loss Study: A randomized trial. *Journal of the American Medical Association, 297*, 969–977.

Greaves, C. J., Sheppard, K. E., Abraham, C., Hardeman, W., Roden, M., ... The IMAGE Study Group. (2011). Systematic review of reviews of intervention components associated with increased effectiveness in dietary and physical activity interventions. *BMC Public Health, 11*, 119–130.

Heymsfield, S. B., van Mierlo, C. A., van der Knapp, H. C., Heo, M., & Frier, H. I. (2003). Weight management using a meal replacement strategy: Meta and pooling analysis from six studies. *International Journal of Obesity and Related Metabolic Disorders, 27*, 537–549.

Look AHEAD Research Group. (2010). Long-term effects of a lifestyle intervention on weight and cardiovascular risk factors in individuals with type 2 diabetes mellitus: Four-year results of the Look AHEAD trial. *Archives of Internal Medicine, 170*, 1566–1575.

McLaren, L. (2007). Socioeconomic status and obesity. *Epidemiologic Reviews, 29*, 29–48.

Metz, J. A., Stern, J. S., Kris-Etherton, P., Reusser, M. E., Morris, C. D., ... McCarron, D. A. (2000). A randomized trial of improved weight loss with a prepared meal plan in overweight and obese patients: Impact on cardiovascular risk reduction. *Archives of Internal Medicine, 160*, 2150–2158.

Misra, A., & Khurana, L. (2011). Obesity-related non-communicable diseases: South Asians vs white Caucasians. *International Journal of Obesity, 35*, 167–187.

National Institutes of Health. (1998). Clinical guidelines on the identification, evaluation, and treatment of overweight and obesity in adults—The evidence report. *Obesity Research, 6*(Suppl 2), 51S–209S.

Padwal, R., Klarenbach, S., Wiebe, N., Birch, D., Karmali, S., ... Tonelli, M. (2011). Bariatric surgery: A systematic review and network meta-analysis of randomized trials. *Obesity Reviews, 12*, 602–621.

Perri, M. G., McAllister, D. A., Gagne, J. J., Jordan, R. C., McAdoo, G., & Nezu, A. M. (1988). Effects of four maintenance programs on the long-term management of obesity. *Journal of Consulting and Clinical Psychology, 56*, 529–534.

Razak, F., Anand, S. S., Shannon, H., Vuksan, V., Davis, B., ... Yusuf, S. (2007). Defining obesity cut points in a multiethnic population. *Circulation, 115*, 2111–2118.

Romero-Corral, A., Caples, S. M., Lopez-Jimenez, F., & Somers, V. K. (2010). Diagnostic performance of body mass index to identify obesity as defined by body adiposity: A systematic review and meta-analysis. *International Journal of Obesity, 34*, 791–799.

Rucker, D., Padwal, R., Li, S. K., Curioni, C., & Lau, D. C. (2007). Long-term pharmacotherapy for obesity and overweight: Updated meta-analysis. *British Medical Journal, 335*, 1194–1199.

Sharp, T. A., Bell, M. L., Grunwald, G. K., Schmitz, K. H., Sidney, S., ... Hill, J. O. (2002). Differences in resting metabolic rate between white and African American young adults. *Obesity Research, 10*, 726–732.

Sjöström, L., Lindroos, A. K., Peltonen, M., Torgerson, J., Bouchard, C., ... Swedish Obese Subjects Study Scientific Group. (2004). Lifestyle, diabetes, and cardiovascular risk factors 10 years after bariatric surgery. *New England Journal of Medicine, 351*, 2683–2693.

Sobal, J., & Stunkard, A. J. (1989). Socioeconomic status and obesity: A review of the literature. *Psychological Bulletin, 105*, 260–275.

Turner-McGrievy, G., & Tate, D. (2011). Tweets, apps, and pods: Results of the 6-month Mobile Pounds Off Digitally (Mobile POD) randomized weight-loss intervention among adults. *Journal of Medical Internet Research, 20*, e120.

Wadden, T. A., Berkowitz, R. I., Womble, L. G., Sarwer, D. B., Phelan, S., ... Stunkard, A. J. (2005). *New England Journal of Medicine, 353*, 2111–2120.

Wadden, T. A., Volger, S., Sarwer, D. B., Vetter, M. L., Tsai, A. G., ... Moore, R. H. (2011). *New England Journal of Medicine, 365*, 1969–1979.

Walker, R. E., Keane, C. R., & Burke, J. G. (2010). Disparities and access to healthy food in the United States: A review of food deserts literature. *Health & Place, 16*, 876–884.

CHAPTER 48

Research

Baskin, M. L., Ahluwalia, H. K., & Resnicow, K. (2001). Obesity intervention among African-American children and adolescents. *Pediatric Clinics of North America, 48*(4), 1027–1039. doi: 10.1016/S0031-3955(05)70355-2

Beech, B. M., Klesges, R. C., Kumanyika, S. K., Murray, D. M., Klesges, L., … Pree-Cary, J. (2003). Child- and parent-targeted interventions: The Memphis GEMS pilot study. *Ethnicity disease, 13*(1 Suppl 1), S40–S53.

Berenson, G. S., Srinivasan, S. R., Wattigney, W. A., & Harsha, D. W. (1993). Obesity and cardiovascular risk in children. *Annals of the New York Academy of Sciences, 699*, 93–103.

Braet, C., Mervielde, I., & Vandereycken, W. (1997). Psychological aspects of childhood obesity: A controlled study in a clinical and nonclinical sample. *Journal of Pediatric Psychology, 22*(1), 59–71.

Brownell, K. D., Kelman, J. H., & Stunkard, A. J. (1983). Treatment of obese children with and without their mothers: Changes in weight and blood pressure. *Pediatrics, 71*(4), 515–523.

Brownell, K. D., & Wadden, T. A. (1991). The heterogeneity of obesity: Fitting treatments to individuals. *Behavior Therapy, 22*(2), 153–177. doi: 10.1016/S0005-7894(05)80174-1

Clay, D. L. (2002). Empirically supported treatments in pediatric psychology: Where is the diversity? *Journal of Pediatric Psychology, 27*, 325–337. doi: 10.1093/jpepsy/27.4.325

Coates, T. J., Killen, J. D., & Slinkard, L. A. (1982). Parent participation in a treatment program for overweight adolescents. *International Journal of Eating Disorders, 1*(3), 37–48.

Crawford, P. B., Story, M., Wang, M. C., Ritchie, L. D., & Sabry, Z. I. (2001). Ethnic issues in the epidemiology of childhood obesity. *Pediatric Clinics of North America, 48*(4), 855–878. doi: 10.1016/S0031-3955(05)70345-X

Dalton, W. T., & Kitzmann, K. M. (2011). A preliminary investigation of stimulus control, self-monitoring, and reinforcement in lifestyle interventions for pediatric overweight. *American Journal of Lifestyle Medicine, 6*(1), 75–89. doi: 10.1177/1559827611402582

Dietz, W. H. (1998). Health consequences of obesity in youth: Childhood predictors of adult disease. *Pediatrics, 101*(3 Pt 2), 518–525.

Ebbeling, C. B., Leidig, M. M., Sinclair, K. B., Hangen, J. P., & Ludwig, D. S. (2003). A reduced-glycemic load diet in the treatment of adolescent obesity. *Archives of Pediatriatrics & Adolescent Medicine, 157*(8), 773–779. doi: 10.1001/archpedi.157.8.773

Epstein, L. H., Klein, K. R., & Wisniewski, L. (1994). Child and parent factors that influence psychological problems in obese children. *The International Journal of Eating Disorders, 15*(2), 151–158.

Epstein, L. H., Paluch, R. A., & Raynor, H. A. (2001). Sex differences in obese children and siblings in family-based obesity treatment. *Obesity, 9*, 746–753. doi: 10.1038/oby.2001.103

Epstein, L. H., Paluch, R. A., Roemmich, J. N., & Beecher, M. D. (2007). Family-based obesity treatment, then and now: Twenty-five years of pediatric obesity treatment. *Health Psychology, 26*, 381–391. doi: 10.1037/0278-6133.26.4.381

Epstein, L. H., Valoski, A. M., Vara, L. S., McCurley, J., Wisniewski, L., … Shrager, L. R. (1995). Effects of decreasing sedentary behavior and increasing activity on weight change in obese children. *Health Psychology, 14*(2), 109–108. doi: 10.1037/0278-6133.14.2.109

Epstein, L. H., Valoski, A., Wing, R. R., & McCurley, J. (1990). Ten-year follow-up of behavioral, family-based treatment for obese children. *JAMA: The Journal of the American Medical Association, 264*(19), 2519–2523. doi: 10.1001/jama.1990.03450190051027

Epstein, L. H., Valoski, A., Wing, R. R., & McCurley, J. (1994). Ten-year outcomes of behavioral family-based treatment for childhood obesity. *Health Psychology, 13*, 373–383. doi: 10.1037/0278-6133.13.5.373

Epstein, L. H., Wing, R. R., Koeske, R., & Valoski, A. (1984). Effects of diet plus exercise on weight change in parents and children. *Journal of Consulting and Clinical Psychology, 52*, 429–437. doi: 10.1037//0022-006X.52.3.429

Epstein, L. H., Wing, R. R., Koeske, R., & Valoski, A. (1985). A comparison of lifestyle exercise, aerobic exercise, and calisthenics on weight loss in obese children. *Behavior Therapy, 16*(4), 345–356. doi: 10.1016/S0005-7894(85)80002-2

Fitzgibbon, M. L. (2004). Commentary on "Psychiatric aspects of child and adolescent obesity: A review of the past 10 years." *Journal of the American Academy of Child & Adolescent Psychiatry, 43*(2), 151–153. doi: 10.1097/00004583-200402000-00009

Fitzgibbon, M. L., Stolley, M. R., Schiffer, L., Van Horn, L., KauferChristoffel, K., & Dyer, A. (2006). Hip-hop to health jr. for latino preschool children. *Obesity, 14*(9), 1616–1625.

Ford, A. L., Bergh, C., Södersten, P., Sabin, M. A., Hollinghurst, S., ... Shield, J. P. H. (2010). Treatment of childhood obesity by retraining eating behaviour: Randomised controlled trial. *BMJ (Clinical Research Ed.), 340*, b5388.

Freedman, D. S., Mei, Z., Srinivasan, S. R., Berenson, G. S., & Dietz, W. H. (2007). Cardiovascular risk factors and excess adiposity among overweight children and adolescents: The Bogalusa Heart Study. *The Journal of Pediatrics, 150*(1), 12–17.e2. doi: 10.1016/j.jpeds.2006.08.042

Friedman, M. A., & Brownell, K. D. (1995). Psychological correlates of obesity: Moving to the next research generation. *Psychological Bulletin, 117*(1), 3–20.

Germann, J. N., Kirschenbaum, D. S., & Rich, B. H. (2007). Child and parental self-monitoring as determinants of success in the treatment of morbid obesity in low-income minority children. *Journal of Pediatric Psychology, 32*(1), 111–121. doi: 10.1093/jpepsy/jsl007

Golan, M., Kaufman, V., & Shahar, D. R. (2006). Childhood obesity treatment: Targeting parents exclusively V. parents and children. *British Journal of Nutrition, 95*(5), 1008–1015. doi: 10.1079/BJN20061757

Golan, M., Weizman, A., Apter, A., & Fainaru, M. (1998). Parents as the exclusive agents of change in the treatment of childhood obesity. *The American Journal of Clinical Nutrition, 67*(6), 1130–1135.

Gordon-Larsen, P., Adair, L. S., & Popkin, B. M. (2003). The relationship of ethnicity, socioeconomic factors, and overweight in U.S. adolescents. *Obesity, 11*, 121–129. doi: 10.1038/oby.2003.20

Gortmaker, S. L., Must, A., Perrin, J. M., Sobol, A. M., & Dietz, W. H. (1993). Social and economic consequences of overweight in adolescence and young adulthood. *The New England Journal of Medicine, 329*(14), 1008–1012. doi: 10.1056/NEJM199309303291406

Graves, T., Meyers, A. W., & Clark, L. (1988). An evaluation of parental problem-solving training in the behavioral treatment of childhood obesity. *Journal of Consulting and Clinical Psychology, 56*, 246–250. doi: 10.1037/0022-006X.56.2.246

Guo, S. S., Wu, W., Chumlea, W. C., & Roche, A. F. (2002). Predicting overweight and obesity in adulthood from body mass index values in childhood and adolescence. *The American Journal of Clinical Nutrition, 76*(3), 653–658.

Herrera, E. A., Johnston, C. A., & Steele, R. G. (2004). A comparison of cognitive and behavioral treatments for pediatric obesity. *Children's Health Care, 33*, 151–167. doi: 10.1207/s15326888chc3302_5

Inge, T. H., Krebs, N. F., Garcia, V. F., Skelton, J. A., Guice, K. S., ... Daniels, S. R. (2004). Bariatric surgery for severely overweight adolescents: Concerns and recommendations. *Pediatrics, 114*(1), 217–223. doi: 10.1542/peds.114.1.217

Israel, A. C., Stolmaker, L., & Andrian, C. A. G. (1985). The effects of training parents in general child management skills on a behavioral weight loss program for children. *Behavior Therapy, 16*(2), 169–180. doi: 10.1016/S0005-7894(85)80043-5

Israel, A. C., Stolmaker, L., Sharp, J. P., Silverman, W. K., & Simon, L. G. (1984). An evaluation of two methods of parental involvement in treating obese children. *Behavior Therapy, 15*(3), 266–272. doi: 10.1016/S0005-7894(84)80028-3

Jelalian, E., & Saelens, B. E. (1999). Empirically supported treatments in pediatric psychology: Pediatric obesity. *Journal of Pediatric Psychology, 24*(3), 223–248.

Jelalian, E., Mehlenbeck, R., Lloyd-Richardson, E. E., Birmaher, V., & Wing, R. R. (2005). "Adventure therapy" combined with cognitive-behavioral treatment for overweight adolescents. *International Journal of Obesity (London), 30*(1), 31–39.

Jelalian, E., Wember, Y. M., Bungeroth, H., & Birmaher, V. (2007). Practitioner review: Bridging the gap between research and clinical practice in pediatric obesity. *Journal of Child Psychology and Psychiatry, 48*(2), 115–127. doi: 10.1111/j.1469-7610.2006.01613.x

Johnson, W. G., Hinkle, L. K., Carr, R. E., Anderson, D. A., Lemmon, C. R., ... Bergeron, K. C. (1997). Dietary and exercise interventions for juvenile obesity: Long-term effect of behavioral and public health models. *Obesity Research, 5*(3), 257–261.

Johnston, C. A., & Steele, R. G. (2007). Treatment of pediatric overweight: An examination of feasibility and effectiveness in an applied clinical setting. *Journal of Pediatric Psychology, 32*(1), 106–110. doi: 10.1093/jpepsy/jsl010

Kiess, W., Galler, A., Reich, A., Müller, G., Kapellen, T., ... Kratzsch, J. (2001). Clinical aspects of obesity in childhood and adolescence. *Obesity Reviews: An Official Journal of the International Association for the Study of Obesity, 2*(1), 29–36.

Kirk, S., Scott, B. J., & Daniels, S. R. (2005). Pediatric obesity epidemic: Treatment options. *Journal of the American Dietetic Association, 105*, 44–51. doi: 10.1016/j.jada.2005.02.013

Kirschenbaum, D. S., Harris, E. S., & Tomarken, A. J. (1984). Effects of parental involvement in behavioral weight loss therapy for preadolescents. *Behavior Therapy, 15*(5), 485–500. doi: 10.1016/S0005-7894(84)80051-9

Kitzmann, K. M., & Beech, B. M. (2006). Family-based interventions for pediatric obesity: Methodological and conceptual challenges from family psychology. *Journal of Family Psychology, 20*, 175–189. doi: 10.1037/0893-3200.20.2.175

Kitzmann, K. M., Dalton III, W. T., & Buscemi, J. (2008). Beyond parenting practices: Family context and the treatment of pediatric obesity. *Family Relations, 57*(1), 13–23. doi: 10.1111/j.1741-3729.2007.00479.x

Krebs, N. F., Himes, J. H., Jacobson, D., Nicklas, T. A., Guilday, P., & Styne, D. (2007). Assessment of child and adolescent overweight and obesity. *Pediatrics, 120*, S193–S228. doi: 10.1542/peds.2007-2329D

Kumanyika, S. K. (2008). Environmental influences on childhood obesity: Ethnic and cultural influences in context. *Physiology & Behavior, 94*, 61–70. doi: 10.1016/j.physbeh.2007.11.019

Luzier, J., Berlin, K., & Weeks, J. (2010). Behavioral treatment of pediatric obesity: Review and future directions. *Children's Health Care, 39*, 312–334. doi: 10.1080/02739615.2010.516202

McLean, N., Griffin, S., Toney, K., & Hardeman, W. (2003). Family involvement in weight control, weight maintenance and weight-loss interventions: A systematic review of randomised trials. *International Journal of Obesity and Related Metabolic Disorders: Journal of the International Association for the Study of Obesity, 27*(9), 987–1005. doi: 10.1038/sj.ijo.0802383

Müller, M. J., Mast, M., Asbeck, I., Langnäse, K., & Grund, A. (2001). Prevention of obesity – Is it possible? *Obesity Reviews, 2*(1), 15–28. doi: 10.1046/j.1467-789x.2001.00012.x

Must, A., & Strauss, R. S. (1999). Risks and consequences of childhood and adolescent obesity. *International Journal of Obesity and Related Metabolic Disorders: Journal of the International Association for the Study of Obesity, 23*(Suppl 2), S2–S11.

Nemet, D., Barkan, S., Epstein, Y., Friedland, O., Kowen, G., & Eliakim, A. (2005). Short- and long-term beneficial effects of a combined dietary–behavioral–physical activity intervention for the treatment of childhood obesity. *Pediatrics, 115*(4), e443–e449. doi: 10.1542/peds.2004-2172

Nova, A., Russo, A., & Sala, E. (2001), Long-term management of obesity in pediatric office practice: Experimental evaluation of two different types of intervention. *Ambulatory Child Health, 7*(3–4), 239–247. doi: 10.1046/j.1467-0658.2001.00135.x

Ogden, C., & Carroll, M. (2010, June). Prevalence of obesity among children and adolescents: United States, Trends 1963–1965 through 2007–2008. *Children, 17*, 1–5.

Ogden, C. L., Carroll, M. D., Curtin, L. R., Lamb, M. M., & Flegal, K. M. (2010). Prevalence of high body mass index in US children and adolescents, 2007-2008. *JAMA: The Journal of the American Medical Association, 303*(3), 242 –249 doi: 10.1001/jama.2009.2012

Oude Luttikhuis, H., Baur, L., Jansen, H., Shrewsbury, V. A., O'Malley, C., … Summerbell, C. D. (2009). Cochrane review: Interventions for treating obesity in children. *Evidence Based Child Health: A Cochrane Review Journal, 4*(4), 1571–1729. doi: 10.1002/ebch.462

Parker, L., Spear, M., Holovach, N. F., & Olson, S., Rapporteur; Standing Committee on Childhood Obesity Prevention; Institute of Medicine. (2011). *Legal strategies in childhood obesity prevention: Workshop summary*. Washington, D.C.: The National Academies Press.

Reinehr, T., Kersting, M., Alexy, U., & Andler, W. (2003). Long-term follow-up of overweight children: After training, after a single consultation session, and without treatment. *Journal of Pediatric Gastroenterology and Nutrition, 37*(1), 72–74.

Resnicow, K., Yaroch, A. L., Davis, A., Wang, D. T., Carter, S., … Baranowski, T. (2000). Go Girls!: Results from a nutrition and physical activity program for low-income, overweight African American adolescent females. *Health Education & Behavior, 27*(5), 616–631. doi: 10.1177/109019810002700507

Shilts, M. K., Horowitz, M., & Townsend, M. S. (2004). Goal setting as a strategy for dietary and physical activity behavior change: A review of the literature. *American Journal of Health Promotion: AJHP, 19*(2), 81–93.

Sothern, M., Gordon, S. T., & Almen, T. K. V. (2006). *Handbook of pediatric obesity: Clinical management*. Boca Raton, FL: CRC Press.

Spear, B. A., Barlow, S. E., Ervin, C., Ludwig, D. S., Saelens, B. E., … Taveras, E. M. (2007). Recommendations for treatment of child and adolescent overweight and obesity. *Pediatrics, 120*, S254–S288. doi: 10.1542/peds.2007-2329F

Stern, M., Mazzeo, S. E., Gerke, C. K., Porter, J. S., Bean, M. K., & Laver, J. H. (2007). Gender, ethnicity, psychosocial factors, and quality of life among severely overweight, treatment-seeking adolescents. *Journal of Pediatric Psychology, 32*(1), 90–94. doi: 10.1093/jpepsy/jsl013

Stice, E., Shaw, H., & Marti, C. N. (2006). A meta-analytic review of obesity prevention programs for children and adolescents: The skinny on interventions that work. *Psychological Bulletin, 132*(5), 667–691. doi: 10.1037/0033-2909.132.5.667

Stolley, M. R., & Fitzgibbon, M. L. (1997). Effects of an obesity prevention program on the eating behavior of African American mothers and daughters. *Health Education & Behavior, 24*(2), 152–164. doi: 10.1177/109019819702400204

Striegel-Moore, R. H., Silberstein, L. R., & Rodin, J. (1986). Toward an understanding of risk factors for bulimia. *The American Psychologist, 41*(3), 246–263.

Summerbell, C. D., Ashton, V., Campbell, K. J., Edmunds, L., Kelly, S., & Waters, E. (2003). Interventions for treating obesity in children. *Cochrane Database of Systematic Reviews (Online)*, (3), CD001872. doi: 10.1002/14651858.CD001872

Treadwell, J. R., Sun, F., & Schoelles, K. (2008). Systematic review and meta-analysis of bariatric surgery for pediatric obesity. *Annals of Surgery, 248*(5), 763–776. doi: 10.1097/SLA.0b013e31818702f4

van den Akker, E. L. T., Puiman, P. J., Groen, M., Timman, R., Jongejan, M. T. M., & Trijsburg, W. (2007). A cognitive behavioral therapy program for overweight children. *The Journal of Pediatrics, 151*, 280–283. doi: 10.1016/j.jpeds.2007.03.042

Wadden, T. A., Stunkard, A. J., Rich, L., Rubin, C. J., Sweidel, G., & McKinney, S. (1990). Obesity in Black adolescent girls: A controlled clinical trial of treatment by diet, behavior modification, and parental support. *Pediatrics, 85*(3), 345–352.

Wilson, P., O'Meara, S., Summerbell, C., & Kelly, S. (2003). The prevention and treatment of childhood obesity. *Quality & Safety in Health Care, 12*(1), 65–74. doi: 10.1136/qhc.12.1.65

Zametkin, A. J., Zoon, C. K., Klein, H. W., & Munson, S. (2004). Psychiatric aspects of child and adolescent obesity: A review of the past 10 years. *Journal of the American Academy of Child & Adolescent Psychiatry, 43*(2), 134–150. doi: 10.1097/00004583-200402000-00008

Clinician Application

Anderson, S. E., Cohen, P., Naumova, E. N., Jacques, P. F., & Must, A. (2007). Adolescent obesity and risk for subsequent major depressive disorder and anxiety disorder: Prospective evidence. *Psychosomatic Medicine, 69*, 740–747.

Barlow, S. E., & The Expert Committee. (2007). Expert committee recommendations regarding the prevention, assessment, and treatment of child and adolescent overweight and obesity: Summary report. *Pediatrics, 120*, S164–S192.

Coppins, D. F., Margetts, B. M., Fa, J. L., Brown, M., Garrett, F., & Huelin, S. (2011). Effectiveness of a multidisciplinary family-based programme for treating childhood obesity (The Family Project). *European Journal of Clinical Nutrition, 65*, 903–909.

Delamater, A. M., Jent, J., Moine, C. T., & Rios, J. (2008). Empirically supported treatment of overweight adolescents. In E. Jelalian & R. Steele (Eds.), *Handbook of child and adolescent obesity.* New York, NY: Springer.

Ellis, D., Janisse, H., Naar-King, S., Kolmodin, K., Jen, K., ... Marshall, S. (2010). The effects of multisystem therapy on family support for weight loss among obese African-American adolescents: Findings from a randomized controlled trial. *Journal of Developmental & Behavioral Pediatrics, 31*, 461–468.

Gerards, S. M. P. L., Sleddens, E. F. C., Dagnelie, P. C., de Vries, N. K., & Kremers, S. P. J. (2011). Interventions addressing general parenting to prevent or treat childhood obesity. *International Journal of Pediatric Obesity, 6*, 28–45.

Germann, J. N., Krischenbaum, D. S., Rich, B. H., & O'Koon, J. C. (2006). Long-term evaluation of multidisciplinary treatment of morbid obesity in low-income minority adolescents: La Rabida children's hospital's Fit Matters program. *Journal of Adolescent Health, 39*, 553–561.

Golley, R. K., Magarey, A. M., Baur, L. A., Steinbeck, K. S., & Daniels, L. A. (2007). Twelve-month effectiveness of a parent-led, family-focused weight-management program for prepubertal children: A randomized, controlled trial. *Pediatrics, 119*, 517–525.

Hart, C. N., & Jelalian E. (2008). Shortened sleep duration is associated with pediatric overweight. *Behavioral Sleep Medicine, 6*, 251–167.

Kalavainen, M., Korppi, M., & Nuutinen, O. (2011). Long-term efficacy of group-based treatment for childhood obesity compared with routinely given individual counseling. *International Journal of Obesity, 35*, 530–533.

Lambiase, M. (2009). Treating pediatric overweight through reductions in sedentary behavior: A review of the literature. *Journal of Pediatric Health Care, 23*, 29–36.

Lowry, K. W., Sallinen, B. J., & Janicke, D. M. (2007). The effects of weight management programs on self-esteem in pediatric overweight populations. *Journal of Pediatric Psychology, 32*, 1179–1195.

Lumeng, J. C., Forrest, P., Appugliese, D. P., Kaciroti, N., Corwyn, R. F., & Bradley, R. H. (2010). Weight status as a predictor of being bullied in third through sixth grades. *Pediatrics, 125*, e1301–e1307.

Michalsky, M., Kramer, R. E., Fullmer, M. A., Polfuss, M., Porter, R., ... Reichard, K. W. (2011). Developing criteria for pediatric/adolescent bariatric surgery specialty centers. *Pediatrics, 128*(Suppl 2), S65–S70.

Safer, D., Couturier, J., & Lock, J. (2007). Dialectical behavior therapy modified for adolescent binge eating disorder: A case report. *Cognitive and Behavioral Practice, 14*, 157–167.

Sato, A. F., Jelalian, E., Hart, C. N., Lloyd-Richardson, E. E., Mehlenbeck, R. S., ... Wing, R. R. (2011). Associations between parent behavior and adolescent weight control. *Journal of Pediatric Psychology, 36*, 451–460.

Striegel-Moore, R. H., Franko, D. L., & Garcia, J. (2009). Validity and clinical utility of night eating syndrome. *International Journal of Eating Disorders, 42*, 720–738.

Striegel-Moore, R. H., Franko, D. L., Thompson, D., Affenito, S., May, A., & Kraemer, H. C. (2008). Exploring the typology of night eating syndrome. *International Journal of Eating Disorders, 41*, 411–418.

Tanofsky-Kraff, M. (2008). Binge eating among children and adolescents. In E. Jelalian & R. Steele (Eds.), *Handbook of child and adolescent obesity.* New York, NY: Springer.

Tanofsky-Kraff, M., Wilfley, D. E., Young, J. F., Mufson, L., Yanovski, S. Z., ... Salaita, C. G. (2007). Preventing excessive weight gain in adolescents: Interpersonal psychotherapy for binge eating. *Obesity, 15*, 1345–1355.

Ward-Begnoche, W. L., Gance-Cleveland, B., & Portilla, M. (2009). Circumventing communication barriers with Spanish-speaking patients regarding pediatric obesity. *Journal of Pediatric Health Care, 23*, 272–280.

Ward-Begnoche, W. L., Pasold, T., O'Neill, V. S., Peck, D., Razzaq, S., & Young, K. (2008). Childhood obesity treatment literature review. In *Treating obesity across the lifespan* (pp. 5–20). Springer Press.

Ward-Begnoche, W. L., & Thompson, J. (2008). Family-centered care: Assessing and surmounting barriers to eating and activity changes in overweight youth. *Journal of Specialists in Pediatric Nursing, 13*(3), 229–234.

Wildermuth, S., Mesman, G. R., & Ward-Begnoche, W. L. (Under review). Binge eating disorder, boredom eating, emotional eating, and night eating syndrome in pediatric patients. *Journal of Pediatric Healthcare.* Submitted February 2011.

Wilfley, D., Kolko, R., & Kass, A. (2011).Cognitive-behavioral therapy for weight management and eating disorders in children and adolescents. *Child and Adolescent Psychiatric Clinics North America, 20*, 271–285.

Wilfley, D. E., Tibbs, T. L., VanBuren, D. J., Reach, K. P., Walker, M. S., & Epstein, L. H. (2007). Lifestyle interventions in the treatment of childhood overweight: A meta-analytic review of randomized controlled trials. *Health Psychology, 26*, 521–532.

Zeller, M. H., & Modi, A. C. (2006). Predictors of health-related quality of life in obese youth. *Obesity, 14*, 122–130.

CHAPTER 49

Research

Cooper, P. J., Murray, L., Wilson, A., & Romaniuk, H. (2003). Controlled trial of the short- and long-term effect of psychological treatment of post-partum depression. *British Journal of Psychiatry, 182*, 412–419.

Forman, D., O'Hara, M. W., Stuart, S., Gorman, L., Larsen, K., & Coy, K. C. (2007). Effective treatment for postpartum depression is not sufficient to improve the developing mother-child relationship. *Development and Psychopathology, 19*, 585–602.

Grote, N. K., Swartz, H. A., Geibel, S. L., Zuckoff, A., Houck, P. R., & Frank E. (2009), A randomized controlled trial of culturally relevant, brief interpersonal psychotherapy for perinatal depression. *Psychiatric Services, 60*, 313–321.

Holden, J. M., Sagovsky, R., & Cox, J. L. (1989). Counselling in a general practice setting: Controlled study of health visitor intervention in treatment of postnatal depression. *British Medical Journal, 298*, 223–226.

Milgrom, J., Negri, L. M., Gemmill, A. W., McNeil, M., & Martin, P. R. (2005). A randomized controlled trial of psychological interventions for postnatal depression. *British Journal of Clinical Psychology, 44*, 529–542.

Misri, S. R., Reebye, P., Corral, M., & Mills, L. (2004). The use of paroxetine and cognitive-behavioral therapy in postpartum depression and anxiety: A randomized controlled trial. *Journal of Clinical Psychiatry, 65*, 1236–1241.

Nylen, K. J., O'Hara, M. W., Brock, R., Moel, J., Gorman, L., & Stuart, S. (2010). Predictors of the longitudinal course of postpartum depression following Interpersonal Psychotherapy. *Journal of Consulting and Clinical Psychology, 78*, 757–763.

O'Hara, M. W. (2009). Postpartum depression: What we know. *Journal of Clinical Psychology, 65*, 1258–1269.

Segre, L. S., Stasik, S. M., O'Hara, M. W., & Arndt, S. (2010). Listening visits: an evaluation of the effectiveness and acceptability of a home-based depression treatment. *Psychotherapy Research, 20*, 712–721.

Stuart, S., O'Hara, M. W., & Gorman, L. L. (2003). The prevention and treatment postpartum depression. *Archives of Women's Mental Health, 6*(Suppl 2), S57–S69.

Stuart, S., & Robertson, M. (2003). *Interpersonal Psychotherapy: A clinician's guide.* London, UK: Hodder Education Group.

Tandon, S. D., Perry, D. F., Mendelson, T., Kemp, K., & Leis, J. A. (2011). Preventing perinatal depression in low-income home visiting clients: A randomized controlled trial. *Journal of Consulting and Clinical Psychololgy, 79*, 707–712.

Wenzel, A. (2011). *Anxiety disorders in childbearing women: Diagnosis and treatment.* Washington, DC: APA Books.

CHAPTER 50

Research

Akechi, T., Okuyama, T., Onishi J., Morita, T., & Furukawa, T. A. (2008). Psychotherapy for depression among incurable cancer patients. *Cochrane Database of Systematic Reviews,* (2), CD005537. doi: 10.1002/14651858. CD005537.pub2

Andrykowski, M. A., & Manne, S. L. (2006). Are psychological interventions effective and accepted by cancer patients? I. Standards and levels of evidence. *Annals of Behavioral Medicine, 32*, 93–97.

Boyes, A., Girgis, A., Zucca, A., & Lecathelinais, C. (2009). Anxiety and depression among long-term survivors of cancer in Australia: Results of a population-based survey. *The Medical Journal of Australia, 190*, S94–S98.

Brintzenhofe-Szoc, K. M., Levin, T. T., Li, Y., Kissane, D. W., & Zabor, J. R. (2009). Mixed anxiety/depression symptoms in a large cancer cohort: Prevalence by cancer type. *Psychosomatics, 50*, 383–391.

Carlson, L. E., Angen, M., Cullum, J., Goodey, E., Koopmans, J., ... Bultz, B. D. (2004). High levels of untreated distress and fatigue in cancer patients. *British Journal of Cancer, 90*, 2297–2304.

Culver, J. L., Arena, P. L., Antoni, M. H., & Carver, C. S. (2002). Coping and distress among women under treatment for early stage breast cancer: Comparing African-Americans, Hispanics, and non-Hispanic Whites. *Psycho-Oncology, 11*, 495–504.

Coyne, J. C., Lepore, S. J., & Palmer, S. C. (2006). Efficacy of psychosocial interventions in cancer care: Evidence is weaker than it first looks. *Annals of Behavioral Medicine, 32*, 104–110.

Coyne, J. C., Stefanek, M., & Palmer, S. C. (2007). Psychotherapy and survival in cancer: The conflict between hope and evidence. *Psychological Bulletin, 133*, 367–394.

Duijts, S. F. A., Faber, M. M., Oldenburg, M. S. A., & van Beurden, M. (2010). Effectiveness of behavioral techniques and physical exercise on psychosocial functioning and health-related quality of life in breast cancer patients and survivors—A meta-analysis. *Psycho-Oncology, 20*, 115–126.

Edwards, A. G. K., Hulbert-Williams, N., & Neal, R. D. (2008). Psychological interventions for women with metastatic breast cancer. *Cochrane Database of Systematic Reviews*, (3), CD004253. doi: 10.1002/14651858. CD004253.pub3

Giese-Davis, J., Collie, K., Rancourt, K. M. S., Neri, E., Kraemer, H. C., & Spiegel, D. (2010). Decrease in depression symptoms is associated with longer survival in patients with metastatic breast cancer: A secondary analysis. *Journal of Clinical Oncology, 29*, 413–420.

Helgeson, V. S., Snyder, P., & Seltman, H. (2004). Psychological and physical adjustment to breast cancer over 4 years: Identifying distinct trajectories of change. *Health Psychology, 23*, 3–15.

Ledesma, D., & Kumano, H. (2009). Mindfulness-based stress reduction and cancer: A meta-analysis. *Psycho-Oncology, 18*, 571–579.

Linden, W., & Satin, J. R. (2007). Avoidable pitfalls in behavioural medicine research. *Annals of Behavioral Medicine, 33*, 143–147.

Linden, W., Vodermaier, A., MacKenzie, R., & Greig, D. (2012). Anxiety and depression after cancer diagnosis: Prevalence rates by cancer type, gender, and age. *Journal of Affective Disorders, 141*, 343–351. doi: 10.1016/j.jad.2012.03.025

Lipsey, M. W., & Wilson, D. B. (1993). The efficacy of psychological, educational, and behavioral treatment. *American Psychologist, 48*, 1181–1209.

Luebbert, K., Dahme, B., & Hasenbring, M. (2001). The effectiveness of relaxation training in reducing treatment-related symptoms and improving emotional adjustment in acute non-surgical cancer treatment: A meta-analytic review. *Psycho–Oncology, 10*, 490–502.

Meyer, T. J., & Mark, M. M. (1995). Effects of psychosocial interventions with adult cancer patients: A meta-analysis of randomized experiments. *Health Psychology, 14*, 101–108.

Mitchell, A. J., Chan, M., Bhatti, H. C., Halton, M., Grassi, L., ... Meader, N. (2011). Prevalence of depression, anxiety, and adjustment disorder in oncological, haematological, and palliative-care settings: A meta-analysis of 94 interview-based studies. *The Lancet Oncology, 12*, 160–174.

National Comprehensive Cancer Network (NCCN). (2007). *NCCN clinical practice guidelines in oncology: Distress management*. Retrieved from http://www.nccn.org/professional/physicians_gls/PDF/distress/pdf

Osborn, R. L., Demoncada, A. C., & Feuerstein, M. (2006). Psychosocial interventions for depression, anxiety, and quality of life in cancer survivors: A meta-analysis. *International Journal of Psychiatry in Medicine, 38*, 13–34.

Pinquart, M., & Duberstein, P. R. (2010). Depression and cancer mortality: A meta-analysis. *Psychological Medicine, 40*, 1797–1810.

Satin, J., Linden, W., & Phillips, M. J. (2009). Depression as a predictor of disease progression and mortality in cancer patients: A meta-analysis. *Cancer, 115*, 5349–5361.

Schneider, S., Moyer, A., Knapp-Oliver, S., Sohl, S., Cannella, D., & Targhetta, V. (2010). Pre-intervention distress moderates the efficacy of psychosocial treatments for cancer patients: A meta-analysis. *Journal of Behavioral Medicine, 33*, 1–14.

Sheard, T., & Maguire, P. (1999). *The effect of psychological interventions on anxiety and depression in cancer patients: Results of two meta-analyses. British Journal of Cancer, 80*, 1770–1780.

Smedley, B. D., Stith, A. Y., & Nelson, A. R. (Eds.). (2003). *Unequal treatment: Confronting racial and ethnic disparities in health care*. Washington, DC: National Research Council.

Tatrow, K., & Montgomery, G. H. (2006). Cognitive-behavioral therapy techniques for distress and pain in breast cancer patients: A meta-analysis. *Journal of Behavioral Medicine, 29*, 17–27.

Thomas, B. C., NandaMohan, V., Nair, M. K., & Pandey, M. (2010). Gender, age and surgery as a treatment modality leads to higher distress in patients with cancer. *Supportive Care in Cancer, 19*, 239–250.

van't Spijker, A., Trijsburg, R. W., & Duivenvoorden, H. J. (1997). Psychological sequelae of cancer diagnosis: A meta-analytical review of 58 studies after 1980. *Psychosomatic Medicine, 59*, 280–293.

CHAPTER 51

Research

Agboola, S., McNeill, A., Coleman, T., & Leonardi Bee J. (2010). A systematic review of the effectiveness of smoking relapse prevention interventions for abstinent smokers. *Addiction, 105*, 1362–1380.

Brandon, T. H., Meade, C. D., Herzog, T. A., Chirikos, T. N., Webb, M. S., & Cantor, A. B. (2004). Efficacy and cost-effectiveness of a minimal intervention to prevent smoking relapse: Dismantling the effects of content versus contact. *Journal of Consulting & Clinical Psychology, 72*, 797–808.

Centers for Disease Control and Prevention. (2011). Current cigarette smoking among adults—United States, 2011. *Morbidity and Mortality Weekly Report, 61*, 889–894.

Cinciripini, P. M., Lapitsky, L. G., Seay, S., Wallfisch, A., Kitchens, K., & Van Vunakis, H. (1995). The effects of smoking schedules on cessation outcome: Can we improve on common methods of gradual and abrupt nicotine withdrawal? *Journal of Consulting & Clinical Psychology, 63*, 388–399.

Cokkinides, V. E., Halpern, M. T., Barbeau, E. M., Ward, E., & Thun, M. J. (2008). Racial and ethnic disparities in smoking-cessation interventions: Analysis of the 2005 National Health Interview Survey. *American Journal of Preventive Medicine, 34*, 404–412.

Dresler, C., & Leon, M. (2007). *Reversal of risk after quitting smoking*. IARC Handbooks of Cancer Prevention: Vol .11, Tobacco Control. World Health Organization.

Godfrey C., & Parrott, S. (2006). Cost effectiveness of smoking cessation interventions. In N. K. Syrigos, C. M. Nutting, & C. Roussos (Eds.), *Tumors of the chest: Biology, diagnosis, and treatment* (pp. 641–648). Berlin, Germany: Springer.

Clinician Application

Burns, D. D., & Burns, S. (2003). *Tools, not schools, of therapy*. Los Altos Hills, CA: Author.

FDA News Release. (2009, July 1). *Boxed Warning on Serious Mental Health Events to be Required for Chantix and Zyban, U.S. Food and Drug Administration*.

Fiore, M. C., Jaen, C. R, Baker, T. B., Bailey, W. C., Benowitz, N. L., ... Wewers, M. E. (2008). *Treating tobacco use and dependence. 2008 update*. Clinical Practice Guideline. Rockville, MD: US Department of Health and Human Services, Public Health Service.

Foulds, J., Veldheer, S., & Berg, A. (2011), Electronic cigarettes (e-cigs): Views of aficionados and clinical/public health perspectives. *International Journal of Clinical Practice, 65*, 1037–1042. doi: 10.1111/j.1742-1241.2011.02751.x

Gottlieb, A., Killen, J., Marlatt, G. A., & Taylor, C. B. (1987), Psychological and pharmacological influences in cigarette smoking withdrawal: Effects of nicotine gum and expectancies on smoking withdrawal symptoms and relapse. *Journal of Consulting and Clinical Psychology, 55*, 606–608.

Gottlieb, A. (1998). Smoking cessation. In J. Roitman, M. Kelsey, & American College of Sports Medicine (Eds.), *Resource manual for guidelines for exercise testing and prescription*. Baltimore, MD: Williams & Wilkins.

Hall, R. G., Sachs, P. L., Hall, S. M., & Benowitz, N. M. (1984). Two year efficacy and safety of rapid smoking therapy in patients with cardiac and pulmonary disease. *Journal of Consulting and Clinical Psychology, 52*, 574–581.

Lichtenstein, E., & Rodrigues, M. P. (1977). Long-term effects of rapid smoking treatment for dependent cigarette smokers. *Addictive Behaviors, 2*, 109–112.

Lichtenstein E. (2002). From rapid smoking to the Internet: Five decades of cessation research. *Nicotine and Tobacco Research, 4*, 139–145.

Stead, L. F., Perera, R., Bullen, C., Mant, D., & Lancaster, T. (2008). Nicotine replacement therapy for smoking cessation. *Cochrane Database of Systematic Reviews*, (1), CD000146. doi: 10.1002/14651858.CD000146.pub3

CHAPTER 52

Research

Altamura, A. C., Carta, M. G., Tacchini, G., Musazzi, A., Pioli, M. R., & The Italian Collaborative Group on Somatoform Disorders. (1998). Prevalence of somatoform disorders in a psychiatric population: An Italian nationwide survey. *European Archives of Psychiatry and Clinical Neuroscience, 248*, 267–271.

American Psychiatric Association. (1994). *Diagnostic and statistical manual of mental disorders* (4th ed.). Washington, DC: Author.

American Psychiatric Association. (2010). *DSM-5*. Retrieved June 15, 2011, DSM5.org

Barsky, A. J., Wyshak, G., Klerman, G. L., & Latham, K. S. (1990). The prevalence of hypochondriasis in medical outpatients. *Social Psychiatry and Psychiatric Epidemiology, 25*, 89–94.

Escobar, J. I., Waitzkin, H., Silver, R. C., Gara, M., & Holman, A. (1998). Abridged somatization: A study in primary care. *Psychosomatic Medicine, 60*, 466–472.

Faravelli, C., Salvatori, S., Galassi, F., Aiazzi, L., Drei, C., & Cabras, P. (1997). Epidemiology of somatoform disorders: A community survey in Florence. *Social Psychiatry and Psychiatric Epidemiology, 32*, 24–29.

Gureje, O., Simon, G. E., Ustun, T., & Goldberg, D. P. (1997). Somatization in cross-cultural perspective: A World Health Organization study in primary care. *American Journal of Psychiatry, 154*, 989–995.

Hahn, S. R. (2001). Physical symptoms and physician-experienced difficulty in the physician-patient relationship. *Annals of Internal Medicine, 134*, 897–904.

Lin, E. H., Katon, W., Von Korff, M., Bush, T., Lipscomb, R., ... Wagner, E. (1991). Frustrating patients: Physician and patient perspectives among distressed high users of medical services. *Journal of General Internal Medicine, 6*, 241–246.

Regier, D., Boyd, J., Burke, J., Rae, D. S., Myers, J. K., ... Locke, B. Z. (1988). One-month prevalence of mental disorders in the US: Based on five epidemiological catchment area sites. *Archives of General Psychiatry, 45*, 977–986.

Smith, G. R., Monson, R. A., & Ray, D. C. (1986). Patients with multiple unexplained symptoms: Their characteristics, functional health, and health care utilization. *Archives of Internal Medicine, 146*, 69–72.

Thomson, A. B., & Page, L. A. (2007). Psychotherapies for hypochondriasis. *Cochrane Database of Systematic Reviews, 4*, CD006520.

Woolfolk, R. L., & Allen, L. A. (2007). *Treatment of somatization: A cognitive-behavioral approach*. New York, NY: Guilford.

CHAPTER 53

Research

American Diabetes Association. (2011). Standards of medical care in diabetes—2011. *Diabetes Care, 34*, S11–S61.

Anderson, B., Ho, J., Brackett, J., Finkelstein, D., & Laffel, L. (1997). Parental involvement in diabetes management tasks: Relationships to blood glucose monitoring adherence and metabolic control in young adolescents with insulin-dependent diabetes mellitus. *Journal of Pediatrics, 130*, 257–265.

Centers for Disease Control and Prevention. (2011). National diabetes fact sheet: National estimates and general information on diabetes and prediabetes in the United States, 2011. Retrieved from http://www.cdc.gov/diabetes/pubs/pdf/ndfs_2011.pdf

Channon, S. J., Huws-Thomas, M. V., Rollnick, S., Hood, K., Cannings-Johns, R. L., ... Gregory, J. W. (2007). A multicenter randomized controlled trial of motivational interviewing in teenagers with diabetes. *Diabetes Care, 30*, 1390–1395.

Ellis, D., Naar-King, S., Templin, T., Frey, M., Cunningham, P., ... Idalski, A. (2008). Multisystemic therapy for adolescents with poorly controlled type 1 diabetes. *Diabetes Care, 31*, 1746–1747.

Ellis, D. A., Yopp, J., Templin, T., Naar-King, S., Frey, M., ... Niec, L. N. (2007). Family mediators and moderators of treatment outcomes among youths with poorly controlled type 1 diabetes: Results from a randomized controlled trial. *Journal of Pediatric Psychology, 32*, 194–205.

Grey, M., Boland, E. A., Davidson, M., Li, J., & Tamborlane, W. V. (2000). Coping skills training for youth with diabetes mellitus has long-lasting effects on metabolic control and quality of life. *Journal of Pediatrics, 137*, 107–113.

Harris, M. A., Freeman, K. A., & Beers, M. (2009). Family therapy for adolescents with poorly controlled diabetes: Initial test of clinical significance. *Journal of Pediatric Psychology, 34*, 1097–1107.

Holmes, C. S., Chen, R., Kumar, A., Mackey, E., Grey, M., & Streisand, R. (2011). A coping skills and family teamwork program to prevent deterioration in adolescent T1D care: Feasibility pilot data. *Diabetes* (Suppl 1) (60), 824-P.

Holmes, C., Chen, R., Streisand, R., Marschall, D., Souter, S., ... Peterson, C. (2006). Predictors of youth diabetes care behaviors and metabolic control: A structural equation modeling approach. *Journal of Pediatric Psychology, 31*, 770–784.

Hood, K. K., Huestis, S., Maher, A., Butler, D., Volkening, L., & Laffel, L. M. (2006). Depressive symptoms in children and adolescents with type 1 diabetes: Association with diabetes-specific characteristics. *Diabetes Care, 29*, 1389–1391.

Jaser, S. S., Whittemore, R., Ambrosino, J. M., Lindemann, E., & Grey, M. (2009). Coping and psychosocial adjustment in mothers of young children with type 1 diabetes. *Children's Health Care, 38*, 91–106.

McGrady, M. E., Laffel, L., Drotar, D., Repaske D., & Hood K. K. (2009). Depressive symptoms and glycemic control in adolescents with type 1 diabetes: Mediational role of blood glucose monitoring. *Diabetes Care, 32*, 804–406.

Silverstein, J., Klingensmith, G., Copeland, K. C., Plotnick, L., Kaufman, F., … Clark, N. (2005). Care of children and adolescents with type 1 diabetes mellitus: A statement of the American diabetes association. *Diabetes Care, 28*, 186–212.

Wysocki, T., Harris, M. A., Buckloh, L. M., Mertlich, D., Lochrie, A. S., … White, N. H. (2007). Randomized trial of behavioral family systems therapy for diabetes: Maintenance of effects on diabetes outcomes in adolescents. *Diabetes Care, 30*, 555–560.

CHAPTER 54

Research

Arkowitz, H., Hinton, R., Perl, J., & Himadi, W. (1978). Treatment strategies for dating anxiety in college men based on real-life practice. *Counseling Psychologist, 7*, 41–46. doi: 10.1177/001100007800700410

Barry, C. M., Madsen, S. D., Nelson, L. J., Carroll, J. S., & Badger, S. (2009). Friendship and romantic relationship qualities in emerging adulthood: Differential associations with identity development and achieved adulthood criteria. *Journal of Adult Development, 16*, 209–222. doi: 10.1007/s10804-009-9067-x

Carver, K., Joyner, K., & Udry, R. J. (2003). National estimates of adolescent romantic relationships. In P. Florsheim (Ed.), *Adolescent romantic relations and sexual behavior: Theory, research, and practical implications* (pp. 23–56). Mahwah, NJ: Lawrence Erlbaum.

Chorney, D. B., & Morris, T. L. (2008). The changing face of dating anxiety: Issues in assessment with special populations. *Clinical Psychology Science & Practice, 15*, 224–238. doi: 10.1111/j.1468-2850.2008.00132.x

Connolly, J., Furman, W., & Konarski, R. (2000). The role of peers in the emergence of heterosexual romantic relationships in adolescence. *Child Development, 71*, 1395–1408.

Erikson, E. H. (1963). *Childhood and society.* New York, NY: Norton.

Glickman, A. R., & La Greca, A. M. (2004). The Dating Anxiety Scale for Adolescents: Scale development and associations with adolescent functioning. *Journal of Clinical Child and Adolescent Psychology, 33*, 566–578. doi: 10.1207/s15374424jccp3303_14

Grossman, K. S., McNamara, J. R., & Dudley, K. (1991). Treatment effectiveness of a self-help manual for dating anxiety. *Journal of College Student Psychotherapy, 6*, 85–106. doi: 10.1300/J035v06n01_07

Grover, R. L., & Nangle, D. W. (2003). Adolescent perceptions of problematic heterosocial situations: A focus study group. *Journal of Youth & Adolescence, 32*, 129–140.

Grover, R. L., Nangle, D. W., & Zeff, K. R. (2005). The measure of adolescent heterosocial competence: Development and initial validation. *Journal of Clinical Child and Adolescent Psychology, 34*, 282–291. doi: 10.1207/s15374424jccp3402_7

Hansen, D. J., Christopher, J. S., & Nangle, D. W. (1992). Adolescent heterosocial interactions and dating. In V. B. Van Hasselt & M. Hersen (Eds.), *Handbook of social development: A life span perspective* (pp. 371–394). New York, NY: Plenum Press.

La Greca, A. M., & Mackey, E. R. (2007). Adolescents' anxiety in dating situations: The potential role of friends and romantic partners. *Journal of Clinical Child and Adolescent Psychology, 36*, 520–531. doi: 10.1080/15374410701662097

Leck, K. (2006). Correlates of minimal dating. *The Journal of Social Psychology, 146*, 549–567. doi: 10.3200/SOCP.146.5.549-567

Raffaelli, M., & Ontai, L. (2001). 'She's 16 years old and there's boys calling over to the house': An exploratory study of sexual socialization in Latino families. *Culture, Health & Sexuality, 3*, 295–310. doi: 10.1080/13691050152484722

Stevens, S. B., & Morris, T. L. (2007). College dating and social anxiety: Using the internet as a means of connecting to others. *CyberPsychology & Behavior, 10*, 680–688. doi: 10.1089/cpb.2007.9970

Sullivan, H. S. (1953). *The interpersonal theory of psychiatry.* New York, NY: Norton.

Clinician Application

Palmiter, D. J. (2009). Child clinician's corner: Monitoring outside of the home. *The Independent Practitioner, 29*, 228–230.

Palmiter, D. J. (2010). Using our screw ups to help our kids [Blog post]. Retrieved from http://hecticparents.wordpress.com/2010/08/06/using-our-screw-ups-to-help-our-kids/

Palmiter, D. J. (2011). *Working parents, thriving families: 10 strategies that make a difference.* North Branch, MN: Sunrise River Press.

CHAPTER 55

Research

Bancroft, J. (2008). Sexual behavior that is "out of control": A theoretical conceptual approach. *Psychiatric Clinics of North America, 31*, 593–601.

Bancroft, J., & Vukadinovic, Z. (2004). Sexual addiction, sexual compulsivity, sexual impulsivity, or what? Toward a theoretical model. *Journal of Sex Research, 41*, 225–234.

Black, D. W., Kehrberg, L. D., Flumerfelt, D. L., & Schlosser, S. S. (1997). Characteristics of 36 subjects reporting compulsive sexual behavior. *American Journal of Psychiatry, 154*(2), 243–249.

Carnes, P. J., Green, B. A., Merlo, L. J., Polles, A., Carnes, S., & Gold, M. (2012). PATHOS: A brief screening application for assessing sexual addiction. *Journal of Addiction Medicine, 6*, 29–34.

Chaney, M. P., & Blalock, A. C. (2006). Boredom proneness, social connectedness, and sexual addiction among men who have sex with male internet users. *Journal of Addictions & Offender Counseling, 26*(2), 111–122.

Coleman, E. (1992). Is your patient suffering from compulsive sexual behavior? *Psychiatric Annals, 22*, 320–325.

Coleman, E., Horvath, K. J., Miner, M., Ross, M. W., Oakes, M., & Rosser, B. R. S. (2010). Compulsive sexual behavior and risk for unsafe sex among internet using men who have sex with men. *Archives of Sexual Behavior, 39*, 1045–1053.

Dodge, B., Reece, M., Cole, S. L., & Sandfort, T. G. M. (2004). Sexual compulsivity among heterosexual college students. *Journal of Sex Research, 41*(4), 343–350.

Friedman, H. R. (1999). A Gestalt approach to sexual compulsivity. *Sexual Addiction and Compulsivity, 6*(1), 63–75.

Goodman, A. (2001). What's in a name? Terminology for designating a syndrome of driven sexual behavior. *Sexual Addiction and Compulsivity, 8*(3–4), 191–213.

Grant J. E., & Kim S. W. (2001). A case of kleptomania and compulsive sexual behavior treated with naltrexone. *Annals of Clinical Psychiatry, 13*, 205–207.

Hook, J. N., Reid, R. C., Penberthy, J. K., Davis, D. E., & Jennings, D. J. (in press). Methodological review of treatments for non-paraphilic hypersexual behavior. *Journal of Sex & Marital Therapy*.

Kafka, M. P. (2010). Hypersexual Disorder: A proposed diagnosis for DSM-V. *Archives of Sexual Behavior, 39*(2), 377–400.

Kafka, M., & Prentky, R. (1992). Fluoxetine treatment of nonparaphilic sexual addictions and paraphilias in men. *Journal of Clinical of Psychiatry, 53*(10), 351–358.

Kafka, M. P., & Prentky, R. A. (1994). Preliminary observations of DSM-III–R Axis I comorbidity in men with paraphilias and paraphilia-related disorders. *Journal of Clinical Psychiatry, 55*(11), 481–487.

Kaplan, M. S., & Krueger, R. B. (2010). Diagnosis, assessment, and treatment of hypersexuality. *Journal of Sex Research, 47*(2–3), 181–198.

Kingston, D. A., & Firestone, P. (2008). Problematic hypersexuality: A review of conceptualization and diagnosis. *Sexual Addiction & Compulsivity, 15*(4), 284–310.

Kor, A., Fogel, Y. A., Reid, R. C., & Potenza, M. N. (2013). Should hypersexual disorder be classified as an addiction? *Sexual Addiction & Compulsivity, 20*(1-2), 27–47.

Lanstrom, N., & Hanson, R. K. (2006). High rates of sexual behavior in the general population: Correlates and predictors. *Archives of Sexual Behavior, 35*(1), 37–52.

Marshall, L. E., & Briken, P. (2010). Assessment, diagnosis, and management of hypersexual disorders. *Current Opinion in Psychiatry, 23*(6), 570–573.

Naficy, H., Samenow, C. P., Fong, T. W. (2013). A review of pharmacological treatments for hypersexual disorder. *Sexual Addiction & Compulsivity, 20*(1-2), 139–153.

Opitz, D. M., Tsytsarev, S. V., & Froh, J. (2009). Women's sexual addiction and family dynamics, depression, and substance abuse. *Sexual Addiction & Compulsivity, 16*, 324–340.

Parker, J., & Guest, D. (2002). The integration of psychotherapy and 12-step programs in sexual addiction treatment. In P. J. Carnes & K. M. Adams (Eds.), *Clinical management of sex addiction* (pp. 115–124). New York, NY: Brunner-Routledge.

Parsons, J. T., Kelly, B. C., Bimbi, D. S., DiMaria, L., Wainberg, M. L., & Morgenstern, J. (2008). Explanations for the origins of sexual compulsivity among gay and bisexual men. *Archives of Sexual Behavior, 37*, 817–826.

Raymond, N. C., Coleman, E., & Miner, M. H. (2003). Psychiatric comorbidity and compulsive/impulsive traits in compulsive sexual behavior. *Comprehensive Psychiatry, 44*(5), 370–380.

Raymond, N. C., Grant, J. E., & Coleman, E. (2010). Augmentation with naltrexone to treat compulsive sexual behavior: A case series. *Annals of Clinical Psychiatry, 22*(1), 56–62.

Raymond, N. C., Grant, J. E., Kim, S. W., & Coleman, E. (2002). Treatment of compulsive sexual behaviour with naltrexone and serotonin reuptake inhibitors: Two case studies. *International Clinical Psychopharmacology, 17*(4), 201–205.

Reid, R. C., Carpenter, B. N., Draper, E. D., & Manning, J. C. (2010). Exploring psychopathology, personality traits, and marital distress among women married to hypersexual men. *Journal of Couple & Relationship Therapy, 9*(3), 203–222.

Reid, R. C., Carpenter, B. N., Gilliland, R., & Karim, R. (2011). Problems of self-concept in a patient sample of hypersexual men with attention-deficit disorder. *Journal of Addiction Medicine, 5*(2), 134–140.

Reid, R. C., Carpenter, B. N., Spackman, M., & Willes, D. L. (2008). Alexithymia, emotional instability, and vulnerability to stress proneness in patients seeking help for hypersexual behavior. *Journal of Sexual and Marital Therapy, 34*(2), 133–149.

Reid, R. C., Garos, S., & Carpenter, B. N. (2011). Reliability, validity, and psychometric development of the Hypersexual Behavior Inventory in an outpatient sample of men. *Sexual Addiction & Compulsivity, 18*(1), 30–51.

Reid, R. C., Stein, J. A., & Carpenter, B. N. (2011). Understanding the roles of shame and neuroticism in a patient sample of hypersexual men. *Journal of Nervous and Mental Disease, 199*(4), 263–267.

Reid, R. C., & Woolley, S. R. (2006). Using Emotionally Focused Therapy for couples to resolve attachment ruptures created by hypersexual behavior. *Sexual Addiction & Compulsivity, 13*(1), 219–239.

Reid, R. C., Davtian, M., Lenartowicz, A., Torrevillas, R. M., & Fong, T. W. (2013). Perspectives on the assessment and treatment of adult ADHD in hypersexual men. *Neuropsychiatry, 3*(3), 295-308.

Reid, R. C. (2013). Personal perspectives on hypersexual disorder. *Sexual Addiction & Compulsivity, 20*(1-2), 4–18.

Rinehart, N. J., & McCabe, M. P. (1997). Hypersexuality: Psychopathology or normal variant of sexuality? *Sexual & Marital Therapy, 12*(1), 45–60.

Rinehart, N. J., & McCabe, M. P. (1998). An empirical investigation of hypersexuality. *Sexual & Marital Therapy, 13*(4), 369–384.

Shepherd, L. (2010). Cognitive behavior therapy for sexually addictive behavior. *Clinical Case Studies, 9*, 18–27.

Skegg, K., Nada-Raja, S., Dickson, N., & Paul, C. (2010). Perceived "out of control" sexual behavior in a cohort of young adults from the Dunedin Multidisciplinary Heath and Development Study. *Archives of Sexual Behavior, 39*, 968–978.

Stein, D. J. (2008). Classifying hypersexual disorders: Compulsive, impulsive, and addictive models. *Psychiatric Clinics of North America, 31*(4), 587–591.

Twohig, M. P., & Crosby, J. M. (2010). Acceptance and commitment therapy as a treatment for problematic internet pornography viewing. *Behavior Therapy, 41*(3), 285–295.

Winters, J., Christoff, K., & Gorzalka, B. B. (2010). Dysregulated sexuality and high sexual desire: Distinct constructs? *Archives of Sexual Behavior, 39*, 1029–1043.

Zapf, J. L., Greiner, J., & Carroll, J. (2008). Attachment styles and male sex addiction. *Sexual Addiction & Compulsivity, 15*(2), 158–175.

CHAPTER 56

Research

Allen, E. S., Atkins, D. C., Baucom, D. H., Snyder, D. K., Gordon, K. C., & Glass, S. P. (2005). Intrapersonal, interpersonal, and contextual factors in engaging in and responding to extramarital involvement. *Clinical Psychology: Science and Practice, 12*, 101–130.

Amato, P. R., & Rogers, S. J. (1997). A longitudinal study of marital problems and subsequent divorce. *Journal of Marriage and the Family, 59*, 612–624.

Baucom, D. H., Gordon, K. C., Snyder, D. K., Atkins, D. C., & Christensen, A. (2006). Treating affair couples: Clinical considerations and initial findings. *Journal of Cognitive Psychotherapy, 20*, 375–392.

Baucom, D. H., Snyder, D. K., & Gordon, K. C. (2009). *Helping couples get past the affair*. New York, NY: Guilford Press.

Glass, S., & Wright, T. (1997). Reconstructing marriages after the trauma of infidelity. In W. K. Halford & H. J. Markman (Eds.), *Clinical handbook of marriage and couples interventions* (pp. 471–507). Chichester, UK: John Wiley & Sons.

Gordon, K. C., & Baucom, D. H. (1999). A multitheoretical intervention for promoting recovery from extramarital affairs. *Clinical Psychology: Science and Practice, 6*, 382–399.

Gordon, K. C., Baucom, D. H., & Snyder, D. K. (2004). An integrative intervention for promoting recovery from extramarital affairs. *Journal of Marital and Family Therapy, 30*, 213–231.

Janus, S. S., & Janus, C. L. (1993). *The Janus report on sexual behavior*. New York, NY: John Wiley & Sons.

Laumann, E. O., Gagnon, J. H., Michael, R. T., & Michaels, S. (1994). *The social organization of sexuality*. Chicago, IL: University of Chicago Press.

Snyder, D. K., Baucom, D. H., & Gordon, K. C. (2007). *Getting past the affair: A program to help you cope, heal, and move on – together or apart.* New York, NY: Guilford.

Snyder, D. K., Baucom, D. H., & Gordon, K. C. (2008). Treating infidelity: An integrative approach to resolving trauma and promoting forgiveness. In P. R. Peluso (Ed.), *In love's debris: A practitioner's guide to addressing infidelity in couples therapy* (pp. 95–125). New York, NY: Routledge.

Snyder, D. K., Castellani, A. M., & Whisman, M. A. (2006). Current status and future directions in couple therapy. *Annual Review of Clinical Psychology, 57,* 317–344.

Snyder, D. K., Gordon, K. C., & Baucom, D. H. (2004). Treating affair couples: Extending the written disclosure paradigm to relationship trauma. *Clinical Psychology: Science and Practice, 11,* 155–160.

Whisman, M. A., Dixon, A. E., & Johnson, B. (1997). Therapists' perspectives of couple problems and treatment issues in the practice of couple therapy. *Journal of Family Psychology, 11,* 361–366.

CHAPTER 57

Research

Avis, N. E., Zhao, C., Johannes, C. B., Ory, M., Brockwell, S., & Greendale, G. A. (2005). Correlates of sexual function among multi-ethnic middle-aged women: Results from the Study of Women's Health Across the Nation (SWAN). *Menopause: Journal of the North American Menopause Society, 12,* 385–398.

Brotto, L. A., Basson, R., & Luria, M. (2008). A mindfulness-based group psychoeducational intervention targeting sexual arousal disorder in women. *Journal of Sexual Medicine, 5,* 1646–1659.

DeRogatis, L., Rosen, R. C., Goldstein, I., Werneburg, B., Kempthorne-Rawson, J., & Sand, M. (2012). Characterization of hypoactive sexual desire disorder (HSDD) in men. *Journal of Sexual Medicine, 9,* 812–820. doi: 10.1111/j.1743-6109.2011.02592.x

Hawton, K., & Catalan, J. (1986). Prognostic factors in sex therapy. *Behaviour Research and Therapy, 24,* 377–385.

Hawton, K., Catalan, J., & Fagg, J. (1991). Low sexual desire: Sex therapy results and prognostic factors. *Behaviour Research and Therapy, 29,* 217–224.

Hurlbert, D. F., White, L. C., Powell, R. D., & Apt, C. (1993). Orgasm consistency training in the treatment of women reporting hypoactive sexual desire: An outcome comparison of women-only groups and couples-only groups. *Journal of Behavior Therapy & Experimental Psychiatry, 24,* 3–13.

Laumann, E. O., Nicolosi, A., Glasser, D. B., Paik, A., Gingell, C., Moreira, E., & Wang, T. (2005). Sexual problems among women and men aged 40-80 y: Prevalence and correlates identified in the Global Study of Sexual Attitudes and Behaviors. *International Journal of Impotence Research, 17,* 39–57.

Leiblum, S. R. (Ed.). (2010). *Treating sexual desire disorders: A clinical casebook.* New York, NY: Guilford Press.

Leiblum, S. R., Koochaki, P. E., Rodenberg, C. A., Barton, I. P., & Rosen R. C. (2006). Hypoactive sexual desire disorder in postmenopausal women: US results from the Women's International Study of Health and Sexuality (WISHeS). *Menopause, 13,* 46–56.

Masters, W. H., & Johnson, V. E. (1970). *Human sexual inadequacy.* Boston, MA: Little, Brown.

Maurice, W. L. (2007). Sexual desire disorders in men. In S. R. Leiblum (Ed.), *Principles and practice of sex therapy* (4th ed.). New York, NY: Guilford Press.

McCabe, M. (1992). A program for the treatment of inhibited sexual desire in males. *Psychotherapy: Theory, Research, Practice, Training, 29,* 288–296.

McCabe, M. (2001). Evaluation of a cognitive behavior therapy program for people with sexual dysfunction. *Journal of Sex & Marital Therapy, 27,* 259–271.

McCarthy, B. W. (1984). Strategies and techniques for the treatment of inhibited sexual desire. *Journal of Sex & Marital Therapy, 10,* 97–104.

Mercer, C. H., Fenton, K. A., Johnson, A. M., Wellings, J., Macdowall, W., ... Erens, B. (2003). Sexual function problems and help seeking behavior in Britain: National probability sample survey. *BMJ, 327,* 426–427.

Petersen, J. L., & Hyde, J. S. (2010). A meta-analytic review of research on gender differences in sexuality, 1993-2007. *Psychological Bulletin, 136,* 21–38.

Sarwer, D. B., & Durlak, J. A. (1997). A field trial of the effectiveness of behavioral treatment for sexual dysfunction. *Journal of Sex & Marital Therapy, 23,* 87–97.

Schover, L. R., & LoPiccolo, J. (1982). Treatment effectiveness for dysfunctions of sexual desire. *Journal of Sex & Marital Therapy, 8,* 179–197.

Simons, J., & Carey, M. P. (2001). Prevalence of sexual dysfunctions: Results from a decade of research. *Archives of Sexual Behavior, 30,* 177–219.

Trudel, G., Marchand, A., Ravart, M., Aubin, S., Turgeon, L., & Fortier, P. (2001). The effect of a cognitive-behavioral group treatment program on hypoactive sexual desire in women. *Sexual and Relationship Therapy, 16,* 145–164.

West, S. L., D'Aloisio, A. A., Agans, R. P., Kalsbeek, W. D., Borisoc, N. N., & Thorp, J. M. (2008). Prevalence of low sexual desire and hypoactive sexual desire disorder in a nationally representative sample of US women. *Archives of Internal Medicine, 168*, 1441–1449.

Zimmer, D. (1987). Does marital therapy enhance the effectiveness of treatment for sexual dysfunctions? *Journal of Sex & Marital Therapy, 13*, 193–209.

Clinician Application

Mintz, L. B., Balzer, A. M., Zhao, X., & Bush, H. E. (2012). Bibliotherapy for low sexual desire: Evidence for effectiveness. *Journal of Counseling Psychology, 59*, 471–478.

Wincze, J. P., & Carey M. P. (2001). *Sexual dysfunction: A guide for assessment and treatment*. New York, NY: The Guilford Press.

CHAPTER 58

Research

Althof, S., Abdo, C., Dean, J., Hackett, G., McCabe, M., ... Tan, H. (2010). International Society for Sexual Medicine's Guidelines for the Diagnosis and Treatment of Premature Ejaculation. *Journal of Sexual Medicine, 7*, 2947–2969.

Kaplan, H. (1974). *The new sex therapy*. New York, NY: Brunner/Mazel.

Laumann, E., Gagnon, J., Michael, R., & Michaels, S. (1994). *The social organization of sexuality: Sexual practices in the United States*. Chicago, IL: University of Chicago Press.

Laumann, E. O., West, S., Glasser, D., Carson, C., Rosen, R., & Jeong-han, K. (1997). Prevalence and correlates of erectile dysfunction by race and ethnicity among men aged 40 or older in the United States: From the male attitudes regarding sexual health survey. *Journal of Sexual Medicine, 4*, 57–65.

Lue, T. (Ed.). (2004). *Atlas of male sexual health*. Philadelphia, PA: Current Medicine.

Master, V., & Turek, P. (2001). Ejaculatory physiology and dysfunction. *Urologic Clinics of North America, 28*, 363–375.

McMahon, C., Althof, S., Waldinger, M., Porst, H., Dean, J., ... Segraves, R. (2008). An evidence-based definition of lifelong premature ejaculation: Report of the International Society for Sexual Medicine Ad Hoc Committee for the Definition of Premature Ejaculation. *British Journal of Urology International, 102*, 338–350. doi: 10.1111/j.1464-410X.2008.07755.x

Montorsi, F., Basson, R., Adaikan, G., Becher, E., Clayton, A., ... Sharlip, I. (2010). Sexual medicine: Sexual dysfunctions in men. *Journal of Sexual Medicine, 7*, 3572–3588.

National Institute of Health (NIH) Consensus Conference. (1992). "Impotence." Bethesda, Maryland.

Patrick, D., Althof, S., Pryor, J., Rosen, R., Rowland, D., ... Jamieson, C. (2005). Premature ejaculation: An observational study of men and their partners. *Journal of SexualMedicine, 2*, 358–367. doi: 10.1111/j.1743-6109.2005.20353.x

Perelman, M. (2005). Psychosocial evaluation and combination treatment of men with erectile dysfunction. *Urologic Clinics of North America, 32*, 431–445, vi. doi: 10.1016/j.ucl.2005.08.010

Perelman, M. (2006). A new combination treatment for premature ejaculation: A sex therapist's perspective. *Journal of Sexual Medicine, 3*, 1004–1012. doi: 10.1111/j.1743-6109.2006.00238.x

Perelman, M. (2008). Integrated sex therapy: A psychosocial-cultural perspective integrating behavioral, cognitive, and medical approaches. In C. Carson, R. Kirby, I. Goldstein, & M. Wyllie (Eds.), *Textbook of erectile dysfunction* (2nd ed., pp. 298–305). London, UK: Informa Healthcare.

Perelman, M. (2009). The sexual tipping point: A mind/body model for sexual medicine. *Journal of Sexual Medicine, 6*, 629–632. doi: 10.1111/j.1743-6109.2008.01177.x

Perelman, M., & Rowland, D. (2006). Retarded ejaculation. *World Journal of Urology, 24*, 645–652.

Rowland, D., Perelman, M., Althof, S., Barada, J., McCullough, A., ... Ho, K. (2004). Self-reported premature ejaculation and aspects of sexual functioning and satisfaction. *Journal of Sexual Medicine, 1*, 225–232.

Segraves, R. (2010). Considerations for an evidence-based definition of premature ejaculation in the DSM-V. *Journal of Sexual Medicine, 7*(2 Pt 1), 672–679. doi: 10.1111/j.1743-6109.2009.01682.x

Strassberg, D. (1994). A physiologically based model of early ejaculation: A solution or a problem? *Journal of Sex Education & Therapy, 20*, 215–217.

Strassberg, D., deGouveia Brazao, C., Rowland, D., Tan, P., & Slob, A. (1999). Clomiprimane in the treatment of rapid (premature) ejaculation. *Journal of Sex & Marital Therapy, 25*, 89–102.

Waldinger, M., & Olivier, B. (2005). Animal models of premature and retarded ejaculation. *World Journal of Urology, 23*, 115–118.

Zilbergeld, B. (1999). *The new male sexuality* (Revised Edition ed.). New York, NY: Bantam Books.

Clinician Application

Hall, K. S. K. & Graham, C. A. (2013). Introduction. In K. S. K. Hall & C.A. Graham (Eds.), *The cultural context of sexual pleasure and problems: Psychotherapy with diverse clients.* New York, NY: Routledge.

Kleinplatz, P. J. (2012). Advancing sex therapy or is that the best you can do? In P. J. Kleinplatz (Ed.), *New directions in sex therapy: Innovations and alternatives* (2nd ed.). New York, NY: Routledge.

Watter, D. N. (2012). The medicalization of sex therapy: Better living through chemistry? *Journal of Ethics in Mental Health,* 7 (Supplement: Sexual Behaviours).

CHAPTER 59

Research

Alexander, P. C., Morris, E., Tracy, A., & Frye, A. (2010). Stages of change and the group treatment of batterers: A randomized clinical trial. *Violence and Victims, 25,* 571–587.

Archer, J. (2000). Sex differences in aggression between heterosexual partners: A meta-analytic review. *Psychological Bulletin, 126,* 651–680.

Babcock, J. C., Green, C. E., & Robie, C. (2004). Does batterer's treatment work? A meta-analytic review of domestic violence treatment. *Clinical Psychology Review, 23,* 1023–1053. doi: 10.1016/j.cpr.2002.07.001

Bennett, L. W., Stoops, C., Call, C., & Flett, H. (2007). Program completion and re-arrest in a batterer intervention system. *Research on Social Work Practice, 17,* 42–54.

Black, M. C., Basile, K. C., Breiding, M. J., Smith, S. G., Walters, M. L., ... Stevens, M. R. (2011). The National Intimate Partner and Sexual Violence Survey (NISVS): 2010 summary report. Atlanta, GA: National Center for Injury Prevention and Control, Centers for Disease Control and Prevention.

Capaldi, D., Knoble, N. B., Shortt, J. W., & Kim, H. K. (2012). A systematic review of risk factors for intimate partner violence. *Partner Abuse, 3,* 1–27.

Chase, K. A., O'Leary, K. D., & Heyman, R. E. (2001). Categorizing partner-violent men within the reactive-proactive typology model. *Journal of Consulting and Clinical Psychology, 69,* 567–572.

Davis, R. C., & Taylor, B. G. (1999). Does batterer treatment reduce violence? *Women & Criminal Justice, 10,* 63–93.

Dunford, F. W. (2000). The San Diego navy experiment: An assessment of interventions for men who assault their wives. *Journal of Consulting and Clinical Psychology, 68,* 468–476.

Dutton, D. G. (2007). *The abusive personality: Violence and control in intimate relationships* (2nd ed.). New York, NY: Guilford Press.

Dutton, D. G., & Corvo, K. (2006). Transforming a flawed policy: A call to revive psychology and science in domestic violence research and practice. *Aggression and Violent Behavior, 11,* 457–483.

Dutton, D. G., & Nicholls, T. L. (2005). The gender paradigm in domestic violence research and theory. *Aggression and Violent Behavior, 10,* 680–714.

Easton, C. J., Mandel, D. L., Hunkele, K. A., Nich, C., Rounsaville, B. J., & Carroll, K. M. (2007). A cognitive behavioral therapy for alcohol-dependent domestic violence offenders: An integrated substance abuse–domestic violence treatment approach (SADV). *American Journal on Addictions, 16,* 24–31.

Eckhardt, C. I. (2007). Effects of alcohol intoxication on anger experience and expression among partner assaultive men during anger arousal. *Journal of Consulting and Clinical Psychology, 75,* 61–71.

Eckhardt, C. I., Murphy, C. M., Black, D., & Suhr, L. (2006). Intervention programs for perpetrators of intimate partner violence: Conclusions from a clinical research perspective. *Public Health Reports, 121,* 369–381.

Eckhardt, C. I., Samper, R., & Murphy, C. (2008). Anger disturbances among perpetrators of intimate partner violence: Clinical characteristics and outcomes of court-mandated treatment. *Journal of Interpersonal Violence, 23,* 1600–1617.

Eckhardt, C., & Schram, J. (2009). Cognitive behavioral interventions for partner abusive men. In P. Lehmann (Ed.), *Interventions for intimate partner violence: A strengths approach.* New York, NY: Springer.

Ehrensaft, M. K., Moffitt, T. E., & Caspi, A. (2004). Clinically abusive relationships in an unselected birth cohort: Men's and women's participation and developmental antecedents. *Journal of Abnormal Psychology, 113,* 258–271.

Feder, L., & Wilson, D. B. (2005). A meta-analytic review of court-mandated batterer intervention programs: Can courts affect abusers' behavior? *Journal of Experimental Criminology, 1,* 239–262.

Felson, R. B. (2002). *Violence and gender reexamined.* Washington, DC: American Psychological Association.

Finkel, E., & Eckhardt, C. (2013). Intimate partner violence. In J. Simpson & L. Campbell (Eds.), *Oxford handbook of close relationships* (chap. 20). New York, NY: Oxford University Press.

Finkel, E. J. (2007). Impelling and inhibiting forces in the perpetration of intimate partner violence. *Review of General Psychology, 11,* 193–207.

Golding, J. M. (1999). Intimate partner violence as a risk factor for mental disorders: A meta-analysis. *Journal of Family Violence, 14*(2), 99–132.

Gondolf, E. W. (2004). Evaluating batterer counseling programs: A difficult task showing some effects and implications. *Aggression and Violent Behavior, 9*, 605–631.

Gondolf, E. W. (2007). Culturally-focused batterer counseling for African-American men. *Criminology & Public Policy, 6*, 341–366.

Holtzworth-Munroe, A., & Stuart, G. L. (1994). Typologies of male batterers: Three subtypes and the differences among them. *Psychological Bulletin, 116*, 476–497.

Huesmann, L. R. (1988). An information processing model for the development of aggression. *Aggressive Behavior, 14*, 13–24.

Jacobson, N. S., Gottman, J. M., Waltz, J., Rushe, R., Babcock, J., & Holtzworth-Munroe, A. (1994). Affect, verbal content, and psychophysiology in the arguments of couples with a violent husband. *Journal of Consulting and Clinical Psychology, 62*, 982–988.

Johnson, M. P. (2008). *A typology of domestic violence: Intimate terrorism, violent resistance, and situational couple violence*. Boston, MA: Northeastern University Press.

Jones, A. S., & Gondolf, E. W. (2002). Assessing the effect of batterer program completion on reassault: An instrumental variables analysis. *Journal of Quantitative Criminology, 18*, 71–98.

Labriola, M., Rempel, M., & Davis, R. C. (2008). Do batterer programs reduce recidivism? Results from a randomized trial in the Bronx. *Justice Quarterly, 25*, 252–282.

Leonard, K. (2001). Alcohol and substance abuse in marital violence and child maltreatment. In C. Wekerle & A. Wall (Eds.), *The violence and addiction equation* (pp. 194–219). New York, NY: Brunner-Routledge.

Maiuro, R. D., & Eberle, J. A. (2008). State standards for domestic violence perpetrator treatment: Current status, trends, and recommendations. *Violence and Victims, 23*, 133–155.

Maxwell, C. D., Davis, R. C., & Taylor, B. G. (2010). The impact of length of domestic violence treatment on the patterns of subsequent intimate partner violence. *Journal of Experimental Criminology, 6*, 465–497.

Mbilinyi, L. F., Neighbors, C., Walker, D. D., Roffman, R. A., Zegree, J., … O'Rourke, A. (2011). A telephone intervention for substance-using adult male perpetrators of intimate partner violence. *Research on Social Work Practice, 21*, 43–56.

Morrel, T. M., Elliott, J. D., Murphy, C. M., & Taft, C. T. (2003). Cognitive behavioral and supportive group treatments for partner-violent men. *Behavior Therapy, 34*, 77–95.

Murphy, C. M., & Ting, L. A. (2010). Interventions for perpetrators of intimate partner violence: A review of efficacy research and recent trends. *Partner Abuse, 1*, 26–44.

Musser, P. H., Semiatin, J. N., Taft, C. T., & Murphy, C. M. (2008). Motivational interviewing as a pregroup intervention for partner-violent men. *Violence and Victims, 23*, 539–557.

Norlander, B., & Eckhardt, C. (2005). Anger, hostility, and male perpetrators of intimate partner violence: A meta-analytic review. *Clinical Psychology Review, 25*, 119–152.

O'Leary, K. D. (1988). Physical aggression between spouses: A social learning perspective. In V. B. Van Hasselt, R. Morrison, A. Bellack, & M. Hersen (Eds.), *Handbook of family violence* (pp. 31–55). New York, NY: Plenum.

O'Leary, K. D., Heyman, R. E., & Neidig, P. H. (1999). Treatment of wife abuse: A comparison of gender-specific and conjoint approaches. *Behavior Therapy, 30*, 475–505.

Pence, E., & Paymar, M. (1993). *Education groups for men who batter: The Duluth model*. New York, NY: Springer.

Rempel, M., Labriola, M., & Davis, R. C. (2008). Does judicial monitoring deter domestic violence recidivism?: Results of a quasi-experimental comparison in the Bronx. *Violence Against Women, 14*, 185–207.

Saunders, D. G. (1996). Feminist-cognitive-behavioral and process-psychodynamic treatments for men who batter: Interaction of abuser traits and treatment models. *Violence and Victims, 11*, 393–414.

Schafer, J., Caetano, R., & Clark C. L. (1998). Rates of intimate partner violence among U.S. couples. *American Journal of Public Health, 88*, 1702–1704.

Schumacher, J. A., Feldbau-Kohn, S., Slep, A. M. S., & Heyman, R. E. (2001). Risk factors for male-to-female partner physical abuse. *Aggression and Violent Behavior, 6*, 281–352.

Scott, K., King, C., McGinn, H., & Hosseini, N. (2011). Effects of motivational enhancement on immediate outcomes of batterer intervention. *Journal of Family Violence, 26*, 139–149. doi: 10.1007/s10896-010-9353-1

Smedslund, G., Dalsbo, T. K., Steiro, A., Winsvold, A., & Clench-Aas, J. (2011). Cognitive behavioural therapy for men who physically abuse their female partner. *The Cochrane Library, 2*, 1–32.

Sonkin, D. J., Martin, D., & Walker, L. E. (1985). *The male batterer: A treatment approach*. New York, NY: Springer.

Stith, S. M., Rosen, K. H., McCollum, E. E., & Thomsen, C. J. (2004). Treating intimate partner violence within intact couple relationships: Outcomes of multi-couple versus individual couple therapy. *Journal of Marital and Family Therapy, 30*, 305–318.

Stith, S. M., Smith, D. B., Penn, C. E., Ward, D. B., & Tritt, D. (2004). Intimate partner physical abuse perpetration and victimization risk factors: A meta-analytic review. *Aggression and Violent Behavior, 10*, 65–98.

Stosny, S. (1995). *Treating attachment abuse: A compassionate approach*. New York, NY: Springer.

Stover, C. S., Meadows, A. L., & Kaufman, J. (2009). Interventions for intimate partner violence: Review and implications for evidence-based practice. *Professional Psychology: Research and Practice, 40*, 223–233.

Straus, M. (2011). Gender symmetry and mutuality in perpetration of clinical-level partner violence: Empirical evidence and implications for prevention and treatment. *Aggression and Violent Behavior, 16*, 279–288.

Straus, M. A. (2004). Prevalence of violence against dating partners by male and female university students worldwide. *Violence Against Women, 10*, 790–811.

Straus, M. A., & Gelles, R. J. (1992). How violent are American families? In M. A. Straus & R. J. Gelles (Eds.), *Physical violence in American families* (pp. 95–108). New Brunswick, NJ: Transaction Publishers.

Stuart, R. B. (2005). Treatment for partner abuse: Time for a paradigm shift. *Professional Psychology: Research and Practice, 36*, 254–263.

Sugarman, D. B., & Frankel, S. L. (1995). Patriarchal ideology and wife-assault: A meta-analytic review. *Journal of Family Violence, 11*, 13–40.

Taylor, B. G., Davis, R. C., & Maxwell, C. D. (2001). The effects of a group batterer treatment program: A randomized experiment in Brooklyn. *Justice Quarterly, 18*, 171–201.

Wathen, C. N., & MacMillan, H. L. (2003). Interventions for violence against women. *Journal of the American Medical Association, 289*, 589–600.

Wexler, D. B. (2006). *Stop domestic violence: Innovative skills, techniques, options, and plans for better relationships.* New York, NY: W. W. Norton & Company Ltd.

Woodin, E. M., & O'Leary, K. D. (2010). A brief motivational intervention for physically aggressive dating couples. *Prevention Science, 11*, 371–383.

Clinician Application

Capaldi, D. M., Knoble, N. B., Shortt, J. W., & Kim, H. K. (2012). A systematic review of risk factors for intimate partner violence. *Partner Abuse, 3*, 231–280.

Capaldi, D. M., Shortt, J. W., Kim, H. K., Wilson, J., Crosby, L., & Tucci, S. (2009). Official incidents of domestic violence: Types, injury, and association with nonofficial couple aggression. *Violence & Victims, 24*, 502–519.

Desmarais, S. L., Reeves, K. A., Nicholls, T. L., Telford, R., & Fiebert, M. S. (2012a). Prevalence of physical violence in intimate Relationships—Part 1: Rates of male and female victimization. *Partner Abuse, 3*, 140–169.

Desmarais, S. L., Reeves, K. A., Nicholls, T. L., Telford, R. & Fiebert, M. S. (2012b). Prevalence of physical violence in intimate relationships—Part 2: Rates of male and female perpetration. *Partner Abuse, 3*, 170–198.

Geffner, R., & Mantooth, C. (2000). *Ending spouse/partner abuse: A psychoeducational approach for individuals and couples.* New York, NY: Springer.

Gottman, J. (1999). *The marriage clinic: A scientifically-based marital therapy.* New York, NY: W.W. Norton.

Hamel, J. (2007). Gender inclusive family interventions in domestic violence: An overview. In J. Hamel & T. Nicholls (Eds.), *Family interventions in domestic violence: A handbook of gender-inclusive theory and treatment* (pp. 247–274). New York, NY: Springer.

Hamel, J. (2008). Beyond ideology: Alternative therapies for domestic violence. In J. Hamel (Ed.), *Intimate partner and family abuse: A casebook of gender inclusive therapy* (pp. 3–26). New York, NY: Springer.

Hazelwood, L. (2007), Systems considerations in working with court-ordered domestic Violence offenders. In J. Hamel & T. Nicholls (Eds.), *Family interventions in domestic violence: A handbook of gender-inclusive theory and treatment* (pp. 341–361). New York, NY: Springer.

Langhinrichsen-Rohling, J., Misra, T. A., Selwyn, C., & Rohling, M. L. (2012). Rates of bi-directional versus unidirectional intimate partner violence across samples, sexual orientations, and race/ethnicities: A comprehensive review. *Partner Abuse, 3*, 199–230.

Neidig, P., & Friedman, D. (1984). *Spouse abuse: A treatment program for couples.* Champaign, IL: Research Press.

Potter-Efron, R. (2005). *Handbook of anger management: Individual, couple, family and group approaches.* New York, NY: Haworth Press.

Sonkin, D. (2007). Domestic violence and attachment theory: Clinical applications to treatment with perpetrators. In N. Jackson (Ed.), *The encyclopedia of domestic violence.* New York, NY: Routledge.

Stacey, W., Hazelwood, L., & Shupe, A. (1994). *The violent couple.* Westport, CT: Praeger.

Stith, S., McCollum, E., & Rosen, K. (2011). *Couples therapy for domestic violence: Finding safe solutions.* Washington, DC: American Psychological Association.

CHAPTER 60

Research

Berliner, L. (2011). Child sexual abuse: Definitions, prevalence, and consequences. In J. E. B. Myers (Ed.), *The APSAC handbook on child maltreatment – Third Edition* (pp. 215–232), Los Angeles, CA: Sage.

Bisson, J., & Andrew, M. (2007). Psychological treatment of post-traumatic stress disorder (PTSD). *Cochrane Database of Systematic Reviews*, (3), CD003388.

Briere, J. (1996). *Therapy for adults molested as children* (Revised and Expanded Edition). New York, NY: Springer.

Cahill, S. P., Rothbaum, B. O., Resick, P. A., & Follette, V. M. (2009). Cognitive-behavioral therapy for adults. In E. B. Foa, T. M. Keane, M. J. Friedman, & J. A. Cohen (Eds.), *Effective treatments for PTSD: Practice guidelines from the International Society for Traumatic Stress Studies* (pp. 139–222). New York, NY: The Guilford Press.

Cloitre, M., Cohen, L. R., & Koenen, K. C. (2006). *Treating survivors of childhood abuse: Psychotherapy for the interrupted life*. New York, NY: Guilford Press.

Crowder, A. (1995). *Opening the door: A treatment model for therapy with male survivors of sexual abuse*. New York, NY: Brunner/Mazel.

Diller, J. V. (1999). *Cultural diversity: A primer for the human services*. Belmont, CA: Wadsworth Publishing Company.

Dimock, P. T. (1988). Adult males sexually abused as children: Characteristics and implications for treatment. *Journal of Interpersonal Violence, 3*, 203–221.

Dube, S. R., Anda, R. F., Whitfield, C. L., Brown, D. W., Felitti, V. J., … & Giles, W. H. (2005). Long-term consequences of childhood sexual abuse by gender of victim. *American Journal of Preventive Medicine, 28*, 430–438.

Foa, E. B., Hembree, E. A., & Rothbaum, B. O. (2007). *Prolonged exposure therapy for PTSD: Emotional processing of traumatic experiences: Therapist guide*. Oxford, UK: Oxford University Press.

Foa, E. B., Keane, T. M., Friedman, M. J., & Cohen, J. A. (Eds.). (2009a). *Effective treatments for PTSD: Practice guidelines from the International Society for Traumatic Stress Studies*. New York, NY: The Guilford Press.

Foa, E. B., Keane, T. M., Friedman, M. J., & Cohen, J. A. (2009b). Introduction. In E. B. Foa, T. M. Keane, M. J. Friedman, & J. A. Cohen (Eds.), *Effective treatments for PTSD: Practice guidelines from the International Society for Traumatic Stress Studies* (pp. 1–20). New York, NY: The Guilford Press.

Freedman, S. A., Gluck, N., Tuval-Mashiach, R., Brandes, D., Peri, T., & Shalev, A. Y. (2002). Gender differences in responses to traumatic events: A prospective study. *Journal of Traumatic Stress, 15*, 407–413.

Friedman, M. J., Davidson, J. R. T., & Stein, D. J. (2009). Psychopharmacotherapy for adults. In E. B. Foa, T. M. Keane, M. J. Friedman, & J. A. Cohen (Eds.), *Effective treatments for PTSD: Practice guidelines from the International Society for Traumatic Stress Studies* (pp. 245–268). New York, NY: The Guilford Press.

Garnefsky, N., & Arends, E. (1998). Sexual abuse and adolescent maladjustment: Differences between male and female victims. *Journal of Adolescence, 21*, 99–107.

Gartner, R. B. (1999). *Betrayed as boys: Psychodynamic treatment of sexually abused men*. New York, NY: Guilford Press.

Holmes, W. C., & Slap, G. B. (1998). Sexual abuse of boys: Definition, prevalence, correlates, sequelae, and management. *Journal of the American Medical Association, 280*, 1855–1862.

Hopper, J. (2007). *Sexual abuse of males: Prevalence, possible lasting effects, & resources*. Retrieved August 4, 2011, from http://www.jimhopper.com/male-ab/

Hopton, J., & Huta, V. (2012) Evaluation of an intervention designed for men who were abused in childhood and are experiencing symptoms of posttraumatic stress. *Psychology of Men and Masculinity*.

Lew, M. (2004). *Victims no longer: The classic guide for men recovering from sexual child abuse* (2nd ed.). New York, NY: Harper.

Maikovich, A. K., Koenen, K. C., & Jaffee, S. R. (2009). Posttraumatic stress symptoms and trajectories in child sexual abuse victims: An analysis of sex differences using the National Survey of Child and Adolescent Well-Being. *Journal of Abnormal Child Psychology, 37*, 727–737.

Maniglio, R. (2009). The impact of child sexual abuse on health: A systematic review of reviews. *Clinical Psychology Review, 29*, 647–657.

Najavits, L., Ryngala, D., Back, S. E., Bolton, E., Mueser, K. T., & Brady, K. T. (2009). Treatment of PTSD and comorbid disorders. In E. B. Foa, T. M. Keane, M. J. Friedman, & J. A. Cohen (Eds.), *Effective treatments for PTSD: Practice guidelines from the International Society for Traumatic Stress Studies* (pp. 508–535). New York, NY: The Guilford Press.

Najavits, L. M. (2002). *Seeking safety: A treatment manual for PTSD and substance abuse*. New York, NY: Guilford Press.

Pereda, N., Guilera, G., Forns, M., & Gómez-Benito, J. (2009). The prevalence of child sexual abuse in community and student samples: A meta-analysis. *Clinical Psychology Review, 29*, 328–338.

Romano, E., & De Luca, R. V. (2001). Male sexual abuse: A review of effects, abuse characteristics, and links with later psychological functioning. *Aggression and Violent Behavior, 6*, 55–78.

Romano, E., & De Luca, R. V. (2005). An individual treatment programme for sexually abused adult males: Description and preliminary findings. *Child Abuse Review, 14*, 40–56.

Romano, E., & De Luca, R. V. (2006). Evaluation of a treatment program for sexually abused adult males. *Journal of Family Violence, 21*, 75–88.

Schulte, J. G., Dinwiddie, S. H., Pribor, E. F., & Yutzy, S. H. (1995). Psychiatric diagnoses of adult male victims of childhood sexual abuse. *Journal of Nervous and Mental Disease, 183*, 111–113.

Spataro, J., Mullen, P. E., Burgess, P. M., Wells, D. L., & Moss, S. A. (2004). Impact of child sexual abuse on mental health: Prospective study in males and females. *The British Journal of Psychiatry, 184*, 416–421.

Spiegel, J. (2003). *The sexual abuse of males.* New York, NY: Brunner-Routledge.

Sue, D. W., Arredondo, P., & McDavis, R. J. (1992). Multicultural counseling competencies and standards: A call to the profession. *Journal of Counseling & Development, 70*, 477–486.

Suzuki, L. A., Ponterotto, J. G., & Meller, P. J. (Eds.). (2001). *Handbook of multicultural assessment: Clinical, psychological, and educational applications* (2nd ed.). San Francisco, CA: Jossey-Bass.

CHAPTER 61

Research

Bennice, J. A., & Resick, P. A. (2002). A review of treatment and outcome of post-trauma sequelae in sexual assault survivors. In J. Petrak & B. Hedge (Eds.), *The trauma of sexual assault: Treatment, prevention, and practice* (pp. 69–97). London, UK: Johns Wiley & Sons Limited.

Cahill, S. P., Rothbaum, B. O., Resick, P. A., & Follette, V. M. (2009). Cognitive-behavioral therapy for adults. In E. B. Foa, T. M. Keane, M. J. Friedman, & J. A. Cohen (Eds.), *Effective treatments for PTSD* (2nd ed., pp. 139–222). New York, NY: Guilford Press.

Chard, K. M. (2005). An evaluation of cognitive processing therapy for the treatment of posttraumatic stress disorder related to childhood sexual abuse. *Journal of Consulting and Clinical Psychology, 73*, 965–971. doi: 10.1037/0022-006X.73.5.965

Ellis, E. M., Atkeson, B. M., & Calhoun, K. S. (1981). An assessment of long-term reaction to rape. *Journal of Abnormal Psychology, 90*, 263–266. doi: 10.1037/0021-843X.90.3.263

Foa, E. B., Dancu, C. V., Hembree, E. A., Jaycox, L. H., Meadows, E. A., & Street, G. P. (1999). A comparison of exposure therapy, stress inoculation training, and their combination for reducing posttraumatic stress disorder in female assault victims. *Journal of Consulting and Clinical Psychology, 67*, 194–200. doi: 10.1037//0022-006X.67.2.194

Foa, E. B., Rothbaum, B., Riggs, D., & Murdock, T. (1991). Treatment of posttraumatic stress disorder in rape victims: A comparison between cognitive-behavioral procedures and counseling. *Journal of Consulting and Clinical Psychology, 59*, 715–723. doi: 10.1037/0022-006X.59.5.715

Gallagher, M. W., & Resick, P. A. (2012). Mechanisms of change in cognitive processing therapy and prolonged exposure therapy for PTSD: Preliminary evidence for the differential effects of hopelessness and habituation. *Cognitive Therapy and Research, 36*, 750–755.

Galovski, T. E., Monson, C., Bruce, S. E., & Resick, P. A. (2009). Does cognitive-behavioral therapy for PTSD improve perceived health and sleep impairment? *Journal of Traumatic Stress, 22*, 197–204.

Heiskanen, M. (2010). Trends in police recorded crime. In S. Harrendorf, M. Heiskanen, & S. Malby (Eds.), *International statistics on crime and justice* (pp. 21–47). Helsinki, Finland: European Institute for Crime Prevention and Control, affiliated with the United Nations.

Kessler, R. C., Sonnega, A., Bromet, E., Hughes, M., & Nelson, C. B. (1995). Posttraumatic stress disorder in the National Comorbidity Survey. *Archives of General Psychiatry, 52*, 1048–1060. doi: 10.1001/archpsyc.1995 .03950240066012

Kilpatrick, D. G., Best, C. L., Veronen, L. J., Amick, A. E., Villeponteaux, L. A., & Ruff, G. A. (1985). Mental health correlates of criminal victimization: A random community survey. *Journal of Consulting and Clinical Psychology, 53*, 866–873. doi: 10.1037/0022-006X.53.6.866

Kilpatrick, D. G., Saunders, B. E., Veronen, L. J., Best, C. L., & Von, J. M. (1987). Criminal victimization: Lifetime prevalence, reporting to police, and psychological impact. *Crime and Delinquency, 33*, 479–489. doi: 10.1177/0011128787033004005

Kilpatrick, D. G., Veronen, L. J., & Resick, P. A. (1982). Psychological sequelae to rape: Assessment and treatment strategies. In D. M. Doleys, R. L. Meredith & A. R. Ciminero (Eds.), *Behavioral medicine: Assessment and treatment strategies* (pp. 473–497). New York, NY: Plenum Press.

Koss, M. P. (1985). The hidden rape victim: Personality, attitudinal, and situational characteristics. *Psychology of Women Quarterly, 9*, 193–212. doi: 10.1111/j.1471-6402.1985.tb00872.x

Koss, M. P., Gidycz, C. A., & Wisniewski, N. (1987). The scope of rape: Incidence and prevalence of sexual aggression and victimization in a national sample of higher education students. *Journal of Consulting and Clinical Psychology, 55*, 162–170. doi: 10.1037/0022-006X.55.2.162

Logan, T. K., Cole, J., & Capillo, A. (2007). Differential characteristics of intimate partner, acquaintance, and stranger rape survivors examined by a sexual assault nurse examiner (SANE). *Journal of Interpersonal Violence, 22*, 1066–1076.

Petrick, J. (2002). Rape: History, myths, and reality. In J. Petrak & B. Hedge (Eds.), *The trauma of sexual assault: Treatment, prevention and practice* (pp. 1-18). London, UK: Johns Wiley & Sons Limited.

Resick, P. A. (1990). Victims of sexual assault. In A. J. Lurigio, W. G. Skogan & R. C. Davis (Eds.), *Victims of crime: Problems, policies, and programs* (Vol. 25). Newbury Park, CA: Sage publications.

Resick, P. A., Galovski, T. E., Uhlmansiek, M. O., Scher, C. D., Clum, G., & Young-Xu, Y. (2008). A randomized clinical trial to dismantle components of cognitive processing therapy for posttraumatic stress disorder in female victims of interpersonal violence. *Journal of Consulting & Clinical Psychology, 76*, 243–258. doi: 10.1037/0022-006X.76.2.243

Resick, P. A., & Jordan, C. G. (1988). Group stress inoculation training for victims of sexual assault: A therapist manual. In P. A. Keller & S. R. Heyman (Eds.), *Innovations in clinical practice: A source book* (Vol. 7, pp. 99–111). Sarasota, FL; England: Professional Resources Exchange, Inc.

Resick, P. A., Nishith, P., & Griffin, M. G. (2003). How well does cognitive-behavioral therapy treat symptoms of complex PTSD? An examination of child sexual abuse survivors within a clinical trial. *CNS Spectrums, 8*, 340–355. Retrieved from http://www.cnsspectrums.com/

Resick, P. A., Nishith, P., Weaver, T. L., Astin, M. C., & Feuer, C. A. (2002). A comparison of cognitive processing therapy, prolonged exposure and a waiting condition for the treatment of posttraumatic stress disorder in female rape victims. *Journal of Consulting and Clinical Psychology, 70*, 867–879. doi: 10.1037//0022-006X.70.4.867

Resick, P. A., Williams, L. F., Suvak, M. K., Monson, C. M., & Gradus, J. L. (2012). Long-term outcomes of cognitive-behavioral treatments for posttraumatic stress disorder among female rape survivors. *Journal of Consulting and Clinical Psychology, 80*, 201–210.

Riggs, D. S., Cahill, S. P., & Foa, E. B. (2006). Prolonged exposure treatment of posttraumatic stress disorder. In V. M. Follette & J. I. Ruzek (Eds.), *Cognitive-behavioral therapies for trauma* (2nd ed., pp. 65–95). New York, NY: Guilford Press.

Shipherd, J. C., Street, A. E., & Resick, P. A. (2006). Cognitive therapy for posttraumatic stress disorder. In V. M. Follette & J. I. Ruzek (Eds.), *Cognitive-behavioral therapies for trauma* (2nd ed., pp. 96–116). New York, NY: Guilford Press.

Steketee, G., & Foa, E. B. (1987). Rape victims: Post-traumatic stress responses and their treatment: A review of the literature. *Journal of Anxiety Disorders, 1*, 69–86. doi: 10.1016/0887-6185(87)90024-7

Tjaden, P., & Thoennes, N. (2000). *Full report of the prevalence, incidence, and consequences of violence against women: Findings from the National Violence Against Women Survey*. Washington, DC: U.S. Department of Justice, National Institute of Justice.

CLINICIAN APPLICATION

Asukai, N., Saito, A., Tsuruta, N., Ogami, R., & Kishimoto, J. (2008). Pilot study on prolonged exposure of Japanese patients with posttraumatic stress disorder due to mixed traumatic events. *Journal of Traumatic Stress, 21*, 340–343. doi: 10.1002/jts.20337

Nacasch, N., Foa, E. B., Huppert, J. D., Tzur, D., Fostick, L., … Zohar, J. (2011). Prolonged exposure therapy for combat- and terror-related posttraumatic stress disorder: A randomized control comparison with treatment as usual. *Journal of Clinical Psychiatry, 72*, 1174–1180. doi: 10.4088/JCP.09m05682blu

CHAPTER 62

Research

Begg, D., & Landley, J. (2001). Changes in risky behavior from age 21 to 26 years. *Journal of Safety Research, 32*, 491–499.

Clayton, A. B. & Mackay, G. M. (1972). Aetiology of traffic accidents. *Health Bulletin, 31*, 277–280.

Deffenbacher, J. L., Filetti, L. B., Lynch, R. S., Dahlen, E. R., & Oetting, E. R. (2002). Cognitive-behavioral treatment of high anger drivers. *Behaviour Research and Therapy, 40*, 895–910.

Deffenbacher, J. L., Huff, M. E., Lynch, R. S., Oetting, E. R., & Salvatore, N. F. (2000). Characteristics and treatments of high-anger drivers. *Journal of Consulting Psychology, 47*, 5–17.

Deffenbacher, J. L., White, G. S., & Lynch, R. S. (2004). Evaluation of two new scales assessing driver anger: The Driving Anger Expression Inventory and the Driver's Angry Thoughts Questionnaire. *Journal of Psychopathology and Behavioral Assessment, 26*, 87–99.

Galovski, T. E., & Blanchard, E. B. (2002a). Psychological characteristics of aggressive drivers with and without Intermittent Explosive Disorder. *Behaviour, Research and Therapy, 40*, 1157–1168.

Galovski, T. E., & Blanchard, E. B. (2002b). The effectiveness of a brief, psychological intervention on aggressive driving. *Behaviour, Research and Therapy, 40*, 1385–1402.

Galovski, T. E., & Blanchard, E. B. (2005). Psychological treatments of angry and aggressive drivers. In D. A. Hennessy & D. L. Wiesenthal (Eds.), *Contemporary issues in traffic research and road user safety*. New York, Nova Science Publishers, Inc.

Galovski, T. E., Blanchard, E. B., & Veazey, C. (2002). Intermittent Explosive Disorder and other psychiatric comorbidity among court-referred and self-referred aggressive drivers. *Behaviour, Research and Therapy, 40*(6), 641–651.

Galovski, T. E., Malta, L. S., & Blanchard, E. B. (2006). *Road rage: Assessment and treatment of the angry, aggressive driver*. Washington DC: APA Books.

Gulian, E., Debney, L. M., Glendon, A. I., Davies, D. R., & Matthews, G. (1989). Coping with driver stress. In M. G. McGuigan & W. E. Sime (Eds.), *Stress and tension control* (Vol. 3, pp. 173–186). New York, NY: Plenum Press.

Gulian, E., Matthews, G., Glendon, A. I., Davies, D. R., & Debney, L. M. (1989). Dimensions of driver stress. *Ergonomics, 32*, 585–602.

Hennessy, D. A., & Wiesenthal, D. L. (1999). Traffic congestion, driver stress and driver aggression. *Aggressive Behavior, 25*, 409–423. doi: 10.1002/(SICI)1098-2337(1999)25:6<409::AID-AB2>3.0.CO;2-0

Hennessy, D. A., & Wiesenthal, D. L. (2001). Gender, driver aggression, and driver violence: An applied evaluation. *Sex Roles, 44*, 661–676. doi: 10.1023/A:1012246213617

Lajunen, T., & Parker, D. (2001). Are aggressive people aggressive drivers? A study of the relationship between self-reported general aggressiveness, driver anger, and aggressive driving. *Accident Analysis and Prevention, 33*, 243–255.

Larson, J. A. (1996). *Steering clear of highway madness: A driver's guide to curbing stress and strain*. Oregon: BookPartners, Inc.

Larson, J. A., Rodriquez, C., & Galvan-Henkin, A. (1998). *Pilot study: Reduction in "road rage" and aggressive driving through one day cognitive therapy seminar*. Represented at New York State Symposium on Aggressive Driving, May 13, 1998, Albany, NY.

Lennon, A., & Watson, B. (2011). "Teaching them a lesson?" A qualitative exploration of underlying motivations for driver aggression. *Accident Analysis and Prevention, 43*, 2200–2208. doi: 10.1016/j.aap.2011.06.015

Maiuro, R. (Summer, 1998). *Recovery: Rage on the road* [On-line].

Mann, R. E., Zhaos, J., Stoduto, G., Adlaf, E. M., Smart, R. G., & Donovan, J. E. (2007). Road rage and collision involvement. *American Journal of Health Behavior, 31*(4), 384–391.

Martinez, R. (1997). The statement of the Honorable Recardo Martinez, M. D., Administrator, National Highway Traffic Safety Administration before the Sub-Committee on Surface Transportation, Committee on Transportation and Infrastructure, U.S. House of Representatives, July 17, 1997.

Mizell, L. (1997). *Aggressive driving*. In AAA Foundation for Traffic Safety (Ed.), Aggressive Driving: Three Studies [On-line].

Shinar, D., & Compton, R. (2004). Aggressive driving: An observational study of driver, vehicle, and situational variables. *Accident Analysis and Prevention, 36*, 429–437.

Snyder, D. S. (1997). The statement of David S. Snyder, Assistant General Counsel, American Insurance Association, representing advocates for highway and auto safety before the Sub-Committee on Surface Transportation, Committee on Transportation and Infrastructure, U.S. House of Representatives, July 17, 1997.

Stradling, S. G., & Parker, D. (1997). Extending the theory of planned behaviour: The role of personal norm, instrumental beliefs, and affective beliefs in predicting driving violations. In J. A. Rothengatter & E. Carbonell (Eds.), *Traffic and transport psychology: Theory and application* (pp. 367–374). Amsterdam, The Netherlands: Pergamon.

Tillmann, W. A., & Hobbs, G. E. (1949). The accident-prone driver. *American Journal of Psychiatry, 106*, 321–331.

Clinician Application

Deffenbacher, J. L. (2013). Cognitive behavioral therapy for angry drivers. In E. Fernandez (Ed.), *Treatment for anger in specific populations: Theory, applications, and outcome*. New York, NY: Oxford University Press.

Deffenbacher, J. L., Filetti, L. B., Richards, T. L., Lynch, R. S., & Oetting, E. R. (2003). Characteristics of two groups of angry drivers. *Journal of Counseling Psychology, 50*, 123–132.

CHAPTER 63

Research

Andrews, D. A., & Bonta, J. (1994). *The psychology of criminal conduct*. Cincinnati, OH: Anderson.

Andrews, D. A., & Bonta, J. (1998). *The psychology of criminal conduct* (2nd ed.). Cincinnati, OH: Anderson.

Andrews, D. A., & Bonta, J. (2003). *The psychology of criminal conduct* (3rd ed.). Cincinnati, OH: Anderson.

Andrews, D. A., & Bonta, J. (2006). *The psychology of criminal conduct* (4th ed.). New Providence, NJ: LexisNexis.

Andrews, D. A., & Bonta, J. (2010a). *The psychology of criminal conduct* (5th ed.). New Providence, NJ: LexisNexis.

Andrews, D. A., & Bonta, J. (2010b). Rehabilitating criminal justice policy and practice. *Psychology, Public Policy and Law, 16*, 39–55.

Andrews, D. A., Bonta, J., & Wormith, J. S. (2011). The risk-need-responsivity (RNR) model: Does adding the good lives model contribute to effective crime prevention? *Criminal Justice and Behavior, 38*, 735–755.

Andrews, D. A., Zinger, I., Hoge, R. D., Bonta, J., Gendreau, P., & Cullen, F. T. (1990). Does correctional treatment work? A clinically-relevant and psychologically informed meta-analysis. *Criminology, 28*, 369–404.

Banyard, V. L., Williams, L. M., & Siegel, J. A. (2001). The long-term mental health consequences of child sexual abuse: An exploratory study of the impact of multiple traumas in a sample of women. *Journal of Traumatic Stress, 14*, 697–715.

Barbaree, H. E., Langton, C. M., Blanchard, R., & Cantor, J. M. (2009). Aging versus stable enduring traits as explanatory constructs in sex offender recidivism: Partitioning actuarial prediction into conceptually meaningful components. *Criminal Justice and Behavior, 36*, 443–465.

Becker, J. V., Skinner, L. J., & Abel, G. G. (1986). Level of postassault sexual functioning in rape and incest victims. *Archives of Sexual Behavior, 15*, 37–49.

Beech, A. R., & Hamilton-Giachritsis, C. E. (2005). Relationship between therapeutic climate treatment outcome in group-based sexual offender treatment programs. *Sexual Abuse: A Journal of Research and Treatment, 17*, 127–140.

Beggs, S. M., & Grace, R. C. (2011). Treatment gain for sexual offenders against children predicts reduced recidivism: A comparative validity study. *Journal of Consulting and Clinical Psychology, 79*, 182–192.

Blanchard, R., Klassen, P., Dickey, R., Kuban, M. E., & Blak, T. (2001). Sensitivity and specificity of the phallometric test for pedophilia in nonadmitting sex offenders. *Psychological Assessment, 13*, 118–126.

Boer, D. P., Hart, S. D., Kropp, P. R., & Webster, C. D. (1997). *Manual for the Sexual Violence Risk-20: Professional guidelines for assessing risk of sexual violence.* Vancouver, BC: Institute Against Family Violence and the Mental Health, Law, and Policy Institute, Simon Fraser University.

Browne, A., & Finkelhor, D. (1986). Impact of sexual abuse: A review of the research. *Psychological Bulletin, 99*, 66–77.

Catalano, S., Smith, E., Snyder, H., & Rand, M. (2009, September). Female victims of violence. *Bureau of Justice Statistics Selected Findings.* Washington, DC: U.S. Department of Justice.

Correctional Service of Canada. (2009). *Facts and figures: Aboriginal community development in corrections.* Retrieved from http://www.csc-scc.gc.ca/text/prgrm/abinit/know/4-eng.shtml

Cortoni, F., Hanson, R. K., & Coache, M. (2010). The recidivism rates of female sexual offenders are low: A meta-analysis. *Sexual Abuse: A Journal of Research and Treatment, 22*, 387–401.

Cuevas, C. A. (n.d.). Working with Latino sex offenders. Retrieved from http://www.newdirectionsacs.com/what-to-know-when-working-with-latino-sex-offenders

Dallam, S. J., Gleaves, D. H., Cepeda-Benito, A., Silberg, J. L., Kraemer, H. C., & Spiegel, D. (2001). The effects of child sexual abuse: Comment on Rind, Tromovitch, and Bauserman (1998). *Psychological Bulletin, 127*, 715–733.

Douglas, E. M., & Finklehor, D. (2005). *Childhood sexual abuse fact sheet.* Retrieved from: http://www.unh.edu/ccrc/factsheet/pdf/CSA-FS20.pdf

Douglas, K. S., & Kropp, P. R. (2002). A prevention-based paradigm for violence risk assessment: Clinical and research applications. *Criminal Justice and Behavior, 29*, 617–658.

Gallagher, C. A., Wilson, D. B., Hirschfield, P., Coggeshall, M. B., & MacKenzie, D. L. (1999). A quantitative review of the effects of sex offender treatment on sexual reoffending. *Corrections Management Quarterly, 3*, 19–29.

Hall, G. C. (1995). Sex offender recidivism revised: A meta-analysis of recent treatment studies. *Journal of Consulting and Clinical Psychology, 63*, 802–809.

Hall, G. C. N., Shondrick, D. D., & Hirshman, R. (1993). The role of sexual arousal in sexually aggressive behavior: A meta-analysis. *Journal of Consulting and Clinical Psychology, 61*, 1091–1095.

Hanson, R. K. (1997). How to know what works with sexual offenders. *Sexual Abuse: A Journal of Research and Treatment, 9*, 129–145.

Hanson, R. K., Bourgon, G., Helmus, L., & Hodgson, S. (2009). The principles of effective correctional treatment also apply to sexual offenders. *Criminal Justice and Behavior, 36*, 865–891.

Hanson, R. K., & Bussière, M. T. (1998). Predicting relapse: A meta-analysis of sexual offender recidivism studies. *Journal of Consulting and Clinical Psychology, 66*, 348–362.

Hanson, R. K., Gordon, A., Harris, A. J. R., Marques, J. K., Murphy, W., ... Seto, M. C. (2002). First report of the Collaborative Data Outcome Project on the effectiveness of psychological treatment for sexual offenders. *Sexual Abuse: A Journal of Research and Treatment, 14*, 169–194.

Hanson, R. K., & Morton-Bourgon, K. (2005). The characteristics of persistent sexual offenders: A meta-analysis of recidivism studies. *Journal of Consulting and Clinical Psychology, 73*, 1154–1163.

Hanson, R. K., & Morton-Bourgon, K. E. (2009). The accuracy of recidivism risk assessments for sexual offenders: A meta-analysis of 118 prediction studies. *Psychological Assessment, 21*, 1–21.

Helmus, L., Thornton, D., Hanson, R. K., & Babchishin, K. M. (2012). Improving the predictive accuracy of Static-99 and Static-2002 with older offenders: Revised age weights. *Sexual Abuse: A Journal of Research and Treatment, 24*, 64–101.

Hudson, S. M., Wales, D. S., Bakker, L., & Ward, T. (2002). Dynamic risk factors: The Kia Marama evaluation. *Sexual Abuse: A Journal of Research and Treatment, 14*, 103–119.

Johnston, P., Hudson, S. M., & Marshall, W. L. (1992). The effects of masturbatory conditioning with nonfamilial child molesters. *Behaviour Research and Therapy, 30*, 559–561.

Jung, S., & Gulayets, M. (2011). Using clinical variables to evaluate treatment effectiveness in programmes for sexual offenders. *Journal of Sexual Aggression, 17*, 166–180.

Kilgust, A. R. (2009). Sentencing and risk characteristics of Latino sexual offenders. *School of Professional Psychology.* Paper 96. Retrieved from http://commons.pacificu.edu/spp/96

Launay, G. (1999). The phallometric assessment of sex offenders: An update. *Criminal Behavior and Mental Health, 9*, 254–274.

Laws, D. R., Hudson, S. M., & Ward, T. (Eds.). (2000). *Remaking relapse prevention: A sourcebook.* Thousand Oaks, CA: Sage.

Löesel, F. & Schmucker, M. (2005). The effectiveness of treatment for sexual offenders: A comprehensive meta-analysis. *Journal of Experimental Criminology, 1*, 117–146.

Marques, J. K., Wienderanders, M., Day, D. M., Nelson, C., & van Ommeren, A. (2005). Effects of a relapse prevention program on sexual recidivism: California's Sex Offender Treatment and Evaluation Project (SOTEP). *Sexual Abuse: A Journal of Research and Treatment, 17*, 79–107.

Marshall, W. L., Anderson, D., & Fernandez, Y. (1999). *Cognitive behavioural treatment of sexual offenders.* Chichester, UK: Wiley.

Marshall, W. L., Bryce, P., Hudson, S. M., Ward, T., & Moth, B. (1996). The enhancement of intimacy and the reduction of loneliness among child molesters. *Journal of Family Violence, 11*, 219–235.

Marshall, W. L., Champagne, F., Sturgeon, C., & Bryce, P. (1997). Increasing the self-esteem of child molesters. *Sexual Abuse: A Journal of Research & Treatment, 9*, 321–333.

Marshall, W. L., Marshall, L. E., Serran, G, A., & O'Brien, M. D. (2011). *Rehabilitating sexual offenders: A strength based approach.* Washington, DC: American Psychological Association.

McGrath, R. J., Cumming, G. F., Buchard, B. L., Zeoli, S., & Ellerby, L. (2010). *Current practices and emerging trends in sexual abuser management: The Safer Society 2009 North American Survey.* Brandon, VT: Safer Society Press.

Miller, W. R., & Rollnick, S. (Eds.). (2002). *Motivational interviewing: Preparing people for change* (2nd ed.). New York, NY: Guilford.

New Zealand Department of Corrections. (2011). *How corrections manages offenders in prison.* Retrieved from www.corrections.govt.nz/about-us/fact-sheets/managing-offenders.html

Nunes, K. L., Babchishin, K. M., & Cortoni, F. (2011). Measuring treatment changes in sex offenders: Clinical and statistical significance. *Criminal Justice and Behavior, 38*, 157–173.

Olver, M. E., Stockdale, K. C., & Wormith, J. S. (2011). A meta-analysis of predictors of offender treatment attrition and its relationship to recidivism. *Journal of Consulting and Clinical Psychology, 79*, 6–21.

Olver, M. E., Wong, S. C. P., Nicholaichuk, T., & Gordon, A. (2007). The validity and reliability of the Violence Risk Scale-Sexual Offender version: Assessing sex offender risk and evaluating therapeutic change. *Psychological Assessment, 19*, 318–329.

Perrault, S., & Brennan, S. (2010). Criminal victimization in Canada, 2009. Ottawa, Canada: Canadian Centre for Justice Statistics, Report 30 (2).

Prentky, R. A. (1997). Arousal reduction in sexual offenders: A review of antiandrogen interventions. *Sexual Abuse: A Journal of Research and Treatment, 9*, 335–347.

Prentky, R. A., Janus, E., Barbaree, H. E., Schwartz, B. K., & Kafka, M. P. (2006). Sexually violent predators in the courtroom: Science on trial. *Psychology, Public Policy, and Law, 12*, 357–393.

Public Safety Canada. (n.d.). Successful projects: Mamowichihitowin Community Wellness Program, Ahousaht Circle of Healing, Biidaaban: The Mnjikaning Community Healing Model, and Relatives Working Together. Retrieved from http://www.publicsafety.gc.ca/prg/cor/ac/su-pr-eng.aspx

Public Safety Canada Portfolio Corrections Statistics Committee. (2011) Corrections and Conditional Release Statistical Overview Annual Report. Public Safety Canada. Ottawa.

Quinsey, V., Harris, G. T., Rice, M. E., & Cormier, C. A. (2005). *Violent offenders: Appraising and managing risk* (2nd ed.). Washington, DC: American Psychological Association.

Tamatea, A. J., Webb, M., & Boer, D. P. (2011). The role of culture in sexual offender rehabilitation: A New Zealand perspective. In D. P. Boer, R. Eher, L. A. Craig, M. H. Miner, & F. Pfäfflin (Eds.), *International perspectives on the assessment and treatment of sexual offenders: Theory, practice, and research* (pp. 313–329). Chichester, UK: Wiley.

Ward, T., & Hudson, S. M. (1998). A model of the relapse process in sex offenders. *Journal of Interpersonal Violence, 13,* 700–725.

Ward, T., Mann, R. E., & Gannon, T. A. (2007). The good lives model of offender rehabilitation: Clinical implications. *Aggression and Violent Behavior, 12,* 87–107.

Wilson, R. J., Cortoni, F., & McWhinnie, A. J. (2009). Circles of support & accountability: A Canadian national replication of outcome findings. *Sexual Abuse: A Journal of Research and Treatment, 21,* 412–430.

Wong, S. C. P., Olver, M. E., & Stockdale, K. C. (2009). The utility of static and dynamic factors in risk assessment, prediction, and treatment. In J. Andrade (Ed.), *Handbook of violence risk assessment and treatment: New approaches for mental health professionals* (pp. 83–120). New York, NY: Springer.

Wormith, J. S. (1986). Assessing deviant sexual arousal: Physiological and cognitive aspects. *Advances in Behaviour Research & Therapy, 8,* 101–137.

CHAPTER 64

Research

American Academy of Child and Adolescent Psychiatry. (1998). Practice parameters for the diagnosis and treatment of posttraumatic stress disorder in children and adolescents. *Journal of the American Academy of Child and Adolescent Psychiatry, 37*(Suppl. 10), 4S–26S.

Association for the Treatment of Sexual Abusers (ATSA). (2006). *Report of the Task Force on Children with Sexual Behavior Problems.* Author

Berliner, L., & Elliott, D. M. (2002). Sexual abuse of children. In J. E. B. Myers, L. Berliner, J. Briere, C. T. Hendrix, C. Jenny, & T. Reid (Eds.), *The APSAC handbook on child maltreatment* (2nd ed., pp. 55–78). Thousand Oaks, CA: Sage Publications.

Bolen, R. M., & Scannapieco, M. (1999). Prevalence of child sexual abuse: A corrective meta-analysis. *Social Service Review, 73*(3), 281–313.

Chaffin, M., Letourneau, E., & Silovsky, J. F. (2002). Adults, adolescents, and children who sexually abuse children: A developmental perspective. In J. E. B. Myers, L. Berliner, J. Briere, C. T. Hendrix, C. Jenny, & T. Reid (Eds.), *The APSAC handbook on child maltreatment* (2nd ed., pp. 205–232). Thousand Oaks, CA: Sage Publications.

Cohen, J. A., Deblinger, E., Mannarino, A. P., & Steer, R. A. (2004). A multisite, randomized controlled trial for children with sexual abuse-related PTSD symptoms. *Journal of the American Academy of Child and Adolescent Psychiatry, 43,* 393–402.

Davies, D. (2004). *Child development: A practitioner's guide.* New York, NY: The Guilford Press.

Felliti, V. J., Anda, R. F., Nordenberg, D., Williamson, D. F., Spitz, A. M., … Marks, J. S. (1998). Relationship of childhood abuse and household dysfunction to many of the leading causes of death in adults: The Adverse Childhood Experiences (ACE) Study. *American Journal of Preventive Medicine, 14*(4), 245–258.

Finkelhor, D. (2008). *Childhood victimization.* New York, NY: Oxford University Press.

Finkelhor, D., Hotaling, G., Lewis, I., & Smith, C. (1990). Sexual abuse in a national survey of adult men and women: Prevalence, characteristics, and risk factors. *Child Abuse and Neglect, 14,* 19–28.

Finkelhor, D., Jones, L., & Shattuck, A. (2011). *Updated trends in child maltreatment 2010.* Retrieved from http://www.unh.edu/ccrc/pdf/CV203_Updated%20trends%202010%20FINAL_12-19-11.pdf

Fontes, L. A. (1995). Introduction. In L. A. Fontes (Ed.), *Sexual abuse in nine North American cultures: Treatment and prevention* (pp. 1–9). Thousand Oaks, CA: Sage.

Fontes, L. A., & Plummer, C. (2010). Cultural issues in disclosures of child sexual abuse. *Journal of Child Sexual Abuse, 19,* 491–518.

Friedrich, W. N. (2007). *Children with sexual behavior problems: Family-based attachment-focused therapy.* New York, NY: Norton.

Grave, J., & Blissett, J. (2004). Is cognitive behavior therapy developmentally appropriate for young children? A critical review of the evidence. *Clinical Psychology Review, 24,* 399–420.

Hetzel-Riggin, M. D., Brausch, A. M., & Montgomery, B. S. (2007). A meta-analytic investigation of therapy modality outcomes for sexually abused children and adolescents: An exploratory study. *Child Abuse & Neglect, 31,* 125–141.

London, K., Bruck, M., Ceci, S. J., & Shuman, D. W. (2005). Disclosure of child sexual abuse: What does the research tell us about the ways that children tell? *Psychology, Public Policy, and Law, 11*(1), 194–226.

Lyon, T. D. (2007). False denials: Overcoming methodological biases in abuse disclosure research. In M. E. Pipe, M. E. Lamb, Y. Orbach, & A. C. Cederborg (Eds.), *Disclosing abuse: Delays, denials, retractions and incomplete accounts* (pp. 41–62). Mahwah, NJ: Erlbaum.

Lyon, T. D., & Ahern, E. C. (2011). Disclosure of child sexual abuse. In J. E. B. Myers (Ed.), *The APSAC handbook on child maltreatment* (3rd ed., pp. 233–252). Newbury Park, CA: Sage.

Putnam, F. W. (2003). Ten year research update review: Child sexual abuse. *Journal of the American Academy of Child and Adolescent Psychiatry, 42*, 269–278.

Sanchez-Meca, J., Rosa-Alcazar, A. I., Lopez-Soler, C. (2011). The psychological treatment of sexual abuse in children and adolescents: A Meta-analysis. *International Journal of Clinical and Health Psychology, 11*, 67–93.

Saunders, B. E., Berliner, L., & Hanson, R. F. (Eds.). (2001, April 26). *Child physical and sexual abuse: Guidelines for treatment* (Revised report). Charleston, SC: National Crime Victims Research and Treatment Center.

Scannapieco, M., & Connell-Carrick, K. (2005). *Understanding child maltreatment: An ecological and developmental perspective.* New York, NY: Oxford University Press.

Sedlak, A. J., Mettenburg, J., Basena, M., Petta, I., McPherson, K., … Li, S. (2010). Fourth National Incidence Study of Child Abuse and Neglect (NIS–4): Report to Congress. Washington, DC: U.S. Department of Health and Human Services, Administration for Children and Families. Retrieved from http://www.acf.hhs.gov/programs/opre/abuse_neglect/natl_incid/reports/natl_incid/nis4_report_congress_full_pdf_jan2010.pdf

Smith, D. W., Letourneau, E. J., Saunders, B. E., Kilpatrick, D. G., Resnick, S. H., & Best, C. L. (2000). Delay in disclosure of childhood rape: Results from a national survey. *Child Abuse and Neglect, 24*, 273–287.

St. Amand, A., Bard, D. E., & Silovsky, J. F. (2008). Meta-analysis of treatment for child sexual behavior problems: Practice elements and outcomes. *Child Maltreatment, 13*, 145–166.

U.S. Department of Health and Human Services, Administration on Children, Youth and Families. (2011). Child Maltreatment 2010. Retrieved from http://www.acf.hhs.gov/programs/cb/pubs/cm10/index.htm

Clinician Application

Cary, C. E., & McMillen, J. C. (2012). The data behind the dissemination: A systematic review of trauma-focused cognitive behavioral therapy for use with children and youth. *Children and Youth Services Review, 34*, 748–757.

Deblinger, E., Mannarino, A. P., Cohen, J. A., Runyon, M. K., & Steer, R. A. (2011), Trauma-focused cognitive behavioral therapy for children: Impact of the trauma narrative and treatment length. *Depression and Anxiety, 28*, 67–75.

Deblinger, E., Mannarino, A. P., Cohen, J. A., & Steer, R. A. (2006). A follow-up study of a multisite, randomized, controlled trial for children with sexual abuse-related PTSD symptoms. *Journal of the American Academy of Child and Adolescent Psychiatry, 45*, 1474–1484.

Margolin, G., Vickerman, K. A., Ramos, M. C., Serrano, S. D., Gordis, E. B., … Spies, L. A. (2009). Youth exposed to violence: Stability, co-occurrence, and context. *Clinical Child and Family Psychology Review, 12*, 39–54.

CHAPTER 65

Research

Bhandari, S., Winter, D., Messer, D., & Metcalfe, C. (2011). Family characteristics and long-term effects of childhood sexual abuse. *British Journal of Clinical Psychology, 50*, 435–451.

Briere, J., & Elliot, D. M. (1993). Sexual abuse, family environment, and psychological symptoms: On the validity of statistical control. *Journal of Consulting and Clinical Psychology, 61*, 284–288.

Briere, J., & Elliott, D. M. (2003). Prevalence and psychological sequelae of self-reported childhood physical and sexual abuse in a general population sample of men and women. *Child Abuse and Neglect, 27*, 1205–1222.

Briere, J., & Jordan, C. E. (2009). Childhood maltreatment, intervening variables, and adult psychological difficulties in women. *Trauma, Violence, & Abuse, 10*, 375–388.

Callahan, K. L., Price, J. L., & Hilsenroth, M. J. (2004). A review of interpersonal-psychodynamic group psychotherapy outcomes for adult survivors of childhood sexual abuse. *International Journal of Group Psychotherapy, 54*, 491–519.

Chard, K. M. (2005). An evaluation of cognitive processing therapy for the treatment of posttraumatic stress disorder related to childhood sexual abuse. *Journal of Consulting and Clinical Psychology, 73*, 965–971.

Classen, C. C., Palesh, O. G., Cavanaugh, C. E., Koopman, C., Kaupp, J. W., … Spiegel, D. (2011). A comparison of trauma-focused and present-focused group therapy for survivors of childhood sexual abuse: A randomized controlled trial. *Psychological Trauma: Theory, Research, Practice, and Policy, 3*, 84–93.

Cloitre, M., Stovall-McClough, K. C., Nooner, K., Zorbas, P., Cherry, S., … Petkova, E. (2010). Treatment for PTSD related to childhood abuse: A randomized controlled trial. *American Journal of Psychiatry, 167*, 915–924.

de Jong, T. L., & Gorey, K. M. (1996). Short-term versus long-term group work with female survivors of childhood sexual abuse: A brief meta-analytic review. *Social Work with Groups, 19*, 19–27.

Draucker, C. B., & Martsolf, D. S. (2006). *Counselling survivors of childhood sexual abuse* (3rd ed.). London, UK: Sage.

Edmond, T., Rubin, A., & Wambach, K. G. (1999). The effectiveness of EMDR with adult female survivors of childhood sexual abuse. *Social Work Research, 23*, 103–116.

Elklit, A. (2009). Traumatic stress and psychological adjustment in treatment-seeking women sexually abused in childhood: A follow-up. *Scandinavian Journal of Psychology, 50*, 251–257.

Fergusson, D. M., Boden, J. M., & Horwood, L. J. (2008). Exposure to childhood sexual and physical abuse and adjustment in early adulthood. *Child Abuse and Neglect, 32*, 607–619.

Finkelhor, D. (1997). Child sexual abuse. In O. W. Barnett, C. L. Miller-Perrin, & R. D. Perrin (Eds.), *Family violence across the lifespan* (pp. 69–104). Thousand Oaks, CA: Sage.

Harper, K., Richter, N. L., & Gorey, K. M. (2009). Group work with female survivors of childhood sexual abuse: Evidence of poorer outcomes among those with eating disorders. *Eating Behaviors, 10*, 45–48.

Hébert, M., & Bergeron, M. (2007). Efficacy of a group intervention for adult women survivors of sexual abuse. *Journal of Child Sexual Abuse, 16*, 37–61.

Jepsen, E. K. K., Svagaard, T., Thelle, M. I., McCullough, L., & Martinsen, E. W. (2009). Inpatient treatment for adult survivors of childhood sexual abuse: A preliminary outcome study. *Journal of Trauma & Dissociation, 10*, 315–333.

Jonas, S., Bebbington, P., McManus, S., Meltzer, H., Jenkins, R., ... Brugha, T. (2011). Sexual abuse and psychiatric disorder in England: Results from the 2007 Adult Psychiatric Morbidity Survey. *Psychological Medicine, 41*, 709–719.

Jumper, S. A. (1995). A meta-analysis of the relationship of child sexual abuse to adult psychological adjustment. *Child Abuse and Neglect, 19*, 715–728.

Jung, K., & Steil, R. (2012). The feeling of being contaminated in adult survivors of childhood sexual abuse and its treatment via a two-session program of cognitive restructuring and imagery modification: A case study. *Behavior Modification, 36*, 67–86.

Kessler, M. R. H., & Goff, B. S. N. (2006). Initial treatment decisions with adult survivors of childhood sexual abuse: Recommendations from clinical experts. *Journal of Trauma Practice, 5*, 33–56.

Kessler, M. R. H., White, M. B., & Nelson, B. A. (2003). Group treatments for women sexually abused as children: A review of the literature and recommendations for future outcome research. *Child Abuse and Neglect, 27*, 1045–1061.

Kimbrough, E., Magyari, T., Langenberg, P., Chesney, M., & Berman, B. (2010). Mindfulness intervention for child abuse survivors. *Journal of Clinical Psychology, 66*, 17–33.

Kreidler, M. (2005). Group therapy for survivors of childhood sexual abuse who have chronic mental illness. *Archives of Psychiatric Nursing, 19*, 176–183.

Lau, M., & Kristensen, E. (2007). Outcome of systemic and analytic group psychotherapy for adult women with history of intrafamilial childhood sexual abuse: A randomized controlled study. *Acta Psychiatrica Scandinavica, 116*, 96–104.

Lundqvist, G., & Öjehagen, A. (2001). Childhood sexual abuse: An evaluation of a two-year group therapy in adult women. *European Psychiatry, 16*, 64–67.

Lundqvist, G., Svedin, C. G., Hansson, K., & Broman, I. (2006). Group therapy for women sexually abused as children: Mental health before and after group therapy. *Journal of Interpersonal Violence, 21*, 1665–1677.

MacIntosh, H. B., & Johnson, S. (2008). Emotionally focused therapy for couples and childhood sexual abuse survivors. *Journal of Marital and Family Therapy, 34*, 298–315.

MacMillan, H. L., Fleming, J. E., Streiner, D. L., Lin, E., Boyle, M. H., ... Beardslee, W. R. (2001). Childhood abuse and lifetime psychopathology in a community sample. *American Journal of Psychiatry, 158*, 1878–1883.

Martsolf, D. S., & Draucker, C. B. (2005). Psychotherapy approaches for adult survivors of childhood sexual abuse: An integrative review of outcome research. *Issues in Mental Health Nursing, 26*, 801–825.

McDonagh, A., Friedman, M., McHugo, G., Ford, J., Sengupta, A., ... Descamps, M. (2005). Randomized trial of cognitive-behavioral therapy for chronic posttraumatic stress disorder in adult female survivors of childhood sexual abuse. *Journal of Consulting and Clinical Psychology, 73*, 515–524.

Molnar, B. E., Buka, S. L., & Kessler, R. C. (2001). Child sexual abuse and subsequent psychopathology: Results from the National Comorbidity Survey. *American Journal of Public Health, 91*, 753–760.

Noll, J. G. (2008). Sexual abuse of children: Unique in its effects on development? *Child Abuse & Neglect, 32*, 603–605.

Owens, G. P., & Chard, K. M. (2003). Comorbidity and psychiatric diagnoses among women reporting child sexual abuse. *Child Abuse and Neglect, 27*, 1075–1082.

Paivio, S. C., Jarry, J. L., Chagigiorgis, H., Hall, I., & Ralston, M. (2010). Efficacy of two versions of emotion-focused therapy for resolving child abuse trauma. *Psychotherapy Research, 20*, 353–366.

Pereda, N., Guilera, G., Forns, M., & Gómez-Benito, J. (2009). The prevalence of child sexual abuse in community and student samples: A meta-analysis. *Clinical Psychology Review, 29*, 328–338.

Price, J. L., Hilsenroth, M. J., Petretic-Jackson, P. A., & Bonge, D. (2001). A review of individual psychotherapy outcomes for adult survivors of childhood sexual abuse. *Clinical Psychology Review, 21*, 1095–1121.

Putnam, F. W. (2003). Ten-year research update review: Child sexual abuse. *Journal of the American Academy of Child and Adolescent Psychiatry, 42*, 269–278.

Resick, P. A., Galovski, T. E., Uhlmansiek, M. O., Scher, C. D., Clum, G. A., & Young-Xu, Y. (2008). A randomized clinical trial to dismantle components of cognitive processing therapy for posttraumatic stress disorder in female victims of interpersonal violence. *Journal of Consulting and Clinical Psychology, 76*, 243–258.

Rieckert, J., & Möller, A. T. (2000). Rational-emotive behavior therapy in the treatment of adult victims of childhood sexual abuse. *Journal of Rational-Emotive and Cognitive-Behavior Therapy, 18*, 87–101.

Rind, B., Tromovitch, P., & Bauserman, R. (1998). A meta-analytic examination of assumed properties of child sexual abuse using college samples. *Psychological Bulletin, 124*, 22–53.

Ryan, M., Nitsun, M., Gilbert, L., & Mason, H. (2005). A prospective study of the effectiveness of group and individual psychotherapy for women CSA survivors. *Psychology and Psychotherapy: Theory, Research and Practice, 78*, 465–479.

Stalker, C. A., & Fry, R. (1999). A comparison of short-term group and individual therapy for sexually abused women. *Canadian Journal of Psychiatry, 44*, 168–174.

Stalker, C. A., Palmer, S. E., Wright, D. C., & Gebotys, R. (2005). Specialized inpatient trauma treatment for adults abused as children: A follow-up study. *American Journal of Psychiatry, 162*, 552–559.

Steil, R., Dyer, A., Priebe, K., Kleindienst, N., & Bohus, M. (2011). Dialectical behaviour therapy for posttraumatic stress disorder related to childhood sexual abuse: A pilot study of an intensive residential treatment program. *Journal of Traumatic Stress, 24*, 102–106.

Talbot, N. L., O'Hara, M. W., Chaudron, L. H., Tu, X., Ward, E. A., ... Stuart, S. (2011). A randomized effectiveness trial of interpersonal psychotherapy for depressed women with sexual abuse histories. *Psychiatric Services, 62*, 374–380.

World Health Organization. (1999, March). *Report of the Consultation on Child Abuse Prevention.* Geneva: World Health Organization, Social Change and Mental Health, Violence and Injury Prevention.

Wright, D. C., Woo, W. L., Muller, R. T., Fernandes, C. B., & Kraftcheck, E. R. (2003). An investigation of trauma-centered inpatient treatment for adult survivors of abuse. *Child Abuse and Neglect, 27*, 393–406.

Zlotnick, C., Shea, T. M., Rosen, K., Simpson, E., Mulrenin, K., ... Pearlstein, T. (1997). An affect-management group for women with posttraumatic stress disorder and histories of childhood sexual abuse. *Journal of Traumatic Stress, 10*, 425–436.

Clinician Application

Allen, J. (2001). *Traumatic relationships and serious mental disorders.* Chichester, UK: John Wiley & Sons.

Allen, J. G., & Fonagy, P. (Eds.). (2006). *Handbook of mentalizing-based treatment.* New York, NY: John Wiley & Sons.

Bertolino, B., & O'Hanlon, B. (2002). *Even from a broken web: Brief, respectful solution-oriented therapy for sexual abuse and trauma.* New York, NY: W. W. Norton.

Briere, J. (1996). *Therapy for adults molested as children: Beyond survival* (2nd ed.). New York, NY: Springer.

Briere, J. (2002). A self-trauma model for treating adult survivors of severe child abuse. In J. Briere, L. Berliner, J. A. Bulkley, C. Jenny, & T. Reid (Eds.), *The APSAC handbook on child maltreatment* (2nd ed., pp. 51–71). Thousand Oaks, CA: Sage.

Briere, J., & Scott, C. (2006). *Principles of trauma therapy: A guide to symptoms, evaluation, and treatment.* Thousand Oaks, CA: Sage.

Chu, J. (1998, 2011). *Rebuilding shattered lives: The responsible treatment of complex post-traumatic and dissociative disorders* (2nd ed.). New York, NY: John Wiley & Sons.

Cloitre, M., Cohen, L. R., & Koenen, K. C. (2006). *Treating survivors of childhood abuse: Psychotherapy for the interrupted life.* New York, NY: Guilford Press.

Cloitre, M., Courtois, C. A., Charuvastra, A., Carapezza, R., Stolbach, B. C., & Green, B. L. (2011). Treatment of complex PTSD: Results of the ISTSS expert clinician survey on best practices. *Journal of Traumatic Stress, 24*, 615–627.

Van der Kolk, B. A., & Courtois, C. A. (October, 2005). Editorial comments: Complex developmental trauma. *Journal of Traumatic Stress, 18*, 5(special section on complex trauma).

Index